COMMON ELEMENTS

Name	Symbol	Approx. at. wt.	Common ox. nos.	Name	Symbol	Approx. at. wt.	Common ox. nos.
aluminum	Al	27.0	+3	magnesium	Mg	24.3	+2
antimony	Sb	121.8	+3,+5	manganese	Mn	54.9	+2,+4,+7
arsenic	As	74.9	+3,+5	mercury	Hg	200.6	+1,+2
barium	Ba	137.3	+2	nickel	Ni	58.7	+2
bismuth	Bi	209.0	+3	nitrogen	N	14.0	−3,+3,+5
bromine	Br	79.9	−1,+5	oxygen	O	16.0	−2
calcium	Ca	40.1	+2	phosphorus	P	31.0	+3,+5
carbon	C	12.0	+2,+4	platinum	Pt	195.1	+2,+4
chlorine	Cl	35.5	−1,+5,+7	potassium	K	39.1	+1
chromium	Cr	52.0	+2,+3,+6	silicon	Si	28.1	+4
cobalt	Co	58.9	+2,+3	silver	Ag	107.9	+1
copper	Cu	63.5	+1,+2	sodium	Na	23.0	+1
fluorine	F	19.0	−1	strontium	Sr	87.6	+2
gold	Au	197.0	+1,+3	sulfur	S	32.1	−2,+4,+6
hydrogen	H	1.0	−1,+1	tin	Sn	118.7	+2,+4
iodine	I	126.9	−1,+5	titanium	Ti	47.9	+3,+4
iron	Fe	55.8	+2,+3	tungsten	W	183.8	+6
lead	Pb	207.2	+2,+4	zinc	Zn	65.4	+2

COMMON IONS AND THEIR CHARGES

Name	Symbol	Charge	Name	Symbol	Charge
aluminum	Al^{+++}	+3	lead(II)	Pb^{++}	+2
ammonium	NH_4^+	+1	magnesium	Mg^{++}	+2
barium	Ba^{++}	+2	mercury(I)	Hg_2^{++}	+2
calcium	Ca^{++}	+2	mercury(II)	Hg^{++}	+2
chromium(III)	Cr^{+++}	+3	nickel(II)	Ni^{++}	+2
cobalt(II)	Co^{++}	+2	potassium	K^+	+1
copper(I)	Cu^+	+1	silver	Ag^+	+1
copper(II)	Cu^{++}	+2	sodium	Na^+	+1
hydronium	H_3O^+	+1	tin(II)	Sn^{++}	+2
iron(II)	Fe^{++}	+2	tin(IV)	Sn^{++++}	+4
iron(III)	Fe^{+++}	+3	zinc	Zn^{++}	+2

Name	Symbol	Charge	Name	Symbol	Charge
acetate	$C_2H_3O_2^-$	−1	hydrogen sulfate	HSO_4^-	−1
bromide	Br^-	−1	hydroxide	OH^-	−1
carbonate	CO_3^{--}	−2	hypoc	ClO^-	−1
chlorate	ClO_3^-	−1	iodid		−1
chloride	Cl^-	−1	nitra		
chlorite	ClO_2^-	−1	nitrit		
chromate	CrO_4^{--}	−2	oxid		
cyanide	CN^-	−1	per		
dichromate	$Cr_2O_7^{--}$	−2	per		
fluoride	F^-	−1	peroxide		
hexacyanoferrate(II)	$Fe(CN)_6^{----}$	−4	phosphate	PO_4^{---}	
hexacyanoferrate(III)	$Fe(CN)_6^{---}$	−3	sulfate	SO_4^{--}	−2
hydride	H^-	−1	sulfide	S^{--}	−2
hydrogen carbonate	HCO_3^-	−1	sulfite	SO_3^{--}	−2

The Holt Modern Chemistry Program

Metcalfe, Williams, and Castka
Modern Chemistry (Student Text)
Modern Chemistry (Teacher's Guide)
Laboratory Experiments in Chemistry
Exercises and Experiments in Chemistry
Tests in Chemistry
Alternate Tests in Chemistry

Supplementary Materials

Scientific Experiments in Chemistry, Manufacturing Chemists' Association
Semimicro Chemistry, DeBruyne, Kirk, and Beers
Chemistry Problems, Castka

H. Clark Metcalfe
John E. Williams
Joseph F. Castka

Modern Chemistry

HOLT, RINEHART AND WINSTON, INC.
New York • London • Toronto • Sydney

H. Clark Metcalfe

P.O. Box V2, Wickenburg, Arizona, 85358; formerly teacher of chemistry at Winchester-Thurston School, Pittsburgh, Pennsylvania and Head of the Science Department, Wilkinsburg Senior High School, Wilkinsburg, Pennsylvania.

John E. Williams

Formerly teacher of chemistry and physics at Newport Harbor High School, Newport Beach, California and Head of the Science Department, Broad Ripple High School, Indianapolis, Indiana.

Joseph F. Castka

Assistant Principal for the Supervision of Physical Science, Martin Van Buren High School, New York City; formerly Adjunct Associate Professor of General Science and Chemistry, C. W. Post College, Long Island University.

Charles E. Dull

Author of the Original editions of MODERN CHEMISTRY, deceased, was Head of the Science Department, West Side High School; and Supervisor of Science, Junior and Senior High Schools, Newark, New Jersey.

The cover photograph is by Manfred Kage. To make this picture, magnesium sulfate was dissolved in water. The magnesium sulfate recrystallized as it dried on a glass surface forming mountain-like microformations. The photograph was taken with a Zeiss "Universal-Pol" microscope using polarized light and a "Polychromator" compensator (designed by Manfred Kage). The lenses used were a 6x objective and an 8x ocular attached to a Planbel camera. Exposure was made on 4x5 Kodak "Type B" film.

The photograph on page ii, courtesy of Pittsburgh Plate Glass Company, is an enlarged view of industrial fiber glass fabric photographed under colored lights.

Photographs on pages 9, 41, 61, 92, 115, 163, 303, 306, 443, 505, 568, 574, and 602 are from the CHEM Study films named. These photographs are used with the permission of the Chemical Education Material Study, University of California, Berkeley.

Credits for other photographs appear under the photograph. Photographs not credited are the property of Holt, Rinehart and Winston.

Preface

MODERN CHEMISTRY is a textbook written to meet the various curriculum requirements for an introductory course in chemistry. This revision continues the sound policy of classroom development which has characterized MODERN CHEMISTRY from its first edition. The subject matter of chemistry is organized for a modern theoretical development. The presentation of chemical theory occupies nearly the first two-thirds of the text; descriptive chemistry, with emphasis on the structure and periodicity of the elements, follows the theoretical material. A single unit on organic chemistry appears near the middle of the text.

The most significant change in the 1974 edition of MODERN CHEMISTRY is readability. The manuscript was computer analyzed by Dr. Milton Jacobson, Director of the Bureau of Educational Research, University of Virginia. Based upon this analysis: (1) technical vocabulary words were identified and specially treated, (2) nontechnical vocabulary words were simplified and limited in grade level, and (3) complex sentences were simplified. The reading level on the Fry scale of the first nine chapters (excluding technical vocabulary words) is late 7th grade. This reading level score was computed by Paul Greenfield, Professor of Reading at Dutchess Community College and First President, North East Area Two-Year College Reading Association. The list of technical vocabulary words is given in the Teacher's Guide and is listed according to chapter of first occurrence. Each of these words is printed in the text in *bold face italics* and is carefully defined where it is first used. Refresher definitions of these words occur at appropriate intervals in the text.

Significant content changes in this edition of MODERN CHEMISTRY include revision of the presentation of evidence for current atomic structure theory; molecular shapes; van der Waals forces; freezing-point depression and boiling-point elevation of solvents; hydration of ions; ionization of covalent compounds; acids, bases, and salts; molar solutions and chemical equivalents; the unit on organic chemistry; heat of formation and heat of combustion; reaction rates; chemical equilibrium; chemical equivalents of oxidizing and reducing agents; electrode potentials; metallic and nonmetallic element technologies. Included also is a revised Table of Standard Electrode Potentials. In this table half-reactions are presented as reduction reactions and electrode potentials are listed as reduction potentials. This is the form recommended by the International Union of Pure and Applied Chemistry.

Teachers will find ample material in MODERN CHEMISTRY for an outstanding college-preparatory course, or for an introductory course at the junior college level. For those students who do not plan to go beyond this course in science, there is sufficient elementary theory and interest-arousing descriptive material for a complete and thorough program. It has been the authors' purpose to include more material than can be covered in one year, thus permitting a wide choice of topics and allowing for selective emphasis. Teachers should feel free to choose those topics which best meet their needs.

The material for each chapter includes Sample Problems where appropriate. At the end of each chapter there are suitable questions and problems. The questions, which are based on the text itself, are graded according to difficulty in Groups A and B. The problems are similarly graded. The average student should master all the Group A questions and problems; the better student will be able to do both. The Appendix in the back of the book, contains tables of useful data.

Because of their clarity and great learning value, line drawings are used extensively. The text is also illustrated with many fine photographs, some of which were taken expressly for this edition.

The text was written by H. Clark Metcalfe and John E. Williams. Joseph F. Castka was mainly responsible for the preparation of all supplementary materials to accompany the text, including the Teacher's Guide, EXERCISES AND EXPERIMENTS IN CHEMISTRY, LABORATORY EXPERIMENTS IN CHEMISTRY, and TESTS and ALTERNATE TESTS IN CHEMISTRY.

The following persons have been kind enough to read the entire manuscript or special parts of it, and have offered assistance by their helpful criticism: Courtland L. Agre, Professor of Chemistry, Augsburg College; Leo Schubert, Chairman of the Chemistry Department, The American University; Elbert C. Weaver, presently associated with undergraduate student work at the Yale University chemistry laboratories and formerly Teacher of Chemistry at Phillips Academy at Andover; Peter E. Yankwich, Professor of Chemistry, University of Illinois.

The authors also acknowledge with thanks the work of Felix Cooper who prepared the text illustrations, Sibyl Weil who obtained many of the photographs, David W. Ridgway, Executive Director of CHEM Study who provided the color photographs from CHEM Study films and supervised photography of student laboratory activities taken at Berkeley High School.

Our special thanks to Harry Choulett, of Berkeley High School for cooperating with Carolyn Polese, photographer for the student laboratory activities, and to Mary P. Connolly and Ella Mae Clark for providing the facilities for the special color photographs that were taken at John F. Kennedy Memorial High School. Also, our special thanks to Harriet Ehrhard and Garry Brown of the Dade County Public Schools as well as Dale Onderak and Theodore Herrick of the Nordonia High School for cooperating with Dr. Jacobson's readability study of the text.

H. Clark Metcalfe, John E. Williams, Joseph F. Castka

Contents

vii

Chapter 1

The Science of Chemistry

INTRODUCTION

1.1 Chemistry: a physical science

You are beginning your study of chemistry at a time when growing numbers of people are concerned about the declining quality of life. Chemistry can help you gain a deeper and more satisfying understanding of your environment than you have now. If you are curious and wish to know more about natural processes, minerals of the earth, water and solutions, and gases of the atmosphere, the activities in chemistry beckon to you.

The solutions to many serious problems related to the increasing consumption of fuels can be found through chemistry. For example, the oxides of nitrogen and sulfur are major atmospheric pollutants. Chemists are now perfecting methods for changing the nitrogen oxides in automobile exhaust gases to harmless nitrogen and oxygen before they are released to the air. Chemical processes are also being developed for removing sulfur oxides from stack gases of coal- and oil-burning power plants.

Some complex problems of pollution, nutrition, and population growth can be solved with the scientific knowledge we already have. Other problems might be solved as chemists and other scientists discover new knowledge. Where there are alternate solutions to environmental problems, the choice is dictated largely by consumers. If these choices are to favor the environment, we, as consumers, must be aware of natural chemical processes. An understanding of basic concepts in chemistry helps us recognize and appreciate the order in nature.

Irene Fertik

Fig. 1-1. A chemist conducting a chemical analysis.

It is convenient to group all sciences into two large divisions: *1.* the *biological sciences* which are concerned with living things, and *2.* the *physical sciences* which deal with the natural relationships about us.

Chemistry is one of the physical sciences. It is a body of systematized knowledge gained from observation, study, and experimentation—as opposed to guesswork or opinion. Chemistry deals with the structure and composition of matter that constitutes living things and their environment. Furthermore, it deals with changes in matter, the mechanisms by which these changes occur, the products formed, and the energy changes encountered.

Chemists are concerned with structures as simple as an atom of hydrogen or as complex as a molecule of hemoglobin which consists of more than 10,000 atoms. Chemists may have special interests which range from the structure of water or the nature of combustion to the colors of flowers or the chemical warfare waged by insects.

Physics is another physical science which is concerned primarily with matter and energy and their relationship in the universe. Physicists seek the basic simplicities that lie hidden beneath the magnificent complexities of nature.

Mathematics is the science of our number system. It gives us a means of expressing the relationships we observe in nature and of performing useful and necessary computations. Mathematics is often called the *language of science*. It is both a tool and a medium of expression of the chemist.

Chemical knowledge is separated into parts in order to make the study of chemistry and the gathering of new chemical knowledge easier. For example, *analytical chemistry* is concerned with identification of the kinds of matter, and the quantity of each, that compose complex substances. *Organic chemistry* is the chemistry of carbon compounds. Originally, substances containing carbon were thought to be found only in living matter. *Physical chemistry* combines the principles and techniques of chemistry and physics. Chemists working in this branch of chemistry may be concerned with the mechanisms or the way reactions occur, how fast they occur, or the structure of materials. Mathematics is used extensively in physical chemistry.

During the present century, chemistry has played an important part in the study of the biological sciences. Biologists and chemists have worked together to understand complex chemical structures and chemical reactions associated with life processes. This division is the realm of *biochemistry,* a blend of biology and chemistry.

1.2 Keystones of modern chemistry

The skilled workers of long ago undoubtedly used some practical chemical knowledge in their work with bronze, in the recovery of iron from its ore, and in making pigments and pottery.

The practice of alchemy in the Middle Ages was generally secretive, often mystic, and sometimes deceiving. The change from alchemy to chemistry had begun by the seventeenth century. This change was helped by two developments: *1.* Quantitative measurements could be made more reliably. *2.* These measurements were used to challenge the beliefs of the alchemists.

In 1669 **John Becher** of Germany introduced the *phlogiston* (flo-*jis*-tun) *theory of combustion*. He assumed that all combustible materials contained a mystical substance called *phlogiston*. During the combustion process the phlogiston was released in the form of heat or flame. Becher explained that a body lost weight during combustion because the phlogiston escaped.

Although the phlogiston theory was easily understood and applied, some early scientists doubted its correctness. They argued that if it were true that Becher's phlogiston left a material during combustion, the ash that remained must always weigh less than the original material. These doubters challenged the phlogiston theory experimentally. They showed that the "ashes" of burned metals were heavier than the metals themselves. Despite such strong challenges, this entirely wrong idea about the nature of fire dominated all chemical thought for more than a century. It was the last important generalization of the alchemy era.

The basic idea of modern chemistry, that elements are the stuff of which things are made, was growing in France at about the time of the American Revolution. In 1778, **Antoine Lavoisier** (la-*vwah*-zee-ay) demonstrated that oxygen was the part of the air actively involved in ordinary burning processes. This discovery set the stage for a better understanding of chemical reactions. A determined search for chemical elements began. Through the efforts of many investigators, about ninety elements were eventually recognized. By 1920, most of these elements had been isolated and their properties studied.

Lavoisier was followed closely by **John Dalton** of England who, in 1808, conceived the idea of a different kind of *atom* for each element. Dalton believed that this idea was the key to understanding chemistry. In 1811, the Italian physicist, **Amedeo Avogadro,** formulated some general laws describing the behavior of combined atoms, or molecules. Then, in 1852, Great Britain's **Sir Edward Frankland** first explained how atoms combine and form molecules. Chemists soon became concerned with the architecture of molecules.

The first great chemical architect was **Friedrich Kekulé** of Germany. He showed how atoms of carbon can unite and form chains. In 1858, he proposed the carbon-chain structure for molecules of a large family of organic compounds. Six years later Kekulé suggested a six-carbon ring for the molecule of benzene, an important part of coal tar. From this beginning, organic chemists have learned to construct a great variety of molecules useful as drugs, dyes, explosives, fibers, plastics, and solvents.

Fig. 1-2. A chemical engineer may specialize in processing problems, marketing, or production. This engineer is studying results from a trial run in a miniature plant.

Allied Chemical Corporation

In 1869 the Russian chemist, **Dmitri Mendeleyev** (men-deh-*lay*-eff), succeeded in arranging the known elements in a table so that their properties were repeated in a regular way. His arrangement suggested that regularities in the properties of elements were related to the structure of atoms. We now understand these regularities in terms of the modern electronic theory of atoms. The development of this theory began in the United States with the work of **Irving Langmuir** and **Gilbert N. Lewis.**

The first Nobel prize in chemistry was awarded to **Jacobus H. van't Hoff** of Holland in 1901 for his pioneering work in developing the laws of reactions and solutions. Germany's **Emil Fischer** received the second Nobel prize in chemistry in 1902 for his work on the structure of sugars and proteins. Sweden's **Svante Arrhenius** was awarded the third Nobel prize in 1903 for his theory explaining the behavior of electrolytes in solution. You will learn more about Arrhenius and electrolytes in Chapter 13.

In 1909, the Nobel prize went to the German chemist, **Wilhelm Ostwald,** for his work in catalysis. Catalysis is a technique for altering the rate of specific chemical reactions. It is very important in industrial chemistry. The Swiss chemist, **Alfred Werner,** received the prize in 1913 for his studies of the structure of complex compounds. The first American chemist to win the Nobel prize was **Theodore Richards.** He was selected in 1914 for his precise determination of atomic weights. In 1920 a German, **Walther Nernst,** was awarded the Nobel prize for his discoveries concerning the role of energy in chemical reactions.

Marie Curie, a Polish chemist working in France, was awarded the Nobel prize in 1911 for her discovery of the radioactive elements radium and polonium. This discovery was probably the most important contribution to chemistry since Lavoisier introduced the modern concept of elements. No longer could the atom be considered a simple unit of matter. Here were atoms of elements which burst apart, giving off tiny particles and high-energy radiations. Thus Madame Curie, a chemist, opened the structure within the atom for exploration by physicists. In 1939 two German chemists, **Otto Hahn** and **Fritz Strassman,** discovered atomic fission of uranium and set the stage for the nuclear age.

The list of Nobel prizes gives a rough indication of the creative efforts in chemistry being made by scientists in various nations. Up to the end of World War II, only three American chemists had been awarded this prize. In the twenty-seven years that followed, however, sixteen Americans have been selected for Nobel prizes in chemistry.

Marie Sklodowska Curie (1867–1934) was born in Warsaw, Poland, where her father was a professor of physics. She studied chemistry and physics at Warsaw and at the Sorbonne in Paris. In 1898 she discovered the element polonium. That same year Madame Curie and her husband, Pierre Curie, discovered the element radium. Madame Curie shared the Nobel prize in physics with her husband and A. H. Becquerel in 1903. She was the first woman scientist to win the Nobel prize in chemistry (1911) and was the first person to share in two Nobel prizes.

1.3 Methods of science

Some important scientific discoveries have come about quite by accident. Others have been the result of brilliant new ideas. Most of our scientific knowledge, however, is the result of carefully planned work carried on by trained scientists. Their techniques are known as **scientific methods**. These methods are simply *logical approaches to the solution of problems which lend themselves to investigation*. Scientific methods require honesty, the ability to withhold a decision until all evidence is in, and a desire for truth.

Scientists believe there is order in nature. They believe that everything in the universe behaves in an orderly way and that man can discover laws that describe the behavior of nature. Chemists, like other scientists, strive to explain a large number of related observations in terms of broad principles or *generalizations*. All basic scientific research is devoted to the discovery of these principles. *The generalizations which describe behavior in nature are called **laws** or **principles**.* Unlike civil or moral laws which require and restrict, natural laws tell us what *does* occur in nature. The laws of science may be expressed by concise statements or by means of mathematical formulas.

One of the distinguishing qualities of man is his curiosity. It causes him to ask two important questions: *"what?"* and *"why?"* When a scientist observes an event or situation in nature, called a *phenomenon,* he seeks the answers to these questions by carrying out systematic, disciplined, and persistent investigations.

We usually recognize four distinct phases in the application of scientific methods: *observing, generalizing, theorizing,* and *testing*.

1.   Observing. The scientist accumulates as much reliable data as possible about an observed phenomenon. His initial interest lies in discovering *what* actually occurs. These data may come from direct observations, from a search of scientific literature for information previously reported, and from well-planned and skillfully performed experiments.

Observations are of little value unless they are made carefully and skillfully. Chemists know that observing is most productive when the conditions which affect the observations are brought under·their control. Thus, observing is generally done in the *laboratory* where conditions can be controlled by the observer. *A sequence of observations carried out under controlled conditions is called an **experiment**.* Experimentation provides the foundation upon which modern science is built.

2.   Generalizing. The scientist organizes the accumulated data and looks for relationships among them. Relationships that he discovers may enable him to formulate a broad generalization describing what does occur. When well established by abundant supporting data, this generalization may be recognized as a new law or principle that describes the behavior.

3.   Theorizing. When the scientist knows *what* occurs, he is ready to move on to the more stimulating task of determining *why* the phenomenon occurs. A creative imagination may enable him to develop a reasonable explanation. It may also enable him to construct a simple physical or mental model which relates the observed behavior to familiar and well-understood phenomena.

Dr. Christian B. Aufinsen, National Institute of Health

Dr. William H. Stein, Rockefeller University

Dr. Stanford Moore, Rockefeller University

Fig. 1-3. Recipients of the 1972 Nobel prize in chemistry, the most prestigious award in science. American chemists have been awarded 19 Nobel gold medals, 16 of these since 1946. The United States stands second in total number of Nobel Laureate chemists. Leading with 22 Nobel Laureates is Germany, which dominated chemistry during the first 30 years of Nobel awards.

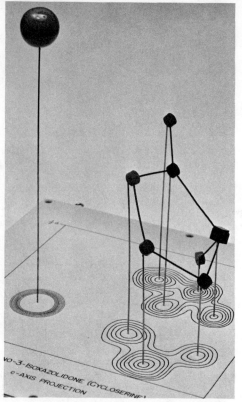

Ray Pepinsky, Crystal Research Laboratory

Fig. 1-4. A physical model is often used by chemists to help them understand the behavior of matter.

A plausible explanation of an observed natural phenomenon in terms of a model with familiar properties is called a **theory.**

4. *Testing.* Once a seemingly satisfactory theory is developed, it must be tested and retested to establish its soundness. In fact, scientists continually test observational and experimental data and predictions based on known principles. They do this testing by subjecting the data and predictions to new and ingenious experiments. A theory is retained only as long as it is useful. It may be discarded or modified as a result of new experimentation. A theory that stands up under scientific testing is valuable to scientists. It stimulates the imagination and serves as a basis for predicting behavior not previously investigated. This testing and predicting is the heart of the methods of science and the real stimulus for the tremendous growth of scientific knowledge.

The principles of chemistry are studied and understood best by the use of a general theory. A general theory about the behavior of matter may be made up of two parts. One part may be the scientific laws. The other part may be the experimental evidence related to the scientific laws. The term "theory" is often used by chemists in this broad sense. Some examples of such chemical theories are the *kinetic theory,* the *atomic theory,* and the *theory of ionization.*

MATTER AND ENERGY

1.4   Concept of matter

All materials about us consist of matter. With our senses—sight, touch, taste, and smell—we recognize various kinds of matter. This book, your desk, the air you breathe, the water you drink are examples of matter. Some kinds of matter are easily observed. A stone or a piece of wood may be seen and held in the hand. Other kinds of matter, such as the air or even water in a quiet pool, are recognized less readily. We ride on compressed air in automobile tires. We know of the tremendous damage which can be caused by the rapidly moving air in a hurricane.

We say that **matter** *is anything which occupies space and has mass.* Matter may be acted upon by *forces* which may set it in motion, or change its motion. Matter possesses **inertia,** a resistance to change of position or motion. The concept of inertia as a property of matter is important in the study of physics and chemistry. Imagine a basketball being used in a bowling alley as a substitute for a bowling ball. The effect on the pins would not be the same at all. Although they are approximately the same size, the bowling ball contains more matter than the basketball. Its inertia is correspondingly higher and thus its tendency to remain in motion, once set in motion, is greater.

While all these statements are descriptive of matter, they do not provide us with a completely satisfactory definition. Scientists, with their great knowledge of the properties and behavior of matter, are not able to define it precisely.

1.5 Mass and weight

The quantity of matter which a body possesses is known as its **mass**. If we move an object which is at rest, we notice that it resists our effort. If we stop the object once it is moving, we notice that it resists this effort also. The object's mass is the measure of this resistance to change of position or motion. Thus *mass is the measure of the inertia of the body* and is responsible for it.

Mass is also responsible for the *weight* of the body. **Weight is** *the measure of the earth's attraction for a body*. If we attach an object to a spring balance we find that it weighs less at high altitudes than it does at sea level. On the other hand, its mass remains unchanged; *the mass of a body is constant*.

Mass is usually measured by comparison with known masses (see Figure 1-5). If the masses of two bodies are the same they have equal weights while in the same location. Thus the mass of a body, when determined by "weighing" it on a platform balance, is sometimes incorrectly referred to as its "weight." The measurement of mass by "weighing" is common throughout chemistry

Fig. 1-5. The combined mass of the material on the left pan is 9.7 grams because they counter-balance this known mass indicated by the slider position on the beam.

11.34 $\frac{g}{cm^3}$

Lead

1.00 $\frac{g}{cm^3}$

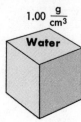

Water

0.24 $\frac{g}{cm^3}$

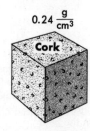

Cork

0.0013 $\frac{g}{cm^3}$

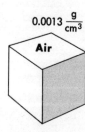

Air

0.000090 $\frac{g}{cm^3}$

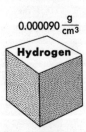

Hydrogen

Fig. 1-6. Equal volumes of different materials do not necessarily have the same mass.

and is not confusing if the meanings of the terms *mass* and *weight* are understood. Chemists are primarily concerned with measurements of mass, and we shall use the term *mass* in its proper meaning.

1.6 Density of matter varies

Matter occupies space and therefore has volume. From our everyday experiences we recognize that materials have different masses. We say that lead is heavy and that cork is light. This statement has little meaning unless we have in mind equal volumes of lead and cork. *The mass of a unit volume of a material is called its **density***. Density is expressed by the equation

$$D = \frac{m}{V}$$

where m is the mass of a material and V is its volume, D is its density. The basic unit of mass in chemistry is the *gram* (g). The basic unit of volume that we shall use is the *cubic centimeter* (cm³). Thus, density may have the dimensions g/cm³.

By comparing the masses of equal volumes of materials we find that the density of different kinds of matter varies. Thus one cubic centimeter of lead, having a mass of 11.34 grams, is nearly 50 times more dense than one cubic centimeter of cork having a mass of 0.24 gram (see Figure 1-6).

$$D_{\text{lead}} = \frac{m}{V} = \frac{11.34 \text{ g}}{\text{cm}^3}$$

$$D_{\text{cork}} = \frac{m}{V} = \frac{0.24 \text{ g}}{\text{cm}^3}$$

1.7 Three phases of matter

We call a block of ice a solid. It may melt and form a liquid. As it evaporates, liquid water changes into a vapor or gas. Iron, too, is a solid but it may be melted and converted into a liquid. When iron is boiled it forms iron vapor. Materials exist either in the *solid, liquid,* or *gaseous* phase (or state) and may undergo a change from one phase to another under suitable conditions.

A block of wood placed on a table keeps its shape and its volume. To change its shape or its volume you would have to use considerable external force on the block. A solid does not need lateral (side) support to prevent it from losing its shape. *Solids have both a definite volume and a definite shape.*

Suppose we pour water onto the top of a table. It flows out over the surface because liquids are not rigid. To hold the water, we must provide it with lateral (side) support. If we try to pour a quart of milk into a pint bottle, we observe that a liquid has a definite volume. Therefore, we conclude that **liquids** have a definite volume, and that they take the shape of their containers.

If we inflate an automobile tire, we find that the air takes the shape of the tire, which is its container. The tire is really full of air, but if a blow-out occurs, the escaping air expands in volume. A pint of liquid does not expand and form a quart if it is put into a quart bottle. However, a pint of air would expand and occupy all the space if it were placed in a really empty quart bottle. *Gases have neither a definite volume nor a definite shape*. This behavior makes it difficult to measure the volume of gases. If they are heated they expand, but their volume is reduced when the pressure on them is increased. In measuring gas volumes, we must specify *both the temperature and the pressure* of the gas.

Both liquids and gases are known as **fluids**. Liquid and gaseous materials flow readily and require vessels to contain them. We think of solids as being rigid, yet none is perfectly rigid. Given two different solids of the same size and shape, one is likely to be more flexible (less rigid) than the other. Similarly, there are no perfectly fluid materials. Molasses, water, and carbon dioxide all may flow, but certainly at different rates.

Because liquids have a definite volume, they may have a free surface, that is, a surface not confined by the container. Thus water may be contained in an open vessel. The free (upper) surface of a liquid lies in a plane perpendicular to the force acting on it. In the normal case of a liquid at rest, this force is gravity and the free surface of the liquid lies in the horizontal plane. For ordinary purposes, matter in the gaseous phase must be confined on all sides by a container. Gases are fluids which do not have a free surface.

Fluids which cannot exist as liquids having a free surface at ordinary conditions of temperature and pressure are correctly termed *gases*. **Vapor** is the term used for the gaseous phase of materials which normally exist as liquids or solids. Thus we speak of water *vapor* and oxygen *gas*.

The particles of a solid are usually arranged in a regular pattern. They are closely packed and are rigidly held in fixed positions. This structure gives a solid its definite size and shape.

The particles of a liquid are also closely packed (when a solid melts, its volume changes very little). The particles of a liquid, however, are not bound in fixed positions. A liquid has fluidity; its structure is less orderly than that of a solid and is without shape.

The particles of a gas are widely dispersed (separated) in a random, disorganized fashion. On the average, the attraction between such particles is so small that it can be disregarded.

Gas, liquid, and solid are often referred to as the three "states" of matter. In chemistry, however, the meaning of "state" is more definite than this reference implies. A system is in a given state only as long as the conditions which define that state remain constant. Thus a gas can exist in different states as a gas. A "phase" is a homogeneous part of a system which is separated from other homogeneous parts by boundary faces. Ice in water represents a two-phase system, a solid phase and a liquid phase.

Fig. 1-7. Water is shown in the solid and the liquid phase. The compound carbon dioxide and the element mercury are shown in the solid phase. How would each of these substances appear in some other phase?

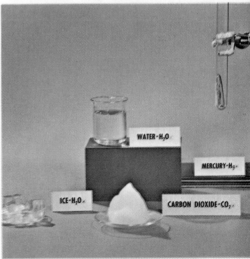

From CHEM Study Film, *Molecular Motions*

1.8   Properties of matter

We identify matter and determine its usefulness by studying its properties. Many liquids, including water, are colorless. Some colorless liquids have distinctive odors; water is odorless. Water freezes at 0° Celsius (also called Centigrade) and boils at 100° Celsius (at standard pressure). It has a density of 1 gram per cubic centimeter at 4° Celsius. Since no other liquid exhibits exactly these properties, we can use them to identify liquid water. *Properties of matter which are useful in identifying it, are called* **specific** *(or characteristic)* **properties.** The most useful specific properties are those that lend themselves to quantitative measurements and can be expressed as a number of measurement units.

The specific properties of materials can be organized under two general headings: *physical* and *chemical.* Physical properties include *color, odor, solubility, density, hardness, melting* and *boiling points,* and *crystalline* or *amorphous* (non-crystalline) *forms.* These physical properties do not apply equally to all phases of matter. For example, hardness and crystalline form are not properties of fluids. Similarly, odor is of little value in describing many solids. **Physical properties** *are those which can be determined without causing a change in the identity of a material.*

Chemical properties include *chemical activity,* or behavior with other materials. Some materials are *active,* reacting vigorously with others. Some other materials are *inactive.* These inactive materials do react, but not very readily with others. Still other materials, said to be *inert,* do not react under ordinary conditions of chemical reactions. In our study of chemical properties, we shall want to know whether a material burns. We shall also want to know how it reacts with air, with water, with acids, and with alkalies. **Chemical properties** *are those which describe the behavior of a material in reactions that alter its identity.*

1.9   Concept of energy

We have the same difficulty in defining energy as we did in defining matter. Scientists know a great deal about energy and how it may be used, but they cannot define it precisely. **Energy is** *usually defined as the capacity for doing work.* It is associated with matter, but is not a form of matter. We have no knowledge of matter which does not possess energy.

1.10   Forms of energy

The most common forms of energy are *mechanical energy* and *heat energy.* Mechanical energy may be of two types: **potential energy** or the *energy of position,* and **kinetic energy** or the *energy*

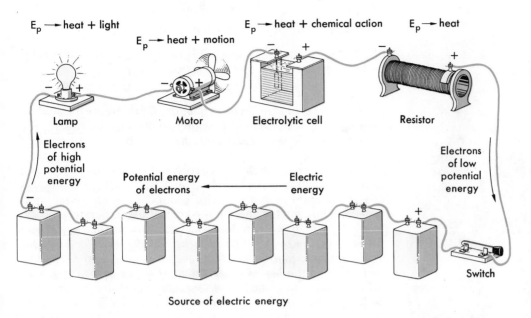

$E_p \rightarrow$ heat + light $E_p \rightarrow$ heat + motion $E_p \rightarrow$ heat + chemical action $E_p \rightarrow$ heat

Lamp Motor Electrolytic cell Resistor

Electrons of high potential energy

Electrons of low potential energy

Potential energy of electrons ← Electric energy

Source of electric energy

Switch

Fig. 1-8. Energy transformation.

of motion. Water held behind a dam has potential energy because of its elevated position. As the water is released from the dam it acquires kinetic energy because of its motion. Heat energy is released when fuels are burned. Practically all industrial power is provided by the heat energy from burning fuel or the kinetic energy of falling water.

Other forms of energy are *electric energy, chemical energy, radiant energy,* and *nuclear energy.* Chemical energy is a basic concern of chemistry. Radio waves, infrared and ultraviolet radiations, visible light, X rays, and gamma rays are examples of radiant energy. Nuclear energy is being developed as a source of electric power.

We may convert or *transform* one form of energy into another. As an example, coal is burned to supply energy. Some of the chemical energy of the coal and the oxygen of the air is released as heat energy during the combustion. The heat energy is transferred to water and it is converted to steam. The steam then drives a turbine producing mechanical energy. The turbine turns a generator which produces electric energy. We can transform this electric energy into heat and radiant (light) energy in an incandescent lamp or carbon arc. Or we can transform it into mechanical energy in an electric motor which drives a clock or a locomotive. It is the *transformation* of energy that is usually observed. We measure the energy change during an energy transformation.

1.11 Conservation of matter and energy

In 1905, Albert Einstein (1879–1955) suggested that matter and energy are related. His famous equation

$$E = mc^2$$

shows this relationship. In this equation, E represents the amount of energy and m the amount of matter; c is a constant equal to the speed of light. Many experiments have established the truth of this relationship.

Matter can be converted to energy and energy to matter. The conversion factor, c^2, is involved in both transformations. Indeed, the amount of matter is changed if the amount of energy is changed. Thus matter and energy are not two different physical quantities, which we can define independently. Instead, *matter and energy may be considered to be two different forms of the same physical quantity.* The facts are formulated into a scientific law known as the ***law of conservation of matter and energy.*** This law may be stated formally: *matter and energy are interchangeable; the total matter and energy in the universe is constant.*

Chemical reactions are always accompanied by an energy change. Either energy is released or it is acquired. Only in nuclear reactions involving a tremendous quantity of energy, such as the explosion of a hydrogen bomb, does the amount of matter transformed into energy become significant. Ordinary chemical reactions involve such small matter changes that they go undetected. For all ordinary purposes such matter losses may be ignored. Thus we recognize the following generalization: *in an ordinary chemical change, the total mass of the reacting materials is equal to the total mass of the products.* It follows that, in such changes, *energy is conserved.*

U.S. Atomic Energy Commission

Fig. 1-9. The law of conservation of matter and energy is demonstrated in the explosion of this nuclear device.

MEASUREMENTS IN CHEMISTRY

1.12 Metric system

The study of science could not be precise without a suitable system of measurement. The English system, which we use in our daily activities, presents many·disadvantages in scientific measurements. It is a system which, in a sense, just grew up. Its chief disadvantage is that there are no simple numerical relationships between the different units.

The *metric system,* with which you may already be familiar, was developed in France near the end of the eighteenth century. It is used in scientific work throughout the world. It is also in general use in practically all countries except the United States,

National Bureau of Standards

Fig. 1-10. The new home of the National Bureau of Standards at Gaithersburg, Maryland. A prime concern of the bureau is the development of measurement standards and techniques.

Great Britain, and other English-speaking countries. Great Britain has started a long-range program for conversion to metric measurements. Certain industries in the United States have adopted the metric system. Our National Bureau of Standards recommended to the Congress a program for the gradual conversion to metric measurements in the United States. At the time of this writing, the Congress is preparing legislation for a 10-year voluntary conversion program.

The metric system is a decimal system that has simple numerical relationships between units. The disadvantage in its everyday usage is that the basic units do not have the practical size of English-system units. Also, metric units do not lend themselves to the convenient custom of dividing into halves and quarters.

1.13 Units of the metric system

The metric system provides units for measuring many physical quantities. In chemistry we measure chiefly **length, capacity,** and **mass.** The basic unit of length is the *meter* (m), of capacity is the *liter* (liter), and of mass is the *gram* (g). Prefixes are used with basic units to complete the system. Latin prefixes are employed to identify *descending* multiple values. Examples are *deci-* (0.1), *centi-* (0.01), and *milli-* (0.001). Greek prefixes are used to identify *ascending* multiple values. Examples are *deka-* (10), *hecto-* (100), and *kilo-* (1000). Common prefixes are shown in Table 1-1 together with their symbols.

You will use the relationships shown in the brief table of metric equivalents, Table 1-2, throughout your study of chemistry. It will be helpful to memorize them. Observe that the liter is always spelled out when used as an uncombined unit.

As originally conceived, the metric system was based on natural standards with the meter as the fundamental unit. The originators of the metric system intended that the meter should be one ten-millionth of the distance from the North Pole to the Equator along the line of longitude passing through Paris. However, they found later that they could compare two meter bars more precisely than they could relate a meter bar to the distance

Table 1-1

COMMON PREFIXES OF THE METRIC SYSTEM

Factor	Prefix	Symbol
10^6	mega	M
10^3	kilo	k
10^2	hecto	h
10	deka	da
10^{-1}	deci	d
10^{-2}	centi	c
10^{-3}	milli	m
10^{-6}	micro	μ (mu)

Table 1-2

COMMON METRIC EQUIVALENTS

Length

10 millimeters (mm)	= 1 centimeter (cm)
100 centimeters	= 1 meter (m)
1000 meters	= 1 kilometer (km)

Capacity

1000 milliliters (ml)	= 1 liter
1000 liters	= 1 kiloliter (kl)

Mass

1000 milligrams (mg)	= 1 gram (g)
1000 grams	= 1 kilogram (kg)

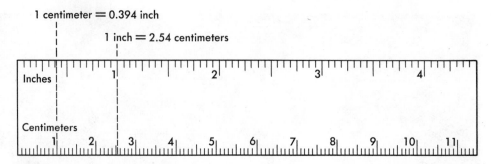

1 centimeter = 0.394 inch

1 inch = 2.54 centimeters

Fig. 1-11. The centimeter is nearly 0.4 of an inch in length. One inch equals 2.54 centimeters.

Fig. 1-12. These are some comparisons between the English and metric systems. The liter is slightly larger than the U.S. liquid quart, and the kilogram is more than twice as heavy as the avoirdupois pound.

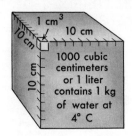

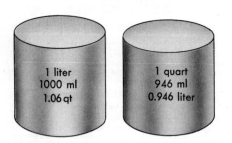

from the North Pole to the Equator. Accordingly, *the standard meter is the distance between two parallel lines engraved on a special metal bar preserved at the International Bureau of Weights and Measures near Paris.*

The standard-meter bar is a physical instrument. If it should be damaged, lost, or destroyed, there would be no primary standard of this fundamental metric unit. Accordingly, the International Conference on Weights and Measures has defined a *nondestructible* standard meter. Any laboratory that has the proper equipment can reproduce this meter as a primary standard. By this new definition, the meter is described in terms of the orange-red spectral line of light given off by excited atoms of an isotope of krypton (krypton-86). The meter is 1,650,763.73 times the wavelength of this line. One meter (m) is slightly longer than the English yard, being equal to 39.37 inches or 3.28 feet. One inch equals exactly 2.54 centimeters (cm), by definition.

One gram (g) was intended to be the mass of 1 cubic centimeter (cm^3) of water at 4° Celsius, the temperature at which it is most dense. Again scientists found it more precise to compare the masses of two metal kilogram cylinders than to compare a cylinder with the mass of 1000 cubic centimeters of water. *The gram is now defined as one thousandth of the mass of the standard kilogram resting in the International Bureau of Weights and Measures.*

The liter is a special name for a cubic decimeter. A cubic decimeter (dm^3) is equal to 1000 cubic centimeters (cm^3). Therefore, a container having a capacity of 1 liter holds 1000 cm^3 of liquid when full. One milliliter (1 ml) is then equivalent to one cubic centimeter (1 cm^3).

$$1 \text{ liter} = 1 \text{ dm}^3$$
$$1 \text{ ml} = 1 \text{ cm}^3$$

Because the volumes of liquids and gases are commonly measured in flasks and other containers graduated in capacity units, their measured volumes are most conveniently expressed in milli-

---

Table 1-3.
VOLUME-MASS RELATIONS FOR WATER

---

1 liter of water has 1000 cm³ volume and a mass of 1 kg
1 ml of water has 1 cm³ volume and a mass of 1 g

---

liter, liter, and kiloliter (capacity) units. This practice is standard in chemistry and will be followed in this book. Because water is a universal standard, the remarkable simplicity of the metric system can be seen in Table 1-3.

Density is a measurable property of matter which we can employ to illustrate the use of metric units. It has been defined in Section 1.6 as the *mass per unit volume* of a material. If mass is measured in *gram* units and volume in *cubic centimeter* units, density is expressed in *grams per cubic centimeter* (g/cm³).

Suppose the mass of 10.0 cubic centimeters of iron is determined to be 78.7 grams and the mass of the same volume of mercury (a *liquid* metal) is found to be 136 grams. Their densities are

$$D_{\text{iron}} = \frac{m}{V} = \frac{78.7 \text{ g}}{10.0 \text{ cm}^3} = \frac{7.87 \text{ g}}{\text{cm}^3}$$

$$D_{\text{mercury}} = \frac{m}{V} = \frac{136 \text{ g}}{10.0 \text{ cm}^3} = \frac{13.6 \text{ g}}{\text{cm}^3}$$

Matter in the gaseous phase has a very low density compared to solids and liquids. Consequently, in the case of gases, expressions of density in grams per cubic centimeter involve inconveniently small numbers. Chemists prefer to state the densities of gases in *grams per liter*. For example, under standard conditions of temperature and pressure, oxygen gas has a density of 1.43 g/liter and air (a mixture of gases) has an average density of 1.29 g/liter.

$$D_{\text{oxygen}} = \frac{m}{V} = \frac{1.43 \text{ g}}{\text{liter}}$$

$$D_{\text{air}} = \frac{m}{V} = \frac{1.29 \text{ g}}{\text{liter}}$$

The unit structure of a measured quantity indicates its *dimensions*. Thus, density has the dimensions "g/cm³" when expressed as a property of a solid or liquid. It has the dimensions "g/liter" when expressed as a property of a gas.

1.14 Temperature and heat

Temperature and heat are different, but related, physical quantities. It is important to understand the subtle distinction between them. Just as we may push an object to estimate its mass or lift it to estimate its weight, we may touch an object to determine its *hotness* or *coldness*. We then describe the sensation with a term

---

Table 1-4
METRIC-ENGLISH EQUIVALENTS

Metric to English

---

1 cm = 0.3937 in = 3.281 X 10^{-2} ft
1 m = 39.37 in = 3.218 ft = 1.094 yd
1 cm³ = 0.0610 in³ = 3.53 X 10^{-5} ft³
1 liter = 1.06 qt = 3.53 X 10^{-2} ft³

English to Metric

---

1 in = 2.54 cm = 2.54 X 10^{-2} m
1 ft = 30.5 cm = 0.305 m
1 yd = 91.4 cm = 0.914 m
1 qt = 946 ml = 0.946 liter

such as hot, warm, cool, or cold. Thus our sense perceptions of hotness and coldness are used to assign a property called *temperature* to the object.

Our temperature sense, while generally useful, may be unreliable under some conditions. If you place one hand in cold water and then in cool water, the cool water feels warm. If your hand had been in hot water first, however, the cool water would feel cold.

This experiment suggests that the temperature sensation depends on the transfer of heat energy to the hand or away from it. If a system, a body of matter, has a higher temperature than its surroundings, energy flows away from the system. If the temperature of the system is lower than its surroundings, energy flows to the system. This energy, *while in transit,* is called *heat.* **Heat** *is the energy transferred between two systems that is associated exclusively with the difference in temperature between the systems. The* **temperature** *of a system is a measure of its ability to transfer heat to, or acquire heat from, other systems.*

When two systems with different temperatures are in contact, heat energy flows from one to the other. *Temperature* is the property that determines the direction of the heat transfer. The warmer system cools as it gives up heat and the cooler system warms as it acquires heat (as long as neither system experiences a change of phase). When the temperatures of the two systems become equal, no further transfer of heat occurs. The two systems are now said to be in *thermal (heat) equilibrium.* It follows that *systems in thermal equilibrium have the same temperature.*

Heat and temperature are different physical quantities that can be sensed qualitatively. However, to determine them quantitatively we must perform operations which involve measurable quantities and are independent of our sense perceptions. Heat is measured as a *quantity of energy,* whereas temperature indicates the *heat intensity* of a body of matter. A burning match and a camp fire might be at the same *temperature* but the quantities of *heat* given off are quite different.

1.15 Measuring temperature

A number of properties of matter vary with temperature and can be used to measure temperature. For example, most materials expand when they are warmed and contract when cooled. Our most familiar temperature-measuring instrument is the mercury thermometer. It is based on the nearly linear expansion and contraction of liquid mercury with changing temperature.

Mercury thermometers for scientific use are commonly marked with the Celsius temperature scale. This scale was devised by a Swedish astronomer, Anders Celsius (1701-1744). He established his thermometer scale by defining two *fixed points* and dividing the interval between them into 100 equal parts or *degrees.*

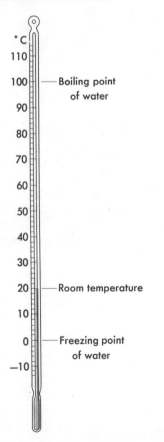

Fig. 1-13. The Celsius thermometer is widely used in scientific work. Compare the temperatures shown here with those on the common Fahrenheit thermometer.

Celsius selected the normal freezing point of water as the lower fixed point and marked it **0 degrees** (0° C). He used the normal boiling point of water as the upper fixed point and marked it **100 degrees** (100° C). By extending the same scale divisions beyond the two fixed points, he could measure temperatures below 0° and above 100°. See Figure 1-13.

In modern temperature measurements, one standard fixed point is defined for establishing an *absolute* (thermodynamic) temperature scale. We will discuss the construction of an absolute temperature scale from the standard fixed point in our study of gases in Chapter 9.

1.16 Measuring heat

When heat is transferred to a material, the temperature of the material rises (as long as its phase does not change). If heat is given up by the material, its temperature falls. We measure quantities of heat to determine various *thermal* properties of matter. Among these properties are heat capacity, heat of fusion, heat of vaporization, heat of combustion, heat of reaction, heat of formation, and heat of solution. The measurement of thermal properties is called *calorimetry.*

The unit of heat energy commonly used by chemists to measure a quantity of heat is the *calorie.* It is defined rigorously in terms of a unit of work. For our purposes, *the **calorie** (cal) is the quantity of heat required to raise the temperature of 1 gram of water through 1 Celsius degree.*

This calorie is a very small unit of heat and is sometimes inconvenient to use. A larger unit, the *kilocalorie,* is often used in chemistry. *The **kilocalorie** (kcal) is the quantity of heat required to raise the temperature of 1 kilogram of water through 1 Celsius degree.*

$$1 \text{ kcal} = 10^3 \text{ cal}$$

The kilocalorie is the large Calorie used in nutritional studies to measure the energy value of foods.

1.17 Uncertainty in measurements

Chemistry is an experimental science. The measurement of numerous physical quantities such as length, mass, volume, and temperature is vital to the experimental process. Unfortunately, *the measurement of any physical quantity is subject to some uncertainty.* If a measurement is to have any worth, we must have some idea regarding its *reliability.* Consequently, the complete expression of a measured quantity must include the number, the unit, and some indication of how reliable the number is.

Contributions to uncertainty occur in two ways. There are limitations in the *accuracy* of any measurement. There are also limitations in the *precision* of any measurement. These two terms, *accuracy* and *precision,* have distinctly different meanings with regard to measurement. If you wish to become competent in making measurements or in interpreting measurement data, you must understand this distinction.

Accuracy means the nearness of a measurement to its accepted value. It refers to the correctness of measurement data. Accuracy is expressed in terms of *error*. Errors may be *absolute* **or** *relative*.

An *absolute error* can be expressed by

$$E_a = O - A$$

where the absolute error E_a is the difference between the observed value O and the accepted value A. In quantitative laboratory experiments we shall refer to absolute errors as *experimental errors*.

Suppose you are asked to decompose a 10.00-gram sample of potassium chlorate in a laboratory experiment and determine the mass of oxygen in the sample. From your experiment, you find that the sample contains 3.80 g of oxygen. The actual mass of oxygen in this quantity of potassium chlorate is 3.92 g. Thus, 3.80 g is your *observed* value whereas 3.92 g is the *accepted* value. Your experimental (absolute) error is

$$E_a = O - A = 3.80 \text{ g} - 3.92 \text{ g} = -0.12 \text{ g}$$

The negative sign merely indicates that your experimental result is lower than the accepted value.

Observe that the dimensions of absolute errors are those of the observed and accepted values. If O and A are expressed in grams, degrees Celsius, or milliliters, the E_a has grams, Celsius degrees, or milliliters as its dimension.

Relative error is generally a more useful quantity than absolute error. Relative error is the ratio of an absolute error to the accepted value. It is expressed as a percentage. In laboratory experiments, relative errors are referred to as *percentage errors*. The relative error E_r is calculated as follows:

$$E_r = \frac{E_a}{A} \times 100\%$$

Consider again the data from which we determined the absolute error. The percentage (relative) error is

$$E_r = \frac{E_a}{A} \times 100\% = \frac{-0.12 \text{ g}}{3.92 \text{ g}} \times 100\% = -3.2\%$$

As in the case of absolute errors, the sign of the relative error merely indicates whether the result is low or high.

Observe that the true or accepted value of a measured quantity is used to determine both the absolute error and the relative error. Thus, we can determine the accuracy of a measurement *only* if the accepted value of that measurement is available.

Precision *is the agreement between the numerical values of two or more measurements that have been made in the same way.* Precision refers to the reproducibility of measurement data or to the degree of detail. That is, precision is related to the $\pm$ uncertainty involved. It conveys nothing about accuracy. Precision is expressed in terms of *deviation*. We will consider two simple forms of deviation, *absolute* and *relative*.

An *absolute deviation* D_a is the difference between an observed value O and the arithmetic mean (average) M for the set of several measurements made in the same way.

$$D_a = O - M$$

Consider an experiment similar to the one described previously. Suppose three identical samples of potassium chlorate are decomposed. The mass of oxygen is determined to be 3.87 g, 3.95 g, and 3.89 g for the set. Assuming that there is an equal chance for the individual values to be high and low, we will take the average for the set as the "best" value. This is found to be 3.90 g.

The deviations of the individual values *from this average* can be calculated from the expression for D_a given above. The average of these deviations provides us with a measure of the precision of the experiment. These results are presented in Table 1-5. The uncertainty in the measurements data is ± 0.03 g. The mass of oxygen derived from the set of experimental data can be expressed as 3.90 ± 0.03 g.

Table 1–5 AVERAGE DEVIATION OF A SET OF MEASUREMENTS		
Sample	*Mass of oxygen*	*Deviation*
1	3.87 g	0.03 g
2	3.95 g	0.05 g
3	3.89 g	0.01 g
Average	3.90 g	0.03 g

Ohaus Scale Corp.

Fig. 1-14. A laboratory balance with 10-milligram sensitivity.

Table 1–6
TYPICAL UNCERTAINTIES

Instrument	Uncertainty
platform balance	±0.1 g
centigram balance	±0.01 g
50 ml buret	±0.10 ml
50 ml gas measuring tube	±0.10 ml
10 ml graduated cylinder	±0.1 ml
50 ml graduated cylinder	±0.4 ml
5 ml pipet	±0.01 ml
50 ml pipet	±0.02 ml
15 cm ruler (grad. in mm)	±0.01 cm
–1 to 101°C thermometer	±0.1 C°
100 ml volumetric flask	±0.08 ml
250 ml volumetric flask	±0.12 ml
1000 ml volumetric flask	±0.30 ml

A *relative deviation* D_r may also be used to express the precision of the set of experimental data. This is calculated as a *percentage average deviation* based on the average value M for the set.

$$D_r = \frac{D_{a(av)}}{M} \times 100\%$$

$$D_r = \frac{0.03 \text{ g}}{3.90 \text{ g}} \times 100\% = 0.8\%$$

The uncertainty can now be expressed as ±0.8% and the mass of oxygen may be recorded as 3.90 g ±0.8%. Uncertainties in measured quantities of different magnitudes can be compared more clearly when expressed as relative rather than absolute deviations.

If several different measurements are combined to yield a final result, the manner in which the individual deviations affect the result depends on the nature of the computation. When measured quantities are added or subtracted, the uncertainty in the result is the sum of the *absolute* deviations of the individual measurements. In multiplication and division, the uncertainty in the result is the sum of the *relative* deviations of the individual measurements.

The reproducibility of a measurement does not ordinarily exceed the *tolerance* of the instrument used. The tolerance of a measuring instrument is the limit of deviation from a standard permitted in the scale markings of the instrument. Known tolerances of laboratory instruments indicate the precision that can be obtained with these instruments. A list of common laboratory instruments is given in Table 1-6. Typical tolerances are shown as ± uncertainties.

1.18   Significant figures

Suppose the mass of a sample is measured on a platform balance as 25.2 g. The balance is precise to the nearest 0.1 g. We can show the precision of the measurement by recording the mass as 25.2 ± 0.1 g. The deviation of ±0.1 g indicates the amount of uncertainty in the first decimal place of the measurement. The digits to the left of the decimal point are certain.

As a matter of convenience, the ±0.1 is often omitted *with the understanding* that there is uncertainty in the *last digit* of the measurement. The recorded value, 25.2 g, then consists entirely of figures that have physical significance—that is, *significant figures*. **Significant figures** *in a number comprise all digits known with certainty plus the first digit that is uncertain.* The position of the decimal point is irrelevant.

The use of significant figures provides us with a third way to indicate the precision of a measurement. Because the amount of uncertainty in the last digit is not specified, this method is less informative than our previous methods. However, the method of significant figures is very convenient and is widely used. It is satisfactory for our purposes in chemistry and is the method we shall use.

If we lack qualifying information about a measuring instrument, such as its tolerance, we may assume that the last digit (the uncertain digit) of a measurement is known to within plus or minus one unit.. For example, the value for π expressed to three significant figures is *3.14*. The digit in the second decimal place is uncertain. We recognize that the true value lies somewhere between *3.13* and *3.15*.

We have seen how the precision of the average value for a set of measurements can be expressed in terms of average deviation (Section 1.17). The average deviation also reveals the number of digits we may include in the average value of the set when its precision is indicated by the method of significant figures.

To illustrate this, assume that a set of measurements includes the following individual values: 36.64 g, 36.55 g, 36.62 g, and 36.41 g. The average for the set appears to be 36.555 g. The average deviation of the individual values from this mean value is ±0.075 g. Clearly, the digit in the second decimal place of the mean is subject to uncertainty. If we are uncertain about the value in the second decimal place, we can have no notion whatsoever about values in succeeding decimal places. Therefore, we are forced to round off the average value to the second decimal place. Will this be 36.55 g or 36.56 g? A good rule to follow when the number you are dropping is *exactly* 5 is: *always round to the nearest even number*. Thus 36.56 g is the "best" value for the set. The last digit has uncertainty and limits the precision of the value to four significant figures.

Suppose you wish to determine the volume of a metal block. Your measuring instrument is a meter stick having 1-millimeter (mm) divisions. You find the sides to be 3.54 cm, 4.85 cm, and 5.42 cm, estimating the value of the last digit in each case. You may be reasonably sure of these measurements. However, you can have no idea of the digit which should occupy the next decimal place. Each measurement thus consists of two *certain figures* and one *doubtful figure,* or three *significant figures.* The area of one surface is

$$3.54 \times 4.85 \text{ cm} = 17.\mathbf{1690} \text{ cm}^2$$

We recognize that the product of anything multiplied by a doubtful figure is also doubtful. Also, only one such figure may be carried. Therefore, the result is rounded to 17.2 cm².

The volume of the block then becomes

$$17.\mathbf{2} \text{ cm}^2 \times 5.42 \text{ cm} = 93.\mathbf{224} \text{ cm}^3$$

Again the result is properly expressed as 93.2 cm³, the volume of the metal block. Had all of the doubtful figures been retained

Mettler Instrument Corp.

Fig. 1-15. A modern analytical balance which provides high precision and rapid readout. Its sensitivity may be 0.0001 gram.

throughout the computation, the volume would be expressed as 93.**055980** cm³. Obviously this precision, millionths of a cubic centimeter, cannot be obtained with a meter stick graduated in tenths of a centimeter. *Merely assuming more decimal places does not improve the accuracy or the precision of the measurement.*

In the measurements and computations given, the number of significant figures is easily recognized because all figures used are nonzero digits. It is not so easy to determine when the zeros in an expression are significant. For example, the mean distance to the moon is known to six significant figures to be 238,856 miles. This distance is more commonly expressed as 239,000 miles and is precise to *three* significant figures. The three zeros which follow the 9 merely serve to locate the (understood) decimal point. Similarly, a measured length of 0.00531 cm is precise to *three* significant figures, the zeros being used to locate the decimal point. However, the measurements 104.06 m (meters) and 100.60 m contain *five* significant figures. The question naturally arises: when are zeros significant?

Of course, the person who reads an instrument while making a measurement knows whether a zero appearing in his expression is significant. He must, however, follow accepted rules concerning significant figures if he is to communicate the information properly to others. To avoid difficulties of communication where zeros are included in the expression of a measured quantity, the following rules for determining the number of significant figures have been established. They will be used throughout this book:

*1. All nonzero digits **are** significant;* 127.34 g contains *five* significant figures.

*2. All zeros between two nonzero digits **are** significant;* 120.007 m contains *six* significant figures.

3. Zeros to the right of a nonzero digit, but to the left of an understood decimal point, are not significant unless specifically indicated to be significant. The rightmost such zero which is significant is indicated by a bar placed above it: 109,000 km contains *three* significant figures; 109,0$\overline{0}$0 km contains *five* significant figures.

*4. All zeros to the right of a decimal point but to the left of a nonzero digit **are not** significant:* 0.00476 kg contains *three* significant figures. (The single zero conventionally placed to the left of the decimal point in such an expression is never significant.)

*5. All zeros to the right of a decimal point and to the right of a nonzero digit **are** significant:* 0.04060 cm and 30.00 mg (milligrams) contain *four* significant figures.

Uncertainty is present in any experimental procedure. Accuracy of a measurement can be determined only if true or accepted values of the measurement are known. However, precision can always be expressed by the proper use of significant figures. Judgment based on precision alone must be considered with caution.

1.19   Exponential notation

In science we often encounter numbers which are extremely large or exceedingly small. The speed of light is approximately 30,000,000,000 centimeters per second. The speed of light in a vacuum, generally accepted as accurate to *seven* significant figures, is 29,979,250,000 cm/sec. The mass of the earth is about 6,000,000,000,000,000,000,000,000,000 grams. The mass of an electron is 0.000,000,000,000,000,000,000,000,000,910,96 gram. The wavelength of yellow light is about 0.000059 cm. These numbers have little meaning in the ordinary sense. To save having to write many zeros, we can express such numbers as powers of 10. This *exponential notation* has the form

$$M \times 10^n$$

where M is a number having one digit to the left of the decimal point and n is a positive or negative whole number.

We may write the unusual quantities already given in exponential form as shown in Table 1-7.

To change a number into exponential notation form:

1. Determine M by moving the decimal point so that you leave only one nonzero digit to the left of it.

2. Determine n by counting the number of places you have moved the decimal point; if moved to the left, n is positive; if to the right, n is negative. The laws of exponents apply in computations involving numbers expressed in exponential form. You will see examples of computations in which the laws of exponents are used in Section 1.20.

When a measurement is written in the form $M \times 10^n$ all digits, zero and nonzero, expressed in M *are significant.* This fact enables us to tell at a glance the number of significant figures in the indicated measurement.

We can express the distance from the earth to the sun, 93,005,000 mi, in ordinary notation to three significant figures as 93,$\overline{0}$00,000 mi. Using the exponential notation, however, we can express this distance to three significant figures more clearly and simply as 9.30×10^7 mi.

Table 1-7
NUMBERS IN EXPONENTIAL-NOTATION FORM

$$30,000,000,000 \text{ cm/sec} = 3 \times 10^{10} \text{ cm/sec}$$
$$29,979,250,000 \text{ cm/sec} = 2.997925 \times 10^{10} \text{ cm/sec}$$
$$6,000,000,000,000,000,000,000,000,000 \text{ g} = 6 \times 10^{27} \text{ g}$$
$$0.000,000,000,000,000,000,000,000,000,910,96 \text{ g} = 9.1096 \times 10^{-28} \text{ g}$$
$$0.000059 \text{ cm} = 5.9 \times 10^{-5} \text{ cm}$$
$$100\overline{0} \text{ ml} = 1.000 \times 10^3 \text{ ml}$$
$$1000 \text{ ml} = 1 \times 10^3 \text{ ml}$$
$$10\overline{0}0 \text{ ml} = 1.00 \times 10^3 \text{ ml}$$

1.20 Operations with significant figures

The results of mathematical operations involving laboratory measurements can be no more precise than the measurements themselves. Accordingly, certain precautions must be observed when performing calculations. The precautions are necessary to avoid implying greater precision in the results than was originally obtained in the measurements. The following rules are practical for most purposes. They should be adopted where the context does not indicate otherwise.

1. Addition and subtraction. Recall that the rightmost significant figure in a measurement is uncertain. Therefore, *the rightmost significant figure in a sum or difference occurs in the leftmost place at which the doubtful figure occurs in any of the measurements involved.* The example of an addition which follows will help you to visualize this rule.

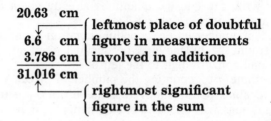

The sum 31.016 cm should then be recorded as 31.0 cm, the best expression for the answer to this addition problem.

For another example, suppose the leftmost place where a doubtful figure occurs is in the hundredths place (second place to the right of the decimal point). The sum or difference, therefore, should be rounded to the nearest hundredth. When working with numbers expressed in exponential notation, all terms must be converted to the same power of ten before adding or subtracting.

2. Multiplication and division. Three points discussed in Section 1.18 must be remembered in operations involving multiplication and division: (*a*) The rightmost significant figure in a measurement is uncertain. (*b*) The product of any number multiplied by a doubtful digit is also uncertain. (*c*) Only one doubtful digit is retained in the result. Therefore, *the product or quotient is precise to the number of significant figures contained in the least precise factor.* The result in either operation is rounded to the same number of significant figures contained in the factor having the least number of significant figures.

In multiplication or division operations with numbers expressed in exponential form, the *M* portions are handled as described above. Keep in mind that *all* digits are significant. The laws of exponents govern the multiplication and division of the 10^n terms. In multiplication, the exponents are added:

$$10^3 \times 10^4 = 10^7$$
$$10^6 \times 10^{-2} = 10^4$$
$$10^4 \times 10^{-6} = 10^{-2}$$

In division, change the sign of the exponent of the divisor and add exponents.

$$10^3 \div 10^2 = 10^1$$
$$10^4 \div 10^{-3} = 10^7$$
$$10^{-5} \div 10^2 = 10^{-7}$$

Number expressions that are not measurements should not be interpreted as having limited accuracy. When such numbers are included in a computation with measurements, they have no influence on the number of significant figures in the result. As an example, the freezing point of water is *defined* as 0° C. It is exactly zero. It could be written with as many zero digits to the right of the decimal point as desired. A thermometer *reading,* of course, is a measurement. As such, it has limited precision and is recorded with the number of significant figures the instrument is capable of yielding. Similarly, a triangle has *exactly* three sides. Suppose one side of an equilateral triangle is measured to a precision of four significant figures. If it is then multiplied by the number of sides, the number of significant figures in the product remains the same as that of the original measurement.

1.21 Operations with units

Measurements are always expressed as a significant number of some kind of units: 12.5 g, 6.7 cm, 10.0 sec, 42.1° C, 0.09 g/liter, etc. Both the number and the unit are essential parts of the expression since the choice of unit affects the magnitude of the number. A measurement determined to three significant figures to be 1.30 m could be written as $13\bar{0}$ cm.

$$1.30 \text{ m} \times \frac{100 \text{ cm}}{\text{m}} = 13\bar{0} \text{ cm}$$

Observe that the expression 100 cm/m is arrived at by definition, not by measurement. Thus, it is exactly 100 cm per meter and it does not affect the significance of the measurement. A measurement determined to two significant figures to be 1.3 m would be written as 130 cm when converted to the centimeter unit.

$$1.3 \text{ m} \times \frac{100 \text{ cm}}{\text{m}} = 130 \text{ cm}$$

Thus, 1.30 m is equivalent to $13\bar{0}$ cm and 1.3 m is equivalent to 130 cm. Similarly, 130.0 cm is equivalent to 1.300 m.

$$130.0 \text{ cm} \times \frac{\text{m}}{100 \text{ cm}} = 1.300 \text{ m}$$

Because there are many different units and because the expression of a physical measurement requires *both* a number and a unit, *always* write the unit with the number to which it belongs. Usually the "cancellation" of units in an expression leads directly to the proper unit for the answer. The technique of unit cancellation is referred to as *dimensional analysis*. This method of writing and solving expressions, illustrated in the following sample problems, is used in problem work in this book.

Sample Problem

A chemistry student was required to determine the density of an irregularly shaped sample of lead. He first weighed it on a balance sensitive to 0.01 g and found its mass to be 49.33 g. He then immersed the lead in water contained in a cylinder graduated in one-tenth millimeter divisions and observed that it displaced 4.35 ml of water (the 0.05 ml being estimated).

Solution

The student recalled from his study of general science that a body immersed in a liquid displaces its own volume. Since the volume of a solid is normally expressed in cubic measure, he used the equivalency of the milliliter and the cubic centimeter to convert the volume to cubic centimeters.

By definition:

$$1 \text{ cm}^3 = 1 \text{ ml}$$

$$4.35 \text{ ml} \times \frac{1 \text{ cm}^3}{\text{ml}} = 4.35 \text{ cm}^3$$

Observe that the indicated division has been carried to the hundredths place. It should next be rounded to the nearest tenth to give the proper number of significant figures in the answer.

A more appropriate way to set up this solution would be as follows:

$$D = \frac{m}{V}$$

$$D = \frac{49.33 \text{ g}}{4.35 \text{ ml} \times 1 \text{ cm}^3/\text{ml}} = 11.3 \text{ g/cm}^3$$

Sample Problem

What is the concentration of sodium chloride (table salt), in grams of salt per gram of solution, if $40\bar{0}$ mg of the salt is dissolved in $10\bar{0}$ ml of water measured at 65° C?

Solution

The problem requires that the concentration be expressed in grams of salt per gram of solution. The mass of solution is the sum of the mass of the water used and the mass of the salt added. As a result, the volume of water must be converted to mass of water. To make this conversion the density of water at 65° C must be known.

The table in a chemistry handbook giving density of water over a range of temperatures shows that water has a density of 0.981 g/ml at 65° C.

By definition:
$$D = \frac{m}{V}$$

Solving for m:
$$m = DV$$

Substituting:
$$m = 0.981 \, \frac{g}{ml} \times 10\bar{0} \, ml = 98.1 \, g$$

(Observe that the ml units "cancel" leaving g which is the proper unit for the answer.)

The mass of the salt is given in milligrams and the mass of the water is in grams. Since milligrams and grams cannot be added, the milligrams of salt must be converted to grams.

By definition:
$$1 \, mg = 0.001 \, g$$

$$40\bar{0} \, mg \times \frac{0.001 \, g}{mg} = 0.400 \, g \text{ of salt added}$$

(Observe that 0.001 g is an exact number derived by definition and is not a measurement precise only to one significant figure.)

$$\text{mass of solution} = 98.1 \, g + 0.400 \, g = 98.5 \, g$$

(Recall the rule for addition of significant figures to recognize that the sum is 98.5 g and *not* 98.500 g.)

Since 0.400 g of salt is present in 98.5 g of solution, there is

$$\frac{0.400 \, g}{98.5} \text{ of salt in 1 g of solution}$$

or

$$\textbf{0.00406 g salt/g solution}$$

QUESTIONS

Group A

1. Why is chemistry considered to be a fundamental science?
2. What distinguishes (*a*) a solid from a liquid? (*b*) a liquid from a gas?
3. What properties of materials are classed as physical properties?
4. What properties of materials are classed as chemical?
5. What three basic units of the metric system are used in chemistry?
6. Name six prefixes used in the metric system and indicate what each one means.
7. Why is the study of chemistry concerned with energy?
8. In scientific work what are the advantages of the metric system over the English system?
9. What metric units would you use to represent: (*a*) the area of the cover of this book; (*b*) a family's daily milk supply; (*c*) your own weight; (*d*) the length of the eye of a darning needle; (*e*) the speed of a moving automobile?
10. What disadvantage would we encounter in everyday use of the metric system instead of our English system of weights and measure?
11. Distinguish between accuracy and precision as they pertain to measurements.
12. (*a*) What is the distinction between heat and temperature? (*b*) In what unit is each measured?

Group B

13. Prepare a list of new chemical products which you have read about in newspapers and magazines.
14. (*a*) List five common materials used in the kitchen in your home. (*b*) What properties does each have which makes it suitable for its particular use?
15. Why are both liquids and gases considered to be fluids?
16. What determines whether a certain property of a material is classed as physical or chemical?
17. Why does our sense of touch give us the most direct evidence of the existence of matter?
18. A weighing was made on a platform balance which was graduated in 0.1 g units and was sensitive to 0.01 g. The mass was recorded as 73.14 g. (*a*) How many significant figures are in the measurement? (*b*) Which digit would be called an uncertain figure?
19. Volume is a property of a material. (*a*) Is it a specific property? (*b*) Is mass a specific property? (*c*) Is the ratio of mass to volume a specific property? Explain.
20. Your laboratory partner was given the task of measuring the length of a box (approximately 5 in) as accurately as possible, using a meter stick graduated in millimeters. He supplied you with the following measurements: 12.65, 12.6 cm, 12.65 cm, 12.655 cm, 126.55 mm, 12 cm. (*a*) State which one of the measurements you would accept, giving the reason. (*b*) Give your reason for rejecting each of the others.
21. Copy each of these measurements and underscore all significant figures in each (*do not mark in this book*): (*a*) 127.50 km; (*b*) 1200 m; (*c*) 90027.00 cm^3; (*d*) 0.0053 g; (*e*) 670 mg; (*f*) 0.0730 g; (*g*) 43.050 liters; (*h*) 300900 kg; (*i*) 0.147 cm; (*j*) 6271.9 cm^2.
22. Explain why the unit of any measurement should be written in a mathematical expression with the number to which it belongs.

23. A thermometer is graduated in 1° intervals. In the absence of any tolerance data, what uncertainty would you assume to be associated with each temperature reading?

24. You may use a laboratory balance that has a sensitivity of 0.01 g. Does this indicate an uncertainty in terms of a limitation in accuracy or precision? Explain.

PROBLEMS

Group A

1. How many millimeters are there (a) in 1 centimeter? (b) in 1 meter? (c) in 1 kilometer?

2. How many centimeters are there (a) in 1 foot? (b) in 2 meters? (c) How many inches are there in 1 meter?

3. How many milliliters are there in (a) 2 liters? (b) 10 liters? (c) How many liters are there in 1 m³?

4. Calculate the number of milligrams (a) in 0.4 kilogram; (b) in 1 pound. (c) How many grams are there in 2 kilograms?

5. (a) What is your height in meters? (b) What is your mass in kilograms?

6. A Florence flask has a capacity of 2.50×10^2 ml. (a) What part of a liter is this? (b) How many grams of water will the flask hold?

7. The distance to the sun is approximately 93,000,000 miles. Express this in exponential notation form.

8. The thickness of an oil film on water is about 0.0000005 cm. Express this in exponential notation form.

Group B

9. A cubic box holds $100\overline{0}$ g of water. (a) What is the volume of the box in milliliters? (b) in cubic centimeters? (c) What is the length of one side in centimeters? (d) in meters?

10. A test tube in a laboratory is 125 mm long and 25.0 mm in diameter. (a) Neglecting the fact that the bottom of the test tube is rounded, calculate its capacity in milliliters. (b) How many grams of water will it hold?

11. Each member of a class of 24 students needs 8.600 g of sodium chloride for an experiment. The instructor sets out a new one-pound jar of the salt. How many grams should be left at the end of the laboratory period?

12. A 1-liter graduated cylinder has an inside diameter of 8.24 cm. There is a 52-mm ungraduated portion at the top. What is the total height of the cylinder in centimeters?

13. The density of mercury, to three significant figures, is 13.6 g/ml. (a) What is the mass of 8.20 ml of mercury? (b) What volume would $12\overline{0}$ g of mercury occupy?

14. Express the distance 152.20 cm in each of the following units, showing the conversion computation in each case: (a) meters; (b) millimeters; (c) kilometers; (d) inches.

15. Chemists have determined that 18.0 g of water consists of 6.02×10^{23} molecules. Assuming that a teaspoon holds 3.70 ml of water, determine the number of water molecules the teaspoon can hold.

16. Suppose that you are able to remove individual molecules of water from the teaspoon of Problem 15 at the rate of 1 molecule per second. How many years would be required to empty the spoon?

Chapter **2**

Matter and Its Changes

COMPOSITION OF MATTER

2.1 Three general classes of matter

We are familiar with many different kinds of materials. It would be very difficult and time-consuming to study materials without first organizing them into similar groups. Chemists have found that all forms of matter may be divided into three general groups on the basis of their properties. These three general classes of matter are *elements, compounds,* and *mixtures.*

2.2 Mixtures

If we examine a common rock, granite, closely with a hand lens, we can see three different crystalline materials: quartz, feldspar, and mica. The properties of each differ greatly. *A material which has parts with different properties is said to be* **heterogeneous** (het-er-oh-*jee*-nee-us). The properties of quartz are the same regardless of its source. One part of a piece of quartz has the same properties as every other part. This is also true of feldspar and mica. *A material which has similar properties throughout is said to be* **homogeneous** (hoh-muh-*jee*-nee-us). Heterogeneous materials are *mixtures* of homogeneous materials.

A mixture does not have a set of unique properties. Instead, it possesses a combination of the properties of the homogeneous materials of which it is composed. However, all mixtures are not heterogeneous. When sugar is dissolved in water, the resulting

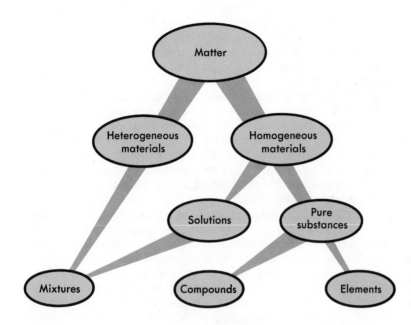

Fig. 2-1. All matter is divided into three general classes: elements, compounds, and mixtures. Solutions are homogeneous mixtures.

solution has similar properties throughout. Thus the solution is homogeneous. We may increase the amount of sugar or water, but we still will have a homogeneous mixture of the two materials. The solution has the sweet taste of the sugar it contains. The water may be removed by evaporation and the sugar recovered in its original form. Solutions are homogeneous mixtures.

Air is a gaseous solution. It is a mixture composed principally of nitrogen, oxygen, argon, carbon dioxide, and water vapor. Each gas present in the air displays its own unique properties. Alloys, combinations of metals (or certain nonmetals), are usually solid solutions. *A **mixture** is a material consisting of two or more kinds of matter, each keeping its own characteristic properties.*

2.3 Substances include compounds and elements

It has already been stated that materials with similar properties throughout are homogeneous. In chemistry, *a **substance** is a homogeneous material consisting of one particular kind of matter.* Both the sugar and the water of a sugar-water solution are substances in this sense. Granite is not a substance because it has a combination of the properties of quartz, feldspar, and mica. On the other hand, the properties of sugar cannot be attributed to anything but the sugar itself. They are caused by its particular composition. *A substance has a definite chemical composition.*

Suppose we place a small quantity of sugar in a test tube and heat it over a low flame. The substance melts and changes color.

Finally a black substance remains in the bottom of the test tube. Drops of a clear colorless liquid appear around the cool open end. The black substance has the properties of carbon and the liquid has the properties of water. The properties of the sugar no longer exist. In fact, the sugar no longer exists. Instead, we have two different substances, carbon and water.

Each time the experiment is repeated, the sugar decomposes in the same way yielding the same proportions of carbon and water. Sugar is recognized as a complex substance showing a consistent composition. It is an example of a *compound. A compound is a substance which may be decomposed into two or more simpler substances by ordinary chemical means.*

Chemists are able to decompose water into two simpler substances, hydrogen and oxygen. Thus water is also a compound. Chemists have not succeeded in decomposing carbon, hydrogen, or oxygen into any simpler substances. We conclude that these are elementary substances or *elements. Elements are substances which cannot be further decomposed by ordinary chemical means.* Elementary substances cannot be broken down or simplified by the usual methods used to cause chemical change. These methods include application of heat, light, or electric energy.

2.4 The known elements

One of the fascinating facts of science is that all known matter is composed of approximately 100 elements. A few elementary substances such as gold, silver, copper, and sulfur, have been known since ancient times. During the Middle Ages and the Renaissance, more elements were discovered. Through the years, improved research techniques have enabled scientists to add to the list of elements.

There are 105 known elements at the time of this writing. Nuclear scientists believe that the list of elements may eventually extend to 110 or possibly 114, based on existing theories.

The 92 elements ranging from hydrogen to uranium are traditionally known as *natural* elements. They make up the pre-Atomic-Age list of elements.

In the decade before World War II, a great experimental study of atomic structure was undertaken. Enrico Fermi, an Italian theoretical physicist, stated that it should be possible to prepare the ninety-third and ninety-fourth elements from uranium. Element 93 was first produced in the laboratories of the University of California (Berkeley) in 1940. It was named *neptunium* for the planet Neptune. This planet is beyond the planet Uranus just as element 93 is beyond uranium (element 92) on the list of elements. Later, element 94 was produced in the same laboratories. It was given the name *plutonium* for the planet Pluto, which is beyond Neptune.

Fig. 2-2. Plutonium being prepared for fabrication into atomic reactor fuel.

General Electric

These triumphs were followed by the production of *americium* (am-er-*ih*-see-um) named for America, *curium* (*ku*-ree-um) named in honor of Madame Curie, *berkelium* (*berk*-lee-um) for Berkeley (the site of the University of California), and *californium* for the University and the State. More recently *einsteinium* named after Albert Einstein, *fermium* named for Enrico Fermi, and *mendelevium* (men-del-*ev*-eeum) named for Dmitri Mendeleyev brought the total to 101.

In 1957, a team of American, British, and Swedish scientists working at the Nobel Institute in Sweden announced the discovery of element 102. They suggested the name *nobelium*. Careful experiments by other scientists, however, failed to confirm their discovery.

In 1958, a research group at Lawrence Radiation Laboratory of the University of California produced *nobelium* and identified it by chemical means. This group kept the name *nobelium* for element 102, to honor Alfred Nobel. Nobel made a great contribution to the advancement of science through his Nobel Prizes.

In 1961, element 103 was produced by scientists at the Lawrence Radiation Laboratory. The name *lawrencium* has been assigned to element 103. It honors Dr. Ernest O. Lawrence, the inventor of the cyclotron (a kind of "atom smasher") and founder of the laboratory in which the element was first produced.

Russian scientists reported the production of element 104 in 1964. They suggested the name *kurchatovium* for the Russian physicist I. V. Kurchatov. However, other scientists have not succeeded in duplicating the Russian experiments and so the report remains unproved. The Lawrence Radiation Laboratory group produced element 104 in 1968 by several different methods. They proposed the name *rutherfordium* after Ernest Rutherford, a British atomic scientist. Both *kurchatovium* and *rutherfordium* are unofficial names for element 104. A permanent name will be assigned when it is determined which group of scientists actually first produced the element.

A similar situation exists at the time of this writing with respect to element 105. In February 1970, Russian scientists reported the production of this element. In April of that same year, American scientists at the Lawrence Radiation Laboratory reported producing element 105. The American group proposed the name *hahnium* after Otto Hahn, a German physical chemist who was one of the discoverers of nuclear fission. Thus, *hahnium* is an unofficial name for element 105.

2.5   The earth's elemental composition

Approximately 90 elements are known to occur in a free or combined state in the earth's crust in measurable amounts. The atmosphere consists almost entirely of two elements, nitrogen and oxygen. Water, which covers a great portion of the surface

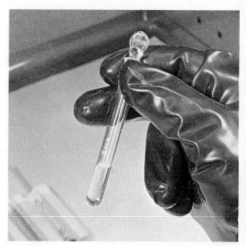

USAEC, Oak Ridge, Tennessee

Fig. 2-3. A vial containing californium, element number 98. This transuranium element is produced by bombarding plutonium with neutrons in a nuclear reactor.

Table 2-1
COMPOSITION OF SURFACE ENVIRONMENT

Element	Distribution
oxygen	49.5%
silicon	25.8%
aluminum	7.5%
iron	4.7%
calcium	3.4%
sodium	2.6%
potassium	2.4%
magnesium	1.9%
hydrogen	0.9%
titanium	0.6%
all other elements	0.7%

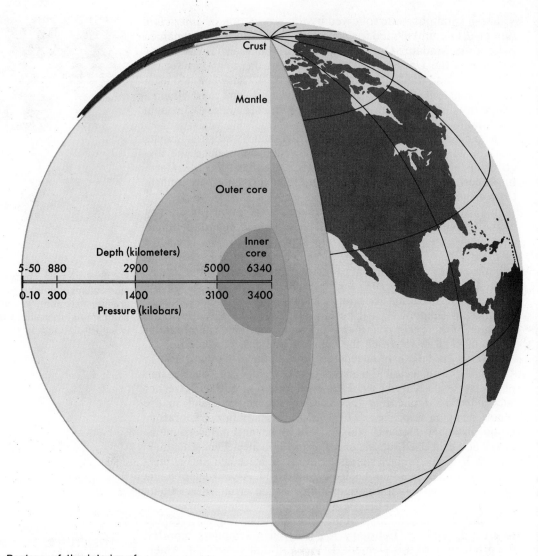

Fig. 2-4. Regions of the interior of the earth.

of the earth, is a compound of hydrogen and oxygen. Natural water also contains many dissolved substances.

Only about 30 elements are fairly common. Table 2-1 shows the relative distribution (by weight) of the 10 most abundant elements in the atmosphere, lakes, rivers, oceans, and the solid earth's crust.

Some elements in Table 2-1 would change positions relative to other elements if the table were based on factors other than weight. On a basis of relative number of particles, for example, hydrogen would appear ahead of aluminum.

The solid crust of the earth is the foundation of all of man's existence. Yet it makes up only about 0.4% of the total mass of the earth and less than 1% of its volume. See Figure 2-4. The

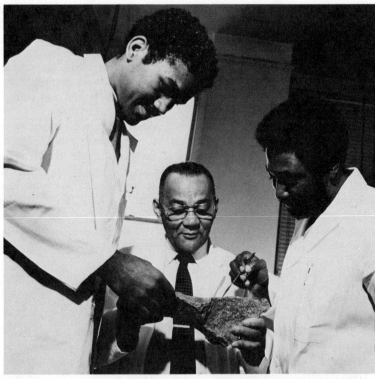

US Geological Survey, Dept of the Interior

Fig. 2-5. Scientists of the United State Department of the Interior Geological Survey, examine a rock specimen.

mantle accounts for about 67.2% and the core 32.4% of the earth's total mass.

The two major elements in the solid crust are oxygen and silicon (in combined form). Together they account for almost 75% of the weight of the continental crust. Eight elements (in combined form) make up over 98% of the weight of the continental crust. These are listed in Table 2-2.

These eight common elements, along with the less common ones, combine in many ways to produce the more than 2000 different minerals that are found in the solid earth's crust.

Scientists of the Smithsonian Institution have estimated that five elements account for more than 94% of the weight of the total solid earth. (This includes the continental crust, mantle, and core.) These elements are given in Table 2-3.

The mantle is believed to consist almost entirely of compounds of four elements—magnesium, iron, silicon, and oxygen. Most earth scientists agree that the earth's core contains about 85% elemental iron, about 7% nickel, and 8% of a mixture of silicon, cobalt, and sulfur.

2.6 Two general classes of elements

Elements differ enough in their properties so that chemists recognize two general classes, *metals* and *nonmetals*.

Table 2-2
COMPOSITION OF THE CONTINENTAL CRUST

Element	Distribution
oxygen	46.6%
silicon	27.7%
aluminum	8.1%
iron	5.0%
calcium	3.6%
sodium	2.8%
potassium	2.6%
magnesium	2.1%

Table 2-3
COMPOSITION OF THE SOLID EARTH

Element	Distribution
iron	34.6%
oxygen	29.5%
silicon	15.2%
magnesium	12.7%
nickel	2.4%

top and bottom—Fritz Goro for LIFE
Magazine © Time Inc.; center—ALCOA

Fig. 2-6. Sulfur (top) is a nonmetallic element that occurs as yellow rhombic crystals in its ordinary form. The metallic element gallium (center) occurs as gray-black orthorhombic crystals. Mercury (bottom) is the only metallic element that is liquid at room temperature.

Metals. Some elements have a *luster* (shine like polished steel or silver). They reflect heat and light readily. They conduct heat and electricity remarkably well. Some are *ductile* (can be drawn into wire). Some are *malleable* (can be hammered into thin sheets). Elements which have such properties are known as **metals.** Some examples of metals are: gold, silver, copper, zinc, sodium, potassium, titanium, magnesium, calcium, and aluminum. At room temperature, mercury is a liquid metal.

Nonmetals. These elements are usually poor conductors of heat and electricity. They cannot be hammered into sheets or drawn into wire because they are usually too brittle. Sulfur is an example of a nonmetal. Some nonmetals such as iodine, carbon, and phosphorus are solid at room temperature. Bromine is a liquid nonmetal. Others, such as oxygen, nitrogen, chlorine, and neon are gases.

Some elements have certain properties characteristic of metals and other properties characteristic of nonmetals. Arsenic, antimony, silicon, and germanium are examples. They are sometimes called ***metalloids.***

2.7   Chemical symbols

Jöns Jaköb Berzelius (1779–1848), a Swedish chemist, was the first to use letters as symbols for elements. These letter symbols replaced the small circles containing identifying marks which John Dalton used to indicate different elements. Berzelius used the first letter of the name of an element as its symbol. For example, the letter O represents oxygen, and the letter H represents hydrogen.

There are over 100 elements and only twenty-six letters in our alphabet. Thus, the names of several elements must begin with the same letter. In such cases, Berzelius added a second letter whose sound is conspicuous when the name of the element is pronounced. For example, the symbol for carbon is C; for calcium, Ca; for chlorine, Cl; for chromium, Cr; and for cobalt, Co. The first letter of a symbol is *always* capitalized, but the second letter of a symbol is *never* capitalized. For example, Co is the symbol for cobalt; CO is the formula for a compound called carbon monoxide. This compound is composed of the elements carbon and oxygen.

In several cases, the symbol for an element is derived from the Latin name of the element. For example, the symbol for iron is Fe, from the Latin *ferrum.* Pb, the symbol for lead, comes from the Latin *plumbum.* The symbols for silver, Ag, and sodium, Na, come from the Latin, *argentum* and *natrium.*

2.8   Significance of a symbol

A chemical symbol is more than an abbreviation; it has quantitative significance. When we use the symbol O, it not only means oxygen but also stands for *one atom* of oxygen. The expression **2O** means 2 atoms of oxygen; **5O** means 5 atoms of oxygen. Similarly, **Fe** means 1 atom of iron; **3Fe**, 3 atoms of iron; and **10Fe**, 10 atoms of iron. The atom is the smallest unit of an element that can enter into combination with other elements. The chemist uses different kinds of atoms to build chemical compounds. The symbol of an element will acquire additional meaning for you as your study of chemistry progresses.

2.9 Compounds differ from mixtures

When matter is made up of two or more elements, the elements are either mixed mechanically or combined chemically. The material is either a *mixture* or a *compound,* depending on what has happened to the elements. If the material is a mixture, the properties used to recognize each element present will persist. On the other hand, if the elements are chemically combined, a complex substance with its own characteristic properties is observed.

Suppose some powdered sulfur and iron powder are mixed thoroughly on a sheet of paper. There is no evidence of a chemical reaction; neither light nor heat is produced. The two substances may be mixed in any proportion. It is possible to use a large amount of iron and a small amount of sulfur or a large portion of sulfur and a small portion of iron.

As the paper containing this mixture is moved back and forth over a strong magnet, the iron particles separate from the sulfur. When a small portion of the mixture is put in hydrochloric acid, the iron reacts with the acid and disappears from view, leaving the sulfur unaffected. When another portion of the mixture is put in liquid carbon disulfide, the sulfur dissolves, leaving the iron powder unchanged.

In each of these tests the properties of iron and sulfur persist. This is typical of a mixture; the *components* (substances of which it is made) do not lose their identity. They may be mixed in any proportion without evidence of chemical activity.

It is possible to cause the iron and sulfur to unite chemically and form a compound. Suppose these two elements are mixed in the ratio of 7 g iron to 4 g sulfur and the mixture is heated strongly in a test tube over a bunsen flame. With a rise in temperature the mixture begins to glow. Even after its removal from the flame, the mixture continues to react and the whole mass soon becomes red hot. *Both heat and light are produced during the chemical reaction in which sulfur and iron combine and form a compound.*

After the reaction has ceased and the product has been removed, careful examination shows that it no longer resembles either the iron or the sulfur. Each element has lost its characteristic properties. The iron cannot be removed by a magnet. The sulfur cannot be dissolved out of the product with carbon disul-

Analysis is the process of decomposing or breaking down a compound into two or more simpler substances. The process may involve determining the identity and proportion of the constituent elements.

Table 2-4

DIFFERENCES BETWEEN A MIXTURE AND A COMPOUND

Mixture	*Compound*
1. In a mixture, the components may be present in any proportion.	1. In a compound, the constituents always have a definite proportion by weight.
2. In the preparation of a mixture, there is no evidence of any chemical action taking place.	2. In the preparation of a compound, evidence of chemical action is usually apparent (light, heat, etc.)
3. In a mixture, the components do not lose their identity. They may be separated by physical means.	3. In a compound, the constituents lose their identity. They can be separated by chemical means only.

fide. In the original mixture, hydrochloric acid reacted chemically with the iron and odorless hydrogen gas was produced. Hydrochloric acid also reacts chemically with this new product and a gas is again produced. However, in this reaction, the gas has a distinctive (decayed egg) odor. The odor is characteristic of hydrogen sulfide. This different gas product gives evidence that a *new substance with a new set of properties* has been formed as a result of the reaction between the iron and sulfur.

Each time this new product is formed it is found to be made up of iron and sulfur in the same weight relationship. *A compound is always composed of the same elements in a definite proportion by weight*. For example, the compound we are now discussing, which is called *iron sulfide,* is composed of 63.5% iron and 36.5% sulfur. This composition represents a weight ratio of 7 parts iron to 4 parts sulfur. If we had started the reaction with eight parts of iron and four parts of sulfur, one part by weight of iron would remain as an unused surplus after the reaction was completed. Differences between mixtures and compounds are summarized in Table 2-4.

2.10   Law of definite composition

Louis Proust (1755–1826), a French chemist, was one of the first to observe that elements always combine with one another in a definite ratio by weight. About fifty years later, Jean Servais Stas, a Belgian chemist, performed a series of precise experiments which confirmed this observation. We now recognize Proust's observation as the **law of definite composition:** *Every compound has a definite composition by weight.*

Using the law of definite composition, a manufacturer of chemical compounds can determine the precise amount of each ingredient needed to prepare a specific compound.

2.11   Common examples of mixtures and compounds

In Section 2.2, we described air as a mixture. Its composition varies somewhat in different localities. Other familiar examples-of mixtures include substances such as baking powders, concrete, and various kinds of soil. There is practically no limit to the number of possible mixtures. They may be made up of two or more elements, of two or more compounds, or of both elements and compounds. For example, brass is a mixture of two elements, copper and zinc. Common gunpowder is a mixture of two elements, carbon and sulfur, with a compound, potassium nitrate. A solution of common salt is a mixture of two compounds, sodium chloride and water.

Some large dictionaries define almost a half-million words. All of these words are formed from one or more of the 26 letters of our alphabet. Try to imagine the number of compounds possible from different combinations of 100 or more elements. Of course, some elements do not unite readily with others and form compounds. Three elements (helium, neon, and argon) form no known compounds. Enough elements do combine, however, to make possible several million compounds known to chemists. Water, table salt, sugar, alcohol, baking soda, ether, glycerol, cellulose, nitric acid, and sulfuric acid are some examples of common compounds.

The simplest compounds are made up of two different elements. Iron sulfide is such a compound. Carbon dioxide is composed only of carbon and oxygen. Table salts consists of sodium combined with chlorine. Sodium is an active metallic element which must be protected from contact with air and water. Chlorine is a poisonous gas. But when combined chemically, the two form common table salt.

Many compounds are composed of no more than three different elements. Carbon, hydrogen, and oxygen are the elements that make up sugar. These same three elements occur combined in different proportions in many other compounds having decidedly different properties.

CHANGES IN MATTER

2.12 Physical changes

Ice melts, water boils, liquids freeze, glass breaks, and sugar dissolves in water. We may heat a wire made of the metal platinum until it glows. In all these cases matter undergoes some change and some quantity of energy is involved. The form of the matter may be different or it may have experienced a change of phase. However, in no case has the matter lost its identity. In some cases, a reversal of the action which caused the change, restores the material to its original form. Then its identifying properties are again readily recognized. An example is the case of water that turns to steam when heated. If the steam loses heat, it returns to the original liquid form and the properties of water are again recognized.

These examples illustrate *physical changes*. In such changes, only physical properties are altered. No new substances are formed. ***Physical changes** are those in which the identifying properties of substances remain unchanged.*

Modern ideas concerning solutions suggest that some types of physical changes may involve intermediate processes which are not physical in nature. These ideas will be treated in Chapter 12.

2.13 Chemical changes

You know that wood burns, iron rusts, silver tarnishes, milk sours, plants decay, and acids react with metals. In each of these actions, the identifying properties of the original substance disappear. New substances with different properties are formed. Changes occurred which have altered the composition of matter. ***Chemical changes** are those in which different substances with new properties are formed.*

Chemical changes may involve: *1.* forming compounds from elementary substances, *2.* breaking down complex substances into simpler compounds or into the elements which compose them. Compounds may react with other compounds or elements. New and different compounds are then formed. To recognize and control these processes, chemists need to understand chemical reactions. What they usually observe are changes in the properties of substances in bulk. They try to interpret and understand these changes in terms of the behavior of the particles of the substances involved.

2.14 Chemical reactions involve energy

Every change in matter, physical or chemical, involves energy. Thus, chemical reactions are always accompanied by energy changes. Substances possess energy because of their composition and structure. This is a kind of potential energy which chemists generally refer to as *chemical energy*. The products of chemical reactions are different in composition and structure from the original substances. Consequently, they have larger or smaller amounts of chemical energy than the original substances. If the amount is smaller, energy is given off or *liberated* during the reaction. Usually this energy is in the form of heat. If the amount of chemical energy is larger, energy is *absorbed* during the change.

Calcium carbide, a compound formed of the elements calcium and carbon, is produced in the intense heat of an electric furnace. The compound carbon disulfide is formed when hot sulfur vapor is passed over white-hot carbon in an electric furnace. Heat energy is absorbed continuously while such chemical reactions are taking place. *Any chemical reaction which absorbs energy as it progresses is said to be **endothermic**.*

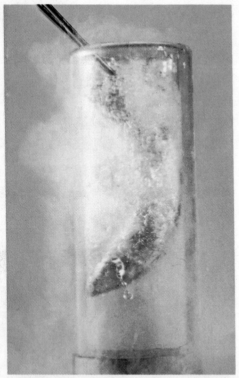

Werner Wolff; Black Star

Fig. 2-7. After a banana is dipped in liquid nitrogen at −195.8°C, it can be used as a hammer.

Some chemical changes are important because of their products. Others are important because of the energy which is released. When fuels are burned, large amounts of heat energy are released rapidly. Many similar changes occur in nature but take place so slowly that the release of heat is not noticed. *Any chemical reaction which liberates energy as it proceeds is said to be exothermic.* Most, but not all, chemical reactions which occur spontaneously in nature are exothermic. One important exception is the photosynthesis process. In this process, carbon dioxide and water are changed to a simple sugar in green plants. Photosynthesis is an endothermic reaction because radiant energy from the sun is converted to chemical energy in sugar.

When fuels are burned, light energy usually accompanies the release of heat. A photoflash lamp is designed to release a maximum amount of energy as light. The final proof that a chemical reaction has taken place rests with the analysis of the products. However, the release of heat and light usually indicates that a chemical reaction is taking place.

The explosion of dynamite or gunpowder is an exothermic chemical reaction that is used to produce *mechanical energy.* Similarly, burning a mixture of gasoline vapor and air in the cylinder of an automobile engine produces mechanical energy.

In a flashlight cell, the zinc cup is involved in a chemical reaction when the cell is in use. *Electric energy* is produced by this reaction. The electricity gives evidence of the chemical reaction taking place within the cell.

The *production of a gas* usually indicates that a chemical reaction is taking place. However, we must avoid mistaking the boiling of a liquid, the escaping of a dissolved gas from solution, or the escaping of gas from the surface of a solid for chemical action.

In many cases when one solution is added to another, an *insoluble* solid (one that is not dissolved in the liquid) is formed. *Such an insoluble solid is called a **precipitate**.* Formation of a precipitate may show that a chemical reaction has taken place as the solutions are mixed.

Chemists use several agents to bring about chemical changes or to control those which have already started. Some form of energy is often involved.

1. Heat energy. A match is kindled by rubbing it over a rough surface to warm it by friction. By holding the lighted match to a piece of paper, we may start the paper burning. The heat from the burning match is used to start this chemical change. It is, however, an exothermic reaction. We do not need to continue furnishing heat in order to keep the paper burning. Many chemical reactions which occur in the preparation of foods are endothermic. Heat is supplied to keep these reactions going. As a rule, increasing temperature increases the rate of chemical reactions. *Each increase in temperature of 10 C° approximately doubles the rate of many chemical reactions.*

From the CHEM Study film: *Molecular Motion*

Fig. 2-8. The elements, sulfur and zinc, mixed at room temperature (top) do not react until heat is applied to the mixture (bottom).

2. Light energy. The process of photosynthesis, by which green plants manufacture food, requires light energy. When we open the shutter of a camera for only a fraction of a second, light falls on the sensitive film. This exposure to light forms an invisible image on the film by a chemical reaction. From this image we can then develop a picture at some later time.

3. Electric energy. If a direct current of electricity is passed through water containing a little acid, the water decomposes into hydrogen and oxygen. We use this method of bringing about a chemical reaction when we charge a storage battery. Electric energy is used in plating one metal on another. It is used in extracting aluminum and other metals from their ores, and in purifying some metals. Electricity is also used to produce heat for thermal processes. The use of an electric furnace in the production of calcium carbide and carbon disulfide was mentioned earlier in this section.

4. Solution in water. Baking powder is a mixture of two or more compounds. No chemical reaction occurs as long as the powder is kept *dry*. However, when water is added to baking powder, chemical reaction begins immediately and a gas is released. Many chemicals which do not react in the *dry* state begin to react as soon as they are dissolved in water.

5. Catalysis (kuh-*tal*-uh-sis). Some chemical reactions are promoted by *catalysts* (*kat*-uh-lists). These are specific agents which promote reactions that would otherwise be difficult or impractical to carry out. A catalyst does not start a chemical reaction which would not occur of itself. For example, oxygen can be prepared in the laboratory by heating a mixture of potassium chlorate and manganese dioxide. Without the manganese dioxide, the preparation would have to be carried out at a higher temperature. Also, the gas would be produced more slowly. The manganese dioxide aids the action by its presence. It can be recovered in its original form at the conclusion of the experiment. *A **catalyst** is a substance or combination of substances which increases the rate of a chemical reaction without itself being permanently changed.*

Many chemical processes, such as the production of vegetable shortening, the manufacture of rubber, and the preparation of high-octane gasoline, depend on catalysis for their successful operation.

2.15　Reaction tendencies

We are not surprised to see a ball roll unaided down an incline. This is just what would be expected. The ball gives up potential energy in this process and achieves a more stable position at a lower energy level. We would be surprised, however, if the ball rolled up the incline by itself. Our experiences with nature have taught us to recognize a basic rule for natural processes: *There is a tendency for processes to occur which lead to a lower energy state*. This tendency in nature is toward greater *stability* (resistance to change) of a system.

The great majority of chemical reactions in nature are exothermic. Energy is liberated as they proceed and the products have less energy than the original *reactants* or starting substances. With the above rule in mind, we expect exothermic reactions *to occur **spontaneously***. That is, we expect them *to have the potential to proceed without outside help*.

It should follow that endothermic reactions, in which energy is absorbed, would not occur spontaneously. They would proceed only with outside help. Certainly, we must expend energy on the ball to roll it up the incline. At the top of the incline its potential energy is high and its stability is low.

We do not have to look very far to find endothermic reactions which take place spontaneously with the absorption of energy. For example, when steam is passed over hot carbon, carbon monoxide and hydrogen gases are produced. Heat is absorbed and the products are in a higher energy state than the reactants. The spontaneous reaction is endothermic and our rule appears to have failed. Apparently the tendency of a reaction to proceed of and by itself is not determined exclusively by this energy-change rule.

An ice cube melts spontaneously at room temperature. As the ice melts it acquires energy. The well-ordered form of the ice crystal is lost. The less orderly liquid water, a state of higher energy, is formed. Why does this occur?

Fig. 2-9. Changes of phase.

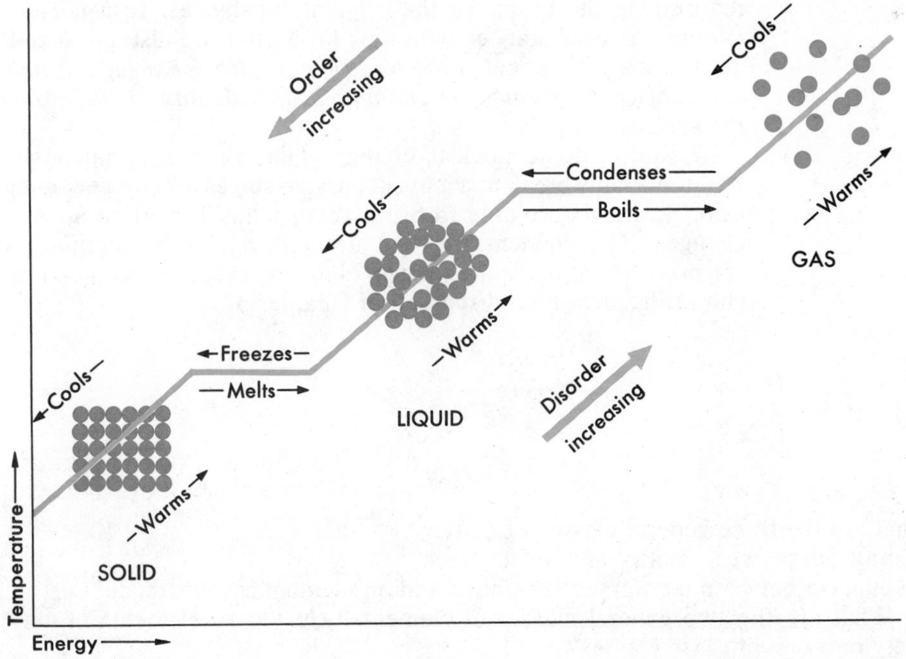

What we observe here is a tendency for the ice to move into the less orderly liquid phase. This observation suggests a second basic rule for natural processes: *There is a tendency for processes to occur which lead to a less orderly or a more disordered state.* This tendency in nature is toward greater disorder in a system. A disordered system is one that lacks a regular arrangement of its parts. *That property which describes the disorder of a system is called* **entropy.** The more disordered or random the state, the *higher* is the entropy. Liquid water has higher entropy than ice.

Thus, processes in nature are driven in two ways: toward *lowest* energy and toward *highest* entropy. Where these two oppose each other, the dominant factor determines the direction of the spontaneous change. In the steam-plus-hot-carbon reaction, the temperature is so high that the entropy factor overcomes the unfavorable energy-change factor. The spontaneous endothermic reaction occurs.

If the ice cube is subjected to a temperature below 0° C, it will not melt. Liquid water placed in this environment freezes. The temperature is low enough for the energy-change factor to overcome the entropy-change factor. Heat is given up by the water (lower energy) and the well-ordered ice crystal is formed (lower entropy). Entropy as a factor in reaction systems will be considered in more detail in Section 19.7.

2.16 Nuclear changes

New substances are produced during a chemical reaction by rearranging the atoms of the original substances. In a *nuclear change,* new substances with new properties are also produced. There is a difference, however. *In a* **nuclear change,** *the new substances are formed by changes in the identity of the atoms themselves.*

In nature, some nuclear changes take place spontaneously. Radium atoms break apart in successive stages, finally becoming lead. Scientists are able to bring about many important nuclear changes. The elements beyond uranium named in Section 2.4 are products of nuclear changes. Nuclear reactions, both natural and artificial, will be discussed in Chapter 30.

QUESTIONS

Group A

1. What are the three general classes of matter?
2. Distinguish between matter and a substance.
3. Distinguish between a complex substance and an elementary substance.
4. (*a*) What are the two general classes of elements? (*b*) Do all elements fit definitely into one of these classes?

5. Distinguish between a compound and a mixture.
6. What are the five most abundant elements in the earth's surface environment?
7. (a) What are the properties of metals? (b) of nonmetals?
8. (a) How many elements are known? (b) How many were known prior to the beginning of the Atomic Age?
9. What is the meaning of a chemical symbol?
10. (a) List five familiar substances which are elements. (b) List five which are compounds. (c) List five familiar mixtures.
11. What is the difference between a physical change and a chemical change?
12. How can a chemist usually increase the speed of a chemical change?
13. If two or more elements have symbols beginning with the same letter, how do we distinguish them?
14. If a symbol has two letters, (a) what is always true of the first letter? (b) what is always true of the second letter?

Group B

15. What difference in the properties of white sand and sugar enables you to separate a mixture of the two substances?
16. How would you carry out the separation of the sand-sugar mixture of Question 15?
17. Why is a solution recognized as a mixture?
18. What is the meaning of the phrase "definite composition by weight"?
19. Why is the law of definite composition very important to chemists?
20. Consult the complete list of known elements appearing on the inside of the back cover of this book and compile a list of those about which you already have some knowledge. Give the name, symbol, and the pertinent bit of knowledge in column form.
21. Given two liquids, one a solution and the other a compound, how would you distinguish the solution from the compound?
22. Suppose you heat three different solids in open vessels and then allow them to cool. The first gains weight, the second loses weight, and the third remains the same. How can you reconcile these facts with the generalization that, in an ordinary chemical reaction, the total mass of the reacting materials is equal to the total mass of the products?
23. How can you explain the fact that gold, silver, and copper were known long before such metals as iron and aluminum?
24. Suppose you were given a sample of iodine crystals, a sample of antimony metal, and a sample of a mixture of iodine and antimony which had been ground together to form a fine powder of uniform consistency. Look up the physical and chemical properties of both iodine and antimony. Then list those properties of each element that you believe would be useful in separating and recovering them from the mixture. On the basis of these properties, devise a procedure which would enable you to separate the two elements from the mixture and recover the separate elements.
25. Which of these changes are physical and which are chemical? (a) burning coal; (b) tarnishing silver; (c) magnetizing steel; (d) exploding gunpowder; (e) boiling water; (f) melting shortening.
26. Which of the chemical changes listed in Question 25 are also exothermic?
27. Show by example how each form of energy produces chemical changes: (a) heat energy; (b) light energy; (c) electric energy.

28. What evidences usually indicate chemical reaction?
29. Can you suggest a reason why iron and sulfur unite in definite proportions when iron sulfide is formed?
30. How do you decide whether a certain change is physical or chemical?
31. What two basic tendencies in nature appear to influence reaction processes?
32. An ice cube melts at room temperature and water freezes at temperatures below 0° C. From these facts, what can you infer concerning the relationship between the temperature of a system and the influence of the entropy factor on the change which the system undergoes?

PROBLEMS

Group B

(Show unit operations in problem solutions as presented in Section 1.21)

1. What is the volume of an iron sphere which has a mass of 4.05 kg? (See Appendix Table 15 for the density of iron.)
2. How many kilocalories of heat are needed to raise the temperature of $45\overline{0}$ g of water from 21.0° C to 100.0° C? (Neglect the slight variation in heat requirement with changing temperature of water. See Section 1.16.)
3. If 1.25 liters of water absorb 45.5 kcal of heat, how much does the temperature of the water rise?
4. Einstein's equation $E = mc^2$ (Section 1.11) shows that 1.0 g of matter is the equivalent of 2.1×10^{10} kcal of energy. When 2.0 g of hydrogen reacts with 16 g of oxygen and forms 18 g of water, 68 kcal of heat energy is given up. To what loss of mass in the reaction system described is this quantity of energy equivalent?
5. Ordinary table salt is the compound sodium chloride. It can be formed by burning metallic sodium in an atmosphere of chlorine gas. According to the Law of Definite Composition, the compound always consists of 39.3% sodium and 60.7% chlorine. What quantity of the compound could you produce if you started with 10.0 g of sodium and 20.0 g of chlorine? (A percentage as given here may be interpreted as meaning *grams of element per* $10\overline{0}$ *g of compound.*)

Chapter 3

Atomic Structure

3.1 Particles of matter

The idea that matter consists of basic, indivisible particles is a very old one. Some Greek thinkers, as early as 400 B.C., believed that matter could not be destroyed. They also thought that it could be divided into smaller and smaller particles until a basic particle was reached which could not be divided. These basic particles were thought to be the smallest particles of matter that existed. Democritus called such particles *atoms*, from a Greek word meaning "indivisible."

When you crush a lump of sugar, you can see that it is made up of many small particles of sugar. You may grind these particles into very fine powder, but each tiny piece is still sugar. Now suppose you dissolve the sugar in water. The tiny particles disappear completely. Even if you look at the sugar-water solution through a microscope, you cannot see any sugar particles. However, if you taste the solution, you know that the sugar is still present.

If you open a laboratory gas valve, you can smell the escaping gas, to which a small amount of odorant has been added. Yet you cannot see gas particles in the air of the room, even if you use the most powerful microscope. These observations and many others like them have led scientists to believe that the basic particles of matter must be very, very small.

Democritus (deh-mock-writ-us) (460–370 B.C.) was a Greek thinker. He believed that the hard atoms of the four primitive elements (earth, air, water, and fire) moved in a vacuum. The shape and size of these atoms explained some of their properties. For example, the atoms of fire were tiny spheres which, because of their smooth surfaces, did not link with the atoms of the other elements. The atoms of earth, air, and water had shapes which enabled them to connect with each other and form visible matter.

3.2 The atomic theory

The idea of basic particles, or atoms of matter, did not add to the growth of science until the beginning of the nineteenth cen-

John Dalton (1766–1844) was an English schoolmaster. He was interested in the composition and properties of the gases in the atmosphere. He kept a daily record of the weather from 1787 until 1844.

tury. Between 1803 and 1808, John Dalton performed many physical and chemical experiments, particularly with gases. Dalton credited these experiments with giving him new ideas about atoms. Dalton was the first to realize that the nature and properties of atoms were related to two observations about matter. The nature and properties of atoms were suggested by:

1. the law of definite composition.
2. the way and the proportions in which substances react with one another.

These are the main ideas of Dalton's *atomic theory.*

The atomic theory today includes a much wider field of knowledge than Dalton's original theory. Modern atomic theory includes information about:

1. the structure and properties of atoms;
2. the kinds of compounds which atoms form;
3. the properties of compounds which atoms form;
4. the mass, volume, and energy relationships of reactions between atoms.

An atom is the smallest unit of an element that can exist either alone or in combination with other atoms like it or different from it. No one has ever directly observed atoms. However, the chemical and physical properties of matter lead scientists to believe the following statements about atoms and their properties are true.

1. All matter is made up of very small particles called *atoms.*
2. Atoms of the *same element* are *chemically alike;* atoms of *different elements* are *chemically different.*
3. Individual atoms of an element may not all have the same mass. However, *the atoms of an element,* as it occurs naturally, *have,* for practical purposes, *a definite average mass that is characteristic of the element.*
4. Individual atoms of different elements may have nearly identical masses. However, *the atoms of different naturally occurring elements have different average masses.*
5. Atoms are not subdivided in *chemical reactions.* Right now, statements 3 and 4 may be a bit puzzling. Later in Section 3.13, we shall make their meaning clearer.

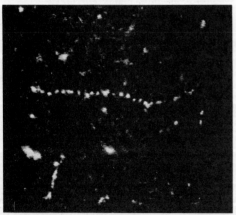

Fig. 3-1. The bright spots in a "chain" in the center of this photograph are the images of single atoms of thorium. The images of the atoms are enlarged more than a million times by a high-resolution scanning electron microscope designed and built by A.V. Crewe of the University of Chicago.

Albert V. Crewe, University of Chicago
Division of Physical Sciences

3.3 The structure of the atom

For about eighty years, scientists have been gathering evidence about the structure of atoms. Some of this evidence has come from the study of radioactive elements such as radium and uranium. Particle accelerators, the mass spectrograph, the X-ray tube, the spectroscope, and a variety of other electronic devices have given additional information. From all this information scientists have developed a theory of atomic structure. As indicated in Section 1.3, this theory includes an explanation of the observed phenomena in terms of a model with familiar properties. This atomic structure model will be described in the following sections of this chapter and in Chapter 4. Remember, as you read, that this explanation is based on the best present understanding of experiments on atomic structure. Further experiments may make changes in the model necessary.

At the present time, scientists know that atoms are not simple indivisible particles. Instead, they are composed of several different kinds of still smaller particles arranged in a rather complex way.

An atom consists of two main parts. *The positively charged central part is called the **nucleus.*** It is very small and very dense. Its diameter is about 10^{-12} cm. A more useful unit for measuring atomic sizes is the angstrom.

$$1 \text{ angstrom (Å)} = 10^{-8} \text{ cm}$$

To get some idea of the extreme smallness of the angstrom, consider the fact that 1 cm is the same fractional part of 10^3 km (about 600 miles) as 1 Å is of 1 cm. We have just given the diameter of a nucleus as about 10^{-12} cm, or about 10^{-4} Å. This is about one ten-thousandth of the diameter of the atom itself, since atoms range from 1 Å to 5Å in diameter.

The idea that an atom has a nucleus was the result of experiments conducted about 1910. These experiments were under the direction of the English physicist Ernest Rutherford (1871–1937). Rutherford used an evacuated tube (a tube from which the gas has been pumped). In it, a thin sheet of gold was bombarded (hit) with many high-speed positively charged particles. Most of the particles passed straight through the gold. A few were slightly deflected (turned away from a straight course) as they passed through the gold. A very few were greatly deflected back from the gold. These very few great deflections were explained by means of an assumption. It was assumed that the positively charged particles were bounced back if they approached a positively charged atomic nucleus head-on. The few slight deflections were explained by assuming that the particles were turned from their paths in near misses of nuclei. But most of the particles passed straight through the gold foil. Therefore, the experimenters reasoned, most of an atom must consist of

Fig. 3-2. A schematic diagram of Rutherford's experiment. Most of the high-speed positively charged particles passed through the gold foil. A few were slightly deflected, while a very few were greatly deflected. The screens emit a flash of light when struck by a charged particle.

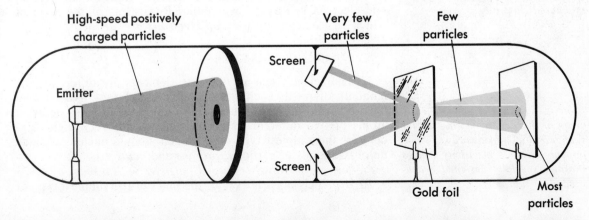

United Press International

Fig. 3-3. The Danish scientist Niels Bohr theorized in 1913 that electrons move about the nucleus of an atom in orbits much as the planets revolve about the sun.

Electrons were discovered in 1897 by an English scientist, J. J. Thomson (1856–1940). This discovery was the result of investigations of the flow of electricity through an evacuated glass tube.

Protons were discovered in the early years of this century during the investigation of "positive rays" which appear when electricity flows through specially designed evacuated glass tubes.

space through which such particles could move readily. In fact, since a vast majority of the particles went undeflected, the nucleus must occupy a very, very small portion of the volume of an atom.

The other part of the atom lies outside the central nucleus. It is made up of negatively charged particles called *electrons*. Electrons move about the nucleus with different energies. Several electrons having similar energies comprise a **shell** and are said to be in the same **energy level**. About 1913, the Danish scientist Niels Bohr (1885–1962) compared the movement of electrons about the nucleus of an atom with the revolution of the planets around the sun. The paths of the electrons are now believed to be much less definite than the orbits of the planets. Electrons move about the nucleus of an atom much as bees move about in the area near their hive. Sometimes the electrons are near the nucleus; sometimes they are farther away. In this way, the electrons seem to occupy the relatively vast empty space around the nucleus. The positions of the electrons may be visualized as an electron cloud about the nucleus. This electron cloud gives the atom its volume and keeps out other atoms. Each atom is electrically neutral. This electric neutrality shows that the total positive charge of the nucleus must equal the total negative charge of the electrons in the shells or energy levels. The experimental evidence for the existence of electrons and for their location and motion within atoms will be described in Sections 3.4 and 4.3.

3.4   The characteristics of electrons

Electrons are negatively charged particles with a mass of 9.110 × 10^{-28} g. The mass of an electron is $\frac{1}{1837}$ of the mass of the most common type of hydrogen atom. The most common type of hydrogen atom has the simplest structure and the least mass of any atom.

The electron is a very small particle. Its radius is 2.818 × 10^{-13} cm, or 2.818 × 10^{-5} Å. Electrons are negatively charged particles. No smaller quantity of electric charge than that on one electron has ever been found. Regardless of the atom of which an electron is a part, *all electrons are identical.*

3.5   The nucleus of the atom

The nuclei of atoms of different elements are different. The amounts of positive charge are always different. Nuclei also have different masses, although the difference in mass between atoms of two different elements is sometimes very slight. Except for the simplest type of hydrogen atom, a nucleus is made up of two kinds of particles, *protons* and *neutrons*.

Protons are positively charged particles with a mass of 1.673 × 10^{-24} g. This mass is $\frac{1836}{1837}$ of the mass of the simplest type of

Table 3-1
PARTICLES IN AN ATOM

Name	Mass	Atomic mass (See Section 3.11)	Mass number (See Section 3.6)	Charge
electron	9.110×10^{-28} g	0.0005486	0	−1
proton	1.673×10^{-24} g	1.007277	1	+1
neutron	1.675×10^{-24} g	1.008665	1	0

hydrogen atom. This atom consists of a single-proton nucleus with a single electron moving about it. While a proton has much more mass than an electron, it is believed to be smaller. The charge on the proton has the same size as that on an electron, but is positive in sign. In any atom, the number of electrons and protons is equal. Since protons and electrons have equal but opposite electric charges, an atom is electrically neutral.

Neutrons are neutral particles with a mass of 1.675×10^{-24} g, which is about the same mass as a proton. They have no electric charge.

Particles that have the same electric charge generally repel one another. Nevertheless, as many as one hundred protons can exist close together in a nucleus. This close existence of protons in the nucleus can occur when up to about one hundred fifty neutrons are also present. When a proton and a neutron are very close to each other, there is a strong attraction between them. Proton-proton attractive forces and neutron-neutron attractive forces exist when such pairs of particles are very close together. These short-range proton-neutron, proton-proton, and neutron-neutron forces hold the nuclear particles together. They are referred to as *nuclear forces*.

Neutrons were discovered by the English scientist, James C. Chadwick, (b. 1891) in 1932. The experiment during which this discovery was made is described in Sec. 30.13.

3.6 Hydrogen atoms

The most common type of hydrogen is sometimes called *protium*. Its atoms have the simplest possible composition. The nucleus of a protium atom consists of one proton. This proton has one electron moving about it. This electron could most probably be found at a distance from the nucleus corresponding to the innermost shell, or lowest energy level, which an electron can have. This shell or energy level is called the *K shell* or *1st energy level*. Scientists discover how electrons are arranged in atoms of an element by studying the chemical properties of the element and its spectrum. To better understand the sizes and distances between the particles of the protium atom, we might picture the nucleus (a proton) as being the size of a pinhead, 0.25 cm in diameter. Comparatively, the electron, which is somewhat larger, moves about this nucleus at an average distance of about 12 m. The electron moves rapidly about the nucleus, effectively occupying the surrounding space.

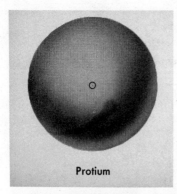

Protium

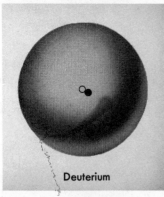

Deuterium

Tritium

Fig. 3-4. Tentative models of the three isotopes of hydrogen: protium, deuterium, and tritium. Each has one proton in the nucleus and one electron moving about the nucleus in the 1st energy level. The only structural difference between them is the number of neutrons in the nucleus of each atom. In these diagrams the nuclei are enlarged in proportion to the size of the atom to show their composition.

*The **atomic number** of an atom is the number of protons in the nucleus of that atom.* An element consists of atoms all of which have the same number of protons in each nucleus. Hence, all atoms of the same element have the same atomic number. (All unexcited neutral atoms of an element have the same arrangement of electrons about their nuclei, too.) The atoms of the element hydrogen have one proton in each nucleus. Their atomic number, therefore, is 1. Any atom having the atomic number 1 contains one proton in its nucleus, and is a hydrogen atom.

In addition to protium, which makes up 99.985% of naturally occurring hydrogen, there are two other known forms of hydrogen atoms. One of these is *deuterium,* which occurs to the extent of 0.015% in nature. Each deuterium atom has a nucleus containing one proton and one neutron, with one electron moving about it.

The third form of hydrogen is *tritium.* Tritium is a radioactive form. It exists in nature in very small amounts, but can be prepared artificially by a nuclear reaction. Each tritium atom has a nucleus composed of one proton and two neutrons, with one electron moving about it.

These three kinds of atoms are all hydrogen atoms, since each has a nucleus containing one proton. The atomic number of each is 1. However, because their nuclei contain different numbers of neutrons, these atoms have different masses. *Atoms of the same element which have different masses are called* **isotopes.**

All elements have two or more isotopes. Isotopes of an element may occur naturally, or they may be prepared artificially. While isotopes have different masses, they do not differ significantly in chemical properties. See Table 2 in the Appendix for a list of both natural and radioactive isotopes of some of the elements.

*Each different variety of atom as determined by the composition of its nucleus is called a **nuclide**.* Nuclides having the same atomic number are isotopes. The three hydrogen isotopes are the nuclides protium, deuterium, and tritium.

In addition to their names, hydrogen nuclides may also be distinguished by their *mass numbers. The **mass number** of an atom is the sum of the number of protons and neutrons in its nucleus.* The mass number of protium is 1 (1 proton + 0 neutron). That of deuterium is 2 (1 proton + 1 neutron). That of tritium is 3 (1 proton + 2 neutrons). Sometimes these isotopes are named hydrogen-1, hydrogen-2, and hydrogen-3, respectively.

3.7　Helium atoms

At the time of this writing, 105 different elements are known or reported to exist. Their atomic numbers range from 1 to 105. The elements may be arranged in the order of increasing atomic number. This arrangement simplifies the understanding of atomic structure. If the elements are arranged in this way, the nuclei of the atoms of one element differ from those of the preceding element by one additional proton per nucleus. (The number of neutrons per nucleus may or may not change from atom to atom.)

The second element in order of complexity is helium. Since each helium nucleus contains two protons, the atomic number of helium is 2. Natural helium exists as a mixture of two isotopes. Helium-3 occurs to the extent of $1.34 \times 10^{-4}\%$. Helium-4 accounts for practically 100% of natural helium. These helium nuclides respectively contain 1 neutron and 2 neutrons per nucleus. (Note that the number of neutrons in the nucleus of an atom may be determined by subtracting the atomic number from the mass number.) Moving about each helium nucleus are two electrons, both in the *1st energy level*. The chemical properties and spectrum of helium indicate that the 1st energy level may contain a *maximum* of two electrons. Thus, helium atoms have a *filled* 1st energy level.

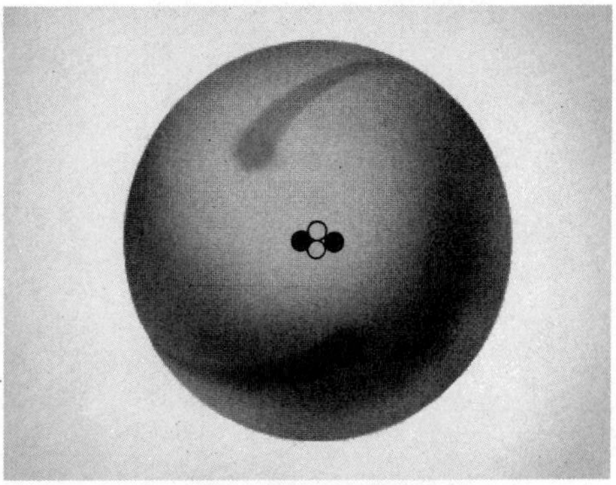

The atoms of hydrogen have one 1st-energy level electron. The atoms of helium have two (the maximum number). Hydrogen and helium, then, form the first *series* of elements.

3.8 Lithium atoms

Lithium exists in nature as two isotopes. Each atom of one isotope contains 3 protons, 3 neutrons, and 3 electrons. Each atom of the other isotope contains 3 protons, 4 neutrons, and 3 electrons. By the composition of these atoms, we know that the atomic number of lithium is 3 (3 protons). The mass number of the first isotope is 6 (3 protons + 3 neutrons). The mass number of the second isotope is 7 (3 protons + 4 neutrons). These isotopes are lithium-6 and lithium-7.

The chemical properties of lithium and a study of its spectrum help us learn its electron arrangement. Two of the three electrons in a lithium atom move in the 1st energy level. The third moves about the nucleus at a greater distance and with higher energy than the other two. It moves in the next larger shell or next higher energy level. This is called the *L-shell* or *2nd energy level*. The 1st energy level contains no more than two electrons. When it has this maximum of two electrons, additional electrons occupy higher energy levels at greater distances from the nucleus.

3.9 Other atoms of the second series

The element with atomic number 4 is beryllium. Naturally occurring beryllium consists of only one nuclide, beryllium-9. Beryllium nuclei consist of four protons and five neutrons. The four electrons are arranged with two in the 1st energy level and two in the 2nd energy level. Next in order of atomic structure are the elements boron, carbon, nitrogen, oxygen, fluorine, and

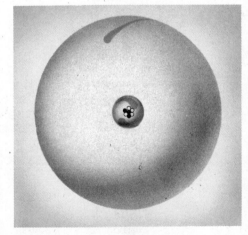

Fig. 3-5. Tentative model of a helium-4 atom. Its nucleus consists of two protons and two neutrons. Its two electrons move about this nucleus and completely fill the 1st energy level of the atom.

Fig. 3-6. Tentative model of a lithium-7 atom. This atom has a nucleus consisting of three protons and four neutrons. Two electrons are in the 1st energy level and one is in the 2nd energy level. Lithium is the first element in the second series.

neon. The atoms of each successive element have one additional proton per nucleus and may have one or two additional neutrons per nucleus. Each successive element has one additional electron in the 2nd energy level of each of its atoms. The atoms of the element neon have eight electrons in the 2nd energy level. The chemical properties and spectrum of neon indicate that the 2nd energy level may contain a maximum of eight electrons. So neon completes the second series of elements.

Table 3-2 contains information about the composition of nuclei and electron configurations (arrangements) of atoms in the first and second series.

3.10   The atoms of the third series

The elements in the third series are sodium, magnesium, aluminum, silicon, phosphorus, sulfur, chlorine, and argon. The

Table 3–2
NATURALLY OCCURRING NUCLIDES
(First and Second Series of Elements)

Name of nuclide	Abundance	Atomic number	Mass number	Composition of nucleus		Electron configuration	
				Protons	Neutrons	1st energy level (K shell)	2nd energy level (L shell)
hydrogen-1 (protium)	99.985%	1	1	1	0	1	
hydrogen-2 (deuterium)	0.015%	1	2	1	1	1	
helium-3	0.00013%	2	3	2	1	2	
helium-4	99.99987%	2	4	2	2	2	
lithium-6	7.42%	3	6	3	3	2	1
lithium-7	92.58%	3	7	3	4	2	1
beryllium-9	100%	4	9	4	5	2	2
boron-10	19.78%	5	10	5	5	2	3
boron-11	80.22%	5	11	5	6	2	3
carbon-12	98.89%	6	12	6	6	2	4
carbon-13	1.11%	6	13	6	7	2	4
nitrogen-14	99.63%	7	14	7	7	2	5
nitrogen-15	0.37%	7	15	7	8	2	5
oxygen-16	99.759%	8	16	8	8	2	6
oxygen-17	0.037%	8	17	8	9	2	6
oxygen-18	0.204%	8	18	8	10	2	6
fluorine-19	100%	9	19	9	10	2	7
neon-20	90.92%	10	20	10	10	2	8
neon-21	0.257%	10	21	10	11	2	8
neon-22	8.82%	10	22	10	12	2	8

atoms of these elements have a filled 1st energy level of two electrons and a filled 2nd energy level of eight electrons. Successive electrons occupy the **M shell** or **3rd energy level.** This level contains eight electrons in the atoms of the element argon.

3.11 Atomic mass

The actual mass of a single atom is very small. An atom of oxygen-16 has a mass of 2.65×10^{-23} g. A hydrogen-1 atom has a mass of 1.67×10^{-24} g. These numbers are not very easy to use in chemical arithmetic problems. Therefore, a system has been worked out for expressing the masses of atoms in numbers on a relative scale. These relative numbers are easier to use.

A relative scale consists of numbers without units. These relative-scale numbers must also be directly proportional to the magnitude of some property of matter we can measure. An example will make this definition clearer. Suppose we wish to set up a relative scale of weights of the members of your class. First, we must select the weight of one member of the class and give this weight a simple numerical value. In theory, it does not make any difference whose weight we select or what numerical value we assign to this weight. In practice, our choices should be made on the basis of convenience and usefulness.

Suppose we select the weight of a 125-lb (pound) pupil and assign this weight a value of 5.00. Now we may calculate the *relative* weights of the other members of the class by comparing their *actual* weights with that of the 125-lb pupil. A $15\overline{0}$-lb pupil has a weight which is $\dfrac{15\overline{0} \text{ lb}}{125 \text{ lb}}$ or 1.20 times that of the 125-lb pupil. Since the 125-lb pupil has an assigned weight of 5.00 on our relative weight scale, the $15\overline{0}$-lb pupil will have a relative weight of $1.20 \times 5.00 = 6.00$. We could have calculated this relative weight in one step by using the expression $\dfrac{15\overline{0} \text{ lb}}{125 \text{ lb}}$ $\times 5.00 = 6.00$. Similarly, the weight of a $20\overline{0}$-lb pupil will have a value of $\dfrac{20\overline{0} \text{ lb}}{125 \text{ lb}} \times 5.00 = 8.00$ on the relative scale. The weight of a $10\overline{0}$-lb pupil will have a value of $\dfrac{10\overline{0} \text{ lb}}{125 \text{ lb}} \times 5.00 = 4.00$ on the relative scale. These relative weights, 5.00, 6.00, 8.00, and 4.00, are directly proportional to the actual weights of 125 lb, $15\overline{0}$ lb, $20\overline{0}$ lb, and $10\overline{0}$ lb, respectively. If we are concerned only with *relationships* between these weights, it does not matter whether we use the actual weights or the relative weights. In the example we have given, the actual weights and the relative weights are probably equally convenient to use. But the very small numbers which express the actual masses of atoms in grams are not convenient to use.

Atomic masses are measured using a mass spectrograph. This device was developed by F. W. Aston, an English scientist, in 1919.

In order to set up a relative scale of masses of atoms, one atom is chosen and assigned a relative mass value. The masses of all other atoms are then expressed in relation to this defined relative mass. Such a system of relative masses was set up by the world organizations of chemists and physicists. In this system, the carbon-12 atom was chosen and assigned a relative mass of exactly 12. An atom such as the hydrogen-1 atom has a mass about $\frac{1}{12}$ that of the carbon-12 atom. So it has a relative mass of about $\frac{1}{12}$ of 12 or about 1. The accurate value for the relative mass of hydrogen-1 atoms is 1.007825. *The mass of an atom expressed relative to the "carbon-12 = exactly 12" scale is called the **atomic mass** of the atom.* Thus, 1.007825 is the atomic mass of hydrogen-1.

The atomic mass of a hydrogen-2 atom is found to be 2.01410, about $\frac{1}{6}$ that of a carbon-12 atom. An oxygen-16 atom has about $\frac{4}{3}$ the mass of a carbon-12 atom. Careful measurements show its atomic mass to be 15.99491. The mass of a magnesium-24 atom is found to be slightly less than double that of a carbon-12 atom. Its accurate atomic mass is 23.98504. In the same way the atomic mass of any nuclide is determined by comparison with the mass of a carbon-12 atom. Atomic masses are very accurately known, as the values given as examples above indicate. We have learned that the *mass number* is the total number of protons and neutrons in the nucleus of an atom. We can now see that it is also *the whole number closest to the atomic mass.*

The masses of the sub-atomic particles may also be expressed on the atomic-mass scale. The atomic mass of the electron is 0.0005486. That of the proton is 1.007277 and that of the neutron is 1.008665.

3.12   The Avogadro number and the mole

The number of atoms in the atomic mass of a nuclide taken in grams is an important unit of measure in chemistry. This is the number of carbon-12 atoms in exactly 12 grams of this nuclide. It is also the number of atoms in 1.007825 g of hydrogen-1. It is also the number of atoms in 15.99491 g of oxygen-16. You should recognize that the number of atoms in these three cases must be identical. This is a fact because atomic masses are directly proportional to actual masses of nuclides.

Scientists have developed many direct and indirect ways for determining this number. Its best present value is 6.022169×10^{23}. This means that scientists have learned that there are 6.022169×10^{23} carbon-12 atoms in exactly 12 g of this nuclide; 6.022169×10^{23} hydrogen-1 atoms in 1.007825 g of hydrogen-1; 6.022169×10^{23} oxygen-16 atoms in 15.99491 g of oxygen-16; and so on. This quantity, 6.022169×10^{23}, is so important in science that it has been given a special name. It is called the **Avogadro number,** after an Italian chemist and physicist, Amedeo Avogadro (1776–1856). This constant is quite useful and should be remembered to at least three significant figures: 6.02×10^{23}.

The amount of substance containing the Avogadro number of any kind of chemical unit is called a **mole** *of that substance.* Thus, exactly 12 g of carbon-12 is a mole of carbon-12 atoms; 1.007825 g of hydrogen-1 is a mole of hydrogen-1 atoms; 15.99491 g of oxygen-16 is a mole of oxygen-16 atoms; and so on. Note that *mole* is the name of the quantity containing a convenient number (6.02×10^{23}) of chemical units. Here the chemical unit is the atom. "Mole" is used by chemists the way a grocer uses "dozen" or a stationer uses "gross." A dozen of eggs is the quantity 12 eggs; a gross of pencils is the quantity 144 pencils; a mole of atoms is the quantity 6.02×10^{23} atoms. The mole is a very important unit of measure in chemistry. It will be used throughout this text. See Table 3-3.

1 mole of carbon atoms
6.02×10^{23} atoms
12.0 g C

Table 3-3
MOLAR QUANTITIES OF NUCLIDES

Nuclide	Atomic mass	Molar quantity	Number of atoms	Mass
C-12	12 exactly	1 mole	6.02×10^{23}	12 g exactly
H-1	1.007825	1 mole	6.02×10^{23}	1.007825 g
O-16	15.99491	1 mole	6.02×10^{23}	15.99491 g

1 mole of copper atoms
6.02×10^{23} atoms
63.5 g Cu

3.13 Atomic weight

Naturally occurring elements usually exist as a mixture of several isotopes. The percentage of each isotope in the naturally occurring element is nearly always the same, no matter where the element is found. Hence, the mass in grams of one mole of the *naturally occurring atoms* of an element indicates the average relative mass of these atoms on the same "carbon-12 = exactly 12" scale used for atomic masses. *The mass in grams of one mole of naturally occurring atoms of an element is called the* **gram-atomic weight** *of the element. The numerical portion of this quantity is the* **atomic weight** *of the element.*

Naturally occurring hydrogen consists of 99.985% hydrogen-1 atoms, atomic mass 1.007825; and 0.015% hydrogen-2 atoms, atomic mass 2.01410. In one mole of atoms of this mixture of isotopes, there will be 0.99985 mole of hydrogen-1 atoms and 0.00015 mole of hydrogen-2 atoms. The mass of 0.99985 mole of hydrogen-1 atoms is

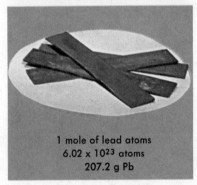

Fig. 3-7. The mass in grams of one mole of atoms of an element, 6.02 x 10^{23} atoms, is the gram-atomic weight of the element. The numerical portion ot this quantity is the atomic weight of the element.

$$0.99985 \text{ mole} \times \frac{1.007825 \text{ g}}{1 \text{ mole}} = 1.00767 \text{ g}$$

and the mass of 0.00015 mole of hydrogen-2 atoms is

$$0.00015 \text{ mole} \times \frac{2.01410 \text{ g}}{1 \text{ mole}} = 0.00030 \text{ g}$$

1 mole of lead atoms
6.02×10^{23} atoms
207.2 g Pb

The mass of one mole of atoms of this mixture is therefore

$$1.00767 \text{ g} + 0.00030 \text{ g} = 1.00797 \text{ g}$$

This mass is the gram-atomic weight of hydrogen. The numerical portion, 1.00797, is the atomic weight of hydrogen. Similarly, naturally occurring carbon consists of 98.89% carbon-12, atomic mass exactly 12 (by definition), and 1.11% carbon-13, atomic mass 13.00335. One mole of atoms of this **mixture** has a mass of 12.01115 g. Thus, 12.01115 g is the gram-atomic weight of carbon and 12.01115 is its atomic weight.

Atomic weights are important to the chemist because they indicate relative mass relationships between reacting elements. They enable him to predict the quantities of materials which will be involved in chemical reactions.

Atomic weights appear in the periodic table on the inside back cover of this book and in Table 4, page 630, of the Appendix. They include the most recent accurate figures. They are still revised occasionally when new data become available. You need not memorize them. Approximate atomic weights are given on the inside of the front cover (and in Table 5 of the Appendix). These are accurate enough for use in solving problems in high school chemistry. Your instructor may ask you to memorize some or all of these approximate values. For more advanced chemical work, the accurate atomic weights in the periodic table or Table 4 on page 630 must always be used.

Sample Problem

What is the mass in grams of 3.50 moles of copper atoms?

Solution

The atomic weight of copper from the table inside the back cover or from Table 4 in the Appendix is 63.546. Therefore, the gram-atomic weight of copper, or the mass of one mole of copper atoms, is 63.546 g. The mass of 3.50 moles of copper atoms is

$$3.50 \text{ moles} \times \frac{63.546 \text{ g Cu}}{\text{mole}} = 222 \text{ g Cu}$$

Since the number of moles of copper atoms is expressed in the problem to only three significant figures, the approximate atomic weight of copper found in the table inside the front cover or in Table 5 in the Appendix, 63.5 could have been used in the solution. The same answer is obtained.

$$3.50 \text{ moles} \times \frac{63.5 \text{ g Cu}}{\text{mole}} = 222 \text{ g Cu}$$

Sample Problem

How many moles of atoms are there in 6.195 g of phosphorus?

Solution

Since the mass of phosphorus is given to four significant figures, we must use the atomic weight of phosphorus given in the table inside the back cover to at least four significant figures. Rounded to four significant figures, 30.9738 is 30.97. Thus there is one mole of phosphorus atoms in 30.97 g of phosphorus. Then 6.195 g of phosphorus contains

$$\textbf{6.195 g P} \times \frac{\textbf{1 mole}}{\textbf{30.97 g P}} = \textbf{0.2000 mole}$$

Note that significant-figure rules permit an answer calculated to four significant figures.

QUESTIONS
Group A

1. What evidence is there that the particles of matter are very small?
2. What topics in chemistry are today included in the atomic theory?
3. What general statements may be made about the atoms of the elements and their properties?
4. (a) What are the main parts of an atom? (b) What particles are found in each part? (c) Describe each type of particle.
5. How does the size of the nucleus of an atom compare with the size of an atom?
6. What is a shell or energy level?
7. Describe the movement of electrons about the nucleus of an atom.
8. Describe the structure of each of the three isotopes of hydrogen.
9. (a) What is the atomic number of an atom? (b) How is it related to the number of electrons in a neutral atom?
10. (a) What are nuclides? (b) What are isotopes?
11. If you know the number and kinds of particles in an atom, how can you calculate its mass number?
12. An atomic nucleus which contains 8 protons and 9 neutrons is surrounded by 8 electrons: 2 in the 1st energy level and 6 in the 2nd energy level. (a) What is the atomic number of this nuclide? (b) What is its mass number? (c) What is the name of this nuclide?
13. Which among the first ten elements exist naturally as a single nuclide?
14. What is the atomic mass of an atom?
15. (a) How many atoms are there in exactly 12 g of carbon-12? (b) What name is given to this number? (c) What name is given to the amount of substance containing this number of chemical units?
16. What is the atomic weight of an element?
17. What nuclide is the standard for the atomic weight scale?
18. Why are atomic weights important to the chemist?
19. From the Table of Atomic Weights, find the atomic numbers and atomic weights of: (a) silver; (b) gold; (c) copper; (d) sulfur; (e) uranium.
20. What is the mass in grams of: (a) 2.00 moles of helium atoms; (b) 5.00 moles of boron atoms; (c) 0.500 mole of neon atoms; (d) 0.250 mole of magnesium atoms;

(e) 0.100 mole of silicon atoms? Use the Table of Atomic Weights and follow the rules for significant figure calculations.

21. How many moles of atoms are there in: (a) 20.823 g of lithium; (b) 160.93 g of sodium; (c) 3.995 g of argon; (d) 8.016 g of sulfur; (e) 20.24 g of aluminum?

Group B

22. What two observations about matter did Dalton believe could suggest the nature and properties of atoms?

23. In one of the Rutherford experiments, it was found that 1 high-speed positively charged particle in 8000 was deflected by 90° or more when directed at a thin sheet of platinum. What does this observation indicate about the structure of platinum atoms?

24. If you arrange the elements in order of increasing atomic number, how do the atoms of successive elements differ in: (a) number of protons? (b) number of electrons? (c) number of neutrons?

25. Describe the electron configurations of the atoms of the elements in the second series.

26. Copy and complete the following table *on a separate sheet of paper.*

Name of nuclide	Atomic number	Mass number	Composition of nucleus		Electron configuration		
			Protons	Neutrons	K	L	M
sodium-23	11						
magnesium-24	12						
aluminum-27	13						
silicon-28	14						
phosphorus-31	15						
sulfur-32	16						
chlorine-35	17						
argon-40	18						

27. Chlorine exists in nature as chlorine-35, atomic mass 34.96885, and chlorine-37, atomic mass 36.96590. Its atomic weight is 35.453. What must be the approximate abundance in nature of these two isotopes?

28. The elements sodium, aluminum, and phosphorus have only one naturally occurring nuclide. How will the atomic mass of this nuclide and the atomic weight of the element compare?

29. (a) What is the relationship between an atom containing 10 protons, 10 neutrons, and 10 electrons, and one containing 10 protons, 11 neutrons, and 10 electrons? (b) What is the relationship between an atom containing 10 protons, 11 neutrons, and 10 electrons and one containing 11 protons, 10 neutrons, and 11 electrons?

30. How can the mass in grams of a single atom of a nuclide be calculated if the atomic mass of the nuclide is known?

31. What is the significance of the quotient obtained by dividing the gram-atomic weight of an element by the Avogadro number?

32. Calculate the atomic weight of oxygen. The naturally occurring element consists of 99.759% O-16, atomic mass 15.99491; 0.037% O-17, atomic mass 16.99914; and 0.204% O-18, atomic mass 17.99916.

Chapter 4

Arrangement of Electrons in Atoms

4.1 The nucleus and moving electrons

We have already described the atom as a nucleus, containing protons and usually neutrons, surrounded by electrons. The electrons move about the nucleus in regions called shells or energy levels. Now we must consider the structure of the atom in more detail. We must learn how the electrons are arranged and held within the atom.

We recall that the nucleus has a positive charge because of its protons. We also know that a neutral atom contains an equal number of protons and negatively charged electrons. Thus we might expect electrons to be held in an atom by the attraction between oppositely charged particles. This arrangement would be similar to the orbiting of a satellite around the earth. Instead of gravitational attraction which holds a satellite in orbit, the attraction of oppositely charged particles would hold an electron in its path.

However, scientists have observed that electrically charged particles moving in curved paths give off energy. If an electron moving about a nucleus continually gave off energy, it should slow down. It should gradually move nearer to the nucleus, and eventually fall into it. This behavior would be like the slowing down of a satellite by friction with the earth's upper atmosphere. As this slowing down occurs, the satellite falls toward the earth, and eventually burns up in the earth's atmosphere. But we know that atoms do not collapse. Electrons do not fall into the nucleus. Thus, the attraction of oppositely charged particles may partly explain how electrons are held by the nucleus of an atom. But it is not satisfactory for explaining the motion of electrons about the nucleus.

Fig. 4-1. Hydrogen atoms are excited when high-voltage electricity is passed through a glass tube containing hydrogen gas. The lavender glow is characteristic of hydrogen.

From the CHEM Study Film, *Chemical Bonding*

61

4.2 Electromagnetic radiation

Visible light is one kind of electromagnetic radiation. Other kinds of electromagnetic radiation are X rays, ultraviolet and infrared light, and radio waves. Electromagnetic radiations are forms of energy which travel through space as waves. They move at the rate of 3.00×10^8 m/sec, the speed of light in a vacuum. For any wave motion, the speed equals the product of the *frequency* (the number of waves passing a given point in one second) and the *wavelength*. For electromagnetic radiation $c = f\lambda$ where c is the speed of light, f is the frequency, and λ (lambda) is the wavelength. Since c is the same for all electromagnetic radiation, the product $f\lambda$ is a constant; and λ is inversely proportional to f.

Electromagnetic radiation, in addition to its wave characteristics, also has some properties of particles. Electromagnetic radiation is transferred to matter in units or *quanta* of energy called **photons**. The energy of a photon is proportional to the frequency of the radiation. The energy of a photon and the frequency of the radiation are related by $E = hf$. Here, E is the energy of the photon, h is a proportionality constant called *Planck's constant,* and f is the frequency of the radiation. Planck's constant is the same for all types of electromagnetic radiation. Since f multiplied by Planck's constant equals E, f and E are directly proportional.

We have already stated that energy is transferred to matter in photon units. Therefore, the absorption of a photon by an atom increases its energy by a definite quantity, hf. An atom which has absorbed energy in this way is called an *excited* atom. When excited atoms radiate energy, the radiation must be given off in photon units also.

4.3 Spectra of atoms

Atoms may be excited by heating them in a flame or in an electric arc. Such excited atoms give off light of a characteristic color as they return to their normal energy states. An example is the yellow-orange light given off by sodium atoms in a glass rod heated in a burner flame. Atoms of gases can be excited by passing high-voltage electricity through the gas contained inside a glass tube. The red light of neon advertising signs is a familiar example. If hydrogen gas is used in such a tube, it glows with a characteristic lavender color. (See Figure 4-1 on page 61.)

Suppose we observe this lavender-colored light of hydrogen gas through a spectroscope. We find that it consists of lines of particular colors as shown in Figure 4-4. Such a spectrum is called a bright-line spectrum. It indicates that the light given off by excited atoms has only certain wavelengths. Light of a particular wavelength has a definite *frequency* ($c = f\lambda$) and a characteristic color. Also, a definite frequency means a definite energy ($E = hf$). Hence the bright-line hydrogen spectrum shows that

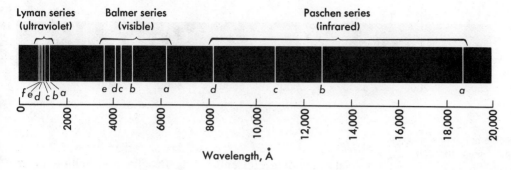

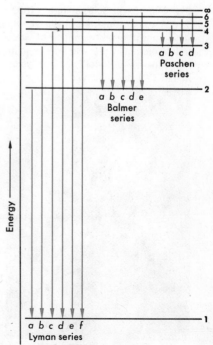

excited hydrogen atoms emit (give off) photons having only certain energies. Now, recall the proportionality relationship between λ, f, and E described in Section 4.2. Because of this relationship, a long wavelength is associated with a small quantity of energy and a short wavelength is associated with a large quantity of energy. (See question 15 at the end of this chapter.)

We have found that emitted photons have only certain energies. Further, these energies represent differences between the energies of atoms before and after radiation. Therefore, these energies of atoms are fixed and definite quantities. And because each species of atom has its own characteristic spectrum, each atom must have its own characteristic energy possibilities. This evidence also means that the energy changes which occur from time to time within an atom involve definite amounts of energy rather than a continuous flow of energy.

Suppose we assume that the energy changes of an excited atom returning to its normal energy state are actually changes in the energy of its electrons. Then we can devise a diagram which shows the electron energy levels of the atom. Since the hydrogen atom is a simple atom with a simple spectrum, it was thoroughly studied in the early years of this century. Figure 4-2 includes lines in the ultraviolet and infrared regions of the hydrogen spectrum. Figure 4-3 gives the corresponding electron energy levels of the hydrogen atom. It also shows some of the transitions which are possible in this atom.

The idea of electron energy levels in the hydrogen atom was developed by Niels Bohr in 1913. The definite energy levels of the atom indicate two things about the electron orbiting the hydrogen nucleus. First, it can move only at certain distances from the nucleus. Second, it can move with only certain speeds.

This model works well in explaining the spectra of one-electron particles like the hydrogen atom. But it does not explain satisfactorily the spectra of more complex atoms.

4.4   Wave-mechanics concept of an atom

During the past half century, scientists have used mathematics widely in the study of atomic structure. The work of theoretical

Fig. 4-2. Representative lines in the hydrogen spectrum. The small letter below each line indicates which of the energy-level transitions in Figure 4-3 produces it.

Fig. 4-3. An electron energy-level diagram for hydrogen showing some of the transitions which are possible in this atom. Transitions which leave an electron in a particular final energy level belongs to a particular spectrum series. Some of these series are named for the men who discovered them.

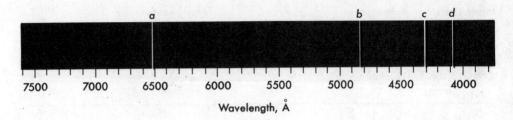

Wavelength, Å

Fig. 4-4. The visible bright-line spectrum of hydrogen seen through a spectroscope.

Fig. 4-5. Erwin Schroedinger (1887-1961) was an Austrian physicist who developed the mathematics of wave mechanics in 1926. He was a joint recipient of the Nobel Prize in physics in 1933 for this achievement.

The Bettmann Archive, Inc.

physicists including Heisenberg, de Broglie, and Schroedinger, helped develop a complex mathematical picture of atomic structure by the use of wave mechanics. We cannot go into detail about the basic ideas of wave mechanics in this text. But we can explain briefly some of the conclusions.

The motion of an electron about an atom is not in a definite path like that of the earth about the sun. In fact, it is impossible to determine an electron's path without changing that path. So we can give an electron's location only in terms of probabilities. This location is described by a *space orbital*. A space orbital may be thought of as a highly probable location in which an electron may be found. The path of the single hydrogen electron is thought to lie within a hollow sphere of somewhat indefinite thickness. This sphere surrounds the nucleus. The average radius of the sphere represents the most probable distance of the electron from the nucleus. This sphere is sometimes referred to as an *electron cloud*. The electron cloud gives size and shape to an atom. It also prevents two free atoms (or portions of free atoms) from occupying the same space.

4.5 Quantum numbers

The mathematics of wave mechanics shows that the energy state of an electron in an atom may be described by a set of four numbers. These are called *quantum numbers*. These quantum numbers describe the space orbital in which the electron moves in terms of (1) distance from the nucleus, (2) shape, (3) position with respect to the three axes in space, and (4) the direction of spin of the electron in the orbital.

The *principal quantum number,* symbolized by n, indicates the average distance of the electron from the nucleus of the atom. It is a positive whole number, having values 1, 2, 3, and so on. The principal quantum number is the main energy-level designation, or identifying number, of an orbital. The 1st energy level is closest to the nucleus with others at increasing distances. Electrons in the 1st energy level have the lowest energies. Electrons in higher energy levels have increasingly greater energies. Sometimes, the energy levels are designated by letters instead of numbers. These designations are K shell, L shell, M shell, N shell, O shell, etc.

Table 4-1
QUANTUM NUMBER RELATIONSHIPS IN ATOMIC STRUCTURE

Principal quantum number (Energy level) (n)	Orbital quantum number (n orbital shapes) (n sublevels)	Number of orbitals per sublevel	Number of orbitals per energy level (n^2)	Number of electrons per sublevel	Number of electrons per energy level ($2n^2$)
1	s	1	1	2	2
2	s	1	4	2	8
	p	3		6	
3	s	1	9	2	18
	p	3		6	
	d	5		10	
4	s	1	16	2	32
	p	3		6	
	d	5		10	
	f	7		14	

The *orbital quantum number* indicates the shape of the orbital in which the electron moves. The number of possible shapes is equal to the value of the principal quantum number. In the 1st energy level, an orbital of only one shape is possible. In the 2nd energy level, orbitals of two shapes are possible. In the 3rd energy level, orbitals of three shapes are possible. In the *n*th energy level, orbitals of *n* shapes are possible. The letter designations for the first four orbital quantum numbers are *s*, *p*, *d*, and *f*. These are listed in order of ascending energies. For a particular energy level, the *s* orbital has the lowest energy. The *p* orbitals have higher energy than the *s* orbitals, the *d* orbitals have higher energy than the *p* orbitals, and so on. Sometimes the *s* orbital is called the *s* sublevel, the *p* orbitals the *p* sublevel, the *d* orbitals the *d* sublevel, etc.

The *magnetic quantum number* indicates the position about the three axes in space of the orbital. There is only one position in the space around the nucleus for an *s* orbital. There are three positions for a *p* orbital, five positions for a *d* orbital, and seven positions for an *f* orbital. See Figures 4-6 and 4-7.

The *spin quantum number* indicates a property of the electron described by just two conditions. These conditions may be thought of as being like the right-handed or left-handed conditions of a glove. By similarity with the earth-sun system, this property is called *electron spin*. Scientists often refer to the two possibilities for spin as clockwise and counterclockwise. Thus each of the *positions of orbitals in the space around the nucleus* described by the first three quantum numbers can be occupied by

Fig. 4-6. Position in the space about the nucleus of s orbitals.

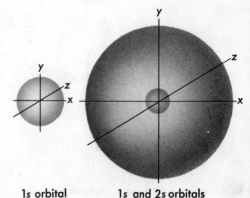

1s orbital   1s and 2s orbitals

Editor's note: In Section 4.6 and throughout the rest of the book, where the authors refer to electrons occupying various orbitals in a definite order, they are referring to an imaginary electron arrangement for each element that can be built starting with the orbital structure of a hydrogen atom. We have confidence that these electron structures accurately represent reality because they can be used to explain the chemical properties of each element.

Fig. 4-7. The three spatial positions of *p* orbitals.

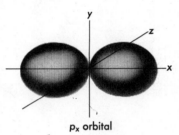

p_x orbital

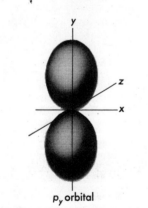

p_y orbital

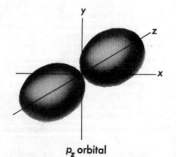

p_z orbital

only two electrons and these must have opposite spins. No two electrons in an atom therefore can have exactly the same set of four quantum numbers. This agrees with the observation that no two electrons in an atom have exactly the same energy.

4.6 Electron configuration of atoms of first three series

The quantum numbers which describe the arrangement of electrons about an atom are related to the energies of the electrons. The energies associated with the various electron orbitals as they become occupied by electrons are shown in Figure 4-8. The most stable state of an atom is called its *ground state*. In this condition, the electrons have the lowest possible energies. If we know the number of electrons in an atom, we can describe the arrangement of electrons, or the *electron configuration,* of its ground state. We can do this because electrons occupy the various orbitals in a reasonably definite order starting with those of lowest energy.

Hydrogen atoms have only one electron. In the ground state this electron moves in the 1*s* sublevel, the *s* sublevel of the 1st energy level. The two electrons of helium atoms both occupy the 1*s* sublevel. This may be shown in *orbital notation* as

$$\text{H} \quad \overset{1s}{\oslash} \qquad \text{He} \quad \overset{1s}{\otimes}$$

Here, the occupation of a space orbital by one electron is represented as $\oslash$. The occupation of a space orbital by two electrons is represented as $\otimes$. An empty circle, $\bigcirc$, indicates an unoccupied space orbital. The two helium electrons occupying the same space orbital must have opposite spins. Two such electrons of opposite spin in the same space orbital are called an *electron pair*.

In *electron-configuration notation* hydrogen has the designation $1s^1$. This designation shows that hydrogen has one electron (represented by the superscript) in the *s* sublevel of the 1st energy level. Helium's electron structure is represented as $1s^2$. This means that helium has two electrons (represented by the superscript) in the *s* sublevel of the 1st energy level.

In *electron-dot notation,* hydrogen and helium are designated as

$$\text{H}\cdot \qquad \text{He:}$$

In this notation, the symbol represents the element, and the dots indicate the number of outer-shell electrons. Two dots written together, as in the helium notation, represent an *electron pair*.

The elements in the second series have electrons occupying the 2nd energy level. Their ground-state electron arrangements may be represented by orbital notation, electron-configuration notation, and electron-dot notation as shown in Table 4-2. Note

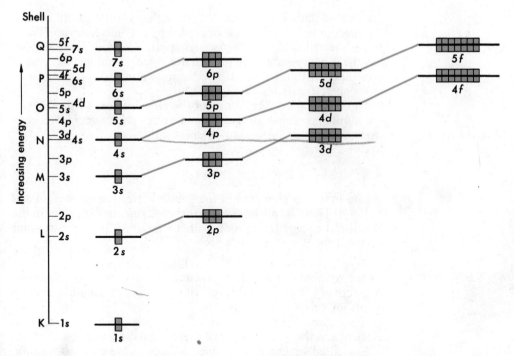

Fig. 4-8. This chart shows the approximate relative energies of the atomic sublevels as they are occupied by electrons.

that the orbital notations and electron-configuration notations show *all* of the electrons in the atom. However, the electron-dot notations show only the electrons in the *outer* (highest numbered) energy level or shell.

Table 4–2

ELECTRON NOTATIONS OF ATOMS IN THE SECOND SERIES

	Orbital notation			Electron-configuration notation	Electron-dot notation
	1s	*2s*	*2p*		
Li	⊗	⊘	○ ○ ○	$1s^2 2s^1$	Li·
Be	⊗	⊗	○ ○ ○	$1s^2 2s^2$	Be:
B	⊗	⊗	⊘ ○ ○	$1s^2 2s^2 2p^1$	Ḃ:
C	⊗	⊗	⊘ ⊘ ○	$1s^2 2s^2 2p^2$	·Ċ:
N	⊗	⊗	⊘ ⊘ ⊘	$1s^2 2s^2 2p^3$	·Ṅ:
O	⊗	⊗	⊗ ⊘ ⊘	$1s^2 2s^2 2p^4$	·Ö:
F	⊗	⊗	⊗ ⊗ ⊘	$1s^2 2s^2 2p^5$	:Ḟ:
Ne	⊗	⊗	⊗ ⊗ ⊗	$1s^2 2s^2 2p^6$	:Ṅe:

Observe that electrons do not pair up in p orbitals until each of the three p space orbitals is occupied by a single electron. These single electrons also have parallel spins. An atom such as neon has the s and p sublevels of its outer (highest numbered) energy level filled with eight electrons. Such an atom is said to have an outer shell consisting of an *octet*.

The electron configurations of the elements of the third series are similar to those of the second series with successive electrons occupying the $3s$ and $3p$ space orbitals.

See Question 20 at the end of this chapter.

4.7 Atoms of the fourth series

The first two elements in the fourth series are potassium and calcium. Their atoms have the same electron configuration in the first three energy levels as argon, $1s^22s^22p^63s^23p^6$. Electron-dot symbols for these elements are

$$\textbf{K}\cdot \qquad \textbf{Ca:}$$

These symbols show the presence of one and two electrons respectively in the $4s$ sublevel. In the atoms of the next ten elements of this fourth series, the $3d$ sublevel is occupied in successive steps by the addition of electrons. The distribution of electrons in the ground state of these atoms is given in Table 4-3.

Half-filled or completely filled sublevels have extra stability. The structures of both the chromium and copper atoms given in Table 4-3 appear to be irregular. Chromium would be expected

Table 4–3
STRUCTURE OF ATOMS IN THE FOURTH SERIES

Name	Symbol	Atomic number	Number of electrons in sublevels							
			1s	2s	2p	3s	3p	3d	4s	4p
potassium	K	19	2	2	6	2	6		1	
calcium	Ca	20	2	2	6	2	6		2	
scandium	Sc	21	2	2	6	2	6	1	2	
titanium	Ti	22	2	2	6	2	6	2	2	
vanadium	V	23	2	2	6	2	6	3	2	
chromium	Cr	24	2	2	6	2	6	5	1	
manganese	Mn	25	2	2	6	2	6	5	2	
iron	Fe	26	2	2	6	2	6	6	2	
cobalt	Co	27	2	2	6	2	6	7	2	
nickel	Ni	28	2	2	6	2	6	8	2	
copper	Cu	29	2	2	6	2	6	10	1	
zinc	Zn	30	2	2	6	2	6	10	2	
gallium	Ga	31	2	2	6	2	6	10	2	1
germanium	Ge	32	2	2	6	2	6	10	2	2
arsenic	As	33	2	2	6	2	6	10	2	3
selenium	Se	34	2	2	6	2	6	10	2	4
bromine	Br	35	2	2	6	2	6	10	2	5
krypton	Kr	36	2	2	6	2	6	10	2	6

to have four $3d$ electrons and two $4s$ electrons. Instead it has
five $3d$ electrons and one $4s$ electron. This $3d^54s^1$ structure must
have higher stability and lower energy than the expected $3d^44s^2$
structure. Apparently a half-filled $3d$ sublevel provides greater
stability than a $3d$ sublevel with only four electrons. This greater
stability occurs even though the electron-pair in the $4s$ sublevel
is broken up. Copper would be expected to have nine $3d$ electrons and two $4s$ electrons. Instead, it has ten $3d$ electrons and
one $4s$ electron. Here the filled $3d$ sublevel provides greater
stability.

With the element zinc, the 3rd energy level is completely filled.
Also there are two electrons in the 4th energy level. The remaining six elements in the fourth series are gallium, germanium,
arsenic, selenium, bromine, and krypton. They all have completely filled 1st, 2nd, and 3rd energy levels. The electrons in the
$4s$ and $4p$ sublevels are shown in these electron-dot symbols:

$$\text{Ga:} \quad \cdot\text{Ge:} \quad \cdot\overset{\displaystyle\cdot}{\text{As:}} \quad \cdot\overset{\displaystyle\cdot\cdot}{\text{Se:}} \quad :\overset{\displaystyle\cdot\cdot}{\text{Br:}} \quad :\overset{\displaystyle\cdot\cdot}{\underset{\displaystyle\cdot\cdot}{\text{Kr:}}}$$

Krypton is the last member of the fourth series. It is a gas that
has an octet (two s and six p electrons) in its 4th energy level. Its
electron-configuration notation is $1s^22s^22p^63s^23p^63d^{10}4s^24p^6$. Observe that in this notation all the sublevels of an energy level are
grouped together in s, p, d, and f order.

4.8 Atoms of the fifth series

The fifth series of elements, like the fourth, consists of eighteen
elements. The first two of these are rubidium and strontium.
These elements have inner shells like krypton, and one and two
electrons respectively in the $5s$ sublevel.

$$\text{Rb}\cdot \qquad \text{Sr:}$$

In the atoms of the next ten elements the five $4d$ sublevel orbitals become occupied by the successive addition of electrons
to the atom structure.

The atoms of the element cadmium have completely filled 1st,
2nd, and 3rd energy levels. The $4s$, $4p$, and $4d$ sublevels are also
filled, and there are two electrons in the $5s$ sublevel. The atoms
of the remaining six elements of the fifth series are indium, tin,
antimony, tellurium, iodine, and xenon. The first four energy
levels of these elements are similar to those of cadmium, but successive electrons occupy the $5p$ sublevel, which has the next
higher energy.

$$\text{In:} \quad \cdot\text{Sn:} \quad \cdot\overset{\displaystyle\cdot}{\text{Sb:}} \quad \cdot\overset{\displaystyle\cdot\cdot}{\text{Te:}} \quad :\overset{\displaystyle\cdot\cdot}{\text{I:}} \quad :\overset{\displaystyle\cdot\cdot}{\underset{\displaystyle\cdot\cdot}{\text{Xe:}}}$$

Thus the addition of electrons to sublevels of two different
energy levels proceeds in the fifth series as it did in the fourth
series. Xenon, the last member of the series, has an octet in its
5th energy level, and $4s$, $4p$ and $4d$ sublevels filled.

Table 4–4
STRUCTURE OF ATOMS IN THE FIFTH SERIES

Name	Symbol	Atomic number	Number of electrons in sublevels										
			1s	2s	2p	3s	3p	3d	4s	4p	4d	5s	5p
rubidium	Rb	37	2	2	6	2	6	10	2	6		1	
strontium	Sr	38	2	2	6	2	6	10	2	6		2	
yttrium	Y	39	2	2	6	2	6	10	2	6	1	2	
zirconium	Zr	40	2	2	6	2	6	10	2	6	2	2	
niobium	Nb	41	2	2	6	2	6	10	2	6	4	1	
molybdenum	Mo	42	2	2	6	2	6	10	2	6	5	1	
technetium	Tc	43	2	2	6	2	6	10	2	6	5	2	
ruthenium	Ru	44	2	2	6	2	6	10	2	6	7	1	
rhodium	Rh	45	2	2	6	2	6	10	2	6	8	1	
palladium	Pd	46	2	2	6	2	6	10	2	6	10		
silver	Ag	47	2	2	6	2	6	10	2	6	10	1	
cadmium	Cd	48	2	2	6	2	6	10	2	6	10	2	
indium	In	49	2	2	6	2	6	10	2	6	10	2	1
tin	Sn	50	2	2	6	2	6	10	2	6	10	2	2
antimony	Sb	51	2	2	6	2	6	10	2	6	10	2	3
tellurium	Te	52	2	2	6	2	6	10	2	6	10	2	4
iodine	I	53	2	2	6	2	6	10	2	6	10	2	5
xenon	Xe	54	2	2	6	2	6	10	2	6	10	2	6

4.9 Atoms of the sixth series

The sixth series of atoms is much longer than the others. It consists of thirty-two elements. The atoms of the first two, cesium and barium, have inner energy levels like xenon and successive electrons in the 6s sublevel.

Cs·   Ba:

At lanthanum the lowest energy d-sublevel (here 5d) begins to fill, as 4d began to fill at yttrium and 3d began to fill at scandium. But with the very next element, cerium, something different happens. In the atoms of cerium and the next twelve elements of the sixth series, the seven orbitals of the 4f sublevel are occupied by the addition of successive electrons. In atoms of the element ytterbium, the 4th energy level has all of its sublevels filled with 32 electrons.

The atoms of the next ten elements of the sixth series have successive electrons occupying the five orbitals of the 5d sublevel, which have the next higher energies.

The atoms of the remaining six elements of this series are thallium, lead, bismuth, polonium, astatine, and radon. They have the first four energy levels complete, and filled 5s, 5p, and 5d sublevels. The 6s and 6p electrons are shown in these electron-dot symbols:

Table 4–5
STRUCTURE OF ATOMS IN THE SIXTH SERIES

Name	Symbol	Atomic number		Number of electrons in sublevels						
				4d	4f	5s	5p	5d	6s	6p
cesium	Cs	55		10		2	6		1	
barium	Ba	56		10		2	6		2	
lanthanum	La	57		10		2	6	1	2	
cerium	Ce	58		10	2	2	6		2	
praseodymium	Pr	59		10	3	2	6		2	
neodymium	Nd	60		10	4	2	6		2	
promethium	Pm	61		10	5	2	6		2	
samarium	Sm	62		10	6	2	6		2	
europium	Eu	63		10	7	2	6		2	
gadolinium	Gd	64		10	7	2	6	1	2	
terbium	Tb	65		10	9	2	6		2	
dysprosium	Dy	66		10	10	2	6		2	
holmium	Ho	67		10	11	2	6		2	
erbium	Er	68	krypton	10	12	2	6		2	
thulium	Tm	69	structure	10	13	2	6		2	
ytterbium	Yb	70	plus	10	14	2	6		2	
lutetium	Lu	71		10	14	2	6	1	2	
hafnium	Hf	72		10	14	2	6	2	2	
tantalum	Ta	73		10	14	2	6	3	2	
tungsten	W	74		10	14	2	6	4	2	
rhenium	Re	75		10	14	2	6	5	2	
osmium	Os	76		10	14	2	6	6	2	
iridium	Ir	77		10	14	2	6	7	2	
platinum	Pt	78		10	14	2	6	9	1	
gold	Au	79		10	14	2	6	10	1	
mercury	Hg	80		10	14	2	6	10	2	
thallium	Tl	81		10	14	2	6	10	2	1
lead	Pb	82		10	14	2	6	10	2	2
bismuth	Bi	83		10	14	2	6	10	2	3
polonium	Po	84		10	14	2	6	10	2	4
astatine	At	85		10	14	2	6	10	2	5
radon	Rn	86		10	14	2	6	10	2	6

Tl: ·Pb: ·Bi: ·Po: :At: :Rn:

Radon, the last member of the sixth series, has an octet in its 6th energy level, and 5s, 5p, and 5d sublevels filled.

4.10 Atoms of the seventh series

The seventh series of elements is an incomplete series of which only 19 elements are known. Table 4-6 shows what is believed to be the arrangement of electrons in the 5th, 6th, and 7th energy

Table 4–6

STRUCTURE OF ATOMS IN THE SEVENTH SERIES

Name	Symbol	Atomic number		Number of electrons in sublevels						
				4f	5d	5f	6s	6p	6d	7s
francium	Fr	87		14	10		2	6		1
radium	Ra	88		14	10		2	6		2
actinium	Ac	89		14	10		2	6	1	2
thorium	Th	90		14	10		2	6	2	2
protactinium	Pa	91		14	10	2	2	6	1	2
uranium	U	92		14	10	3	2	6	1	2
neptunium	Np	93		14	10	4	2	6	1	2
plutonium	Pu	94	xenon	14	10	6	2	6		2
americium	Am	95	structure	14	10	7	2	6		2
curium	Cm	96	plus	14	10	7	2	6	1	2
berkelium	Bk	97		14	10	8	2	6	1	2
californium	Cf	98		14	10	10	2	6		2?
einsteinium	Es	99		14	10	11	2	6		2?
fermium	Fm	100		14	10	12	2	6		2?
mendelevium	Md	101		14	10	13	2	6		2?
nobelium	No	102		14	10	14	2	6		2?
lawrencium	Lr	103		14	10	14	2	6	1	2?
		104		14	10	14	2	6	2	2?
		105		14	10	14	2	6	3	2?

levels. Appendix Table 7, Electronic Arrangement of the Elements, gives the complete electron configurations for all of the elements.

QUESTIONS

Group A

1. (a) What are electromagnetic radiations? (b) Give examples of forms of electromagnetic radiation.
2. (a) In what form do electromagnetic radiations travel through space? (b) In what form are they transferred to matter?
3. How is an excited atom produced?
4. (a) The red line in the visible spectrum of hydrogen has a wavelength of 6563 Å. From Figures 4-2 and 4-3 identify the electron-energy-level transition which produces this line. (b) Which electron-energy-level transition produces the blue line having a wavelength of 4861 Å?
5. What are the principle characteristics of the Bohr model of the hydrogen atom?
6. What is a space orbital?
7. (a) What is an electron cloud? (b) What properties does it give an atom?
8. What are the four kinds of quantum numbers and what does each indicate?

9. (a) What is the shape of an s orbital? (b) How many s orbitals can there be in an energy level? (c) How many electrons can occupy such an orbital? (d) What characteristic must these electrons have? (e) Which is the lowest energy level having an s orbital?
10. (a) What is the shape of a p orbital? (b) How many p orbitals can there be in an energy level? (c) How are they arranged with respect to one another? (d) Which is the lowest energy level having p orbitals?
11. (a) May two electrons in the same atom have exactly the same set of quantum numbers? (b) May two electrons occupy the same space orbital in an atom? (c) Under what conditions?
12. Distinguish between an atom in its ground state and an excited atom.
13. (a) What is an electron pair? (b) What is an octet?

Group B

14. What aspect of the attraction between oppositely charged particles makes it unsatisfactory for explaining how electrons move in an atom?
15. Derive the relationship between λ and E for electromagnetic radiation.
16. Why must energy transitions within an atom occur in definite amounts rather than as a continuous flow?
17. (a) From Figures 4-2 and 4-3, determine the approximate wavelength of the radiation produced by an electron transition in a hydrogen atom from the 4th energy level to the 1st energy level; (b) from the 4th energy level to the 3rd energy level.
18. (a) How many d orbitals can there be in an energy level? (b) How many d electrons can there be in an energy level? (c) Which is the lowest energy level having d orbitals?
19. (a) How many f orbitals can there be in an energy level? (b) How many f electrons can there be in an energy level? (c) Which is the lowest energy level having f orbitals?
20. On a separate sheet of paper copy and complete the following table for the atoms in the third series. *Do not write in this book.*

Chemical symbol	Orbital notation	Electron-configuration notation	Electron-dot notation
Na			
Mg			
Al			
Si			
P			
S			
Cl			
Ar			

21. How many electron pairs are there in the outer shell of each of the following atoms: (a) carbon; (b) krypton; (c) oxygen; (d) arsenic; (e) iodine?
22. Which of the atoms in Question 21 has an octet as an outer shell?
23. How many energy levels are partially or fully occupied in the mendelevium atom?

24. Why do the fourth and fifth series of elements contain 18 elements, rather than 8 as in the second and third series?

25. Why does the sixth series of elements contain 32 elements, rather than 18 as in the fourth and fifth series?

26. (*a*) Which energy level corresponds to the N shell? (*b*) What types of space orbitals can be found in this energy level? (*c*) How many of each type? (*d*) How many electrons can occupy each of these types of space orbitals? (*e*) How many electrons are needed to completely fill the N shell?

27. Which sublevels of the 3rd energy level are filled (*a*) in the element argon; (*b*) in the element krypton?

28. What is a probable electron configuration for element 106?

Chapter 5

The Periodic Law

5.1 Mendeleyev's periodic table

Suppose you had to study the properties of each of the 105 chemical elements to have even an elementary knowledge of chemistry. The task would be very great. But suppose some elements had similar properties. If these elements could be grouped together systematically, it would not be too difficult to remember the distinguishing properties of the group. It might even be possible to remember variations in properties among the members of the group, if the variations occurred fairly regularly.

About 1869, the Russian chemist Dmitri Mendeleyev (men-deh-*lay*-eff) (1834–1907) devised a useful classification system for the elements. Mendeleyev called this classification system the *Periodic Table of the Elements*. In this table, consisting of rows and columns, elements are placed in order. The sequence is like that of words on a printed page, left to right, top to bottom. The particular order Mendeleyev used was that of increasing atomic weight. He selected the width of the table (the number of columns) so that elements with similar properties occupied positions in the same column. Other scientists tried other arrangements of the elements. But their arrangements now have only historical importance, because Mendeleyev's arrangement was more useful. The periodic tables we use today are based largely upon the pioneer work done by Mendeleyev.

When Mendeleyev first prepared his periodic table, he realized that all the elements were probably not yet discovered. For example, the elements scandium, gallium, and germanium were unknown in Mendeleyev's day. He carefully studied the properties of the known elements. Based upon his study, Mendeleyev

You may be interested in looking up the chemical element classifications of J.W. Dobereiner, J.A. Newlands, and L. Meyer.

Fig. 5-1. Dmitri Mendeleyev, a Russian chemist, worked out the first useful Periodic Table of the chemical elements.

USSR Embassy, Department of Information

75

left gaps in his table and predicted that new elements would be discovered that would fill these gaps. He also predicted the properties of these new elements. His predictions were later found to be very accurate when compared with the actual properties of these elements.

Mendeleyev noticed that when the elements are arranged in order of increasing atomic weight, their chemical properties follow a pattern. Similar chemical properties occur again at definite intervals. Mendeleyev concluded that "the properties of the elements are in periodic dependence on their atomic weights."

In Mendeleyev's table, the first two rows (or *series,* or *periods*) had seven elements before elements with similar properties occurred again. In the third and fourth periods, Mendeleyev found that there were seventeen elements before similar properties occurred again. The noble gases, neon, argon, krypton, and xenon, were discovered by Sir William Ramsay (1852–1916) during the 1890's. Together with the earlier discovered element, helium, these gases added an additional element to each period in Mendeleyev's table.

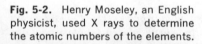

5.2   Moseley determines atomic numbers

About 45 years after Mendeleyev's work on the periodic table, an important discovery was made which helped improve the classification of the elements. In Chapter 3 it was stated that the atomic number of an element indicates the number of protons in the nuclei of its atoms. Henry Gwyn-Jeffreys Moseley (1887–1915), a brilliant young English scientist, performed some X-ray experiments which showed how the number of protons per nucleus varied progressively from element to element.

X rays are electromagnetic radiations. They are similar to light in this regard. But, unlike light, *X rays are not visible and are of higher frequency and shorter wavelength than light.* X rays are produced when high-speed electrons strike a metal target in an evacuated tube (one from which the gas has been pumped). Moseley found that the wavelengths of the X rays produced depend on the kind of metal used as the target. He used as targets various metals ranging in atomic weight from aluminum to gold. He found that the wavelengths of X rays became shorter as he used elements with more protons in their nuclei. The higher the atomic number of an element, the shorter is the wavelength of the X rays produced when that element is used as the target in an X-ray tube.

Moseley found in some cases an unusual variation in the wavelengths of X rays between two successive elements. The variation was twice as great as his calculations indicated. He concluded that in such cases an element was missing from the periodic table. Several elements have since been discovered which fill the gaps that Moseley indicated.

Fig. 5-2. Henry Moseley, an English physicist, used X rays to determine the atomic numbers of the elements.

Brown Brothers

5.3   The periodic law

When the elements in a periodic table are placed in the order of increasing atomic numbers instead of increasing atomic weights, some of the problems of arrangement disappear. Arranged according to increasing atomic weights, potassium precedes argon. Yet, when arranged according to properties in the table, potassium follows argon. This is in agreement with the atomic numbers: argon, 18, and potassium, 19. A similar case is that of tellurium, 52, and iodine, 53.

As stated in Section 5.1, Mendeleyev concluded that the properties of elements are in periodic dependence on their atomic weights. Today, evidence shows that atomic numbers are better standards for establishing the order of the elements. Mendeleyev's conclusion is now restated as the *periodic law: The physical and chemical properties of the elements are periodic functions of their atomic numbers*. In other words, (1) the properties of elements go through a pattern of change; (2) elements of similar properties occur at certain intervals, provided the elements are arranged in a periodic table in the order of increasing atomic number.

5.4   Arrangement of the modern periodic table

The modern periodic table is shown on pages 78-79. Frequent reference to these pages as you study this section will help you to understand the periodic table and its importance in chemistry.

Each element is assigned a separate block in the table. In the center of the block is the chemical symbol for the element. Below the symbol is the atomic number of the element. Above the symbol is the atomic weight. To the right of each symbol are numbers. These numbers indicate the distribution of electrons in the shells of the atoms of this element. A horizontal row of blocks on the table is called a *period* or *series*. A vertical column is called a *group* or *family*.

Hydrogen, atomic number 1, is placed at the top of the table by itself because of its many unique properties. It is in the first column at the left of the table because its atoms have one electron in the outermost shell. Helium, atomic number 2, is at the top of the extreme right-hand column. Helium is classified as an inert gas because it does not react with other elements. It is the simplest member of the group of elements known as the *noble gases*. Note that helium atoms have two electrons in the K shell or 1st energy level, and that with these two electrons, the K shell is complete. Hydrogen and helium compose the first period of elements.

The second period consists of eight elements: (1) *Lithium*, a soft, silvery, active metal, whose atoms have one electron in their outer shell, the L shell or 2nd energy level. (2) *Beryllium*, a silvery

PERIODIC TABLE

METALS

Period	I	II							
1	1.0080 **H** 1								

	I	II							
2	6.941 **Li** 3 (2,1)	9.01218 **Be** 4 (2,2)							
3	22.9898 **Na** 11 (2,8,1)	24.305 **Mg** 12 (2,8,2)							
4	39.102 **K** 19 (2,8,8,1)	40.08 **Ca** 20 (2,8,8,2)	44.9559 **Sc** 21 (2,8,9,2)	47.90 **Ti** 22 (2,8,10,2)	50.9414 **V** 23 (2,8,11,2)	51.996 **Cr** 24 (2,8,13,1)	54.9380 **Mn** 25 (2,8,13,2)	55.847 **Fe** 26 (2,8,14,2)	58.9332 **Co** 27
5	85.4678 **Rb** 37 (2,8,18,8,1)	87.62 **Sr** 38 (2,8,18,8,2)	88.9059 **Y** 39 (2,8,18,9,2)	91.22 **Zr** 40 (2,8,18,10,2)	92.9064 **Nb** 41 (2,8,18,12,1)	95.94 **Mo** 42 (2,8,18,13,1)	98.9062 **Tc** 43 (2,8,18,13,2)	101.07 **Ru** 44 (2,8,18,15,1)	102.9055 **Rh** 45
6	132.9055 **Cs** 55 (2,8,18,18,8,1)	137.34 **Ba** 56 (2,8,18,18,8,2)	Lanthanide Series / 174.97 **Lu** 71 (2,8,18,32,9,2)	178.49 **Hf** 72 (2,8,18,32,10,2)	180.9479 **Ta** 73 (2,8,18,32,11,2)	183.85 **W** 74 (2,8,18,32,12,2)	186.2 **Re** 75 (2,8,18,32,13,2)	190.2 **Os** 76 (2,8,18,32,14,2)	192.22 **Ir** 77
7	[223] **Fr** 87 (2,8,18,32,18,8,1)	226.0254 **Ra** 88 (2,8,18,32,18,8,2)	Actinide Series / [257] **Lr** 103 (2,8,18,32,32,9,2)	[261] **104** (2,8,18,32,32,10,2)	[260] **105** (2,8,18,32,32,11,2)				

Lanthanide Series

138.9055 **La** 57 (2,8,18,18,9,2)	140.12 **Ce** 58 (2,8,18,20,8,2)	140.9077 **Pr** 59 (2,8,18,21,8,2)	144.24 **Nd** 60 (2,8,18,22,8,2)	[147] **Pm** 61 (2,8,18,23,8,2)	150.4 **Sm** 62 (2,8,18,24,8,2)	151.96 **Eu** 63

Actinide Series

[227] **Ac** 89 (2,8,18,32,18,9,2)	232.0381 **Th** 90 (2,8,18,32,18,10,2)	231.0359 **Pa** 91 (2,8,18,32,20,9,2)	238.029 **U** 92 (2,8,18,32,21,9,2)	237.0482 **Np** 93 (2,8,18,32,22,9,2)	[244] **Pu** 94 (2,8,18,32,24,8,2)	[243] **Am** 95

OF THE ELEMENTS

Noble gases

	III	IV	V	VI	VII	VIII
						4.00260 **He** 2 — (2)
	10.81 **B** 5 (2,3)	12.011 **C** 6 (2,4)	14.0067 **N** 7 (2,5)	15.9994 **O** 8 (2,6)	18.9984 **F** 9 (2,7)	20.179 **Ne** 10 (2,8)
	26.9815 **Al** 13 (2,8,3)	28.086 **Si** 14 (2,8,4)	30.9738 **P** 15 (2,8,5)	32.06 **S** 16 (2,8,6)	35.453 **Cl** 17 (2,8,7)	39.948 **Ar** 18 (2,8,8)

			III	IV	V	VI	VII	VIII
58.71 **Ni** 28 (2,8,16,2)	63.546 **Cu** 29 (2,8,18,1)	65.37 **Zn** 30 (2,8,18,2)	69.72 **Ga** 31 (2,8,18,3)	72.59 **Ge** 32 (2,8,18,4)	74.9216 **As** 33 (2,8,18,5)	78.96 **Se** 34 (2,8,18,6)	79.904 **Br** 35 (2,8,18,7)	83.80 **Kr** 36 (2,8,18,8)
106.4 **Pd** 46 (2,8,18,18,0)	107.868 **Ag** 47 (2,8,18,18,1)	112.40 **Cd** 48 (2,8,18,18,2)	114.82 **In** 49 (2,8,18,18,3)	118.69 **Sn** 50 (2,8,18,18,4)	121.75 **Sb** 51 (2,8,18,18,5)	127.60 **Te** 52 (2,8,18,18,6)	126.9045 **I** 53 (2,8,18,18,7)	131.30 **Xe** 54 (2,8,18,18,8)
195.09 **Pt** 78 (2,8,18,32,17,1)	196.9665 **Au** 79 (2,8,18,32,18,1)	200.59 **Hg** 80 (2,8,18,32,18,2)	204.37 **Tl** 81 (2,8,18,32,18,3)	207.2 **Pb** 82 (2,8,18,32,18,4)	208.9806 **Bi** 83 (2,8,18,32,18,5)	[210] **Po** 84 (2,8,18,32,18,6)	[210] **At** 85 (2,8,18,32,18,7)	[222] **Rn** 86 (2,8,18,32,18,8)

ARE EARTH ELEMENTS

157.25 **Gd** 64 (2,8,18,25,9,2)	158.9254 **Tb** 65 (2,8,18,27,8,2)	162.50 **Dy** 66 (2,8,18,28,8,2)	164.9303 **Ho** 67 (2,8,18,29,8,2)	167.26 **Er** 68 (2,8,18,30,8,2)	168.9342 **Tm** 69 (2,8,18,31,8,2)	173.04 **Yb** 70 (2,8,18,32,8,2)
[245] **Cm** 96 (2,8,18,32,25,9,2)	[247] **Bk** 97 (2,8,18,32,26,9,2)	[249] **Cf** 98 (2,8,18,32,28,8,2)	[254] **Es** 99 (2,8,18,32,29,8,2)	[255] **Fm** 100 (2,8,18,32,30,8,2)	[256] **Md** 101 (2,8,18,32,31,8,2)	[254] **No** 102 (2,8,18,32,32,8,2)

A value given in brackets denotes the mass number of the isotope of longest known half-life.

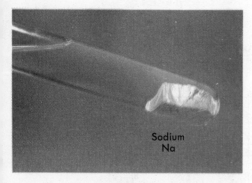

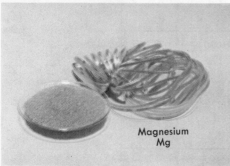

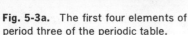

Fig. 5-3a. The first four elements of period three of the periodic table.

metal, less active than lithium, whose atoms have two electrons in their L shell. (3) *Boron*, a black solid with few metallic properties, whose atoms have three electrons in their L shell. (4) *Carbon*, a solid element with very distinctive chemical properties intermediate between those of metals and nonmetals, four electrons in the L shell. (5) *Nitrogen*, a colorless gas, nonmetallic properties, five electrons in the L shell. **(6)** *Oxygen*, a colorless gas, strong nonmetallic properties, six electrons in the L shell. (7) *Fluorine*, a pale-yellow gas, very strong nonmetallic properties, seven electrons in the L shell. (8) *Neon*, a colorless, inert (unreactive) gas, eight electrons in the L shell. Refer to Appendix Table 7, Electron Arrangement of the Elements.

It should be noted that these elements range from an active metallic element (Li) through two metalloids (Be, B whose properties are between those of the typical metal and nonmetal) to an active nonmetallic element (F), while the last element in the period (Ne) is inert. This variation in properties from metallic through metalloidal to nonmetallic is accompanied by an increase in the number of L-shell electrons from 1 to 7. The inert element neon has 8 electrons, an octet, in the L shell.

The third period also consists of eight elements: (1) *Sodium*, a soft, silvery, active metal similar to lithium, one electron in the outermost shell (the M shell or 3rd energy level). (2) *Magnesium*, a silvery metal similar in properties to beryllium, two electrons in the M shell. (3) *Aluminum*, a silvery metal with some nonmetallic properties, three electrons in the M shell. (4) *Silicon*, a dark-colored nonmetallic element with some properties resembling carbon, four electrons in the M shell. (5) *Phosphorus*, a nonmetallic solid element which forms compounds similar to those of nitrogen, five electrons in the M shell. (6) *Sulfur, a* yellow nonmetallic solid element, six electrons in the M shell. (7) *Chlorine*, a yellow-green gas with strong nonmetallic properties resembling those of fluorine, seven electrons in the M shell. (8) *Argon*, a colorless, inert gas, eight electrons in the M shell. Figure 5-3 illustrates the variations in the properties of these third-period elements. Again the elements range from strong metallic through metalloidal to strong nonmetallic properties as the number of electrons in the outer shell varies from 1 to 7. The element with an octet as its outer shell is a noble gas.

Notice that elements with similar properties have a similar arrangement of outer-shell electrons. They fall into the same group in the periodic table.

In Group I of the periodic table, we find the *sodium family,* a group of six similar, very active, metallic elements. Their atoms all have only one electron in the outermost shell. *Francium* is the most complex member of the sodium family. The position of Francium in the periodic table indicates that it is probably the most active metal.

Group II also consists of six active metals whose chemical properties are very much alike. The atoms of each have two electrons in their outer shell. This is the *calcium family*. The most chemically active member of this family is *radium*.

The properties of elements in Group III vary from nonmetallic to metallic as the atoms become more complex. The atoms of this group have three electrons in their outer shell.

The elements of Group IV vary in similar fashion. Their atoms have four electrons in the outer shell. Atoms of elements in both of Group III and Group IV have very stable inner shells.

Group V is the *nitrogen family*. *Nitrogen* and *phosphorus*, the elements in this family at the top of the table, are nonmetallic. The element *bismuth* at the bottom of the table is metallic. *Arsenic* and *antimony* exhibit both metallic and nonmetallic properties. The atoms of each of these elements have five electrons in the outer shell, and have very stable inner shells.

Group VI is the *oxygen family*. The properties of elements in this family vary from active nonmetallic to metallic as the atoms become more complex. The atoms of each of these elements has six electrons in the outer shell and they have very stable inner shells.

The elements in Group VII, the *halogen family,* are very active nonmetals. Their atoms each have seven electrons in the outer shell, and have very stable inner shells. The most active member of the halogen family is its simplest element, *fluorine*. Thus we see that the activity of the elements ranges from the most active metal at the lower left corner of the periodic table to the most active nonmetal at the upper right corner.

Group VIII is the *noble-gas family*. With the exception of *helium* atoms, which have a pair of electrons as their outer shell, atoms of these elements have an octet as their outer shell. This is the greatest number of electrons found in an outer shell. No compounds of helium, neon, and argon are known. A few compounds of krypton, xenon, and radon have been prepared.

The fourth period consists of eighteen elements. It is the first long period. In addition to the eight elements in Groups I to VIII, there are also ten *transition elements*. These are metallic elements whose atoms have one or two electrons in the outer shell. Successive electrons usually occupy the group of 5 space orbitals of the 3d sublevel.

The fifth period also consists of eighteen elements. It includes ten transition elements, in which successive electrons occupy the group of 5 space orbitals of the 4d sublevel. The transition elements are all metals.

The sixth period consists of thirty-two elements. In addition to the elements in Groups I to VIII and the ten transition elements, there is a group of fourteen *rare earth elements*. These elements have almost identical chemical properties. They compose the *lanthanide series*. The two outer shells of these atoms are almost the same. The outermost shell contains two electrons. The next-inner shell contains either eight or nine electrons. Successive electrons occupy the group of 7 space orbitals of the 4f

Phosphorus
P

Sulfur
S

Chlorine
Cl

Argon
Ar

Fig. 5-3b. The last four elements of period three of the periodic table.

SUBLEVEL BLOCKS OF THE PERIODIC TABLE

Period	Sublevels being filled	s sublevel block																	p sublevel block					
		I	II															III	IV	V	VI	VII	VIII
1	1s	H 1	He 2																				
2	2s 2p	Li 3	Be 4															B 5	C 6	N 7	O 8	F 9	Ne 10
3	3s 3p	Na 11	Mg 12				TRANSITION ELEMENTS d sublevel block											Al 13	Si 14	P 15	S 16	Cl 17	Ar 18
4	4s 3d 4p	K 19	Ca 20	Sc 21	Ti 22	V 23	Cr 24	Mn 25	Fe 26	Co 27	Ni 28	Cu 29	Zn 30					Ga 31	Ge 32	As 33	Se 34	Br 35	Kr 36
5	5s 4d 5p	Rb 37	Sr 38	Y 39	Zr 40	Nb 41	Mo 42	Tc 43	Ru 44	Rh 45	Pd 46	Ag 47	Cd 48					In 49	Sn 50	Sb 51	Te 52	I 53	Xe 54
6	6s 4f 5d 6p	Cs 55	Ba 56	Lu 71	Hf 72	Ta 73	W 74	Re 75	Os 76	Ir 77	Pt 78	Au 79	Hg 80					Tl 81	Pb 82	Bi 83	Po 84	At 85	Rn 86
7	7s 5f 6d 7p	Fr 87	Ra 88	Lr 103	104	105																	

RARE EARTH ELEMENTS
f sublevel block

Period	Sublevels	series														
6	4f	Lanthanide series	La 57	Ce 58	Pr 59	Nd 60	Pm 61	Sm 62	Eu 63	Gd 64	Tb 65	Dy 66	Ho 67	Er 68	Tm 69	Yb 70
7	5f	Actinide series	Ac 89	Th 90	Pa 91	U 92	Np 93	Pu 94	Am 95	Cm 96	Bk 97	Cf 98	Es 99	Fm 100	Md 101	No 102

Fig. 5-4. The periodic table consists essentially of blocks of elements whose structures add support to our modern atomic theory.

sublevel, as the number of electrons in the 4th energy level increases from 18 to 32.

The seventh period of elements is at present an incomplete period. It is assumed to be similar to the sixth period. The rare earth elements in this period compose the *actinide series*. At present, nineteen members of the seventh period are known or reported.

In the periodic table the elements are roughly divided into metals, nonmetals, and noble gases. The line separating the metals from the nonmetals is a zigzag line. It runs diagonally down and to the right near the right end of the table. The elements which border this zigzag line are the *metalloids*. These elements show both metallic and nonmetallic properties under different conditions.

5.5 Size of atoms: a periodic property

We recognized in Chapter 3 that an atom consists of a central nucleus with electrons moving about it. It was noted that the nucleus has a diameter which is about one ten-thousandth that of the atom. We concluded that most of the volume of an atom is the result of the complex motion of the electrons. By their motion and their negative charge, electrons seem to occupy the space around the nucleus. They form a spherical electron cloud which gives the atom its volume and excludes other atoms.

The volume of an atom is not a completely definite quantity because the boundary of an atom's electron cloud is not a distinct surface. Rather, it is somewhat fuzzy and indefinite. An atom may be rather easily distorted when it combines with other atoms. But very great force must be used if it is to be compressed.

The reported "size" of an atom varies somewhat with the dimension measured and the method used to measure it. Scientists have measured the distance between adjacent nuclei in the crystalline forms of elements and in the molecules of gaseous elements. One-half of this distance is used, with slight correction, as the radius of one atom. The radius of an atom, and thus its volume, do *not* increase regularly with atomic number. Such an increase might be expected from the regular addition of an electron in successive elements. But atomic size varies in a periodic fashion as shown in Figure 5-5. This figure is a miniature periodic table with element symbols and atomic numbers in black. Atomic radii are shown in color. The radii of atoms of the elements are

Fig. 5-5. Periodic table showing radii of the atoms of the elements in angstrom units.

PERIODIC TABLE OF ATOMIC RADII

I	II											III	IV	V	VI	VII	VIII
0.32 **H** 1																	0.31 **He** 2
1.23 **Li** 3	0.89 **Be** 4											0.82 **B** 5	0.77 **C** 6	0.75 **N** 7	0.73 **O** 8	0.72 **F** 9	0.71 **Ne** 10
1.54 **Na** 11	1.36 **Mg** 12											1.18 **Al** 13	1.11 **Si** 14	1.06 **P** 15	1.02 **S** 16	0.99 **Cl** 17	0.98 **Ar** 18
2.03 **K** 19	1.74 **Ca** 20	1.44 **Sc** 21	1.32 **Ti** 22	1.22 **V** 23	1.18 **Cr** 24	1.17 **Mn** 25	1.17 **Fe** 26	1.16 **Co** 27	1.15 **Ni** 28	1.17 **Cu** 29	1.25 **Zn** 30	1.26 **Ga** 31	1.22 **Ge** 32	1.20 **As** 33	1.17 **Se** 34	1.14 **Br** 35	1.12 **Kr** 36
2.16 **Rb** 37	1.91 **Sr** 38	1.62 **Y** 39	1.45 **Zr** 40	1.34 **Nb** 41	1.30 **Mo** 42	1.27 **Tc** 43	1.25 **Ru** 44	1.25 **Rh** 45	1.28 **Pd** 46	1.34 **Ag** 47	1.48 **Cd** 48	1.44 **In** 49	1.40 **Sn** 50	1.40 **Sb** 51	1.36 **Te** 52	1.33 **I** 53	1.31 **Xe** 54
2.35 **Cs** 55	1.98 **Ba** 56	1.56 **Lu** 71	1.44 **Hf** 72	1.34 **Ta** 73	1.30 **W** 74	1.28 **Re** 75	1.26 **Os** 76	1.27 **Ir** 77	1.30 **Pt** 78	1.34 **Au** 79	1.49 **Hg** 80	1.48 **Tl** 81	1.47 **Pb** 82	1.46 **Bi** 83	1.46 **Po** 84	1.45 **At** 85	**Rn** 86
Fr 87	2.20 **Ra** 88	**Lr** 103	104	105													

1.69 **La** 57	1.65 **Ce** 58	1.64 **Pr** 59	1.64 **Nd** 60	1.63 **Pm** 61	1.62 **Sm** 62	1.85 **Eu** 63	1.62 **Gd** 64	1.61 **Tb** 65	1.60 **Dy** 66	1.58 **Ho** 67	1.58 **Er** 68	1.58 **Tm** 69	1.70 **Yb** 70
2.0 **Ac** 89	1.65 **Th** 90	**Pa** 91	1.42 **U** 92	**Np** 93	**Pu** 94	**Am** 95	**Cm** 96	**Bk** 97	**Cf** 98	**Es** 99	**Fm** 100	**Md** 101	**No** 102

Atomic radii mostly from R.T. Sanderson, INORGANIC CHEMISTRY, Reinhold Publishing Corporation, New York, 1967

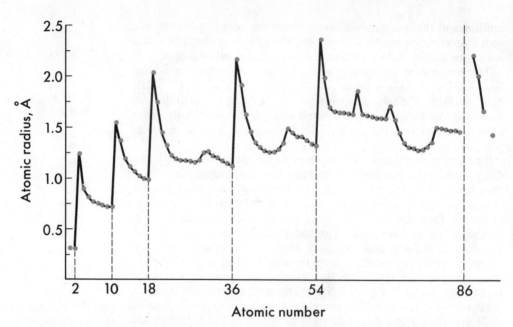

Fig. 5-6. Graph showing atomic radius plotted as a function of atomic number.

given in angstroms. Figure 5-6 shows the atomic radius plotted as a function of the atomic number.

From this chart and graph two conclusions about the relationship between atomic radius and the periodic table may be drawn:

1. The atomic radius increases with atomic number in a particular group or family of elements. Each element in a group has one more shell or energy level than the element above it. The increased nuclear charge decreases the radii of the electron shells by drawing them closer. But the addition of a shell more than counteracts this effect.

2. From Group I to Group VIII in a period, there is a general decrease in the atomic radii of the elements. Since the atomic number increases across a period from left to right, each element has a greater positive nuclear charge than the one before it. This greater charge results in a greater total force of attraction between the electrons and the nucleus. This greater force of attraction may explain why the electrons of the elements across a period are successively closer to the nucleus.

Since the number of protons in the nucleus of the elements increases in any one period from left to right, so does the number of electrons in the outermost orbitals about the nucleus. As the number of electrons increases, the force of repulsion between them also increases. Irregularities in the atomic radius pattern may be caused by patterns in this force of repulsion.

5.6 Ionization energy

A negatively-charged electron is held in an atom mainly by the attraction of the positively charged protons in the nucleus. By supplying energy, it is possible to remove an electron from an atom. Suppose we use **A** as a symbol for an atom of any element and → to mean "yields." Then this electron removal may be shown in equation form as

$$A + energy \rightarrow A^+ + e^-$$

The particle, A^+, remaining after the removal of an electron, e^-, is an *ion* with a single positive charge. *An ion is an atom* (or sometimes a group of atoms) *which has a net positive or negative charge.* This net charge results from unequal numbers of positively charged protons and negatively charged electrons. *The energy required to remove an electron from an atom is its* ***ionization energy.*** The chart, Figure 5-7, shows the ionization energy required to remove one electron from an atom of each element. One unit in which ionization energy is expressed is kcal/mole. The first ionization energy of oxygen, for example, is 312 kcal/mole. This means that 312 kcal of energy must be supplied to remove one electron from each atom in one mole of oxygen atoms. (Recall that one mole of oxygen atoms is 6.02×10^{23}

Fig. 5-7. Periodic table showing first ionization energies of the elements in kilocalories per mole.

PERIODIC TABLE OF IONIZATION ENERGIES

I	II												III	IV	V	VI	VII	VIII
314 **H** 1																		566 **He** 2
124 **Li** 3	215 **Be** 4												191 **B** 5	260 **C** 6	335 **N** 7	312 **O** 8	402 **F** 9	498 **Ne** 10
119 **Na** 11	176 **Mg** 12												138 **Al** 13	188 **Si** 14	254 **P** 15	239 **S** 16	300 **Cl** 17	363 **Ar** 18
100 **K** 19	141 **Ca** 20	151 **Sc** 21	158 **Ti** 22	155 **V** 23	156 **Cr** 24	171 **Mn** 25	182 **Fe** 26	181 **Co** 27	176 **Ni** 28	178 **Cu** 29	216 **Zn** 30	138 **Ga** 31	187 **Ge** 32	242 **As** 33	225 **Se** 34	273 **Br** 35	323 **Kr** 36
96 **Rb** 37	131 **Sr** 38	152 **Y** 39	160 **Zr** 40	156 **Nb** 41	166 **Mo** 42	172 **Tc** 43	173 **Ru** 44	178 **Rh** 45	192 **Pd** 46	174 **Ag** 47	207 **Cd** 48	133 **In** 49	169 **Sn** 50	199 **Sb** 51	208 **Te** 52	241 **I** 53	280 **Xe** 54
90 **Cs** 55	120 **Ba** 56	115 **Lu** 71	127 **Hf** 72	140 **Ta** 73	184 **W** 74	181 **Re** 75	201 **Os** 76	212 **Ir** 77	208 **Pt** 78	212 **Au** 79	241 **Hg** 80	141 **Tl** 81	171 **Pb** 82	184 **Bi** 83	196 **Po** 84	**At** 85	248 **Rn** 86
Fr 87	122 **Ra** 88	**Lr** 103	104	105													

129 **La** 57	159 **Ce** 58	133 **Pr** 59	145 **Nd** 60	**Pm** 61	129 **Sm** 62	131 **Eu** 63	142 **Gd** 64	155 **Tb** 65	157 **Dy** 66	**Ho** 67	**Er** 68	**Tm** 69	143 **Yb** 70
162 **Ac** 89	**Th** 90	**Pa** 91	92 **U** 92	**Np** 93	**Pu** 94	**Am** 95	**Cm** 96	**Bk** 97	**Cf** 98	**Es** 99	**Fm** 100	**Md** 101	**No** 102

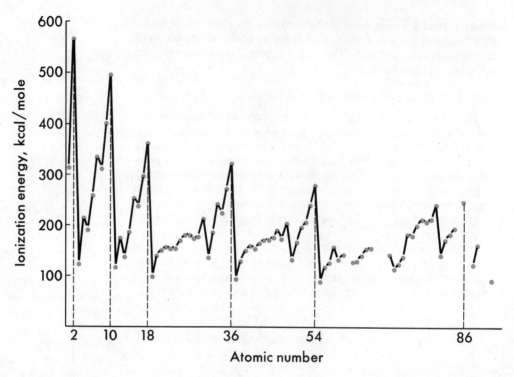

Fig. 5-8. Graph showing first ionization energy as a function of atomic number.

atoms.) Figure 5-8 is a graph showing first ionization energy plotted as a function of atomic number. From these data the following conclusions can be drawn:

1. Low ionization energy is characteristic of a metal. *High ionization energy* is characteristic of a nonmetal. An *intermediate ionization energy* is characteristic of a metalloid. The chemical inertness of the noble gases is strong evidence for the unusual stability, or resistance to change, of the outer-shell octet. As might be expected, the noble gases have unusually high ionization energies.

2. Within a group of elements, the ionization energy generally decreases with increasing atomic number. This is because, within a group, increasing atomic number is accompanied by increasing atomic radius. The outer-shell electrons of the elements of higher atomic number within a group are farther from the nucleus. Thus, they are attracted less by it. The ionization energy for removal of one such electron is therefore less as the atomic number of the atom is greater.

3. Ionization energy does not vary uniformly from element to element within a series. Instead, it is a *periodic* property. In each series or period, the ionization energy increases from Group I to Group VIII. But the increase is not regular. There is a decrease in ionization energies between Groups II and III in Periods 2 and 3. This decrease occurs as the *s* sublevel is filled and the *p* sublevel is started. In these periods there is also a decrease between Groups V and VI as the *p* sublevel becomes half-filled. In Periods 4, 5, and 6, there is a sharp decrease in the ionization energy between the last transition element and Group III. This decrease occurs as the *d* sublevel has become filled and the *p* sublevel is started. These irregularities apparently are caused by the extra stability of completed and half-completed sublevels.

5.7   Ionization energy to remove successive electrons

It is, of course, possible to remove more than one electron from many-electron atoms.

Na + ionization energy 1st electron → Na⁺ + e⁻

Na⁺ + ionization energy 2nd electron → Na⁺⁺ + e⁻

Na⁺⁺ + ionization energy 3rd electron → Na⁺⁺⁺ + e⁻

Table 5-1 shows the electron configurations of sodium, magnesium, and aluminum atoms. It also gives the ionization energies required to remove successive electrons from atoms of these elements. Notice the increase in energy for each successive electron removed.

It is not surprising that the ionization energy increases with each electron removed from an atom. After all, each successive electron must be removed from a particle with an increasingly greater net positive charge. But let us examine the variation in ionization energies still more closely.

For sodium atoms, there is a great increase between the first and second ionization energies. The first electron, a $3s$ electron, is rather easily removed. But to remove the second electron, almost ten times as much energy is needed. This increase occurs because the second electron is a $2p$ electron in a much lower energy level. The lower the energy level, the greater the energy needed to remove an electron from the attraction of the nucleus. See Figure 5-9.

The removal of electrons from magnesium atoms requires little ionization energy for the first two electrons, since both are $3s$

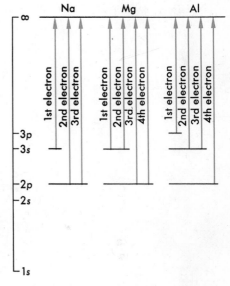

Fig. 5-9. Energy-level transitions for the removal of successive electrons from sodium, magnesium, and aluminum atoms.

Table 5–1

ELECTRON CONFIGURATIONS AND IONIZATION ENERGIES OF SODIUM, MAGNESIUM, AND ALUMINUM

Elements	Electron configuration	Ionization energy (kcal/mole)			
		1st electron	2nd electron	3rd electron	4th electron
Na	$1s^2 2s^2 2p^6 3s^1$	119	1085	1630	
Mg	$1s^2 2s^2 2p^6 3s^2$	176	345	1837	2510
Al	$1s^2 2s^2 2p^6 3s^2 3p^1$	138	432	653	2752

electrons. More energy is required to remove the first $3s$ electron from magnesium atoms than the first $3s$ electron from sodium atoms. This increase occurs because the magnesium atoms have a greater nuclear charge and the $3s$ electrons are paired. But to remove the third electron from magnesium atoms requires between five and six times as much energy as is needed to remove the second. This increase occurs because the third electron is a $2p$ electron. Since $2p$ electrons of magnesium are at a much lower energy level than $3s$ electrons, there is a great increase in ionization energy.

It is easy to remove the first three electrons from aluminum atoms. In fact, it is easier to remove the first electron from aluminum atoms than it is to remove the first electron from magnesium atoms. A look at the electron configuration indicates that the first aluminum electron is a $3p$ electron. It is in a slightly higher energy sublevel than the first magnesium electron, which is a $3s$ electron. There is a great increase in ionization energy between the third and fourth aluminum electrons. This increase is explained by the fact that the fourth electron is a $2p$ electron. This electron is in a much lower energy level than the first three electrons, which were all 3rd energy-level electrons.

The order in which electrons are removed from atoms by ionization is not the same as the order in which electrons occupy orbitals in the structures described in Sections 4.6-4.10. This difference is caused by the shifting of the relative positions of energy sublevels as they are occupied by electrons. Electrons are removed from atoms by ionization in the reverse of the order given by the electron-configuration notation. The electron-configuration notation of iron is $1s^2 2s^2 2p^6 3s^2 3p^6 3d^6 4s^2$. The first electron removed from iron atoms is a $4s$ electron. So is the second. The third electron is a $3d$ electron. So are the fourth, fifth, sixth, and so on.

See Question 28 at the end of this chapter.

5.8 Electron affinity

Some neutral atoms have a tendency to acquire additional electrons. The measure of this tendency is the *electron affinity*. **Electron affinity** *is the energy released when an electron is added to a neutral atom.* When an electron is added to a neutral atom, an ion with a single negative charge is formed. An amount of energy, the electron affinity, is released. In equation form, this electron transfer may be expressed as follows:

$$\mathbf{A + e^- \rightarrow A^- + energy}$$

Like ionization energy, electron affinity may be measured in kcal/mole. The electron affinity indicates how tightly an additional electron is bound to an atom. If the electron affinity is low, the electron is weakly bound. If the electron affinity is high, the electron is strongly bound. Table 5-2 gives the electron affinities for four members of the halogen family. The halogens have rela-

Table 5-2
ELECTRON AFFINITIES OF THE HALOGENS

Element	Electron affinity (kcal/mole)
fluorine	82.1
chlorine	86.6
bromine	82.6
iodine	71.0

tively high electron affinities. This is to be expected because the addition of one electron to these atoms gives them a stable outer-shell octet. It is also to be expected that the electron affinities would decrease with increasing atomic number. This decrease occurs because the added electron occupies shells which are increasingly farther from the nucleus. There is no simple explanation for the low electron affinity of fluorine. However, the atoms of second-period elements are relatively small in size. Because of the small size of their atoms, many of these elements show irregularities in properties when compared with other elements in their group. Also, the determination of electron affinity is difficult, and data are available for only a few elements.

The concepts of ionization energy and electron affinity are helpful in understanding how compounds are formed from atoms of metallic and nonmetallic elements. This topic is discussed in greater detail in parts of Chapter 6.

5.9   Value of the periodic table.

In former years the periodic table served as a check on atomic weight determinations. It also was used in the prediction of new elements. These uses are now outdated. Today, the periodic table serves as a useful and systematic classification of elements according to their properties. The occurrence at regular intervals of properties such as atomic size, ionization energy, and electron affinity has already been described. This information is valuable in determining the types of compounds which certain elements form. The periodic table, though not perfect, makes the study of chemistry easier.

QUESTIONS

1. (a) On what basis did Mendeleyev arrange the elements in his periodic table?   **Group A**
   (b) On what basis are they arranged today?
2. What use did Mendeleyev make of his study of the known elements?
3. How are X rays used to determine the atomic number of an element?
4. What is the periodic law?
5. (a) What information is given in each block of the periodic table? (b) How are these data arranged in each block?
6. (a) What is a group or family of elements? (b) What position does a family occupy in the periodic table?
7. (a) What is a series or period of elements? (b) What position does a period occupy in the periodic table?
8. (a) Name the elements in the second period. (b) How does the number of electrons in the outer shell vary in these elements? (c) How do their properties compare?
9. What is similar about the electron configurations of elements with similar properties?
10. How do the elements at the left of the periodic table vary in activity?
11. How do the elements in Group VII vary in activity?

12. What name is given to the elements which border the line dividing the metals from the nonmetals?
13. Why is the radius of an atom not a definitely fixed quantity?
14. (a) How do the atomic radii of the Group I elements compare with the radii of other elements of their period? (b) Why?
15. (a) Write an equation to represent the removal of the single outer shell electron from a potassium atom. (b) Write an equation to represent the addition of an electron to a neutral bromine atom. (c) What particles are produced from the neutral atoms by these reactions?
16. (a) Why do metals have low ionization energies? (b) Why are the ionization energies of nonmetals high?

Group B

17. What family of elements was missing from Mendeleyev's periodic table?
18. (a) What are X rays? (b) How are they produced?
19. (a) How did Mendeleyev know where to leave gaps for undiscovered elements in his periodic table? (b) How did Moseley know where to leave gaps for undiscovered elements?
20. (a) Why is hydrogen placed separately in the periodic table? (b) Why is it placed above Group I?
21. (a) What are transition elements? (b) In which periods of elements do they appear?
22. (a) What are rare earth elements? (b) In which periods of elements do they appear?
23. (a) How does atomic size vary with atomic number within a family of elements? (b) Why does it vary this way?
24. (a) How does atomic size generally vary with atomic number within a period of elements? (b) Why does it vary this way?
25. (a) How would you expect the ionization energies of two atoms of about equal size but different atomic number to compare? (b) Why?
26. (a) If energy must be supplied to remove an outer shell electron from an atom, which is more stable, the atom or the resulting ion? (b) If energy is released during the addition of an electron to a neutral atom, which is more stable, the atom or the resulting ion?
27. What determines the number of elements in each period of the periodic table?
28. On a separate sheet of paper, copy and complete the following table. *Do not write in this book.*

Chemical element	Electron-configuration notation	Ionization energy (kcal/mole)			
		1st electron	2nd electron	3rd electron	4th electron
K		$10\overline{0}$	$73\overline{0}$	1070	
Ca		141	272	1175	1610
Ga		138	436	705	1470

On the basis of the electron configuration, explain the variation in ionization energies for successive electrons for the atoms given.
29. How many 5th energy-level orbitals would be filled theoretically in element 118?
30. What is the present value of the periodic table?

Chapter 6

Chemical Bonds

6.1 Elements form compounds

In Chapter 2 it was stated that elements *could* form compounds during a chemical change. In the chapters that followed, the theory of the atomic structure of the elements was described. Now, we are ready to use this theory to explain *how* atoms form the other particles of substances.

A chemical analysis of the compound formed of the elements hydrogen and chlorine reveals that the ratio of hydrogen atoms to chlorine atoms is one to one. Analysis of the compound formed of the elements sodium and chlorine reveals that the ratio of sodium atoms to chlorine atoms is one to one. However, analysis of one compound formed of the elements hydrogen and oxygen reveals that there are two hydrogen atoms for each oxygen atom. Furthermore, in a compound formed of the elements calcium and chlorine, there are two chlorine atoms for each calcium atom. In a compound of hydrogen and nitrogen, there are three hydrogen atoms for each nitrogen atom. A compound of aluminum and chlorine has three chlorine atoms for each atom of aluminum. The results of these and other analyses are summarized in the following series of formulas.

Analysis means the separation of a material into its component parts to determine its composition.

$$HCl \quad\quad NaCl$$
$$H_2O \quad\quad CaCl_2$$
$$NH_3 \quad\quad AlCl_3$$
$$CH_4 \quad\quad CCl_4$$

In each case the formula represents the simplest ratio of the number of atoms of each element in the compound. For example, the

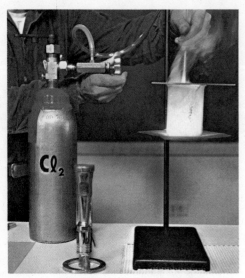

From the CHEM Study film, *Chemical Families*

Fig. 6-1. Sodium metal, heated in the beaker, combines directly with chlorine gas and forms the compound sodium chloride.

Recall from Section 2.15 that the products of exothermic reactions have less energy and are more stable than the reactants. The products of endothermic reactions have more energy and are less stable than the reactants.

Some experimental evidence for electron transfer is described in Section 21.6.

formula $AlCl_3$ indicates that for each aluminum atom in the compound, there are three chlorine atoms.

The series of formulas of well-known compounds given above shows that different numbers of hydrogen atoms and of chlorine atoms are found in combination with single atoms of other elements. Why is there this difference in the number of hydrogen and chlorine atoms per atom of another element? Is there any relation between the structure of an atom and the number of other atoms found in combination with it?

6.2 Valence electrons and chemical bonds

The electrons in the outermost shell of an atom play a very important part in the formation of compounds. The electrons in an *incomplete* outer shell are called **valence electrons**. The remainder of the atom, excluding the valence electrons, is called the **kernel** of the atom. In the formation of chemical compounds from the elements, *valence electrons are usually either transferred from the outer shell of one atom to the outer shell of another atom, or shared among the outer shells of the combining atoms.* This transfer or sharing of electrons produces **chemical bonds**. (The formation of some chemical bonds involves not only outer shell electrons but also those of an incomplete next inner shell.)

*Electron transfer results in **ionic bonding** while electron sharing produces **covalent bonding**.* When an atom of one element combines chemically with an atom of another element, both atoms usually attain a stable outer shell consisting of an octet. (Hydrogen either shares its single $1s$ electron or attains a stable outer shell of two $1s$ electrons. Lithium loses its single $2s$ electron and attains a stable outer shell of two electrons.) *This kind of electron structure, resembling that of the noble gases, has chemical stability.*

Energy changes are always involved in the process of electron transfer or electron sharing. In *most* cases, when compounds are formed from the elements, energy is given off. The process of electron transfer is *always* exothermic and that of electron sharing is *usually* exothermic. In a *few* cases of compound formation by electron sharing, energy is absorbed. The process of electron sharing may sometimes be endothermic.

6.3 Ionic bonding (electrovalence)

In the formation of a compound by ionic bonding, electrons are actually transferred from the outer shell of one atom to the outer shell of a second atom. By this process both atoms usually attain outer shells containing eight electrons. For example, sodium reacts with chlorine and forms sodium chloride. The single $3s$ electron of a sodium atom is transferred to the singly occupied $3p$ orbital of a chlorine atom.

	1s	2s	2p	3s	3p
Na	⊗	⊗	⊗⊗⊗	⦵	◯◯◯
Cl	⊗	⊗	⊗⊗⊗	⊗	⊗⊗⦸

The sodium, now deficient in one electron, has the stable electron configuration of neon. The chlorine, now with one excess electron, has the stable electron configuration of argon. Only 1 atom of each element is required for the electron transfer which produces these stable electronic configurations. Thus, the *formula* of the compound is **NaCl**. *A chemical formula is a shorthand method of using chemical symbols to represent the composition of a substance.*

The particles produced by this transfer of an electron are no longer electrically neutral atoms of sodium and chlorine. They are: (1) a *sodium ion* with a single excess positive charge, and (2) a *chloride* ion with a single excess negative charge.

	1s	2s	2p	3s	3p
Na$^+$	⊗	⊗	⊗⊗⊗	◯	◯◯◯
Cl$^-$	⊗	⊗	⊗⊗⊗	⊗	⊗⊗⊗

These ions are arranged systematically in crystals of sodium chloride in the ratio of 1 sodium ion to 1 chloride ion. See Figure 6-2.

The formula NaCl which represents the composition of the compound, sodium chloride, is an ***empirical formula.*** An empirical formula indicates: (1) the kinds of atoms in the compound formed, and (2) the simplest whole-number ratio of the atoms in the compound. The formula $Na_{17}Cl_{17}$ shows the kinds and ratio of atoms that make up the compound, sodium chloride. But the empirical formula NaCl represents this information in the simplest way.

Table 6-1 shows the number of protons and electrons in the atoms and ions of sodium and chlorine and the charges that result. It also shows their electrovalent symbols, and their radii in angstroms.

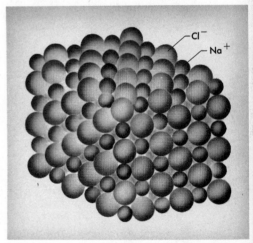

Fig. 6-2. This diagram shows the arrangement of the sodium and chloride ions in a portion of a sodium chloride crystal.

Table 6-1
DATA ON ATOMS AND IONS OF SODIUM AND CHLORINE

	Sodium atom	Sodium ion	Chlorine atom	Chloride ion
number of protons	11	11	17	17
number of electrons	11	10	17	18
net charge	0	+1	0	−1
symbol	Na	Na$^+$	Cl	Cl$^-$
radius, Å	1.54	0.97	0.99	1.81

Using only the 3rd energy level electrons, the electron-dot symbol for an atom of sodium is

$$\text{Na}\circ$$

That for an atom of chlorine is

$$\cdot\overset{\cdot\cdot}{\underset{\cdot\cdot}{\text{Cl}}}:$$

After reaction, the electron-dot formula for sodium chloride may be written as

$$\text{Na}^+ \:\overset{\cdot\cdot}{\underset{\cdot\cdot}{\text{Cl}}}:^-$$

or as a simpler ionic formula, Na^+Cl^-.

Note the symbols for electrons ∘ and · which are used here and in other electron-dot formulas in this chapter. These symbols are used only to show the origin of the electrons in the completed shells. They *do not mean* that electrons from different atoms are different from each other. All electrons, regardless of the atom from which they originate, are identical. However, when two electrons occupy the same space orbital, we can tell something more about them because of electron spin. If the orbital is to be occupied in a stable way, the electrons must have opposite spins.

6.4 Energy change in ionic bonding

Sodium ions and chloride ions in a common salt crystal can be formed from widely separated sodium and chlorine atoms. In order *to study the energy change involved,* this chemical change can be assumed to consist of three separate reactions. The first reaction, the removal of one electron from each sodium atom, is endothermic. The amount of energy required is the *ionization energy* of sodium. For one mole of sodium atoms,

$$1 \text{ mole Na} + 119 \text{ kcal} \rightarrow 1 \text{ mole Na}^+ + 1 \text{ mole e}^-$$

Only one electron can be readily removed from each sodium atom because a great increase in ionization energy occurs between the first and second electrons. (See Section 5.7.)

The second reaction is the addition of one electron to each neutral chlorine atom. This reaction is exothermic. The energy given off is the *electron affinity* of chlorine. For one mole of chlorine atoms,

$$1 \text{ mole Cl} + 1 \text{ mole e}^- \rightarrow 1 \text{ mole Cl}^- + 85 \text{ kcal}$$

The third reaction is the taking up by the oppositely charged sodium ions and chloride ions of their equilibrium positions in the sodium chloride crystal. This reaction is also exothermic.

$$1 \text{ mole Na}^+ + 1 \text{ mole Cl}^- \rightarrow 1 \text{ mole Na}^+\text{Cl}^- + 187 \text{ kcal}$$

The first reaction requires energy (119 kcal). This is less than the sum of the energies given off in the second and third reactions (85 kcal and 187 kcal). The overall effect is that energy is given off. [(85 kcal + 187 kcal) − (119 kcal) = 153 kcal]. The summation of these three separate reactions is

$$1 \text{ mole Na} \ \ + 119 \text{ kcal} \ \ \rightarrow \cancel{1 \text{ mole Na}^+} \ \ + \cancel{1 \text{ mole e}^-}$$
$$1 \text{ mole Cl} \ \ + \cancel{1 \text{ mole e}^-} \ \rightarrow \cancel{1 \text{ mole Cl}^-} \ \ + 85 \text{ kcal}$$
$$\cancel{1 \text{ mole Na}^+} + \cancel{1 \text{ mole Cl}^-} \rightarrow 1 \text{ mole Na}^+\text{Cl}^- + 187 \text{ kcal}$$
$$\overline{1 \text{ mole Na} \ \ + 1 \text{ mole Cl} \ \rightarrow 1 \text{ mole Na}^+\text{Cl}^- + 153 \text{ kcal}}$$

The net process of electron transfer is exothermic. The formation of all ionic compounds from their elements is exothermic.

6.5   Oxidation and reduction

Let us now consider still another aspect of the reactions by which sodium ions and chloride ions are produced. We may consider the formation of a sodium ion from a sodium atom to involve the loss of an electron:

$$\textbf{Na} - \textbf{e}^- \rightarrow \textbf{Na}^+ \textbf{ (Loss of electron: Oxidation)}$$

Any chemical reaction which involves the loss of one or more electrons by an atom or ion is called **oxidation.** The particle which loses the electron(s) is said to be *oxidized.* In the reaction above, the sodium atom is oxidized to a sodium ion, since it loses one electron. The reaction is an *oxidation.*

The *oxidation state* of an element is represented by a signed number, called an **oxidation number.** This number indicates the number of electrons which can be assumed to be lost, gained, or shared by an atom in forming a compound. Oxidation numbers are assigned according to a set of seven rules. These rules will be introduced as needed in this chapter.

Rule 1.   *The oxidation number of an atom of a free element is zero.*

Rule 2.   *The oxidation number of a monatomic (one-atomed) ion is equal to its charge.*

From these rules we see: (1) The oxidation number of elementary sodium is zero: $\overset{0}{\textbf{Na}}$. (2) The oxidation number of sodium ion is plus one: $\overset{+1}{\textbf{Na}^+}$. Note that an oxidation number is written above a symbol, while an ion charge is written as a right superscript. The formation of a chloride ion from a chlorine atom involves the gain of an electron:

$$\textbf{Cl} + \textbf{e}^- \rightarrow \textbf{Cl}^- \textbf{ (Gain of electron: Reduction)}$$

A chemical reaction which involves the gain of one or more electrons by an atom or ion is called **reduction.** The particle which gains the electron(s) is said to be *reduced*. The chlorine atom is reduced to a chloride ion since it gains an electron. The reaction is a *reduction*. The oxidation number of elementary chlorine is zero: $\overset{0}{\text{Cl}}$ (Rule 1). The oxidation number of chloride ion is minus one: $\overset{-1}{\text{Cl}^-}$ (Rule 2).

In the reaction

$$\overset{0}{\text{Na}} + \overset{0}{\text{Cl}} \rightarrow \overset{+1}{\text{Na}^+}\overset{-1}{\text{Cl}^-}$$

elementary sodium is oxidized and elementary chlorine is reduced. *The substance which is reduced* has received electrons from the oxidized substance and is called the **oxidizing agent.** At the same time, *the substance which is oxidized* has transferred electrons to the reduced substance and is called the **reducing agent.** **NaCl** is the correct empirical formula for the compound sodium chloride. Note that the algebraic sum of the oxidation numbers written above this formula is zero.

Rule 3.   *The algebraic sum of the oxidation numbers of all the atoms in the formula of a compound is zero.*

6.6   Formation of magnesium bromide from its elements

In the formation of magnesium bromide, the two $3s$ electrons of the magnesium are transferred. *Both* $3s$ electrons must be transferred if magnesium is to acquire the stable electron configuration of the noble gas, neon. Recall that the ionization energies of the two $3s$ electrons in magnesium are low. But there is a great increase in ionization energy between the second and third electrons. Hence, only two electrons may be removed chemically. The 4th energy level of the bromine atom already contains seven electrons. (Eight, of course, is the number needed for an octet.) Thus, a single bromine atom has a place for only one of the two electrons which the magnesium atom transfers. So two bromine atoms are needed to react with one magnesium atom. Each bromine atom gains one electron. The diagram representing this electron transfer is

Table 6–2
DATA ON ATOMS AND IONS OF MAGNESIUM AND BROMINE

	Magnesium atom	Magnesium ion	Bromine atom	Bromide ion
number of protons	12	12	35	35
number of electrons	12	10	35	36
net charge	0	+2	0	−1
symbol	Mg	Mg^{++}	Br	Br^-
radius, Å	1.36	0.66	1.14	1.96

The empirical formula for the compound magnesium bromide is **MgBr₂**. The magnesium ions in this compound each have two excess positive charges. The bromide ions each have a single excess negative charge. These particles are arranged in orderly fashion in crystals of magnesium bromide. The ratio of the particles is 2 bromide ions to 1 magnesium ion (see Table 6-2 and also Figure 6-3). The subscript₂ following Br in the formula indicates that there are two bromide ions to each magnesium ion in the compound. When no subscript is used, as with the Mg, one atom or monatomic ion is understood.

The electron-dot symbols for atoms of magnesium and bromine are

$$\mathbf{Mg\!:} \qquad \cdot\ddot{\mathbf{Br}}\!:$$

The electron-dot formula for magnesium bromide is then

$$:\!\ddot{\mathbf{Br}}\!:^- \; \mathbf{Mg}^{++} \; \overset{\cdot}{\underset{\cdot\cdot}{\mathbf{Br}}}\!:^-$$

and the ionic formula is $Mg^{++}Br_2^-$. Note that in the formula $Mg^{++}Br_2^-$ the subscript ₂ applies to *both* the symbol **Br** and its charge⁻. It shows that there are two **Br⁻** ions with each **Mg⁺⁺** ion in the formula.

Energy is required to remove two electrons from one magnesium atom. But this energy is less than the electron affinity of two bromine atoms plus the energy released when one magnesium ion and two bromide ions take up their equilibrium positions in a magnesium bromide crystal. Thus, the formation of the compound magnesium bromide from widely separated magnesium and bromine atoms is another example of the exothermic nature of electron transfer.

In forming the compound magnesium bromide, elemental magnesium atoms are oxidized from $\overset{0}{\mathbf{Mg}}$ to $\overset{+2}{\mathbf{Mg}^{++}}$.

$$\overset{0}{\mathbf{Mg}} - 2e^- \rightarrow \overset{+2}{\mathbf{Mg}^{++}}$$

At the same time, for each magnesium atom oxidized, two elemental bromine atoms are reduced from $\overset{0}{\mathbf{Br}}$ to $\overset{-1}{\mathbf{Br}^-}$.

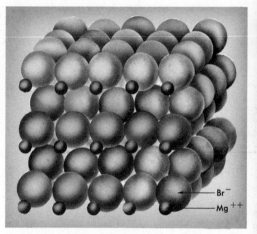

Fig. 6-3. This diagram shows the arrangement of the magnesium and bromide ions in a portion of magnesium bromide crystal.

See Problem 3 at the end of the chapter.

$$\overset{0}{2Br} + 2e^- \rightarrow \overset{-1}{2Br^-}$$

Bromine is the oxidizing agent; magnesium is the reducing agent.

In the formula $\overset{+2}{Mg^{++}}\overset{-1}{Br_2^-}$ the algebraic sum of $+2$ and $2 (-1)$ equals zero. Note how the algebraic sum of the oxidation numbers of the atoms in a formula is determined. Each oxidation number must be multiplied by the number of atoms or monatomic ions having that oxidation number. The formulas of ionic compounds merely indicate the relative numbers of positive and negative ions which combine. Therefore, *all formulas for ionic compounds are empirical.*

6.7 Elements with several oxidation numbers

Many elements exhibit more than one oxidation state. Some differences in the oxidation number of an element depend on the kind of bond which it forms with other elements. However, another factor is important. Transition elements, with four or five electron energy levels, can readily transfer the electrons in the outermost level. Many of them, with very little additional energy, can also transfer one or two electrons from the next-to-outermost level. The electrons in excess of an octet in the next-to-outermost energy level are those available for transfer. Iron is such a transition element. In forming compounds, it can transfer two $4s$ electrons. Sometimes, in more energetic reactions, a $3d$ electron can also be transferred. Thus its oxidation number can be $+2$ or $+3$. This variable number of transferable electrons accounts for the variable oxidation state of many of the transition metals.

6.8 Relative sizes of atoms and ions

Once again, look at Tables 6-1 and 6-2 accompanying Sections 6.3 and 6.6. These tables give the radii of the atoms and ions of sodium, magnesium, chlorine, and bromine. Notice the great difference in radius between an atom and the ion formed from it.

It is characteristic of metals to form positive ions. *Positive ions are called cations.* It is to be expected that metallic ions would be smaller than the corresponding metallic atoms since the outer shell electrons are no longer present. As a result, the remaining electrons are drawn closer to the nucleus by its unbalanced positive charge.

Nonmetallic elements form negative ions. *Negative ions are called anions.* Nonmetallic ions are larger than the corresponding nonmetallic atoms. Electrons have been added, making the outer shell an octet. Since the total positive charge of the nucleus remains the same, the average force of attraction for each electron decreases because there are more electrons.

Table 6–3
RADII OF REPRESENTATIVE ATOMS AND IONS IN ANGSTROMS

	Group I		Group II		Group III		Group VI		Group VII	
Period 2	Li	1.23	Be	0.89	B	0.82	O	0.73	F	0.72
	Li^+	0.68	Be^{++}	0.35	B^{+++}	0.23	O^{--}	1.40	F^-	1.33
Period 3	Na	1.54	Mg	1.36	Al	1.18	S	1.02	Cl	0.99
	Na^+	0.97	Mg^{++}	0.66	Al^{+++}	0.51	S^{--}	1.84	Cl^-	1.81
Period 4	K	2.03	Ca	1.74	Ga	1.26	Se	1.17	Br	1.14
	K^+	1.33	Ca^{++}	0.99	Ga^{+++}	0.62	Se^{--}	1.98	Br^-	1.96
Period 5	Rb	2.16	Sr	1.91	In	1.44	Te	1.36	I	1.33
	Rb^+	1.47	Sr^{++}	1.12	In^{+++}	0.81	Te^{--}	2.21	I^-	2.20
Period 6	Cs	2.35	Ba	1.98	Tl	1.48				
	Cs^+	1.67	Ba^{++}	1.34	Tl^{+++}	0.95				

Table 6-3 shows the sizes of representative atoms and ions. From these data and the generalizations given above, it will be seen that:

1. Within a group or family of elements, the ion size increases with atomic number because of shell addition.

2. Within a period of elements, the Group I, II, and III cations show a sharp decrease in size. On the other hand, the Group VII anion is only slightly smaller than the Group VI anion. Group I and II cations have the same electron configurations, but the Group II cation's greater nuclear charge draws the electrons much closer. Group VI and VII anions have identical electron configurations, too. The Group VII anion's greater nuclear charge draws the electrons somewhat closer.

Figures 6-2 and 6-3 show the arrangement of ions in crystals of the compounds sodium chloride and magnesium bromide. Such arrangements depend on the relative numbers and sizes of each kind of ion present. Crystals are described in more detail in Chapter 11.

6.9   Covalent bonding (covalence)

In covalent bonding, electrons are not transferred from one atom to another. Instead, they are *shared* by the bonded atoms. In forming a single covalent bond, two atoms mutually share one of their electrons. These two shared electrons (with opposite spins) effectively fill an orbital in each atom. They make up a *covalent·electron pair* that forms the bond between these two atoms.

The atoms of the common elemental gases, hydrogen, oxygen, nitrogen, fluorine, and chlorine, form stable diatomic (two-

PERIODIC TABLE OF

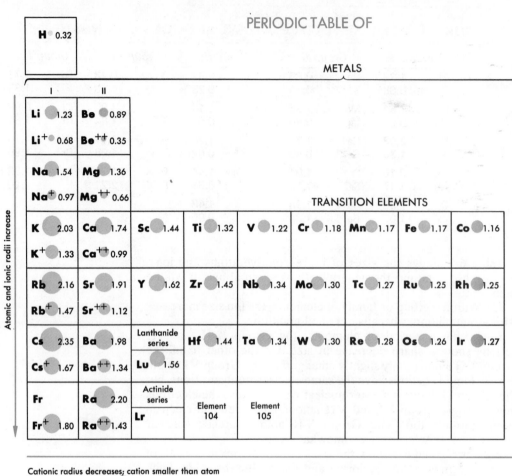

METALS

H 0.32

TRANSITION ELEMENTS

Atomic and ionic radii increase

I	II							
Li 1.23	Be 0.89							
Li⁺ 0.68	Be⁺⁺ 0.35							
Na 1.54	Mg 1.36							
Na⁺ 0.97	Mg⁺⁺ 0.66							
K 2.03	Ca 1.74	Sc 1.44	Ti 1.32	V 1.22	Cr 1.18	Mn 1.17	Fe 1.17	Co 1.16
K⁺ 1.33	Ca⁺⁺ 0.99							
Rb 2.16	Sr 1.91	Y 1.62	Zr 1.45	Nb 1.34	Mo 1.30	Tc 1.27	Ru 1.25	Rh 1.25
Rb⁺ 1.47	Sr⁺⁺ 1.12							
Cs 2.35	Ba 1.98	Lanthanide series	Hf 1.44	Ta 1.34	W 1.30	Re 1.28	Os 1.26	Ir 1.27
Cs⁺ 1.67	Ba⁺⁺ 1.34	Lu 1.56						
Fr	Ra 2.20	Actinide series	Element 104	Element 105				
Fr⁺ 1.80	Ra⁺⁺ 1.43	Lr						

Cationic radius decreases; cation smaller than atom

Lanthanide series	La 1.69	Ce 1.65	Pr 1.64	Nd 1.64	Pm 1.63	Sm 1.62	Eu 1.85
Actinide series	Ac 2.0	Th 1.65	Pa	U 1.42	Np	Pu	Am

ATOM AND ION SIZES

NONMETALS

						Noble gases VIII
	III	IV	V	VI	VII	He ●0.31
	B ●0.82 B^{+++}0.23	C 0.77	N 0.75 N^{---}1.71	O 0.73 O^{--}1.40	F 0.72 F$^-$1.33	Ne ●0.71
	Al ●1.18 Al^{+++}0.51	Si ●1.11	P 1.06 P^{---}2.12	S 1.02 S^{--}1.84	Cl 0.99 Cl$^-$1.81	Ar ●0.98
Ni ●1.15 Cu ●1.17 Zn ●1.25	Ga ●1.26 Ga^{+++}0.62	Ge ●1.22	As ●1.20	Se 1.17 Se^{--}1.98	Br 1.14 Br$^-$1.96	Kr ●1.12
Pd ●1.28 Ag ●1.34 Cd ●1.48	In ●1.44 In^{+++}0.81	Sn ●1.40	Sb ●1.40	Te ●1.36 Te^{--}2.21	I 1.33 I$^-$2.20	Xe ●1.31
Pt ●1.30 Au ●1.34 Hg ●1.49	Tl ●1.48 Tl^{+++}0.95	Pb ●1.47	Bi ●1.46	Po ●1.46	At ●1.45	Rn

Atomic radius generally decreases →

Anionic radius decreases; anion larger than atom →

Gd ●1.62	Tb ●1.61	Dy ●1.60	Ho ●1.58	Er ●1.58	Tm ●1.58	Yb ●1.70
Cm	Bk	Cf	Es	Fm	Md	No

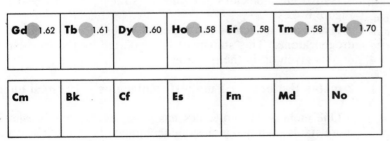

(Atomic radii mostly from R. T. Sanderson, INORGANIC CHEMISTRY, Reinhold Publishing Corporation, New York, 1967.)

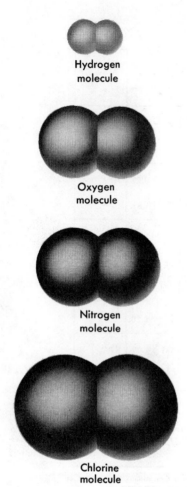

Fig. 6-4. The molecules of the common gases, such as those of hydrogen, nitrogen, oxygen, and chlorine represented here, consist of two atoms joined by covalent bonding. These are all linear molecules.

atomed) *molecules* by covalent bonding. *A molecule is the smallest chemical unit of a substance which is capable of stable independent existence.* For these elemental gases, the smallest chemical units capable of stable independent existence are diatomic units. Single atoms of the five gases listed above are chemically unstable. Hence, these diatomic units make up molecules of these gases.

In diatomic hydrogen molecules, each hydrogen atom shares its single $1s$ valence electron with the other. These two electrons move about both nuclei, so that each atom, in effect, has its $1s$ orbital filled. In effect, each hydrogen atom has the stable electron configuration of a helium atom.

$$1s$$

$$\text{H} \quad \boxed{\oslash}$$
$$\text{H} \quad \boxed{\oslash}$$

The *electron-dot formula* for a molecule of hydrogen is

$$\text{H}\!:\!\text{H}$$

Frequently chemists indicate a shared pair of electrons by a dash (—) instead of the symbol (:). Thus the formula for a molecule of hydrogen may be written

$$\text{H}\!-\!\text{H}$$

This type of formula is called a *structural formula*.

The *molecular formula* for hydrogen is H_2. The numerical subscript indicates the number of atoms per molecule. *A formula which indicates the actual composition of a molecule is called a molecular formula.*

Hydrogen molecules are linear (straight-line) as shown in Figure 6-4.

Hydrogen molecules have greater stability than separate hydrogen atoms. This statement is supported by the fact that energy is given off in the reaction

2 moles H atoms $\rightarrow$ 1 mole H_2 molecules + 104 kcal energy

One mole of H_2 molecules has lower energy and is therefore more stable than two moles of uncombined H atoms. The reverse reaction is that of separating hydrogen molecules into the atoms that make them up. Energy must be supplied for this reaction.

1 mole H_2 + 104 kcal $\rightarrow$ 2 moles H

The energy required, 104 kcal/mole, is called the *bond energy* of the **H—H** bond. *Bond energy is the energy required to break chemical bonds.* It is usually expressed in kcal per mole of bonds broken.

Diatomic chlorine molecules can be formed in the same manner as hydrogen molecules. Each atom shares one electron with the other, filling, in effect, an incomplete $3p$ orbital in each. This gives both atoms the stable electron arrangement of the noble gas, argon. Both atoms have, in effect, an octet in the 3rd energy level.

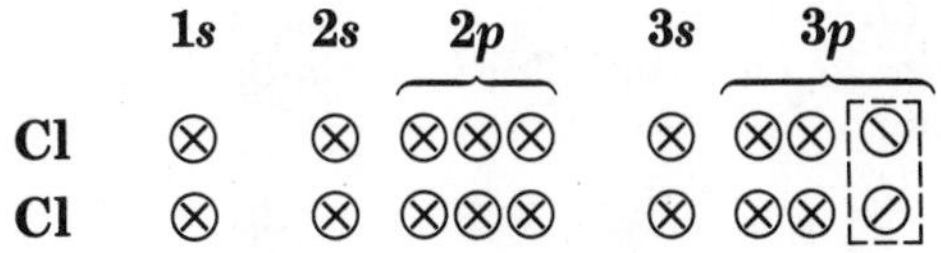

	$1s$	$2s$	$2p$	$3s$	$3p$
Cl	⊗	⊗	⊗⊗⊗	⊗	⊗⊗ ⊙̄
Cl	⊗	⊗	⊗⊗⊗	⊗	⊗⊗ ⊘

The electron-dot formula for a molecule of chlorine is

$$: \overset{\circ\circ}{\underset{\circ\circ}{Cl}} \circ \overset{\cdot\cdot}{\underset{\cdot\cdot}{Cl}} :$$

Its structural formula is

$$Cl\text{---}Cl$$

and its molecular formula is Cl_2. Chlorine molecules are linear (straight-line) like those of hydrogen. (See Figure 6-4.)

Energy is required to separate chlorine molecules into the atoms of which they are made.

$$\textbf{1 mole } Cl_2 + \textbf{58 kcal} \rightarrow \textbf{2 moles Cl}$$

Hence, the bond energy of the Cl—Cl bond is 58 kcal/mole, and the chlorine molecules are more stable than separate chlorine atoms.

Diatomic molecules of the other halogens have similar formulas and shapes. Their bond energies are given in Table 6-4.

Oxygen also exists as diatomic molecules. But the bonding in an oxygen molecule is rather complex. It is not shown very satisfactorily by orbital and electron-dot formulas. A possible orbital notation for an oxygen molecule is

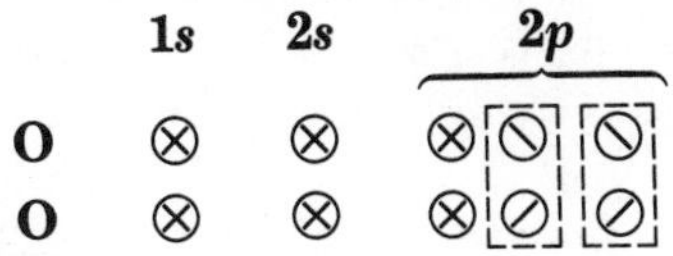

	$1s$	$2s$	$2p$
O	⊗	⊗	⊗ ⊙̄ ⊙̄
O	⊗	⊗	⊗ ⊘ ⊘

The corresponding electron-dot formula is

$$\overset{\circ\circ}{\underset{\circ\circ}{O}} \circ\circ \overset{\cdot\cdot}{\underset{\cdot}{O}}$$

Its structural formula is

$$O=O$$

and its molecular formula is O_2.

Table 6-4	
BOND ENERGIES	
Bond	*Energy* (kcal/mole)
H–H	104
N–N	37
N≡N	227
O–O	34
O=O	119
Cl–Cl	58
Br–Br	46
I–I	36
C–H	98
N–H	92
O–H	111
Cl–H	103
Br–H	87
I–H	71
C–Cl	78
C–Br	66

Note that *two pairs* of electrons are shared in the oxygen molecule. This sharing of two electron pairs makes a *double covalent bond*. A double covalent bond is represented in a structural formula by a double dash. The oxygen molecule is linear. The bond energy of the O=O bond is 119 kcal/mole. Oxygen molecules are more stable than separate oxygen atoms.

The structure of the nitrogen molecule indicates the sharing of *three pairs* of electrons. Nitrogen molecules contain a *triple covalent bond*.

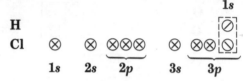

The electron-dot formula for the nitrogen molecule is

$$\overset{\circ}{\underset{\circ}{N}}\,\vdots\,\vdots\,\vdots\,\overset{}{N}\colon$$

Its structural formula is

$$N\equiv N$$

and its molecular formula is N_2. Note that a triple covalent bond is represented in a structural formula by a triple dash. Nitrogen molecules are linear molecules. The bond energy of the N≡N bond is 227 kcal/mole. With such a high bond energy, nitrogen molecules are much more stable than individual atoms.

Diatomic molecules of elements are considered to be free elements. Thus, each atom in the molecule may be assigned a zero oxidation number (Rule 1).

6.10 Covalent bonding of unlike atoms

Atoms of different elements may combine by covalent bonding. A hydrogen atom and a chlorine atom combine by covalent bonding and form a hydrogen chloride molecule. In this molecule the 1s hydrogen electron and a 3p chlorine electron complete a space orbital, as shown below.

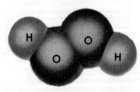

The electron-dot formula for hydrogen chloride is

$$H\overset{\circ}{\underset{\circ\circ}{\colon}}\overset{\cdot\cdot}{Cl}\colon$$

Its structural formula is

$$H\!-\!Cl$$

Fig. 6-5. Hydrogen chloride, water, and hydrogen peroxide are compounds whose simplest particles are molecules composed of covalently bonded atoms. Hydrogen chloride molecules are linear; water molecules are bent molecules; hydrogen peroxide molecules are double bent molecules.

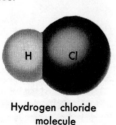

Hydrogen chloride
molecule

Water
molecule

Hydrogen peroxide
molecule

and its molecular formula is **HCl**. The HCl molecule is linear as shown in Figure 6-5.

To separate HCl molecules into H and Cl atoms requires energy.

$$\textbf{1 mole HCl + 103 kcal} \rightarrow \textbf{1 mole H + 1 mole Cl}$$

Hence, hydrogen chloride molecules are more stable than separate hydrogen and chlorine atoms. The bond energy of the **H—Cl** bond is 103 kcal/mole.

Rule 4: *In compounds, the oxidation number of hydrogen is +1.* By Rule 4, the oxidation number of hydrogen in hydrogen chloride is +1. By Rule 3 (Section 6.5) the oxidation number of chlorine must be −1.

Bond energies can be used to calculate the approximate energy of a chemical reaction. (See Table 6-4). This method of calculation assumes that the energy change in a reaction is the net result of the breaking and making of chemical bonds.

The reaction for the formation of one mole of hydrogen chloride molecules may be used as an example. One-half mole of hydrogen molecules and one-half mole of chlorine molecules combine as follows:

$$\textbf{$\tfrac{1}{2}$ mole H$_2$ + $\tfrac{1}{2}$ mole Cl$_2$ $\rightarrow$ 1 mole HCl}$$

This reaction may be considered for calculation purposes to occur in three steps. The first step is the breaking of bonds in one-half mole of hydrogen molecules:

$$\textbf{$\tfrac{1}{2}$ mole H$_2$ + 52 kcal $\rightarrow$ 1 mole H}$$

(The equation is written for one-half mole of H_2 molecules. The energy needed is one-half the bond energy per mole, 104 kcal.)

The second step is the breaking of bonds in one-half mole of chlorine molecules:

$$\textbf{$\tfrac{1}{2}$ mole Cl$_2$ + 29 kcal $\rightarrow$ 1 mole Cl}$$

(Again the energy involved is one-half the bond energy per mole, 58 kcal.)

The third reaction is the reverse of the **H—Cl** bond energy reaction written earlier in this section:

$$\textbf{1 mole H + 1 mole Cl $\rightarrow$ 1 mole HCl + 103 kcal}$$

Combining these three equations and adding them algebraically:

$$
\begin{array}{l}
\tfrac{1}{2}\text{ mole H}_2 + 52\text{ kcal} \quad \rightarrow \cancel{1\text{ mole H}} \\
\tfrac{1}{2}\text{ mole Cl}_2 + 29\text{ kcal} \quad \rightarrow \cancel{1\text{ mole Cl}} \\
\underline{\cancel{1\text{ mole H}} + \cancel{1\text{ mole Cl}} \rightarrow 1\text{ mole HCl} + 103\text{ kcal}} \\
\tfrac{1}{2}\text{ mole H}_2 + \tfrac{1}{2}\text{ mole Cl}_2 \rightarrow 1\text{ mole HCl} + \ \ 22\text{ kcal}
\end{array}
$$

For review purposes, use the statement of this rule in Section 6.19 since an exception is described later in this chapter.

Thus, we see that the reaction is exothermic. The amount of energy released is 22 kcal.

The common compound, water, consists of molecules formed by covalent bonding of two hydrogen atoms with one oxygen atom. The orbital representation of this bonding is

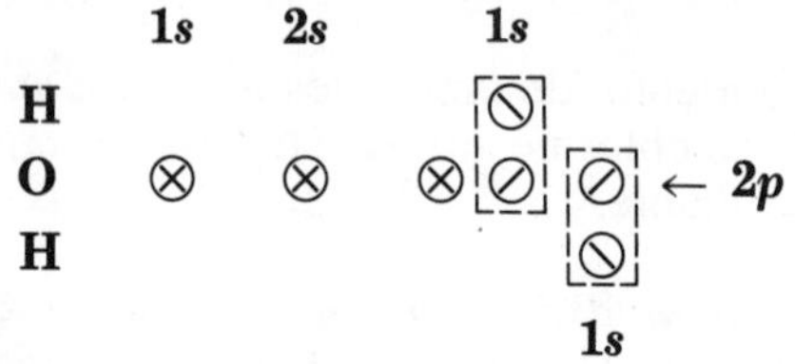

The electron-dot formula for water is

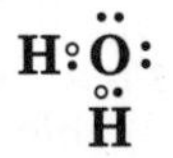

$$H \overset{..}{\underset{\overset{\displaystyle ..}{H}}{O}}:$$

Its structural formula is

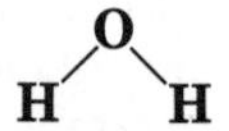

and its molecular formula is H_2O.

A molecule containing three atoms can have one of only two shapes. Either (1) the atoms lie on the same straight line and form a linear molecule, or (2) the atoms do not lie on one straight line and form a bent molecule. Figure 6-5 shows that the hydrogen atoms and oxygen atom in a water molecule do not lie on the same straight line. Water molecules are bent molecules. Very careful measurements reveal that the distances between the oxygen atom and each of the two hydrogen atoms are the same. This evidence suggests that the two hydrogen atoms act the same way in the molecule. One explanation of the bent shape of the water molecule can be found in Figure 4-7. This figure shows that the electrons with which the oxygen atom forms bonds by sharing are in p space orbitals. These orbitals point in directions 90° apart.

Energy is required to break up water molecules into the atoms of which they are made.

$$\textbf{1 mole } H_2O + \textbf{222 kcal} \rightarrow \textbf{2 moles H} + \textbf{1 mole O}$$

Water molecules, therefore, have lower energy and are more stable than separate hydrogen and oxygen atoms. Two H—O bonds are broken per molecule of water decomposed. Therefore, the H—O bond energy is 111 kcal/mole or one-half that shown in the equation.

It is possible for more than one kind of molecule to be formed from the same kinds of atoms. A second compound which may be formed from hydrogen and oxygen is hydrogen peroxide, a well-known bleaching and oxidizing agent. The orbital notation of hydrogen peroxide is

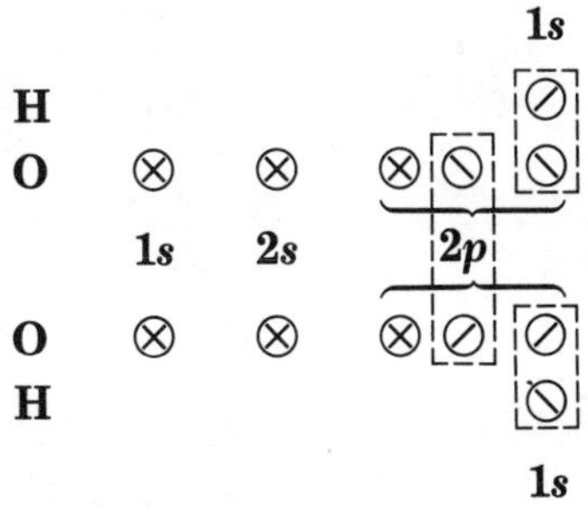

1s

H

O   ⊗   ⊗   ⊗ ⊘ ⊘

   1s   2s   2p

O   ⊗   ⊗   ⊗ ⊘ ⊘

H

1s

Its electron-dot formula is

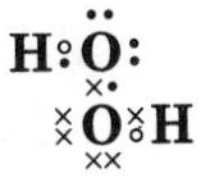

$$H\!:\!\overset{\cdot\cdot}{\underset{\times}{O}}\!:$$
$$\times\overset{\times}{\underset{\times\times}{O}}\overset{\times}{}H$$

Its structural formula is

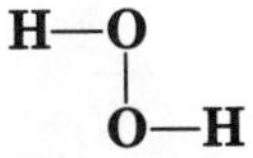

$$\begin{array}{c} H{-}O \\ \quad | \\ \quad O{-}H \end{array}$$

Its molecular formula is H_2O_2. Experimental evidence indicates that the hydrogen peroxide molecule is a double-bent shaped molecule. (See Figure 6-5.)

Rule 5: *In compounds, the oxidation number of oxygen is −2. One exception to this rule is that, in peroxides, the oxidation number of oxygen is −1. Thus we see that, in water, the oxidation number of hydrogen is +1 and of oxygen is −2. On the other hand, in hydrogen peroxide, the oxidation number of hydrogen is +1, and of oxygen is −1. (Use Rule 3 to check this result.)*

For review purposes, use the statement of this rule in Section 6.19 since a further exception is discussed later in this chapter.

Table 6-5 gives some examples of covalent bonding between hydrogen and nitrogen, and between hydrogen and carbon. The oxidation number of hydrogen in each molecule is +1. But note that the oxidation numbers of nitrogen and carbon vary from molecule to molecule.

Ammonia, NH_3, molecules have three hydrogen atoms so spaced about a nitrogen atom that the molecule has the shape of a pyramid. Think of the hydrogen atoms as forming the base of the pyramid, with the nitrogen atom at the peak. In methane, CH_4, the hydrogen atoms are symmetrically spaced in three dimensions about the carbon atom. Methane molecules have a regular tetrahedral shape. A regular tetrahedron is a solid figure that has four sides, each side an equilateral triangle.

Consider the examples of covalent bonding illustrated thus far. Except for hydrazine (Table 6-5), all of the bonded atoms are more stable because they have filled orbitals. They have lower energy than the unbonded atoms. Thus, the reactions in which these molecules are formed from atoms are exothermic.

Table 6-5
DATA ON SOME REPRESENTATIVE MOLECULES

	Ammonia	Hydrazine	Methane	Ethane
molecular formula	NH_3	N_2H_4	CH_4	C_2H_6
structural formula	H H \\ / N | H	H H \\ / N—N / \\ H H	H | H—C—H | H	H H | | H—C—C—H | | H H
electron-dot formula	H o· 8N°H ·o H	H H o· x· 8N°N× ·o ·x H H	H o· H8C°H ·o H	H H o· x· H8C°C×H ·o ·x H H
oxidation numbers	H = +1 N = −3	H = +1 N = −2	H = +1 C = −4	H = +1 C = −3
model of molecule				

Only the combination of nitrogen and hydrogen atoms forming hydrazine, N_2H_4, is endothermic.

The neutral particle which results from the covalent bonding of atoms is a molecule. Its composition is represented by a molecular formula.

6.11 Resonance

If we attempt to draw an electron-dot formula for the molecular compound sulfur dioxide, we find that two formulas may be written. Each formula gives all three atoms in the molecule an octet.

From these formulas, we might suspect that the two sulfur-oxygen bonds in the molecule are different. Experimental evidence, however, indicates that these bonds are identical. Hence, neither of the formulas we have written can be correct. Unfortunately, *we cannot satisfactorily represent this bond identity by any single formula using the electron-dot notation system and keeping the octet rule.* To describe such situations we make use of a concept called *resonance*.

Sulfur dioxide molecules may be considered to have a structure intermediate between the two electron-dot structures given.

In this sense, the electron arrangement in the molecule is a *resonance hybrid* of the written structures. The term "resonance" is not really very accurate in this connection. It encourages the wrong idea that the structure of the molecule switches from one electron-dot formula to the other and that a pair of electrons is sometimes part of one bond and sometimes part of the other.

Sulfur dioxide molecules have only one real structure. The properties of a resonance hybrid do not switch from those of one electron-dot structure to those of the other. The properties are definite and are characteristic of the hybrid structure. The concept of resonance is an attempt to make up for deficiencies in the electron-dot structures of certain molecules. Difficulties occur when the electron-pair and electron-octet rules are used to write the structures of these molecules. The difficulties lie in our method of writing formulas, not in the molecules which we are trying to represent.

6.12   Hybridization

In a methane molecule, CH_4, one carbon atom is covalently bonded to four hydrogen atoms. The hydrogen atoms are symmetrically arranged as if at the vertices of a regular tetrahedron with the carbon atom at the center. The carbon-hydrogen bond angles in this molecule are all 109.5°. See Figure 6-6.

The electron configuration of a carbon atom, $1s^2 2s^2 2p^2$, indicates that the valence electrons should be two $2s$ and two $2p$ electrons. However, when carbon atoms combine, it is believed that one of the $2s$ electrons acquires enough energy to occupy a $2p$ orbital. The electron configuration $1s^2 2s^1 2p^3$ results. Thus, the bonding electrons of a carbon atom are one $2s$ electron and three $2p$ electrons. A carbon atom therefore, can form four covalent bonds, as it does with hydrogen atoms in the methane molecule.

We have noted that one of the valence electrons of the carbon atom is a $2s$ electron and the other three are $2p$ electrons. Hence, we might expect one of the carbon-hydrogen bonds in methane to be different from the other three. Experimentally, however, this is not the case. All the bonds are equivalent. We can explain this difference by assuming that *hybridization* of the one $2s$ and three $2p$ orbitals occurs. Four equivalent orbitals are produced.

Hybridization is the combining of two or more orbitals of nearly the same energy into new orbitals of equal energy. The hybrid orbitals of the carbon atom are called sp^3 (read sp-three) orbitals. Hybrid orbitals result from the combination of one s orbital and three p orbitals. As mentioned, these four sp^3 orbitals point toward the corners of a regular tetrahedron from the carbon atom at their center. This arrangement permits the maximum separation of four orbitals grouped about a given point. This arrangement accounts for the regular tetrahedral shape of methane molecules.

Fig. 6-6. In the methane molecule, CH_4, a carbon atom is covalently and symmetrically bonded to four hydrogen atoms. The tetrahedral shape is the result of sp^3 hybridization of the carbon-atom orbitals.

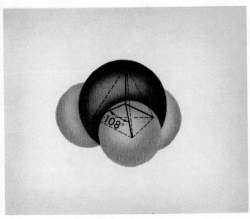

Fig. 6-7. The pyramidal shape of the ammonia molecule, NH₃, may be explained by the *sp*³ hybridization of nitrogen-atom orbitals.

The idea of hybrid tetrahedral orbitals can also account for the observed shape of the ammonia molecule. This is true even though ammonia has only three hydrogen atoms attached to a central nitrogen atom. The electron-dot symbol for a nitrogen atom is

$$\cdot \ddot{\mathbf{N}} \colon$$

Let us imagine that the electrons in the four positions about the symbol are distributed among four equivalent tetrahedral orbitals. This arrangement gives one orbital with a pair of electrons, and three orbitals with single electrons which can be shared with the electron from each of three hydrogen atoms. The result is a structure that resembles a pyramid as shown in Figure 6-7. The three hydrogen atoms form the base of the pyramid. The unshared pair of nitrogen electrons forms the peak. The angles between the N—H bonds in ammonia are known to be 108°. This agrees well with the tetrahedral angle of 109.5°.

We may extend this idea to the structure of the water molecule. The electron-dot formula for this molecule is

$$\mathbf{H} \colon \ddot{\underset{\cdot\cdot}{\mathbf{O}}} \colon$$
$$\mathbf{H}$$

Here we may imagine four tetrahedral hybrid orbitals. Two of these form the oxygen-hydrogen bonds. The other two are each a pair of unshared oxygen electrons. See Figure 6-8. The bond angle in the water molecule is only 105°. The unshared electron pairs on the oxygen atom tend to repel each other more than the shared electrons repel each other. These unequal opposing repulsions make the angle between the shared pairs decrease slightly in size.

Other types of hybridization are described in Chapter 17.

Fig. 6-8. The bent shape of the water molecule, H₂O, may be explained by the considerable *sp*³ hybridization of oxygen-atom orbitals.

6.13 More about particles of matter

Free and isolated atoms are rarely found in nature. Instead, atoms of most elements combine with one another at ordinary temperatures and form larger structural particles. Notable exceptions are the noble elements: helium, neon, argon, krypton, xenon, and radon. The atoms of these noble gases do not combine with each other and form larger particles. There is no distinction, therefore, between the atoms and molecules of these gases. We may say that a molecule of helium is monatomic (one-atomed), and is written as **He**.

We have already mentioned that the atoms of some elements combine naturally and form pairs that exist as simple diatomic molecules. Atmospheric oxygen and nitrogen are two examples. Their molecules are represented respectively as **O₂** and **N₂**.

Observe that O_2 means two atoms of oxygen are bonded together and form one oxygen molecule. On the other hand, $2O$ means two separate unbonded oxygen atoms. $3O_2$ means three molecules of oxygen, each of which consists of two oxygen atoms bonded together. The other elemental gases, hydrogen, fluorine, and chlorine, also exist as diatomic molecules, H_2, F_2, and Cl_2 respectively. The nonmetal bromine, a liquid at ordinary temperatures, exists as diatomic molecules, Br_2. Another element in the same group, iodine, forms molecular crystals in which each molecular particle is diatomic, I_2.

Other elements may form groups consisting of a larger number of atoms. Phosphorus may form molecules consisting of four atoms, written P_4. Sulfur molecules may be eight-atom particles, or S_8. The metallic elements generally exhibit crystalline structures. Their atoms are closely packed in regular patterns which show no simple molecular units. In these instances, each individual crystal can be considered to be a single giant molecule.

Some compounds have distinct unit structures composed of simple molecules. Water is a familiar example. Water molecules consist of two hydrogen atoms and one oxygen atom represented as H_2O. The expression $2H_2O$ represents two molecules of water, each containing two atoms of hydrogen and one atom of oxygen. Similarly, $5H_2O$ signifies five molecules of water. When no other coefficient (the number before the formula) is used, it is understood that the coefficient is 1. Molecules of compounds range from a minimum of two atoms to large numbers of atoms.

Some substances show complex unit structures formed by groups of molecules or molecular aggregates. Still others have no molecular organization at all. Ordinary table salt, sodium chloride, consists of sodium and chloride ions distributed in a regular crystalline lattice pattern that is continuous to each face of the salt crystal. Simple molecules of sodium chloride do not exist except in the vapor state at very high temperatures. In general, *a coefficient of a symbol or formula gives the number of particles whose composition is given by the symbol or formula; a subscript gives the number of atoms of a particular kind in the particle.*

6.14   Size of molecules

Molecules are very small. It is estimated that if a drop of water could be magnified to the size of the earth, the molecules composing it would be about one meter in diameter. But molecules vary greatly in size. The simple molecules of gases, consisting of one, two, or three atoms, have diameters of about 3×10^{-8} cm. Some virus protein molecules consist of about 7.5×10^5 atoms and have diameters of about 2.3×10^{-6} cm. These molecules have been photographed with an electron microscope. On the angstrom scale, this range of molecular diameters is from 3 Å to 230 Å.

6.15 Electronegativity

In ionic bonding, electrons are *completely transferred* from the outer shells of metallic atoms to the outer shells of non-metallic atoms. In covalent bonding, electrons are *shared* in the outer shells of the bonded atoms.

If two covalently bonded atoms are alike, their attractions for the shared electrons are equal. The electrons are most probably distributed equally about both atoms. Each atom remains electrically neutral, even though they are bonded together. *A covalent bond in which there is an equal attraction for the shared electrons and a resulting balanced distribution of charge is called a **pure, or nonpolar, covalent bond**.* If two different atoms are covalently bonded, one atom may attract the shared electron pair more strongly than the other atom does. Then, the electrons are not equally shared, but are more closely held by the atom with stronger attraction. This atom is not electrically neutral. Instead it is slightly negative, though not as negative as a singly charged anion. The other atom is then left slightly positive, though not as positive as a singly charged cation. *A covalent bond in which there is an unequal attraction for the shared electrons and a resulting unbalanced distribution of charge is called a **polar covalent bond**.* Polar covalent bonds thus are intermediate in nature between ionic bonds and pure covalent bonds. In ionic bonds, electron transfer is complete. In pure covalent bonds, electron sharing is equal. Polar covalent bonds are part covalent and part ionic in character.

Ionization energy is a measure of the strength with which a neutral atom holds an outer-shell electron. Electron affinity indicates the strength of the attraction between a neutral atom and an additional electron. Linus Pauling (b. 1901) and other chemists considered these two values, together with certain properties of molecules. They derived an arbitrary scale which indicates *the attraction of an atom for the shared electrons forming a bond between it and another atom. This property is called **electronegativity**.* Atoms with high electronegativity have a strong attraction for electrons they share with another atom. Atoms with low electronegativity have a weak attraction for electrons they share with another atom. The relative electronegativities of two atoms give an indication of the type of bonding which can exist between them.

The chart, Figure 6-10, gives the electronegativity values of the elements. A study of this chart leads to these conclusions:

1. Low electronegativity is characteristic of metals. The lower the electronegativity, the more active the metal. Thus, the lowest electronegativities are found at the lower left of the periodic table.

2. High electronegativity is characteristic of nonmetals. Thus, the highest electronegativities are found at the upper

Fig. 6-9. Linus Pauling is an outstanding chemistry teacher and research director. He has made notable contributions to our understanding of the structure of molecules, from simple ones like hydrogen molecules to very complex ones like those of proteins. He was awarded the Nobel prize in chemistry in 1954 and the Nobel peace prize in 1963.

California Institute of Technology

PERIODIC TABLE OF ELECTRONEGATIVITIES

I	II											III	IV	V	VI	VII	VIII
2.1 H 1																	He 2
1.0 Li 3	1.5 Be 4											2.0 B 5	2.5 C 6	3.0 N 7	3.5 O 8	4.0 F 9	Ne 10
0.9 Na 11	1.2 Mg 12											1.5 Al 13	1.8 Si 14	2.1 P 15	2.5 S 16	3.0 Cl 17	Ar 18
0.8 K 19	1.0 Ca 20	1.3 Sc 21	1.5 Ti 22	1.6 V 23	1.6 Cr 24	1.5 Mn 25	1.8 Fe 26	1.8 Co 27	1.8 Ni 28	1.9 Cu 29	1.6 Zn 30	1.6 Ga 31	1.8 Ge 32	2.0 As 33	2.4 Se 34	2.8 Br 35	3.0 Kr 36
0.8 Rb 37	1.0 Sr 38	1.2 Y 39	1.4 Zr 40	1.6 Nb 41	1.8 Mo 42	1.9 Tc 43	2.2 Ru 44	2.2 Rh 45	2.2 Pd 46	1.9 Ag 47	1.7 Cd 48	1.7 In 49	1.8 Sn 50	1.9 Sb 51	2.1 Te 52	2.5 I 53	2.6 Xe 54
0.7 Cs 55	0.9 Ba 56	1.2 Lu 71	1.3 Hf 72	1.5 Ta 73	1.7 W 74	1.9 Re 75	2.2 Os 76	2.2 Ir 77	2.2 Pt 78	2.4 Au 79	1.9 Hg 80	1.8 Tl 81	1.8 Pb 82	1.9 Bi 83	2.0 Po 84	2.2 At 85	2.4 Rn 86
0.7 Fr 87	0.9 Ra 88	Lr 103	104	105													

1.1 La 57	1.1 Ce 58	1.1 Pr 59	1.1 Nd 60	1.1 Pm 61	1.1 Sm 62	1.1 Eu 63	1.1 Gd 64	1.1 Tb 65	1.1 Dy 66	1.1 Ho 67	1.1 Er 68	1.1 Tm 69	1.1 Yb 70
1.1 Ac 89	1.3 Th 90	1.5 Pa 91	1.7 U 92	1.3 Np 93	1.3 Pu 94	1.3 Am 95	1.3 Cm 96	1.3 Bk 97	1.3 Cf 98	1.3 Es 99	1.3 Fm 100	1.3 Md 101	1.3 No 102

right of the periodic table. Fluorine is the most electronegative element. Oxygen is second.

3. Electronegativity generally decreases within the numbered groups or families with increasing atomic number. In the transition element groups, there is usually only a slight variation in electronegativity.

4. Electronegativity increases within a period or series through the middle of the periodic table. It decreases slightly in the remaining metals, and then increases usually to a maximum in Group VII or VIII.

Fig. 6-10. Periodic table showing the electronegativities of the elements on an arbitrary scale.

6.16 Electronegativity difference and chemical bonding

The electronegativity difference between two elements is related to the percentage of ionic character of a single bond between atoms of the two elements. Table 6-6 gives values for this useful approximate relationship.

Bonds with more than 50% ionic character are considered to be largely ionic. Thus, the bonds between metallic elements and the distinctly nonmetallic elements are largely ionic. Sodium chloride, NaCl, electronegativity difference $3.0 - 0.9 = 2.1$, is

Table 6–6
RELATIONSHIP BETWEEN ELECTRONEGATIVITY DIFFERENCE AND IONIC CHARACTER

Electronegativity difference		Percentage of ionic character
0.2	nonpolar	1
0.4	covalent bond	4
0.6		9
0.8		15
1.0	polar covalent bond	22
1.2		30
1.4		39
1.6		47
1.8		55
2.0		63
2.2		70
2.4	ionic bond	76
2.6		82
2.8		86
3.0		89
3.2		92

a compound with ionic bonds. Similarly $CaBr_2$ and BaO are examples of compounds with ionic bonds.

Bonds with less than 50% ionic character are considered to be largely covalent. Below 5% ionic character, a bond is considered nonpolar covalent. Between 5% and 50% ionic character, a bond is considered polar covalent. The nonmetallic elements have rather similar electronegativity values. So the bonding between nonmetallic elements is largely covalent. The hydrogen-oxygen bonds in water, electronegativity difference $3.5 - 2.1 = 1.4$, are 39% ionic. Thus these are polar covalent bonds, with the oxygen being somewhat negative and the hydrogen being somewhat positive.

Bonds between like atoms are found in molecules of elements such as oxygen or chlorine. These bonds have no ionic character since the electronegativity difference is zero.

We have classed chemical bonds as ionic bonds or covalent bonds. But it is apparent that these classifications are not clear and distinct. On the periodic table, the type of bonding gradually changes. Bonds are essentially ionic between the active metals of Groups I and II and oxygen or the halogens. But they are essentially covalent between metalloids and nonmetals as well as between two nonmetals. A third type of bonding, metallic bonding, occurs between atoms of metals. It will be described in Chapter 11.

The noble gases have electron configurations which are chemically very stable. It is possible, however, to produce several stable compounds of krypton, xenon, and radon with fluorine.

We are now ready to introduce the sixth rule for assigning oxidation numbers.

Rule 6: *In combinations involving nonmetals, the oxidation number of the less electronegative element is positive, and that of the more electronegative element is negative.*

Rule 6 leads us to two further exceptions to the rules as already stated. First, hydrogen forms some ionic compounds with very active metals, such as lithium and sodium. In these compounds, the hydrogen atom gains an electron from the metal and forms a *hydride* ion, H^-. In hydrides, the oxidation number of hydrogen is -1. Second, in compounds with fluorine, oxygen is the less electronegative element. Oxygen, therefore, must have a positive oxidation number $+2$.

6.17 Molecular polarity

If all the bonds in a molecule are nonpolar, the valence electrons are equally shared by the bonding atoms. Thus, there is a uniform distribution of electrons on the exterior of the molecule. This uniform distribution occurs regardless of the number of bonds and their direction in space. A molecule with such characteristics is a *nonpolar molecule*. Molecules such as H_2, Cl_2, O_2, N_2, CH_4, and C_2H_6 are nonpolar because all of the bonds in such molecules are nonpolar.

Diatomic molecules like HCl and HBr have only one bond and it is a polar bond. These molecules have one somewhat more negative end and a somewhat less negative end. On the more negative end, the electron density (probability of finding electrons) is greater than on the less negative end. Molecules with such unbalanced electron distributions are *polar molecules*. Because polar molecules have two regions of different electric charge, they are sometimes also called *dipolar molecules*, or simply *dipoles*.

If a molecule has more than one polar bond, the molecule as a whole may be nonpolar or polar depending on the arrangement in space of the bonds in the molecule. If the polar bonds in a molecule are all alike, the polarity of the molecule as a whole depends only on the arrangement in space of the bonds. Thus, water molecules are polar due to a bent structure.

Fig. 6-11. Thin streams of falling water deflected by charged rods.

But carbon dioxide is nonpolar due to a linear structure.

$$O=C=O$$

Triangular boron trifluoride molecules

are nonpolar, but pyramidal ammonia molecules

are polar.

6.18 Polyatomic ions

Some covalently bonded groups of atoms act like single atoms in forming ions. These charged groups of covalently bonded atoms are called *polyatomic* (many-atomed) *ions*. Some common polyatomic ions are the sulfate ion, SO_4^{--}, the nitrate ion,

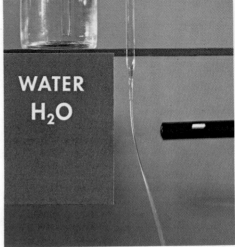

From the CHEM Study Film: *Shapes and Polarities of Molecules*

NO_3^-, and the phosphate ion, PO_4^{---}. The bonds within these polyatomic ions are largely covalent. But the groups of atoms have an excess of electrons when combined, and thus are negative ions. There is only one common positive polyatomic ion, the ammonium ion, NH_4^+. It is produced when a molecule of ammonia, NH_3, acquires a proton. Electron-dot representations of these polyatomic ions are:

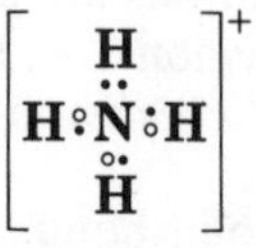

ammonium ion

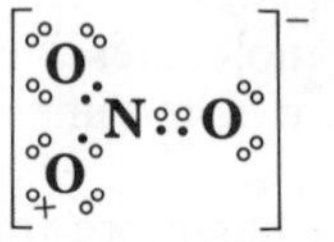

nitrate ion

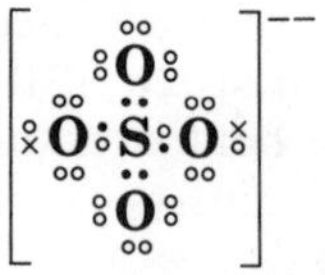

sulfate ion

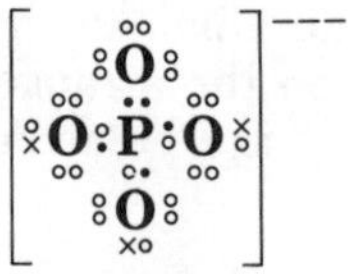

phosphate ion

There are some covalent bonds in which both electrons that form the bond between two atoms come from only one of the bonded atoms. Each of the electron-dot formulas shown here has at least one such bond. Let us use the ammonium ion as an example. In this ion, three of the covalent nitrogen-hydrogen bonds consist of one shared electron from nitrogen and one shared electron from hydrogen. The other covalent nitrogen-hydrogen bond consists of two electrons, both of which are supplied by a nitrogen atom. A hydrogen ion (proton) can thus bond at this position and produce the single net positive charge of the NH_4^+ ion. Looking at the structure another way, there are eleven protons (seven in the nitrogen nucleus and one in each of four hydrogen nuclei) in the ammonium ion. There are only ten electrons (two $1s$ electrons of the nitrogen atom, and eight valence electrons shown). With eleven protons and only ten electrons, an ammonium ion has a net charge of $+1$.

Rule 7: *The algebraic sum of the oxidation numbers of the atoms in the formula of a polyatomic ion is equal to its charge.*

In an ammonium ion, the oxidation number of hydrogen is $+1$ (Rules 4 and 6). But the algebraic sum of the oxidation numbers must equal $+1$ (Rule 7). Using x as the oxidation number of nitrogen:

$$\overset{x\quad +1}{[NH_4]^+}$$

$$x + 4(+1) = +1 \quad \text{and} \quad x = -3$$

The bonding, charges, and oxidation numbers of the elements in the other polyatomic ions can be examined in similar fashion. The electrons represented by small crosses are acquired by the ion from other elements through electron transfer.

The electron-dot formula shown for the nitrate ion is only one of several possible formulas which can be written. Nitrate ions have a resonance-hybrid structure.

6.19 Summary of oxidation-number rules

1. The oxidation number of an atom of a free element is zero.

2. The oxidation number of a monatomic ion is equal to its charge.

3. The algebraic sum of the oxidation numbers of the atoms in the formula of a compound is zero.

4. In compounds, the oxidation number of hydrogen is +1, *except* in metallic hydrides where its oxidation number is −1.

5. In compounds, the oxidation number of oxygen is −2, *except* in peroxides, where its oxidation number is −1. In compounds with fluorine, oxygen is the less electronegative element and has a positive oxidation number, +2.

6. In combinations involving nonmetals, the oxidation number of the less electronegative element is positive, and that of the more electronegative element is negative.

7. The algebraic sum of the oxidation numbers of the atoms in the formula of a polyatomic ion is equal to its charge.

QUESTIONS

1. (*a*) What part of the atom is involved in the production of a chemical bond? **Group A**
   (*b*) How are such bonds formed?
2. (*a*) What are the types of chemical bonding? (*b*) What particles result from each type of bonding?
3. (*a*) What kind of outer electron shell does an atom usually attain when it combines with other atoms? (*b*) Why is this electron structure chemically stable?
4. Which type of energy changes may occur (*a*) in electron transfer? (*b*) in electron sharing?
5. (*a*) What is a chemical formula? (*b*) Distinguish between an empirical formula and a molecular formula.
6. Which type of formula is used to represent the composition of (*a*) an ionic compound? (*b*) a covalent compound?
7. Draw an electron-dot symbol for (*a*) a potassium atom; (*b*) a potassium ion.
8. Draw an electron-dot symbol for (*a*) a sulfur atom; (*b*) a sulfide ion.
9. Using electron-dot symbols, represent a compound of potassium and sulfur.
10. (*a*) State the general definition for oxidation; (*b*) for reduction.

11. (a) Why is a substance which undergoes oxidation a reducing agent? (b) Why may a substance which undergoes reduction be considered an oxidizing agent?

12. Explain: A barium atom is larger than a calcium atom.

13. Explain: A bromide ion is larger than a chloride ion.

14. For a fluorine molecule, draw: (a) its orbital notation; (b) its electron-dot formula; (c) its molecular formula.

15. Distinguish between an atom and a molecule.

16. What is the difference between a symbol and a formula?

17. (a) From a comparison of the bond energies of H_2, N_2, O_2, and Cl_2, which is the most stable molecule? (b) Which is the least stable molecule?

18. (a) What gaseous elements have diatomic molecules? (b) By what symbol or formula is each represented?

19. (a) What gaseous elements have monatomic molecules? (b) By what symbol or formula is each represented?

20. How many atoms of each element are represented by the following formulas: sugar, $C_{12}H_{22}O_{11}$; sand, SiO_2; salt, $NaCl$; hydrogen peroxide, H_2O_2; soap, $C_{17}H_{35}COONa$?

21. What does each of the following represent? (a) Ar; (b) $4N_2$; (c) HI; (d) $6H_2SO_4$; (e) 3Cu; (f) $2K^+Cl^-$; (g) CO; (h) Co.

22. What is electronegativity?

23. What electronegativity difference is there between atoms which form (a) ionic bonds; (b) polar covalent bonds; (c) bonds with no ionic character?

24. Assuming chemical union between the following pairs, indicate in each case which element would have the positive oxidation number: (a) hydrogen-sodium; (b) chlorine-fluorine; (c) chlorine-oxygen; (d) hydrogen-lithium; (e) bromine-hydrogen.

25. What is the oxidation number of each element in the following compounds: (a) MnO_2, a dioxide; (b) H_3PO_4; (c) HNO_3; (d) P_4O_{10}; (e) Na^+OH^-?

Group B

26. Draw the orbital notation for (a) a calcium atom; (b) a calcium ion.

27. Draw the orbital notation for (a) a fluorine atom; (b) a fluoride ion.

28. Using orbital notation, show how an ionic compound of calcium and fluorine is formed.

29. Explain why a calcium atom is smaller than a potassium atom.

30. Explain why a sulfide ion is larger than a chloride ion.

31. For a hydrogen-bromide molecule, HBr, draw: (a) its orbital notation; (b) its electron-dot formula.

32. Hydrogen and sulfur form a simple molecular compound. Using both orbital notation and electron-dot notation, show how such a compound may be represented. Then determine its probable molecular formula.

33. Oxygen atoms form a triatomic molecule, O_3, called ozone. (a) Draw an electron-dot formula for this molecule which satisfies the octet rule. (b) Is this the only formula you can draw for this molecule which satisfies the octet rule? (c) What is the explanation of the actual structure of an ozone molecule?

34. (a) From a consideration of the electron-dot notation of phosphorus, what is the shape of a PH_3 molecule? (b) Consider sulfur and H_2S in similar fashion.

35. For each of the following bonds give the percent ionic character and indicate whether the bond is largely ionic, polar covalent, or pure covalent. (a) K—Br; (b) C—O; (c) Na—O; (d) C—H; (e) Br—Br.

36. Classify each of the following as ionic crystal, polar covalent molecule, or non-polar covalent molecule. (a) $MgCl_2$; (b) CF_4, consisting of a central carbon atom and four symmetrically arranged fluorine atoms; (c) HBr; (d) SO_2, consisting of an oxygen atom, a sulfur atom, and a second oxygen atom arranged in a bent molecule; (e) P_4.

37. What is the oxidation state of manganese in: (a) potassium permanganate, $K^+MnO_4^-$; (b) manganese(II) sulfate, $Mn^{++}SO_4^{--}$? (c) If manganese(II) sulfate is one of the products of a reaction in which potassium permanganate was one of the reactants, what kind of change has manganese undergone? (d) What name is given to manganese in this change?

38. The four oxygen acids of chlorine are: hypochlorous acid, HClO; chlorous acid, $HClO_2$; chloric acid, $HClO_3$; and perchloric acid, $HClO_4$. What is the oxidation number of chlorine in each acid of the series?

39. What is the oxidation number of each element in the following polyatomic ions? (a) SO_4^{--}; (b) SO_3^{--}; (c) NO_2^-; (d) CO_3^{--}; (e) CrO_4^{--}.

PROBLEMS

1. From bond-energy data, determine whether the energy change in this reaction is exothermic or endothermic. What is the magnitude, or size, of the energy change?

Group A

$$\tfrac{1}{2} \text{ mole } H_2 + \tfrac{1}{2} \text{ mole } Br_2 \rightarrow 1 \text{ mole HBr}$$

2. From bond-energy data, determine the kind and amount of energy change for the reaction:

$$1 \text{ mole } H_2 + \tfrac{1}{2} \text{ mole } O_2 \rightarrow 1 \text{ mole } H_2O$$

3. Calculate the energy change for the reaction:

Group B

$$1 \text{ mole Mg} + 2 \text{ moles Br} \rightarrow 1 \text{ mole } Mg^{++}Br_2^-$$

As described in Section 6.6, this reaction may be assumed to consist of three separate reactions.

$$1 \text{ mole Mg} + \text{energy} \rightarrow 1 \text{ mole } Mg^{++} + 2 \text{ moles } e^-$$

The energy required for this reaction is the sum of the ionization energies for removing the first and second electrons from a magnesium atom. Obtain energy data from Chapter 5.

$$2 \text{ moles Br} + 2 \text{ moles } e^- \rightarrow 2 \text{ moles } Br^- + \text{energy}$$

The energy released is the electron affinity of *two* moles of bromine atoms. Obtain energy data from Chapter 5.

$$\text{1 mole Mg}^{++} + \text{2 moles Br}^- \rightarrow \text{1 mole Mg}^{++}\text{Br}^-_2 + 575 \text{ kcal}$$

Set up these three equations in suitable form and do the required calculations. Is the overall reaction exothermic or endothermic?

4. From bond-energy data, determine the kind and amount of energy change for the reaction:

$$\text{1 mole H}_2 + \text{1 mole O}_2 \rightarrow \text{1 mole H}_2\text{O}_2$$

Assume four reaction steps: (1) breaking bonds in H_2 molecules; (2) breaking bonds in O_2 molecules; (3) combining of H atoms and O atoms into H—O groups; (4) combining of H—O groups into H_2O_2 molecules by forming O—O bonds between them.

5. From bond-energy data, determine the kind and magnitude of the energy change for the reaction:

$$\text{1 mole N}_2 + \text{2 moles H}_2 \rightarrow \text{1 mole N}_2\text{H}_4 \text{ (hydrazine)}$$

Chapter 7

Chemical Composition

7.1 Table of ions and their charges

A knowledge of the charges of common ions is very important in chemistry. They are given in Table 7-1. Cations other than am-

---

Table 7-1
COMMON IONS AND THEIR CHARGES

+1	+2	+3
ammonium, NH_4^+	barium, Ba^{++}	aluminum, Al^{+++}
copper (I), Cu^+	calcium, Ca^{++}	chromium (III), Cr^{+++}
potassium, K^+	copper (II), Cu^{++}	iron (III), Fe^{+++}
silver, Ag^+	iron (II), Fe^{++}	
sodium, Na^+	lead (II), Pb^{++}	
	magnesium, Mg^{++}	
	mercury (I), Hg_2^{++}	
	mercury (II), Hg^{++}	
	nickel (II), Ni^{++}	
	zinc, Zn^{++}	

−1	−2	−3
acetate, $C_2H_3O_2^-$	carbonate, CO_3^{--}	phosphate, PO_4^{---}
bromide, Br^-	chromate, CrO_4^{--}	
chlorate, ClO_3^-	dichromate, $Cr_2O_7^{--}$	
chloride, Cl^-	oxide, O^{--}	
fluoride, F^-	peroxide, O_2^{--}	
hydrogen carbonate, HCO_3^-	sulfate, SO_4^{--}	
hydrogen sulfate, HSO_4^-	sulfide, S^{--}	
hydroxide, OH^-	sulfite, SO_3^{--}	
iodide, I^-		
nitrate, NO_3^-		
nitrite, NO_2^-		

Table 7-2

METALLIC ION NAME EQUIVALENTS

Old system		New system	
chromic	Cr^{+++}	chromium (III)	Cr^{+++}
ferrous	Fe^{++}	iron (II)	Fe^{++}
ferric	Fe^{+++}	iron (III)	Fe^{+++}
cuprous	Cu^+	copper (I)	Cu^+
cupric	Cu^{++}	copper (II)	Cu^{++}
mercurous	Hg^+	mercury (I)	Hg_2^{++}
mercuric	Hg^{++}	mercury (II)	Hg^{++}

Fig. 7-1. During the early nineteenth century, Jöns Jakob Berzelius invented alphabetical chemical symbols for the elements and conducted careful chemical analyses which resulted in the first systematic determination of atomic weights.

Swedish Information Service

monium have names which are the same as the elements from which they are derived. If a metallic atom forms more than one ion, the name of the ion includes its oxidation number in Roman numerals in parentheses. You may find it helpful to *memorize* Table 7-1 in order to be able to work with formulas and equations more easily.

An older system of naming metallic ions is still in use. Table 7-2 will help you convert the name of a compound in the older system to the newer system used in this book.

7.2   Writing chemical formulas

Formulas for chemical compounds are determined by chemical analysis. How this is done is explained in Section 7.12. As a consequence of the atomic theory, however, the formulas for many ionic compounds can be easily derived from the table of ions and their charges. This table enables us to write formulas for many common compounds without becoming involved in the details of chemical analysis, atomic structure, and chemical bonding. The procedure we shall use for writing formulas is called the *ion-charge method*.

Let us use *sodium chloride* as our first example. Sodium ion is represented by Na^+, while chloride ion is represented by Cl^-. When formulas for ionic compounds are written, *the total charge of the first (positive) part of the compound must be equal and opposite to the total charge of the second (negative) part of the compound. The total charge of an ion is found by multiplying the charge of the ion by the number of that ion taken.* The charge of one sodium ion is equal and opposite to the charge of one chloride ion. So the formula for sodium chloride, *NaCl,* indicates one of each ion.

Using the same method, we can derive the formula for *calcium chloride.* Calcium ion is represented by Ca^{++}. Chloride ion is represented by Cl^-. The total charge of the negative part of the compound must be equal and opposite to that of the positive part of the compound. So two chloride ions will be needed with one calcium ion. One calcium ion has a charge of $+2$ and the total charge of two chloride ions is -2. The formula is written $CaCl_2$. The subscript $_2$ indicates that two chloride ions per calcium ion is the composition of calcium chloride. No subscript is used with Ca since only one calcium ion is needed in the formula. When no subscript is written, a subscript $_1$ is always understood.

What is the formula for *aluminum bromide?* Aluminum ion is Al^{+++}. Bromide ion is Br^-. Three bromide ions are needed to balance the positive charge of one Al^{+++} ion. The formula is $AlBr_3$.

Observe that this ion-charge method of formula writing yields only an empirical formula. You will recall that an empirical formula shows the simplest whole-number ratio of atoms in a compound.

7.3 Writing the formulas for other compounds

The formula for *lead(II) sulfate* is easy to write. Lead(II) ion is Pb^{++}. Sulfate ion is SO_4^{--}. The charges are already equal and opposite. So the simplest formula for lead(II) sulfate includes just one lead ion and one sulfate ion, $PbSO_4$.

In the formula for *magnesium hydroxide,* a polyatomic ion must be used more than once. Magnesium ion is Mg^{++}. Hydroxide ion, a polyatomic ion, is written OH^-. Two hydroxide ions are needed for a negative charge equal and opposite to the positive charge of one magnesium ion. In writing the formula for magnesium hydroxide, parentheses are used to enclose the formula for the hydroxide ion, (OH). Then the subscript $_2$ is written outside the parentheses, $(OH)_2$. This way of representing the composition shows that the *entire* OH^- ion is taken twice. The complete formula for *magnesium hydroxide* is $Mg(OH)_2$. This formula must **not** be written $MgOH_2$. The incorrect formula $MgOH_2$ represents two hydrogen atoms and one oxygen atom instead of two hydroxide ions. Chemists put the subscript number outside the parentheses to indicate that the polyatomic ion inside the parentheses is taken that many number of times in the formula. *Parentheses are not used when a polyatomic ion is taken only once in a formula.* For example, the formula for potassium hydroxide represents one K^+ ion and one OH^- ion. The formula is written KOH. No parentheses are used.

Let us work out another similar formula, that for *lead(II) acetate*. Lead(II) ion is Pb^{++}. The acetate ion is $C_2H_3O_2^-$. For each lead ion, two acetate ions must be represented by the formula. Following the same system used in writing the formula for magnesium hydroxide, the formula for lead(II) acetate becomes $Pb(C_2H_3O_2)_2$. Note that in order to represent two acetate ions in the formula, $C_2H_3O_2$ is enclosed in parentheses, and the subscript $_2$ is placed outside.

Ammonium sulfate has two polyatomic ions in its formula. Ammonium ion is NH_4^+ and sulfate ion is SO_4^{--}. In order to make the total charges equal and opposite, two ammonium ions must be used with one sulfate ion. To represent these in the formula, the NH_4 is enclosed in parentheses with the subscript $_2$ outside. The formula is then written $(NH_4)_2SO_4$.

Finally, let us write the formula for *iron(III) carbonate*. Iron(III) ion is Fe^{+++} and the carbonate ion is CO_3^{--}. Again the total charge of the positive part of the formula must be equal and opposite to that of the negative part of the formula. So for every two Fe^{+++} ions, three CO_3^{--} ions must be used. Six charges of each sign are involved—six positive charges on the two Fe^{+++} ions and six negative charges on the three CO_3^{--} ions. The formula is $Fe_2(CO_3)_3$.

As a beginner in chemistry you must be warned that the ion-charge method has limitations. A formula can give no more information than that required to write it. It is possible to write the formula for a compound and then learn that such a compound does not exist! On the other hand, there are many covalent compounds which *do* exist but whose formulas cannot be written using the ion-charge method.

7.4 Naming compounds from their formulas

The names of many chemical compounds consist of two words: the name of the first part of the formula and the name of the second part. $BaSO_4$ is called barium sulfate (Ba^{++} represents the barium ion; SO_4^{--} represents the sulfate ion). $FeCl_3$ is the formula for iron(III) chloride. Notice that there are two possible oxidation states for iron. One is iron(II), with an oxidation number of $+2$; the other is iron(III), with an oxidation number of $+3$. There are 3 chloride ions associated with one iron ion in the formula, $FeCl_3$. Therefore, the iron ion has a charge of $+++$, and the compound is *iron(III) chloride*. $FeCl_2$ is *iron(II) chloride*.

The use of Roman numerals to indicate oxidation states does not always provide simple and useful names for all known or possible compounds. Hence, another system, using Greek numerical prefixes, is sometimes used for certain binary covalent compounds. **Binary compounds** are those which consist of only *two elements*. Binary compounds are named by the following steps.

1. The first word of the name is made up of: (*a*) a prefix indicating the number of atoms of the first element appearing in the formula, if more than one; and (*b*) the name of the first element in the formula.

2. The second word of the name is made up of: (*a*) a prefix indicating the number of atoms of the second element appearing in the formula, if there exists more than one compound of these two elements; (*b*) the root of the name of the second element; and (*c*) the suffix *-ide,* which means that *only* the two elements named are present.

Carbon monoxide is written CO. Only one atom of the first element appears in the formula, so no prefix is used with the first word. It consists only of the name of the first element, *carbon.* The prefix *mon-* is used in the second word of the name because only one atom of oxygen appears in this formula, but more than one compound of carbon and oxygen exists. *Ox-* is the root of the name of the element oxygen. Then comes the suffix *-ide.*

In like manner, CO_2 is *carbon dioxide*. The prefix indicating three is *tri-;* for four it is *tetra-;* and for five it is *pent-* or *penta-.* These prefixes can be used with both the first and second words in the name. Some examples of the use of Greek numerical prefixes are: $SbCl_3$, *antimony trichloride;* CCl_4, *carbon tetrachloride;* and As_2S_5, *diarsenic pentasulfide.*

7.5   Significance of chemical formulas

We have learned to write formulas for many chemical compounds, using our knowledge of the charges of the ions composing them. When it is known that a substance exists as simple molecules, its formula represents one molecule of the substance. Such a formula is known as a *molecular formula.*

The molecular structure of some substances is not known. Other substances have no simple molecular structure. For these substances, the formula represents (*1*) the elements in the substances and (*2*) the simplest whole-number ratio of the atoms of these elements. In these cases, the formula is called an *empirical,* or simplest, *formula.*

Let us examine some chemical formulas to learn their full significance. The compound water has the molecular formula H_2O. This molecular formula represents *one molecule* of water. It shows that each molecule of water is made up of *two atoms of hydrogen* and *one atom of oxygen.*

The atomic weight of hydrogen is 1.0 and the atomic weight of oxygen is 16.0. Hence this molecular formula signifies that the *formula weight of water* is 18.0. The calculation is (1.0, the atomic weight of hydrogen, $\times$ 2 atoms of hydrogen) + (16.0, the atomic weight of oxygen, $\times$ 1 atom of oxygen) = 18.0, the formula weight of water. The *formula weight* of any compound is *the sum of the atomic weights of all of the atoms represented in the formula.*

The compound sodium chloride, table salt, has the empirical formula **NaCl**. It is a crystalline solid which has no molecular structure. It is composed of an orderly arrangement of sodium and chloride ions. This empirical formula tells us the relative number of atoms of each element present in the compound, sodium chloride. It shows that for each sodium atom there is one chlorine atom. The atomic weight of sodium is 23.0 and that of chlorine is 35.5. So the empirical formula signifies that the formula weight of sodium chloride is 23.0 + 35.5, or 58.5.

7.6   Molecular weight

We have seen that a molecular formula represents one molecule of a substance. The formula H_2O is a molecular formula. It represents one molecule of water. The formula weight, 18.0, is then the relative weight of *one molecule* of water. *The formula weight of a molecular substance is its **molecular weight.***

In the strictest sense it is not correct to speak of the molecular weight of a nonmolecular substance, such as sodium chloride, which is represented by an empirical formula. The term *formula weight* is a more general term than *molecular weight* and therefore is preferred by chemists. However, both terms are used. In elementary chemical calculations the distinction is not important.

7.7   Formula weight of a compound

To find the total weight of all the members of your chemistry class, you must add the weights of the individual members of the class. Similarly, to find the formula weight of any substance for which a formula is given, you must add the atomic weights of all the atoms represented in the formula. Let us use the formula for cane sugar, $C_{12}H_{22}O_{11}$, as an example. The approximate atomic weights found inside the front cover and in Table 5 of the Appendix can be used.

Number of atoms	Atomic weight	Total weight
12 of C	12.0	$12 \times 12.0 = 144.0$
22 of H	1.0	$22 \times 1.0 = 22.0$
11 of O	16.0	$11 \times 16.0 = 176.0$
		formula weight (molecular weight) $= 342.0$

The formula for calcium hydroxide is $Ca(OH)_2$. The subscript $_2$ following the parentheses indicates that there are two hydroxide groups per calcium atom in calcium hydroxide. Thus the formula $Ca(OH)_2$ shows one calcium atom, two oxygen atoms, and two hydrogen atoms.

Number of atoms	Atomic weight	Total weight
1 of Ca	40.1	$1 \times 40.1 = 40.1$
2 of O	16.0	$2 \times 16.0 = 32.0$
2 of H	1.0	$2 \times 1.0 = 2.0$
		formula weight $= 74.1$

The atomic weights of the elements are relative weights. They are based on the fact that an atom of carbon-12 has been assigned a value of exactly 12. In the quantitative study of chemical reactions, the atomic weights and formula weights are very useful. They tell us the relative weights of elements or compounds that combine or react. We can convert these relative weights to any desired units. Thus atomic weights, formulas, and formula weights play a very important part in chemical calculations.

7.8   Percentage composition of a compound

Frequently it is important to know the composition of a compound in terms of the *mass percentage* of each element of which it is made. We may want to know the percentage of iron in the compound, iron(III) oxide. Or, we may want to know the percentage of oxygen in potassium chlorate. This knowledge enables us to determine the amount of potassium chlorate needed to supply enough oxygen for a laboratory experiment.

The chemical formula for a compound can be used directly to determine its formula weight. This is done simply by adding the atomic weights of all the atoms represented. The formula weight represents *all,* or 100 percent, of the composition of the substance as indicated by the formula. The part of the formula weight contributed by each element represented in the formula is the *total atomic weight* of that element (atomic weight $\times$ number of atoms). The *fractional part* due to each element is

$$\frac{\textbf{total atomic weight of the element}}{\textbf{formula weight of the compound}}$$

or

$$\frac{\textbf{(atomic weight} \times \textbf{number of atoms) of the element}}{\textbf{formula weight of the compound}}$$

The percentage of each element present in the compound is therefore a fractional part of 100 percent of the compound.

$$\frac{\textbf{(atomic weight} \times \textbf{number of atoms) of the element}}{\textbf{formula weight of the compound}} \times \textbf{100\% of the compound}$$

Remember that atomic weights and formula weights are relative weights. They are expressed by numbers without dimensions, that is, numbers without units of measure. The relationship for the percentage of an element by mass in a compound is dimensionally correct when expressed as follows:

$$\frac{\textbf{(atomic weight} \times \textbf{number of atoms) element}}{\textbf{formula weight compound}} \times \textbf{100\% compound} = \textbf{\% element by mass}$$

Let us consider the compound iron(III) oxide, mentioned earlier. The formula is Fe_2O_3. What is the percentage of each of the elements in this compound?

1. *Formula weight of Fe_2O_3*

$$\begin{array}{l} \textbf{total atomic weight Fe} = 2 \times 55.8 = 111.6 \\ \underline{\textbf{total atomic weight O}\ \ = 3 \times 16.0 = \ \ 48.0} \\ \qquad\qquad \textbf{formula weight Fe}_2\textbf{O}_3 = 159.6 \end{array}$$

2. *Percentage of Fe*

$$\frac{\textbf{total atomic weight Fe}}{\textbf{formula weight Fe}_2\textbf{O}_3} \times \textbf{100\% Fe}_2\textbf{O}_3 = \textbf{\% Fe by mass}$$

Using three significant figures,

$$\frac{\textbf{112 Fe}}{\textbf{160 Fe}_2\textbf{O}_3} \times \textbf{100\% Fe}_2\textbf{O}_3 = \textbf{70.0\% Fe}$$

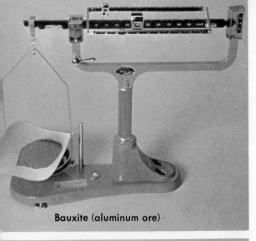

Bauxite (aluminum ore)

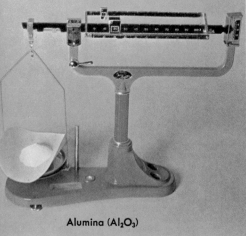

Alumina (Al_2O_3)

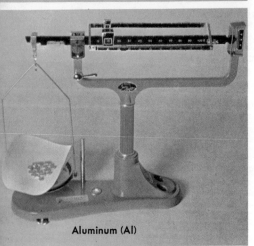

Aluminum (Al)

Fig. 7-2. Industrially, 40 g of bauxite (aluminum ore) produces 20 g of alumina (Al_2O_3) which produces 10 g of aluminum (Al). The extra mass shown is the mass of the filter paper. Chemically, what is the percentage by mass of aluminum in alumina?

3. *Percentage of O*

$$\frac{\text{total atomic weight O}}{\text{formula weight Fe}_2\text{O}_3} \times 100\% \text{ Fe}_2\text{O}_3 = \% \text{ O by mass}$$

$$\frac{48.0 \text{ O}}{16\overline{0} \text{ Fe}_2\text{O}_3} \times 100\% \text{ Fe}_2\text{O}_3 = 30.0\% \text{ O}$$

Of course, since there is no third element present, the percentage of oxygen is $100.0\% - 70.0\% = 30.0\%$.

Observe that when dimensional analysis (Section 1.21) is applied to these simple computations, the result is the label we expect for the answer. Many errors in the solutions to problems in chemistry can be avoided by consistently labeling each quantity properly. We must also remember to solve the expression for both the numerical value and the label of the result.

As a second example, let us use a crystallized form of sodium carbonate: $Na_2CO_3 \cdot 10H_2O$. (The raised period indicates that these crystals contain 10 molecules of water for each 2 sodium ions or for each carbonate ion. The formula does not tell us how the water molecules are placed with respect to the sodium and carbonate ions in the crystal.) To find the percentage composition of this crystalline material (to 3 significant figures), we proceed as before:

1. *Formula weight $Na_2CO_3 \cdot 10H_2O$*

2 Na	$2 \times 23.0 =$	46.0	
1 C	$1 \times 12.0 =$	12.0	
3 O	$3 \times 16.0 =$	48.0	
10 H₂O $\left\{\begin{array}{l} 20 \text{ H} \\ 10 \text{ O} \end{array}\right.$	$\begin{array}{l} 20 \times 1.0 = \\ 10 \times 16.0 = \end{array}$	$\left.\begin{array}{l} 2\overline{0} \\ 16\overline{0} \end{array}\right\}$	$18\overline{0}$

$$\text{formula weight} = 286$$

2. *Percentage of Na*

$$\frac{46.0 \text{ Na}}{286 \text{ Na}_2\text{CO}_3 \cdot 10\text{H}_2\text{O}} \times 100\% \text{ Na}_2\text{CO}_3 \cdot 10\text{H}_2\text{O} = 16.1\% \text{ Na}$$

3. *Percentage of C*

$$\frac{12.0 \text{ C}}{286 \text{ Na}_2\text{CO}_3 \cdot 10\text{H}_2\text{O}} \times 100\% \text{ Na}_2\text{CO}_3 \cdot 10\text{H}_2\text{O} = 4.2\% \text{ C}$$

4. *Percentage of O (in $CO_3{}^{--}$ ion)*

$$\frac{48.0 \text{ O}}{286 \text{ Na}_2\text{CO}_3 \cdot 10\text{H}_2\text{O}} \times 100\% \text{ Na}_2\text{CO}_3 \cdot 10\text{H}_2\text{O} = 16.8\% \text{ O}$$

5. *Percentage of H_2O*

$$\frac{18\overline{0}\ H_2O}{286\ Na_2CO_3 \cdot 10H_2O} \times 100\%\ Na_2CO_3 \cdot 10H_2O = 62.9\%\ H_2O$$

Approximate atomic weights usually have no more than two or three significant figures. The accuracy of a result cannot be improved by carrying out the computations beyond the accuracy of the data used. The sum of the mass percentages, therefore, may only approximate 100 percent. Such results do not make us doubt the chemistry involved. Rather, they properly reflect the approximations employed in the computations.

7.9 Law of definite composition and the atomic theory

The law of definite composition (Section 2.10) states, in effect, that the percentage composition of a chemical compound is always the same. This law is true regardless of the source of the compound. We have just learned how to calculate the percentage composition of chemical compounds. We are now ready to understand how this law may be explained by the atomic theory.

The fact that the percentage composition of a compound does not change depends upon two things: (*1*) The relative mass of the atoms of an element is constant, and (*2*) the proportion in which atoms are present in a compound is constant. The idea that, under most conditions, atomic weights are constant is basic to the atomic theory. For practical purposes, the atomic weight we use for an element is the average relative mass of the naturally occurring mixture of its isotopes. (This fact was discussed in Section 3.13.) For example, the average relative mass (atomic weight) of a hydrogen atom is 1.0080. That of a chlorine atom is 35.453.

The atomic theory explains how atoms combine in a constant proportion by mass. Individual atoms can lose, gain, or share only a definite number of electrons. Therefore, the mass of one element that can combine with a given mass of another element is limited. In forming hydrogen chloride, for example, only one hydrogen atom can combine with one chlorine atom. One hydrogen atom can share only 1 electron. One chlorine atom has room for only 1 electron to complete its octet of 3rd energy level electrons. So the ratio of these two atoms which combine can be only 1 to 1. It cannot be 1 to 2, or 3 to 2, or any other ratio. Consequently, a molecule of hydrogen chloride always consists of one atom of hydrogen, atomic weight 1.0080, and one atom of chlorine, atomic weight 35.453. The molecule has a molecular weight of 36.461. Furthermore, hydrogen chloride always contains $\frac{1.0080}{36.461}$ parts by weight of hydrogen or 2.765% hydrogen, and $\frac{35.453}{36.461}$ parts by weight of chlorine, or 97.235% chlorine.

7.10 Law of multiple proportions

Hydrogen and oxygen are present in an unvarying ratio in all samples of water. This ratio is approximately 1 to 8, *by mass.* There is also another compound of hydrogen and oxygen, hydrogen peroxide. The composition of hydrogen peroxide is 1 part of hydrogen to 16 parts of oxygen by mass. Note that for the same mass of hydrogen in the two compounds, 8 is to 16 just as 1 is to 2. In other words, the relative masses of the second element (oxygen) in the two compounds can be expressed as a ratio of small whole numbers. It is not uncommon in chemistry for two or more compounds to be composed of the same two elements. For example,

H_2O	1 g of H	and	8 g of O
H_2O_2	1 g of H	and	16 g of O
$FeCl_2$	56 g of Fe	and	71 g of Cl
$FeCl_3$	56 g of Fe	and	106.5 g of Cl

The mass of the hydrogen in the first pair of compounds is fixed, or constant. The mass of iron in the second pair of compounds is also constant. The masses of oxygen, 8 and 16, in the first case are in the simple ratio of 1 to 2. The masses of chlorine, 71 and 106.5, in the second case are in the simple ratio of 2 to 3. It would be possible to give other examples, but in every case the *law of multiple proportions* is found to describe such pairs of compounds. *If two or more different compounds composed of the same two elements are analyzed, the masses of the second element combined with a fixed mass of the first element can always be expressed as a ratio of small whole numbers.*

This law was first proposed by John Dalton, in connection with his atomic theory. He recognized the possibility that two kinds of atoms could combine in more than one way and in more than one proportion. But only whole atoms could be involved in such combinations. Therefore, Dalton reasoned, the masses of the second atom combined with fixed masses of the first atom would have to be in the ratio of small whole numbers. This ratio is the same as the ratio of the actual numbers of atoms of the second element combined with a fixed number of atoms of the first element. The information summarized in the law of multiple proportions is one of the strongest supports for the atomic theory.

Today scientists recognize two reasons for the truth of the law of multiple proportions. (1) Some elements exist in more than one oxidation state. (2) Some elements combine in more than one way with another element. Iron can exist in compounds as iron(II) ions with an oxidation number of $+2$ or as iron(III) ions with an oxidation number of $+3$. The elements iron and chlorine can be found combined in two different compounds: $FeCl_2$, iron(II) chloride, and $FeCl_3$, iron(III) chloride. The ratio of the numbers of atoms of chlorine combined with a single atom of iron is 2 to 3. As recognized by Dalton, the relative numbers of atoms which combine is proportional to the masses which combine. Therefore, the ratio of the masses of chlorine combined with a fixed mass of iron in these two compounds is also 2 to 3.

Analysis of the composition and molecular structure of water and hydrogen peroxide lead to these electron-dot formulas:

$$H\!:\!\overset{..}{\underset{..}{O}}\!:$$
$$H$$

$$\overset{H}{:\!\overset{..}{O}\!:\!\overset{..}{O}\!:}$$
$$H$$

water   **hydrogen peroxide**

These two formulas represent the two different patterns in which these two kinds of atoms can combine. Each molecule of water contains 2 hydrogen atoms combined with only 1 oxygen atom. Each molecule of hydrogen peroxide contains 2 hydrogen atoms combined with 2 oxygen atoms. The numbers of atoms combined are proportional to the masses combined. So the ratio of the masses of oxygen combined with the same mass of hydrogen in these two compounds is 1 to 2, a ratio of small whole numbers.

7.11 Mole concept

Imagine that all the people on the earth were assigned the task of counting the molecules in a tablespoon of water. If each person counted at the rate of one molecule each second, it would take approximately 8×10^6 years to complete the project. The number of molecules involved is so large that it staggers the imagination!

Fortunately, chemists are not ordinarily faced with the problem of weighing out a certain number of molecules of a compound or atoms of an element. They do frequently need to weigh out equal numbers of atoms or molecules of different substances. A knowledge of the atomic weights of the elements allows this to be done very simply.

In Sections 3.12 and 3.13, we recognized four important quantitative definitions.

1. The number of carbon-12 atoms in the defined quantity of exactly 12 grams of this nuclide is the *Avogadro number,* approximately 6.02×10^{23}.

2. The amount of substance containing the Avogadro number of any kind of chemical unit is called a *mole* of that substance.

3. The mass in grams of one mole of naturally occurring atoms of an element is the *gram-atomic weight* of the element.

4. The numerical portion of the gram-atomic weight of an element is the *atomic weight* of the element.

From these definitions, we see that if we wish to weigh out an Avogadro number (one mole) of carbon atoms, we must take one gram-atomic weight of carbon, 12 g. If we wish to weigh out an Avogadro number (one mole) of hydrogen atoms, we must

Fig. 7-3. The compounds formed from two elements combined in different proportions frequently have strikingly different chemical properties. The H_2O (top beaker) has no reaction with the green felt. The H_2O_2 (bottom beaker) readily bleaches the green dye of the felt.

Table 7–3

THE MOLE CONCEPT

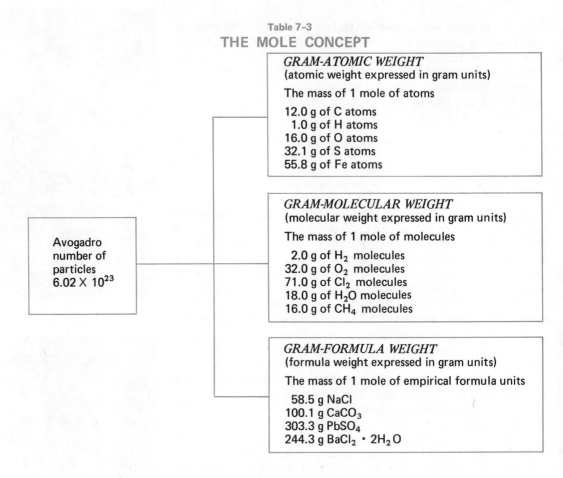

Avogadro number of particles 6.02×10^{23}

GRAM-ATOMIC WEIGHT
(atomic weight expressed in gram units)

The mass of 1 mole of atoms

12.0 g of C atoms
 1.0 g of H atoms
16.0 g of O atoms
32.1 g of S atoms
55.8 g of Fe atoms

GRAM-MOLECULAR WEIGHT
(molecular weight expressed in gram units)

The mass of 1 mole of molecules

 2.0 g of H_2 molecules
32.0 g of O_2 molecules
71.0 g of Cl_2 molecules
18.0 g of H_2O molecules
16.0 g of CH_4 molecules

GRAM-FORMULA WEIGHT
(formula weight expressed in gram units)

The mass of 1 mole of empirical formula units

 58.5 g NaCl
100.1 g $CaCO_3$
303.3 g $PbSO_4$
244.3 g $BaCl_2 \cdot 2H_2O$

take one gram-atomic weight of hydrogen, 1.0 g. These two quantities, 12 g of carbon and 1.0 g of hydrogen, contain the same number of atoms. Thus, any given masses of carbon and hydrogen which are in the ratio of 12:1 (the ratio of their atomic weights) must also have the same number of atoms.

To obtain 5.0 moles of oxygen atoms, we must weigh out 5.0×16 g $= \overline{80}$ g of oxygen. To obtain 5.0 moles of sulfur atoms, we must take 5.0×32 g $= 160$ g of sulfur. The $\overline{80}$ g of oxygen and 160 g of sulfur contain the same number of atoms. Note that the ratio of these masses equals the ratio of the atomic weights of the elements:

$$\frac{\overline{80} \text{ g}}{160 \text{ g}} = \frac{16}{32} = \frac{1}{2}$$

By similar reasoning, using the atomic weights of other elements, we can recognize the following important generalization:

If the quantities of two elements are in the same ratio by weight as their atomic weights, they contain the same number of atoms.

Chemists measure quantities of substances in gram (mass) units. They sometimes refer to these masses of substances as "weights" because "weighing" methods are used to determine them. However, it should be recognized that quantities measured in gram units are, in fact, mass quantities. Atomic weights are most useful when expressed in gram units. *The gram-atomic weight of an element is the mass of one mole of atoms of the element.* Thus the mass of one mole of O atoms is 16 g of oxygen, of one mole of S atoms is 32 g of sulfur, and of one mole of Fe atoms is 56 g of iron.

Let us extend our concept of a mole of atoms of an element to a mole of diatomic molecules of an element. One mole of O_2 molecules contains two moles of O atoms. We know that two moles of O atoms has a mass of 2×16 g $= 32$ g. Hence a mole of O_2 molecules must have this same mass, 32 g. But we recognize that this is the molecular weight of O_2, 32, expressed in gram units. *The mass of a molecular substance in grams equal to its molecular weight is its **gram-molecular weight**.* Similar reasoning leads us to see that a mole of H_2 molecules has a mass of 2.0 g, and a mole of Cl_2 molecules has a mass of 71.0 g. *Thus the gram-molecular weight of a diatomic molecular element is the mass of one mole of molecules of the element.* Note that one mole of O atoms has a mass of 16 g, but one mole of O_2 molecules has a mass of 32 g, and so on. Also note that 16 g of O atoms, 32 g of O_2 molecules, 1.0 g of H atoms, 2.0 g of H_2 molecules, 35.5 g of Cl atoms, and 71.0 g of Cl_2 molecules all contain the same number of *particles*—atoms or molecules as the case may be.

One mole of H_2O molecules contains two moles of H atoms and one mole of O atoms. Two moles of H atoms has a mass of 2.0 g; one mole of O atoms has a mass of 16 g. Thus, by addition, one mole of H_2O molecules has a mass of 18 g. This mass is the gram-molecular weight of water. One mole of methane, CH_4, contains one mole of C atoms and four moles of H atoms. One mole of C atoms has a mass of 12 g; four moles of H atoms has a mass of 4 g. One mole of CH_4 molecules has a mass, then, of 16 g, its gram-molecular weight. From these examples, we see that the *gram-molecular weight of a molecular substance is the mass of one mole of molecules of the substance.* There are the same number of molecules in 32 g of O_2, 18 g of H_2O, and 16 g of CH_4. Moles of all molecular substances contain the same number of molecules, the Avogadro number, 6.02×10^{23} molecules per mole. Further, any masses of oxygen, water, and methane which are in the ratio of 32:18:16 will contain the same number of molecules.

The mole concept can also be extended to substances which do not have molecules but are expressed by empirical formulas. For example, the **gram-formula weight** (the formula weight in grams) of sodium chloride is 58.5 g of sodium chloride. One mole of sodium atoms has a mass of 23.0 g; one mole of chlorine atoms has a mass of 35.5 g. Thus, 58.5 g is the mass of one mole of sodium chloride.

Not only does the symbol for an element stand for one atom of that element, but *in quantitative relationships,* it stands for the mass of one mole of atoms of that element. A formula for a diatomic molecule may represent one molecule of the element. But it also may represent the mass of one mole of such molecules. Similarly, the formula for a compound may represent the composition of the compound and the mass of one mole of that compound.

7.12 Determining the empirical formula of a compound

We have learned (Section 7.8) how to determine the percentage composition of a compound if we are given its formula. Now let us calculate the ratio of the number of atoms of the elements combined in a compound from its percentage composition. The elements of a compound and their smallest whole-number ratio are used to write the empirical formula for the compound.

This is the method by which most formulas are originally determined. A compound is analyzed to identify the elements present

---

Table 7-4
MASS-MOLE RELATIONSHIPS

1 gross = 144 objects

If we compare

144 erasers @	10.0 g each =	1440 g
144 pencils @	5.0 g each =	720 g
144 tablets @	30$\overline{0}$ g each =	43200 g

The masses of the gross-quantity packages are different because the mass of each kind of object is different. However, the ratios between the masses of the packages, 1440 g: 720 g: 43200 g, are the same as the ratios between the masses of the individual objects, 10.0 g: 5.0 g: 30$\overline{0}$ g, since each package contains the same number of objects.

1 mole = 6.02 × 10^{23} particles

If we compare

6.02 × 10^{23} helium atoms	= 4.0 g
6.02 × 10^{23} hydrogen molecules =	2.0 g
6.02 × 10^{23} water molecules	= 18.0 g
6.02 × 10^{23} NaCl formula units	= 58.5 g

The mass of the mole varies just as the mass of the gross varies. It depends upon what the particles are. However, the ratios between the masses of the moles are the same as the ratios between the masses of the individual particles since each mole contains the same number of particles.

and to determine their mass ratios or the percentage composition. The empirical formula is then calculated from this information. The gram-atomic weight (mass per mole of atoms) of each element is used to reduce the mass ratios to atom ratios.

Edward W. Morley (1838–1923) of Western Reserve University found that 1.0000 part by weight of hydrogen combines with 7.9396 parts by weight of oxygen and forms 8.9396 parts by weight of water vapor. Every 8.9396 parts of water formed requires 1.0000 part of hydrogen and 7.9396 parts of oxygen. Thus, water consists of

$$\frac{1.0000 \text{ part H}}{8.9396 \text{ parts water}} \times 100\% \text{ water} = 11.186\% \text{ hydrogen}$$

and

$$\frac{7.9396 \text{ parts O}}{8.9396 \text{ parts water}} \times 100\% \text{ water} = 88.814\% \text{ oxygen}$$

We can easily determine the relative number of atoms of hydrogen and oxygen in water. This is done by comparing the mass percentages of the elements, or their actual masses by analysis, to their respective gram-atomic weights (masses per mole of atoms).

Number of moles of atoms of an element =

$$\frac{\text{mass of the element}}{\text{mass of 1 mole of atoms of the element}}$$

1. From percentage composition data. The simplest way to think of percentage composition is in terms of *parts per hundred.* Morley's experiments show that (rounding to 3 significant figures) 11.2% of water is hydrogen and 88.8% is oxygen. In other words, 100.0 parts of water consists of 11.2 parts hydrogen and 88.8 parts oxygen. Similarly, there are 11.2 g of hydrogen and 88.8 g of oxygen per 100.0 g of water. How many moles of hydrogen and oxygen atoms are present in 100.0 g of water?

$$\text{H:} \quad \frac{11.2 \text{ g H}}{1.01 \text{ g/mole}} = 11.1 \text{ moles H}$$

$$\text{O:} \quad \frac{88.8 \text{ g O}}{16.0 \text{ g/mole}} = 5.55 \text{ moles O}$$

You will remember that 1 mole of atoms of one element is the same number of atoms as 1 mole of atoms of any other element (the Avogadro number). Therefore, the relative number of atoms is

$$\text{H : O} = 11.1 : 5.55$$

Case Western Reserve

Fig. 7-4. Edward Williams Morley was a skillful chemical analyst. His determination of the density of oxygen and of hydrogen and of the mass ratio in which oxygen and hydrogen combine, published in 1895, were the result of twelve years of research.

2. *From relative mass data.* Since the table of approximate atomic weights is used, we may round off the relative masses given. We then have 1.00 part hydrogen and 7.94 parts oxygen in 8.94 parts of water. Accordingly, each 8.94-g quantity of water produced requires 1.00 g of hydrogen and 7.94 g of oxygen. We can determine the number of moles of hydrogen and oxygen atoms in 8.94 g of water and reduce this to the relative number of atoms of each as before.

$$\text{H:} \quad \frac{1.00 \text{ g H}}{1.01 \text{ g/mole}} = 0.990 \text{ mole H}$$

$$\text{O:} \quad \frac{7.94 \text{ g O}}{16.0 \text{ g/mole}} = 0.496 \text{ mole O}$$

The relative number of atoms is

$$\text{H} : \text{O} = 0.990 : 0.496$$

From these calculations, we can write the empirical formula of water as

$$\text{H}_{11.1}\text{O}_{5.55} \quad \text{or} \quad \text{H}_{0.990}\text{O}_{0.496}$$

Both formulas show the correct ratio of hydrogen atoms to oxygen atoms in the compound water. However, according to the atomic theory, only whole atoms combine chemically. We need to convert these atom ratios to their simplest whole-number values. This is accomplished by dividing each ratio by its smaller term, shown as

$$
\begin{array}{ccc}
\text{H} & : & \text{O} \\
\dfrac{11.1}{5.55} & : & \dfrac{5.55}{5.55} \\
2.00 & : & 1.00
\end{array}
$$

and

$$
\begin{array}{ccc}
\text{H} & : & \text{O} \\
\dfrac{0.990}{0.496} & : & \dfrac{0.496}{0.496} \\
2.00 & : & 1.00
\end{array}
$$

The empirical formula for water is therefore H_2O.

Sometimes the operation just performed does not yield a simple whole-number ratio. In such instances the simplest whole-number ratio can be found by expressing the result as fractions and clearing. **CAUTION:** In some problems, dividing by the smallest term may result in such ratios as 1:2.01, 1:2.98, or 1:3.99. Remember that results obtained by using approximate atomic weights can be no more accurate than these values. You should not attempt to clear the fractions in such instances; simply round off to 2, 3, or 4 respectively. These operations are illustrated further in the Sample Problems which follow.

Sample Problem

A compound is found by analysis to contain 75.0% carbon and 25.0% hydrogen. What is the empirical formula?

Solution

Since the compound is 75.0% carbon (75.0 parts per 100.0), 75.0 g per 100.0 g is carbon. Similarly 25.0 g per 100.0 g of the compound is hydrogen. The number of moles of atoms of each element in 100.0 g of the compound is determined by the following relation:

Number of moles of atoms of an element =

$$\frac{\textbf{mass of the element}}{\textbf{mass of 1 mole of atoms of the element}}$$

$$\text{C:} \quad \frac{75.0 \text{ g C}}{12.0 \text{ g/mole}} = 6.25 \text{ moles C}$$

$$\text{H:} \quad \frac{25.0 \text{ g H}}{1.01 \text{ g/mole}} = 24.8 \text{ moles H}$$

Relative number of atoms, C:H = 6.25:24.8

$$\textbf{Smallest ratio of atoms} = \frac{6.25}{6.25} : \frac{24.8}{6.25} = 1:4$$

Empirical formula = CH$_4$

Sample Problem

A compound contains carbon, 81.7%, and hydrogen, 18.3%. Find the empirical formula.

Solution

Each 100.0-g quantity of the compound contains 81.7 g of carbon and 18.3 g of hydrogen as shown by the percentage composition.

Number of moles of atoms of an element =

$$\frac{\textbf{mass of the element}}{\textbf{mass of 1 mole of atoms of the element}}$$

$$\text{C:} \quad \frac{81.7 \text{ g C}}{12.0 \text{ g/mole}} = 6.81 \text{ moles C}$$

$$\text{H:} \quad \frac{18.3 \text{ g H}}{1.01 \text{ g/mole}} = 18.1 \text{ moles H}$$

Relative number of atoms, C:H = 6.81:18.1

$$\text{Smallest ratio of atoms} = \frac{6.81}{6.81} : \frac{18.1}{6.81} = 1:2.66$$

Simplest whole number ratio $= 1:2.66 = 1:2\frac{2}{3} = \frac{3}{3}:\frac{8}{3} = 3:8$

Empirical formula = C_3H_8

Sample Problem

The decomposition of 11.47 g of a compound of copper and oxygen yields 9.16 g of copper. What is the empirical formula for the compound?

Solution

Since the compound is composed of only copper and oxygen, the mass of oxygen removed in the decomposition process must be

$$\textbf{11.47 g} - \textbf{9.16 g} = \textbf{2.31 g oxygen}$$

Number of moles of atoms of an element =

$$\frac{\textbf{mass of the element}}{\textbf{mass of 1 mole of atoms of the element}}$$

$$\text{Cu:} \quad \frac{\textbf{9.16 g Cu}}{\textbf{63.5 g/mole}} = \textbf{0.144 mole Cu}$$

$$\text{O:} \quad \frac{\textbf{2.31 g O}}{\textbf{16.0 g/mole}} = \textbf{0.144 mole O}$$

Relative number of atoms, Cu:O = 0.144:0.144

Smallest ratio of atoms = 1:1

Empirical formula = CuO

7.13 Finding the molecular formula

The analysis of a substance enables us to determine its empirical formula. This simplest formula may or may not be the molecular formula. We calculated the empirical formula for the gas, methane, and found it to be CH_4. Any multiple of CH_4, such as C_2H_8, C_3H_{12}, or C_nH_{4n}, represents the same ratio of carbon and hydrogen atoms. How then can we know which is the correct molecular formula?

It is not possible to decide which is the true formula unless the molecular weight of the substance has been determined. Some substances lend themselves to known methods of determining molecular weights and some do not. These methods will be discussed in Chapters 10 and 12. But, if the molecular weight is known, it is a simple matter to decide which multiple of the empirical formula is the molecular formula.

Let us represent the correct multiple of the empirical formula by the subscript x. Then

(empirical formula)$_x$ = molecular formula

and (empirical formula weight)$_x$ can then be equated to the known molecular weight.

(empirical formula weight)$_x$ = molecular weight

In the case of methane, the molecular weight is known to be 16.0. The equation is

$$\textbf{(CH$_4$ weight)}_x \textbf{ = 16.0}$$
$$\textbf{[12.0 + 4(1.0)]}_x \textbf{ = 16.0}$$
$$x \textbf{ = 1}$$
$$\textbf{molecular formula = (CH$_4$)$_1$ or CH$_4$}$$

Hence the empirical formula for methane is also the molecular formula. We have seen that this is true also in the case of water. For another example, see the Sample Problem which follows.

Sample Problem

Hydrogen peroxide is found by analysis to consist of 5.9% hydrogen and 94.1% oxygen. Its molecular weight is determined to be 34.0. What is the correct formula?

Solution

1. The empirical formula, determined from the analysis by the method described in Section 7.12, is

HO

2. The molecular formula determined from the empirical formula and molecular weight is

$$\textbf{(HO weight)}_x \textbf{ = 34.0}$$
$$\textbf{(1.0 + 16.0)}_x \textbf{ = 34.0}$$
$$x \textbf{ = 2}$$
$$\textbf{molecular formula = (HO)$_2$ or H$_2$O$_2$}$$

QUESTIONS

Group A

1. What is the full significance of the molecular formula for ammonia, NH_3?
2. Why is *formula weight* a more general term than *molecular weight?*
3. What is the symbol and charge of (*a*) sodium ion; (*b*) copper(I) ion; (*c*) iron(III) ion; (*d*) nickel(II) ion; (*e*) lead(II) ion?
4. What are the names and charges of these polyatomic ions: (*a*) NH_4; (*b*) SO_4; (*c*) NO_3; (*d*) CO_3; (*e*) $C_2H_3O_2$?
5. What is the symbol or formula and charge of (*a*) hydrogen carbonate ion; (*b*) bromide ion; (*c*) chromate ion; (*d*) sulfite ion; (*e*) phosphate ion?
6. Write formulas for these compounds: (*a*) barium chloride; (*b*) calcium oxide; (*c*) magnesium sulfate; (*d*) silver bromide; (*e*) zinc carbonate.
7. Name these compounds: (*a*) $NaHCO_3$; (*b*) K_2O_2; (*c*) $HgCl_2$; (*d*) $Fe(OH)_3$; (*e*) $Ni(C_2H_3O_2)_2$.
8. Write the formulas for these compounds: (*a*) ammonium nitrate; (*b*) aluminum sulfide; (*c*) copper(II) hydroxide; (*d*) lead(II) phosphate; (*e*) iron(III) sulfate.
9. Name these compounds: (*a*) $CuCl_2$; (*b*) CaS; (*c*) $KHSO_4$; (*d*) $NaNO_2$; (*e*) $Ni_3(PO_4)_2$.
10. Write the formulas for these compounds: (*a*) chromium(III) fluoride; (*b*) nickel(II) chlorate; (*c*) potassium hydrogen carbonate; (*d*) calcium chromate; (*e*) mercury(II) iodide.
11. Name these compounds: (*a*) Na_2O_2; (*b*) NH_4NO_2; (*c*) $Mg_3(PO_4)_2$; (*d*) $FeSO_4$; (*e*) Ag_2CO_3.
12. Write the formulas for (*a*) sodium hydrogen sulfate; (*b*) lead(II) chromate; (*c*) copper(I) chloride; (*d*) mercury(I) nitrate; (*e*) iron(II) oxide.
13. Name the following: (*a*) K_2SO_4; (*b*) $BaCr_2O_7$; (*c*) $Cr(OH)_3$; (*d*) $PbBr_2$; (*e*) HgI_2.
14. What is the formula for: (*a*) aluminum hydroxide; (*b*) copper(I) oxide; (*c*) ammonium sulfide; (*d*) lead(II) acetate; (*e*) iron(III) bromide?
15. Write the formulas for: (*a*) magnesium hydrogen carbonate; (*b*) silver sulfide; (*c*) potassium sulfite; (*d*) chromium(III) sulfate; (*e*) sodium phosphate.

Group B

16. How are percentage composition, the law of definite composition, and the atomic theory related?
17. How is the law of multiple proportions related to the atomic theory?
18. Write the names for these compounds according to the system for naming binary compounds: (*a*) SO_3; (*b*) $SiCl_4$; (*c*) PBr_3; (*d*) As_2O_5; (*e*) PbO.
19. Write the formulas for these compounds: (*a*) sulfur dioxide; (*b*) bismuth trichloride; (*c*) manganese dioxide; (*d*) arsenic pentiodide; (*e*) carbon tetraiodide.
20. Name these compounds: (*a*) CO; (*b*) CO_2; (*c*) CBr_4; (*d*) N_2O_3; (*e*) N_2O_5.

PROBLEMS

Group A

1. What is the formula weight of hydrazine, N_2H_4?
2. Find the formula weight of sulfuric acid, H_2SO_4.
3. Dextrose, or grape sugar, has the formula $C_6H_{12}O_6$. Determine its formula weight.
4. Find the formula weight of ethyl alcohol, C_2H_5OH.

5. Calcium phosphate has the formula $Ca_3(PO_4)_2$. Determine the formula weight.
6. Crystallized magnesium sulfate, or Epsom salts, has the formula $MgSO_4 \cdot 7H_2O$. What is its formula weight?
7. Determine the formula weight for each of these compounds: (a) HNO_3; (b) $NaOH$; (c) HgO; (d) $CuSO_4 \cdot 5H_2O$; (e) $HC_2H_3O_2$; (f) $MgBr_2$; (g) Al_2S_3; (h) $Ca(NO_3)_2$; (i) $Fe_2(Cr_2O_7)_3$; (j) $KMnO_4$.
8. Vinegar contains acetic acid, $HC_2H_3O_2$. Find its percentage composition.
9. All baking powders contain sodium hydrogen carbonate, $NaHCO_3$. Calculate its percentage composition.
10. What is the percentage composition of a soap having the formula $C_{17}H_{35}COONa$?
11. What is the percentage composition of each of these compounds: (a) SO_2; (b) $Ca(OH)_2$; (c) $Ca(H_2PO_4)_2 \cdot H_2O$; (d) $MgSO_4 \cdot 7H_2O$?
12. Which of these compounds contains the highest percentage of nitrogen: (a) $Ca(NO_3)_2$; (b) $CaCN_2$; or (c) $(NH_4)_2SO_4$?
13. A strip of pure copper, mass 6.356 g, is heated with oxygen until it is completely converted to a compound of copper and oxygen, mass 7.956 g. What is the percentage composition of the compound?
14. Calculate the mass of (a) 1.00 mole of chlorine atoms; (b) 5.00 moles of nitrogen atoms; (c) 3.00 moles of bromine molecules; (d) 6.00 moles of hydrogen chloride; (e) 10.00 moles of magnesium sulfate.
15. You are given 25.00 g of each of these compounds: (a) CaO; (b) $Na_2CO_3 \cdot 10H_2O$; (c) $BaCl_2 \cdot 2H_2O$; (d) $(NH_4)_2SO_4$; (e) $Fe(NO_3)_3 \cdot 6H_2O$. How many moles of each do you have?
16. How many moles of iron may be recovered from 1.000 metric ton $(100\overline{0}$ kg) of Fe_3O_4?
17. Cinnabar, an ore of mercury, has the formula HgS. Calculate the number of moles of mercury recovered from 1.00 kg of cinnabar.
18. Calculate the percentage of copper in each of these minerals: cuprite, Cu_2O; malachite, $CuCO_3 \cdot Cu(OH)_2$; and cubanite, $CuFe_2S_4$.
19. Calculate the percentage of CaO in $CaCO_3$.
20. Calculate the percentage of H_2O in $CuSO_4 \cdot 5H_2O$.

21. One compound of platinum and chloride is known to consist of 42.1% chlorine. Another consists of 26.7% chlorine. What are the two empirical formulas? **Group B**
22. What is the empirical formula for silver fluoride, which is 85% silver?
23. What is the percentage composition of the drug Chloromycetin, $C_{11}H_{12}N_2O_5Cl_2$?
24. Analysis: phosphorus, 43.67%; oxygen, 56.33%. What is the empirical formula?
25. Analysis: potassium, 24.58%; manganese, 34.81%; oxygen, 40.50%. What is the empirical formula?
26. Calculate the empirical formula for a compound having 37.70% sodium, 22.95% silicon, and 39.34% oxygen.
27. A compound has the composition: sodium, 28.05%; carbon, 29.26%; hydrogen, 3.66%; oxygen, 39.02%. What is the empirical formula?
28. The analysis of a compound shows: nitrogen, 21.20%; hydrogen, 6.06%; sulfur, 24.30%; oxygen, 48.45%. Find the simplest formula.
29. A compound has the composition: potassium, 44.82%; sulfur, 18.39%; oxygen, 36.79%. Determine its empirical formula.
30. A compound has the composition: calcium, 24.7%; hydrogen, 1.2%; carbon 14.8%; oxygen, 59.3%. What is its empirical formula?

31.   An oxide of iron has the composition: Fe = 72.4%, O = 27.6%. Determine its empirical formula.

32.   The analysis of a gas reveals this composition: carbon, 92.3%; hydrogen, 7.7%. Its molecular weight is 26.0. What is the molecular formula?

33.   Analysis of a compound reveals this composition: 80% carbon and 20% hydrogen. Its molecular weight is 30.0. What is its molecular formula?

34.   The percentages by weight of carbon in its two oxides are 42.8% and 27.3%. Use these data to illustrate the law of multiple proportions.

Chapter 8

Chemical Equations

8.1 Formula equations

A simple way to represent chemical change is by the use of *word equations*. Such equations enable us to state briefly our observations of chemical reactions. Word equations give the names of the substances that enter into chemical reactions and the names of the substances that are produced. Thus, word equations have only *qualitative* significance.

From experiments, chemists know that water is formed by the combustion of hydrogen in the oxygen of the air. The word equation for this reaction is

hydrogen + oxygen → water

We read, hydrogen and oxygen react and yield water. This equation signifies that when hydrogen and oxygen react as indicated, water is the only product. Thus, it briefly states an experimental fact. It does not tell us the circumstances under which the reaction occurs, or the quantities involved.

In our discussion of the law of conservation of matter and energy (Section 1.11), we recognize a very useful generalization: *In ordinary chemical changes, the total mass of the reacting substances is equal to the total mass of the products.* This may be thought of in terms of the **law of conservation of atoms.**

Suppose we replace the names of the *reactants,* hydrogen and oxygen, and the name of the *product,* water, with their respective formulas. We can now write the equation as a *balanced formula equation* which agrees with the law of conservation of atoms.

$$2H_2 + O_2 \rightarrow 2H_2O$$

143

This agreement is verified by comparing the total number of atoms of hydrogen and oxygen on the left side of the reaction sign ($\rightarrow$) to their respective totals on the right. Two molecules of hydrogen contain 4 atoms of hydrogen; two molecules of water also contain 4 hydrogen atoms. One molecule of oxygen contains 2 atoms of oxygen; two molecules of water also contain 2 oxygen atoms. Thus a chemical equation is similar to an algebraic equation. *They both express an equality. Until it is balanced a chemical equation cannot express an equality and is not a true equation.* The yields sign ($\rightarrow$) has the meaning of an equals sign ($=$). In addition the yields sign indicates the direction in which the reaction proceeds.

Our formula equation now signifies much more than the word equation.

   1. It tells us the relative proportions of the reactants, hydrogen and oxygen, and the product, water.

   2. It tells us that *2 molecules* of hydrogen react with *1 molecule* of oxygen and *2 molecules* of water are formed.

And since there is an Avogadro number of molecules in each mole of a molecular substance, most importantly,

   3. It tells us that 2 moles of hydrogen molecules react with 1 mole of oxygen molecules and 2 moles of water are formed.

The mass of a mole of a molecular substance is its gram-molecular weight.

   4. It tells us that *4 g* of hydrogen reacts with *32 g* of oxygen and *36 g* of water is formed.

Furthermore, these masses are only relative masses. Hence,

   5. It tells us that any masses of hydrogen and oxygen which are in the ratio of 1:8 respectively and which react and form only water will yield a mass of water which is related to the masses of hydrogen and oxygen as 1:8:9.

Finally, in any equation, the equality exists in both directions. If $x + y = z$, then $z = x + y$. So our formula equation

   6. Tells us that *2 moles* of water, if decomposed, yield *2 moles* of hydrogen molecules and *1 mole* of oxygen molecules.

From these six statements, it is clear that formula equations have *quantitative* significance. Formula equations represent facts concerning reactions which have been established by experiments or other means. They indicate the nature and relative masses of reactants and products. But equations reveal nothing about the mechanism by which the reactants are converted into the products. Important reaction conditions are sometimes written near the yields sign.

It is possible to write an equation for a reaction which does not occur. Gold and oxygen do not combine directly to form gold(III) oxide, Au_2O_3. But we can write a word equation which says gold and oxygen react and yield gold(III) oxide. The corresponding formula equation can even be balanced to conform to the law of conservation of atoms. However, these would be false equations, since they are contrary to known facts.

8.2   Factors in equation writing

A chemical equation has no value unless it is correct in every detail. Three factors must be considered in writing a balanced equation.

1.   The equation must represent the facts. If we are to write the equation for a reaction, we must know the facts concerning the reaction. We must know all the reactants and all the products. The chemist relies upon analysis for facts.

2.   The equation must include the symbols and formulas of all elements and compounds which are used as reactants or formed as products. We must know these symbols and formulas and must be sure that they are correctly written. The elements which exist as diatomic molecules are oxygen, hydrogen, nitrogen, fluorine, chlorine, bromine, and iodine. Others are usually considered to be monatomic (one-atomed) in equation writing. Our knowledge of the oxidation states of the elements and the ion-charge method of writing correct formulas usually will enable us to satisfy this requirement. We will not need extensive experience with experiments or analyses.

3.   The law of conservation of atoms must be satisfied. There must be the same number of atoms of each kind represented on each side of the equation. A new species of atom cannot be represented on the product side and no species of atom can disappear from the reactant side. These are the *balancing requirements.* They are met by adjusting the *coefficients* of the formulas of reactants and products. We must adjust these coefficients to the *smallest possible whole numbers* which satisfy the law of conservation of atoms.

8.3   Procedure in writing equations

Let us consider some simple chemical reactions and write the chemical equations which represent them. We must proceed in steps which satisfy the three factors in equation writing.

1.   Represent the facts.

2.   Write correct formulas of compounds balanced as to oxidation number or ion charge. (Formulas for elemental gases with diatomic molecules also must be correctly written.)

3.   Balance the equation according to the law of conservation of atoms.

Passing an electric current through a slightly acid solution of water produces the elements hydrogen and oxygen. You may already have done this experiment in the laboratory. Let us write the word equation and write and balance the formula equation for this reaction.

Step 1: What are the facts? The only reactant is water and the only products are hydrogen and oxygen. We can represent these facts by the word equation

water → hydrogen + oxygen

Now let us substitute the formulas for these substances.

$$H_2O → H_2 + O_2 \quad \text{(not balanced)}$$

Step 2: Are the formulas correctly written? The oxidation number of hydrogen is +1 and of oxygen −2. So the formula for water is correctly written as H_2O. Both hydrogen and oxygen exist in the free state as diatomic molecules. So the formulas of molecular hydrogen and molecular oxygen are correctly written as H_2 and O_2.

Step 3: Is the equation balanced as to atoms? On the left, one molecule of water is represented. It consists of 2 hydrogen atoms and 1 oxygen atom. To the right of the yields sign (→) one molecule of hydrogen consisting of 2 atoms and one molecule of oxygen made up of 2 atoms are represented. *But there is only 1 atom of oxygen on the left.* How may we adjust this difference? We may not add a subscript $_2$ to the oxygen of the water formula, for this would change a formula which we know to be correctly written. Once we write the formulas of the substances correctly, we may not change the subscripts. This rule results because the *number of atoms in the molecule,* based upon experimental analysis, cannot be changed. But a change in the *number of molecules* may be represented by changing the coefficients. Suppose we increase the number of water molecules to two. This change can be represented by placing the coefficient 2 ahead of the formula H_2O, making it $2H_2O$. Thus, we have represented two molecules of water, each having 1 oxygen atom. This representation gives us the necessary 2 atoms of oxygen on the left.

$$2H_2O → H_2 + O_2 \quad \text{(not balanced)}$$

Two molecules of water have a total of 4 atoms of hydrogen. We must now move to the right side of the equation and adjust the number of hydrogen atoms represented to 4. We can do this by placing the coefficient 2 ahead of the hydrogen molecule, making it $2H_2$. We now have a total of 4 atoms of hydrogen represented on the right, and our equation reads

$$2H_2O → 2H_2 + O_2$$

We have represented the same number of atoms of each element on both sides of the equation. Furthermore, we have used the lowest whole-number ratio of coefficients possible. Thus, the equation is balanced.

If we wish to indicate the physical phases of the reactant and products, we may write the balanced equation

$$2H_2O(l) \rightarrow 2H_2(g) + O_2(g)$$

The abbreviations commonly used in this way are (s), solid; (l), liquid; (g), gas; and (aq), water solution. In this text, these abbreviations are used *only* when they contribute to a better understanding of the reaction represented by the equation. Frequently they are used only to designate solid or gaseous products.

Oxygen is one of the most active elements. Oxygen's high activity is related to its high electronegativity. Oxygen combines with other elements and forms compounds called *oxides. An oxide is a compound consisting of oxygen and usually one other element.* When oxides are formed by direct combination of the elements, the reaction is exothermic. Generally, oxides are very stable compounds. Nonmetals such as hydrogen, carbon, and sulfur burn in oxygen and form oxides. Experiments indicate that these oxides are bonded covalently and exist as molecules. This fact supports the atomic theory because the electronegativity difference between these nonmetals and oxygen is small.

The relationship between electronegativity difference and type of bonding between elements was explained in Section 6.16.

In the burning of sulfur, oxygen gas combines with solid sulfur and forms sulfur dioxide gas. These are the facts, so we may write

sulfur + oxygen → sulfur dioxide

$$S(s) + O_2(g) \rightarrow SO_2(g)$$

Molecular oxygen is diatomic, O_2, and the binary name "sulfur dioxide" indicates that its formula is SO_2. All formulas are correctly written. The numbers of atoms of sulfur and oxygen are the same on both sides of the equation. No further adjustments are required; the equation is balanced.

Oxygen can be prepared in the laboratory by heating solid mercury(II) oxide. The facts are: heating mercury(II) oxide yields liquid metallic mercury and oxygen gas.

mercury(II) oxide → mercury + oxygen

Substituting the proper symbols and formulas, we write

$$HgO \rightarrow Hg + O_2 \quad \text{(not balanced)}$$

Mercury(II) has an oxidation number of +2 and oxygen has an oxidation number of −2. So the formula of mercury(II) oxide is correctly written. However, the equation is not balanced with respect to oxygen. To balance it we must represent two molecules of HgO decomposing and yielding the 2 atoms making up the diatomic molecule of oxygen. After making this adjustment we see that we must also represent 2 atoms of mercury on the right. The balanced equation is

$$2HgO(s) \rightarrow 2Hg(l) + O_2(g)$$

In your laboratory work you may have learned that zinc reacts with hydrochloric acid (a water solution of hydrogen chloride gas). This reaction produces hydrogen gas and a solution of zinc chloride. These facts may be represented by the word equation

zinc + hydrochloric acid → zinc chloride + hydrogen

With proper consideration for oxidation numbers and ion charges we may write

$$Zn + HCl \rightarrow ZnCl_2 + H_2 \quad \text{(not balanced)}$$

In balancing atoms, we must represent two molecules of HCl supplying the 2 chlorine atoms of $ZnCl_2$ and the 2 hydrogen atoms of the diatomic hydrogen molecule. Thus our balanced equation is

$$Zn(s) + 2HCl(aq) \rightarrow ZnCl_2(aq) + H_2(g)$$

One of the most common mistakes that beginners make in balancing equations is that of destroying the ion charge or oxidation number balance of a formula in order to get the required number of atoms. Do not become discouraged at this time if equations offer considerable difficulty. The trouble lies not in the method of balancing but in the large number of facts that must be known. As you continue to make progress in class and gain experience in the laboratory, the equations that now seem difficult will prove to be simple.

Let us try an equation for a reaction that occurs in a process of water purification. Aluminum sulfate and calcium hydroxide are added to water containing unwanted suspended matter. These two substances react in water and produce two insoluble products, aluminum hydroxide and calcium sulfate. These products settle out, taking the suspended matter with them. The reaction may be represented by the word equation

aluminum sulfate + calcium hydroxide →
aluminum hydroxide + calcium sulfate

By ion-charge balancing to assure correct formulas we may write

$$Al_2(SO_4)_3 + Ca(OH)_2 \rightarrow Al(OH)_3 + CaSO_4 \quad \text{(not balanced)}$$

We now begin at the left, with $Al_2(SO_4)_3$, to balance atoms. Two Al atoms are indicated. To represent 2 Al atoms on the right we place the coefficient 2 ahead of $Al(OH)_3$. Three SO_4 groups are indicated, so we place the coefficient 3 in front of $CaSO_4$. Our equation now reads:

$$Al_2(SO_4)_3 + Ca(OH)_2 \rightarrow 2Al(OH)_3 + 3CaSO_4 \quad \text{(not balanced)}$$

Next we observe that there must be 3 Ca atoms on the left to equal the 3 Ca atoms now on the right. We place the coefficient 3 in front of $Ca(OH)_2$. This gives us 6 OH groups on the left and we observe that there are 6 OH groups on the right. We now have a balanced equation.

$$Al_2(SO_4)_3 + 3Ca(OH)_2 \rightarrow 2Al(OH)_3(s) + 3CaSO_4(s)$$

(The (s) indicates those products which are insoluble and leave the reaction environment as *precipitates*. A precipitate is an insoluble solid that separates from a solution.)

To write chemical equations correctly:

1. You must know the symbols of the common elements.

2. You must know the usual oxidation numbers or ionic charges of the common elements and polyatomic (many-atomed) ions.

3. You must know the facts relating to the reaction for which an equation is to be written.

4. You must be sure that all formulas are correctly written before attempting to balance the equation.

5. You must balance the equation for atoms of all elements represented. You must do this using the lowest ratio of whole-number coefficients possible.

8.4   General types of chemical reactions

There are several different ways of classifying chemical reactions. No single scheme is entirely satisfactory. In elementary chemistry it is helpful to recognize reactions which fall into the main categories given below. Later (in Units 5 and 7) you will learn other ways in which chemical reactions can be classified. The main types of reactions are:

1. Composition reactions, in which two or more substances combine and form a more complex substance. Composition reactions have the general form

$$A + X \rightarrow AX$$

Examples:
Iron and sulfur combine and form iron(II) sulfide

$$Fe + S \rightarrow FeS$$

Water and sulfur trioxide combine and form hydrogen sulfate (sulfuric acid).

$$H_2O + SO_3 \rightarrow H_2SO_4$$

Fig. 8-1. A composition reaction.

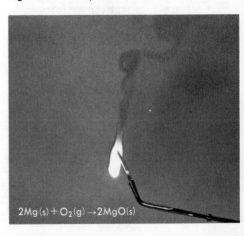

$2Mg(s) + O_2(g) \rightarrow 2MgO(s)$

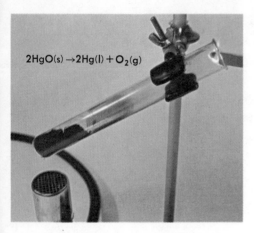

$$2HgO(s) \rightarrow 2Hg(l) + O_2(g)$$

Fig. 8-2. A decomposition reaction.

$$Cu(s) + 2AgNO_3(aq) \rightarrow Cu(NO_3)_2(aq) + 2Ag(s)$$

Fig. 8-3. A replacement reaction.

2. *Decomposition reactions,* the reverse of the first type. Here one substance breaks down and forms two or more simpler substances. Decomposition reactions have the general form

$$\mathbf{AX \rightarrow A + X}$$

Examples:
Water is decomposed, yielding hydrogen and oxygen.

$$\mathbf{2H_2O \rightarrow 2H_2(g) + O_2(g)}$$

Potassium chlorate is decomposed, yielding potassium chloride and oxygen.

$$\mathbf{2KClO_3 \rightarrow 2KCl + 3O_2(g)}$$

3. *Replacement reactions,* in which one substance is replaced in its compound by another substance. Replacement reactions have the general form

$$\mathbf{A + BX \rightarrow AX + B}$$

or

$$\mathbf{Y + BX \rightarrow BY + X}$$

Examples:
Iron replaces copper in a solution of copper(II) sulfate yielding iron(II) sulfate and copper.

$$\mathbf{Fe + CuSO_4 \rightarrow FeSO_4 + Cu(s)}$$

Chlorine replaces iodine in a solution of potassium iodide yielding potassium chloride and iodine.

$$\mathbf{Cl_2 + 2KI \rightarrow 2KCl + I_2}$$

In these first three types of reactions some change in the sharing of electrons occurs or there is a transfer of electrons from one atom to another.

4. *Ionic reactions* involve no transfer of electrons. Instead, ions in solution combine and form a product that leaves the reaction environment. Ionic reactions may have the general form

$$\mathbf{A^+(aq) + B^-(aq) \rightarrow AB}$$

Example:
A solution of sodium chloride, containing sodium ions and chloride ions, is added to a solution of silver nitrate, containing silver ions and nitrate ions. A reaction occurs between the silver ions and chloride ions. A white precipitate of silver chloride is formed.

$$\mathbf{Ag^+ + Cl^- \rightarrow Ag^+Cl^-(s)}$$

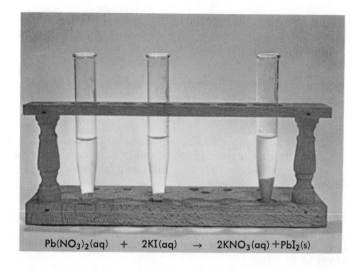

$$Pb(NO_3)_2(aq) \quad + \quad 2KI(aq) \quad \rightarrow \quad 2KNO_3(aq) + PbI_2(s)$$

Fig. 8-4. An ionic reaction.

The sodium ions and nitrate ions remain uncombined in solution. But they can be recovered as sodium nitrate by evaporating the water. The sodium ions and silver ions may be regarded as having exchanged places. For this reason, ionic reactions are sometimes called *exchange* reactions.

When we wish to show what substances are used to bring about ionic reactions, we may write formula equations. The equations have the general form

$$\textbf{AX} + \textbf{BY} \rightarrow \textbf{AY} + \textbf{BX}$$

In this sense, the ionic reaction just described may be written

$$\textbf{NaCl} + \textbf{AgNO}_3 \rightarrow \textbf{NaNO}_3 + \textbf{AgCl(s)}$$

In order for an ionic reaction to occur, a product must be formed that separates ions from the reaction environment (the solution). The product may be a solid precipitate, an insoluble gas, or a new molecular species. These reactions will be studied extensively in Units 5 and 7.

8.5 Six kinds of decomposition reactions

Decomposition reactions are promoted by heat or electricity. The kinds generally recognized are as follows:

1. Metallic carbonates, when heated, form metallic oxides and carbon dioxide. Calcium carbonate, $CaCO_3$, on being heated, forms calcium oxide, CaO. Carbon dioxide, CO_2, is given off as a gas.

$$\textbf{CaCO}_3 \rightarrow \textbf{CaO} + \textbf{CO}_2\textbf{(g)}$$

Ammonium carbonate, $(NH_4)_2CO_3$, because of the nonmetallic nature of the ammonium ion, decomposes in a special manner. The equation for this reaction is

$$(NH_4)_2CO_3 \rightarrow 2NH_3(g) + H_2O(g) + CO_2(g)$$

Ammonia, steam, and carbon dioxide are produced.

2. *Many metallic hydroxides, when heated, decompose into metallic oxides and water.* If we strongly heat calcium hydroxide, $Ca(OH)_2$, steam is given off and calcium oxide, CaO, remains.

$$Ca(OH)_2 \rightarrow CaO + H_2O(g)$$

Sodium hydroxide and potassium hydroxide are common exceptions to this rule.

3. *Metallic chlorates, when heated, decompose into metallic chlorides and oxygen.* This is the type of reaction used to prepare oxygen from potassium chlorate.

$$2KClO_3 \rightarrow 2KCl + 3O_2(g)$$

4. *Some acids, when heated, decompose into nonmetallic oxides and water.* Acids may be formed by the reaction of certain nonmetallic oxides and water. The reactions described below involve the reverse process—the decomposition of the acid. Examples are: Carbonic acid yields water and carbon dioxide gas.

$$H_2CO_3 \rightarrow H_2O + CO_2(g)$$

Sulfurous acid yields water and sulfur dioxide gas.

$$H_2SO_3 \rightarrow H_2O + SO_2(g)$$

The two reactions above take place quite readily at room temperature. The following reaction occurs at elevated temperatures.

$$H_2SO_4 \rightarrow H_2O + SO_3(g)$$

5. *Some oxides, when heated, decompose.* Most oxides are very stable compounds. There are only a few of them which decompose on heating. Two of these oxides and the reactions for their decomposition are

$$2HgO \rightarrow 2Hg + O_2(g)$$
$$2PbO_2 \rightarrow 2PbO + O_2(g)$$

6. *Some decomposition reactions are produced by electricity.*
The reactions represented by the following equations are typical.

$$2H_2O \xrightarrow{\text{(electricity)}} 2H_2(g) + O_2(g)$$

$$2NaCl \xrightarrow{\text{(electricity)}} 2Na + Cl_2(g)$$

8.6 Four kinds of replacement reactions

The quantities of energy involved in replacement reactions are
generally smaller than in composition and decomposition reactions. The possibility of reaction depends on the relative activities of the elements involved. We generally use an experimentally
derived *activity series* much like the one discussed in Section
8.8 in writing replacement equations. We will consider four
kinds of replacement reactions.

1. *Replacement of a metal in a compound by a more active
metal.* One reaction of this type involves zinc and a solution of
copper(II) sulfate, $CuSO_4$. Zinc replaces the copper in the solution. From this reaction we conclude that zinc is a more active
metal than copper.

$$Zn + CuSO_4 \rightarrow ZnSO_4 + Cu(s)$$

2. *Replacement of hydrogen in water by metals.* The very
active metals, such as potassium, calcium, and sodium, react
vigorously with water. They replace half the hydrogen and form
metallic hydroxides. The reaction represented by the following
equation is typical.

$$Ca + 2H_2O \rightarrow Ca(OH)_2 + H_2(g)$$

Less active metals, such as magnesium, zinc, and iron, react
at elevated temperatures with water (steam) and replace hydrogen. Because of the high temperature involved, oxides rather
than hydroxides are formed. Metals less active than iron do not
react measurably with water.

3. *Replacement of hydrogen in acids by metals.* Many metals
react with certain acids, such as hydrochloric acid and dilute
sulfuric acid. These metals replace hydrogen in the acids and
form the corresponding metallic compounds. You may have
used this method for the laboratory preparation of hydrogen by
reacting sulfuric acid with zinc.

$$Zn + H_2SO_4 \rightarrow ZnSO_4 + H_2(g)$$

4. *Replacement of halogens.* The halogens are the elements
in Group VII of the periodic table. They have somewhat similar

properties. These elements are fluorine, chlorine, bromine, and iodine. Experiments show that fluorine is the most active halogen; it replaces the other three halogens in their compounds. Chlorine replaces bromine and iodine in their compounds. Bromine replaces only iodine. An example of a halogen replacement reaction is chlorine replacing bromine in a potassium bromide solution.

$$\text{Cl}_2 + 2\text{KBr} \rightarrow 2\text{KCl} + \text{Br}_2$$

Chlorine replaces iodide, forming the corresponding chloride.

$$\text{Cl}_2 + 2\text{NaI} \rightarrow 2\text{NaCl} + \text{I}_2$$

Bromine replaces iodide, but not so vigorously as does chlorine.

$$\text{Br}_2 + 2\text{KI} \rightarrow 2\text{KBr} + \text{I}_2$$

8.7 Many reactions are reversible

Frequently, the products of a chemical reaction can react and produce the original reactants. Hydrogen can be used as a reducing agent to separate certain metals from their oxides. If dry hydrogen gas is passed over hot magnetic iron oxide, iron and steam are produced.

$$4\text{H}_2 + \text{Fe}_3\text{O}_4 \rightarrow 3\text{Fe} + 4\text{H}_2\text{O(g)}$$

If the procedure is reversed and steam is passed over hot iron, magnetic iron oxide and hydrogen are formed.

$$3\text{Fe} + 4\text{H}_2\text{O} \rightarrow \text{Fe}_3\text{O}_4 + 4\text{H}_2\text{(g)}$$

Such reactions are said to be reversible. They may be indicated by two yields signs pointing in opposite directions ($\leftrightarrows$)

$$3\text{Fe} + 4\text{H}_2\text{O} \leftrightarrows \text{Fe}_3\text{O}_4 + 4\text{H}_2$$

Conditions may be such as to allow both reactions to occur at the same time. That is, if none of the products leaves the field of action, they may react and form the original reactants. Under such circumstances, an equilibrium (state of balance) may develop between the two reactions. After equilibrium is reached, the quantities of all the reactants remain constant. The subject of equilibrium reactions will be discussed in Chapter 20.

8.8 The activity series of the elements

In general, the ease with which the atoms of a metal lose electrons determines the ease with which the metal forms compounds. In the replacement reaction

$$A + BX \rightarrow AX + B$$

metal **A** gives up electrons to **B** and replaces it. Thus we know that **A** is more active than **B**. If metal **B** is immersed in a solution of the compound **AX**, **B** does not replace **A**. Atoms of a more active metal lose electrons to positively charged ions of a less active metal under proper reaction conditions. Similarly, atoms of more active nonmetals acquire electrons from negatively charged ions of less active nonmetals.

Many exothermic chemical reactions can be carried out in such a way that electric energy is given off. From a study of such reactions, chemists are able to devise an activity series of elements to help predict the course of replacement reactions. Some composition and decomposition reactions can likewise be predicted with the aid of an activity series. The series presented in Table 8-1 lists the most important common elements in descending order of their metallic and nonmetallic activities.

The relative positions of the elements in the activity series enable us to apply some of the following generalizations to appropriate composition, decomposition, and replacement reactions.

1.   Each element in the list displaces from a compound any of the elements below it. The larger the interval between elements in the series, the more vigorous the action.
2.   All metals above hydrogen displace hydrogen from hydrochloric acid or dilute sulfuric acid.
3.   Metals near the top of the series vigorously displace hydrogen from water. Magnesium displaces hydrogen from steam.
4.   Metals above silver combine directly with oxygen; those near the top do so rapidly.
5.   Metals below mercury form oxides only indirectly.
6.   Oxides of metals below mercury decompose with mild heating.
7.   Oxides of metals below chromium easily undergo reduction to metals by heating with hydrogen.
8.   Oxides of metals above iron resist reduction by heating with hydrogen.
9.   Elements near the top of the series are never found free in nature.
10. Elements near the bottom of the series are often found free in nature.

8.9   Stoichiometric relations

The determination of empirical formulas of compounds is always the result of experimentation. Empirical formulas are derived from the relative numbers of moles of atoms of the elements present in compounds. Therefore, they indicate the

Table 8-1

ACTIVITY SERIES OF THE ELEMENTS

Metals	Nonmetals
lithium	fluorine
potassium	chlorine
calcium	bromine
sodium	iodine
magnesium	
aluminum	
zinc	
chromium	
iron	
nickel	
tin	
lead	
HYDROGEN	
copper	
mercury	
silver	
platinum	
gold	

relative numbers of atoms present. An empirical formula tells us nothing about the nature of the association of the atoms or the make-up of the molecular structure. It does not even tell us whether a substance actually exists in simple molecular units. Nevertheless, empirical formulas are very useful in calculations involving the combining and reacting relationships among substances.

The branch of chemistry which deals with the numerical relationships of elements and compounds and the mathematical proportions of reactants and products in chemical changes is known as **stoichiometry** (stoy-key-*om*-eh-tree). The determination of the percentage composition of compounds and of empirical formulas was discussed in Chapter 7. The calculations for these determinations are based upon *stoichiometric relations.* We are now going to learn to solve stoichiometric problems involving the mass relations of reactants and products in chemical reactions. To do this, you will need an understanding of the mole concept and some skill in writing and balancing chemical equations. The concept of mole volumes of gases is introduced in Chapter 10. This concept will enable you to solve a great number of problems involving mass and volume relations of gaseous reactants and products by means of very simple computations. Simple mass and volume relations exist only for gases.

8.10   Mole relations of reactants and products

When carbon burns in the oxygen of the air, carbon dioxide, a covalent molecular gas, is produced.

$$C + O_2 \rightarrow CO_2(g)$$

The balanced equation indicates the mole proportions of the reactants and products. It also gives the composition of each substance in terms of the kinds of elements and the relative number of each kind of atom present. Thus, the equation signifies that 1 mole of carbon combines with 1 mole of oxygen molecules and yields 1 mole of carbon dioxide. This may be indicated as follows:

$$
\begin{array}{cccc}
C & + & O_2 & \rightarrow & CO_2(g) \\
1 \text{ mole} & & 1 \text{ mole} & & 1 \text{ mole} \\
= 12.0 \text{ g} & & = 32.0 \text{ g} & & = 44.0 \text{ g}
\end{array}
$$

The mole proportions of reacting substances and products convert readily to equivalent mass quantities as shown above. An equation is used in this way when we wish to determine the mass of one substance that reacts with, or is produced from, a definite mass of another. This is one of the common problems chemists are called upon to solve.

8.11   Mole method of solving mass-mass problems

The mole concept is quite important and practical in chemistry. Mole quantities can be used in a variety of problem situations. We will describe the mole method of solving mass-mass problems.

Suppose we wish to determine the mass of calcium oxide produced by heating 50.0 g of calcium carbonate. Observe that the mass of the reactant is given and the mass of a product is required. From the data given in the problem and the facts known concerning this reaction, we can *set up the problem*. This can be accomplished in four steps.

Step 1. Write the balanced equation.

Step 2. Show the problem specifications: what is given and what is required. To do this we write the mass of calcium carbonate, 50.0 g, above the formula $CaCO_3$. Letting **X** represent the unknown mass of calcium oxide produced, we write **X** above the formula CaO.

Step 3. Show the mole proportions established by the balanced equation. We do this by writing under each substance in the problem the number of *moles* indicated by the equation.

Step 4. Determine the mass of 1 mole of each substance involved in the problem. These masses should be written below the equation set up. The problem is now ready to be solved.

$$
\begin{array}{llll}
\textit{Step 2:} & 50.0 \text{ g} & \textbf{X} & \\
\textit{Step 1:} & CaCO_3 & \rightarrow \quad CaO & + \quad CO_2(g) \\
\textit{Step 3:} & 1 \text{ mole} & 1 \text{ mole} &
\end{array}
$$

$$
\begin{array}{ll}
\textit{Step 4:} & 1 \text{ mole } CaCO_3 = 100.1 \text{ g} \\
& 1 \text{ mole } CaO \quad = \quad 56.1 \text{ g}
\end{array}
$$

The number of moles of $CaCO_3$ *given in the problem* is found by multiplying the given mass of $CaCO_3$, 50.0 g, by the fraction $\dfrac{\text{mole}}{100.1 \text{ g}}$, or

$$
50.0 \text{ g } CaCO_3 \times \frac{\text{mole}}{100.1 \text{ g}} = \textbf{number moles } CaCO_3
$$

The balanced equation indicates that for each mole of $CaCO_3$ decomposed, 1 mole of CaO is produced. So from the given mass of $CaCO_3$ we can produce

$$
50.0 \text{ g } CaCO_3 \times \frac{\text{mole}}{100.1 \text{ g}} \times \frac{1 \text{ mole } CaO}{1 \text{ mole } CaCO_3} = \textbf{number moles } CaO
$$

To determine the mass of CaO produced, we next multiply by the mass of 1 mole of CaO.

$$
50.0 \text{ g } CaCO_3 \times \frac{\text{mole}}{100.1 \text{ g}} \times \frac{1 \text{ mole } CaO}{1 \text{ mole } CaCO_3} \times \frac{56.1 \text{ g}}{\text{mole}} = \textbf{g } CaO
$$

It is always wise to make a preliminary estimate of the answer to a problem before starting your computations. Thus you may avoid accepting an answer as correct which actually is quite absurd due to errors in computation or in operations with units. In this problem, a check of the units indicates that they are correct. The numerical result of the first multiplication is $\frac{1}{2}$, the numerical value of the second fraction is 1, and that of the third fraction is about 60. So we estimate the numerical answer to be $\frac{1}{2} \times 1 \times 60 = 30$. We are now ready to perform the arithmetic calculations

$$X = 50.0 \text{ g CaCO}_3 \times \frac{\text{mole}}{100.1 \text{ g}} \times \frac{1 \text{ mole CaO}}{1 \text{ mole CaCO}_3} \times \frac{56.1 \text{ g}}{\text{mole}} = 28.0 \text{ g CaO}$$

This calculated answer is in good agreement with our estimate.

Note that solving a mass-mass problem by the mole method involves four operations following the problem set-up.

1. Determine the number of moles of the substance whose mass is given in the problem by multiplying its mass by the fraction $\frac{\text{mole}}{\text{mass of one mole}}$ of the substance.

2. Determine the number of moles of substance whose mass is required. To do this, multiply the expression from operation 1 by the ratio of the number of moles of substance whose mass is required and the number of moles of substance whose mass is given. This ratio is indicated by the balanced equation.

3. Determine the mass of the substance required. To do this, multiply the expression from operation 2 by the number of grams per mole of the substance required.

4. Check the units assigned to make sure they yield the proper units for the answer, and estimate the answer. Perform the arithmetic operations. Compare the calculated result with your estimated one.

See the Sample Problems.

Sample Problem

How many grams of potassium chlorate must be decomposed to yield 30.0 g **of** oxygen?

Solution

We set up the problem *first*, by writing the balanced equation. *Second*, we write the specifications of the problem above the equation. *Third*, we write the number of moles of each specified substance under its formula. And *fourth*, we calculate the mass/mole of each of the specified substances. We will let X represent the mass of potassium chlorate decomposed.

Step 2:   X   30.0 g

Step 1: $2KClO_3$ $\rightarrow$ $2KCl$ + $3O_2(g)$

Step 3:   2 moles   3 moles

Step 4:   1 mole $KClO_3 = 122.6$ g

           1 mole O_2 $= \ \ 32.0$ g

$$X = 30.0 \text{ g } O_2 \times \frac{\text{mole}}{32.0 \text{ g}} \times \frac{2 \text{ moles } KClO_3}{3 \text{ moles } O_2} \times \frac{122.6 \text{ g}}{\text{mole}} = 76.6 \text{ g } KClO_3$$

Operation 1 gives expression for no. moles O_2 given	Operation 2 gives expression for no. moles $KClO_3$ required	Operation 3 gives expression for no. grams $KClO_3$ required	Operation 4 involves unit check, estimate of answer, and arithmetic operations

Sample Problem

(a) How many grams of oxygen are required to oxidize $14\overline{0}$ g of iron to iron(III) oxide? (b) How many moles of iron(III) oxide are produced?

Solution

The problem set-up for Parts (a) and (b) is:

Step 2: $14\overline{0}$ g   X   Y

Step 1:   4Fe   + $3O_2$ $\rightarrow$ $2Fe_2O_3$

Step 3:   4 moles   3 moles   2 moles

Step 4:   1 mole Fe   =   55.8 g

           1 mole O_2 =   32.0 g

The solution set-up for Part (a) is

$$X = 14\overline{0} \text{ g Fe} \times \frac{\text{mole}}{55.8 \text{ g}} \times \frac{3 \text{ moles } O_2}{4 \text{ moles Fe}} \times \frac{32.0 \text{ g}}{\text{mole}} = 60.2 \text{ g } O_2$$

The solution set-up for Part (b) is

$$Y = 14\overline{0} \text{ g Fe} \times \frac{\text{mole}}{55.8 \text{ g}} \times \frac{2 \text{ moles } Fe_2O_3}{4 \text{ moles Fe}} = 1.25 \text{ moles } Fe_2O_3$$

EQUATIONS

Group A

Write balanced formula equations for these reactions and identify the type of reaction. *Do not write in this book.*

1. zinc + sulfur → zinc sulfide.
2. potassium chloride + silver nitrate → silver chloride(s) + potassium nitrate.

3. calcium oxide + water → calcium hydroxide.
4. sodium hydroxide + hydrochloric acid(HCl) → sodium chloride + water.
5. magnesium bromide + chlorine → magnesium chloride + bromine.
6. sodium chloride + sulfuric acid (H_2SO_4) → sodium sulfate + hydrogen chloride(g).
7. aluminum + iron(III) oxide → aluminum oxide + iron.
8. ammonium nitrite → nitrogen(g) + water.
9. silver nitrate + copper → copper(II) nitrate + silver(s).
10. hydrogen + nitrogen → ammonia (NH_3)(g).

Complete the word equation and write the balanced formula equation. Give a reason for the product(s) in each case. Consult the activity series (Table 8-1) and Table 12, Solubility Chart, in the Appendix as necessary.

Composition reactions:

11. sodium + iodine →
12. magnesium + oxygen →
13. hydrogen + chlorine →

Decomposition reactions:

14. nickel(II) chlorate →
15. barium carbonate →
16. zinc hydroxide →

Replacement reactions:

17. aluminum + sulfuric acid →
18. potassium iodide + chlorine →
19. iron + copper(II) nitrate → iron(II) nitrate +

Ionic reactions:

20. silver nitrate + zinc chloride →
21. copper(II) hydroxide + acetic acid ($HC_2H_3O_2$) →
22. iron(II) sulfate + ammonium sulfide →

Group B

Where the word equation is complete, write and balance the formula equation. Where the word equation is incomplete, complete it, write and balance the formula equation, tell the type of reaction, and give a reason for the product(s).

23. barium chloride + sodium sulfate →
24. calcium + hydrochloric acid →
25. iron(II) sulfide + hydrochloric acid → hydrogen sulfide(g) +
26. zinc chloride + ammonium sulfide →
27. ammonia + oxygen → nitric acid (HNO_3) + water.
28. magnesium + nitric acid →
29. potassium + water →
30. sodium iodide + bromine →
31. silver + sulfur →
32. sodium chlorate →
33. carbon + steam (H_2O) → carbon monoxide(g) + hydrogen(g).

34. zinc + lead(II) acetate →
35. iron(III) hydroxide →
36. iron(III) oxide + carbon monoxide → iron + carbon dioxide(g).
37. lead(II) acetate + hydrogen sulfide →
38. aluminum bromide + chlorine →
39. magnesium carbonate →
40. iron(III) chloride + sodium hydroxide →
41. calcium oxide + diphosphorus pentoxide → calcium phosphate.
42. chromium + oxygen →
43. sodium + water →
44. calcium carbonate + hydrochloric acid →
45. calcium hydroxide + phosphoric acid (H_3PO_4) →
46. sodium carbonate + nitric acid →
47. aluminum hydroxide + sulfuric acid →
48. copper + sulfuric acid → copper(II) sulfate + water + sulfur dioxide(g).
49. calcium hydroxide + ammonium sulfate → calcium sulfate + water + ammonia(g).
50. sodium sulfite + sulfuric acid →

PROBLEMS

Group A

1. Mercury(II) oxide (25.0 g) is to be decomposed by heating. (a) How many moles of mercury(II) oxide are given? (b) How many moles of oxygen can be prepared? (c) How many grams of oxygen can be prepared?
2. Potassium chlorate (25.0 g) is to be decomposed by heating. (a) How many moles of potassium chlorate are given? (b) How many moles of oxygen can be prepared? (c) How many grams of oxygen can be prepared?
3. A quantity of zinc reacts with sulfuric acid and produces 0.10 g of hydrogen. (a) How many moles of hydrogen are produced? (b) How many moles of zinc are required? (c) How many grams of zinc are required?
4. Sodium chloride reacts with 10.0 g of silver nitrate in water solution. (a) How many moles of silver nitrate react? (b) How many moles of sodium chloride are required? (c) How many grams of sodium chloride are required?
5. (a) How many moles of silver chloride are precipitated in the reaction of Problem 4? (b) How many grams of silver chloride is this?
6. In a reaction between sulfur and oxygen, 80.0 g of sulfur dioxide is formed. How many grams of sulfur were burned?
7. How many grams of hydrogen are required to completely convert 25 g of hot magnetic iron oxide (Fe_3O_4) to elemental iron? Steam is the other product of the reaction.
8. What mass of copper(II) oxide in grams is formed by oxidizing 1.00 kg of copper?
9. What mass of silver in grams is precipitated when 40.0 g of copper reacts with silver nitrate in solution?
10. Suppose 10.0 g of iron(II) sulfide is treated with enough hydrochloric acid so that the iron(II) sulfide completely reacts. How many grams of hydrogen sulfide gas will be given off?

Group B

11. An excess of sulfuric acid reacts with $15\overline{0}$ g of barium peroxide. (*a*) How many moles of hydrogen peroxide are produced? (*b*) How many moles of barium sulfate are formed?

12. Approximately 130 g of zinc was added to a solution containing $10\overline{0}$ g of HCl. After the action ceased, 41 g of zinc remained. How many moles of hydrogen were produced?

13. A mixture of 10.0 g of powdered iron and 10.0 g of sulfur is heated to its reaction temperature in an open crucible. (*a*) How many grams of iron(II) sulfide are formed? (*b*) The reactant in excess is oxidized. How many grams of its oxide are formed?

14. What mass of calcium hydroxide in grams can be produced from 1.00 kg of limestone, calcium carbonate? (Decomposition of calcium carbonate by heating produces calcium oxide and carbon dioxide. Calcium hydroxide is formed by the reaction of calcium oxide and water.)

15. How many grams of air are required to complete the combustion of 93 g of phosphorus to diphosphorus pentoxide, assuming the air to be 23% oxygen by mass?

16. How many metric tons of carbon dioxide can be produced from the combustion of 1.00 metric ton ($100\overline{0}$ kg) of coke which is $9\overline{0}\%$ carbon?

17. (*a*) What mass of H_2SO_4 in grams is required in a reaction with an excess of aluminum to produce 0.50 mole of aluminum sulfate? (*b*) How many moles of hydrogen are also produced?

18. A certain rocket uses butane, C_4H_{10}, as fuel. How many kilograms of liquid oxygen should be carried for the complete combustion of each 1.00 kg of butane to carbon dioxide and water vapor?

19. When 45 g of ethane gas, C_2H_6, is burned completely in air, carbon dioxide and water vapor are formed. (*a*) How many moles of carbon dioxide are produced? (*b*) How many moles of water are produced?

20. (*a*) How many grams of sodium sulfate are produced in the reaction between $15\overline{0}$ g of sulfuric acid and an excess of sodium chloride? (*b*) How many grams of sodium chloride are used? (*c*) How many grams of hydrogen chloride are also produced?

Chapter 9

The Gas Laws

9.1 Kinetic theory

In Chapter 1 we recognized that matter exists in three physical phases—gas, liquid, and solid. Then we learned that the particles that make up various substances are atoms, molecules, or ions. The *kinetic theory* helps explain the properties of gases, liquids, and solids in terms of *(1)* the forces between the particles of matter, and *(2)* the energy these particles possess.

Most of the data in support of the kinetic theory comes from indirect observation. It is almost impossible to observe the behavior of individual particles of matter. Scientists, however, can observe the behavior of large groups of particles. From the results of these observations, they can then describe the average behavior of the particles under study.

The three basic assumptions of the *kinetic theory* are:

1. Matter is composed of very tiny particles. The chemical properties of the particles of matter depend on their composition. Their physical properties depend on the forces they exert on each other and the distance separating them.

2. The particles of matter are in continual motion. Their average kinetic energy (energy of motion) depends on the temperature.

3. The particles of matter do not lose energy in collisions. When particles collide with each other or with the walls of their container, there is no loss of energy. Collisions of this type are said to be perfectly *elastic.*

Fig. 9-1. The rate of diffusion of bromine vapor in air. Diffusion has occurred for 2 minutes in the left cylinder. Diffusion has occurred for 20 minutes in the right cylinder.

From the CHEM Study Film: *Molecular Motion*

163

9.2 Observed properties of gases

A study of gases reveals four characteristic properties:

1. Expansion. A gas does not have a definite shape or a definite volume. It completely fills any container into which it is introduced.

2. Pressure. When we inflate a toy balloon, it becomes larger because we increase the pressure on its inside surface. If we let air escape, the balloon becomes smaller because the pressure is decreased. If we raise the temperature of the air in the balloon by warming it carefully, the balloon becomes larger. This observation indicates that pressure increases with an increase in temperature. On the other hand, if we cool the balloon, its size decreases as the pressure decreases.

3. Low density. The density of a gas is about $\frac{1}{1000}$ of the density of the same substance in the liquid or solid phase. Oxygen gas has a density of 1.429 g/liter (0.001429 g/ml) at 0° C and 1 atmosphere pressure. Liquid oxygen has a density of 1.149 g/ml at −183° C and solid oxygen has a density of 1.426 g/ml at −252.5° C. Hydrogen gas has a density of 0.0899 g/liter (0.0000899 g/ml) at 0° C and 1 atmosphere pressure. Liquid hydrogen has a density of 0.0708 g/ml at −253° C. Solid hydrogen has a density of 0.0807 g/ml at −262° C.

4. Diffusion. If the stopper is removed from a container of ammonia, the irritating effects of this gas on the eyes, nose, and throat soon become evident throughout the room. When the chemistry class makes the foul-odored hydrogen sulfide gas in the laboratory, objections may come from other students and teachers in all parts of the building. This process of spreading out spontaneously (without additional help) to occupy a space uniformly, is characteristic of all gases. It is known as *diffusion*.

9.3 Kinetic-theory description of a gas

According to the kinetic theory, a gas consists of very small independent particles. These particles move at random in space and experience perfectly elastic collisions. This theoretical description is of an imaginary gas called the ***ideal gas***.

The particles of substances which are gases at room temperature are molecules. Some of these molecules consist of a single atom (He, Ne, Ar). Many consist of two atoms (O_2, H_2, HCl, etc.). Others consist of several atoms (NH_3, CH_4, C_2H_2, etc.). Matter in the gaseous phase occupies a volume of the order of 1000 times that which it occupies in the liquid or solid phases. Thus, molecules of gases are much farther apart than those of liquids or solids. This difference accounts for the much lower density of gases as compared to solids or liquids. Even so, 1 ml of a gas at 0° C and 1 atmosphere pressure contains about 3×10^{19} molecules. Many ordinary molecules have diameters of the order of 4 Å, or 4×10^{-10} m. In gases, these molecules are widely sepa-

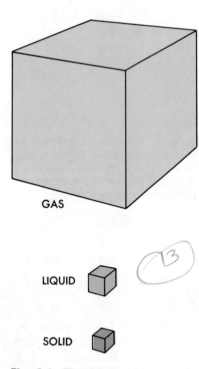

GAS

LIQUID

SOLID

Fig. 9-2. The density of many substances in the gaseous phase is about 1/1000 of their density in the liquid and solid phases. This diagram shows the relative volumes of 1.5 g of oxygen as a gas, a liquid, and a solid. The oxygen gas occupies 1050 ml, while liquid oxygen occupies 1.3 ml and solid oxygen occupies 1.0 ml.

rated. They are, on an average, about 4×10^{-9} m (or about 10 diameters) apart at 0° C and 1 atmosphere pressure. The kinetic energy of the molecules of a gas (except near its condensing temperature) overcomes the attractive forces between them. The molecules of a gas are on the average essentially independent particles. These molecules travel in random directions at high speed. This speed is of the order of 10^3 m/sec at 0° C and 1 atmosphere pressure. At this speed, molecules of a gas travel about 10^{-7}·m before colliding with other gas molecules or with the walls of the container. They undergo about 5×10^9 collisions per second.

Fig. 9-3. Molecules of a gas are widely separated and move rapidly.

The expansion and diffusion of gases are both explained by the fact that gas molecules are essentially independent particles. They move through space until they strike other gas molecules or the walls of the container. A gas moves very rapidly into an evacuated container. Gaseous diffusion is slowed down, but not prevented, by the presence of other gases. The rate of diffusion of one gas through another depends on three properties of the intermingling gas molecules:

1. Speed,
2. Diameter,
3. Attractive force.

Gas pressure results from many billions of moving molecules continuously hitting the walls of the container. If we increase the number of molecules within the container, the number which strike any area of the inside surface increases. Therefore, the pressure on the inside surface increases. If the temperature of the gas is raised, the molecules on an average have more kinetic energy. They move more rapidly, and collide more energetically with the walls of the container. These more frequent and more energetic collisions with the container walls increase the pressure. The pressure drops when the number of molecules is decreased or the temperature is lowered.

Figure 9-4 shows the distribution of molecular speeds in a gas at two different temperatures. From these graphs we draw two conclusions:

1. Molecules of a gas do not all have the same speed.
2. An increase in temperature increases the average rate at which gas molecules move.

The kinetic energy of a molecule is related to its speed by the equation.

$$E_k = \tfrac{1}{2}mv^2$$

in which E_k is the kinetic energy of the molecule, m is its mass, and v is its speed. Since the molecules of a gas do not all have the same speed, they will not all have the same kinetic energy. Since the average molecular speed varies with the temperature, the average kinetic energy of the molecules of a gas varies with the temperature. Thus, the temperature of a gas provides an indica-

Fig. 9-4. Molecular speed distribution in a gas at different temperatures.

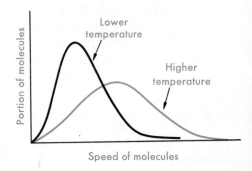

Table 9–1

CONDENSATION TEMPERATURES OF VARIOUS SUBSTANCES

Type of substance	Substance	Condensation temperature (1 atm, °C)
nonpolar covalent molecular	H_2	−253
	O_2	−183
	CH_4	−161
	CCl_4	77
	C_6H_6	80
polar covalent molecular	NH_3	−33
	H_2O	100
ionic	NaCl	1413
	MgF_2	2239
covalent network	$(SiO_2)_x$	2230
	C_x (diamond)	4827
metallic	Hg	357
	Cu	2595
	Fe	3000
	W	5927

Johannes Diderik van der Waals (1837–1923) was a Dutch scientist who helped explain the differences in physical properties between real and the ideal gas.

tion of the average kinetic energy of the molecules. The higher the temperature, the higher the average kinetic energy. The lower the temperature, the lower the average kinetic energy.

9.4 Attractive forces between gas molecules

The lowest temperature at which a substance can exist as a gas at atmospheric pressure is the *condensation temperature* of the gas. At this temperature, the kinetic energy of the gas particles is not sufficient to overcome the forces of attraction between them. The gas condenses to a liquid. The kinetic theory tells us that the temperature of a substance is a measure of the kinetic energy of its particles. So a study of condensation temperatures of various substances should give us an idea of the magnitude (size) of the forces of attraction between particles of matter. Table 9-1 gives selected condensation temperatures.

Substances such as H_2, O_2, and CH_4 (methane) consist of low-molecular-weight nonpolar covalent molecules. They can exist as gases at very low temperatures. Evidently the attractive forces between such molecules in the gaseous phase are very small. More complex substances such as CCl_4 and C_6H_6 (benzene) have condensation temperatures somewhat above room temperature. They have higher-molecular-weight nonpolar molecules. The forces of attraction between such molecules must be greater than those between similar molecules that are less complex.

Ammonia (NH_3) and H_2O consist of polar covalent molecules. Notice that their molecular weights are low and their molecular structures are simple. Even so, their condensation temperatures are considerably above those of nonpolar molecules of the same molecular weight.

The condensation temperatures of ionic compounds such as sodium chloride, covalent network substances such as diamond, and metals are all very high. Evidently the forces between particles of such substances are very strong. The nature of the forces of attraction in these types of substances will be described in Chapter 11.

The attractive forces between molecules are called *van der Waals forces*. These forces are important only when molecules are very close together. Hence van der Waals forces are not important in gases unless the gas molecules are under very high pressure or are at a temperature near their condensation temperature. Van der Waals forces are of two types. One type, called *dispersion interaction*, exists between all molecules. The other type, called *dipole-dipole attraction*, exists between polar molecules only.

The strength of dispersion interaction depends on the number of electrons in a molecule and the tightness with which the electrons are held. The greater the number of electrons and the less tightly they are bound, the more powerful is the attractive force of dispersion interaction. We can observe this effect most easily between nonpolar molecules, where dispersion interaction is the only type of attractive force. Thus, for nonpolar molecules in general, the higher the molecular weight, the higher the condensation temperature. This generalization can be observed in Table 9-1. Compare the condensation temperatures of oxygen, hydrogen, and methane with those of carbon tetrachloride and benzene. The energy associated with dispersion interaction is only a few tenths of a kilocalorie per mole.

Dipole-dipole attraction is the attraction between the oppositely charged portions of neighboring polar molecules. Remember from Section 6.17 that polar molecules are sometimes called dipoles. Dipole-dipole attractive forces as well as dispersion interaction forces act between polar molecules. This combination of forces accounts for the much higher condensation temperatures of polar molecules as compared to nonpolar molecules of similar complexity. For example, methane, ammonia, and water have comparable molecular weights. Yet the condensation temperature of ammonia is about 130 C° higher than that of methane. The condensation temperature of water is over 130 C° higher than that of ammonia. The energy associated with dipole-dipole attraction may be as high as 6 kilocalories per mole.

9.5 Dependence of gas volume on temperature and pressure

A given number of molecules can occupy widely different volumes. The expression "a cubic foot of air" means little unless we know the temperature and pressure at which it is measured. A cubic foot of air can be compressed to a few cubic inches in volume. It can also expand to fill an auditorium. Steel cylinders containing oxygen and hydrogen are widely used in industry. They have an internal volume of two cubic feet. When such cylinders are returned "empty" they still contain two cubic feet of gas, although when they were delivered "full" they may have had 100 times as many molecules of the gas compressed within the cylinder.

We have stated that the temperature of a gas is an indication of the average kinetic energy of its molecules. The higher the temperature of a gas, the more kinetic energy its molecules possess, and the more rapidly they move about. The pressure which a gas exerts on the walls of its container is the result of the collisions of gas molecules with the walls. Thus, if the volume of one mole of gas molecules remains constant, the pressure exerted by the gas increases as its temperature is raised. It follows that the pressure exerted by one mole of gas decreases as the temperature is lowered (Figure 9-5).

Furthermore, if the pressure exerted by one mole of gas molecules is to remain the same as the temperature increases, the vol-

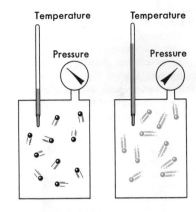

Fig. 9-5. At constant volume, as the temperature of a gas increases, the pressure it exerts increases.

Fig. 9-6. At constant pressure, as the temperature of a gas increases, the volume it occupies increases.

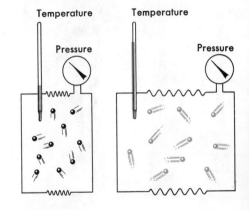

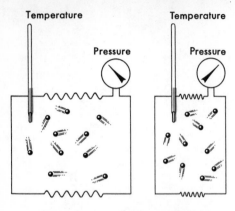

Fig. 9-7. At constant temperature, as the volume of a gas decreases, the pressure it exerts increases.

Fig. 9-8. A barometer is used to measure atmospheric pressure. Left, a laboratory mercurial barometer. Center, a close-up of the top of the mercury column showing the height-measuring scales. Right, the adjustable reservoir with indicator pin for setting the height of the mercury level exposed to the atmosphere.

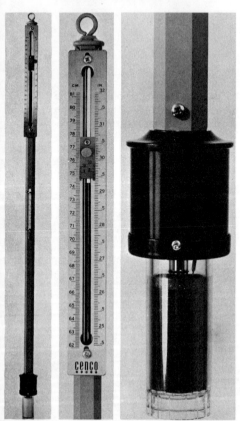

ume which the gas occupies must increase. Since the molecules move faster at higher temperatures, they strike the walls of the container more frequently and with more force. Suppose the area of the wall is increased. Then the force of collisions on a unit area of the wall can remain the same as at the lower temperature, and the pressure will remain the same. The area which the molecules strike can be enlarged by enlarging the volume of the container. On the other hand, if pressure remains constant and the temperature decreases, the volume which one mole of gas molecules occupies must decrease (Figure 9-6).

Finally, suppose the temperature of one mole of gas molecules remains constant. Then the pressure exerted by the gas becomes greater as the volume which the gas occupies becomes smaller. And similarly, the pressure exerted by one mole of gas molecules is less if the volume available to the gas is larger (Figure 9-7). In light of these consequences, the kinetic theory explains satisfactorily how gas volumes are related to the temperature and pressure of the gas. Accordingly, we must consider both temperature and pressure when measuring the volume of a gas.

9.6   Standard temperature and pressure

As explained in Section 9.5, the volume of a gas depends greatly on temperature and pressure. For this reason, it is very helpful to have a standard temperature and a standard pressure for use in measuring or comparing gas volumes. *Standard temperature is defined as exactly zero degrees Celsius.* It is the temperature of melting ice. This temperature was selected because pure water is widely available and the melting temperature of ice is not much affected by pressure changes. *Standard pressure is defined as the pressure exerted by a column of mercury exactly 760 millimeters high.* We use 760 millimeters of mercury as the standard pressure because that is the average atmospheric pressure at sea level. Temperatures are easily measured with an accurate thermometer. The pressure of a gas in simple gas experiments may be determined from properly corrected barometer reading. Standard temperature and pressure are commonly abbreviated as STP.

9.7   Variation of gas volume with pressure: Boyle's law

If a rubber ball filled with air is squeezed, the volume of the gas inside is decreased. But the gas expands again when the pressure is released. Robert Boyle (1627–1691) was the first scientist to make careful measurements showing the relationship between pressures and volumes of gases. He found that doubling the pressure on a gas reduces its volume by one half. Boyle formulated the results of his experiments into a law that bears his name.

Boyle's law is stated: *The volume of a definite quantity of dry gas is inversely proportional to the pressure, provided the temperature remains constant.*

This law is expressed mathematically as

$$\frac{V}{V'} = \frac{p'}{p}$$

V is the original volume, V' the new volume, p the original pressure, and p' the new pressure. Solving the expression for V', we obtain a useful mathematical form of Boyle's law,

$$V' = V\frac{p}{p'}$$

Robert Boyle is considered to be the founder of modern chemistry because (1) he recognized that chemistry is a worthwhile field of learning and not just a branch of medicine or alchemy; (2) he introduced careful experimentation into chemistry; and (3) he defined an element as something which could not be decomposed—a definition which held for over 200 years.

The Bettmann Archive, Inc.

Fig. 9-9. Robert Boyle was an English scientist whose first important experimental work was a study of the properties of air which he reported in 1660.

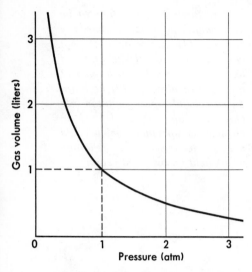

Fig. 9-10. The variation of volume with pressure at constant temperature of 1 liter of an ideal gas measured at 1 atmosphere pressure. The product of pressure and volume is a constant.

9.8 Using Boyle's law

Suppose 40.0 ml of hydrogen gas, collected when the barometer reading is $74\overline{0}$ mm, stands until the barometric pressure has risen to $75\overline{0}$ mm. If the temperature is unchanged, the volume of gas becomes smaller because of the increased pressure. If we measure the new gas volume, we find it to be 39.5 ml.

Using Boyle's law, we can calculate the new volume resulting from the pressure change without actually experiencing the pressure changes. The new volume V' is p/p' or $74\overline{0}$ mm/$75\overline{0}$ mm of the original volume V, 40.0 ml. Substituting in the Boyle's law formula and solving, we obtain

$$V' = Vp/p'$$
$$V' = 40.0 \text{ ml} \times 74\overline{0} \text{ mm}/75\overline{0} \text{ mm}$$
$$V' = 39.5 \text{ ml}$$

Later, if the pressure has fallen to $72\overline{0}$ mm, the new gas volume V' is calculated as

$$V' = 40.0 \text{ ml} \times 74\overline{0} \text{ mm}/72\overline{0} \text{ mm}$$
$$V' = 41.1 \text{ ml}$$

The following Sample Problem gives another example of Boyle's law in use.

Sample Problem

A $20\overline{0}$-ml sample of hydrogen is collected when the pressure is $80\overline{0}$ mm of mercury. What volume will the gas occupy at $76\overline{0}$ mm pressure?

Solution

$$V' = Vp/p'$$
$$V'_{76\overline{0} \text{ mm}} = 20\overline{0} \text{ ml} \times 80\overline{0} \text{ mm}/76\overline{0} \text{ mm}$$
$$V'_{76\overline{0} \text{ mm}} = 211 \text{ ml}$$

9.9 Variation of gas volume with temperature

Bread dough rises when put in a hot oven. The increase in temperature causes the bubbles of carbon dioxide gas within the dough to expand. The rather large increase in the volume of the dough during baking shows that the gas must expand considerably as the temperature increases. In fact, gases expand many times as much per degree rise in temperature as do liquids and solids.

Jacques Charles (1746–1823), a French scientist, was the first to make careful measurements of the changes in volume of gases with changes in temperature. His experiments revealed that:

1. All gases expand or contract at the same rate with changes in temperature, provided the pressure is unchanged.

2. The change in volume amounts to $\frac{1}{273}$ of the original volume at 0° C for each Celsius degree the temperature is changed.

We may start with a definite volume of a gas at 0° C and experiment by heating it. Just as the whole of anything may be considered as made up of two halves, $\frac{2}{2}$, or three thirds, $\frac{3}{3}$, so we can consider this volume as $\frac{273}{273}$. If we warm the gas one Celsius degree, it expands $\frac{1}{273}$ of its original volume. Its new volume is $\frac{274}{273}$. In the same manner, the gas expands $\frac{100}{273}$ when it is heated 100 C°. Such expansion, added to the original volume, makes the new volume $\frac{373}{273}$. Any gas warmed 273 Celsius degrees expands $\frac{273}{273}$. That is, its volume is just doubled, as represented by the fraction $\frac{546}{273}$.

A gas whose volume is measured at 0° C contracts by $\frac{1}{273}$ of this volume if it is cooled 1 C°. Its new volume is $\frac{272}{273}$ of its original volume. Cooling the gas to -100° C reduces the volume by $\frac{100}{273}$. In other words, the gas shrinks to $\frac{173}{273}$ of its original volume. At this rate, if we cooled the gas to -273° C, it would lose $\frac{273}{273}$ of its volume, and its volume would become zero. Such a situation cannot occur, however, because all gases become liquids before such a low temperature is reached. This rate of contraction with cooling applies only to gases.

The Bettmann Archive, Inc.

Fig. 9-11. Jacques Charles formulated the law relating changes in gas volumes to changes in temperature about 1787.

9.10 Kelvin temperature scale

In Section 1.15 the Celsius temperature scale was described. This scale is based on the *triple point* of water. *The **triple point** of pure water is that single temperature and pressure condition at which water exists in all three phases at the same time.* On the Celsius scale, the triple point of water has a temperature of 0.01° C.

From measuring the variation of gas volume with temperature at low pressures, scientists believe that -273.15° C is the lowest possible temperature. At this temperature a body would have lost all the heat that it is possible for it to lose. Scientists have come very close to this lowest possible temperature, but theoretically it is impossible to reach. The interval between the lowest possible temperature, -273.15° C, and the triple point temperature of water, 0.01° C, is 273.16 C°.

The physicist Sir William Thomson (1824–1907), better known by his title, Lord Kelvin, invented the Kelvin temperature scale. A Kelvin degree is the same temperature interval as a Celsius degree. But 0° K is the lowest possible temperature, -273.15° C. The temperature of the triple point of water is 273.16° K. The lowest possible temperature, 0° K, is frequently called *absolute zero*. Temperatures measured on the Kelvin scale are often called *absolute temperatures*.

You may wish to review Section 1.15.

Table 9–2

COMPARISON OF TEMPERATURES ON THE KELVIN AND CELSIUS SCALES

Celsius scale (°C)	Kelvin scale (°K)
$10\overline{0}°$	$373°$
$5\overline{0}°$	$323°$
$2\overline{0}°$	$293°$
$0°$	$273°$
$-10\overline{0}°$	$173°$
$-273°$	$\overline{0}°$

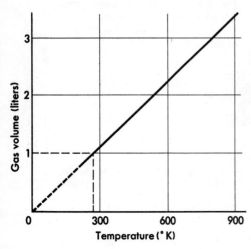

Fig. 9-12. The variation in volume with Kelvin temperature at constant pressure of 1 liter of an ideal gas measured at 273° K. The ratio of volume to Kelvin temperature is a constant.

The normal freezing point of water is 0.01 C° lower than the triple point temperature of water. On the Celsius scale the normal freezing point of water is 0.00° C. Recall that a Kelvin degree is the same temperature interval as a Celsius degree. So the normal freezing point of water is also 0.01 K° lower than the triple point temperature of water, 273.16° K, or 273.15° K. Thus 0.00° C = 273.15° K. In many calculations 273.15° K is rounded off to 273° K. Table 9-2 will help you compare Kelvin and Celsius temperatures.

Kelvin temperature = Celsius temperature + 273°

In section 9.3, you learned that the temperature of a gas provides an indication of the average kinetic energy of the molecules. Since the Kelvin scale starts at what is believed to be the lowest possible temperature, the average kinetic energy of the molecules of a gas is directly proportional to the Kelvin temperature of the gas.

9.11 Charles' law

Thermometers are not graduated (marked) to give Kelvin-scale readings. But use of the Kelvin scale does give results that correspond with actual volume changes observed in gases. In problems dealing with changes in gas volumes as temperatures vary, the Kelvin scale eliminates the use of zero and of negative numbers. Using the Kelvin temperature scale, *Charles' law* can be stated: *The volume of a definite quantity of dry gas varies directly with the Kelvin temperature, provided the pressure remains constant.*

Charles' law may be expressed mathematically as

$$\frac{V}{V'} = \frac{T}{T'}$$

V is the original volume, V' the new volume, T the original *Kelvin* temperature, and T' the new *Kelvin* temperature. Solving the expression for V'

$$V' = V\frac{T'}{T}$$

The Sample Problem below illustrates the use of this formula.

Sample Problem

A 50.0-ml volume of gas is measured at $2\overline{0}°$ C. If the pressure remains unchanged, what will be the volume of the gas at $\overline{0}°$ C?

Solution

Change the Celsius temperatures to Kelvin temperatures:

$$20° C + 273° = 293° K \qquad 0° C + 273° = 273° K$$
$$V' = VT'/T$$
$$V'_{0° C} = 50.0 \text{ ml} \times 273° K/293° K$$
$$V'_{0° C} = 46.4 \text{ ml}$$

9.12   Use of Boyle's and Charles' laws combined

Calculation of the new volume of a gas when both temperature and pressure are changed involves no new principles. The new volume is the same whether the changes in temperature and pressure are done together or in either order. We multiply the original volume first by a ratio of the pressures. In this way, we determine the new volume corrected for pressure alone. Then we multiply this answer by a ratio of the Kelvin temperatures. This gives us the new volume corrected for both pressure and temperature.

Expressed mathematically,

$$V' = V \times \frac{p}{p'} \times \frac{T'}{T}$$

The Sample Problem below illustrates the use of this formula. You will find it much easier to solve gas-law problems if you use logarithms or a slide rule in making your calculations.

Sample Problem

A gas measures 25.0 ml at 20° C and 735 mm pressure. What will be its volume at 15° C and 750 mm pressure?

Solution

$$20° C = 293° K; 15° C = 288° K$$
$$V' = V \times p/p' \times T'/T$$
$$V'_{15° C, 750 \text{ mm}} = 25.0 \text{ ml} \times 735 \text{ mm}/750 \text{ mm} \times 288° K/293° K$$
$$V'_{15° C, 750 \text{ mm}} = 24.1 \text{ ml}$$

9.13   Pressure of a gas collected
by displacement of mercury

We have discussed how gas volume varies with pressure and temperature changes. But we have not considered any practical laboratory methods of making the necessary measurements. We must now explain these laboratory operations. In the laboratory, a gas may be collected and its volume measured by using a long graduated tube closed at one end. This tube is called a *eudiometer* (you-dee-*om*-eh-ter), Figure 9-13.

Suppose some hydrogen is delivered into a eudiometer which was previously filled with mercury. As hydrogen enters the tube, it bubbles to the top, and pushes the mercury down. Suppose

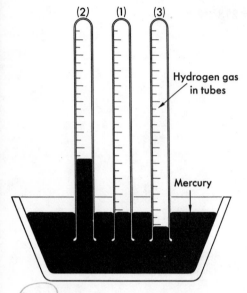

(2) (1) (3)

Hydrogen gas
in tubes

Mercury

Fig. 9-13. In (1) the pressure of the hydrogen is the same as that of the atmosphere. In (2) the pressure of the hydrogen is less than that of the atmosphere. In (3) the pressure of the hydrogen is greater than that of the atmosphere.

enough hydrogen is added to make the level of the mercury inside the tube the same as the level of the mercury in the bowl, as *in (1)*, Figure 9-13. *When these two levels are the same, the pressure of the hydrogen is the same as that of the atmosphere.* This pressure can be found by reading a barometer. The volume of hydrogen is read from the graduations (markings) on the eudiometer.

Suppose, however, that not enough hydrogen is delivered into the eudiometer to make the mercury levels the same even when the eudiometer rests on the bottom of the bowl of mercury. Then the level inside the tube is above the mercury level outside the tube, as in (2), Figure 9-13. The pressure of the gas inside the tube is less than the pressure of the air outside. Otherwise, the enclosed gas would push the mercury down to the same level as that outside the tube. To determine the pressure of the hydrogen, the difference between the levels of the mercury inside and outside the tube must be *subtracted* from the barometer reading. The gas volume is read, as before, from the eudiometer graduations.

Suppose enough hydrogen is delivered into the eudiometer to force the mercury level inside the tube below the outside level. Then the gas inside the tube is under a greater pressure than the air outside, as in (3), Figure 9-13. To determine the pressure of the gas in this case, the difference between the levels of the mercury inside and outside the tube must be *added* to the barometer reading. To make this measurement and that of the gas volume directly would not be practical, since mercury is not transparent. It is easier to raise the eudiometer in the bowl of mercury until the mercury levels inside and outside the tube are the same. Then the gas pressure inside will be the same as that read on the barometer. See the following Sample Problem.

Sample Problem

What is the pressure of the gas in a eudiometer (gas measuring tube) when the mercury level in the tube is 14 mm higher than that outside? The barometer reads 735 mm.

Solution

Since the mercury level inside is higher than that outside, the pressure on the gas in the eudiometer must be less than atmospheric pressure. Accordingly, the difference in levels is subtracted from the barometric pressure to obtain the pressure of the gas,

735 mm − 14 mm = 721 mm, the pressure of the gas

Sample Problem

The volume of oxygen in a eudiometer is 37.0 ml. The mercury level inside the tube is 25.0 mm higher than that outside. The barometer reading is 742.0 mm. The temperature is 24° C. What will be the volume of the oxygen at STP?

Note: When STP conditions are involved, 0° C and 760 mm are considered exact quantities. No bars are required over the zeros. These terms have no effect on the number of significant figures in the calculated result.

1. Correction for difference in levels:

$$742.0 \text{ mm} - 25.0 \text{ mm} = 717.0 \text{ mm}$$

2. Conversion of Celsius temperatures to Kelvin temperatures:

$$24° \text{ C} + 273° = 297° \text{ K}; \; 0° \text{ C} + 273° = 273° \text{ K}$$

3. Correction for change in pressure and temperature:

$$V' = V \times p/p' \times T'/T$$
$$V'_{STP} = 37.0 \text{ ml} \times 717.0 \text{ mm}/760 \text{ mm} \times 273° \text{ K}/297° \text{ K}$$
$$V'_{STP} = 32.0 \text{ ml}$$

9.14   Pressure of a gas collected by water displacement

In elementary work, gases are usually collected by water displacement rather than by mercury displacement. (Mercury is very expensive and poisonous.) Water is 1/13.6 as dense as mercury. Therefore, a given gas pressure will support a column of water 13.6 times as high as an equivalent column of mercury (Figure 9-14). When a gas is collected by water displacement, pressure corrections are made just as with mercury displacement. *But a difference in water levels must first be divided by 13.6 to convert it to its equivalent height in terms of a column of mercury.*

In advanced work, gases are often collected by mercury displacement. The advantage of this method is that mercury does not evaporate measurably at room temperatures. When a gas is bubbled through water, however, the collected gas always has some water vapor mixed with it. Water vapor, like other gases, exerts pressure. Since the gas pressure is the result of the collision of the various gas molecules with the walls of the container, *the total pressure of the mixture of gases* (the collected gas and the water vapor) *is the sum of their partial pressures.* This is a statement of **Dalton's law of partial pressures.** The partial pressure is the pressure each gas would exert if it alone were present. The partial pressure of the water vapor, called *water vapor pressure,* depends only on the temperature of the water. Table 8 in the Appendix gives the pressure of water vapor at different water temperatures. *To determine the partial pressure of the dry gas* (unmixed with water vapor), *the vapor pressure of water at the given temperature is subtracted from the total pressure of the gas within the tube.*

Solution

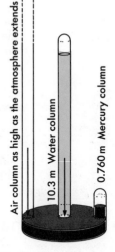

Fig. 9-14. The pressure of the atmosphere supports a column of water 13.6 times as high as the column of mercury it supports.

Fig. 9-15. Because the liquid levels inside and outside this eudiometer are the same, the sum of the partial pressures of the confined gas and water vapor equals atmospheric pressure. To determine the dry gas pressure, the water vapor pressure must be subtracted from the atmospheric pressure.

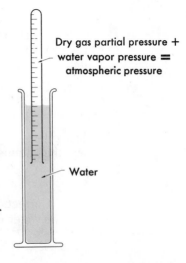

Dry gas partial pressure + water vapor pressure = atmospheric pressure

Water

Sample Problem

Oxygen is collected in a eudiometer by water displacement. The water level inside the tube is 27.2 mm higher than that outside. The temperature is 25.0° C. The barometric pressure is 741.0 mm. What is the partial pressure of the dry oxygen in the eudiometer?

Solution

To convert the difference in water levels to an equivalent difference in mercury levels, the difference in water levels is divided by 13.6.

27.2 mm ÷ 13.6 = 2.0 mm, the equivalent difference in mercury levels

Since the level inside the tube is higher than that outside, the difference in levels must be subtracted from the barometric pressure.

741.0 mm − 2.0 mm = 739.0 mm

To correct for the water vapor pressure, Table 8 in the Appendix indicates that the water vapor pressure at 25.0° C is 23.8 mm. This must be subtracted from the pressure corrected for difference in levels.

739.0 mm − 23.8 mm = 715.2 mm, the partial pressure of the dry oxygen

Sample Problem

A gas-measuring tube contains 38.4 ml of air, collected by water displacement at a temperature of 20.0° C. The water level inside the eudiometer is $14\overline{0}$ mm higher than that outside. The barometer reading is 740.0 mm. Calculate the volume of dry air at STP. (See Figure 9-16.)

Solution

Note that in this problem we were able to measure the barometric pressure to the nearest 0.1 mm, while we measured the water level difference to the nearest unit millimeter.

1. Correction for difference in levels:

$14\overline{0}$ mm ÷ 13.6 = 10.3 mm

Since the water level inside is higher than that outside, the air is under pressure less than atmospheric, and the correction is subtracted:

740.0 mm − 10.3 mm = 729.7 mm

2. Correction for water vapor pressure: Table 8 in the Appendix indicates that the water vapor pressure at 20.0° C is 17.5 mm. This correction is subtracted:

729.7 mm − 17.5 mm = 712.2 mm

3.   Correction for pressure and temperature changes:

$$V' = V \times p/p' \times T'/T$$
$$V'_{STP} = 38.4 \text{ ml} \times 712.2 \text{ mm}/760 \text{ mm} \times 273° \text{ K}/293° \text{ K}$$
$$V'_{STP} = 33.4 \text{ ml}$$

9.15   Behavior of real gases

   Boyle's and Charles' laws describe the behavior of the *ideal gas*. Real gases consist of molecules of finite size which do exert forces on each other. These forces affect the behavior of the molecules. But at temperatures near room temperature and at pressures of less than a few atmospheres, real gases conform closely to the behavior of an ideal gas. Under these conditions of temperature and pressure, the spaces separating the molecules are large enough so that the size of the molecules and forces between them have little effect.

   Boyle's law applies to real gases with a fairly high degree of accuracy. But it does not apply to gases under very high pressure. Under such pressures the molecules are close enough together to attract each other, and the gas is almost at its condensation point.

   Charles' law holds for real gases with considerable accuracy, except at low temperature. Under this condition, gas molecules move more slowly and molecular attraction exerts a greater influence. Thus, Charles' law does not apply at temperatures near the point at which a gas condenses into a liquid.

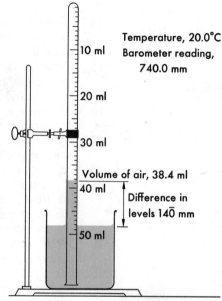

Temperature, 20.0°C
Barometer reading, 740.0 mm

Volume of air, 38.4 ml

Difference in levels 140 mm

Fig. 9-16.   A typical laboratory set-up for a gas-volume conversion problem.

QUESTIONS

1.   What are the three basic assumptions of the kinetic theory?

Group A

2.   Why does the pressure of a gas in a closed vessel remain constant indefinitely under constant conditions?
3.   (*a*) What is the relationship between the temperature of a gas and the kinetic energy of its molecules? (*b*) Do gas molecules all have exactly the same kinetic energy at the same temperature? Explain.
4.   (*a*) What is the condensation temperature of a gas? (*b*) What occurs at this temperature? (*c*) Explain in terms of the kinetic theory.
5.   What two types of attractive forces may exist between the molecules of molecular substances? Explain each.
6.   Why is the term "a cubic foot of air" unsatisfactory?
7.   (*a*) What is standard temperature? (*b*) What is standard pressure?
8.   State Boyle's law (*a*) in words; (*b*) mathematically.
9.   (*a*) What is the Celsius temperature corresponding to 0° K? (*b*) How does any Celsius temperature compare with the corresponding Kelvin temperature?
10.   State Charles' law (*a*) in words; (*b*) mathematically.
11.   If some hydrogen gas is enclosed in a eudiometer, what are three possibilities concerning its pressure compared with that of the air in the room?

Group B

12. In terms of the kinetic theory explain (*a*) expansion of a gas; (*b*) pressure of a gas; (*c*) low density of a gas; (*d*) diffusion of a gas.

13. If we assume that the molecules of a solid or a liquid are in contact with each other, but those of a gas are about 10 diameters apart, why is the volume occupied by a gas about 1000 times that of the solid or liquid?

14. Compare the strength of the attractive forces between the particles of nonpolar covalent molecular substances and polar covalent molecular substances as indicated by their condensation temperatures.

15. Compare the strength of the attractive forces between the particles of molecular substances and the particles of ionic, covalent network, and metallic substances, as indicated by their condensation temperatures.

16. At constant volume, how is the pressure exerted by a gas related to the Kelvin temperature?

17. At constant pressure, how is the volume occupied by a gas related to the Kelvin temperature?

18. At constant temperature, how is the volume occupied by a gas related to its pressure?

19. (*a*) What is meant by the vapor pressure of water? (*b*) What effect does it have on the observed pressure of a gas collected by water displacement? (*c*) How is the observed pressure corrected to obtain the partial pressure of the dry gas?

20. What corrections are applied to the barometer reading: (*a*) gas collected by displacement of mercury, level inside the eudiometer the same as that outside; (*b*) gas collected by displacement of mercury, level inside eudiometer higher than that outside; (*c*) gas collected by displacement of water, level inside eudiometer same as that outside; (*d*) gas collected by displacement of water, level inside eudiometer higher than that outside?

21. Boyle's and Charles' laws describe the behavior of the ideal gas. Under what conditions do they describe the behavior of real gases?

PROBLEMS

Use cancellation whenever possible.

Group A

1. Some oxygen occupies $25\overline{0}$ ml when its pressure is $72\overline{0}$ mm. How many milliliters will it occupy when its pressure is $75\overline{0}$ mm?

2. A gas collected when the pressure is $80\overline{0}$ mm has a volume of $38\overline{0}$ ml. What volume, in milliliters, will the gas occupy at standard pressure?

3. A gas has a volume of $10\overline{0}$ ml when the pressure is 735 mm. How many milliliters will the gas occupy at $70\overline{0}$ mm pressure?

4. A gas has a volume of 240.0 ml at 70.0 cm pressure. What pressure, in centimeters of mercury, is needed to reduce the volume to 60.0 ml?

5. Convert the following temperatures to Kelvin scale: (*a*) $2\overline{0}°$ C; (*b*) $85°$ C; (*c*) $-15°$ C; (*d*) $-19\overline{0}°$ C.

6. Given 90.0 ml of hydrogen gas collected when the temperature is $27°$ C: How many milliliters will the hydrogen occupy at $42°$ C?

7. A gas has a volume of 180 ml when its temperature is 43° C. What change in Celsius temperature reduces its volume to 135 ml?

8. A gas measures $50\overline{0}$ ml at a temperature of −23° C. What will be its volume in milliliters at 23° C?

9. A sample of gas occupies 50.0 liters at 27° C. What will be the volume of the gas in liters at standard temperature?

10. Convert to standard conditions: 2280 ml of gas measured at $3\overline{0}$° C and 808 mm pressure.

11. Convert to standard conditions: $100\overline{0}$ ml of gas at −23° C and $70\overline{0}$ mm pressure.

12. Convert to standard conditions: 1520 ml of gas at −33° C and $72\overline{0}$ mm pressure.

13. A gas collected when the temperature is 27° C and the pressure is 80.0 cm measures $50\overline{0}$ ml. Calculate the volume in milliliters at −3° C and 75.0 cm pressure.

14. Given $10\overline{0}$ ml of gas measured at 17° C and $38\overline{0}$ mm pressure: What volume, in milliliters, will the gas occupy at 307° C and $50\overline{0}$ mm pressure?

Use logarithms or a slide rule.

Group B

15. Hydrogen, 35.0 ml, was collected in a eudiometer by displacement of mercury. The mercury level inside the eudiometer was $4\overline{0}$ mm higher than that outside. The temperature was 25° C and the barometric pressure was 740.0 mm. Convert the volume of hydrogen to STP.

16. A gas collected by displacement of mercury in an inverted graduated cylinder occupies 60.0 ml. The mercury level inside the cylinder is 25 mm higher than that outside; temperature, $2\overline{0}$° C; barometer reading, 715 mm. Convert the volume of gas to STP.

17. Hydrogen is collected by water displacement in a eudiometer. Gas volume, 25.0 ml; liquid levels inside and outside the eudiometer are the same; temperature, 17° C; barometer reading, 720.0 mm. Convert the volume to that of dry gas at STP.

18. Some nitrogen is collected by displacement of water in a gas-measuring tube. Gas volume, 45.0 ml; liquid levels inside and outside the gas-measuring tube are the same; temperature, 23° C; barometer reading, 732.0 mm. Convert the volume to that of dry gas at STP.

19. A volume of 50.0 ml of oxygen is collected by water displacement. The water level inside the eudiometer is 65 mm higher than that outside. Temperature, 25° C; barometer reading, 727.0 mm. Convert the volume to that of dry gas at STP.

20. At 18° C and 745.0 mm barometric pressure, 12.0 ml of hydrogen is collected by water displacement. The liquid level inside the gas-measuring tube is 95 mm higher than that outside. Convert the volume to that of dry gas at STP.

21. The density of carbon dioxide at STP is 1.98 g/liter. What is the mass of exactly one liter of the gas, if the pressure increases by $4\overline{0}$ mm of mercury?

22. The density of oxygen at STP is 1.43 g/liter. Find the mass of exactly one liter of oxygen at a temperature of 39° C, if the pressure remains unchanged.

23. The density of nitrogen is 1.25 g/liter at STP. Find the mass of exactly one liter of nitrogen at a temperature of 27° C and 90.0 cm of mercury pressure.

24. A gas measures $40\overline{0}$ ml at a temperature of 25° C, under a pressure of $80\overline{0}$ mm. To what Celsius temperature must the gas be cooled, if its volume is to be reduced to $35\overline{0}$ ml when the pressure falls to $74\overline{0}$ mm?

Chapter 10

Molecular Composition of Gases

10.1 Law of combining volumes of gases

The law of definite composition, stated by Proust, served as a basis for Dalton's atomic theory. While Dalton investigated the masses of combining substances, his contemporary, the Swedish chemist Berzelius, was developing methods of chemical analysis. During this same period, the French chemist Joseph Louis Gay-Lussac (1778–1850) became interested in the combining volumes of gaseous substances.

Gay-Lussac investigated the reaction between hydrogen and oxygen. He observed that 2 liters of hydrogen reacted with 1 liter of oxygen and formed 2 liters of water vapor, when the volumes of reactants and products were measured at the same temperature and pressure.

2 liters hydrogen + 1 liter oxygen → 2 liters water vapor

We can write this equation in a more general form to show the simple relationship between the volumes of the reactants and the volume of the product.

2 volumes hydrogen + 1 volume oxygen → 2 volumes water vapor

Gay-Lussac also found that 1 liter of hydrogen combined with 1 liter of chlorine and formed 2 liters of hydrogen chloride gas.

1 volume hydrogen + 1 volume chlorine → 2 volumes hydrogen chloride

180

From a third experiment, Gay-Lussac discovered that 1 liter of hydrogen chloride combined with 1 liter of ammonia and produced a white powder. No residue (remainder) of either hydrogen chloride or ammonia was left over.

1 volume hydrogen chloride + 1 volume ammonia → ammonium chloride(s)

Another French chemist, Claude Louis Berthollet (1748–1822), recognized a similar relationship in experiments with hydrogen and nitrogen. He found that 3 liters of hydrogen always combined with 1 liter of nitrogen and formed 2 liters of ammonia.

3 volumes hydrogen + 1 volume nitrogen → 2 volumes ammonia

In 1808, Gay-Lussac summarized the results of these experiments and set forth the principle which bears his name. *Gay-Lussac's law of combining volumes of gases states: Under the same conditions of temperature and pressure, the volumes of reacting gases and of their gaseous products are expressed in ratios of small whole numbers.*

Proust had demonstrated the definite proportion of elements in a compound. Dalton's atomic theory had explained this regularity in the composition of substances. However, Dalton pictured an atom of one element combining with an atom of another element and forming a single particle of the product. He could not explain why *one* volume of hydrogen united with *one* volume of chlorine and formed *two* volumes of hydrogen chloride gas. To explain this volume relationship according to Dalton's theory would require that atoms be subdivided. Dalton had described the atoms of elements as "ultimate particles" and not capable of subdivision. Here was a disagreement between Dalton's theory and Gay-Lussac's observations. Was there an explanation to resolve the difficulty?

10.2 Avogadro's principle

Avogadro proposed a possible explanation for Gay-Lussac's simple ratios of combining gases in 1811. This explanation was to become one of the basic principles of chemistry, although its importance was not understood until after Avogadro's death.

Avogadro's explanation was that *equal volumes of all gases, under the same conditions of temperature and pressure, contain the same number of molecules.* Avogadro decided upon this believable explanation after studying the behavior of gases. He immediately saw its application to Gay-Lussac's volume ratios.

Avogadro further reasoned that the numbers of molecules of all gases, as reactants and products, *must be in the same ratio as their respective gas volumes.* Thus the composition of water vapor

French Embassy, Press and Information Division

Fig. 10-1. Joseph Louis Gay-Lussac, a French chemist, carried out a number of experiments which showed that chemical reactions between gases occur with simple volume ratios. The results of these experiments are summarized in the law of combining volumes of gases.

2 volumes hydrogen + 1 volume oxygen → 2 volumes water vapor

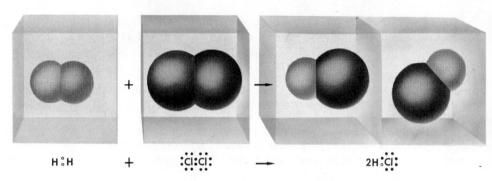

$$H \overset{\circ}{\circ} H \quad + \quad \overset{\cdot\cdot}{\underset{\cdot\cdot}{Cl}} \overset{\cdot\cdot}{\underset{\cdot\cdot}{Cl}} \quad \longrightarrow \quad 2H \overset{\cdot\cdot}{\underset{\cdot\cdot}{Cl}} \cdot$$

Fig. 10-2. As HCl is known to be the correct molecular formula for hydrogen chloride gas, the molecules of hydrogen and chlorine are proved to be diatomic.

could be represented as 2 molecules of hydrogen combining with 1 molecule of oxygen and producing 2 molecules of water vapor.

2 molecules hydrogen + 1 molecule oxygen → 2 molecules water vapor
(Equation 1)

Avogadro saw that the oxygen molecules must somehow be equally divided between the two molecules of water vapor formed. *Thus, each molecule of oxygen must consist of at least two identical parts (atoms).* Avogadro did not reject the atoms of Dalton. He merely stated that they did not exist as independent basic particles. Instead, he said, they were grouped into molecules which consisted of two identical parts. The simplest such molecule would, of course, contain two atoms.

Avogadro's reasoning applied equally well to the combining volumes in the composition of hydrogen chloride gas.

1 volume hydrogen + 1 volume chlorine → 2 volumes hydrogen chloride

1 molecule hydrogen + 1 molecule chlorine → 2 molecules hydrogen chloride
(Equation 2)

Each molecule of hydrogen must consist of two identical parts. One of these parts is found after the reaction in each of the two molecules of hydrogen chloride. Likewise, each chlorine molecule must consist of two identical parts. One of these parts is found in each of the two molecules of hydrogen chloride.

By Avogadro's explanation, the simplest molecules of hydrogen, oxygen, and chlorine each contain two atoms. The simplest possible molecule of water contains two atoms of hydrogen and one atom of oxygen. The simplest molecule of hydrogen chloride contains one atom of hydrogen and one atom of chlorine.

The correctness of Avogadro's explanation is so well recognized today that it has become known as *Avogadro's principle.* It is supported by the kinetic theory of gases. Chemists use it widely in determining molecular weights and molecular formulas.

10.3 Molecules of active gaseous elements are diatomic

By applying Avogadro's principle to Gay-Lussac's law of combining volumes of gases, we can find out the simplest possible makeup of elemental gases. But we also need to know whether the simplest structure of an elemental gas is the correct one. To do this, we must determine the molecular formula for the product of each composition reaction described so far. In Sections 7.12 and 7.13, we discussed empirical and molecular formulas. You will recall that an empirical formula can be determined from percentage composition data obtained by chemical analysis. The molecular formula can then be calculated if the molecular weight is known. We can determine the molecular weights of gases from their densities. We can find the molecular weights of solids and liquids which exist as molecules by measuring the freezing or boiling temperatures of their solutions.

Chemists have analyzed hydrogen chloride gas and, with the aid of atomic weights, have determined its empirical formula to be HCl. The molecular formula could be the same as the empirical formula or it could be any multiple of the empirical formula such as H_2Cl_2, H_3Cl_3, etc. To decide which formula is correct, chemists must experimentally determine the molecular weight. By measuring the density of hydrogen chloride, they have found its molecular weight to be 36.5. So the molecular formula must be HCl. The weight of one atom of hydrogen is 1.0 and the weight of one atom of chlorine is 35.5, giving a calculated molecular weight of 36.5. Any other multiple of the empirical formula gives a calculated molecular weight that is too high compared to the molecular weight determined experimentally. Thus, a molecule of hydrogen chloride contains *only one* atom of hydrogen and *only one* atom of chlorine.

Equation 2 (page 182) indicates that two molecules of hydrogen chloride (2HCl) are formed from one molecule of hydrogen and one molecule of chlorine. But 2HCl contains two atoms of hydrogen. These must have been provided by the one molecule of hydrogen reactant. Therefore this molecule must be a two-atomed, or *diatomic,* molecule, H_2. Similarly, 2HCl contains two atoms of chlorine which must have been provided by the one molecule of chlorine reactant. This chlorine molecule must therefore be a diatomic molecule, Cl_2. We may write the equation correctly as

$$H_2 + Cl_2 \rightarrow 2HCl$$

Similarly, oxygen molecules are proved to be diatomic because H_2O is the known molecular formula of water vapor.

$$2H_2 + O_2 \rightarrow 2H_2O$$

Let us examine one additional gaseous reaction. Berthollet found that *3 volumes* of hydrogen combined with *1 volume* of nitrogen and formed *2 volumes* of ammonia. By Avogadro's principle we conclude that *3 molecules* of hydrogen combine with *1 molecule* of nitrogen and form *2 molecules* of ammonia. Analysis of ammonia reveals that it is composed of 82% nitrogen and 18% hydrogen. The atomic weights of nitrogen and hydrogen are 14 and 1.0 respectively. The molecular weight of ammonia is known from gas density measurements to be 17.0. Therefore, the molecular formula is determined as follows:

$$N: \quad \frac{82 \text{ g N}}{14 \text{ g/mole}} = 5.9 \text{ moles N}$$

$$H: \quad \frac{18 \text{ g H}}{1.0 \text{ g/mole}} = 18 \text{ moles H}$$

$$N:H = \frac{5.9}{5.9} : \frac{18}{5.9} = 1.0 : 3.0$$

Empirical formula $= NH_3$
Molecular formula $= (NH_3)_x$
and $(NH_3 \text{ weight})_x = 17$
thus $\qquad x = 1$
Molecular formula $= NH_3$

Since each molecule of NH_3 contains one nitrogen atom, the two molecules of NH_3 produced must contain a total of two nitrogen atoms. Therefore, two nitrogen atoms must come from the one molecule of nitrogen reactant. Again the two molecules of NH_3 produced must contain a total of six hydrogen atoms. Therefore, these six atoms must come from the three molecules of hydrogen reactant. We may summarize these relations as follows:

3 volumes hydrogen $+$ 1 volume nitrogen $\rightarrow$ 2 volumes ammonia

3 molecules hydrogen $+$ 1 molecule nitrogen $\rightarrow$ 2 molecules ammonia

$$3H_2 \qquad + \qquad N_2 \qquad \rightarrow \qquad 2NH_3$$

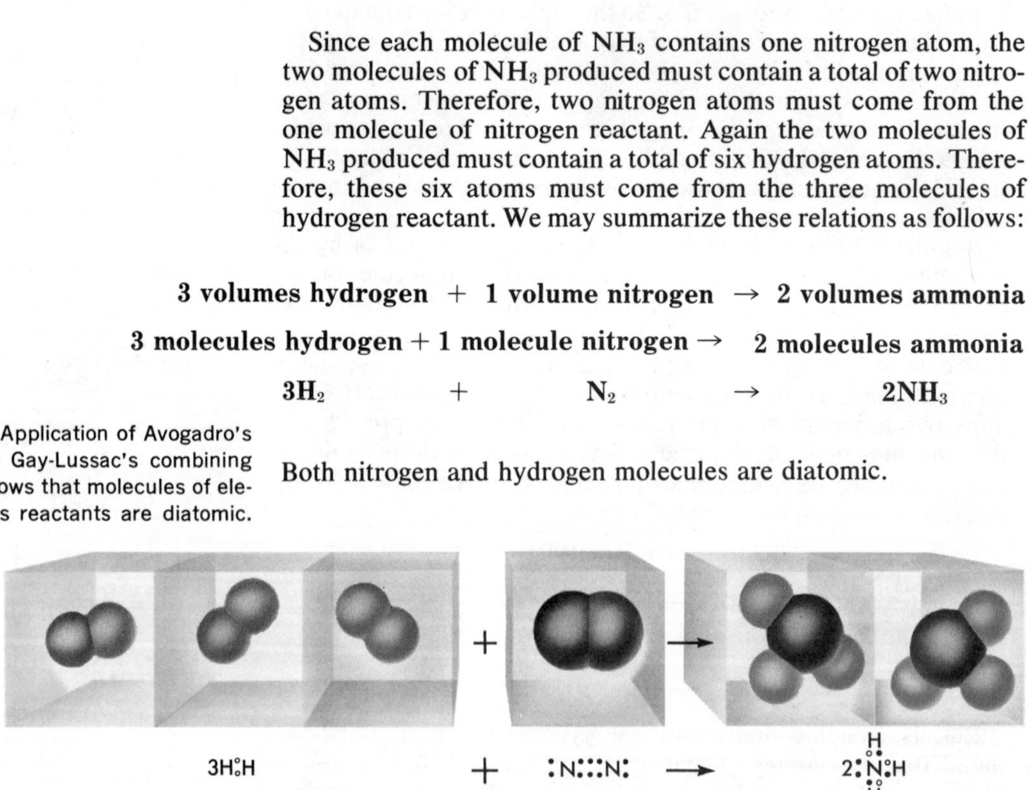

Fig. 10-3. Application of Avogadro's principle to Gay-Lussac's combining volumes shows that molecules of elementary gas reactants are diatomic.

Both nitrogen and hydrogen molecules are diatomic.

3H°H   +   :N::N: →   2 H°N°H (with H above and below)

10.4   Molecules of the noble gases are monatomic

By using the methods described in the preceding sections, we can show that the molecules of all *ordinary* gaseous elements contain *two* atoms. Other methods have shown that the *noble* gaseous elements, such as helium and neon, have only *one* atom to each molecule. None of these methods applies to solids, and may not even apply to the vapors of certain elements which are liquid or solid at room temperature. For example, at high temperatures the molecules of mercury and iodine vapors are known to consist of only one atom each.

10.5   Molar volume of a gas

Oxygen gas consists of diatomic molecules. One mole of O_2 contains the Avogadro number of molecules (6.02×10^{23}) and has a mass of 31.9988 g. One mole of H_2 contains the same number of molecules and has a mass of 2.016 g. Helium is a monatomic gas. One mole of **He** contains the Avogadro number of monatomic molecules and has a mass of 4.003 g. One-mole quantities of all molecular substances contain the Avogadro number of molecules.

*The volume occupied by one mole (or by one gram-molecular weight) of a gas at STP is called its **molar volume**.* Since moles of gases have equal numbers of molecules, Avogadro's principle tells us that they must occupy equal volumes under the same conditions of temperature and pressure. *The molar volumes of all gases are equal under the same conditions.* This has great practical significance in chemistry. Let us see how the molar volume of gases may be determined.

The densities of gases represent the masses of *equal numbers* of their respective molecules measured at STP. Since different gases have different densities, the mass of an *individual molecule* of one gas must be different from the mass of an individual molecule of a different gas.

The density of hydrogen is 0.0899 gram/liter, measured at STP. A mole of hydrogen, or 1 g-mol wt of hydrogen, has a mass of 2.016 g. (G-mol wt is an abbreviation for gram-molecular weight.) Since 0.0899 g of H_2 occupies 1 liter volume at STP, what volume will 2.016 g of H_2 occupy under the same conditions? The molar volume expressed in liters bears the same relation to 1 liter as 2.016 g bears to 0.0899 g. This proportionality may be expressed as follows:

Recall from Section 9.6 that STP means standard temperature and pressure.

$$\frac{\text{molar volume of } H_2}{1 \text{ liter}} = \frac{2.016 \text{ g}}{0.0899 \text{ g}}$$

Solving for molar volume:

$$\text{molar volume of } H_2 = \frac{2.016 \text{ g} \times 1 \text{ liter}}{0.0899 \text{ g}}$$

$$\text{molar volume of } H_2 = 22.4 \text{ liters}$$

The density of oxygen is 1.43 grams/liter. A mole of oxygen has a mass of 31.9988 g. Following our reasoning in the case of hydrogen, we may compute the molar volume of O_2.

$$\frac{\text{molar volume of } O_2}{1 \text{ liter}} = \frac{32.0 \text{ g}}{1.43 \text{ g}}$$

$$\text{molar volume of } O_2 = \frac{32.0 \text{ g} \times 1 \text{ liter}}{1.43 \text{ g}}$$

$$\text{molar volume of } O_2 = 22.4 \text{ liters}$$

Computations with other gases would yield similar results. However, it is clear from Avogadro's principle that this is unnecessary. We may generalize the proportion used above to read as follows:

$$\frac{1 \text{ molar volume}}{1 \text{ liter}} = \frac{\text{g-mol wt}}{\text{mass of 1 liter}}$$

Transposing terms,

$$\frac{\text{mass of 1 liter}}{1 \text{ liter}} = \frac{\text{g-mol wt}}{1 \text{ molar volume}}$$

But

$$\frac{\text{mass of 1 liter}}{1 \text{ liter}} = \text{density } (D) \text{ of a gas}$$

and

$$1 \text{ molar volume} = 22.4 \text{ liters}$$

So

$$D \text{ (of a gas)} = \frac{\text{g-mol wt}}{22.4 \text{ liters}}$$

and

$$\text{g-mol wt} = D \times 22.4 \text{ liters}$$

Thus, the *gram-molecular weight* (mass in grams of one mole) *of a gaseous substance is the mass, in grams, of 22.4 liters of the gas measured at STP.* In other words, it is simply the density of the gas multiplied by the constant, 22.4 liters. Similarly, the density of a gas can be found by dividing its gram-molecular weight by the constant, 22.4 liters.

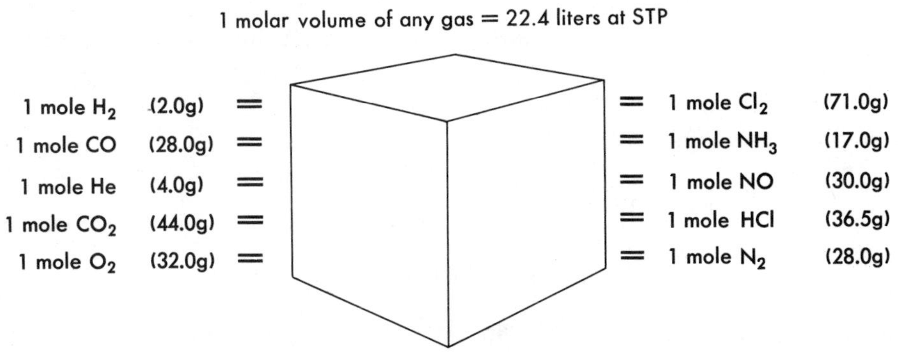

1 molar volume of any gas = 22.4 liters at STP

1 mole H_2 (2.0g) =

1 mole CO   (28.0g) =

1 mole He   (4.0g) =

1 mole CO_2 (44.0g) =

1 mole O_2 (32.0g) =

= 1 mole Cl_2 (71.0g)

= 1 mole NH_3 (17.0g)

= 1 mole NO   (30.0g)

= 1 mole HCl   (36.5g)

= 1 mole N_2 (28.0g)

If we know the molecular formula for a gas, we can determine its density directly from the formula. Let us use sulfur dioxide, SO_2, as an example. The mass of one mole of SO_2 is 64.1 g. Thus

Fig. 10-4. At STP, 22.4 liters of all gases have the same number of molecules, and the mass of each volume in grams is numerically equal to its molecular weight.

$$D_{SO_2} = \frac{64.1 \text{ grams}}{22.4 \text{ liters}} = 2.86 \text{ grams/liter at STP}$$

10.6   Molecular weight of gases determined experimentally

The molecular weights of gases, or of the vapors of substances which vaporize without decomposition, can be determined by the *molar-volume method.*

It is generally impractical in the laboratory to weigh directly a molar volume (22.4 liters) of a gas or vapor at STP. Indeed, some substances, otherwise suitable for this method, are liquids or even solids under STP conditions. Fortunately, we need not weigh a full molar volume of a gas or vapor to find its molecular weight. Any quantity of a gas or vapor which can be weighed to determine its mass precisely may be used. Its volume may be measured under any suitable conditions of temperature and pressure. This volume is then converted to STP and the mass of 22.4 liters is calculated. The Sample Problem shows how this experimental method is used to determine molecular weight.

Sample Problem

A gas sample, mass 0.350 g, is collected by water displacement at $20°$ C and $75\overline{0}$ mm pressure. Its volume is $15\overline{0}$ ml. What is its molecular weight?

Solution

The partial pressure of the gas is the difference between the indicated pressure and the partial pressure due to water vapor, $75\overline{0}$ mm $-$ 17.5 mm, or $(75\overline{0} - 17.5)$ mm. As the pressure is raised the volume will decrease in the ratio

$\dfrac{(75\overline{0} - 17.5)\ \text{mm}}{760\ \text{mm}}$. As the temperature is lowered the volume will decrease in

the ratio $\dfrac{273°\ \text{K}}{293°\ \text{K}}$.

Therefore, the volume at STP is:

$$V_{\text{STP}} = 15\overline{0}\ \text{ml} \times \dfrac{(75\overline{0} - 17.5)\ \text{mm}}{760\ \text{mm}} \times \dfrac{273°\ \text{K}}{293°\ \text{K}}$$

$$V_{\text{STP}} = 135\ \text{ml, or } 0.135\ \text{liter}$$

The quantity of 0.350 g per 0.135 liter at STP is an expression of the density of the gas and may be substituted for it. Thus

$$\textbf{g-mol wt} = D \times 22.4\ \textbf{liters}$$

$$\textbf{g-mol wt} = \dfrac{\textbf{0.350 gram}}{\textbf{0.135 liter}} \times 22.4\ \textbf{liters}$$

$$\textbf{g-mol wt} = \textbf{58.1 g}$$

$$\textbf{mol wt} = \textbf{58.1}$$

We can also calculate the volume occupied by a known mass of a gas under any conditions of temperature and pressure, if we know the molecular formula of the gas. The molecular formula provides the mass of 1 mole of the gas. We know that one mole of any gas occupies the molar volume, 22.4 liters, at STP. By proportion, we can determine the volume of the known mass of the gas at STP. Then by applying the gas laws, we can compute the volume at any temperature and pressure. See the following Sample Problem.

Sample Problem

What is the volume of $1\overline{0}$ g of carbon dioxide gas, CO_2, at $2\overline{0}°$ C and 740 mm?

Solution

The formula CO_2 indicates that the molecular weight is 44. Now 44 g (1 mole) of CO_2 occupies 22.4 liters (1 molar volume) at STP. The volume occupied by $1\overline{0}$ g will be represented as X.

$$\dfrac{\textbf{44 g}}{\textbf{22.4 liters}} = \dfrac{1\overline{0}\ \textbf{g}}{\textbf{X}}$$

Solving for X:

$$\textbf{X} = 1\overline{0}\ \textbf{g} \times \dfrac{\textbf{22.4 liters}}{\textbf{44 g}} = \textbf{5.1 liters, at STP}$$

As the pressure decreases, the volume increases in the ratio $\dfrac{760\ \text{mm}}{740\ \text{mm}}$. As the temperature rises, the volume increases in the ratio $\frac{293°\,K}{273°\,K}$. Thus the volume at $2\bar{0}°$ C and 740 mm is

$$V_{2\bar{0}°\,C,\,740\,mm} = \textbf{5.1 liters} \times \frac{\textbf{760 mm}}{\textbf{740 mm}} \times \frac{\textbf{293° K}}{\textbf{273° K}}$$

$$V_{2\bar{0}°\,C,\,740\,mm} = \textbf{5.6 liters}$$

10.7   Chemical problems involving gases

As shown in Chapter 8, the equation for a chemical reaction expresses quantities of reactants and products in *moles*. The numerical coefficients in the balanced equation tell us the number of moles of each substance.

Frequently, a reactant or a product of a reaction is a gas. Indeed in certain reactions, *all* reactants and products may be gaseous. Avogadro's principle indicates that single moles of all such gases have the same volume under the same conditions of temperature and pressure. At STP a mole of any gas occupies 1 molar volume, 22.4 liters. *Consequently, the mole relationships in the equation are also the volume relationships of gases.*

Remember that the behavior of real gases is not described exactly by the ideal gas laws. Calculations which involve the molar volume as 22.4 liters can give only approximately correct answers.

There are two general types of problems which involve chemical equations and the volumes of gases.

1.   Gas volume–gas volume problems. In these problems, a certain *volume of a gas* reactant or product is given. The *volume of another gas* reactant or product is required.

2.   Mass–gas volume problems. Here a certain *mass* of a reactant or product is given and the *volume of a gas* reactant or product is required, or vice versa.

10.8   Gas volume–gas volume problems

The *volume* of one *gaseous substance* is given in gas volume–gas volume problems. In this type of problem, we are asked to determine the *volume* of another *gaseous substance* involved in the chemical action. We recall that single moles of all gases at the same temperature and pressure occupy the same volume. Thus, in a balanced equation, the volumes of gases are proportional to the number of moles shown by the numerical coefficients. To illustrate:

$$\textbf{2CO(g)} \quad + \quad \textbf{O}_2\textbf{(g)} \quad \rightarrow \quad \textbf{2CO}_2\textbf{(g)}$$

2 moles	1 mole	2 moles
2 volumes	1 volume	2 volumes

The balanced equation signifies that 2 moles of CO reacts with 1 mole of O_2 and produces 2 moles of CO_2. From Avogadro's principle, 2 volumes (liters, milliliters, etc.) of carbon monoxide reacts with 1 volume (liter, milliliter, etc.) of oxygen and produces 2 volumes (liters, milliliters, etc.) of carbon dioxide. (In this relationship we assume, of course, that the temperature and pressure of all three gases are the same.) Thus, 10 liters of CO would require 5 liters of O_2 for complete combustion and would produce 10 liters of CO_2. The volume relationship is 2:1:2 under the same conditions of temperature and pressure.

Since the above reaction is exothermic, the gas that is produced expands because of the rise in temperature. The volume relations apply only after the temperature of the gaseous product has been lowered to that of the reactants at the beginning of the reaction.

We must know the conditions of temperature and pressure in order to determine which substances exist as gases. Whenever the conditions are not stated, they are assumed to be standard. Let us consider the complete combustion of methane.

$$CH_4(g) \quad + \quad 2O_2(g) \quad \rightarrow \quad CO_2(g) \quad + 2H_2O(l)$$

| 1 mole | 2 moles | 1 mole | 2 moles |
| 1 volume | 2 volumes | 1 volume | |

The formula for water is followed by the symbol (1) because water is a liquid at temperatures under $100°$ C. Let us assume that the volumes of the gaseous reactants are measured under ordinary room conditions. If so, water cannot be included in the volume ratio. But the reactants, methane and oxygen, and the product, carbon dioxide, are gases. Their volume relationship is seen to be 1:2:1.

Gas volume–gas volume problems are very simple to solve. The problem set-up is similar to that of mass–mass problems (see Section 8.11). However, it is not necessary to use atomic weights to convert moles of the specified gases to their respective masses as represented in the equation. Once set up, most gas volume-gas volume problems can be solved by inspection. The following example shows how these problems are commonly solved.

Suppose we wish to know the volume of hydrogen which combines with 4.0 liters of nitrogen and forms ammonia gas. We set up the problem this way:

$$\begin{array}{ccc} X & 4.0 \text{ liters} & \\ 3H_2(g) & + \quad N_2(g) & \rightarrow 2NH_3(g) \\ 3 \text{ moles} & 1 \text{ mole} & \end{array}$$

The equation shows that H_2 and N_2 combine in the ratio of 3 moles to 1 mole. From Avogadro's principle, these gases must combine in the ratio of 3 volumes to 1 volume. Thus, 4.0 liters of nitrogen requires 12 liters of hydrogen for complete reaction. Since 2 moles of NH_3 is shown, 8.0 liters of this gas is produced.

Mathematically, the problem may be set up:

$$X = 4.0 \text{ liters } N_2 \times \frac{3 \text{ moles } H_2}{1 \text{ mole } N_2}$$

Solving,

$$X = 12 \text{ liters } H_2$$

See the following Sample Problem.

Sample Problem

Assuming air to be 21.0% oxygen by volume: (a) How many liters of air must enter a carburetor to complete the combustion of 60.0 liters of octane vapor? (b) How many liters of carbon dioxide are formed? (All gases are measured at the same temperature and pressure.)

Solution

Octane has the formula C_8H_{18}. Its complete oxidation produces carbon dioxide and water. Note that it is only the *oxygen* of the air which combines with octane. Therefore we must determine first the volume of oxygen required. Let X be this volume, and Y the volume of CO_2 formed. The problem set-up is:

60.0 liters   X   Y

$$2C_8H_{18}(g) + 25O_2(g) \rightarrow 16CO_2(g) + 18H_2O(l)$$

2 moles   25 moles   16 moles

(a) Solving:

$$X = 60.0 \text{ liters } C_8H_{18} \times \frac{25 \text{ moles } O_2}{2 \text{ moles } C_8H_{18}}$$

$$X = 75\bar{0} \text{ liters } O_2$$

Now $75\bar{0}$ liters of O_2 is 21.0% of the air required. So

$$\text{air required} = 75\bar{0} \text{ liters} \times \frac{100\%}{21.0\%} = 3570 \text{ liters}$$

(b) Solving as before:

$$Y = 60.0 \text{ liters } C_8H_{18} \times \frac{16 \text{ moles } CO_2}{2 \text{ moles } C_8H_{18}}$$

$$Y = 48\bar{0} \text{ liters } CO_2$$

Reminder: The volumes of air and CO_2 computed are those which would be measured at the temperature and pressure of the octane vapor prior to its combustion. Under such conditions, the water formed as water vapor at the reaction temperature would have condensed. Thus, it could not enter the problem as a gas.

10.9 Mass–gas volume problems

This type of problem involves the relation between the *volume of gas* and the *mass* of another substance in a reaction. In some cases, the mass of the substance is given and the volume of the gas is required. In others, the volume of the gas is given and the mass of the substance is required.

As an illustration, let us determine how many grams of calcium carbonate, $CaCO_3$, must be decomposed to produce 4.00 liters of carbon dioxide, CO_2, at STP. The problem set-up is:

$$\begin{array}{ccc} X & & 4.00 \text{ liters} \\ CaCO_3(s) \rightarrow CaO(s) + & & CO_2(g) \\ 1 \text{ mole} & & 1 \text{ mole} \end{array}$$

$$1 \text{ mole } CaCO_3 = 10\bar{0} \text{ g}$$
$$1 \text{ mole } CO_2 = 22.4 \text{ liters}$$

Observe that the molar volume (22.4 liters) is used in place of the mass/mole (44 g/mole) of CO_2. This is possible since each mole of gas occupies 22.4 liters at STP (*and only at STP*). The problem may now be solved by the method used for mass–mass problems.

The volume of CO_2 multiplied by the fraction $\dfrac{\text{mole}}{22.4 \text{ liters}}$ will indicate the number of moles of CO_2 given (operation 1):

$$4.00 \text{ liters } CO_2 \times \frac{\text{mole}}{22.4 \text{ liters}} = \text{number of moles } CO_2$$

Then, after operations 2, 3, and 4 of the solution of a mass–mass problem,

$$X = 4.00 \text{ liters } CO_2 \times \frac{\text{mole}}{22.4 \text{ liters}} \times \frac{1 \text{ mole } CaCO_3}{1 \text{ mole } CO_2} \times \frac{10\bar{0} \text{ g}}{\text{mole}} = 17.9 \text{ g } CaCO_3$$

10.10 Gases not measured at STP

Gases are seldom measured under standard conditions of temperature and pressure. But *only* gas volumes under standard conditions can be placed in a proportion with the molar volume of 22.4 liters. Therefore, *gas reactants measured under conditions other than STP must first be corrected to STP before proceeding with mass–gas volume calculations.* These corrections are performed in agreement with the gas laws in Chapter 9.

For example, suppose that the gas in question is a *product* whose volume is to be measured under conditions other than STP. *We first must calculate the volume at STP from the chemical equation.* We then convert this volume at STP to the required conditions of temperature and pressure by proper application of the gas laws.

Gas volume–gas volume calculations do not require STP corrections since volumes of gases are related to moles rather than to molar volumes. Thus, in gas volume–gas volume problems, it is necessary only that all measurements of gas volumes be made at the same temperature and pressure.

10.11   Gases collected by water displacement

The volume of any gas in a mass–gas volume problem is calculated under STP conditions and must be corrected for any other specified conditions of temperature and pressure. If this gas is collected by water displacement, the vapor pressure of the water must be taken into account. The partial pressure of the gas is the difference between the measured pressure and the partial pressure exerted by water vapor at the specified temperature.

Let us suppose that a gaseous product is collected by water displacement. The volume of this product is to be determined at 29° C and 752 mm pressure by a mass–gas volume calculation. The volume at STP is computed from an appropriate chemical equation. The vapor pressure of water at 29° C is found in the tables to be $3\bar{0}$ mm. Thus

$$V_{29°,\ 752\ \text{mm}} = V_{\text{STP}} \times \frac{760\ \text{mm}}{(752 - 3\bar{0})\ \text{mm}} \times \frac{302°\ \text{K}}{273°\ \text{K}}$$

See the Sample Problem which follows.

Sample Problem

What volume of oxygen, collected by water displacement at $2\bar{0}°$ C and 750.0 mm pressure, can be obtained by the decomposition of 175 g of potassium chlorate?

Solution

A mass is given and a gas volume is required. The volume of the gas at STP may first be found from the chemical equation. The problem set-up is as follows:

$$
\begin{array}{cc}
\textbf{175 g} & \textbf{X} \\
\textbf{2KClO}_3\textbf{(s)} \rightarrow \textbf{2KCl(s)} + & \textbf{3O}_2\textbf{(g)} \\
\textbf{2 moles} & \textbf{3 moles}
\end{array}
$$

$$\textbf{1 mole KClO}_3 = \textbf{122.6 g}$$
$$\textbf{1 mole O}_2 = \textbf{22.4 liters}$$

Solution by moles

$$X = 175 \text{ g } KClO_3 \times \frac{\text{mole}}{122.6 \text{ g}} \times \frac{3 \text{ moles } O_2}{2 \text{ moles } KClO_3} \times \frac{22.4 \text{ liters}}{\text{mole}}$$
$$= 48.0 \text{ liters } O_2 \text{ at STP}$$

The vapor pressure of water at $2\bar{0}°$ C is found to be 17.5 mm. As the pressure is decreased to 750.0 mm, the volume will increase in the ratio $\dfrac{760 \text{ mm}}{750.0 \text{ mm} - 17.5 \text{ mm}}$. As the temperature is increased to $2\bar{0}°$ C, the volume will increase in the ratio $\dfrac{293° \text{ K}}{273° \text{ K}}$. Thus the volume of O_2 at $2\bar{0}°$ C and 750.0 mm pressure is:

$$V_{2\bar{0}° \text{ C}, \, 750.0 \text{ mm}} = 48.0 \text{ liters} \times \frac{760 \text{ mm}}{750.0 - 17.5 \text{ mm}} \times \frac{293° \text{ K}}{273° \text{ K}}$$

$$V_{2\bar{0}° \text{ C}, \, 750.0 \text{ mm}} = 53.5 \text{ liters}$$

10.12   The gas constant

From Avogadro's principle, we know that the volume of a mole is the same for all gases under the same conditions of temperature and pressure. The volume of any gas is directly proportional to the number of moles (n) of the gas, if pressure and temperature are constant. The $\propto$ means "varies directly as."

$$V \propto n \quad (p \text{ and } T \text{ constant})$$

From Boyle's law we know that the volume of a gas is inversely proportional to the pressure applied to it, if the quantity of gas (number of moles of gas) and temperature are constant. The inverse relationship is shown by placing the pressure in the denominator.

$$V \propto \frac{1}{p} \quad (n \text{ and } T \text{ constant})$$

Similarly, from Charles' law, we know that the volume of a gas is directly proportional to the Kelvin temperature, if the pressure and quantity of gas remain constant.

$$V \propto T \quad (p \text{ and } n \text{ constant})$$

Thus,

$$V \propto n \times \frac{1}{p} \times T$$

By insertion of a proportionality constant R of suitable dimensions, this proportion may be restated as an equation.

$$V = nR \left(\frac{1}{p}\right) T$$

or

$$pV = nRT$$

R is the proportionality constant known as the *gas constant*. When the quantity of gas is expressed in moles, R has the same value for all gases. Conventionally the gas volume V is expressed in *liters*, the quantity n in *moles*, the temperature T in *degrees Kelvin*, and the pressure p in *atmospheres* (abbreviated atm). Of course, the standard pressure of 760 mm is *1 atmosphere*. So

$$\frac{\text{pressure in mm Hg}}{760 \text{ mm Hg/atm}} = \text{pressure in atm}$$

Let us determine the dimensional units of the gas constant R from the ideal gas equation.

$$pV = nRT$$

Then,

$$R = \frac{pV}{nT}$$

Using the conventional units stated,

$$R = \frac{\text{atm} \times \text{liters}}{\text{moles} \times {}^{\circ}\text{K}}$$

Thus, R must have the dimensions *liter·atm per mole·°K*.

Careful measurements of the density of oxygen at low pressures yield the molar volume of 22.414 liters. This is accepted as the accurate molar volume of an ideal gas. It represents the volume occupied by exactly 1 mole of ideal gas under conditions of exactly 1 atm and 273.15° K. Substituting in the ideal gas equation and solving the expression for R,

$$R = \frac{pV}{nT} = \frac{1 \text{ atm} \times 22.414 \text{ liters}}{1 \text{ mole} \times 273.15^{\circ} \text{ K}}$$

$$R = 0.082057 \text{ liter·atm/mole·}^{\circ}\text{K}$$

Suppose the properties of an unknown gas are examined at a temperature of 28° C and 74$\overline{0}$ mm pressure. It is found that the mass of 1 liter is 4.62 g under these conditions. We wish to determine the molecular weight of the gas. This calculation can be made directly by using the gas constant R, 0.0821 liter·atm per mole·°K, and the ideal-gas equation, $pV = nRT$. The use of R in the ideal-gas equation enables moles per liter of gas to be computed.

$$T = 273^{\circ} + 28^{\circ} = 301^{\circ} \text{ K}$$

$$V = 1 \text{ liter}$$

$$p = \frac{74\overline{0} \text{ mm}}{760 \text{ mm/atm}} = 0.974 \text{ atm}$$

$$pV = nRT$$

Solving for *n* moles:

$$n = \frac{pV}{RT}$$

$$n = \frac{0.974 \text{ atm} \times 1 \text{ liter}}{\dfrac{0.0821 \text{ liter} \cdot \text{atm}}{\text{mole} \cdot {}^\circ\text{K}} \times 301^\circ \text{ K}}$$

$$n = \frac{0.974 \text{ mole}}{0.0821 \times 301} = 0.0394 \text{ mole}$$

This calculation shows that the experimental mass of 1 liter of the gas, 4.62 g, is 0.0394 mole.

Since 0.0394 mole has a mass of 4.62 g, the mass of 1 mole is

$$1 \text{ mole} \times \frac{4.62 \text{ g}}{0.0394 \text{ mole}} = 117 \text{ g}$$

Therefore, the molecular weight of the gas is 117.

The ideal-gas equation simplifies the solution of mass–gas volume problems under non-standard conditions. The number of moles of gas required is calculated by the mole method. This result may then be substituted in the ideal-gas equation, together with the pressure and temperature conditions. The gas volume is then calculated directly. On the other hand, suppose we know the volume of a gas under non-standard temperature and pressure conditions. We can then use the ideal-gas equation to calculate the *number of moles* of the gas. This quantity may then be used to complete the solution of a gas volume–mass problem by the mole method.

10.13   Real gases and the ideal gas

Precise experiments involving molar volumes of gases show that all gases vary slightly from the ideal-gas characteristics assigned to them by the gas laws and Avogadro's principle. This does not mean that the laws are only approximately true. Rather, it indicates that real gases do not behave as ideal gases over wide ranges of temperature and pressure. They act most like ideal gases at low pressures and high temperatures.

Two factors contribute to the difference between the behavior of real gases and our equations for an ideal gas:

1. Compression of a gas is *limited* by the fact that the molecules themselves occupy space, even though the volume of the molecules is extremely small.

2. Compression of a gas is *aided* by the fact that van der Waals (attractive) forces, however weak, do exist between the molecules.

Only when these two opposing tendencies within the gas exactly balance, will it respond as an ideal gas.

When expressed to five significant figures, the molar volume of an ideal gas is 22.414 liters. Gases such as ammonia and chlorine, which at ordinary temperatures are not far above their condensation points, show rather marked deviations from 22.4 liters as the molar volume. The molar volumes of ammonia and chlorine, measured under normal conditions, are 22.09 liters and 22.06 liters respectively. Gases such as oxygen and nitrogen, which have low condensation points, behave more nearly as ideal gases under ordinary conditions. The molar volumes of oxygen and nitrogen are 22.394 liters and 22.404 liters respectively. For most gases, deviations from ideal-gas performance through ordinary ranges of temperature and pressure do not exceed two percent.

PROBLEMS

In the absence of stated conditions of temperature and pressure, they are assumed to be STP.

Group A

1. Calculate the density of hydrogen chloride gas, HCl, at STP to three significant figures.
2. What is the density of hydrogen sulfide, H_2S, at STP, calculated to three significant figures?
3. What is the mass in grams of 1.00 liter of methane gas, CH_4, at STP?
4. The mass of 1.00 liter of gas at STP is 2.75 g. What is its molecular weight?
5. The mass of 1.00 liter of nitrogen at STP is 1.25 g. (*a*) Calculate the molecular weight of nitrogen from these data. (*b*) From this calculated molecular weight, determine the number of atoms in a molecule of nitrogen.
6. Hydrogen is the gas of lowest density. What is the mass in grams of $30\overline{0}$ ml of hydrogen at STP?
7. At standard conditions, 225 ml of a gas has a mass of 0.6428 g. Calculate the molecular weight of the gas from these data.
8. What is the mass in grams of $75\overline{0}$ ml of CO_2 at STP?
9. If the mass of $25\overline{0}$ ml of methane is 0.179 g at STP, what is its molecular weight?
10. The compounds HBr, PH_3, and N_2O are all gaseous at room temperature. (*a*) Calculate their molecular weights to 3 significant figures. (*b*) What is the density of each?
11. Find the mass in grams of 4.00 liters of: N_2, NH_3, and C_2H_2.
12. How many liters of hydrogen and of nitrogen are required to produce $2\overline{0}$ liters of ammonia gas?
13. Carbon monoxide burns in oxygen and forms carbon dioxide. (*a*) How many liters of carbon dioxide are produced when 15 liters of carbon monoxide burns? (*b*) How many liters of oxygen are required?
14. Acetylene gas, C_2H_2, burns in oxygen and forms carbon dioxide and water vapor. (*a*) How many liters of oxygen are needed to burn 25.0 liters of acetylene? (*b*) How many liters of carbon dioxide are formed?
15. Ethane gas, C_2H_6, burns in air and produces carbon dioxide and water vapor. (*a*) How many liters of carbon dioxide are formed when 12 liters of ethane is burned? How many moles of water are formed?

16. How many liters of air are required to furnish the oxygen to complete the reaction in Problem 15? (Assume the air to be 21% oxygen by volume.)

17. If $40\bar{0}$ ml of hydrogen and $40\bar{0}$ ml of oxygen are mixed and ignited, (a) what volume of oxygen remains uncombined? (b) What volume of water vapor is formed if all gases are measured at $15\bar{0}°$ C?

18. How many grams of sodium are needed to release 4.0 liters of hydrogen from water?

19. (a) How many liters of hydrogen are required to convert 25.0 g of hot copper(II) oxide to metallic copper? (b) How many moles of water are formed?

20. When $13\bar{0}$ g of zinc reacts with $15\bar{0}$ g of HCl, how many liters of hydrogen are formed? (Note: first determine which reactant is in excess.)

21. (a) How many liters of oxygen can be produced by the decomposition of 90.0 g of water? (b) How many liters of hydrogen are produced in the same reaction?

22. (a) How many grams of copper will be produced when hydrogen is passed over 39.75 g of hot copper(II) oxide? (b) How many liters of hydrogen are required?

23. How many liters of hydrogen will be produced by the action of 25 g of calcium metal and an excess of hydrochloric acid? Calcium chloride is the other product of the reaction.

Group B

24. A compound contains: nitrogen, 30.51%; oxygen, 69.49%. The density of the gas is 4.085 grams/liter. Find: (a) its empirical formula; (b) its molecular weight; (c) its molecular formula.

25. It is found that 1.00 liter of a certain gas, collected at a pressure of $72\bar{0}$ mm of mercury and a temperature of 27° C, has a mass of 1.30 g. Calculate its molecular weight.

26. It is found that 1.00 liter of nitrogen combines with 1.00 liter of oxygen in an electric arc and forms 2.00 liters of a gas. By analysis, this gas contains 46.7% nitrogen and 53.3% oxygen. Its density is determined to be 1.34 grams/liter. (a) Find the empirical formula of the product. (b) What is the molecular formula? (c) Using the information of this problem and the arguments of Avogadro, determine the number of atoms per molecule of nitrogen and oxygen.

27. How many liters will 2.0 g of CS_2 vapor occupy at 756 mm pressure and $5\bar{0}°$ C?

28. A 1.00-liter flask filled with a gas at STP is attached to a high vacuum pump and evacuated until the pressure is only 1.00×10^{-4} mm. Assuming no temperature change, how many molecules remain in the flask?

29. A sample of a vapor having a mass of 0.865 g measures 174 ml at $10\bar{0}°$ C and 745 mm. What is the molecular weight?

30. (a) How many liters of sulfur dioxide gas at STP are formed when $5\bar{0}$ g of sulfur burns? (b) What volume will this gas occupy at 25° C and 745 mm pressure?

31. Hydrogen ($40\bar{0}$ ml) measured at 20° C and $74\bar{0}$ mm pressure is to be prepared by reacting magnesium with hydrochloric acid. What mass in grams of magnesium is required?

32. How many liters of hydrogen, collected by water displacement at 25° C and 755.0 mm pressure, can be obtained from 6.0 g of magnesium and an excess of sulfuric acid?

33. What is the mass in grams of 12.0 liters of oxygen collected by water displacement at 23° C and 745.0 mm pressure?

34. A reaction between 5.0 g of aluminum and an excess of dilute sulfuric acid is used as a source of hydrogen gas. What volume of hydrogen is collected by water dis-

placement at $2\overline{0}°$ C and 765 mm pressure? Aluminum sulfate is the other product of the reaction.

35. How many liters of dry air, measured at 29° C and 744 mm pressure, are required to complete the combustion of 1.00 mole of carbon disulfide, CS_2, to carbon dioxide, CO_2, and sulfur dioxide, SO_2?

36. What is the volume of the mixture of CO_2 and SO_2 produced in the reaction of Problem 35, if measured under the same conditions as the air used in the reaction?

37. Chlorine gas may be generated in the laboratory by a reaction between manganese dioxide and hydrogen chloride. The equation is:

$$MnO_2(s) + 4HCl(aq) \rightarrow MnCl_2(aq) + 2H_2O(l) + Cl_2(g)$$

(a) How many grams of MnO_2 are required to produce 1.00 liter of Cl_2 gas at STP? (b) How many grams of HCl are required?

38. In Problem 37, the HCl is available as a water solution which is 37.4% hydrogen chloride by mass. The solution has a density of 1.189 g/ml. What volume of HCl solution (hydrochloric acid) must be supplied to the reaction?

39. How many grams of charcoal, 90.0% carbon, must be burned to produce $10\overline{0}$ liters of CO_2 measured at $2\overline{0}°$ C and 747 mm pressure?

40. How many grams of chlorine gas are contained in a 5.00-liter flask at $2\overline{0}°$ C and $60\overline{0}$ mm pressure?

41. What temperature must be maintained to insure that a 2.50-liter flask containing 0.100 mole of a certain gas will show a continuous pressure of 745 mm?

42. From the ideal-gas equation, $pV = nRT$, and the density of a gas defined as the mass per unit volume, $D = m/V$, prove that the density of a gas at STP is directly proportional to its molecular weight.

43. At 12.0° C and $74\overline{0}$ mm, 1.07 liters of a gas has a mass of 1.98 g. Calculate the molecular weight of the gas from the ideal-gas equation.

Chapter 11

Liquids — Solids — Water

LIQUIDS

11.1 Properties of liquids

All liquids have several easily observed properties in common.

1. Definite volume. A liquid occupies a definite volume; it does not expand and completely fill its container as does a gas. A liquid may have one free surface; its other surfaces must be supported by the container walls.

2. Fluidity. A liquid can be made to flow or can be poured from one container to another. A liquid takes the shape of its container.

3. Noncompressibility. If water at 20° C is subjected to a pressure of 1000 atmospheres, its volume decreases by only 4%. This behavior of water is typical of all liquids. Even under very high pressure, liquids are compressed only slightly.

4. Diffusion. Suppose we slowly pour some ethanol (ethyl alcohol) down the side of a graduated cylinder already half full of water. If we pour carefully, the alcohol can be made to float on the water. At first, a fairly definite boundary exists between the liquids. However, if we let this system stand, the boundary becomes less and less distinct. Some of the water diffuses into the alcohol while at the same time some of the alcohol diffuses into the water. If the cylinder stands undisturbed for some time, the alcohol and water completely mix.

5. Evaporation. If a liquid is left in an open container, it may gradually disappear. Spontaneously, many liquids slowly change into vapors at room temperature.

Fig. 11-1. The attractive forces between the particles of a liquid are strong enough so that a liquid has a definite volume, but are weak enough so that the particles can move with respect to one another.

200

11.2 Kinetic-theory description of a liquid

Liquids are denser than gases. This fact indicates that the particles of liquids are much closer together than those of gases. Further, we know that liquids are practically noncompressible. Therefore, the particles of a liquid must be almost as close together as it is possible for them to be. A liquid has a definite volume and can have one free surface. This observation shows that a body of liquid holds together. Consequently, the attractive forces among the particles of a liquid must be much stronger than those among the particles of a gas.

Liquids are fluid and take the shape of their containers. These observations show that single particles or groups of particles in a liquid move with respect to one another. The kinetic energy of the liquid particles must be large enough to make this motion possible despite the attractive forces among them.

Substances composed of low-molecular-weight nonpolar molecules are liquids only at temperatures below room temperature. Higher-molecular-weight nonpolar molecular substances may be liquids at room temperature. Hence, the forces of attraction among nonpolar molecules are the relatively weak dispersion interaction forces.

Substances composed of polar molecules may be liquids at room temperature. Thus, the attractive forces among polar molecules are the stronger combination of dispersion interaction and dipole-dipole attraction forces.

Most metals, ionic compounds, and covalent network substances are liquids only at temperatures well above room temperature. Therefore, we believe that the attractive forces among the particles of these substances are much stronger than van der Waals forces. Table 11-1 gives the range of temperatures over which examples of each of these kinds of substances exist as liquids.

There is abundant evidence that the particles of liquids are in motion. Very small particles of a solid suspended in water or some other liquid can be viewed through a microscope. They are observed to move about in a random manner. The motion is increased by using smaller particles and higher temperatures. We may conclude that the observed random motion is caused by collisions with molecules of the liquid.

The diffusion of liquid molecules results from the intermingling of such molecules due to their motion. The diffusion of liquids is slower than that of gases because the molecules of liquids move more slowly and are closer together. Their movement in a given direction is thereby hindered.

Water and some other liquids, such as perfume, evaporate fairly rapidly. Evaporation occurs when some molecules acquire enough kinetic energy to escape from the surface into the vapor phase. The vapor molecules of liquids in closed containers exert pressure, as do the molecules of all confined gases. This vapor

Densities of gases and liquids were compared in Section 9.2(3).

Van der Waals forces—dispersion interaction and dipole-dipole attraction—were explained in Section 9.4.

Table 11–1
LIQUID-PHASE TEMPERATURE RANGES OF REPRESENTATIVE SUBSTANCES

Type of substance	Substance	Temperature range of liquid phase (1 atm, °C)
nonpolar covalent molecular	H_2	−259 - −252
	O_2	−218 - −183
	CH_4	−182 - −161
	CCl_4	−23 - 77
	C_6H_6	6 - 80
polar covalent molecular	NH_3	−78 - −33
	H_2O	0 - 100
ionic	NaCl	801 - 1413
	MgF_2	1266 - 2239
covalent network	$(SiO_2)_x$	1610 - 2230
	C_x (diamond)	3500 - 4827
metallic	Hg	−39 - 357
	Cu	1083 - 2595
	Fe	1535 - 3000
	W	3410 - 5927

Fig. 11-2. This enlarged diagram shows the movement of particles of paint as they are bombarded by invisible molecules of the liquid in which they are suspended.

Fig. 11-3. Water evaporates because some molecules acquire sufficient kinetic energy to escape from the surface into the vapor phase. Some rebound into the surface after colliding with molecules of gases in the air or with other water vapor molecules.

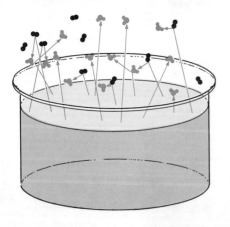

pressure reaches some maximum value depending on the temperature and nature of the substance.

The molecules of the vapors of liquids and solids have properties similar to those of gases. As stated previously, there is no distinction between a vapor and a gas other than the temperatures at which they normally exist. On cooling, gases may condense (become liquids). With further cooling, they may become solids.

11.3   Dynamic equilibrium

Suppose we place a cover over a container partially filled with a liquid. It appears that evaporation of the liquid continues for a while and then ceases. Let us examine this apparent situation in terms of the kinetic theory. The temperature of the liquid is proportional to the average kinetic energy of all the molecules of the liquid. Most of these molecules have energies very close to the average. However, some have very high energies and a few have very low energies at any given time. The motions of all are random.

Some high-energy molecules near the surface are moving toward the surface. These molecules may overcome the attractive forces of the surface molecules completely and escape, or evaporate. But some of them then collide with molecules of gases in the air or other vapor molecules and rebound into the liquid. As the evaporation continues, the concentration of vapor molecules continues to increase. This causes the chance of collisions of escaping molecules with vapor molecules to increase. Consequently, the number of vapor molecules rebounding into the liquid increases.

Eventually, the number of vapor molecules returning to the liquid equals the number of liquid molecules evaporating. Beyond this point, there will be no *net* increase in the *concentration* of vapor molecules. That is, there will be no change in the number of vapor molecules per unit volume of air above the liquid. But the motions of the molecules do not cease. The two actions, evaporation and condensation, do not cease either. They merely continue at equal rates. We may conclude that an *equilibrium* is reached between the rate of liquid molecules evaporating and the rate of vapor molecules condensing. This equilibrium is a dynamic condition in which *opposing* changes occur at *equal* rates. Since this dynamic equilibrium involves only physical changes, it is referred to as ***physical equilibrium:*** *a dynamic state in which two opposing physical changes occur at equal rates in the same system.*

We may represent the evaporation process in the following manner:

$$\textbf{liquid + energy} \rightarrow \textbf{vapor}$$

The condensation process will be, accordingly,

$$\text{vapor} \rightarrow \text{liquid} + \text{energy}$$

We can then represent this state of dynamic equilibrium occurring in a confined space as

$$\text{liquid} + \text{energy} \rightleftarrows \text{vapor}$$

11.4   Equilibrium vapor pressure

We have stated that the vapor molecules of liquids in closed containers exert pressure, as do the molecules of all confined gases. But when equilibrium is reached, there is no further net change in the system. The concentration of vapor molecules in the space above the liquid surface remains constant. Thus, at equilibrium, there is a vapor pressure characteristic of the liquid present in the system. It is known as the *equilibrium vapor pressure* of the liquid. *Equilibrium vapor pressure is the pressure exerted by a vapor in equilibrium with its liquid.*

What is the effect on a liquid-vapor equilibrium system if the temperature of the liquid is raised? Again, let us examine this situation in terms of the kinetic theory. The rise in temperature means that the average kinetic energy of the liquid molecules has been increased. A relatively larger number of liquid molecules now possess enough energy to escape through the liquid surface. Thus, the rate of evaporation is increased. In this way, the liquid-vapor equilibrium is *disturbed*. The concentration of vapor molecules above the liquid surface is increased. More vapor molecules, in turn, increases the chances of collision with escaping molecules and causes an increase in the rate of condensation. Soon the equilibrium is reestablished, but at a *higher equilibrium vapor pressure*. See Figure 11-4.

All liquids have characteristic forces of attraction between their molecules. If the attractive forces are strong, there is less tendency for the liquid to evaporate. The equilibrium vapor pressure of such a liquid is correspondingly low. Glycerol is an example of a liquid with a low equilibrium vapor pressure. On the other hand, the attractive forces between liquid molecules may be relatively weak. Then the liquid tends to evaporate readily, with a resulting high equilibrium vapor pressure. Ether is such a liquid. The amount of equilibrium vapor pressure exerted by a liquid depends on the *nature of the liquid and its temperature.*

11.5   Le Chatelier's principle

In systems that have attained equilibrium, opposing actions occur at equal rates. Any change which alters the rate of either the forward or the reverse action disturbs the equilibrium. It

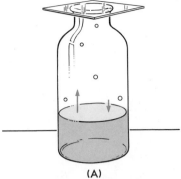

(A)
Before equilibrium

(B)
At equilibrium

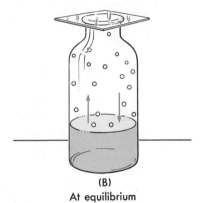

(C)
Equilibrium reestablished
at a higher temperature

Fig. 11-4. An example of physical equilibrium and the influence of temperature. The different lengths of the arrows indicate the relative rates of evaporation (up) and condensation (down). The pressure exerted by the vapor molecules at equilibrium is known as the equilibrium vapor pressure of that particular liquid.

HENRY LOUIS LE CHÂTELIER
1850–1936

Foundations of Chemistry, HRW

Fig. 11-5. Henri Louis Le Chatelier, a French mining engineer and chemist, was a brilliant scientist, teacher, writer, and editor. He did work in the science and technology of metals, high temperature measurement, microscopy, ceramics, cements, chemical mechanics, and the theory of combustion of gases. His important contribution to the understanding of the direction in which a physical or chemical change will occur is now known as Le Chatelier's principle.

is often possible to displace an equilibrium in a desired direction by changing the equilibrium conditions.

In 1888, the French chemist Henri Louis Le Chatelier (luh-*shah*-teh-lee-ay) (1850–1936) published an important principle. This principle is the basis for much of our knowledge of equilibrium. *Le Chatelier's principle* may be stated as follows: *If a system at equilibrium is subjected to a stress, the equilibrium will be displaced in such direction as to relieve the stress.* This principle is a general law which applies to all kinds of dynamic equilibria. Let us apply it to the

$$\textbf{liquid + energy} \rightleftarrows \textbf{vapor}$$

system we have been considering.

We have already learned something about how the kinetic theory applies to this system. We know that the system may reach equilibrium at a given temperature. If the temperature is then raised, equilibrium can be reestablished, but at a greater vapor concentration. *The rise in temperature is a stress on the system.* According to Le Chatelier's principle, the equilibrium is displaced in the direction which relieves this stress. In this case, the forward reaction is endothermic. The forward reaction absorbs heat energy and displaces the equilibrium to the right. This displacement means that the vapor concentration is higher when equilibrium is reestablished. Similarly, we can apply Le Chatelier's principle to a lowering of the temperature of the system at equilibrium. Here, the reverse reaction is favored. Equilibrium is reestablished at the lower temperature with a reduced vapor concentration. Thus, Le Chatelier's principle enables us to predict the dependence of equilibrium vapor pressure on temperature.

Suppose we keep the temperature of the system constant, but alter the volume which the system occupies. This constant-temperature condition means that the vapor pressure at equilibrium remains constant. It also means that the concentration of vapor molecules (density of the vapor) at equilibrium remains constant.

First, let us increase the volume which the system occupies. The volume of the liquid cannot change measurably, but the volume of the vapor can. When the volume of the vapor increases at constant temperature, its pressure must drop (Boyle's law). In order to restore the vapor to its equilibrium concentration, more vapor molecules must be produced. Le Chatelier's principle indicates that the equilibrium must shift to the right, and more liquid must evaporate. Equilibrium is then restored with the same vapor pressure and the same concentration of vapor molecules as before. But with a larger volume of vapor, the actual number of vapor molecules must be greater. The number of liquid molecules is therefore necessarily reduced.

If we reduce the volume which the system occupies, the pressure of the vapor increases. To restore equilibrium, this increased pressure must be reduced to the equilibrium vapor pressure at the same temperature. Le Chatelier's principle indicates that some vapor molecules must condense to liquid molecules. The reverse (right-to-left) reaction, condensation, is favored. Equilibrium is once again established. This time there are fewer vapor molecules and a greater number of liquid molecules. But the same *concentration* of vapor molecules exists as before.

11.6 Boiling of liquids

We now have some understanding of equilibrium and of the way in which equilibrium vapor pressures arise. Let us apply this knowledge to the phenomenon of *boiling*.

We know that pressure exerted uniformly on the surface of a confined liquid is transmitted undiminished in every direction throughout the liquid (Pascal's law). Consider a beaker of water being heated over a Bunsen flame (Figure 11-6). Vapor bubbles first appear at the bottom of the beaker, where the water is hottest. They diminish in size and disappear completely as they rise into cooler water. Atmospheric pressure presses from all directions perpendicular to the surface of the vapor bubble, according to Pascal's law, collapsing it. Only when the equilibrium vapor pressure exerted by the vapor molecules on the liquid at the surface of the bubbles is equal to the atmospheric pressure can the vapor bubble be maintained as it rises through the liquid.

As the temperature of the water increases, the vapor pressure also increases. *Ultimately a temperature is reached at which the equilibrium vapor pressure is equal to the pressure of the atmosphere acting on the surface of the liquid.* At this temperature, the vapor bubbles maintain themselves in the liquid. They present to the liquid a greatly increased liquid-vapor surface. This allows evaporation (a surface phenomenon) to occur at a greatly increased rate. We say that the liquid *boils*. The *boiling point* of a liquid is the temperature at which the equilibrium vapor pressure of the liquid is equal to the prevailing atmospheric pressure. If the pressure on the surface of a liquid is increased, the boiling point of the liquid is raised. If the pressure is decreased, the boiling point of the liquid is lowered.

The boiling point of water is exactly 100° C at *standard atmospheric pressure*. This temperature is known as the *standard* (or *normal*) *boiling point of water*. When the boiling points of liquids are given, standard pressure conditions are understood. Ether, which has a high equilibrium vapor pressure, boils at 34.6° C. The boiling point of glycerol, mentioned earlier (Section 11.4) for its low equilibrium vapor pressure, is 290° C. See Figure 11-7.

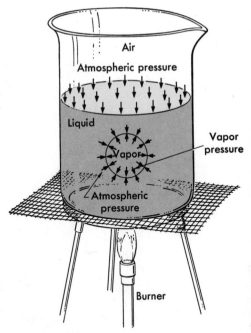

Fig. 11-6. A liquid boils when its equilibrium vapor pressure becomes equal to the prevailing atmospheric pressure.

Fig. 11-7. The equilibrium vapor pressures of some common liquids as a function of temperature.

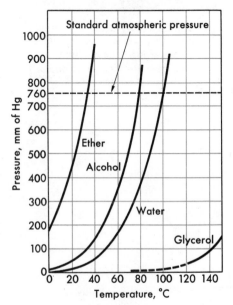

During boiling, the temperature of a liquid remains constant. The temperature of the vapor is the same as that of the liquid. Hence, the kinetic energies of linear motion of liquid and vapor molecules must be the same. But energy must be supplied for boiling to continue. This energy is absorbed by the liquid as it becomes a vapor. The energy separates the molecules in the liquid to the much wider spacing of molecules in the gas. It effects this separation by overcoming the attractive forces between the molecules. Thus, this supplied energy increases the potential energy of the molecules.

The heat energy required to vaporize one mole of liquid at its standard boiling point is its *standard molar heat of vaporization.* Its magnitude is a measure of the degree of attraction between liquid molecules.

11.7 Liquefaction of gases

Michael Faraday (1791–1867) discovered that it is possible to liquefy certain gases by cooling and compressing them at the same time. He used a thick-walled sealed tube of the type shown in Figure 11-8. With this apparatus, Faraday liquefied chlorine, sulfur dioxide, and some other gases. One end of the glass tube containing the chlorine gas was strongly heated. That caused the gas in the heated end of the tube to expand. The expanding gas exerted pressure on the gas in the other end of the tube, which was cooled in a freezing mixture. Cooling and compression in this manner converted the gaseous chlorine into liquid chlorine.

The modern method of liquefying a gas is more complicated. The first step involves compressing the gas and then removing the heat of compression. Compressing a gas always raises its temperature since energy is acquired by the molecules of a gas when work is done to push them closer together. In liquefying gases the heat of compression is absorbed by a suitable coolant. The gas molecules thereby lose the energy acquired during compression. The compressed gas is cooled to the same temperature that it had before compression. The molecules possess the same kinetic energy they had before compression, but are now closer together.

The second step in liquefying a gas is to permit the cool compressed gas to expand without absorbing external energy. When a compressed gas expands, the molecules lose energy as they do work in spreading apart against the force of molecular attraction. This energy loss by the molecules is observed as a decrease in the temperature of the gas. Remember that the temperature of the compressed gas was that which it had *before* compression. So the *expanded* gas is now at a much lower temperature than originally. By repeating this compression, cooling, and expansion cycle, the temperature of the gas is reduced still further.

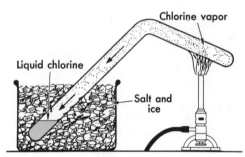

Fig. 11-8. By using a tube like the one shown above, Faraday succeeded in liquefying chlorine, sulfur dioxide, and several other gases which have high critical temperatures.

The increased pressure crowds the gas molecules together. The lowered temperature slows their movement. Ultimately, they are slowed down greatly and crowded together very closely. At this point, the attractive forces between the molecules cause them to condense to a liquid.

Scientists have found that above a certain characteristic temperature it is impossible to liquefy a gas by pressure alone. Above this temperature, the kinetic energy of the molecules is great enough to overcome the attractive forces between them. Thus the gas does not liquefy no matter how great the pressure applied. *The highest temperature at which it is possible to liquefy a gas with any amount of pressure is called its **critical temperature**. The pressure required to liquefy a gas at its critical temperature is called its **critical pressure**. The volume occupied by one mole of a gas under these conditions is called its **critical volume**.* The critical temperature and critical pressure of several common gases are given in Table 11-2.

From these data, we see that two conditions are necessary to liquefy a gas:

1. Its temperature must be lowered to or below its critical temperature.

2. Its pressure must be raised to or above the vapor pressure of the liquefied gas at this temperature.

This combination of conditions enables the attractive forces between the molecules to effect condensation. All gases can be liquefied.

11.8   Critical temperature and molecular attraction

We have defined the critical temperature of a gas as the temperature above which it cannot be liquefied no matter how great the pressure. Thus, the magnitude of the critical temperature of a gas serves as a measure of the attractive forces between its molecules. The higher the critical temperature of a gas, the larger is the attractive force between its molecules. The lower the critical temperature of a gas, the smaller is the attractive force between its molecules.

The high critical temperature of water is shown in Table 11-2. This high critical temperature indicates that the forces of attraction between polar water molecules are very great. In fact, they can cause water vapor to liquefy even at 374° C. The critical temperature of sulfur dioxide is less than that of water. Thus, the attractive forces between sulfur dioxide molecules must be less than those between water molecules. This difference is expected because sulfur dioxide molecules are less polar than water molecules. Consequently, sulfur dioxide can be condensed to a liquid only below 157° C.

Attractive forces also exist between nonpolar covalent molecules such as chlorine, carbon dioxide, oxygen, nitrogen, and

Table 11-2
CRITICAL TEMPERATURES AND PRESSURES

Gas	Critical temperature (°C)	Critical pressure (atm)
water	374.0	217.7
sulfur dioxide	157.2	77.7
chlorine	144.0	76.1
carbon dioxide	31.1	73.0
oxygen	−118.8	49.7
nitrogen	−147.1	33.5
hydrogen	−239.9	12.8

hydrogen. These attractive forces are dispersion interaction forces. Such forces generally increase with an increase in the complexity of a nonpolar molecule. Thus, the higher the molecular weight of such a molecule, the higher its critical temperature. This phenomenon is clearly illustrated in Table 11-2. Notice the descending order of the critical temperatures of chlorine, carbon dioxide, oxygen, nitrogen, and hydrogen.

SOLIDS

11.9 Properties of solids

Some of the general properties of solids which we can easily see are:

1. Definite shape. A solid maintains its shape. Unlike liquids and gases, it does not flow under ordinary circumstances. The shape of a solid is independent of its container.

2. Definite volume. All of the surfaces of a solid are free surfaces. Hence, the volume of a solid is also independent of its container.

3. Noncompressibility. The pressures required to decrease the volumes of solids are even greater than those required for liquids. For all practical purposes, solids are noncompressible. Solids such as wood, cork, sponge, etc. may *seem* to be compressible. But we must remember that these materials are very porous. Compression does not reduce the volume of the solid portion of such substances significantly. It merely reduces the volume of the pores of the solid.

4. Very slow diffusion. Suppose a lead plate and a gold plate are placed in close contact. After several months, particles of gold can be detected in the lead and vice versa. This observation is evidence that diffusion occurs even in solids, although at a *very slow rate.*

5. Crystal formation. Solids may be described as either *crystalline* or *amorphous.* Crystalline solids have a regular arrangement of particles. Amorphous solids have a completely random particle arrangement.

Fig. 11-9. The particles of a solid vibrate about fixed equilibrium positions.

11.10 Kinetic-theory description of a solid

Particles of solids are held close together in fixed positions by forces which are stronger than those between particles of liquids. This is how scientists explain the definite shape and volume of a solid as well as its noncompressibility. Whether the particle arrangement is orderly or not determines whether the solid is crystalline or amorphous. The particles of a solid vibrate weakly back and forth about fixed equilibrium positions.

Their kinetic energy is related to the extent of this vibratory motion. Their kinetic energy is proportional to the temperature of the solid. At low temperatures, the kinetic energy is small. At higher temperatures it is larger. Crystal particles vibrate extensively at high temperatures. But there is relatively little diffusion in any solid, because the vibration is about fixed positions.

11.11 Changes of phase involving solids

The physical change of a liquid to a solid is called *freezing,* and involves a loss of energy by the liquid.

$$\textbf{liquid} \rightarrow \textbf{solid} + \textbf{energy}$$

Since this change occurs at constant temperature, the liquid and solid particles must have the same kinetic energy. The energy loss is a loss of *potential* energy. The particles lose potential energy as the forces of attraction do work on them.

The reverse physical change, *melting,* also occurs at constant temperature.

$$\textbf{solid} + \textbf{energy} \rightarrow \textbf{liquid}$$

It involves a gain of potential energy by the particles of the solid as they do work against the attractive forces in becoming liquid particles.

For pure crystalline solids, the temperatures at which these two processes occur coincide. That is, the freezing point and the melting point are the same. For pure water, both processes occur at 0° C. Ice melts at 0° C and forms liquid water; water freezes at 0° C and forms ice. The heat energy required to melt one mole of solid at its melting point is its *molar heat of fusion.*

If ice gradually disappears in a mixture of ice and water, the melting process clearly is proceeding faster than the freezing process. Suppose, however, that the relative amounts of ice and water remain unchanged in the mixture. Then both processes must be proceeding at equal rates and a state of physical equilibrium is indicated.

$$\textbf{solid} + \textbf{energy} \rightleftarrows \textbf{liquid}$$

Not all particles of a solid have the same energy. A surface particle of a solid may acquire sufficient energy to overcome the attractive forces holding it to the body of the solid. Such a particle may escape from the solid and become a vapor particle.

$$\textbf{solid} + \textbf{energy} \rightarrow \textbf{vapor}$$

Professor Isador Fankuchen,
Polytechnic Institute of Brooklyn

Fig. 11-10. X-ray diffraction photograph of ice. Chemists use X-ray diffraction in their study of crystal structure.

Homogeneous materials, such as crystals, have similar properties throughout.

If a solid is placed in a closed container, vapor particles cannot escape from the system. Eventually they come in contact with the solid and are held by its attractive forces.

$$\text{vapor} \rightarrow \text{solid} + \text{energy}$$

Thus a solid in contact with its vapor can reach an equilibrium.

$$\text{solid} + \text{energy} \rightleftarrows \text{vapor}$$

In such a case, the solid exhibits a characteristic equilibrium vapor pressure. Like that of a liquid, the equilibrium vapor pressure of a solid depends only on the temperature and the substance involved. Some solids like camphor and naphthalene (moth crystals) have fairly high equilibrium vapor pressures. They evaporate noticeably when exposed to air. Solids like carbon dioxide (Dry Ice) and iodine have equilibrium vapor pressures which rise very rapidly as the temperature is raised. The equilibrium vapor pressures of these solids equal atmospheric pressure before the solids melt. In such cases the solid vaporizes directly, without passing through the liquid phase. The change of phase from a solid to a vapor is known as *sublimation*.

11.12 Amorphous solids

The term *amorphous solids* refers to those which appear to have random particle arrangement. But truly amorphous solids are rare. Many solids which scientists once thought were amorphous have been found to have a partially crystalline structure. Charcoal is such a solid. However, materials like glass and paraffin may be considered amorphous. These materials have the properties of solids. That is, they have definite shape and volume and diffuse slowly. But they do not have the orderly arrangement of particles characteristic of crystals. They also lack sharply defined melting points. In many respects, they resemble liquids which flow very slowly at room temperature.

11.13 Nature of crystals

Most substances exist as solids in some characteristic crystalline form. *A **crystal** is a homogeneous portion of a substance bounded by plane surfaces making definite angles with each other, giving a regular geometric form.*

Scientists determine the arrangement of particles composing a crystal by mathematical analysis of its diffraction patterns. These patterns appear clearly on photographs produced when the crystal is illuminated by X rays. An example of an X-ray diffraction photograph is shown in Figure 11-10. Every crystal structure shows a pattern of points which describes the arrangement of its particles. This pattern of points is known as the *crystal lattice*. The smallest portion of the crystal lattice which exhibits the pattern of the lattice structure is called the *unit cell*. The unit cell defines the kind of symmetry to be found throughout a crystalline substance. The kinds of unit cells are shown in Figure 11-11.

The classification of crystals by shape is a part of the science of *crystallography*. Shape classification helps chemists to identify crystals. Any crystal can be placed in one of six crystalline systems:

1. Isometric (or *cubic*). The three axes are at right angles as in a cube, and are of equal length.

2. Tetragonal. The three axes are at right angles to each other, but only the two lateral axes are of equal length.

3. Orthorhombic. Three unequal axes are at right angles to each other.

4. Monoclinic. There are three unequal axes, with one oblique (not a right angle) intersection.

5. Triclinic. There are three unequal axes and three oblique intersections.

6. Hexagonal. Three equilateral axes intersect at angles of 60°. A vertical axis of variable length is at right angles to the equilateral axes. (See Figure 11-12.)

Crystals of common salt, NaCl, are isometric (cubic). This cubic nature can be seen by sprinkling a little table salt on a black surface and examining with a magnifying lens. Alum crystals, $K_2SO_4 \cdot Al_2(SO_4)_3 \cdot 24H_2O$, are also isometric, being formed as *octahedrons* (regular eight-sided solids). Copper(II) sulfate pentahydrate, $CuSO_4 \cdot 5H_2O$, forms blue triclinic crystals.

Crystals of many chemical compounds are formed when their solutions evaporate or when their hot, saturated solutions cool. Crystals also form when certain substances change from the liquid to the solid phase and when others change from the gaseous to the solid phase. Most of us are familiar with snowflake crystals. These are formed when water vapor changes directly to the solid phase. Melted sugar, sulfur, and iron form crystals in a similar manner when they change from the liquid to the solid phase. In some cases, crystals grow from the solid phase.

11.14   Binding forces in crystals

The regularity of crystal structures is their most fascinating feature. When possible, ions or atoms or molecules arrange themselves in positions of least energy. The more opportunity there is for particles to do this during the formation of crystals, the more symmetrical and regular the crystals will be. Thus, the more slowly crystals form, the more closely their shapes approach perfect regularity.

We describe the six crystalline systems in terms related to symmetry. But it is frequently more useful to classify crystals according to the types of lattice structure. Is the crystal lattice

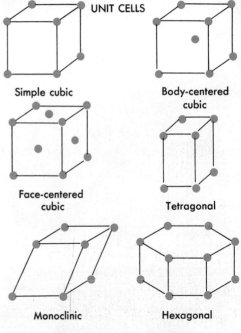

UNIT CELLS

Simple cubic

Body-centered cubic

Face-centered cubic

Tetragonal

Monoclinic

Hexagonal

Fig. 11-11. The kind of symmetry found throughout a crystalline substance is determined by the type of unit cell which generates the lattice structure.

Fig. 11-12. Schematic diagram of the six basic crystal systems.

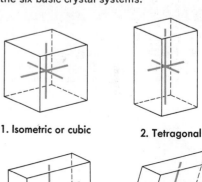

1. Isometric or cubic

2. Tetragonal

3. Orthorhombic

4. Monoclinic

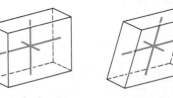
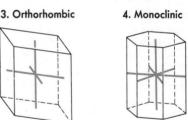

5. Triclinic

6. Hexagonal

B.M. Shaub

Fig. 11-13. A garnet crystal (top) and a group of quartz crystals (bottom) show how crystal structure follows a characteristic pattern.

Table 11-3

MELTING POINTS AND BOILING POINTS OF REPRESENTATIVE TYPES OF SUBSTANCES

Type of substance	Substance	Melting point (°C)	Boiling point (1 atm, °C)
nonpolar covalent molecular	H_2	−259	−252
	O_2	−218	−183
	CH_4	−182	−161
	CCl_4	−23	77
	C_6H_6	6	$8\overline{0}$
polar covalent molecular	NH_3	−78	−33
	H_2O	$\overline{0}$	$10\overline{0}$
ionic	NaCl	801	1413
	MgF_2	1266	2239
covalent network	$(SiO_2)_x$	1610	2230
	C_x (diamond)	3500	4827
metallic	Hg	−39	357
	Cu	1083	2595
	Fe	1535	3000
	W	3410	5927

ionic, covalent network, metallic, or *covalent molecular?* Ionic and covalent molecular crystal lattices represent the two extremes of bonding. Covalent network and metallic crystal lattices are intermediate types. (See Table 11-3.)

1. Ionic crystals. The ionic crystal lattice consists of positive and negative ions arranged in a characteristic regular pattern. No molecular units are evident within the crystal. The strong bonding forces result from the attraction of positive and negative charges. Consequently, ionic crystals are hard and brittle, have rather high melting points, and are good insulators. Generally, ionic crystals result from Group I or Group II metals combining with Group VI or Group VII nonmetals, or the nonmetallic polyatomic ions.

2. Covalent network crystals. The covalent network crystal lattice consists of an array of atoms that shares electrons with neighboring atoms. The binding forces are strong covalent bonds which extend in fixed directions. The resulting crystals are compact, interlocking, covalent network structures. They may be considered to be giant molecules. They are very hard and brittle, have rather high melting points, and are nonconductors. Diamond, silicon carbide, silicon dioxide, and oxides of transition metals are of this type.

3. Metallic crystals. The metallic crystal lattice consists of positive ions surrounded by a cloud of valence electrons. This cloud is commonly referred to as the *electron gas.* The binding force is the attraction between the positive ions of the metal and the electron "gas." The valence electrons are donated by the atoms of the metal and belong to the crystal as a whole. These electrons are free to migrate throughout the crystal lattice. This electron mobility explains the high electric conductivity associated with metals. The hardness (resistance to wear) and melting points of metallic crystals vary greatly for different metals. Sodium, iron, tungsten, copper, and silver are typical examples of metallic crystals that have good electric conductivity. But they are quite different in terms of other characteristics, such as hardness and melting point.

4. Covalent molecular crystals. The covalent molecular crystal lattice consists of an orderly arrangement of individually distinct molecules. If the molecules are nonpolar, the binding force is the relatively weak dispersion interaction force. If the molecules are polar, both types of van der Waals attractions make up the binding force. The covalent chemical bonds which bind the atoms within the molecules are much stronger than the forces which form the crystal lattice. Thus, molecular crystals have low melting points, are relatively soft, volatile (easily vaporized), and good insulators. Iodine, carbon dioxide, water, and hydrogen form crystals of this type. See Section 11.15 for the discussion of ice crystals.

WATER

11.15 Physical properties of water

Pure water is a transparent, odorless, tasteless, and almost colorless liquid. The faint blue or blue-green color of water is apparent only in deep layers.

Any odor or taste in water is caused by impurities such as dissolved mineral matter, dissolved liquids, or dissolved gases. The strong odor and taste of water from some mineral springs is caused by the presence of such substances in detectable quantity.

Water may exist as a vapor, liquid, or solid. Liquid water changes to ice at 0° C under standard pressure, 760 mm of mercury. As water solidifies, it gives off heat and expands one ninth in volume. Consequently, ice has a density of about 0.9 g/cm³. The density of ice increases slightly as ice is cooled below 0° C. The molar heat of fusion of ice at 0° C is 1.44 kcal.

When water at 0° C is warmed, it contracts until its temperature reaches 4° C. Then water gradually expands as its temperature is raised further. *At its temperature of maximum density, 4° C, one milliliter of water has a mass of one gram.*

Fig. 11-14. Solid iodine (top) forms molecular crystals. Compare its molecular structure with that of diamond (bottom) which forms covalent crystals which may be considered to be giant molecules.

When the pressure on the surface of water is *one atmosphere* (760 mm of mercury), water boils at a temperature of 100° C. The molar heat of vaporization of water at 100° C is 9.70 kcal. The steam that is formed by boiling water occupies a much greater volume than the water from which it was formed. When one liter of water evaporates, the steam occupies about 1700 liters at 100° C and 1 atmosphere pressure.

When water is heated in a closed vessel so that the steam cannot escape, the pressure on the water's surface increases. As a result, the boiling temperature of the water is raised above 100° C. But suppose that the air and water vapor above the liquid in a closed vessel are partially removed by means of a vacuum pump. Then the pressure is decreased and the water boils at a lower temperature than 100° C. Pressure cookers are used for cooking food because the higher temperature of the water cooks the food in a shorter time. Vacuum evaporators are used to concentrate milk and sugar solutions. Under reduced pressure, the water boils away at a temperature low enough so that the sugar or milk is not scorched.

11.16   Structure and properties of water molecules

Water molecules are composed of two atoms of hydrogen and one atom of oxygen joined by polar covalent bonds. Studies of the crystal structure of ice indicate that these atoms are not joined in a straight line. Instead, the molecule is bent, with a structure which may be represented as

The angle between the two hydrogen-oxygen bonds is about 105°. This was explained in Section 6.12 as evidence of considerable sp^3 hybridization of the oxygen-atom orbitals.

Since oxygen is more strongly electronegative than hydrogen, the bonds in a water molecule are polar. The electronegativity difference indicates that H—O bonds have about 39% ionic character. Thus, the electrons are not distributed perfectly uniformly about the molecule. On the average, they are clustered slightly about the oxygen nucleus. This gives the oxygen part of the molecule a partial negative charge, and leaves the hydrogen parts with a partial positive charge. Since the polar covalent bonds in this molecule do not lie on the same straight line, the molecule as a whole is polar. Water molecules, being polar, are sometimes called water dipoles.

The polarity of water molecules enables them to be attracted to one another. This mutual attraction causes water molecules to *associate,* or join together into groups of molecules. One slightly positive hydrogen atom of a water molecule may weakly, but effectively, attract the slightly negative oxygen of a second

Philadelphia Electric Co.

Fig. 11-15. The analysis and resulting purification of the water discharged from industrial plants helps to reduce the pollution of streams and rivers.

water molecule. In this way, one hydrogen serves as a link between the oxygen atoms of two water molecules by sharing electrons with them. This situation is an example of a *hydrogen bond*. *A **hydrogen bond** is a weak chemical bond between a hydrogen atom in one polar molecule and a very electronegative atom in a second polar molecule.* A hydrogen of the second water molecule may be attracted to the oxygen of a third water molecule, and so on. In this way, a group of molecules is formed. The number of molecules in such a group decreases with an increase in temperature. But there are usually from four to eight molecules per group in liquid water. The formation of molecular groups by hydrogen bonding causes water to be liquid at room temperature. Other substances, such as methane, CH_4, have nonpolar molecules similar in size and mass to water molecules. But these substances do not undergo hydrogen bonding, and are gases at room temperature. Hydrogen bonding seems to occur only between hydrogen and highly electronegative small nonmetallic atoms such as oxygen, fluorine, and nitrogen.

Ice consists of H_2O molecules arranged in a definite hexagonal structure. They are held together by hydrogen bonds in a rather open hexagonal pattern (Figure 11-16). As heat is applied to ice, the increased energy of the atoms and molecules causes them to vibrate more vigorously. This stretches the hydrogen bonds, and the ice expands as it is heated.

When the melting point of ice is reached, the energy of the atoms and molecules is so great that the rigid open lattice structure of the ice crystals breaks down. The ice turns into

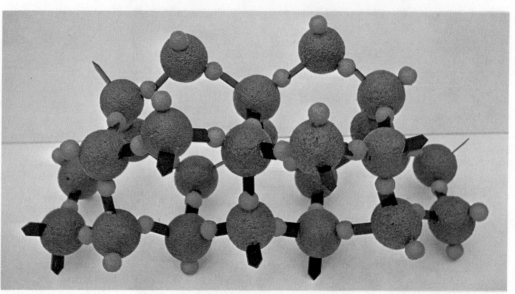

The Chemistry Department, University of Iowa

Fig. 11-16. Model of the crystal structure of ice.

Table 11–4
DENSITY OF WATER

°C	g/ml
0	0.99987
1	0.99993
2	0.99997
3	0.99999
4	1.00000
5	0.99999
6	0.99997
7	0.99993
8	0.99988
9	0.99981
10	0.99973
15	0.99913
20	0.99823
25	0.99707
30	0.99567
40	0.99224
50	0.98807
60	0.98324
70	0.97781
80	0.97183
90	0.96534
100	0.95838

water. The hydrogen bonds in water at 0° C are longer than those in ice. But they are more flexible. Thus, the groups of liquid molecules can crowd together more compactly than those in ice. As a result, H_2O molecules occupy less volume as water than they do as ice. Water is denser than ice.

As water is warmed from 0° C, two phenomena having opposite effects occur:

1. The breaking down of some hydrogen bonds enables water molecules to crowd closer together.

2. The increased energy of the water molecules causes them to overcome molecular attractions more effectively and spread apart.

Up to 4° C, the first effect wins out and water increases in density. Above 4° C, the first phenomenon continues to occur, but the effect of the second becomes much greater. Thus, above 4° C, the density of water decreases.

Groups of water molecules must absorb enough energy to break up into single molecules before water boils. This energy requirement makes the boiling point of water relatively high. It also makes it necessary to use a large amount of heat to vaporize water at its normal boiling point.

11.17 Chemical behavior of water

1. Stability of water. Water is a very **stable compound.** *A stable compound is one which does not break up, or decompose, easily.* Mercury(II) oxide, on the other hand, is a rather **unstable compound.** *This means that it does not require much energy to decompose it into its elements.* Water is so stable that it does not decompose a measurable amount until its temperature reaches about 2700° C. The stability of water is evidence of the strength of the covalent bonds between the oxygen and hydrogen atoms.

2. *Behavior with metals.* Very active metals such as sodium and potassium react with cold water, setting free hydrogen and forming metallic hydroxide solutions.

$$2Na(s) + 2HOH(l) \rightarrow 2NaOH(aq) + H_2(g)$$

Magnesium reacts with boiling water and forms magnesium hydroxide and hydrogen. When heated red hot, iron reacts with steam and forms iron oxide and hydrogen. Aluminum and zinc also react with water at high temperatures.

3. *Behavior with metallic oxides.* The oxides of many metals are insoluble, and water has little or no effect upon them. But water does react with the ionic oxides of the very active metals. The oxides of sodium, potassium, calcium, and barium unite with water and form soluble hydroxides. Soluble metallic hydroxides are compounds whose water solutions have basic properties. Some basic properties of a solution are a slippery feeling, a bitter taste, and the ability to change red litmus to blue. Calcium hydroxide is formed when water is added to calcium oxide, CaO.

$$CaO(s) + H_2O(l) \rightarrow Ca(OH)_2(s)$$

Compounds such as calcium oxide, CaO, are known as *anhydrides.* The word anhydride means "without water." Since it forms a solution with basic properties when water is added to it, calcium oxide is called a *basic anhydride. A **basic anhydride** is the oxide of a metal which unites with water and forms a solution having basic properties.*

4. *Behavior with oxides of nonmetals.* The oxides of such nonmetals as carbon, sulfur, and phosphorus are molecular compounds with polar covalent bonds. They unite with water and form a solution with *acidic* properties. Two acidic properties are a sour taste and the ability to turn blue litmus to red. For example, water unites with carbon dioxide and forms carbonic acid, H_2CO_3.

$$CO_2(g) + H_2O(l) \rightarrow H_2CO_3(aq)$$

Carbon dioxide is an anhydride which, with water, forms a solution having acidic properties. Therefore, it is called an *acid anhydride. An **acid anhydride** is the oxide of a nonmetal which unites with water and forms a solution having acidic properties.*

5. *Water of crystallization.* In some crystals, many positive ions and a few negative ions are surrounded by a definite number of water molecules. These crystals are formed by evapo-

rating the water from their solutions. This water is called *water of crystallization or water of hydration. A crystallized substance that contains water of crystallization is a **hydrate**.* Each hydrate holds a definite proportion of water which is necessary for the formation of its crystal structure. For example, blue crystals of copper(II) sulfate consist of copper(II) ions, sulfate ions, and water molecules. Each copper(II) ion is surrounded by four water molecules. Each sulfate ion is associated with one water molecule. The formula of this substance is written as

$$CuSO_4 \cdot 5H_2O$$

This formula is empirical in two ways:

1. The empirical formula $CuSO_4$ shows the composition of the crystal with respect to copper(II) and sulfate ions.

2. The water of crystallization is shown as the *total* per formula unit of copper(II) sulfate. This total is expressed as $\cdot 5H_2O$. If $CuSO_4 \cdot 5H_2O$ is heated to a temperature slightly above the boiling point of water, the water of crystallization is driven off.

$$CuSO_4 \cdot 5H_2O(s) \rightarrow CuSO_4(s) + 5H_2O(g)$$

The substance which then remains is called an **anhydrous compound.** Anhydrous copper(II) sulfate, $CuSO_4$, is a white powder. It can be prepared by heating the blue $CuSO_4 \cdot 5H_2O$ crystals gently in a test tube. The fact that water turns anhydrous copper(II) sulfate blue may be used as a *test for water.*

Other examples of hydrates are the compounds $ZnSO_4 \cdot 7H_2O$, $CoCl_2 \cdot 6H_2O$, and $Na_2CO_3 \cdot 10H_2O$. Some hydrates have two or more forms which are stable over different temperature ranges. Many other compounds form crystals which do not require water of crystallization. Examples are $NaCl$, KNO_3, and $KClO_3$.

6. Water promotes many chemical changes. One good example of these changes is the reaction of an effervescent (fizzing) alkalizing tablet, which is a dry mixture. As long as the tablet is kept dry, no chemical action occurs. When the tablet is dropped in water, the substances in the mixture dissolve and react immediately. Bubbles of gas are given off (see Figure 11-17). Mixtures of many other dry substances do not react until water is added. The role of water in promoting chemical changes will be more fully explained in Unit 5.

11.18 Efflorescence

Suppose we put ten grams of sodium carbonate crystals, $Na_2CO_3 \cdot 10H_2O$, on a watch glass on one pan of a balance. We add weights to the other pan until both pans are balanced. In a few minutes, the crystals begin to show a loss of mass. At the same time, the crystals lose their glassy luster (shine) and become powdery. By the end of the laboratory period, the loss in mass may amount to a gram or more. This loss in mass results from the loss of some of the molecules of water of crystallization.

$$Na_2CO_3 \cdot 10H_2O(s) \rightarrow Na_2CO_3 \cdot H_2O(s) + 9H_2O(g)$$

The loss of some or all molecules of water of crystallization when a hydrate is exposed to the air is called **efflorescence.**

Efflorescence occurs when the water vapor pressure of the hydrate is greater than the partial pressure of the water vapor in the air surrounding it. Consequently, efflorescence occurs much more rapidly in a warm, dry atmosphere than in one that is cool and moist. The water vapor pressure of hydrates varies greatly. $Na_2CO_3 \cdot 10H_2O$ has a high water vapor pressure and effloresces quite rapidly. $CuSO_4 \cdot 5H_2O$, on the other hand, has a low water vapor pressure. It can be exposed to the air at room temperature without efflorescence.

Fig. 11-17. Water acts to promote some reactions, as shown when effervescent alkalizing tablets are added to water.

11.19 Deliquescence

Suppose we now put ten grams of calcium chloride granules on a watch glass on one pan of a balance. We add weights to the other pan until the pans are just balanced. After the calcium chloride has been exposed to the moist air for half an hour, it shows a decided gain in mass. The granules have become moist; they may even have formed a solution with water from the air. *Certain substances take up water from the air and form solutions. This property is called* **deliquescence.** Deliquescent substances are very soluble in water. Their concentrated solutions have water vapor pressures lower than the normal range of partial pressures of water vapor in the air. Consequently, such substances and their solutions absorb water vapor from the air more rapidly than they give it off. The absorption of water results in a gradual dilution of the solution involved. Absorption and dilution continue until the water vapor pressure of the solution and the partial pressure of water vapor in the surrounding air are equal.

Many insoluble materials such as silk, wool, hair, and tobacco take up water vapor from the air. The water molecules may be held in pores and imperfections of the solid. All such materials, along with deliquescent substances, are classed as *hygroscopic.* Common table salt is hygroscopic only because it contains a small amount of magnesium chloride, a very deliquescent substance. This impurity causes table salt to "cake" and clog the holes of a salt shaker.

Fig. 11-18. Calcium chloride removes water vapor from the air to control the dust on an unpaved road.

Calcium Chloride Institute

11.20 Deuterium oxide

Most water molecules are composed of hydrogen atoms with mass number 1 and oxygen atoms with mass number 16. But there are other possible types of water molecules. There are three isotopes of hydrogen, with mass numbers 1, 2, and 3. There are three isotopes of oxygen, with mass numbers 16, 17, and 18. The possible combinations of these six nuclides give 18 types of water molecules. In liquid water, these molecules are associated most commonly in chains of from four to eight units. In water there is also a very small proportion of hydronium (H_3O^+) ions, hydroxide ions, and oxide ions. These ions are formed from the various isotopes of hydrogen and oxygen. Thus, water is a complex mixture of many kinds of molecules and ions.

Particles other than ordinary water molecules exist in only small traces in a water sample. But one such type of water molecule has been studied rather extensively. This is the *deuterium oxide* molecule, D_2O. The symbol D is used to represent an atom of the isotope of hydrogen with mass number 2. D_2O is separated from H_2O by electricity. D_2O molecules are not as readily decomposed by the passage of electric current as are H_2O molecules. Thus, the concentration of D_2O molecules increases as H_2O molecules are decomposed. From 2400 liters of water, 83 ml of D_2O that is 99% pure can be obtained.

Deuterium oxide is about 10% denser than ordinary water. It boils at 101.42° C, freezes at 3.82° C, and has its maximum density at 11.6° C. Delicate tests have been devised for detecting deuterium oxide. It has been used as a "tracer" in research work on living organisms. By tracing the course of deuterium oxide molecules through such organisms, scientists have gained new information about certain life processes. Deuterium oxide usually produces harmful effects on living things, particularly when present in high concentrations. The most important use of deuterium oxide is in nuclear reactors. You will learn more about this use of deuterium oxide in Chapter 30.

QUESTIONS

Group A
1. How does the kinetic theory explain these properties of liquids: (a) definite volume; (b) fluidity; (c) noncompressibility; (d) diffusion; (e) evaporation?
2. What evidence is there that the particles of a liquid are in constant motion?
3. Describe the conditions prevailing in a system in equilibrium?
4. Would you expect an equilibrium vapor pressure to be reached in the space above a liquid in an open container? Why?
5. Water standing in a covered flask experiences a drop in temperature of $1\overline{0}$ C°. How is the liquid-vapor equilibrium disturbed? Explain.
6. What effect does the pressure on a water surface have on the boiling temperature of the water?
7. Define (a) critical temperature; (b) critical pressure; (c) critical volume.
8. What conditions must be met in order for a gas to be liquefied?
9. How does the kinetic theory explain these properties of solids: (a) definite shape; (b) definite volume; (c) noncompressibility; (d) very slow diffusion; (e) crystal formation?

10. What are the general properties of solids composed of (*a*) ions; (*b*) molecules; (*c*) atoms in a covalent network structure; (*d*) metal ions in an electron "gas"?
11. List six physical properties of water.
12. How does the volume of steam compare with the volume of water from which it was produced?
13. (*a*) Write a formula equation for the melting of one mole of ice at 0° C to water at 0° C, including the quantity of energy involved. (*b*) Similarly write an equation for the boiling of one mole of water at 100° C to steam at 100° C.
14. Describe the structure of the water molecule, and tell why it is a polar molecule.
15. (*a*) What is a hydrogen bond? (*b*) What effect do the hydrogen bonds in water have on its boiling point?
16. (*a*) What is a stable compound? Give an example. (*b*) What is an unstable compound? Give an example.
17. (*a*) List five metals which react with water. (*b*) Give the conditions under which they react.
18. (*a*) What is an anhydride? (*b*) Distinguish between a basic anhydride and an acid anhydride. (*c*) What type of compound may be an acid anhydride? (*d*) What type of compound may be a basic anhydride?
19. What is the significance of the raised dot in $BaCl_2 \cdot 2H_2O$?
20. Give an example of a chemical change which is promoted by the presence of water.
21. A package of washing soda, $Na_2CO_3 \cdot 10H_2O$, labeled "one pound" was found to weigh only 14 ounces. Was the packer necessarily dishonest? Explain.
22. (*a*) Explain why anhydrous calcium chloride may be used to keep the air in a basement dry. (*b*) Suggest a suitable method of accomplishing this.
23. How is deuterium oxide separated from ordinary water?
24. Give some uses for deuterium oxide.

Group B

25. What kinds of particles compose substances which are liquids (*a*) well below room temperature; (*b*) at room temperature; (*c*) well above room temperature?
26. (*a*) Using the curves of Fig. 11-7, determine the temperature at which water in an open vessel will boil when the atmospheric pressure is reduced to 600 mm. (*b*) What is the boiling point of alcohol at this pressure? (*c*) of ether?
27. The system **alcohol(l) + energy $\rightleftarrows$ alcohol(g)** is at equilibrium in a closed container at 50° C. What will be the effect of each of the following stresses on the equilibrium? (*a*) Temperature is raised to 60° C. (*b*) Volume of container is doubled. (*c*) Barometer rises from 720 mm to 740 mm.
28. (*a*) Why does compressing a gas raise its temperature? (*b*) Why does a gas become colder when it is allowed to expand?
29. (*a*) Can carbon dioxide be liquefied at 100° C? (*b*) Can chlorine be liquefied at 100° C? Explain.
30. (*a*) How does the addition of the molar heat of vaporization affect the energy of the particles of one mole of liquid at its standard boiling point? (*b*) How does the addition of the molar heat of fusion affect the energy of the particles of one mole of a solid at its standard melting point?
31. A bottle of alum crystals was erroneously labeled "sodium chloride." How could the error be detected at once by an alert chemistry student?
32. Camphor crystals are soft and volatile. Explain.
33. Explain why ice occupies a greater volume than the water from which it is formed.

34. The system **ice + energy** ⇌ **water** is at equilibrium at $0°$ C in an open vessel. What will be the effect on the system if (*a*) heat is supplied to the system; (*b*) heat is removed from the system; (*c*) the pressure on the system is increased?
35. Explain why water has a point of maximum density at $4°$ C.
36. What does the extreme stability of H_2O molecules indicate about the strength of the covalent bonds between the oxygen and hydrogen atoms?
37. Tobacco growers prefer to handle dried tobacco leaves during damp weather. Explain.
38. What particles are present in pure water besides ordinary H_2O molecules?

PROBLEMS

Group A

1. A mixture of 50.0 ml of hydrogen and 30.0 ml of oxygen is ignited by an electric spark. What gas remains? What is its volume in milliliters?
2. A mixture of 40.0 ml of oxygen and 120.0 ml of hydrogen is ignited. What gas remains and how many milliliters does it occupy?
3. (*a*) How many milliliters of hydrogen are needed for complete reaction with 37.5 ml of oxygen? (*b*) What fraction of a mole of water is produced?
4. A mixture of equal volumes of oxygen and hydrogen has a volume of 100.0 ml. (*a*) After the mixture is ignited, what gas remains, and what is its volume in milliliters? (*b*) How many millimoles of water are formed?
5. How many grams of hydrogen and oxygen are required in order to produce 15.0 moles of water?
6. (*a*) The volume of a water molecule is 15 $Å^3$. From this information calculate the volume in milliliters one mole of water should occupy. (*b*) From the gram-molecular weight of water and its density at $4°$ C, calculate the volume in milliliters actually occupied by one mole of water. (*c*) What is the meaning of the difference between these two results?

Group B

7. How many grams of anhydrous sodium carbonate can be obtained by heating 100 g of $Na_2CO_3 \cdot 10H_2O$?
8. Calculate the percentage of cobalt, chlorine, and water in $CoCl_2 \cdot 6H_2O$.
9. What is the empirical formula of certain hydrated crystals having a composition of 56.14% $ZnSO_4$ and 43.86% water?
10. If 124.8 g of copper(II) sulfate crystals is heated to drive off the water of crystallization, the loss of mass is 45.0 g. What is the percentage of water in hydrated copper(II) sulfate?
11. The anhydrous copper(II) sulfate in Problem 10 was found to contain copper, 31.8 g; sulfur, 16.0 g; and oxygen, 32.0 g. Determine the empirical formula of the hydrated copper(II) sulfate crystals.
12. The density of carbon tetrachloride at $0°$ C is 1.600 g/ml. (*a*) Calculate the volume in milliliters occupied by a single molecule of CCl_4. (*b*) Assuming the molecules to be spherical, calculate the approximate diameter in angstroms of a CCl_4 molecule.
13. Obtain from Figure 5-5 the radius of an atom of mercury. (*a*) If we assume an atom of mercury to be spherical, what is its volume in $Å^3$? (*b*) If we assume that in liquid mercury the atoms are packed in a cubic array with six nearest neighbors, what is the volume in milliliters of 1.00 mole of liquid mercury?

Chapter 12

The Solution Process

12.1 Solutions and suspensions

If a lump of sugar is dropped into a beaker of water, it disappears gradually. The sugar is said to *dissolve* in the water. Even careful examination of the water with a microscope does not reveal the dissolved sugar. By tasting the liquid, however, we can tell that the sugar is present. Eventually, molecules of sugar become uniformly distributed among the molecules of water. Then the same degree of sweetness is detected in all parts of the liquid. Such a mixture of sugar and water is homogeneous throughout. It is an example of a *solution*.

A *solution* is a homogeneous mixture of two or more substances, the composition of which may vary within characteristic limits. The *dissolving medium* is called the **solvent**. The *substance that dissolves* is called the **solute**. The simplest solution consists of molecules of a single solute distributed throughout a single solvent. Now, let us return for a moment to our sugar-water solution. Suppose we continue to add sugar to the liquid. Eventually a point is reached at which no more sugar dissolves. At this point the solution is said to be *saturated*.

Not all substances form true solutions in water. If clay is mixed with water, for example, very little actually dissolves. Particles of clay are huge compared to molecules of water. The result is a muddy, heterogeneous mixture called a *suspension*. Because the components of the mixture have different densities, they readily separate into two distinct phases. However, some

The World of Neglected Dimensions

The colloidal state has been called the world of neglected dimensions. It lies between true solutions and coarse suspensions which separate on standing. Colloidal size ranges between ordinary molecular size great enough to be seen through a microscope. Colloidal particles have dimensions ranging from approximately 10 Å to 10,000 Å. Ordinary simple molecules are only a few angstroms in diameter.

223

Carolyn Polese

Fig. 12-1. A beam of light can be used to distinguish a colloidal suspension from a true solution. The jar at the left contains a water solution of sodium chloride. The jar at the right contains a suspension of gelatine in water.

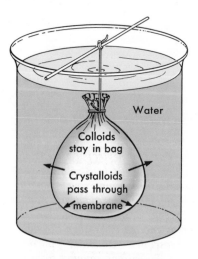

Fig. 12-2. A colloidal suspension is held back by the parchment membrane, permitting it to be separated from substances in solution.

very small particles, though still much larger than water molecules, are kept permanently suspended. They are bombarded from all sides by water molecules and this bombardment keeps them from settling out. Such mixtures may appear to be homogeneous, but careful examination shows that they are not true solutions. Mixtures of this type are called *colloidal suspensions*. See Figure 12-1.

The term *colloid* was originally applied to sticky substances such as starch and glue. *Colloids* are substances that, when mixed with water, do not pass through parchment membranes. In contrast, substances such as sugar and salt form true solutions with water and do pass through parchment membranes. These substances were called *crystalloids*.

Under certain conditions, some substances are nondiffusing and colloidal. Under different conditions, they are crystalloidal in behavior. We now know that *the state of subdivision,* rather than the chemical nature of a substance, determines whether it forms a suspension or a true solution when dispersed (scattered) in a second medium. For example, a colloidal suspension may be formed if sodium ions and chloride ions are brought together in a medium in which sodium chloride is not soluble. Colloidal-sized crystals, each consisting of many sodium ions and chloride ions, may form in the medium.

A true solution is formed when a solute, as molecules or ions, is dispersed throughout a solvent and forms a homogeneous mixture. It consists of a *single phase*. The solute is said to be *soluble* in the solvent. A colloidal suspension, on the other hand, is a *two-phase system*. It has dispersed particles rather than a solute, and a dispersing medium rather than a solvent. The dispersed substance (*internal phase*) is not soluble in the dispersing medium (*external phase*). The system consists of finely divided particles which remain suspended in the medium.

We stated in Section 6.3 that electrovalent solids do not exist as molecules. Instead, each has a crystal lattice composed of ions bound together by the strong electrostatic force of attraction between positive and negative charges. Such substances are called **electrolytes** because their water solutions conduct electricity.

Generally, covalent substances which dissolve in water are present in the solution as neutral molecules. Neutral molecules do not conduct electricity. Such substances are called **nonelectrolytes**. Many acids are exceptions. When undissolved, they are molecular and do not conduct an electric current. However, the water solutions of the stronger acids conduct electricity. These acids are electrolytes.

Solutions of electrolytes have physical properties which are different from solutions of nonelectrolytes. Electrolytes will be considered in detail in Chapters 13 and 14. The remainder of our present discussion of the properties of solutions will deal primarily with solutions of nonelectrolytes.

12.2 Types of solutions

Matter may exist as a solid, liquid, or gas, depending upon temperature and pressure. Therefore, nine different types of solutions are possible. These types of solutions are listed in Table 12-1.

All mixtures of gases are solutions, since they consist of homogeneous systems of different kinds of molecules. Solutions of solids in liquids are very common. Since water is a liquid at ordinary temperatures, we may think of water vapor in air as a liquid-in-gas solution. Solutions of gases in solids are rare. An example is the *condensation* of hydrogen on the surface of paladium and platinum. This phenomenon, called *adsorption,* approaches the nature of a solution.

In general, substances which are alike in their chemical makeup are apt to form solutions. Silver and gold, or alcohol and water, are examples. *Two liquids which are mutually soluble in each other are said to be* **miscible.** Ethanol (ethyl alcohol) and water are miscible in all proportions. Similarly, ether and ethanol are completely miscible. Ether and water, on the other hand, are only slightly miscible. Acetone is completely miscible with water, alcohol, and ether.

12.3 Solvents are selective

High solubility occurs when solutes and solvents are alike structurally. In a very general sense, the *possibility* of solvent action is increased by a similarity in the composition and structure of substances. Chemists believe that the distribution of electronic forces helps to explain why solvents are *selective.* That is, it may explain why solvents dissolve some substances readily and others only to an insignificant extent.

The water molecule is a polar structure with a distinct negative region (the oxygen atom) and a distinct positive region (the hydrogen atoms). It is frequently referred to as the *water dipole.* The two polar covalent O—H bonds in water form an angle of about 105°. Thus, the molecule as a whole is polar and behaves as a dipole (has a negative region and a positive region).

The carbon tetrachloride molecule, CCl_4, contains four polar covalent bonds. Each C—Cl bond is formed by electron sharing between an sp^3 hybrid orbital of the carbon atom and a p orbital of a chlorine atom. The set of four sp^3 orbitals of carbon (see Section 6.12) leads to the regular tetrahedral shape of the CCl_4 molecules (Figure 12-4). Because of the symmetrical arrangement of the four polar bonds, the molecule is nonpolar. On the other hand, gasoline-type compounds, while unsymmetrical in bond arrangement, are practically nonpolar. They are practically nonpolar because the electronegativity difference between the hydrogen and carbon atoms of which they are composed is small.

Table 12-1
TYPES OF SOLUTION

Solute	Solvent	Example
gas	gas	air
gas	liquid	soda water
gas	solid	hydrogen in palladium
liquid	gas	water vapor in air
liquid	liquid	alcohol in water
liquid	solid	mercury in copper
solid	gas	sulfur vapor in air
solid	liquid	sugar in water
solid	solid	copper in nickel

Fig. 12-3. Models of solutions.

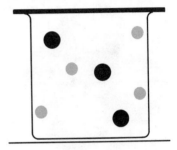

Gaseous solution

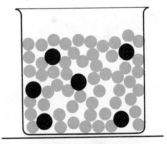

Liquid solution

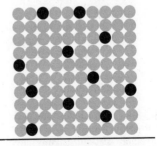

Solid solution

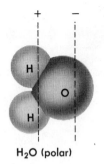

H₂O (polar)

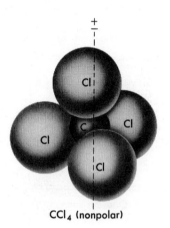

CCl₄ (nonpolar)

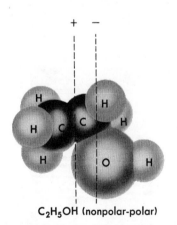

C₂H₅OH (nonpolar-polar)

Fig. 12-4. Molecular models of three common solvents. Differences in molecular structure may help to explain why they are selective.

Suppose we apply the rough rule that *like dissolves like* to these solvents. According to this rule, we would expect water to dissolve polar substances and carbon tetrachloride to dissolve nonpolar substances. Solute crystals composed of polar molecules or ions are held together by strong attractive forces. They are more likely to be attracted away from their solid structures by polar water molecules than by nonpolar solvents. Thus, many crystalline salts like table salt and molecular solids like sugar readily dissolve in water. Compounds which are insoluble in water, such as oils and greases, readily dissolve in nonpolar carbon tetrachloride.

Ethanol, C_2H_5OH, is typical of a group of solvents which dissolve both polar and nonpolar substances.

$$\overset{\displaystyle H \quad H}{\underset{\displaystyle H \quad H}{H\overset{\times}{\underset{\times}{\cdot}}C\overset{\bullet}{\underset{\times}{\cdot}}C\overset{\bullet\times}{\underset{\bullet}{\cdot}}\overset{\circ\circ}{\underset{\circ\circ}{O}}\overset{\circ}{\underset{\circ}{\cdot}}H}}$$

There are five essentially nonpolar carbon-hydrogen bonds. Also, there is one carbon-carbon bond which is completely nonpolar. The carbon-oxygen bond and the hydrogen-oxygen bond are polar. As in water, the oxygen region of an ethanol molecule is more negative than the other regions. Thus, an ethanol molecule has some polar character. As a solvent, it is in an intermediate position between the strongly polar water molecule and the nonpolar carbon tetrachloride molecule. This may account for the fact that ethanol is a good solvent for some polar and some nonpolar substances.

12.4 Hydrogen bonds and properties of solvents

Electronegativity is the measure of the tendency of an atom in a molecule to attract shared electrons (Section 6.15). Hydrogen atoms form distinctly polar covalent bonds with atoms of such highly electronegative elements as fluorine, oxygen, chlorine, and nitrogen. The hydrogen end of such a bond is unique. It consists essentially of an exposed proton. The proton is exposed because the shared electrons are attracted more strongly by the other atom. The somewhat positive hydrogen end of such polar bonds attracts the relatively negative atoms of other molecules. This attraction is strong enough to be recognized as a type of loose chemical bond called the *hydrogen bond* (Section 11.16). By far the most common hydrogen bonds involve oxygen, although those with fluorine are stronger. See Figure 12-5.

We have discussed such properties of water as its abnormally high boiling and melting points. These properties may be attributed in part to the presence of hydrogen bonds between molecules. Also, the formation of hydrogen bonds between a solvent and a solute increases the solubility of the solute. Hydrogen bond

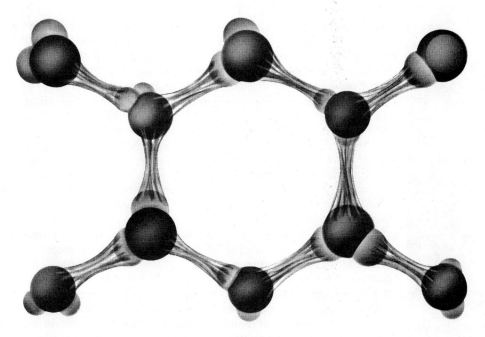

Fig. 12-5. Hydrogen bond formation in an ice crystal.

formation between water and ethanol may partially explain their complete miscibility.

Some elements other than hydrogen tend to lose electrons. However, the loss of the valence electrons by these elements does not expose the nucleus. The nucleus is still surrounded by inner electrons. The end of polar molecules having such elements is slightly positive. Unlike the positive hydrogen end, it does not form a bond with the slightly negative end of another molecule. The inner electrons which shield the nucleus of the atom at the positive end of the molecule repel the highly electronegative regions of other particles.

12.5 Solution equilibrium

We may think of the solution process as being *reversible*. Suppose we again consider the lump of sugar dropped into a beaker of water. The sugar molecules which break away from the crystals and enter the water have completely random motions. Some of these molecules which have broken away come in contact with the undissolved sugar. Here they are attracted by the sugar molecules in the crystal and become part of the crystal structure once more. Thus, the solution process includes both the act of dissolving and the act of crystallizing.

At first, there are no sugar molecules in solutions. The solution process occurs only in the direction of dissolving. Molecules leave the crystal structure and diffuse throughout the water. *As*

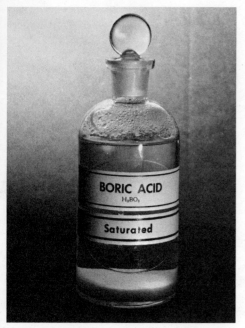

Fig. 12-6. A saturated solution contains the equilibrium concentration of solute, under existing conditions.

Fig. 12-7. A comparison of the masses of three common solutes that can be dissolved in $10\overline{0}$ g of water at 0° C. Convert these quantities to moles of solute per $10\overline{0}$ g of water and compare them.

the solution concentration (number of sugar molecules per unit volume of solution) increases, the reverse process begins. The rate at which the sugar crystals rebuild increases as the concentration of the sugar solution increases. Eventually, if undissolved sugar remains, sugar crystals rebuild as fast as they dissolve.

At this point, the concentration of the solution is the maximum possible under existing conditions. Such a solution is said to be *saturated.* An *equilibrium* is reached between undissolved sugar and sugar dissolved in water. *Solution equilibrium is the physical state in which the opposing processes of dissolving and crystallizing of a solute occur at equal rates. A saturated solution is one in which the dissolved and undissolved solutes are in equilibrium.* (In Figure 12-6, what visible evidence is there that this solution is saturated?)

If more water is added to the sugar solution, it is no longer saturated; the concentration of solute molecules has been decreased. In the language of the Le Chatelier principle, the decrease in concentration of solute particles places a *stress* on the equilibrium. This stress is relieved by an increase in the dissolving rate. More sugar dissolves and restores *the same equilibrium concentration* of solute molecules. Solution equilibrium exists when no more solute can dissolve in a given quantity of solvent. *The solubility of a substance is defined as the maximum amount of that substance which can dissolve in a given amount of a certain solvent under specified conditions.*

12.6 Influence of pressure on solubility

Ordinary changes in pressure affect the solubility of solids and liquids so slightly that we may ignore them altogether. Because

100g of water   100g of water   100g of water

4.90g. of potassium dichromate   31.6g of copper(II) sulfate, pentahydrate   76.7g of cobalt(II) chloride, hexahydrate

all mixtures of gases are homogeneous, the solubility of one gas in another is independent of pressure. The gas laws describe the behavior of mixtures of gases just as they do of individual gases.

The solubility of gases in liquids and solids, on the other hand, is measurably affected by changes in pressure. Carbonated beverages *fizz* or *effervesce* when poured into an open glass tumbler. At the bottling plant, carbon dioxide gas is forced into solution in the flavored water under a pressure of from 5 to 10 atmospheres. While under such pressure, the gas-in-liquid solution is sealed in the bottles. When the cap is removed, the pressure is reduced to 1 atmosphere and some of the carbon dioxide escapes from solution as gas bubbles. *This rapid escape of a gas from a liquid in which it is dissolved is known as **effervescence**.*

Solutions of gases in liquids reach equilibrium in about the same way that solids in liquids do. The attractive forces between gas molecules are insignificant on the average and their motions are relatively free. If a gas is in contact with the surface of a liquid, gas molecules can easily enter the liquid surface. As the concentration of dissolved gas molecules increases, some begin to escape from the liquid. The escaping molecules reenter the gaseous phase above the liquid. An equilibrium is eventually reached between the rates at which gas molecules are dissolving and escaping from solution. After the equilibrium is attained, there is no increase in the concentration of the gaseous solute. Thus, the solubility of the gas is limited to its equilibrium concentration in the liquid under existing conditions.

Suppose the pressure of the gas above the liquid is increased. The equilibrium is then disturbed in accordance with Le Chatelier's principle, and more gas dissolves. This action, of course, increases the concentration of the dissolved gas. The increased concentration, in turn, causes gas molecules to escape from the liquid surface at a faster rate. When equilibrium is restored, there is a higher concentration of solute at the higher external pressure. The increase in gas pressure also increases the concentration of undissolved gas in contact with the solvent. Thus, the solubility of the gas in the liquid is increased. *The solubility of a gas in a liquid is directly proportional to the pressure of the gas above the liquid.* This statement is known as **Henry's law**. It is named after William Henry, an English chemist (1775–1836).

Some gases react chemically with their liquid solvents. Such gases are generally more soluble than those which do not form compounds with the solvent molecules. Oxygen, hydrogen, and nitrogen are only slightly soluble in water. Ammonia, carbon dioxide, and sulfur dioxide are more soluble probably because they form the weak monohydrates $NH_3 \cdot H_2O$, $CO_2 \cdot H_2O$, and $SO_2 \cdot H_2O$ with the water solvent. Such gases do not follow Henry's law as stated above.

If different gases are mixed in a confined space of constant volume and at a definite temperature, *each gas exerts the same pressure as if it alone occupied the space.* The pressure of the mixture as a whole is the *total* of the individual or *partial* pressures of the gases composing the mixture. You will recognize this statement as *Dalton's law of partial pressures,* discussed in Section 9.14. The partial pressure of each gas is proportional to the number of molecules of that gas in the mixture.

If a mixture of gases is in contact with a liquid, the solubility of each gas is proportional to its partial pressure. Let us assume that the gases present in the mixture do not react in any way when in solution. Then each gas dissolves to the same extent that it would if the other gases were not present.

Air is about 20 percent oxygen. When air is bubbled through water, only about 20 percent as much oxygen dissolves as would dissolve if pure oxygen were used instead of air, at the same pressure. Oxygen remains dissolved in the water because it is in equilibrium with the oxygen in the air above the water. If the oxygen were removed from the air above the water, this equilibrium would be disturbed. By Le Chatelier's principle, the dissolved oxygen must eventually escape from the water. This fact is important when we consider the abundance of life that exists in water.

12.7 Temperature and solubility

1. Gases in liquids. A glass of water drawn from the hot water tap often appears milky. Tiny bubbles of air suspended throughout the water cause this cloudiness. The suspended air originally was *dissolved* in cold water. It was driven out of solution as the water was heated.

Raising the temperature of a solution increases the average speed of its molecules. Molecules of dissolved gas leave the solvent at a faster rate than gas molecules enter the solvent. This lowers the equilibrium concentration of the solute. Thus, the solubility of a gas decreases as the temperature of the solvent is increased. Table 11 of the Appendix shows how the solubility of gases varies with the kind of gas and the temperature.

2. Solids in liquids. An excess of sugar added to water results in an equilibrium between the sugar solute and the undissolved crystals. This equilibrium is characteristic of a saturated solution.

If the solution is warmed, the equilibrium is disturbed and solid sugar dissolves as the temperature of the solution rises. It is evident that the solubility of the sugar in water has increased with the rise in temperature. A new solution equilibrium is eventually reached at the higher solution temperature. At this temperature, the solution has a higher equilibrium concentration of solute sugar.

Cooling the solution causes dissolved sugar to separate as crystals. The separation of solute from the solution indicates that solubility diminishes as the temperature falls. No more than the equilibrium concentration of the solute can normally remain in solution. Thus, lowering the temperature disturbs the equilibrium, and sugar crystallizes from solution faster than solid crystals dissolve.

It is possible, however, to cool a hot saturated solution very carefully so that the excess solute does not separate. Such a solution is said to be *supersaturated*. Supersaturated solutions have a strong tendency to reestablish normal equilibrium. Disturbing the solution slightly, or seeding it with a small crystal, causes the excess solute to separate. The equilibrium concentration of the solute is then quickly established.

Increasing the temperature usually increases the solubility of solids in liquids. Sometimes, however, the reverse effect is observed. A certain rise in temperature may result in a large increase in solubility in one case, a slight increase in another case, and a definite decrease in still another. For example, the solubility of potassium nitrate in $10\overline{0}$ g of water at 0° C is 13 g. Solubility increases to nearly 140 g when the temperature is raised to 70° C. Under similar circumstances, the solubility of sodium chloride increases only about 2 g. The solubility of cerium sulfate, on the other hand, decreases nearly 14 g. Typical solubility curves are shown in Figure 12-8. If the solubility curve for cane sugar in water were included, the graph would have to be extended considerably. At 0° C, 179 g of sugar dissolves in $10\overline{0}$ g of water. The solubility increases to 487 g at 100° C. The solubility of solids depends upon the nature of the solid, the nature of the solvent, and the temperature. Solubility data for various substances in water are given in Table 12-2.

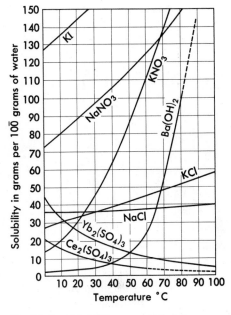

Fig. 12-8. Solubility curves. The solubility of a solute is expressed in grams per $10\overline{0}$ grams of solvent, at a stated temperature.

Table 12–2

SOLUBILITY OF SOLUTES AS A FUNCTION OF TEMPERATURE

(Grams of solute per 100 grams of H_2O)

Substance	0°	20°	40°	60°	80°	100°
$AgNO_3$	122	222	376	525	669	952
$Ba(OH)_2$	1.67	3.89	8.22	20.94	101.4	–
$C_{12}H_{22}O_{11}$	179	204	238	287	362	487
$Ca(OH)_2$	0.185	0.165	0.141	0.116	0.094	0.077
$Ce_2(SO_4)_3$	20.8	10.1	–	3.87	–	–
KCl	27.6	34.0	40.0	45.5	51.1	56.7
KI	128	144	$16\overline{0}$	176	192	208
KNO_3	13.3	31.6	63.9	$11\overline{0}$	169	246
Li_2CO_3	1.54	1.33	1.17	1.01	0.85	0.72
NaCl	35.7	36.0	36.6	37.3	38.4	39.8
$NaNO_3$	73	88	104	124	148	$18\overline{0}$
$Yb_2(SO_4)_3$	44.2	$38.4^{10°}$	$21.0^{30°}$	10.4	6.92	4.67
CO_2 (gas at SP)	0.335	0.169	0.097	0.058	–	–
O_2 (gas at SP)	0.0069	0.0043	0.0031	0.0023	0.0014	0.0000

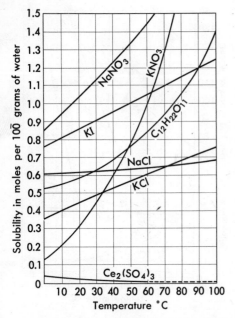

Fig. 12-9. Solubility plotted in moles of solute per 100 g of water as a function of temperature. Compare the relative positions of the curves with those of Fig. 12-8.

When a solid dissolves in a liquid, we may think of the solid as changing in phase to something resembling a liquid. Such a change is endothermic, and heat is absorbed. Thus, we expect the temperature of the solution to be lowered as a solid dissolves. We also expect the solubility of a solid to increase as the temperature is raised. Deviations from this normal pattern may indicate some kind of chemical reaction between solute and solvent.

3. *Liquids in liquids.* Similar logic applies to solutions of liquids in liquids. As no change in phase occurs when such solutions are prepared, we expect little change in temperature.

A great change in temperature, as in the case of sulfuric acid in water, suggests some type of chemical reaction between solute and solvent. When water is the solvent, this reaction may involve *hydration,* a clustering of water dipoles about the solute particles.

12.8   Increasing the rate of dissolving

The rate at which a solid dissolves in a liquid depends on the solid and liquid involved. As a rule, the more nearly the solute and solvent are alike in structure, the more readily solution occurs. We may, however, increase the rate of solution of a solid in a liquid in three ways.

1. *By stirring.* The diffusion of solute molecules throughout the solvent occurs rather slowly. Stirring or shaking the mixture aids in the dispersion of the solute particles. It does so by bringing fresh portions of the solvent in contact with the undissolved solid.

2. *By powdering the solid.* Solution action occurs only at the surface of the solid. By grinding the solid into a fine powder, we greatly increase the surface area. Hence, finely powdered solids dissolve much more rapidly than large lumps or crystals of the same substance.

3. *By heating the solvent.* The rate of dissolving increases with temperature. If we apply heat to a solvent, the molecular activity increases. As a result, the dissolving action is speeded up. At the same time, the solubility of the substance increases if the dissolving process is endothermic.

The first two actions influence the rate of dissolving by increasing the effective contact area between solid and liquid. The third does so by producing a more favorable energy distribution among the particles of the solid. As temperature is raised, the average kinetic energy of the solute particles is also raised. A larger portion of the particles have enough kinetic energy to overcome the binding forces and leave the surface of the solid.

12.9   Dissolving mechanisms

Chemists do not fully understand the actual manner in which substances enter into solution. However, some aspects of the solution process are fairly well understood. Let us examine possible mechanisms by which a solid dissolves in a liquid. Why is this process *spontaneous,* or self-acting? We may assume that at least three important actions occur in the dissolving process:

1. Solute particles must be separated from the solid mass (as a solid changing phase to a liquid). *This action takes up energy.*

2. Solvent particles must be moved apart to allow solute particles to enter the liquid environment. *This action also takes up energy.*

3. Solute particles are attracted to solvent particles. *This action gives up energy.*

The first two of these actions are endothermic and the last one is exothermic. If this exothermic action is less than the combined effect of the first two, the net change is endothermic. Consequently, the temperature of the solution *decreases* as the solid dissolves. This is the usual pattern for solid-in-liquid solutions. In such cases, heating the solution results in an increase in the solubility of the solid. If the net change is exothermic, the temperature of the solution *increases* as the solid dissolves. Heating such solutions results in a decrease in the solubility of the solid. The reasons for these effects will be discussed in Section 12.10.

We may think of dissolving as being aided by the attraction between solute and solvent particles. Solvent molecules move at random. Some may be attracted to surface molecules of undissolved crystals. As they cluster about the surface molecules, enough energy may be released to enable the solvent molecules

Fig. 12-10. A possible mechanism of the solution process.

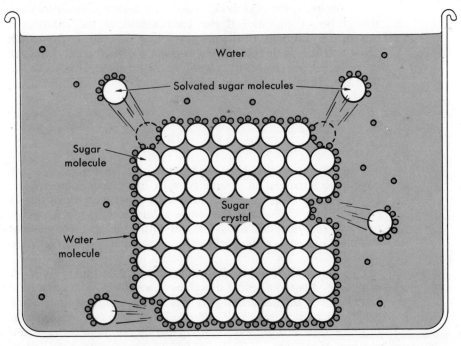

to carry off solute molecules. This process arises from the attraction between unlike molecules of solute and solvent. It is known as *solvation*. If water is the solvent, the solvation process is known more specifically as *hydration*. The solute molecule which leaves the crystal, along with its cluster of solvent molecules, is said to be *solvated*. If water molecules compose the solvent cluster, the solute molecule is said to be *hydrated*.

We have seen that natural processes generally lead to lower energy states (see Section 2.15). Thus, an endothermic energy change cannot account for the fact that the dissolving process occurs spontaneously. Perhaps the entropy change in such instances can account for it.

The mixture of solute and solvent particles in a solution is in a more disordered state (higher entropy) than that of the unmixed solid and liquid. Thus, the mixture is more probable than the unmixed state because of this higher entropy. The favorable entropy change of the dissolving process may cause solution to occur even though the energy change is not toward a lower state.

How well does this logic hold up when it is applied to solutions of gases in liquids? The solute is in a more random state as a gas than when dissolved in the liquid. Thus, the higher entropy of the gaseous state opposes the dissolving process. For dissolving to occur, the energy change must be favorable (to a lower state). It also must be great enough to overcome the unfavorable entropy change.

Accordingly, the dissolving process for a gas-in-liquid solution should be exothermic. If the temperature of the solution is raised, the solubility of the gas should be lowered. Experiments show that this is the case. Heat is given off when a gas dissolves in water. Furthermore, the solubility of the gas decreases as the temperature of the solution is raised.

12.10 Heat of solution

From the previous discussions, it is clear that no single rule covers all changes of solubility with increasing temperature. Gases generally become less soluble in water as temperature is raised. Table 12-2 shows that some solids become more soluble in water as temperature is raised. Other solids become less soluble, and still others experience practically no change in solubility.

In Section 12.9, we learned that heat may be either given off or absorbed when a solute dissolves in a solvent. Thus, the total heat content of a solution may not be the same as that of its separate components. *The difference between the heat content of a solution and the heat contents of its components is called the **heat of solution**.*

solute + solvent → solution + heat   **(exothermic)**

or

solute + solvent + heat → solution   **(endothermic)**

When the dissolving process is exothermic, the total heat content of the solution is less than that of its separate components. The solution warms as dissolving proceeds. The heat of solution is said to be *negative*. When the process is endothermic, the heat content of the solution is *greater* than that of its components. The solution cools as dissolving proceeds and the heat of solution is said to be *positive*.

The dilution of a concentrated solution may cause the release or absorption of heat. Thus, the heat of solution of any system depends upon the concentration of the final solution. For this reason, heat of solution is measured in kilocalories per mole of solute dissolved in a specific number of moles of solvent. Heats of solution for some common substances are given in Table 12-3. How do these data relate to the solubility information of Table 12-2?

Observe that the change in solubility of a substance with temperature is closely related to its heat of solution. The heat of solution of sodium chloride, for example, is nearly zero. The solubility change of sodium chloride with temperature is also very small.

In a saturated solution with undissolved solute, an equilibrium exists between the dissolving and crystallizing processes. Let us consider such a solution of KCl. The symbols (s) and (l) indicate solid and liquid, respectively.

$$KCl(s) + H_2O(l) + heat \rightleftarrows solution$$

The heat of solution is +4.20 kcal/mole. The dissolving process is endothermic. The crystallizing process must then be exothermic. At equilibrium, the tendency toward lower energy (release of heat) as solute crystallizes just balances the tendency toward higher entropy (greater disorder) as crystals dissolve. Consequently, there is no net driving force in the system.

Suppose we now add heat to the solution. The rise in temperature produces a stress on the equilibrium. From Le Chatelier's principle, the system relieves this stress by increasing the rate of the *endothermic* process. Thus, dissolving proceeds faster than crystallizing until the concentration of KCl in solution is increased and the stress is relieved. Solutes with *positive* heats of solution become more soluble as the temperature of their solution is raised.

The effect of temperature on saturated solutions of solutes having *negative* heats of solutions is the reverse of the process just described. Here, the dissolving process is exothermic and the crystallizing process is endothermic. A rise in solution temperature disturbs the equilibrium and the rate of the endothermic process (crystallizing) increases. Solute separates from the solution. Solutes with *negative* heats of solution become less soluble as the temperature of their solution is raised.

Table 12-3

HEATS OF SOLUTION
(kcal/mole solute in 200 moles H_2O)
[(s) = solid, (1) = liquid, (g) = gas at SP]

Substance	Heat of solution
$AgNO_3$ (s)	+5.44
CO_2 (g)	−4.76
$CuSO_4$ (s)	−16.20
$CuSO_4 \cdot 5H_2O$(s)	+2.75
$HC_2H_3O_2$ (l)	−0.38
HCl(g)	−17.74
HI(g)	−7.02
H_2SO_4 (l)	−17.75
KCl(s)	+4.20
$KClO_3$ (s)	+10.04
KI(s)	+5.11
KNO_3 (s)	+8.52
KOH(s)	−13.04
$LiCl$(s)	−8.37
Li_2CO_3 (s)	−3.06
$MgSO_4 \cdot 7H_2O$(s)	+3.80
$NaCl$(s)	+1.02
$NaNO_3$ (s)	+5.03
$NaOH$(s)	−9.94
$Na_2SO_4 \cdot 10H_2O$(s)	+18.76
NH_3 (g)	−8.28
NH_4Cl(s)	+3.88
NH_4NO_3 (s)	+6.08

12.11   Concentration of solutions

The *concentration* of a solution depends upon the relative proportions of solute and solvent. The more solute that is dissolved in a solvent, the more *concentrated* the solution becomes. On the other hand, the more solvent that is added, the more *dilute* the solution becomes.

The terms *dilute* and *concentrated* are qualitative. They are useful in a general sense only. In order to be of value to the chemist, the concentrations of solutions must be known quantitatively. Chemists have developed several methods of expressing concentrations to suit various problems which arise in the laboratory.

We shall use only three methods for expressing the concentrations of solutions quantitatively. One method expresses the *ratio of solute to solvent*. We shall discuss this method immediately. Two other methods will be introduced later, as they are needed. They both express the *ratio of solute to solution,* but in different ways.

If it is important to know the ratio of solute molecules to solvent molecules in a solution, we will state the concentration in terms of *molality. The **molality** of a solution is the number of moles of solute per kilogram of solvent.* The symbol for molality is the small letter *m*.

A one-molal (1-*m*) solution contains *1 mole of solute per kilogram of solvent.* You will recognize that 0.5 mole of solute dissolved in 0.5 kg of solvent, or 0.25 mole of solute in 0.25 kg of solvent also gives a 1-*m* solution. A *half-molal* (0.5-*m*) solution contains *one-half mole* of solute per kilogram of solvent. A *two-molal* (2-*m*) solution has *two moles* of solute in 1 kilogram of solvent. Several exercises for expressing the concentration of solutions in terms of molality are given in Table 12-4.

Molal solutions are important to chemists because (for a given solvent) *two solutions of equal molality have the same ratio of solute to solvent molecules.* (A kilogram, 1000 g, of

Table 12-4
CONCENTRATION OF SOLUTIONS IN MOLALITY

Quantity of solute	Quantity of solvent	Mass solute per mole	Conversion to moles solute	Conversion to kg solvent	Moles solute per kg solvent	Molality
18.2 g HCl	250 g H₂O	$\dfrac{36.5 \text{ g}}{\text{mole}}$	$18.2 \text{ g HCl} \times \dfrac{\text{mole}}{36.5 \text{ g}}$	$250 \text{ g H}_2\text{O} \times \dfrac{\text{kg}}{10^3 \text{ g}}$	$\dfrac{0.499 \text{ mole HCl}}{0.250 \text{ kg H}_2\text{O}}$	$= 2.00 \, m$
2.50 g NH₃	175 g H₂O	$\dfrac{17.0 \text{ g}}{\text{mole}}$	$2.50 \text{ g NH}_3 \times \dfrac{\text{mole}}{17.0 \text{ g}}$	$175 \text{ g H}_2\text{O} \times \dfrac{\text{kg}}{10^3 \text{ g}}$	$\dfrac{0.147 \text{ mole NH}_3}{0.175 \text{ kg H}_2\text{O}}$	$= 0.840 \, m$
15.6 g NaCl	500 g H₂O	$\dfrac{58.5 \text{ g}}{\text{mole}}$	$15.6 \text{ g NaCl} \times \dfrac{\text{mole}}{58.5 \text{ g}}$	$500 \text{ g H}_2\text{O} \times \dfrac{\text{kg}}{10^3 \text{ g}}$	$\dfrac{0.264 \text{ mole NaCl}}{0.500 \text{ kg H}_2\text{O}}$	$= 0.534 \, m$
12.2 g I₂	100 g CCl₄	$\dfrac{254 \text{ g}}{\text{mole}}$	$122.2 \text{ g I}_2 \times \dfrac{\text{mole}}{254 \text{ g}}$	$100 \text{ g CCl}_4 \times \dfrac{\text{kg}}{10^3 \text{ g}}$	$\dfrac{0.0466 \text{ mole I}_2}{0.100 \text{ kg CCl}_4}$	$= 0.480 \, m$

solvent can be expressed in terms of moles since $1000 \text{ g} \div$ number of grams/mole of solvent = number of moles of solvent.) Molality is preferred for expressing the concentration of solutions in procedures in which temperature changes may occur. The following Sample Problems illustrate calculations involving solution concentrations in molalities.

Sample Problem

How many grams of $AgNO_3$ are needed to prepare a $0.125\text{-}m$ solution in $25\overline{0}$ ml of water?

Solution

Molality expresses solution concentration in moles of solute per kilogram of solvent.

$$25\overline{0} \text{ ml } H_2O = 25\overline{0} \text{ g } H_2O$$

The gram-formula weight of $AgNO_3 = 17\overline{0} \text{ g} = $ mass of 1 mole $AgNO_3$. Our $0.125\text{-}m$ $AgNO_3$ solution = 0.125 mole $AgNO_3$/kg H_2O. We wish to determine the mass of $AgNO_3$ required for $25\overline{0}$ g of H_2O to give the $0.125\text{-}m$ concentration. So we must convert moles of $AgNO_3$ to grams and grams of H_2O to kilograms. This is done by unit cancellations as follows:

$$\frac{0.125 \text{ mole } AgNO_3}{\text{kg } H_2O} \times \frac{17\overline{0} \text{ g}}{\text{mole}} \times 25\overline{0} \text{ g } H_2O \times \frac{\text{kg}}{10^3 \text{ g}} = 5.30 \text{ g } AgNO_3$$

Sample Problem

A solution contains 17.1 g of sucrose, $C_{12}H_{22}O_{11}$, dissolved in 125 g of water. Determine the molal concentration.

Solution

The formula weight of $C_{12}H_{22}O_{11} = 342$. Thus, 1 mole has a mass of 342 g. The concentration is 17.1 g sucrose/125 g H_2O. To express in terms of molality, we must convert grams of sucrose to moles, and grams of H_2O to kilograms, giving moles of sucrose per kilogram of water. This is accomplished by unit cancellations as follows:

$$\frac{17.1 \text{ g } C_{12}H_{22}O_{11}}{125 \text{ g } H_2O} \times \frac{\text{mole}}{342 \text{ g}} \times \frac{10^3 \text{ g}}{\text{kg}} = \frac{0.400 \text{ mole } C_{12}H_{22}O_{11}}{\text{kg } H_2O} = 0.400 \text{ } m$$

12.12 Freezing-point depression of solvents

In the preceding sections, we have examined in some detail the nature of the solution process. Now let us see how the addition of a solute affects the properties of the solvent.

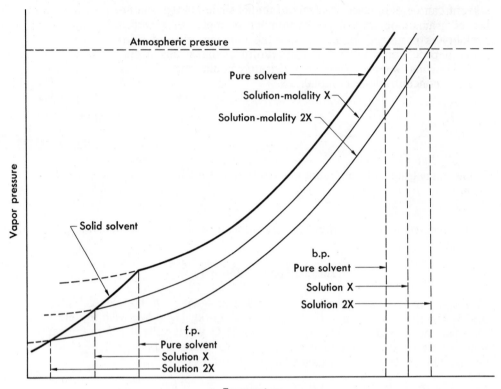

Fig. 12-11. Vapor pressure of solvent as a function of temperature plotted for a pure solvent and dilute solutions of molalities X and 2X. Freezing-point depressions and boiling-point elevations are shown to be proportional to the molal concentrations of the solutions.

An important effect is known from experiments involving vapor pressure. *At any temperature, the vapor pressure of a pure solvent is higher than that of the same solvent when it contains dissolved solute.* We can think of the vapor pressure of a liquid as a measure of the *escaping tendency* of the liquid molecules. Thus, the presence of solute particles in solution lowers the escaping tendency of the solvent molecules. This effect is reasonable if we think of the solute particles in solution as *decreasing the concentration* of solvent molecules.

Figure 12-11 shows plots of vapor pressure of a solvent as a function of temperature. Curves are given for a pure solvent, a dilute solution of molal concentration X, and a dilute solution of molal concentration 2X. Observe that, at any given temperature, the vapor pressure of the solvent decreases in porportion to the concentration of *solute particles*. This decrease in solvent vapor pressure has the effect of extending the liquid range of the solution. That is, the solution can exist in the liquid phase at both higher and lower temperatures than can the pure solvent. What can we conclude from this observation concerning the boiling and freezing points of solutions?

Salt water freezes at a lower temperature than fresh water. Sea water is a dilute solution of common salt, NaCl, and many other minerals. Suppose a sample of sea water is cooled enough for freezing to occur. The crystals produced are those of the *pure solvent* itself (in this case, water), not of the solution. This phenomenon occurs when any dilute solution is cooled enough for freezing to occur. We may conclude that *solutes lower the freezing point of the solvent in which they are dissolved.* We make use of this fact when we add alcohol or ethylene glycol (permanent antifreeze) to the water in an automobile radiator during the winter months.

Chemists have investigated many dilute solutions of nonelectrolytes in water. They have found that the *freezing-point depression* of the water is determined by the *number* of solute particles in a given quantity of water, not by their identity. Dilute solutions of equal molality, but which contain different solutes, yield the same freezing-point depression for water. Dilute solutions of different molality give different freezing-point depressions. These facts suggest that the *lowering of the freezing point of the solvent is directly proportional to the molecular concentration of the solute.*

Freezing-point depressions of solvents are represented by the symbol ΔT_f. They are expressed in Celsius degrees, C°. The Greek letter Δ (delta) signifies "change in." Suppose the freezing point of a quantity of water is lowered from $0.00°$ C to $-0.36°$ C by the addition of a small amount of some molecular solute. The freezing-point depression of the water is indicated to be 0.36 C°.

$$\Delta T_f = 0.36 \text{ C}°$$

The depression of the freezing point has been calculated for a 1-molal solution of any molecular solute in water. It has been found to have the constant value of 1.86 C°. *This freezing-point depression for a 1-molal water solution is called the* **molal freezing-point constant,** K_f, *for water.* It is expressed as 1.86 C°/molal. Since

$$\text{molality} = \frac{\text{moles solute}}{\text{kg solvent}}$$

K_f has the dimensions $\dfrac{\text{C}°}{\text{mole solute/kg solvent}}$.

The molal freezing-point constant for water is

$$K_f = \frac{1.86 \text{ C}°}{\text{molal}} = \frac{1.86 \text{ C}°}{\text{mole solute/kg } H_2O}$$

Using this value of K_f, a molecular solute added to 1 kg of water should lower the freezing point 1.86 C° per mole of solute dissolved. However, this relation holds experimentally only for dilute solutions. Even a 1-molal solution is concentrated enough so that the freezing-point depression is somewhat less than 1.86 C°. All solvents have their own characteristic molal freezing-

The phenomenon of freezing-point change is observed for solvents containing volatile solutes (those which evaporate rapidly) as well as nonvolatile solutes. Alcohol and ammonia are examples of volatile solutes when in water solutions. Sugar is a nonvolatile solute when in water solution.

Table 12-5

MOLAL FREEZING-POINT AND BOILING-POINT CONSTANTS

Solvent	Normal f.p. (°C)	Molal f.p. constant, K_f (C°/molal)	Normal b.p. (°C)	Molal b.p. constant, K_b (°C/molal)
acetic acid	16.6	3.90	118.5	3.07
acetone	−94.8	−	56.00	1.71
aniline	−6.1	5.87	184.4	3.22
benzene	5.48	5.12	80.15	2.53
carbon disulfide	−111.5	3.80	46.3	2.34
carbon tetrachloride	−22.96	−	76.50	5.03
ethanol	−114.5	−	78.26	1.22
ether	−116.3	1.79	34.42	2.02
napthalene	80.2	6.9	218.0	5.65
phenol	40.9	7.27	181.8	3.56
water	0.00	1.86	100.0	0.51

point constants. The values of K_f for some common solvents are given in Table 12-5.

The depression of the freezing point of the solvent in a dilute solution of a molecular solute is directly proportional to the molal concentration of the solution. The freezing-point depression *is equal to the product of the molal freezing-point constant of the solvent and the molality of the solution.*

$$\Delta T_f = K_f m$$

Here K_f is the molal freezing-point constant of the solvent expressed in C°/(mole solute/kg solvent). The quantity m is the molality of the solution expressed in moles of solute/kg of solvent. ΔT_f is the freezing-point depression in C°. The following Sample Problems illustrate the use of the equation.

Sample Problem

A solution is prepared in which 17.1 g of sucrose, $C_{12}H_{22}O_{11}$, is dissolved in $20\overline{0}$ g of water. What is the freezing-point depression of the solvent?

Solution

The gram-molecular weight of $C_{12}H_{22}O_{11} = 342$ g. Thus, for sucrose 342 g = 1 mole.

The mass, 17.1 g of sucrose, must be converted to moles. The mass, $20\overline{0}$ g of water, must be converted to kilograms. These conversions are accomplished by familiar unit-cancellation methods.

$$K_f \text{ for water} = \frac{1.86 \text{ C}°}{\text{molal}} = \frac{1.86 \text{ C}°}{\text{mole solute/kg H}_2\text{O}}$$

Solving for ΔT_f:

$$\Delta T_f = K_f m$$

$$\Delta T_f = \frac{1.86\ C°}{\text{mole } C_{12}H_{22}O_{11}/\text{kg } H_2O} \times \frac{17.1\ \text{g } C_{12}H_{22}O_{11}}{20\bar{0}\ \text{g } H_2O} \times \frac{\text{mole}}{342\ \text{g}} \times \frac{10^3\ \text{g}}{\text{kg}}$$

$$\Delta T_f = 0.465\ C°$$

Observe that the unit-cancellation operations yield the answer unit C°.

$$\Delta T_f = \frac{C°}{\text{mole } \cancel{C_{12}H_{22}O_{11}}/\cancel{\text{kg } H_2O}} \times \frac{\cancel{\text{g}}\ \cancel{C_{12}H_{22}O_{11}}}{\cancel{\text{g}}\ \cancel{H_2O}} \times \frac{\cancel{\text{mole}}}{\cancel{\text{g}}} \times \frac{\cancel{\text{g}}}{\cancel{\text{kg}}}$$

$$\Delta T_f = C°$$

Sample Problem

A water solution of a nonelectrolyte is found to have a freezing point of $-0.23°$ C. What is the molal concentration of the solution?

Solution

The normal freezing point of water is $0.00°$ C, so the freezing-point depression, $\Delta T_f, = 0.23$ C°.

$$K_f\ (\text{water}) = 1.86\ C°/\text{molal}$$
$$\Delta T_f = K_f m$$

Solving for m:

$$m = \frac{\Delta T_f}{K_f} = \frac{0.23\ C°}{1.86\ C°/\text{molal}} = 0.12\ \text{molal}$$

12.13   Boiling-point elevation of solvents

The boiling point of the solvent in a solution is higher than that of the pure solvent alone, provided the solute present is not *volatile*. (A volatile solute is one easily vaporized.) Experiments with dilute solutions of nonvolatile nonelectrolytes have shown that the rise in boiling point of the solvent is directly proportional to the molecular concentration of the solute. This rise in boiling point is called the *boiling-point elevation, ΔT_b,* of the solvent.

The boiling-point elevation for a 1-molal water solution of any molecular solute is determined indirectly. It is derived from the properties of dilute water solutions at standard pressure. This boiling-point elevation has the constant value of 0.51 C°. That is, based on the behavior of dilute water solutions, the boiling point at 1-molal concentration should be raised to $100.51°$ C at 760 mm pressure. *The boiling-point elevation for* a 1-molal water solution is called the **molal boiling-point constant**, K_b, *for water*. It is expressed as 0.51 C°/molal. Thus, the molal boiling-point constant for water is

$$K_b = \frac{0.51\ C°}{molal} = \frac{0.51\ C°}{mole\ solute/kg\ H_2O}$$

The actual elevation of the boiling point in concentrated solutions deviates somewhat from that indicated by K_b. Thus, the proportionality between boiling-point elevation and solution molality is limited to dilute solutions. All solvents have their own characteristic molal boiling-point constants. The values of K_b for some common solvents are given in Table 12-5.

The elevation of the boiling point of a dilute solution of a nonvolatile molecular solute is directly proportional to the molal concentration of the solution. It is equal to the product of the molal boiling-point constant and the molality of the solution.

$$\Delta T_b = K_b m$$

The molal boiling-point constant, K_b, is expressed in the units C°/(mole solute/kg solvent). The molality of the solution, *m,* is expressed in moles of solute/kg of solvent. Thus, ΔT_b is the boiling-point elevation in C°.

The freezing points and boiling points of solutions of electrolytes are also depressed or elevated. However, they do not follow the simple relationships just described. Such solutes are not molecular and our generalizations about molecular substances do not hold for them.

12.14 Molecular weights of solutes

We have applied the Avogadro principle to determine the molecular weights of gases and volatile liquids by the molar-volume method. Now we shall see how molecular weights can be determined for certain other substances. Such substances are those which cannot be vaporized without decomposition, *but which are soluble in water or some other common solvent.* Of course, such solutes must not react with the solvent.

In previous sections we discussed the freezing-point depression and the boiling-point elevation of solvents. We found that both phenomena depend on the relative number of solute molecules mixed with a definite number of solvent molecules. They do *not* depend upon the nature of the solute.

The molal freezing-point constants, K_f, and molal boiling-point constants, K_b, are known for many common solvents. Suppose we know the concentration of a molecular solution in terms of the mass of solute and mass of solvent (for which K_f or K_b is known). The freezing-point depression or boiling-point elevation can be determined experimentally. The molecular weight can then be calculated. The freezing-point method is favored in these molecular-weight determinations.

From Section 12.12, we have the expression

$$\Delta T_f = K_f m$$

$$\text{Molality } m = \frac{\text{moles solute}}{\text{kg solvent}} = \frac{\text{g solute/g-mol wt}}{\text{kg solvent}}$$

Thus,

$$\Delta T_f = K_f \times \frac{\text{g solute/g-mol wt}}{\text{kg solvent}}$$

Solving for gram-molecular weight:

$$\text{g-mol wt} = \frac{K_f \times \text{g solute}}{T_f \times \text{kg solvent}}$$

The following Sample Problem illustrates this method of determining the molecular weight of a solute.

Sample Problem

It is found experimentally that 1.8 g of sulfur dissolved in $10\bar{0}$ g of naphthalene, $C_{10}H_8$, decreases the freezing point of the solvent 0.48 C°. What is the molecular weight of the solute?

Solution

The molal freezing-point constant for naphthalene is 6.9 C°/molal (Table 12-5). Molality is expressed in terms of kilograms of solvent. Therefore, the quantity of naphthalene used must be converted from grams to kilograms, using the factor 10^3 g/kg.

$$\Delta T_f = K_f m$$

$$\text{where } m = \frac{\text{moles solute}}{\text{kg solvent}} = \frac{\text{g solute/g-mol wt}}{\text{kg solvent}}$$

$$\Delta T_f = K_f \times \frac{\text{g solute/g-mol wt}}{\text{kg solvent}}$$

$$\text{g-mol wt} = \frac{K_f \times \text{g solute}}{\Delta T_f \times \text{kg solvent}}$$

$$\text{g-mol wt} = \frac{6.9 \text{ C}° \times 1.8 \text{ g S}}{\text{mole S/kg } C_{10}H_8 \times 0.48 \text{ C}° \times 10\bar{0} \text{ g } C_{10}H_8 \times \text{kg}/10^3 \text{ g}}$$

$$\text{g-mol wt} = 260 \text{ g/mole}$$

$$\text{mol wt} = 260$$

What does this result suggest about the composition of the sulfur molecule?

QUESTIONS

Group A

1. List, by name, five common solvents.
2. Why are the terms *dilute* and *concentrated* not entirely satisfactory as applied to solutions?
3. (*a*) Name the nine different types of solutions possible. (*b*) Which type is the most common?
4. Why does carbonated water effervesce when it is drawn from the soda fountain?
5. What action limits the amount of a solute which can dissolve in a given quantity of solvent under fixed conditions?
6. Explain the difference between *dissolve* and *melt*.
7. What is the influence of pressure on the solubility of: (*a*) a gas in a liquid; (*b*) a solid in a liquid?
8. What is the influence of temperature on the solubility of: (*a*) a gas in a liquid; (*b*) a solid in a liquid?
9. (*a*) What is the difference between *miscible* and *immiscible?* (*b*) Give an example of each?
10. What is the distinguishing characteristic of *polar* molecules?
11. Alcohol is a nonelectrolyte and is soluble in water, yet a molal solution of alcohol in water does not give the molal boiling-point elevation of water. Explain.
12. Explain the expression *saturated solution* in terms of solution equilibrium.

Group A

13. (*a*) What determines the amount of oxygen that remains dissolved in water which is at constant temperature and in contact with the atmosphere? (*b*) Explain what would happen if the oxygen were removed from the air above the water.
14. Suppose you wished to make a concentrated solution of copper(II) sulfate in water, using the crystalline hydrate as the solute. How would you hasten the solution process?
15. The carbon tetrachloride molecule contains four polar covalent bonds yet the molecule as a whole is nonpolar. Explain.
16. How can you explain the fact that alcohol is a solvent for both water and carbon tetrachloride?
17. Why do caps sometimes blow off the tops of ginger ale bottles when they are exposed to direct sunlight for some time?
18. Why is cold water more appropriate than hot water for making a saturated solution of calcium hydroxide?
19. How are the solubility curves like those in Figure 12-7 constructed?
20. Liquid methanol, CH_3OH, and water are miscible in all proportions. When 1 mole of CH_3OH (solute) is mixed with 10 moles of H_2O (solvent), the heat of solution is found to be -1.43 kcal. (*a*) Is the formation of solution accompanied by an increase or decrease in entropy? (State the argument upon which your answer is based.) (*b*) Does the change in entropy favor the separate components or the solution? (*c*) Is the dissolving process endothermic or exothermic? Justify your answer. (*d*) Does the energy change as indicated by the sign of the heat of solution favor the separate components or the solution? (*e*) Are your previous answers consistent with the fact that methanol and water are freely miscible? Explain.

PROBLEMS

1. How many grams of ethanol, C_2H_5OH, are required to prepare a 0.175-m solution in $40\overline{0}$ g of water?
2. Calculate the mass in grams of sucrose, $C_{12}H_{22}O_{11}$, which must be dissolved in $250\overline{0}$ g of water to make up a 0.100-m solution.
3. A solution of glucose, $C_6H_{12}O_6$, is prepared by dissolving 6.75 g of the glucose in 325 g of water. What is the molality of this solution?
4. What is the molality of a solution containing 46.0 g of glycerol, $C_3H_5(OH)_3$, in $75\overline{0}$ g of water?
5. A solution contains 96.0 g of methanol, CH_3OH, in $350\overline{0}$ g of water. Calculate the molality of the solution.
6. How many grams of water must be added to 90.0 g of glucose, $C_6H_{12}O_6$, to make a 0.250-m solution?
7. A 0.400-m solution of naphthalene, $C_{10}H_8$, in benzene, C_6H_6, is needed. If 32.0 g of naphthalene are available, how many grams of the benzene must be used?
8. A solution contains 31.0 g of ethylene glycol, $C_2H_4(OH)_2$, in $10\overline{0}$ g of water. What is the molality of the solution?
9. Calculate the molality of a solution containing 0.762 g of I_2 (solute) in $45\overline{0}$ g of CCl_4 (solvent).
10. A solution consists of 15.0 g sucrose, $C_{12}H_{22}O_{11}$, in 150.0 g of water. What is the freezing point of the water?
11. What is the boiling point of the solution described in Problem 10?
12. What is the freezing point of 250 g of water containing 11.25 g of a nonelectrolyte which has a molecular weight of 180?
13. A solution of iodine in benzene is found to have a freezing point of 4.3° C. What is the molality of the solution?
14. A sucrose-in-water solution raises the boiling point of the solvent to 100.11° C at standard pressure. Determine the molality of the solution.

15. The analysis of a compound yields: carbon, 32.0%; hydrogen, 4.0%; oxygen, 64.0%. It is found that 15.0 g of the compound added to 1.00 kg of water lowers the freezing point of the water 0.186 C°. (a) Find the empirical formula. (b) What is its molecular weight? (c) What is its molecular formula?
16. A compound contains: carbon, 40.00%; hydrogen, 6.6%; oxygen, 53.33%. Tests show that 9.0 g of the compound dissolved in $50\overline{0}$ g of water raises the boiling point of the water 0.051 C°. (a) Find its empirical formula. (b) Find its molecular weight. (c) What is its molecular formula?
17. The analysis of a compound shows: carbon, 30.3%; hydrogen, 1.7%; bromine, 68%. The substance is soluble in benzene and 10.0 g of it lowers the freezing point of $10\overline{0}$ g of benzene 2.1 C°. (a) Find the empirical formula of the solute. (b) Determine its molecular weight. (c) What is its molecular formula?

Group B

Chapter 13

Ionization

13.1 Conductivity of solutions

We have observed that solutions of electrovalent compounds may behave quite differently from those of covalent compounds. These differences in behavior and properties result from differences in the chemical natures of electrovalent and covalent solutes. Electrovalent compounds are ionic, and their water solutions conduct electric currents.

The conductivity of a solution can be tested by the use of the apparatus shown in Figure 13-1. A lamp is connected as in Figure 13-1 with an ammeter (a meter that measures electric currents), a switch, and a pair of electrodes. The electrodes

Fig. 13-1. An apparatus for testing the conductivity of solutions.

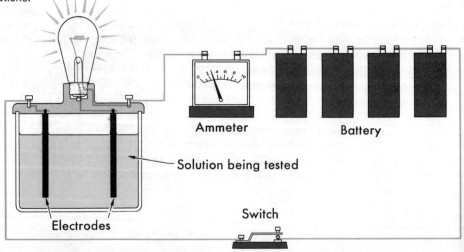

Ammeter

Battery

Solution being tested

Electrodes

Switch

are conductors used to establish electric contact with the test solution when they are dipped into it. A battery or other suitable electric energy supply serves as the source of current.

If the liquid under test is a good *conductor* of electricity, the lamp filament glows brightly when the switch is closed. The meter registers the current in the test circuit. For a liquid which is a poorer conductor, the brightness of the lamp is reduced and the meter shows a smaller current. If a liquid is a very poor conductor, the lamp does not glow and the meter indicates only a feeble current.

When pure water is tested, the lamp does not glow and the meter does not register a measurable current. Pure water is (for all practical purposes) a *nonconductor*. Water solutions of such covalent substances as sugar, alcohol, and glycerin (glycerol) do not conduct electricity. These solutes are *nonelectrolytes*.

Solutions of electrovalent substances such as sodium chloride, copper(II) sulfate, and potassium nitrate are *conductors*. These solutes are *electrolytes*. Hydrogen chloride is one of several covalent compounds which, in water solution, conducts an electric current. These compounds are also called *electrolytes*.

13.2   Electrolytes as solutes

In Chapter 12, we considered the depression of the freezing point of solvents by dissolved nonelectrolytes in dilute solutions. The molal freezing-point constant for water, 1.86 C°, is related to the influence of nonelectrolytes in water solution. *Solutes which are electrolytes have a somewhat greater influence on the freezing point of their solvents.* A 0.1-*m* solution of sodium chloride in water lowers the freezing point *nearly twice* as much as 0.1-*m* solution of sugar. A 0.1-*m* solution of potassium sulfate or calcium chloride lowers the freezing point *nearly three times* as much as a 0.1-*m* solution of sugar. *Electrolytes in water solutions lower the freezing point nearly 2, or 3, or more times as much as nonelectrolytes in water solutions of the same molality.*

The molal boiling-point constant for water is 0.51 C°. Nonvolatile electrolytes in solution have a greater effect on the boiling point of the solvent than do nonelectrolytes. Dilute sodium chloride solutions have boiling-point elevations *almost twice* those of sugar solutions of equal molality. A 0.1-*m* solution of potassium sulfate shows *almost three times* the rise in boiling point as a 0.1-*m* solution of sugar. *Electrolytes in water solutions raise the boiling point nearly 2, or 3, or more times as much as nonelectrolytes in water solutions of the same molality.*

13.3   Behavior of electrolytes explained

Michael Faraday first used the terms *electrolyte* and *nonelectrolyte* in describing his experiments on the conductivity of solutions. He concluded that conducting solutions contained particles which carried electric charges from one electrode to the other. Faraday called these particles *ions*. He assumed that they were produced from molecules by the electric potential difference between the electrodes. Later experiments revealed that electrolytic solutions contained ions regardless of the presence of charged electrodes.

In 1887, the Swedish chemist Svante Arrhenius (1859–1927) published a report on his study of solutions of electrolytes. In this report (written in 1883), he introduced the original *theory of ionization*. Arrhenius believed that ions were produced by the *ionization* of molecules of electrolytes in water solution. He considered the ions to be electrically charged. When molecules ionized, they produced both positive ions and negative ions. The solution as a whole contained equal numbers of positive and negative charges. He considered the ionization to be complete only in very dilute solutions. In more concentrated solutions, the ions were in equilibrium with *un-ionized* molecules of the solute.

These assumptions formed the basis of the theory of solutions for many years. As chemists gained a better understanding of crystals and water molecules, some of the original concepts were modified or replaced. It is a great tribute to Arrhenius that his original theory served for so long. Our present knowledge of the crystalline structure of electrovalent compounds was not available to him when, at the age of 24, he wrote his thesis on ionization.

According to the modern theory of ionization, the solvent plays an important part in the solution process. Water is by far the most important solvent. Knowledge of the polar nature of water molecules helps us understand the solution process. The theory of ionization assumes:

    1.   that electrolytes in solution exist in the form of ions;

    2.   that an ion is an atom or a group of atoms which carries an electric charge;

    3.   that in the water solution of an electrolyte, the total positive ionic charge equals the total negative ionic charge.

13.4   Structure of electrovalent compounds

Electrovalent compounds result from the transfer of electrons from one kind of atom to another. Consequently, electrovalent compounds are not made up of neutral atoms. They consist of atoms which have lost or gained electrons. Atoms which *gained* electrons in forming the compound have a *negative charge*. Those which *lost* electrons have a *positive charge*. Such atoms or groups of atoms which have an electric charge are called *ions*. In forming ions, atoms lose electric neutrality and gain chemical stability.

Swedish Information Service

Fig. 13-2. Svante August Arrhenius investigated the nature of solutions which conduct an electric current when he was a graduate student in chemistry at the University of Stockholm. He decided to solve this problem for his doctor's thesis in spite of opposition from his professors. In 1883, at the age of 24, he presented his thesis on "electrolytic dissociation" and his professors gave him a barely passing mark. Twenty years later he received the Nobel prize in chemistry in recognition of this outstanding contribution to chemistry.

A review of Section 6.3 will be helpful at this point.

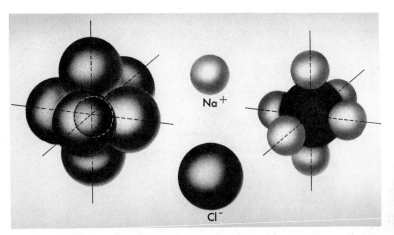

Fig. 13-3. The packing of Na⁺ and Cl⁻ ions in the NaCl crystal.

The properties of ions are very different from those of the atoms from which they were produced. Such differences reflect changes in structure and electron stability which result from the formation of ions. For example, a neutral sodium atom with a single $3s$ electron in the third energy level is different from a sodium ion. The sodium ion does not have the $3s$ electron and thus has one excess positive charge. There is an octet in the second energy level consisting of two $2s^2$ and six $2p^6$ electrons.

We must remember that chemical properties are determined chiefly by the outer electron arrangement of an atom or an ion. If the outer electron structure changes, the properties will change. The loss of the $3s$ electron gives sodium the stable electron configuration of neon. *The charge of a simple ion and its oxidation number are the same.* In fact, the charge of the ion determines its oxidation state.

Electrovalent compounds usually exist as crystals arranged in a very orderly fashion. For example, the cubic structure of crystalline sodium chloride is shown in Figures 13-3, 13-4, and 13-5. By X-ray analysis, these crystals are known to be composed of ions. Other electrovalent compounds crystallize in different patterns. Each has a characteristic lattice structure which depends on the relative size and charge of the ions.

Fig. 13-4. The sodium chloride unit cell showing the lattice arrangement of ions in the crystal.

Fig. 13-5. Model of a portion of a cubic sodium chloride crystal. The lattice structure is composed of sodium ions and chloride ions. Each ion has six neighbors of opposite charge, the arrangement being repeated in each direction to the edge of the crystal.

13.5 Hydration of ions

Suppose a few crystals of sodium chloride are dropped into a beaker of water. The water dipoles exert an attractive force on the ions forming the surfaces of the crystals. The negative oxygen ends of several water dipoles exert an attractive force on a positive sodium ion. Similarly, the positive hydrogen ends of other water dipoles exert an attractive force on a negative chloride ion. These forces weaken the bond by which the sodium and chloride ions are held together in the crystal lattice. The sodium and chloride ions then break away from the crystal lat-

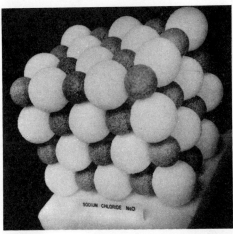

H. Bassow, Germantown Friends School

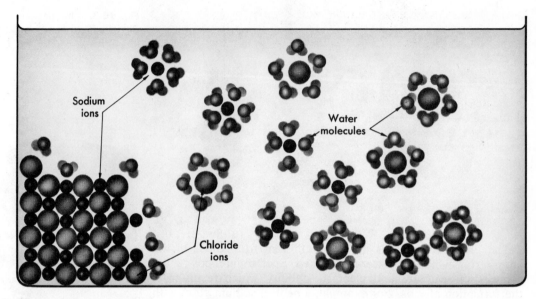

Fig. 13-6. When sodium chloride crystals are dissolved in water, the polar water molecules exert attracting forces which weaken the ionic bonds. The process of solution occurs as the ions of sodium and chloride become hydrated.

tice. They diffuse throughout the solution, loosely bonded to the solvent water molecules. See Figure 13-6.

Other sodium and chloride ions are similarly attracted by solvent molecules and diffuse in the solution. In this way, the salt crystal is gradually dissolved and the ions are dispersed throughout the solution. *The separation of ions from the crystals of ionic compounds during the solution process is called **dissociation**.* We may represent the dissociation of sodium chloride crystals in water by use of an ionic equation:

$$Na^+Cl^- \text{ (solid)} \rightarrow Na^+ \text{ (in water)} + Cl^- \text{ (in water)}$$

Sodium chloride is said to *dissociate* when it is dissolved in water.

We have already used the symbol (s) for (solid). Solutions in water are commonly referred to as "aqueous solutions." In this sense, (aq) is often used for (in water). Thus, the dissociation of an ionic salt in water is usually written as

$$Na^+Cl^-(s) \rightarrow Na^+(aq) + Cl^-(aq)$$

The number of water dipoles which attach themselves to the ions of the crystal depends largely upon the size and charge of the ion. *This attachment of water molecules to ions of the solute is called **hydration**.* The ions are said to be *hydrated*. The degree of hydration of these ions is somewhat indefinite. Water molecules are interchanged continuously from ion to ion. They are also interchanged between ions and solvent.

In certain cases, the water dipoles are not involved in reforming the crystal structure during the evaporation of the solvent. This situation occurs with sodium chloride, whose crystals do not contain water of crystallization. On the other hand, some ions retain a characteristic number of water molecules in re-forming the crystal lattice of their salt in the hydrated form. An example of this is crystalline copper(II) sulfate, $CuSO_4 \cdot 5H_2O$.

Extensive hydration of the solute ions ties up a large portion of the solvent molecules. This reduces the number of *free* water molecules in the spaces separating hydrated ions of opposite charge. Attraction between ions then becomes stronger and the crystal begins to form again. Eventually, the tendency for hydrated ions to reform the crystal lattice reaches an *equilibrium* with a tendency of ions to be hydrated. At this point, the practical limit of solubility is reached.

$$Na^+Cl^-(s) \rightleftarrows Na^+(aq) + Cl^-(aq)$$

Here, the tendency toward minimum energy (crystallizing) equals the tendency toward maximum entropy (dissolving).

Many ionic compounds which exist as crystalline solids are very soluble in water. They dissolve and produce solutions with high concentrations of hydrated ions. The following examples are typical.

$$Ca^{++}Cl_2^-(s) \rightarrow Ca^{++}(aq) + 2Cl^-(aq)$$
$$K^+Cl^-(s) \rightarrow K^+(aq) + Cl^-(aq)$$
$$K^+ClO_3^-(s) \rightarrow K^+(aq) + ClO_3^-(aq)$$
$$Ag^+NO_3^-(s) \rightarrow Ag^+(aq) + NO_3^-(aq)$$

Even ionic compounds of very slight solubility in water show measurable dissociation tendencies. Low concentrations of aqueous ions are present in their water solutions. Silver chloride, AgCl, is such a substance. Its dissociation equation is

$$Ag^+Cl^-(s) \rightarrow Ag^+(aq) + Cl^-(aq)$$

Both KCl and $AgNO_3$ have been described as very soluble ionic compounds. Their aqueous solutions contain hydrated ions which can be present in very high concentrations. These hydrated particles are $K^+(aq)$ and $Cl^-(aq)$ ions for the KCl solute. They are $Ag^+(aq)$ and $NO_3^-(aq)$ ions for the $AgNO_3$ solute. On the other hand, AgCl is only very slightly soluble in water. Its solubility is 1.25×10^{-5} mole/liter at $25°$ C. This means that only very low concentrations of $Ag^+(aq)$ and $Cl^-(aq)$ ions can be present in the water solution.

Suppose we mix fairly concentrated solutions of KCl and $AgNO_3$. In a single solution environment we have the four ionic species: $K^+(aq)$, $Cl^-(aq)$, $Ag^+(aq)$, and $NO_3^-(aq)$. However, the concentrations of Ag^+ and Cl^- ions greatly exceed the solubility of AgCl. Excess Ag^+ and Cl^- ions separate from the solution as a *precipitate* of solid AgCl. *The separation of a solid from a solution is called* **precipitation**.

The empirical equation for this reaction can be written as

$$KCl + AgNO_3 \rightarrow KNO_3 + AgCl(s)$$

The salts KCl, $AgNO_3$, and KNO_2 are all very soluble in water. Only their aqueous ions are present in the solution environment. A more useful representation is the *ionic equation,*

$$K^+(aq) + Cl^-(aq) + Ag^+(aq) + NO_3^-(aq) \rightarrow K^+(aq) + NO_3^-(aq) + Ag^+Cl^-(s)$$

In this form, the equation shows clearly that the $K^+(aq)$ and $NO_3^-(aq)$ ions take no part in the action. We will refer to ions which take no part in a chemical reaction as *"spectator ions."* Suppose we temporarily ignore these spectator ions and retain only the reacting species. The chemical action is then shown most simply by the following *net ionic equation:*

$$Ag^+(aq) + Cl^-(aq) \rightarrow Ag^+Cl^-(s)$$

Sometimes there is no reason to write the complete empirical equation or the complete ionic equation for such a reaction. The net ionic equation, which includes only the participating chemical species, may be the most useful way to represent the reaction.

Ionic compounds can act as conductors of electric charge in another way. Any effect which overcomes the attraction between the ions allows them the mobility to conduct an electric current. We have seen how water as a solvent provides ion mobility through the dissociation process. Heating produces the same effect. If an ionic compound is heated until it melts, or *fuses,* the ions become mobile and can conduct an electric current through the melted substance. Some solid ionic compounds, such as silver nitrate and potassium chlorate, melt at fairly low temperatures. The electric conductivity of such fused salts can be demonstrated easily in the laboratory. Other ionic compounds, such as sodium chloride and potassium fluoride, must be heated to relatively high temperatures before they melt. When melted, they too conduct an electric current.

13.6 Some covalent compounds ionize

Covalent bonds are formed when two atoms share electrons. The shared electrons move about the nuclei of both atoms joined by the covalent bond. However, one of the atoms may be more highly electronegative than the other. If so, the shared electrons may be thought of as spending more time in the vicinity of this atom. Therefore, the covalent bond in such a case is polar. If the two atoms form a molecule, the molecule is a polar structure having a distinctly negative region and a distinctly positive region. How strongly polar the molecule is, depends on the electronegativity difference between the two atoms.

When polar molecules are dissolved in water, the water dipoles may weaken the bonds enough to pull the molecules apart. *These portions of the polar solute molecules become hydrated as ions.* The ions did not exist in the undissolved solute, but were formed

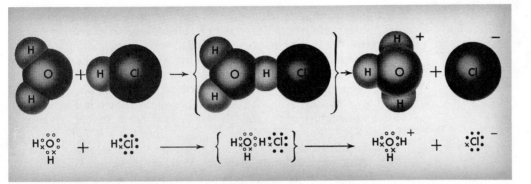

in the hydration process. *The formation of ions from polar solute molecules by the action of the solvent is called* **ionization.**

Let us consider an example of ionization. Hydrogen chloride is molecular in structure. Its single covalent bond is polar. The electronegativity difference between the hydrogen atom and the chlorine atom is 0.9, the chlorine atom being the more electronegative. Thus, the chlorine region of the molecule is negative and the hydrogen region is positive. The hydrogen chloride molecule is polar.

As a pure liquid, hydrogen chloride *does not* conduct an electric current. Dissolved in water, however, hydrogen chloride *does* conduct an electric current. This conductivity indicates that ions have been formed in the solution. On the other hand, a solution of hydrogen chloride in a nonpolar solvent, such as benzene, does not conduct electricity. We may conclude that the water dipoles play a part in this ionization process. The ionization of HCl in water solution is illustrated in Figure 13-7.

Arrhenius believed that the ionization of HCl involved simply the separation of the solute molecule into hydrogen ions and chloride ions on entering the solution. Today, chemists recognize that single hydrogen ions, actually protons, do not exist *free* in a water solution. They do, however, show a strong tendency to become hydrated. Thus, the solvent plays a definite part in the separation of protons from the solute molecules. This relationship is shown in the equation

$$HCl(g) + H_2O(l) \rightarrow H_3O^+(aq) + Cl^-(aq)$$

Neglecting the phases of the reactants and products, we may write the equation more simply as

$$HCl + H_2O \rightarrow H_3O^+ + Cl^-$$

The H_3O^+ *ion is a hydrated proton* $(H^+\cdot H_2O)$ *and is known as the* **hydronium ion.** A model of this ion is shown in Figure 13-8. Because of the ionization, a solution of hydrogen chloride in water has distinctly different properties from hydrogen chloride gas. Consequently, the solution is given the name **hydrochloric acid.**

Fig. 13-7. The polar hydrogen chloride molecule ionizes in water solution and forms the hydronium ion and the chloride ion.

Fig. 13-8. A model of the hydronium ion, H_3O^+.

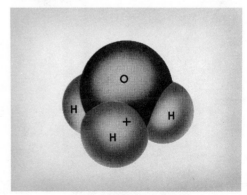

Fig. 13-9. A model of the aluminum chloride molecule, Al_2Cl_6.

Fig. 13-10. The brightness of the lamp filament indicates the conductivity of the tested material. (A) Distilled water, pure solvent, a nonconductor; (B) dilute acetic acid, a poor conductor — contains a weak electrolyte; (C) dilute hydrochloric acid, a good conductor — contains a strong electrolyte.

(A)

(B)

(C)

The aluminum halides, binary compounds of aluminum with a halogen of Group VII, are molecular. The energy required to remove the two $3s$ and one $3p$ electrons from each aluminum atom exceeds the energy available when the elements combine. The bonds are covalent with a partial ionic character.

Aluminum chloride has the structure Al_2Cl_6 in both liquid and vapor phases. A model of this molecule is shown in Figure 13-9. The structure of the solid is less certain, but is thought to consist of $AlCl_3$ units. Thus, the empirical formula $AlCl_3$ is generally used for this halide.

Aluminum chloride in the liquid phase is a very poor conductor of electricity. In water solution, however, it is a good conductor. This change indicates that ionization occurs during the solution process. The aluminum ion has a strong tendency for hydration. The hydration process provides the energy needed to complete the transfer of three electrons from each aluminum atom to three chlorine atoms. The ionization can be represented as follows:

$$Al_2Cl_6 + 12H_2O \rightarrow 2Al(H_2O)_6^{+++} + 6Cl^-$$

or, more simply, using the empirical formula

$$AlCl_3 + 6H_2O \rightarrow Al(H_2O)_6^{+++} + 3Cl^-$$

Other hydrated aluminum ions are probably formed at the same time.

13.7 Strength of electrolytes

The strength of an electrolyte is determined by the concentration of its ions in solution. Electrovalent compounds in the solid phase are crystals composed of ions. Their solutions contain the solute only in the form of dispersed hydrated ions. Such solutions are said to be completely ionized. Hydrogen chloride, a covalent compound, has a strong tendency to ionize in water solution. Even at ordinary dilutions, all of the dissolved hydrogen chloride exists as dispersed hydrated hydrogen and chloride ions. It is considered to be completely ionized. Such substances, when very soluble in water, can form solutions with high concentrations of ions. We call these substances *strong electrolytes*. Their water solutions are good conductors of electricity.

A water solution of acetic acid, $HC_2H_3O_2$, is a poor conductor. Its relative merit as a conductor is shown in Figure 13-10. The fact that the solution does conduct slightly tells us that some ionization has occurred. This ionization is shown in the reversible reaction

$$HC_2H_3O_2 + H_2O \rightleftarrows H_3O^+ + C_2H_3O_2^-$$

We must assume that the ion concentration is low. Acetic acid molecules show only a slight tendency to hydrate as ions. A 0.1-m solution is approximately 1% ionized; a 0.001-m solution is approximately 15% ionized. Such substances are said to be *weak electrolytes*. Solutions of weak electrolytes contain a low concentration of ionic species and a high concentration of molecular species.

We must be careful to avoid confusing the terms *strong* and *weak* with the terms *dilute* and *concentrated*. *Strong* and *weak* refer to the *degree of ionization*. *Dilute* and *concentrated* refer to the *amount of solute dissolved in a solvent*.

13.8   Ionization of water

Water is a polar covalent compound. Its polar molecules exert an attraction on each other. Probably because of this attraction, water ionizes to the extent of about two molecules in a billion. Even though this concentration of ions is low, it is very important in chemistry. Its significance will be discussed further in Chapter 15. We may neglect the slight ionization of water when dealing with substances such as hydrogen chloride, which may ionize completely. It must be considered when dealing with very weak electrolytes.

The ionization of water probably begins with the formation of a hydrogen bond between two water molecules as shown in Figure 13-11. Under the right conditions, this bond may be stronger than the normal covalent bond of the molecule. The result of such a chance situation is the formation of a hydrated proton and a hydroxide ion. This reaction may be expressed as

$$H_2O + H_2O \rightleftarrows H_3O^+ + OH^-$$

Chemically the *hydronium ion*, H_3O^+, acts just like a hydrogen ion, H^+, or proton. In any reaction involving the hydronium ion, the water of hydration is always left behind. This water of hydration often is of little significance in the reaction process. If this is the case, the ion may be written as H^+ or $H^+(aq)$ in the interest of simplicity. *In all such cases, it is understood that this ion exists in hydrated form in aqueous solution.*

Hydronium Ions

Chemists do not know conclusively that H_3O^+ ions exist in water solution in precisely this form. Certainly the proton H^+ is hydrated in water; the smaller an ion and the higher its charge, the stronger the hydration tendency is likely to be. Some evidence suggests a more aquated structure than H_3O^+, such as $H_9O_4^+$, because of hydrogen bonding. When the ion is written as H_3O^+, it is with the understanding that additional water molecules may be associated with it. More information on possible structures for a hydrated proton is given in Section 14.4.

Fig. 13-11. The formation of a hydrogen bond between two water dipoles may be an intermediate step in the ionization of water.

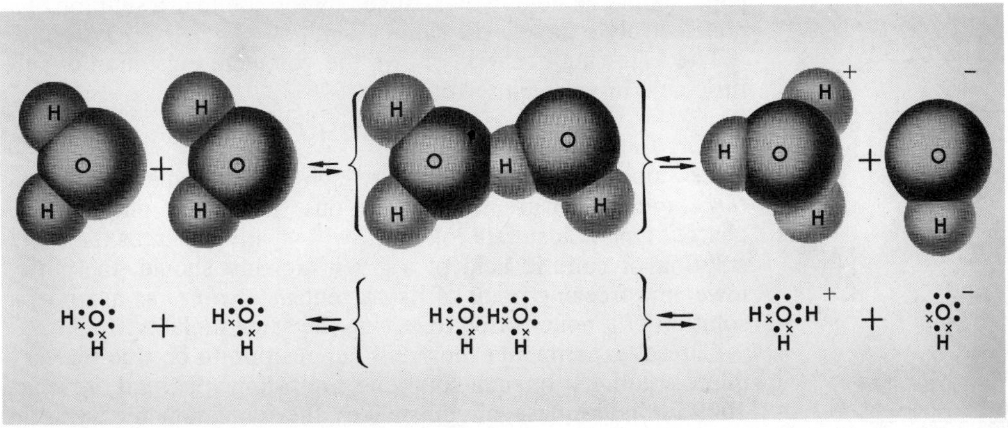

13.9 Substances that do not ionize

We have seen that some substances do not conduct an electric current either as a pure substance or in water solution. Many covalent compounds do not show the polar nature of hydrogen chloride molecules. The electronegativity difference between the atoms forming the covalent bonds may be small and the bond polarity slight. Or, polar bonds may be symmetrically arranged as in the tetrahedral configuration of the carbon tetrachloride molecule. Thus, the structure as a whole is nonpolar. Such covalent substances are nonelectrolytes. If soluble in water, they do not ionize in the water solution.

13.10 Effects of electrolytes on the freezing and boiling points of solvents

Molal solutions have a definite ratio of solute particles to solvent molecules (see Section 12.4). The depression of the freezing point of a solvent by a solute is directly proportional to the number of particles of solute present. The same reasoning applies to the elevation of the boiling point of a solvent by a nonvolatile solute. Why, then, does one mole of hydrogen chloride dissolved in 1 kg of water lower the freezing point more than one mole of sugar does? The greater freezing-point depression is caused by the separation into *two* particles of each molecule of hydrogen chloride that ionizes. This comparison is illustrated in Figure 13-12.

Suppose that, in a concentrated solution, 90 out of every 100 molecules ionize. Then, for every 100 molecules in solution, 190 particles are formed (180 ions and 10 un-ionized molecules). Such a solute therefore lowers the freezing point of its solvent 1.9 (190 ÷ 100) times as much as would a solute which does not ionize.

Suppose 100% of the hydrogen chloride molecules were ionized, as in a more dilute solution. The lowering of the freezing point should be double that caused by the solute in a solution of a nonelectrolyte having the same molality.

The following equation shows the complete ionization of sulfuric acid in very dilute solutions.

$$H_2SO_4 + 2H_2O \rightarrow 2H_3O^+ + SO_4^{--}$$

Every molecule of sulfuric acid which ionizes completely forms *three ions.* Two are hydronium ions, each with one positive charge. One is a sulfate ion with two negative charges. A dilute solution of sulfuric acid of a given molality should, therefore, lower the freezing point of its solvent *three times* as much as a solution of a nonelectrolyte having the same molality.

Careful experiments show this supposition to be true for very dilute solutions. In such solutions, ionization apparently reaches 100%. Under these circumstances the ionization theory is in

Fig. 13-12. Five sugar molecules produce only five particles in solution. Five hydrogen chloride molecules, on the other hand, produce ten particles when dissolved in water.

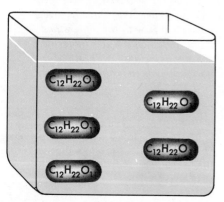

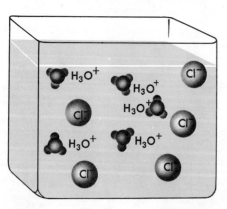

agreement with the facts. Similarly, the theory explains the relatively great rise in the boiling point of a solvent caused by nonvolatile electrolytes in solution. Here, too, ionization increases the number of solute particles present in the solution.

Now let us consider a solution of an ionic substance such as calcium chloride in water. The dissociation equation is

$$Ca^{++}Cl_2^-(s) \rightarrow Ca^{++}(aq) + 2Cl^-(aq)$$

We have seen that a mole of a nonelectrolyte provides one mole of solute particles when dissolved in water. An example is a mole of sugar, which provides the Avogadro number of particles. One mole of $CaCl_2$ dissociates and provides three times the Avogadro number of solute particles in solution. We might expect a $CaCl_2$ solution of a given molality to lower the freezing-point of its solvent three times as much as a nonelectrolyte having the same molality. However, experiments do not bear this out except for very dilute solutions.

13.11 The degree of ionization

The larger the number of ions in a given volume of a solution, the better it conducts electricity. This fact suggests one way of determining the concentration of ions in a solution. Another way is to measure the lowering of the freezing point caused by an ionized solute in a measured amount of solvent. Suppose a 0.1-m solution of an electrolyte such as sodium chloride were to freeze at $-0.372°$ C [$0° - (2 \times 0.186$ C°)]. If so, we could assume the solute to be 100% ionized.

Actual measurements, however, give only an *apparent degree of ionization*. We have seen that electrovalent compounds, by the nature of their structure, must be 100% ionic in solution. Experimental results give an apparent degree of ionization somewhat less than 100%. For example, consider the 0.1-m solution of sodium chloride referred to above. This solution actually freezes at $-0.346°$ C, yielding a freezing-point depression of 0.346 C° instead of the predicted value of 0.372 C°. For many years, such differences prevented chemists from deciding whether or not a compound was completely ionized in water solution.

Today we recognize that attractive forces exist between ions in aqueous solutions. These forces are small compared with those in the crystalline salt. However, they do interfere with the movements of the aqueous ions, even in dilute solutions. Only in very dilute solutions is the average distance between ions great enough, and the attraction between ions small enough, for the aqueous solute ions to move freely. Therefore, the more dilute the sodium chloride solution, the more nearly the freezing-point depression approaches twice the value for a molecular solute.

These observations are in agreement with the Debye-Hückel theory of the attraction between ions. This theory accounts quantitatively for the attraction between dissociated ions of ionic

Peter J. W. Debye (1884–1966) of Holland had a long and productive career in science. Though primarily a physicist, he made his most lasting and fundamental contributions to physical chemistry. Dr. Debye collaborated with E. Hückel in 1923 to investigate the nature of electrolytes. Together, they proposed the Debye-Hückel theory which greatly advanced the quantitative understanding of electrolytic solutions. Debye was awarded the Nobel Prize in Chemistry in 1936 for his research on molecular dipole moments, interatomic distances, X-ray scattering, and the theory of electrolytes. In 1940 he accepted an appointment as professor of chemistry at Cornell University and became an American citizen in 1946.

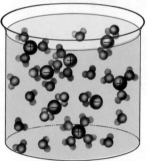

Fig. 13-13. The ions in the dilute solution on the top are far apart and act independently. The activity of the ions in the solution on the bottom is somewhat restricted because of the concentration. Thus the apparent number of ions present may be less than the actual number.

solids in dilute water solutions. According to the Debye-Hückel theory, each ion is surrounded on the average by more ions of opposite charge than of like charge. See Figure 13-13. The effect is to hinder the movements of an ion. Thus, the "ion activity" is less than that expected on the basis of the number of ions known to be present. Table 13-1 gives the observed freezing-point depressions of aqueous solutions of sodium chloride at various concentrations. The table also shows freezing-point depressions per mole of NaCl calculated from the observed values.

In concentrated solutions, an additional effect on the freezing-point depression may arise from a shortage of solvent molecules. There may not be enough water molecules to hydrate completely all solute ions. In such a case, clusters of ions may act as a single solute unit.

Table 13–1

INFLUENCE OF CONCENTRATION ON FREEZING POINT OF AQUEOUS SOLUTIONS OF NaCl

Concentration of NaCl (m)	Freezing-point depression ($C°$)	Freezing-point depression/mole NaCl ($C°$)
0.100	0.346	3.46
0.0100	0.0361	3.61
0.00100	0.00366	3.66
0.000100	0.000372	3.72

QUESTIONS

Group A

1. What is the distinction between an electrolyte and a nonelectrolyte?
2. What effect does the addition of electrolytes have on the boiling points and freezing points of solvents such as water?
3. What theory helps to explain the behavior of electrolytes?
4. What are the important assumptions of this theory?
5. What is an ion?
6. Write the equation for the ionization of water.
7. Explain why the water molecule is a polar molecule.
8. What is the nature of the crystal structure of an electrovalent compound?
9. How does an atom differ from an ion?
10. How may we account for the stability of an ion?
11. (a) How do water molecules cause an electrovalent compound to dissociate? (b) How may the process be reversed?
12. Why is the dissociation of electrovalent compounds 100%?
13. Melted potassium chloride conducts an electric current. Explain.
14. Predict the approximate freezing-point depressions for 0.01-m aqueous solutions of the following substances: (a) KI, (b) C_2H_5OH, (c) $Al_2(SO_4)_3$.

15. (*a*) Explain how the action of water on a polar compound like hydrogen chloride produces ionization. (*b*) Write the equation for the ionization of hydrogen chloride in water solution showing the part played by the water.

Group B

16. What is the distinction between dissociation and ionization?
17. Describe the solution equilibrium in a saturated solution of sodium nitrate containing an excess of the crystals.
18. (*a*) What are symmetrical covalent molecules? (*b*) Why don't they ionize?
19. Explain the abnormal freezing-point lowering and boiling-point elevation of solvents produced by electrolytes in terms of the theory of ionization.
20. (*a*) Write an equation for the dissociation of calcium chloride. (*b*) What is the theoretical freezing point of a one-molal solution of calcium chloride in water?
21. Describe two ways of measuring the apparent degree of ionization.
22. Why does the measurement of the apparent degree of ionization not coincide with the evidence that electrovalent compounds are 100% dissociated in solution?
23. How does a concentrated solution of a weak electrolyte differ from a dilute solution of a strong electrolyte?
24. When potassium nitrate is dissolved in water, the dissolving process is endothermic. (*a*) What temperature change does the solution undergo? (*b*) Which is greater, the hydration energy or the lattice energy? (*c*) To what do you attribute the driving force that causes the dissolving process to proceed?
25. (*a*) How is the solubility of potassium nitrate affected by warming the solution of Question 24? (*b*) Apply the principle of Le Chatelier to account for this change in solubility.
26. Suppose 0.1 mole of a substance dissolved in 1 kg of water lowers the freezing point of the water 0.360 C°. (*a*) What can you predict about the nature of the solution? (*b*) What can you conclude about the oxidation numbers of the particles of solute?

PROBLEMS

1. In a certain experiment it was found that 185 drops of water were required to give a volume of 10.0 ml. (*a*) How many molecules of water are in each drop? (*b*) How many hydronium ions are in each drop? (*c*) How many hydroxide ions are in each drop?

Group B

2. How many grams of copper(II) sulfate pentahydrate must be added to 125 g of water to give a 0.0156-*m* solution?
3. Calculate the freezing point of $60\overline{0}$ g of water to which 12.0 g of ethyl alcohol, C_2H_5OH, has been added.
4. The composition of a substance was determined by analysis to be 10.1% carbon, 0.846% hydrogen, and 89.1% chlorine. It was found to be soluble in benzene and when 2.50 g was dissolved in 100 g of benzene, the freezing point of the benzene was 4.41° C. Determine the molecular formula of the substance.
5. A chemistry student collected 15.0 ml of dry HCl gas at 21.0° C and 748 mm pressure and then dissolved the gas in 1.00 kg of water. Assuming complete ionization and no interionic attraction, calculate the freezing-point depression of the water.

Chapter **14**

Acids, Bases, and Salts

14.1 Importance of acids

Compounds whose water solutions contain ions are traditionally classed as *acids, bases,* or *salts.* Even in ancient times, acids were recognized as a distinct class of materials. Today we encounter them, directly or indirectly, in many of our daily activities.

Nearly all fruits contain acids, and so do many common foods. Lemons, oranges, and grapefruit contain citric acid. Apples contain malic acid. The souring of milk produces lactic acid. Rancid butter contains butyric acid. The fermentation of hard cider forms the acetic acid of vinegar. These acids, because of their origin and nature, are called *organic* acids.

Chemists prepare large quantities of important industrial acids synthetically. Some of these are organic. Others are made by composition reactions directly from the elements. Acids manufactured from minerals are known as *inorganic* acids, or, more commonly, as *mineral* acids. These substances have been known for centuries because their properties are very distinctive. When the term "acid" is used in a very general sense, the reference is usually to these compounds. These substances are, therefore, the traditional acids; their water solutions are called *aqueous acids.* Modern definitions of acids give the name "acid" to many substances which are not acids in the traditional sense.

14.2 Industrial acids

If a manufacturing chemist were asked to name the most important acid, he would probably mention *sulfuric acid.* It is a very versatile mineral acid. It is used in so many technical and manufacturing processes that the consumption of sulfuric acid is an index to a country's industrialization and prosperity. A dye chemist or one who makes explosives would tell you that *nitric acid* is also very important. A third important industrial acid is *hydrochloric acid*. It is used for cleaning metals before they are plated. Hydrochloric acid makes up about 0.4% of the gastric juice in the human stomach and aids in the digestion of foods.

1.   Sulfuric acid. This acid, which has the formula H_2SO_4, is a dense, oily liquid with a high boiling point. *Concentrated* sulfuric acid contains 95% – 98% sulfuric acid (by weight), and the balance is water. Its density is 1.84 g/ml. Ordinary *dilute* sulfuric acid is made by adding 1 volume of concentrated acid to 6 volumes of water. Other dilutions are used also.

2.   Nitric acid. This acid is a volatile liquid which has the formula HNO_3. Pure nitric acid is too unstable for commercial use. Concentrated nitric acid is fairly stable. It is a 70% HNO_3 solution in water and has a density of 1.42 g/ml. Ordinary dilute nitric acid is made by adding 1 volume concentrated acid to 5 volumes water. However, it can be mixed with water in any proportion. A pure solution of nitric acid is colorless, but it may turn brown on standing because of slight decomposition.

3.   Hydrochloric acid. Hydrogen chloride gas, HCl, is extremely soluble in water. It forms the colorless solution known as hydrochloric acid. Concentrated hydrochloric acid is a water solution containing about 36% hydrogen chloride. Its density is 1.19 g/ml. Ordinary dilute hydrochloric acid is prepared by adding 1 volume of concentrated acid to 4 volumes of water. Such a solution contains approximately 7% hydrogen chloride. Hydrochloric acid can be diluted to any concentration.

CAUTION: *Add the sulfuric acid to the water slowly while stirring. Never add the water to the acid because that will cause a violent reaction which produces steam and spatters the acid.*

14.3   Aqueous acids

Arrhenius gave us a clue to the chemical nature of acids in his *Theory of Ionization.* He believed that acids ionize in water solutions and form hydrogen ions.

The three acids we have just described are essentially covalently bonded structures. They have one element in common, *hydrogen.* Sulfuric and nitric acids in pure form are very poor conductors, since they are only very slightly ionized. Liquid hydrogen chloride is a nonconductor of electricity. In water solution, however, each of these substances is highly ionized because of the hydrating action of the water dipoles. We can represent their ionization in water solutions by the equations:

$$H_2SO_4 + H_2O \rightarrow H_3O^+ + HSO_4^-$$
$$HNO_3 + H_2O \rightarrow H_3O^+ + NO_3^-$$
$$HCl + H_2O \rightarrow H_3O^+ + Cl^-$$

Hydronium ions, H_3O^+, are present in all of these solutions. We

Table 14–1

CONCENTRATIONS OF COMMON ACIDS

(Average values for freshly opened bottles)

	Acetic	*Hydrochloric*	*Nitric*	*Sulfuric*
formula	$HC_2H_3O_2$	HCl	HNO_3	H_2SO_4
molecular weight	60.03	36.46	63.02	98.08
density of concentrated reagent, g/cm³	1.06	1.19	1.42	1.84
percentage assay concentrated reagent	99.5	36.0	69.5	96.0
grams active ingredient/ml	1.055	0.426	0.985	1.76
normality of concentrated reagent	17.6	11.7	15.6	35.9
ml concentrated reagent/liner N solution	56.9	85.5	64.0	27.9

can assume that the acid properties of the solutions are due to these H_3O^+ ions.

When a sulfuric acid solution is diluted enough, some HSO_4^- ions may ionize further and contribute additional H_3O^+ ions to the solution.

$$HSO_4^- + H_2O \rightarrow H_3O^+ + SO_4^{--}$$

The ionization of HSO_4^- ions may be complete in very dilute solutions of sulfuric acid. If so, the equation is written

$$H_2SO_4 + 2H_2O \rightarrow 2H_3O^+ + SO_4^{--}$$

Observe that this equation merely summarizes the two partial ionizations that occur with increasing dilution of the sulfuric acid solution.

$$(\text{1st stage}) \quad H_2SO_4 + H_2O \rightarrow H_3O^+ + HSO_4^-$$
$$(\text{2nd stage}) \quad HSO_4^- + H_2O \rightarrow H_3O^+ + SO_4^{--}$$
$$(\text{summary}) \quad H_2SO_4 + 2H_2O \rightarrow 2H_3O^+ + SO_4^{--}$$

Acids which ionize completely, or nearly so, in water solution provide high concentrations of hydronium ions. Such concentrations characterize strong acids. Sulfuric, nitric, and hydrochloric acids are strong mineral acids. Substances which produce few hydronium ions in water solution, such as acetic acid and carbonic acid, are weak acids. They ionize only slightly in water, even in very dilute solutions.

14.4 Modern definition of acids

The hydronium ion is really a hydrated proton. In water solution, it is considered to be in the hydrated form, $H^+ \cdot H_2O$ or H_3O^+. In other words, it is a proton combined with a polar water molecule.

Chemists have found conclusive evidence that H_3O^+ ions exist in hydrated crystals of perchloric acid (a very strong acid) and in concentrated solutions of strong acids. In dilute aqueous solutions of acids, however, the proton hydration may be more extensive. Physical evidence, such as electric and thermal conductivities, suggests the formula $H^+ \cdot 4H_2O$. This formula corresponds to the ionic species $H_9O_4^+$. A model of the $H_9O_4^+$ ion having the spatial structure of a triagonal pyramid is shown in Figure 14-1.

Other species of the hydrated proton have been suggested for dilute aqueous acid solutions. These species are $H^+ \cdot 2H_2O$ and $H^+ \cdot 3H_2O$, corresponding respectively to the species $H_5O_2^+$ and $H_7O_3^+$. Chemists write formulas of this kind only when the degree of hydration is itself the subject of discussion. Otherwise, for simplicity, the hydrated proton in aqueous solutions is written as $H^+(aq)$ or as the hydronium ion, H_3O^+.

When hydrogen chloride is dissolved in a nonpolar solvent, such as toluene, the solution remains a nonconductor. *We conclude that protons (hydrogen ions) are not released by molecules such as HCl unless there are molecules or ions present which can accept them.*

Hydrogen chloride dissolved in ammonia transfers protons to the solvent much as it does in water.

$$HCl + H_2O \rightarrow H_3O^+ + Cl^-$$
$$HCl + NH_3 \rightarrow NH_4^+ + Cl^-$$

The similarity of these reactions is very clear when we write their electron-dot formulas.

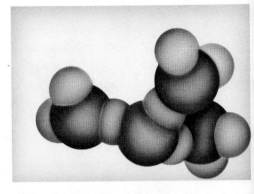

Fig. 14-1. A model of the $H_9O_4^+$ ion which suggests an H_3O^+ ion with three H_2O molecules attached.

$$H\overset{\times}{\cdot}\overset{..}{\underset{..}{Cl}}: + H\overset{oo}{\underset{\underset{H}{ox}}{O}}\overset{o}{_o} \rightarrow H\overset{oo}{\underset{\underset{H}{ox}}{O}}\overset{o}{_o}H^+ + \overset{\times}{\cdot}\overset{..}{\underset{..}{Cl}}:^-$$

$$H\overset{\times}{\cdot}\overset{..}{\underset{..}{Cl}}: + H\overset{oo}{\underset{\underset{H}{ox}}{N}}\overset{\times}{_\times}H \rightarrow H\overset{H^+}{\overset{oo}{\underset{\underset{H}{ox}}{N}}}\overset{\times}{_\times}H + \overset{\times}{\cdot}\overset{..}{\underset{..}{Cl}}:^-$$

A proton is transferred to the ammonia molecule, forming the *ammonium ion,* just as one is transferred to the water molecule, forming the hydronium ion. See Figures 14-2 and 14-3. In each case, the proton is given up by the hydrogen chloride molecule.

Fig. 14-2. When HCl is dissolved in water, a proton is donated by the polar HCl molecule forming the hydronium ion, H_3O^+, and the chloride ion, Cl^-.

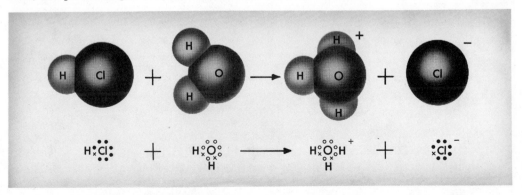

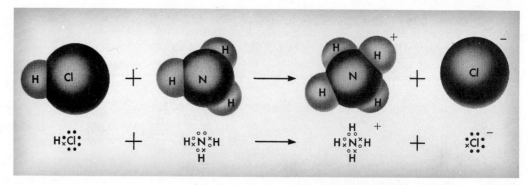

Fig. 14-3. When hydrogen chloride is dissolved in ammonia, a proton is donated by the polar HCl molecule to the NH_3 molecule forming the ammonium ion, NH_4^+, and the chloride ion, Cl^-.

This molecule is said to be a **proton donor.** In the modern theory advanced by J. N. Brønsted, a Danish chemist, *an acid is simply a proton donor.* In other words, *an acid is a species of molecule or ion which gives up protons to another substance.* Thus hydrogen chloride is an acid, according to Brønsted's theory, even though it does not contain hydrogen ions when pure.

According to this general definition, water is an acid when gaseous ammonia is dissolved in it. Some water molecules donate protons to ammonia molecules:

$$NH_3 + H_2O \rightleftarrows NH_4^+ + OH^-$$

Furthermore, in water solutions of the strong mineral acids described in Section 14.3, the hydronium ion, H_3O^+, is the acid. This ion is the actual proton donor in reactions involving the solutions.

This modern definition of acids is very broad. It describes the behavior of substances as sources of protons which combine with the molecules or ions of other substances. Definitions do not alter the facts of chemistry; they are useful if they help us to organize the facts of chemistry.

Fig. 14-4. When ammonia is dissolved in water, water molecules are the proton donors and ammonia molecules are the proton acceptors.

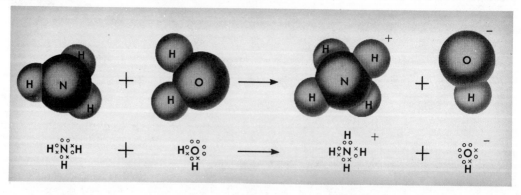

14.5 Properties of aqueous acids

Acids such as hydrochloric, nitric, and sulfuric are quite soluble in water. Their other physical properties differ widely. However, they have many *chemical* properties in common.

1. Acids contain ionizable hydrogen in covalent combination with a nonmetallic element or polyatomic species. The strength of an acid depends upon the *degree* of ionization in water solution, not upon the *amount* of hydrogen in the molecule. Perchloric acid, $HClO_4$, hydrochloric acid, HCl, and nitric acid, HNO_3, are strong acids by this rule. Each donates one proton per molecule. Acetic acid, $HC_2H_3O_2$, is a weak acid. It ionizes only slightly in water and yields one proton and one acetate ion, $C_2H_3O_2^-$, per ionized molecule.

In Section 14.3 we stated that sulfuric acid ionizes in two stages, depending on the amount of dilution:

$$H_2SO_4 + H_2O \rightarrow H_3O^+ + HSO_4^-$$
$$HSO_4^- + H_2O \rightarrow H_3O^+ + SO_4^{--}$$

The first stage is completed in fairly concentrated solutions. In this form sulfuric acid can produce *acid salts,* in which the HSO_4^- ion is presented. Sodium *hydrogen* sulfate, $NaHSO_4$, is an example. The second stage may be completed in more dilute solutions. Here the SO_4^{--} ion is present. Under such conditions *normal salts* are formed. Sodium sulfate, Na_2SO_4, is an example.

The rather weak phosphoric acid ionizes in three stages:

$$H_3PO_4 + H_2O \rightarrow H_3O^+ + H_2PO_4^-$$
$$H_2PO_4^- + H_2O \rightarrow H_3O^+ + HPO_4^{--}$$
$$HPO_4^{--} + H_2O \rightarrow H_3O^+ + PO_4^{---}$$

Only the first stage occurs in solutions of moderate concentrations. This stage produces *dihydrogen phosphate ions,* $H_2PO_4^-$. In more dilute solutions *monohydrogen phosphate ions,* HPO_4^{--}, are formed. In very dilute solutions measurable concentrations of normal *phosphate ions,* PO_4^{---}, may be formed.

2. Acids donate protons when they react with bases. The many common properties of acids depend on this characteristic behavior. Acids which donate only one proton per molecule are called *monoprotic acids.* Examples are HCl, HNO_3, and $HC_2H_3O_2$. Sulfuric acid, H_2SO_4, and carbonic acid, H_2CO_3, are *diprotic,* being capable of donating two protons per molecule. Phosphoric acid, H_3PO_4, is *triprotic.*

3. Acids have a sour taste. Lemons, grapefruit, and limes are sour. These fruits contain weak acids in solution. A solid acid tastes sour as it dissolves in the saliva and forms a water solution. Most laboratory acids are very corrosive (they destroy the skin) and they are powerful poisons.

CAUTION: *Never use the "taste test" in the laboratory.*

4. Acids affect indicators. If a drop of an acid solution is placed on a test strip of blue *litmus,* the *blue* color changes to *red.* Litmus is a dye extracted from certain lichens. Some other substances may be used as indicators. *Phenolphthalein* (fee-nole-*thall*-een) is colorless in the presence of acids. *Methyl orange* turns red in acid solutions.

5. Acids neutralize hydroxides. Solutions of an acid and a metallic hydroxide may be mixed in chemically equivalent quantities. If so, each cancels the properties of the other. This process is called *neutralization* and is an example of an ionic reaction. The products are a salt and water. The salt is recovered in crystalline form by evaporating the water. The acid and the hydroxide neutralize each other.

Suppose a solution containing 1 mole of NaOH is added to a dilute solution containing 1 mole of HCl. The reaction is represented empirically by the following equation:

$$\text{HCl} + \text{NaOH} \rightarrow \text{NaCl} + \text{H}_2\text{O}$$

Since both reactants and the salt product are present as aqueous ions, an ionic equation is more useful:

$$\text{H}^+(\text{aq}) + \text{Cl}^-(\text{aq}) + \text{Na}^+(\text{aq}) + \text{OH}^-(\text{aq}) \rightarrow \text{Na}^+(\text{aq}) + \text{Cl}^-(\text{aq}) + \text{H}_2\text{O}$$

We may wish to represent hydrated protons, $\text{H}^+(\text{aq})$, as hydronium ions, H_3O^+. The ionic equation then becomes

$$\text{H}_3\text{O}^+(\text{aq}) + \text{Cl}^-(\text{aq}) + \text{Na}^+(\text{aq}) + \text{OH}^-(\text{aq}) \rightarrow \text{Na}^+(\text{aq}) + \text{Cl}^-(\text{aq}) + 2\text{H}_2\text{O}$$

Observe that sodium ions and chloride ions remain in solution and actually play no part in the reaction. In writing the simplest ionic equation for this reaction, we eliminate these spectator ions. Only those species which actually participate in the chemical reaction are shown in the net ionic equation.

$$\text{H}^+(\text{aq}) + \text{OH}^-(\text{aq}) \rightarrow \text{H}_2\text{O}$$

or

$$\text{H}_3\text{O}^+(\text{aq}) + \text{OH}^-(\text{aq}) \rightarrow 2\text{H}_2\text{O}$$

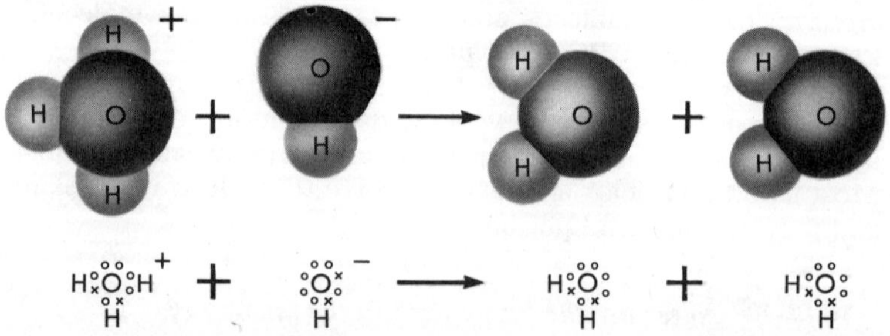

Fig. 14-5. In neutralization reactions, hydronium ions and hydroxide ions combine and form essentially unionized water molecules.

The neutralization reaction is entirely between hydronium ions from the acid and hydroxide ions from the soluble metallic hydroxide. In all neutralizations of very soluble hydroxides by strong acids, the reaction is the same. The nonmetallic ions of the acid and metallic ions of the hydroxide undergo no chemical change. However, we still may prefer to write the complete equation because it shows what pure substances were the original reactants and what salt can be recovered by evaporating the water solvent.

6. *Acids react with many metals.* The reaction products are hydrogen gas and a salt. The equation for the reaction between zinc and sulfuric acid is typical.

$$\mathbf{Zn + H_2SO_4 \rightarrow ZnSO_4 + H_2(g)}$$

Written ionically, the equation is

$$\mathbf{Zn + 2H^+(aq) + SO_4^{--}(aq) \rightarrow Zn^{++}(aq) + SO_4^{--}(aq) + H_2(g)}$$

or simply

$$\mathbf{Zn + 2H^+(aq) \rightarrow Zn^{++}(aq) + H_2(g)}$$

The salt separates from solution as crystals of $ZnSO_4$ on evaporation of the water solvent. Remember that, in solution, such *salts* are simply solutions of hydrated ions.

7. *Acids react with oxides of metals.* They form salts and water. As an example, consider the reaction of copper(II) oxide and sulfuric acid.

$$\mathbf{CuO + H_2SO_4 \rightarrow CuSO_4 + H_2O}$$

Written ionically,

$$\mathbf{CuO + 2H^+(aq) + SO_4^{--} \rightarrow Cu^{++} + SO_4^{--} + H_2O}$$

The net reaction is

$$\mathbf{CuO + 2H^+(aq) \rightarrow Cu^{++} + H_2O}$$

8. *Acids react with carbonates.* These reactions give off carbon dioxide and produce a salt and water.

$$\mathbf{CaCO_3 + 2HCl \rightarrow CaCl_2 + H_2O + CO_2(g)}$$

Ionically:

$$\mathbf{Ca^{++}CO_3^{--} + 2H^+(aq) + 2Cl^- \rightarrow Ca^{++} + 2Cl^- + H_2O + CO_2(g)}$$

Net:

$$\mathbf{Ca^{++}CO_3^{--} + 2H^+(aq) \rightarrow Ca^{++} + H_2O + CO_2(g)}$$

14.6 Naming aqueous acids

Some acids are *binary* compounds. They contain only *two* elements, hydrogen and another nonmetal. Other acids contain oxygen as a third element. They are often referred to as *oxyacids*.

Table 14-2
NAMES OF BINARY ACIDS

Formula	Name of pure substance	Name of acid
HF	hydrogen fluoride	hydrofluoric acid
HCl	hydrogen chloride	hydrochloric acid
HBr	hydrogen bromide	hydrobromic acid
HI	hydrogen iodide	hydroiodic acid
H_2S	hydrogen sulfide	hydrosulfuric acid

1. Binary acids. The name of an acid having only two elements begins with the prefix *hydro*. The root of the name of the nonmetal in combination with hydrogen follows this prefix. The name has the ending *-ic*. This scheme is illustrated by the examples given in Table 14-2. Water solutions of the binary compounds listed are acids known by the names given in the right column.

2. Oxyacids. These acids contain hydrogen, oxygen, and a third element. The formulas and names of the series of oxyacids of chlorine illustrate the general method of naming such acids. The acid name for the water solution of each oxychlorine is shown at the right in the following series.

$$HClO \ldots\ldots\ldots\ldots \textbf{hypo-chlor-ous acid}$$
$$HClO_2 \ldots\ldots\ldots\ldots\ldots \textbf{chlor-ous acid}$$
$$HClO_3 \ldots\ldots\ldots\ldots\ldots \textbf{chlor-ic acid}$$
$$HClO_4 \ldots\ldots\ldots\ldots \textbf{per-chlor-ic acid}$$

In all of these oxyacids, chlorine is the central element. For this reason the root *-chlor-* is used in each case. $HClO_3$ is named *chlor-ic acid*. It contains the chlorate group and no prefix is used. The oxyacid of chlorine which contains *more* oxygen per molecule than chloric acid is called *per-chlor-ic acid*. The prefix *per-* is a contraction of *hyper,* which means *above.* The acid containing *less* oxygen per molecule than chloric acid is called *chlor-ous acid.* The oxyacid of chlorine which contains *still less* oxygen than chlorous acid has the prefix *hypo-,* the root *-chlor-,* and the suffix *-ous.* The prefix *hypo-* means *below.*

To use this scheme, it is only necessary to know the formula and name of one oxyacid in any series. The formula and name of the member of each series that you should remember are listed below.

$$HClO_3 \ldots\ldots\ldots\ldots \textbf{chloric acid}$$
$$HNO_3 \ldots\ldots\ldots\ldots\ldots \textbf{nitric acid}$$
$$HBrO_3 \ldots\ldots\ldots\ldots \textbf{bromic acid}$$
$$H_2SO_4 \ldots\ldots\ldots\ldots \textbf{sulfuric acid}$$
$$H_3PO_4 \ldots\ldots\ldots\ldots \textbf{phosphoric acid}$$

The names of common oxyacids are given in Table 14-3.

Table 14-3
NAMES OF OXYACIDS

Formula	Name of pure substance	Name of acid
$HC_2H_3O_2$	hydrogen acetate	acetic acid
H_2CO_3	hydrogen carbonate	carbonic acid
$HClO$	hydrogen hypochlorite	hypochlorous acid
$HClO_2$	hydrogen chlorite	chlorous acid
$HClO_3$	hydrogen chlorate	chloric acid
$HClO_4$	hydrogen perchlorate	perchloric acid
HNO_2	hydrogen nitrite	nitrous acid
HNO_3	hydrogen nitrate	nitric acid
H_3PO_3	hydrogen phosphite	phosphorous acid
H_3PO_4	hydrogen phosphate	phosphoric acid
H_2SO_3	hydrogen sulfite	sulfurous acid
H_2SO_4	hydrogen sulfate	sulfuric acid

14.7 Acid anhydrides

Only fluorine is more highly electronegative than oxygen. Its compound with oxygen, OF_2, is a fluoride rather than an oxide. Other elements form oxides with oxygen. The oxidation number of oxygen in these compounds is -2. Oxides range structurally from ionic to covalent. The more ionic oxides involve the highly electropositive metals on the left side of the periodic table. The oxides formed with nonmetals on the right side of the periodic table are, in general, covalent molecular structures.

Many of the molecular (nonmetallic) oxides are gases at ordinary temperatures. Examples are carbon monoxide, CO, carbon dioxide, CO_2, and sulfuric dioxide, SO_2. Diphosphorus pentoxide, P_4O_{10}, on the other hand, is a solid. Most nonmetallic oxides react with water and form *oxyacids*.

Oxyacids all contain one or more oxygen-hydrogen (OH) groups in the covalent structure. These are called *hydroxyl* groups. They are not to be confused with oxygen-hydrogen groups existing as OH^- ions, whose compounds are called *hydroxides*. The hydroxyl group is arranged in the molecule in such a manner that it may donate a proton. This arrangement gives the molecule its acid character.

Figure 14-6 shows the electron-dot formulas of the four oxyacids of chlorine. Each formula contains the OH group not as an ion but as a group covalently bonded to the central Cl atom. Aqueous solutions of these solutes are acidic because the OH bond is broken during ionization. The OH group provides the proton donated by the oxychlorine acid molecule.

When carbon dioxide dissolves in water, a very small amount of it reacts chemically with the solvent and forms carbonic acid:

$$CO_2 + H_2O \rightleftharpoons H_2CO_3$$

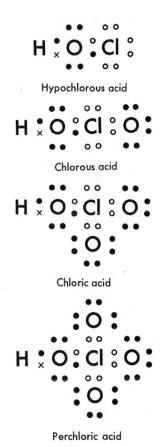

Fig. 14-6. Electron-dot formulas of the four oxyacids of chlorine.

These H_2CO_3 molecules can ionize and give the aqueous solution a very low concentration of H_3O^+ ions.

$$H_2CO_3 + H_2O \rightleftharpoons H_3O^+ + HCO_3^-$$

The net equation which shows the acid-producing behavior of CO_2 in aqueous solution is

$$CO_2 + 2H_2O \rightleftharpoons H_3O^+ + HCO_3^-$$

Carbonic acid and carbon dioxide differ in composition from each other just by a molecule of water. For this reason, carbon dioxide is called the *acid anhydride* of carbonic acid. *Oxides that react with water and form acids, or that are formed by the removal of water from acids, are known as* **acid anhydrides**.

Binary acids do not contain oxygen and do not have an anhydride form. Thus, the reaction between an acid anhydride and water cannot be used to prepare such acids. However, it is an important method of preparing some oxyacids.

Sulfur dioxide is the acid anhydride of sulfurous acid.

$$SO_3 + H_2O \rightleftharpoons H_2SO_4$$

Sulfur trioxide is the acid anhydride of sulfuric acid.

$$SO_2 + H_2O \rightleftharpoons H_2SO_3$$

These anhydrides are important in the manufacture of sulfuric acid. Sulfuric acid, because it is cheap and has a high boiling point, can be used in the laboratory to produce several other acids. Although most hydrochloric acid is now produced commercially by other methods, the reaction for producing hydrogen chloride gas is an example.

$$H_2SO_4 + 2NaCl \rightarrow Na_2SO_4 + 2HCl(g)$$

Nitric acid can be produced by the reaction of sulfuric acid with a nitrate. However, this process is not used commercially for preparing HNO_3 because it is more expensive than other processes.

BASES

14.8   The nature of bases

Several substances long known as bases are commonly found in homes. Household ammonia, an ammonia-water solution, is a familiar cleaning agent. Lye is a commercial grade of sodium hydroxide, $NaOH$, used for cleaning clogged sink drains. Limewater is a solution of calcium hydroxide, $Ca(OH)_2$. Milk of magnesia is a suspension of magnesium hydroxide, $Mg(OH)_2$, in water; it is used as an antacid, a laxative, and an antidote for strong acids. All of these hydroxides are *bases*.

Arrhenius considered a base to be any soluble hydroxide which neutralized an acid when their solutions were mixed. We now know that the only reaction occurring in such a neutralization is between hydronium ions and hydroxide ions. The nonmetal of the acid and the metal of the hydroxide remain in solution as hydrated ions.

Bases are now broadly defined as substances which acquire *protons from another substance.* In this sense, the hydroxide ion is the most common base. Hydronium ions combine with hydroxide ions and form water.

$$H_3O^+(aq) + OH^-(aq) \rightarrow 2H_2O(l)$$

Ammonia-water solutions and water solutions of soluble metallic hydroxides are commonly referred to as *aqueous bases*. They are our most useful basic solutions. Aqueous ammonia solutions are traditionally called *ammonium hydroxide,* NH_4OH. This molecular species probably does not exist in water solutions except possibly through the formation of hydrogen bonds between some NH_3 and H_2O molecules. These solutions are more appropriately called ammonia-water solutions, or simply $NH_3(aq)$ (aqueous ammonia). The most common basic solutions used in the laboratory are those of NaOH, KOH, $Ca(OH)_2$, and $NH_3(aq)$. Chemists refer to these solutions as being *alkaline* in their behavior.

In the Brønsted theory, an acid is simply a *proton donor.* Accordingly, *a base is a **proton acceptor**.* We have noted that OH^- ions are the most common proton acceptors. However, many other particles also may combine with protons. Our general use of the term *base* includes all species which accept protons in solution.

We have stated that hydrogen chloride ionizes in water solution as a result of the hydrating action of the solvent dipoles.

$$HCl + H_2O \rightarrow H_3O^+ + Cl^-$$
$$\text{acid} \qquad \text{base} \qquad \text{acid} \qquad \text{base}$$

Here, the water molecule is the base. It accepts a proton from the HCl molecule, the acid. This reaction forms the H_3O^+ ion which is a weaker acid, and the Cl^- ion which is a weaker base. (The relative strengths of acids and bases are discussed further in Section 14.12.)

Earlier, we described the neutralization reaction between aqueous solutions of HCl and NaOH. Here, the H_3O^+ ion acts as the acid since it, and not the HCl molecule, is the proton donor. The OH^- ion is, of course, the proton acceptor or base.

Fig. 14-7. A space filling model of the hydroxide ion and its electron-dot formula. When it accepts a proton, a water molecule is formed.

When HCl gas is dissolved in liquid ammonia, the ammonia acts as the base.

$$HCl + NH_3 \rightarrow NH_4^+ + Cl^-$$

acid   base   acid   base

When NH_3 gas is dissolved in water, the water donates protons and therefore acts as an acid. Ammonia accepts protons and therefore is the base. A low concentration of NH_4^+ ions and OH^- ions is produced in the reversible reaction.

$$NH_3 + H_2O \rightleftharpoons NH_4^+ + OH^-$$

base   acid   acid   base

This general conception of acids and bases is quite broad. It is very useful, however, in more advanced studies of nonaqueous solutions. In elementary chemistry we deal mostly with aqueous bases. As stated, these include ammonia-water and the water solutions of soluble metallic hydroxides containing OH^- ions.

14.9   Characteristics of hydroxides

1. Hydroxides of the active metals supply OH⁻ ions in solution. Sodium and potassium hydroxides are very soluble in water. They are electrovalent (ionic) compounds and are, therefore, completely ionized in water solution. Their solutions are *strongly alkaline* because of the high concentration of strongly basic OH^- ions. In speaking of such solutions, chemists often attach the property of the ions to the solution itself. Thus, they may speak of "strongly basic solutions."

$$Na^+OH^- \rightarrow Na^+(aq) + OH^-(aq)$$
$$K^+OH^- \rightarrow K^+(aq) + OH^-(aq)$$

Calcium and strontium hydroxides also are ionic compounds. Thus, their water solutions are completely ionized. However, they are only slightly soluble in water. Therefore, they are only *moderately basic.*

$$Ca^{++}(OH^-)_2 \rightarrow Ca^{++}(aq) + 2OH^-(aq)$$
$$Sr^{++}(OH^-)_2 \rightarrow Sr^{++}(aq) + 2OH^-(aq)$$

The strength of the base depends on the *concentration* of OH^- ions *in solution.* It does not depend on the number of hydroxide ions per mole of the compound.

Ammonia-water solutions are *weakly basic* because they have a low concentration of OH^- ions. Ammonia, NH_3, is not a strong base and so does not acquire very many protons from water molecules when in solution. Relatively few NH_4^+ ions and OH^- ions are present.

$$NH_3(aq) + H_2O \rightleftharpoons NH_4^+(aq) + OH^-(aq)$$

2. *Soluble hydroxides have a bitter taste.* Possibly you have tasted limewater and know that it is bitter. Soapsuds also taste bitter because of the presence of hydroxide ions. **CAUTION: *Never use the "taste test" in the laboratory.*** Strongly basic solutions are very caustic (they chemically burn the skin) and the metallic ions in them are sometimes poisonous.

3. *Solutions of hydroxides feel slippery.* The very soluble hydroxides, such as sodium hydroxide, attack the skin and may produce severe caustic burns. Dilute solutions have a soapy, slippery feel when rubbed between the thumb and fingers.

4. *Soluble hydroxides affect indicators.* The basic OH^- ions in solutions of the soluble hydroxides cause *litmus* to turn from *red* to *blue*. This is just the opposite of the color change caused by H_3O^+ ions of acid solutions. In a basic solution, *phenolphthalein* turns *red* and *methyl orange* changes to *yellow*. The insoluble hydroxides, on the other hand, seldom produce enough OH^- ions to affect indicators.

5. *Hydroxides neutralize acids.* The neutralization of HNO_3 by KOH may be represented empirically by the equation:

$$KOH + HNO_3 \rightarrow KNO_3 + H_2O$$

Of course, ionic KOH dissociates in water solution and exists as hydrated K^+ ions and OH^- ions.

$$K^+OH^- \rightarrow K^+ + OH^-$$

In water solution, the covalent HNO_3 is ionized and exists as hydrated protons and nitrate ions.

$$HNO_3 + H_2O \rightarrow H_3O^+ + NO_3^-$$

The complete ionic equation for this neutralization reaction is:

$$H_3O^+ + NO_3^- + K^+ + OH^- \rightarrow K^+ + NO_3^- + 2H_2O$$

Removing the spectator ions, we have

$$H_3O^+ + OH^- \rightarrow 2H_2O$$

This represents the only chemical reaction that takes place in the neutralization process. The hydrated K^+ and NO_3^- ions join as ionic crystals of the salt, KNO_3, only when the water is evaporated.

6. *Hydroxides react with the oxides of nonmetals.* Such reactions form salts and sometimes water. For example, sodium hydroxide reacts with carbon dioxide in different ways. The products may be either carbonate *or* hydrogen carbonate ions, depending on the relative quantities of reactants. Two moles of NaOH per mole of CO_2 forms sodium carbonate, Na_2CO_3, and H_2O.

$$CO_2 + 2NaOH \rightarrow Na_2CO_3 + H_2O$$

Table 14–4
SOLUBILITY OF METALLIC HYDROXIDES

Hydroxide	Solubility (g/100 g H_2O at 20°C)
soluble (>1 g/100 g H_2O)	
KOH	112
NaOH	109
LiOH	12.8
$Ba(OH)_2$	3.89
slightly soluble (>0.1 g/100 g H_2O)	
$Ca(OH)_2$	0.165
insoluble (<0.1 g/100 g H_2O)	
$Pb(OH)_2$	0.016
$Mg(OH)_2$	0.0009
$Sn(OH)_2$	0.0002
$Zn(OH)_2$	negligible
$Cu(OH)_2$	negligible
$Al(OH)_3$	negligible
$Cr(OH)_3$	negligible
$Fe(OH)_3$	negligible

One mole of NaOH per mole of CO_2 forms only sodium hydrogen carbonate, $NaHCO_3$.

$$CO_2 + NaOH \rightarrow NaHCO_3$$

The net reactions are

$$CO_2 + 2OH^- \rightarrow CO_3^{--} + H_2O$$

and

$$CO_2 + OH^- \rightarrow HCO_3^-$$

Carbon dioxide is the acid anhydride of carbonic acid. Therefore, these reactions are essentially neutralization reactions between carbonic acid and sodium hydroxide.

7. *Certain hydroxides are amphiprotic.* The metallic hydroxides, except those of the active metals, are generally insoluble. They are weakly basic in the presence of an acid. They may behave as acids in the presence of a strong base. *Substances which have either acidic or basic properties under appropriate conditions are said to be **amphiprotic*** (am-fih-*proh*-tick). Amphiprotic hydroxides dissolve in solutions that contain an excess of hydroxide ions.

Aluminum hydroxide separates as a jelly-like precipitate when hydroxide ions are added to a solution of an aluminum salt.

$$Al(H_2O)_6^{+++} + 3OH^-(aq) \rightarrow Al(H_2O)_3(OH)_3 + 3H_2O$$

The strongly basic OH^- ions accept protons from three water molecules of each hydrated aluminum ion. In this way, the insoluble hydrated aluminum hydroxide is formed. Disregarding the water of hydration, we can write the above equation more simply as

$$Al^{+++}(aq) + 3OH^-(aq) \rightarrow Al(OH)_3(s)$$

A high concentration of hydroxide ions causes the aluminum hydroxide precipitate to redissolve. The aluminum then exists in the form of soluble, negatively-charged aluminate ions, AlO_2^-.

$$Al(OH)_3(s) + OH^-(aq) \xrightarrow{} AlO_2^-(aq) + 2H_2O$$

This insoluble hydroxide acts as an acid in the presence of the strong base. Suppose we rearrange the formula of the hydroxide into the familiar form of an acid. The acid-base character of the reaction is then more apparent:

$$H_3AlO_3(s) + OH^-(aq) \rightarrow AlO_2^-(aq) + 2H_2O$$

$Al(OH)_3$ and H_3AlO_3 are equivalent formulas. They could lead to different names (*aluminum hydroxide* and *aluminic acid*, respectively) for this single substance.

The amphiprotic aluminum hydroxide dissolves in an excess of hydronium ions. Aluminum ions and water are produced.

$$Al(OH)_3(s) + 3H_3O^+ \rightarrow Al^{+++}(aq) + 6H_2O$$

The equation can be written more simply as

$$Al(OH)_3(s) + 3H^+(aq) \rightarrow Al^{+++}(aq) + 3H_2O$$

Zinc hydroxide is an insoluble, amphiprotic hydroxide of a metal in the $+2$ oxidation state. When zinc hydroxide is added to hydrochloric acid, zinc chloride and water are produced.

$$Zn(OH)_2(s) + 2HCl \rightarrow ZnCl_2 + 2H_2O$$

In the presence of sodium hydroxide solution, $Zn(OH)_2$ acts as an acid. Sodium zincate (the zincate ion is ZnO_2^{--}) and water are formed.

$$H_2ZnO_2(s) + 2NaOH \rightarrow Na_2ZnO_2 + 2H_2O$$

Disregarding all spectator ions, we can write simplified equations for the above reactions. These net equations show proton-transfer, or *protolysis,* reactions. In such reactions, protons are transferred from an acid to a base.

$$Zn(OH)_2(s) + 2H^+(aq) \rightarrow Zn^{++}(aq) + 2H_2O$$

and

$$H_2ZnO_2(s) + 2OH^-(aq) \rightarrow ZnO_2^{--}(aq) + 2H_2O$$

The hydroxides of lead(II), tin(II), chromium(III), and antimony(II) are other common amphiprotic hydroxides. Iron(III) hydroxide is not amphiprotic. This hydroxide does not dissolve in an excess of OH$^-$ ions.

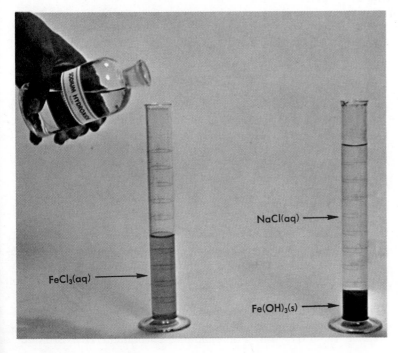

Fig. 14-8. The hydroxides of heavy metals are practically insoluble.

In the Brønsted theory of acids and bases, water is an amphiprotic substance. When a water molecule accepts a proton from hydrogen chloride, it acts as a base. On the other hand, when a water molecule donates a proton to ammonia, it acts as an acid. Indeed, in the slight ionization of water, one water molecule donates a proton to another water molecule. Thus, some of the water molecules behave as an acid while others behave as a base.

$$H_2O + H_2O \rightleftarrows H_3O^+ + OH^-$$

Liquid ammonia undergoes a similar ionization, but to a lesser extent than water. Ammonium ions and amide ions, NH_2^-, are formed.

$$NH_3 + NH_3 \rightleftarrows NH_4^+ + NH_2^-$$

Ammonia is therefore amphiprotic.

14.10 Basic anhydrides

We have stated that the oxides of the active metals are ionic in structure. Like other ionic substances, they are solid at room temperature. They contain O^{--} ions. When placed in water, O^{--} ions react with the water and form basic OH^- ions.

$$O^{--} + H_2O \rightarrow 2OH^-$$

If the metallic hydroxide is soluble in water, the solution is basic because of the presence of OH^- ions.

Oxides of sodium, potassium, calcium, strontium, and barium react vigorously with water. You may have seen a plasterer *slaking* quicklime, CaO, by adding water to it. He was forming *slaked lime,* $Ca(OH)_2$.

$$CaO + H_2O \rightarrow Ca(OH)_2$$

Oxides which react with water and produce solutions containing the basic OH^- ions are called basic anhydrides. The oxides of the active metals are basic anhydrides. In contrast, acid anhydrides are oxides of nonmetals (see Section 14.7); they are covalent compounds which, in the solid state, have molecular crystalline structures.

14.11 Hydroxides and periodic trends

In general, the hydroxides of the active metals are strongly basic. The O—H groups are present as ions and the compounds are usually quite soluble. Other hydroxide compounds may be weakly basic amphiprotic, or acidic. The higher the oxidation state of the atom combined with the O—H group, the more covalent is the bond between this atom and the O—H group. Further, the more covalent the bond, the more difficult it is to remove the OH^- ion. For example, chromium(II) hydroxide is basic, chromium(III) hydroxide is amphiprotic, and chromium(VI) hydroxide is acidic.

With amphiprotic hydroxides, it appears that the O—H bond is as easily broken as the bond between the metal and the O—H group. A strong base acquires a proton by breaking the O—H bond. An acid, on the other hand, donates a proton to the O—H group. In doing so, it breaks the bond between the O—H group and the metal atom.

Hydroxides of atoms having high electronegativity and high oxidation states are acidic. The O—H bond is more easily broken than the bond between the O—H group and the central atom. For example, O_3ClOH is strongly acidic. The chlorine atom is in the +7 oxidation state. It is also the central atom to which three oxygen atoms and one O—H group are bonded. In water solution the molecule donates a proton from its O—H group and forms the negative O_3ClO^- ion.

$$O_3ClOH + H_2O \rightarrow H_3O^+ + O_3ClO^-$$

If we rewrite the formula in the conventional form of acids, O_3ClOH becomes $HClO_4$. We can recognize this formula as *perchloric* acid, an oxyacid. The equation now has a more familiar appearance.

$$HClO_4 + H_2O \rightarrow H_3O^+ + ClO_4^-$$

It may not be apparent from the formula of a substance whether it has acidic or basic properties. We have observed that oxides which react with water form oxygen-hydrogen groups. In general, the oxygen-hydrogen groups formed by ionic oxides (metal oxides) are OH^- ions. Their compounds are hydroxides and their solutions are basic.

Oxygen-hydrogen groups formed by molecular oxides (nonmetal oxides) are not ionic. Instead, they are bonded covalently to another atom in the product molecule. Such groups were identified as hydroxyl groups in Section 14.7. Hydroxyl groups donate protons in aqueous solution. The compounds have acid properties and are oxyacids.

Figure 14-9 shows electron-dot formulas for several molecular substances which contain hydroxyl groups. Considering their structures alone, their molecular formulas could be written $SO_2(OH)_2$, CH_3COOH, $PO(OH)_3$, and C_2H_5OH. However, none has the basic properties characteristic of the OH^- ion in water solution. The first three are oxyacids. This acidic character is recognized by writing their formulas as H_2SO_4, $HC_2H_3O_2$, and H_3PO_4. Experimental evidence must establish the acidic or basic character of a substance.

14.12 Relative strengths of acids and bases

The Brønsted theory of acids and bases provides a broad basis for the study of *protolysis,* or proton-transfer, reactions. Any

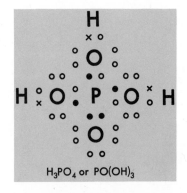

H_3PO_4 or $PO(OH)_3$

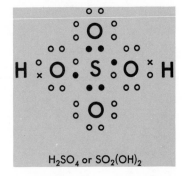

H_2SO_4 or $SO_2(OH)_2$

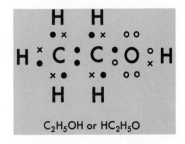

C_2H_5OH or HC_2H_5O

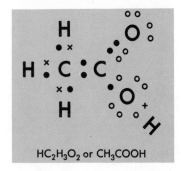

$HC_2H_3O_2$ or CH_3COOH

Fig. 14-9. Molecular formulas alone will not identify acidic or basic properties.

molecule or ion capable of donating a proton is considered to be an acid. Any molecule or ion that can accept the proton is a base.

Suppose that an acid (in the Brønsted sense) gives up a proton. The remainder of the acid particle itself is then capable of accepting a proton. Therefore, we may consider this remaining particle to be a base; it is called a *conjugate base*. *A **conjugate base** is the species that remains after an acid has given up a proton.*

An aqueous solution of sulfuric acid contains H_3O^+ ions and HSO_4^- ions. With further dilution, the HSO_4^- ions may give up protons to H_2O molecules.

$$HSO_4^- + H_2O \rightarrow H_3O^+ + SO_4^{--}$$
$$\text{acid} \qquad \text{base} \qquad \text{acid} \qquad \text{base}$$

The SO_4^{--} ion is what is left of the HSO_4^- after its proton has been removed. It is the conjugate base of the acid HSO_4^-.

The SO_4^{--} ion, as a base, can accept a proton from H_3O^+. When this occurs, the acid HSO_4^- ion is formed.

$$H_3O^+ + SO_4^{--} \rightarrow HSO_4^- + H_2O$$
$$\text{acid} \qquad \text{base} \qquad \text{acid} \qquad \text{base}$$

The HSO_4^- ion can be called the *conjugate acid* of the base SO_4^{--}. *A **conjugate acid** is the species formed when a base takes on a proton.* Thus, in the example given, the HSO_4^- ion and the SO_4^{--} ion are a *conjugate acid-base pair*.

The H_2O molecule also acts as a base in this reaction. It receives the proton given up by the HSO_4^- ion and forms the H_3O^+ ion. Thus, the H_3O^+ ion is the conjugate acid of the base H_2O.

Similarly, the acidic H_3O^+ ion gives up a proton to the basic SO_4^{--} ion and forms the H_2O molecule. Thus, the H_2O molecule is the conjugate base of the H_3O^+ ion. The H_2O molecule and the H_3O^+ ion make up the second conjugate acid-base pair in the reaction.

In the above reaction, each reactant and product is labeled either as an acid or a base. There are two conjugate acid-base pairs.

Conjugate acid-base pair	HSO_4^-	SO_4^{--}
	acid	base

Conjugate acid-base pair	H_2O	H_3O^+
	base	acid

Each acid has one more proton than its conjugate base.

We can apply similar reasoning to the equation for the initial ionization of H_2SO_4. Here, the HSO_4^- ion is the *conjugate* base of H_2SO_4.

$$H_2SO_4 + H_2O \rightarrow H_3O^+ + HSO_4^-$$
$$\text{acid} \qquad \text{base} \qquad \text{acid} \qquad \text{base}$$

The HSO_4^- ion is *both* the conjugate acid of the base SO_4^{--} and the conjugate base of the acid H_2SO_4. Thus, the HSO_4^- ion is amphiprotic.

We know that HCl is highly ionized even in concentrated aqueous solutions. The hydrogen chloride molecule gives up protons readily and is therefore a strong acid. It follows that the Cl^- ion, the conjugate base of this acid, has little tendency to retain the proton. It is, consequently, a weak base.

This observation suggests an important statement that follows naturally from the Brønsted theory of acids and bases: *the stronger an acid, the weaker its conjugate base; and the stronger a base, the weaker its conjugate acid.*

An aqueous solution of the strong acid $HClO_4$ is highly ionized. The reaction to the right is practically complete even in concentrated solutions.

$$\underset{\text{acid}}{\underset{\textbf{stronger}}{HClO_4}} + \underset{\text{base}}{\underset{\textbf{stronger}}{H_2O}} \rightleftarrows \underset{\text{acid}}{\underset{\textbf{weaker}}{H_3O^+}} + \underset{\text{base}}{\underset{\textbf{weaker}}{ClO_4^-}}$$

The ClO_4^- ion is the conjugate base of $HClO_4$. It is too weak a base to compete successfully with the base H_2O in acquiring a proton. The H_3O^+ ion is the conjugate acid of H_2O. It is too weak an acid to compete successfully with the acid $HClO_4$ in donating a proton. Thus, there is little tendency for the reaction to proceed to the left and re-form the $HClO_4$ and H_2O molecules.

Now let us examine the situation in an aqueous solution of acetic acid.

$$\underset{\text{acid}}{\underset{\textbf{weaker}}{HC_2H_3O_2}} + \underset{\text{base}}{\underset{\textbf{weaker}}{H_2O}} \rightleftarrows \underset{\text{acid}}{\underset{\textbf{stronger}}{H_3O^+}} + \underset{\text{base}}{\underset{\textbf{stronger}}{C_2H_3O_2^-}}$$

The H_3O^+ ion concentration is quite low even in dilute solutions. This fact indicates that $HC_2H_3O_2$ is indeed a weak acid. It does not compete very successfully with H_3O^+ ions in donating protons to a base. The H_2O molecules do not compete very successfully with $C_2H_3O_2^-$ ions in accepting protons. The H_3O^+ ion is the stronger acid and the $C_2H_3O_2^-$ ion is the stronger base. Thus, the reaction tends to proceed to the left.

Observe that in each example the stronger acid had the weaker conjugate base and the stronger base had the weaker conjugate acid. Also note that, in each reversible situation, the reaction tended to proceed toward the weaker acid and base.

These observations suggest a second important statement that follows naturally from the Brønsted theory: *protolysis reactions favor the production of the weaker acid and the weaker base.*

We have stated that protolysis occurs when a proton donor and a proton acceptor are brought together in a solution. The extent of this protolysis depends on the relative strengths of the acids and bases involved. For a proton-transfer reaction to approach

Table 14-5
RELATIVE STRENGTHS OF ACIDS AND BASES

	Acid	*Formula*	*Conjugate base*	*Formula*	
Decreasing Acid Strength	perchloric	$HClO_4$	perchlorate ion	ClO_4^-	*Decreasing Base Strength*
	hydrogen chloride	HCl	chloride ion	Cl^-	
	nitric	HNO_3	nitrate ion	NO_3^-	
	sulfuric	H_2SO_4	hydrogen sulfate ion	HSO_4^-	
	hydronium ion	H_3O^+	water	H_2O	
	hydrogen sulfate ion	HSO_4^-	sulfate ion	SO_4^{--}	
	phosphoric	H_3PO_4	dihydrogen phosphate ion	$H_2PO_4^-$	
	acetic	$HC_2H_3O_2$	acetate ion	$C_2H_3O_2^-$	
	carbonic	H_2CO_3	hydrogen carbonate ion	HCO_3^-	
	hydrogen sulfide	H_2S	hydrosulfide ion	HS^-	
	ammonium ion	NH_4^+	ammonia	NH_3	
	hydrogen carbonate ion	HCO_3^-	carbonate ion	CO_3^{--}	
	water	H_2O	hydroxide ion	OH^-	
	ammonia	NH_3	amide ion	NH_2^-	
	hydrogen	H_2	hydride ion	H^-	

completeness, the reactants must be much stronger as an acid and a base than the products.

Table 14-5 shows the relative strengths of several Brønsted acids and of their conjugate bases. Observe that the strongest acid listed, $HClO_4$, has the weakest conjugate base listed, ClO_4^-. The weakest acid, H_2, has the strongest conjugate base, the hydride ion, H^-. A violent protolysis could result from bringing together the strongest acid and the strongest base in certain proportions. Such a reaction would be highly exothermic and very dangerous.

SALTS

14.13 Nature of salts

Common table salt, NaCl, is only one of a large class of compounds which chemists refer to as *salts*. The solution of an aqueous acid contains H_3O^+ ions and negatively charged nonmetal ions (anions). These particles result from ionization of the acid in water. On the other hand, the solution of an aqueous base contains positively charged metal ions (cations) and OH^- ions. These particles result from dissociation of the ionic metallic hydroxide in water. A neutralization reaction between two such solutions removes almost all of the H_3O^+ and OH^- ions. They unite and form water, which is only very slightly ionized. The cations of the hydroxide and the anions of the acid are spectator ions. They have no part in the neutralization reaction.

As an example, let us consider the neutralization reaction between aqueous solutions of HCl and KOH. Aqueous ions are present in the acid solution because of ionization.

$$HCl(g) + H_2O \rightarrow H_3O^+(aq) + Cl^-(aq)$$

Aqueous ions are present in the hydroxide solution because of dissociation.

$$K^+OH^-(s) \rightarrow K^+(aq) + OH^-(aq)$$

Neutralization occurs when the proper quantities of the two solutions are mixed.

$$H_3O^+(aq) + Cl^-(aq) + K^+(aq) + OH^-(aq) \rightarrow K^+(aq) + Cl^-(aq) + 2H_2O$$

Removing all spectator ions, the net equation for the neutralization reaction becomes

$$H_3O^+(aq) + OH^-(aq) \rightarrow 2H_2O$$

As solvent water is evaporated, K^+ cations and Cl^- anions no longer remain separated from each other by water dipoles. They form a characteristic ionic crystalline structure and separate from solution as the *salt* KCl. *A compound composed of the positive ions of an aqueous base and the negative ions of an aqueous acid is called a salt.* All true salts, by this definition, are electrovalent substances. They vary in solubility in water, but their aqueous solutions are simple solutions of hydrated ions. Some useful solubility information regarding salts is summarized in Table 14-6.

14.14 Salt-producing reactions

There are several ways of forming salts, but not all of these ways apply to the formation of every salt.

1. Direct union of the elements. Some metals react directly with certain nonmetals and form a salt. For example, burning sodium in an atmosphere of chlorine gas produces sodium chloride.

$$2Na + Cl_2 \rightarrow 2NaCl$$

Table 14–6
SOLUBILITY OF SALTS

---

1. Common sodium, potassium, and ammonium compounds are soluble in water.
2. Common nitrates, acetates, and chlorates are soluble.
3. Common chlorides are soluble except silver, mercury(I), and lead. (Lead(II) chloride is soluble in hot water.)
4. Common sulfates are soluble except calcium, barium, strontium, and lead.
5. Common carbonates, phosphates, and silicates are insoluble except sodium, potassium, and ammonium.
6. Common sulfides are insoluble except calcium, barium, strontium, magnesium, sodium, potassium, and ammonium.

---

2. Reaction of a metal with an acid. Many metals replace hydrogen in an aqueous acid and form the corresponding salt. Zinc reacts with hydrochloric acid and forms zinc chloride and hydrogen.

$$Zn + 2HCl \rightarrow ZnCl_2 + H_2(g)$$

3. Reaction of a metallic oxide with an aqueous acid. The oxides of some metals react with an acid and form a salt. Magnesium oxide, when treated with hydrochloric acid, forms magnesium chloride and water.

$$MgO + 2HCl \rightarrow MgCl_2 + H_2O$$

If calcium oxide is substituted for magnesium oxide in this reaction, the salt formed is calcium chloride.

$$CaO + 2HCl \rightarrow CaCl_2 + H_2O$$

4. Reaction of a nonmetallic oxide with a base. The oxides of some nonmetals react with a soluble hydroxide and form a salt. Carbon dioxide gas passed into limewater (saturated calcium hydroxide solution) forms insoluble calcium carbonate and water.

$$CO_2 + Ca(OH)_2 \rightarrow CaCO_3(s) + H_2O$$

Additional carbon dioxide converts the calcium carbonate to soluble calcium hydrogen carbonate.

$$CO_2 + H_2O + CaCO_3 \rightarrow Ca(HCO_3)_2$$

The reactions of sulfur dioxide in limewater are similar. Insoluble calcium sulfite, $CaSO_3$, is first formed.

$$SO_2 + Ca(OH)_2 \rightarrow CaSO_3(s) + H_2O$$

When excess sulfur dioxide gas is bubbled through limewater, however, soluble calcium hydrogen sulfite is formed.

$$SO_2 + H_2O + CaSO_3 \rightarrow Ca(HSO_3)_2$$

5. Acid-base neutralization. When an acid neutralizes a soluble hydroxide, a salt may be recovered from the water solvent. This salt corresponds to the metallic ion of the base and the nonmetallic ion of the acid. Many different salts can be prepared by neutralization. An example is the reaction between hydrochloric acid and sodium hydroxide mixed in chemically equivalent quantities. When the solvent water is evaporated, sodium chloride remains.

$$NaOH + HCl \rightarrow NaCl + H_2O$$

6. Ion-exchange reaction. Two salts may be prepared in ionic reactions if one of them is practically insoluble. The equation for the reaction between solutions of sodium sulfate and barium chloride is

$$BaCl_2 + Na_2SO_4 \rightarrow 2NaCl + BaSO_4(s)$$

Since both reactants are dissociated in water solution, the ionic equation is more useful.

$$Ba^{++} + 2Cl^- + 2Na^+ + SO_4^{--} \rightarrow 2Na^+ + 2Cl^- + BaSO_4(s)$$

In this reaction, barium sulfate is only very slightly soluble. It precipitates readily and can be filtered from the solution. The sodium chloride can be obtained by evaporating the solvent water. Sodium chloride thus recovered contains some barium sulfate since precipitates always separate from saturated solutions.

7. *Reaction of an acid with a carbonate.* A salt can be obtained from this reaction because the other products are water and carbon dioxide gas. If hydrochloric acid is added to a solution of sodium carbonate, the following reaction occurs:

$$2HCl + Na_2CO_3 \rightarrow 2NaCl + H_2O + CO_2(g)$$

Carbon dioxide bubbles out of the solution as a gas. Sodium chloride can be recovered by evaporation.

8. *Reaction of a metallic oxide with a nonmetallic oxide.* An oxygen-containing salt may be formed by the reaction between a basic oxide and an acidic oxide. Water is not involved in this process. Instead, the dry oxides are mixed and heated. Metallic carbonates, silicates, and phosphates are typical of the salts produced.

$$MgO + CO_2 \rightarrow MgCO_3$$
$$CaO + CO_2 \rightarrow CaCO_3$$
$$CaO + SiO_2 \rightarrow CaSiO_3$$
$$3CaO + P_2O_5 \rightarrow Ca_3(PO_4)_2$$

14.15 Naming salts

Salts are generally named by combining the names of the ions of which they are composed. For example, the name of $Ba(NO_3)_2$ is *barium nitrate*. By agreement the positive ion, in this case the Ba^{++} ion, is named first. The name of the negative ion, in this case the NO_3^- ion, follows.

Over the years, many difficulties have arisen in the naming of salts. For example, many outdated names of salts have carried over into our present naming system. These old names do not provide for a simple translation from name to formula or from formula to name. In 1940, the International Union of Pure and Applied Chemistry recommended a more logical system for naming inorganic compounds. It is known as the *Stock system*, and it provides the uniformity needed for chemical names.

This text uses the Stock system for naming salts which contain metals *with variable oxidation states*. Several examples of Stock names for salts are given in Table 14-7. Observe that the

Table 14-7
SALT NOMENCLATURE

Formula	Stock name
CuCl	copper (I) chloride
CuCl$_2$	copper (II) chloride
FeO	iron (II) oxide
Fe$_2$O$_3$	iron (III) oxide
Fe$_3$O$_4$	iron (II, III) oxide
MnCl$_2$	maganese (II) chloride
MnCl$_4$	maganese (IV) chloride
PtO$_2$	platinum (IV) oxide
Cr$_2$(SO$_3$)$_3$	chromium (III) sulfite
CoCO$_3$	cobalt (II) carbonate
Co$_2$(SO$_4$)$_3$	cobalt (III) sulfate
Cu$_2$SO$_4$	copper (I) sulfate
CuSO$_4$	copper (II) sulfate
Fe$_3$(PO$_4$)$_2$	iron (II) phosphate
Hg(NO$_3$)$_2$	mercury (II) nitrate
KCaPO$_4$	potassium calcium phosphate
NaHCO$_3$	sodium hydrogen carbonate

Table 14-8
ACID-SALT NOMENCLATURE

Formula	Name of acid	Name of salt anion
HF	hydrofluoric	fluoride
HBr	hydrobromic	bromide
HI	hydriodic	iodide
HCl	hydrochloric	chloride
HClO	hypochlorous	hypochlorite
$HClO_2$	chlorous	chlorite
$HClO_3$	chloric	chlorate
$HClO_4$	perchloric	perchlorate
H_2S	hydrosulfuric	sulfide
H_2SO_3	sulfurous	sulfite
H_2SO_4	sulfuric	sulfate
HNO_2	nitrous	nitrite
HNO_3	nitric	nitrate
H_2CO_3	carbonic	carbonate
H_3PO_3	phosphorous	phosphite
H_3PO_4	phosphoric	phosphate

more electropositive cation is named first in *double salts*. A **double salt** *is one in which two different kinds of metallic ions are present.*

The names of anions (negative ions) take the same root and prefix as the acid in which they occur. However, the acid ending *-ic* is changed to *-ate*, and the ending *-ous* is changed to *-ite*. Salts derived from binary acids take the ending -ide. Table 14-8 shows the names of the anions of salts produced by the reactions of various acids.

Salt anions that are polyatomic and include metallic atoms with variable oxidation states may have rather complex names in the Stock system. For example, polyatomic MnO_4^- anion is the *tetraoxomanganate(VII) ion* in this system. However, its potassium salt, $KMnO_4$, is well known as *potassium permanganate;* it will not likely become *potassium tetraoxomanganate (VII)*.

QUESTIONS

Group A
1. Name the three most important industrial acids and tell why each is important.
2. What ion is responsible for the acidic properties of aqueous acid solutions?
3. Why is an acid thought of as a proton donor?
4. (*a*) What is an acid anhydride? (*b*) a basic anhydride? (*c*) Give an example of each.
5. (*a*) State the rules for naming binary acids. (*b*) for naming oxyacids.
6. A base is defined as a proton acceptor. How do you interpret this definition?
7. Write the net ionic equation for the neutralization reaction between an acid and a base.

8. Aluminum hydroxide has basic properties in the presence of a strong acid, and acidic properties in the presence of a solution which is strongly basic. (*a*) Write the formula for aluminum hydroxide to show its basic properties. (*b*) Rewrite the formula to show its acidic properties. (*c*) What term is used to describe such substances?

9. What is the nature of true salts?

10. How are salts named?

11. What method would you use to prepare a small quantity of calcium sulfate quickly and safely in the laboratory? Explain why you chose the method you did and write the equation.

12. Would barium sulfate be a suitable source of the sulfate ion for an ionic reaction with another salt? Explain.

Group B

13. Explain why a water solution of hydrogen chloride has acidic properties but pure hydrogen chloride does not, in the usual sense.

14. (*a*) How can you justify calling hydrogen chloride an acid when it is dissolved in ammonia? (*b*) Write the equation.

15. (*a*) Explain the manner in which water may be considered to be an acid. (*b*) Write an equation which illustrates this behavior using electron-dot formulas.

16. (*a*) What basic solution would you use for cleaning a greasy sink trap? Explain. (*b*) for removing grease spots from clothing? Explain.

17. What basic solutions would you use for neutralizing acid stains on clothing? Explain.

18. Describe the solubility of the following salts in water: $NaCl$, $CaCO_3$, $BaSO_4$, $(NH_4)_2S$, $Al(C_2H_3O_2)_3$, Ag_2SO_4, $Pb(NO_3)_2$, Hg_2Cl_2, $Mg_3(PO_4)_2$, CuS.

19. Name the following compounds: (*a*) H_2Se, (*b*) HIO_3, (*c*) $Ga(OH)_3$, (*d*) $CsOH$, (*e*) $RaBr_2$.

20. (*a*) When H_2O molecules act as a base, what is the conjugate acid? (*b*) When H_2O molecules act as an acid, what is the conjugate base?

21. (*a*) When NH_3 molecules act as a base, what is the conjugate acid? (*b*) When NH_3 molecules act as an acid, what is the conjugate base?

22. Write the equations that show the amphiprotic character of HSO_3^- ions.

PROBLEMS

Group A

1. Nitric acid can be prepared in the laboratory by the reaction of sodium nitrate with sulfuric acid. Sodium hydrogen sulfate is also formed. (*a*) How many grams of sulfuric acid are required to produce 50.0 g of nitric acid? (*b*) How many grams of sodium hydrogen sulfate are formed?

2. How many liters of carbon dioxide can be collected at $\overline{20}°$ C and 745 mm pressure from a reaction between 25.0 g of calcium carbonate and an excess of hydrochloric acid?

3. What quantity of calcium silicate can be prepared by mixing 75.0 g of calcium oxide and 90.0 g of silicon dioxide and heating the mixture?

4. Suppose 75.0 liters of dry carbon dioxide gas, measured at 25.0° C and 755 mm pressure, are available to convert hot calcium oxide to calcium carbonate. (*a*) What quantity of calcium oxide is required? (*b*) What quantity of calcium carbonate is produced?

Chapter 15

Acid-Base Titration and pH

15.1 Molar solutions

In Chapter 12, we studied the effects of solutes on the freezing and boiling points of solvents. We found that the most important factor was the ratio of solute to solvent molecules. Solution concentrations were stated in terms of *molality, m*. Recall that molal concentration expresses the quantity of solute in moles per kilogram of solvent. For a given solvent, two solutions of equal molality have the same ratio of solute to solvent molecules.

Our present studies deal with the solutions of acids, bases and salts. Here, it will be more useful to express solution concentrations in terms of a *known quantity of solute in a given volume of solution*. It is easier to measure the volume of a solution than to measure its mass.

We can state the quantity of solute in *moles* and the volume of solution in *liters*. This scheme for expressing the concentration of a solution is called *molarity*. The symbol for *molarity* is *M. The molarity of a solution is an expression of the number of moles of solute per liter of solution.*

A *one-molar* (1-*M*) solution contains *1 mole of solute per liter of solution*. Solutions of the same molarity have the same concentration of solute molecules. A 1-*M* solution contains 1 gram-molecular weight of molecular solute per liter of solution. It contains 1 gram-formula weight of an ionic solute per liter of solution.

286

A mole of sodium chloride, NaCl, has a mass of 58.5 g, its gram-formula weight. This quantity of NaCl dissolved in enough water to make exactly 1 liter of solution gives a 1-*M* solution. Half this quantity of NaCl in 1 liter of solution forms a 0.5-*M* solution. Twice this quantity of NaCl per liter of solution yields a 2-*M* solution.

A *volumetric flask* like the one shown in Figure 15-1 is commonly used in preparing solutions of known molarity. A measured quantity of solute is dissolved in a portion of solvent in the flask. Then more solvent is added to fill the flask to the mark on the neck. Thus, the quantity of solute and the volume of solution are known. The molarity of the solution is easily calculated.

As an example, suppose we wish to prepare a 1-*M* solution of sulfuric acid. The molecular weight of H_2SO_4 is 98. Thus, a mole of H_2SO_4 has a mass of 98 g. To prepare 1 liter of the 1-*M* solution, we must use 98 g of H_2SO_4 solute. To make 100 ml of the 1-*M* solution, we must use 9.8 g of H_2SO_4 solute. Similarly, a 0.5-*M* solution requires 0.5 mole (49 g) of H_2SO_4 per liter of solution. A 0.05-*M* solution requires 0.05 mole (4.9 g) of H_2SO_4 per liter of solution.

Observe that *molar* solutions are based on the *volume of solution*. (*Molal* solutions, on the other hand, are based on the *mass of solvent*.) *Equal volumes of molecular solutions of equal molarity have the same number of solute molecules*. Molarity is preferred when volumes of solutions are to be measured.

15.2 Chemical equivalents

Solution concentrations can be expressed in a way that allows *chemically equivalent quantities* of different solutes to be measured very simply. These quantities of solutes are called *equivalents* (equiv). *Equivalents are the quantities of substances that have the same combining capacity in chemical reactions.*

Consider the following equations. They show that 36.5 g (1 mole) of HCl and 49 g (1/2 mole) of H_2SO_4 are chemically equivalent in neutralization reactions with basic KOH.

$$HCl \ + \ KOH \ \rightarrow \ KCl \ + \ H_2O$$
$$\text{1 mole} \quad \text{1 mole} \rightarrow \text{1 mole} \quad \text{1 mole}$$
$$\text{36.5 g} \qquad \text{56 g}$$

or,
$$H_2SO_4 \ + 2KOH \ \rightarrow \ K_2SO_4 \ + \ 2H_2O$$
$$1/2 \ H_2SO_4 + \ KOH \ \rightarrow 1/2 \ K_2SO_4 + \ H_2O$$
$$\text{1/2 mole} \quad \text{1 mole} \qquad \text{1/2 mole} \quad \text{1 mole}$$
$$\text{49 g} \qquad \text{56 g}$$

The equations also reveal that both 36.5 g of HCl and 49 g of H_2SO_4 are chemically equivalent to 56 g (1 mole) of KOH in these neutralization reactions.

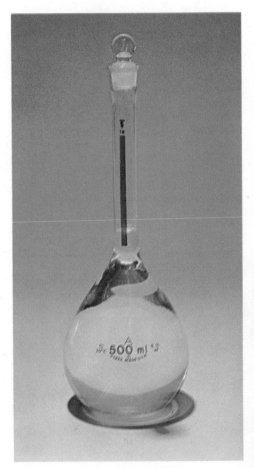

Fig. 15-1. A volumetric flask. When filled to the mark at 20° C it contains 500 ml ± 0.15 ml.

Suppose we replace KOH with $Ca(OH)_2$ in one of the above reactions. The new equation shows that 37 g (1/2 mole) of $Ca(OH)_2$ is equivalent to 56 g (1 mole) of KOH.

$$
\begin{array}{llll}
& 2HCl \;+\; Ca(OH)_2 & \rightarrow & CaCl_2 \;+\; 2H_2O \\
or, & HCl \;+\; 1/2\,Ca(OH)_2 & \rightarrow & 1/2\,CaCl_2 \;+\; H_2O \\
& \;1\;mole \quad\quad 1/2\;mole & & 1/2\;mole \quad 1\;mole \\
& 36.5\;g \quad\quad\quad 37\;g & &
\end{array}
$$

In proton-transfer reactions, *one equivalent of an acid is the quantity, in grams, which supplies one mole of protons (as H_3O^+ ions)*. HCl and H_2SO_4 are the acids in the neutralization reactions we have just considered. We can determine the quantity representing *one equivalent* of each acid in these reactions as follows:

$$
1\ equiv\ HCl = \frac{1\ mole\ HCl}{1\ mole\ H_3O^+} \times \frac{36.5\ g}{mole} = \frac{36.5\ g\ HCl}{mole\ H_3O^+}
$$

$$
1\ equiv\ H_2SO_4 = \frac{1\ mole\ H_2SO_4}{2\ moles\ H_3O^+} \times \frac{98\ g}{mole} = \frac{49\ g\ H_2SO_4}{mole\ H_3O^+}
$$

One equivalent of a base is the quantity, in grams, which accepts one mole of protons (as H_3O^+ ions), or supplies one mole of OH^- ions. For KOH and $Ca(OH)_2$ in the above reactions,

$$
1\ equiv\ KOH = \frac{1\ mole\ KOH}{1\ mole\ OH^-} \times \frac{56\ g}{mole} = \frac{56\ g\ KOH}{mole\ OH^-}
$$

$$
1\ equiv\ Ca(OH)_2 = \frac{1\ mole\ Ca(OH)_2}{2\ moles\ OH^-} \times \frac{74\ g}{mole} = \frac{37\ g\ Ca(OH)_2}{mole\ OH^-}
$$

HCl, HNO_3, and $HC_2H_3O_2$ are monoprotic acids. One mole of each can supply 1 mole of H_3O^+ ions. Therefore, *1 equivalent of a monoprotic acid is the same as 1 mole of the acid*. One mole of a diprotic acid such as H_2SO_4 can supply 2 moles of H_3O^+ ions. Thus, *for complete neutralization, 1 equivalent of a diprotic acid is the same as 1/2 mole of the acid*. H_3PO_4 is triprotic and can furnish 3 moles of H_3O^+ ions per mole of acid. *When completely neutralized, 1 equivalent of a triprotic acid is the same as 1/3 mole of the acid.*

A similar relationship exists between chemical equivalents and moles of bases. One mole of KOH supplies 1 equivalent of OH^- ions. One mole of $Ca(OH)_2$ supplies 2 equivalents of OH^- ions. Therefore, 1 equivalent of KOH is the same as 1 mole of KOH, and 1 equivalent of $Ca(OH)_2$ is the same as 1/2 mole of $Ca(OH)_2$.

In many chemical reactions a diprotic or triprotic acid is not completely neutralized. In such a case, we determine the number of moles of protons supplied per mole of acid by the reaction it undergoes. For example, suppose we add a solution containing 1 mole of H_2SO_4 to a solution containing 1 mole of NaOH. The salt, sodium hydrogen sulfate, is then recovered by evaporating the water solvent. Observe that the neutralization of H_2SO_4 is *not* complete.

$$H_2SO_4 + NaOH \rightarrow NaHSO_4 + H_2O$$

1 mole	1 mole	1 mole	1 mole
98 g	40 g		

One mole of H_2SO_4 supplies 1 mole of protons to the base and forms an "acid salt" containing HSO_4^- ions. Therefore, 1 equivalent of H_2SO_4 is the same as 1 mole of the acid, 98 g, *in this reaction.*

$$1 \text{ equiv } H_2SO_4 = \frac{1 \text{ mole } H_2SO_4}{1 \text{ mole } H_3O^+} \times \frac{98 \text{ g}}{\text{mole}} = \frac{98 \text{ g } H_2SO_4}{\text{mole } H_3O^+}$$

Now, suppose we add a solution containing 1 mole of H_3PO_4 to one containing 1 mole of NaOH. The reaction is

$$H_3PO_4 + NaOH \rightarrow NaH_2PO_4 + H_2O$$

1 mole	1 mole	1 mole	1 mole
98.0 g	40.0 g		

The salt, sodium dihydrogen phosphate, can be recovered by evaporation. One mole of H_3PO_4 supplies 1 mole of protons to the base and forms a salt containing $H_2PO_4^-$ ions. Thus, one equivalent of H_3PO_4 is the same as 1 mole of the acid, 98.0 g, *in this reaction.*

$$1 \text{ equiv } H_3PO_4 = \frac{1 \text{ mole } H_3PO_4}{1 \text{ mole } H_3O^+} \times \frac{98.0 \text{ g}}{\text{mole}} = \frac{98.0 \text{ g } H_3PO_4}{\text{mole } H_3O^+}$$

Suppose the basic solution in the reaction above contained 2 moles of NaOH. The salt recovered by evaporation would then be Na_2HPO_4. One equivalent of H_3PO_4 in this reaction is the same as 1/2 mole of the acid, 49.0 g. Of course, in another reaction, if the neutralization of the triprotic acid is complete, 1 equivalent of H_3PO_4 is the same as 1/3 mole of the acid, 32.7 g.

Now, let us consider a reactant that is neither an acid nor a base. A chemical equivalent of such a reactant is *that quantity, in grams, which supplies or acquires 1 mole of electrons in a chemical reaction.* In the following reaction, a mole of sodium atoms (23 g) loses 1 mole of electrons and forms 1 mole of Na^+ ions.

$$Na - e^- \rightarrow Na^+$$

1 mole	1 mole	1 mole
23 g		23 g

Therefore, 1 equivalent of sodium is the same as 1 mole of sodium atoms, 23 g.

A mole of calcium atoms ($4\bar{0}$ g) supplies 2 moles of electrons when Ca^{++} ions are formed. A mole of aluminum atoms (27 g) supplies 3 moles of electrons when Al^{+++} ions are formed. Thus, 1 equivalent of calcium is the mass of 1/2 mole of calcium atoms, $2\bar{0}$ g. One equivalent of aluminum is the mass of 1/3 mole of aluminum atoms, 9.0 g.

$$
\begin{array}{cccc}
1/2\ \text{Ca} & -\quad e^- & \rightarrow & 1/2\ Ca^{++} \\
1/2\ \text{mole} & 1\ \text{mole} & & 1/2\ \text{mole} \\
2\bar{0}\ \text{g} & & & 2\bar{0}\ \text{g}
\end{array}
$$

and

$$
\begin{array}{cccc}
1/3\ \text{Al} & -\quad e^- & \rightarrow & 1/3\ Al^{+++} \\
1/3\ \text{mole} & 1\ \text{mole} & & 1/3\ \text{mole} \\
9.0\ \text{g} & & & 9.0\ \text{g}
\end{array}
$$

These relationships can be summarized as follows:

$$1\ \text{equiv Na} = \frac{1\ \text{mole Na}}{1\ \text{mole } e^-} \times \frac{23\ \text{g}}{\text{mole}} = \frac{23\ \text{g Na}}{\text{mole } e^-}$$

$$1\ \text{equiv Ca} = \frac{1\ \text{mole Ca}}{2\ \text{moles } e^-} \times \frac{4\bar{0}\ \text{g}}{\text{mole}} = \frac{2\bar{0}\ \text{g Ca}}{\text{mole } e^-}$$

$$1\ \text{equiv Al} = \frac{1\ \text{mole Al}}{3\ \text{moles } e^-} \times \frac{27\ \text{g}}{\text{mole}} = \frac{9.0\ \text{g Al}}{\text{mole } e^-}$$

Oxidating and reducing agents with several common oxidation states are given special attention in connection with oxidation-reduction reactions in Chapter 21.

Observe that when its ions are formed, the numerical *change* in oxidation state for sodium atoms is 1. This change for calcium atoms is 2. For aluminum atoms it is 3. We can ordinarily use such numbers to determine one equivalent of an element for a given reaction. We simply divide the mass of 1 mole of atoms of the element (1 g-at wt) by the *change in oxidation state* these atoms undergo in a chemical reaction.

$$1\ \text{equiv Na} = \frac{23\ \text{g}}{1} = 23\ \text{g}$$

$$1\ \text{equiv Ca} = \frac{4\bar{0}\ \text{g}}{2} = 2\bar{0}\ \text{g}$$

$$1\ \text{equiv Al} = \frac{27\ \text{g}}{3} = 9.0\ \text{g}$$

A somewhat similar method can ordinarily be used to find the mass of 1 equivalent of a salt. The mass of 1 mole of the salt is divided by the *total* positive (or negative) ionic charge indicated by its formula. This total positive charge is determined by multiplying the number of cations (shown in the formula of the salt) by the charge on each cation.

$$1\ \text{equiv (salt)} = \frac{\text{mass of 1 mole of salt}}{\text{total positive charge}}$$

The formula of sodium sulfate is Na_2SO_4 and the mass of 1 mole is 142 g. Each of the two Na^+ ions has a $+1$ charge.

The total positive charge = 2. (Notice that the total negative charge also = 2.)

$$1 \text{ equiv Na}_2\text{SO}_4 = \frac{142 \text{ g}}{2} = 71.0 \text{ g}$$

One mole of calcium phosphate, $Ca_3(PO_4)_2$, has a mass of $31\bar{0}$ g. Each of the three Ca^{++} ions has a +2 charge. The total positive charge = 6. (Note that the total negative charge also = 6.)

$$1 \text{ equiv Ca}_3(\text{PO}_4)_2 = \frac{31\bar{0} \text{ g}}{6} = 51.7 \text{ g}$$

15.3 Normal solutions

We can now express solution concentration based on the volume of solution in a second way. This method involves stating the quantity of solute in equivalents and is called *normality*. The symbol for normality is the capital letter N. The **normality** *of a solution expresses the number of equivalents of solute per liter of solution.*

A one-normal (1-N) solution contains 1 equivalent of solute per *liter of solution.* Equal volumes of solutions of the same normality are chemically equivalent.

Knowing solution concentrations in molarity or normality can be very helpful. Using these expressions, we can take any desired mass of *solute* in the form of its solution. We simply measure out a certain volume of the solution. A disadvantage is that the mass or volume of *solvent* present is not known precisely. The expressions for solution concentration are summarized in Table 15-1.

A mole of the monoprotic hydrogen chloride has a mass of 36.5 g. As a reactant, it can furnish 1 mole of protons. Thus, 1 mole of HCl in 1 liter of aqueous solution provides 1 mole of protons as H_3O^+ ions. This solution has a 1-N concentration.

Suppose we require a solution of HCl which furnishes 0.100 mole of H_3O^+ ions per liter. This is a 0.100-N HCl solution. It is evident that the solute must be 3.65 g of HCl dissolved in

Name	Symbol	Solute unit	Solvent unit	Dimensions
molality	*m*	mole	kilogram solvent	$\dfrac{\text{mole solute}}{\text{kg solvent}}$
molarity	*M*	mole	liter solution	$\dfrac{\text{mole solute}}{\text{liter solution}}$
normality	*N*	equivalent	liter solution	$\dfrac{\text{equiv solute}}{\text{liter solution}}$

Table 15–1
METHODS OF EXPRESSING CONCENTRATION OF SOLUTIONS

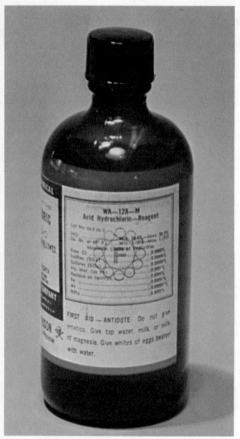

Fig. 15-2. The manufacturer's label on a reagent bottle provides important information to the chemist.

water and diluted to a 1.00-liter volume. However, *this solute is 3.65 g of anhydrous hydrogen chloride in one liter of solution.* It is not 3.65 g of the concentrated hydrochloric acid found in the laboratory.

How can we determine the volume of concentrated hydrochloric acid which contains 3.65 g of hydrogen chloride? First we must know the mass percentage of HCl in the concentrated solution and the density of the concentrated solution. This information is printed on the label of the concentrated hydrochloric acid container. See Figure 15-2. Representative values are

$$\text{percent HCl} = 37.23\%$$
$$\text{density} = 1.19 \text{ g/ml}$$

Thus, we have 37.23 g HCl per $10\overline{0}$ g of concentrated solution. The density of this solution is 1.19 g/ml. From these data we can determine the mass of HCl in each milliliter of concentrated solution.

$$\frac{37.23 \text{ g HCl}}{10\overline{0} \text{ g conc soln}} \times \frac{1.19 \text{ g}}{\text{ml}} = \frac{0.443 \text{ g HCl}}{\text{ml conc soln}}$$

For 1.00 liter of 0.100-N solution, 3.65 g of HCl is required, since

$$\frac{0.100 \text{ equiv HCl}}{\text{liter}} \times \frac{36.5 \text{ g}}{\text{equiv}} \times 1.00 \text{ liter} = 3.65 \text{ g HCl}$$

We now know the mass of HCl per milliliter of concentrated solution and the mass of HCl required. From these data we can calculate the volume of concentrated hydrochloric acid solution required.

$$3.65 \text{ g HCl} \times \frac{\text{ml conc soln}}{0.443 \text{ g HCl}} = 8.24 \text{ ml conc soln}$$

Thus, 8.24 ml of concentrated HCl solution diluted to 1.00 liter with distilled water gives a 0.100-N solution of HCl.

We have already seen that 1 mole of H_2SO_4 contains 2 equivalents of that substance. A 1-M solution contains 98 g of H_2SO_4 per liter of solution. However, a 1-N solution contains 49 g (98 g ÷ 2) of H_2SO_4 per liter of solution. A 5-N solution contains 245 g (49 g × 5) of H_2SO_4 per liter. Similarly, 0.01-N H_2SO_4 contains 0.49 g (49 g ÷ 100) of H_2SO_4 per liter of solution. Concentrated sulfuric acid is usually 95% - 98% H_2SO_4 and has a density of about 1.84 g/ml. Dilutions to desired normalities are calculated as shown above for HCl.

Compounds containing water of crystallization present special problems in preparing solutions. For example, crystalline copper(II) sulfate has the empirical formula

$$CuSO_4 \cdot 5H_2O$$

The formula weight is 249.5. One mole of this hydrate, 249.5 g, contains 1 mole of $CuSO_4$, 159.5 g. This fact must be recognized when moles or equivalents of crystalline hydrates are measured.

A 1-M $CuSO_4$ solution contains 159.5 g of $CuSO_4$ per liter of solution. This 1-M solution is also a 2-N solution because 1 mole of $CuSO_4$ contains 2 equivalents. A 1-N solution requires 79.75 g of $CuSO_4$ per liter. Of course, this solution is 0.5 M.

If a mole of a solute is also 1 equivalent, the molarity and normality of the solution *are the same*. A 1-M HCl solution is also a 1-N solution. If a mole of solute is two equivalents, a 1-M solution is 2 N. A 0.01-M H_2SO_4 solution is therefore 0.02 N. Similarly, a 0.01-M H_3PO_4 solution is 0.03 N if it is completely neutralized. *Solutions of equal normality are chemically equivalent, volume for volume.*

15.4 Ion concentration in water

Water is very weakly ionized by self-ionization. This process is sometimes referred to as *autoprotolysis*. We stated in Section 13.8 that this self-ionization probably starts with hydrogen bond formation. The very poor conductivity of pure water results from the slight ionization of water itself. This fact can be demonstrated by testing water which has been highly purified by several different techniques.

Electric conductivity measurements of very pure water show that, at 25° C, water is very slightly ionized to H_3O^+ and OH^- ions. In fact, the concentrations of these ions in pure water are only

$$\frac{1 \text{ mole } H_3O^+}{10^7 \text{ liters } H_2O} \quad \text{and} \quad \frac{1 \text{ mole } OH^-}{10^7 \text{ liters } H_2O}$$

One liter of water has a mass of 997 g at 25° C (1 liter = 1000 g at 4° C). The mass of 1 mole of water is 18.0 g. Using these quantities, we see that 1 liter contains 55.4 moles of water at 25° C.

$$\frac{997 \text{ g}}{\text{liter}} \times \frac{1 \text{ mole}}{18.0 \text{ g}} = 55.4 \text{ moles/liter}$$

The extent of the ionization can be stated as a percentage if the concentration of H_3O^+ ions (and also OH^- ions) is expressed in moles of ions per mole of water.

$$\frac{1 \text{ mole } H_3O}{10^7 \text{ liters } H_2O} \times \frac{1 \text{ liter}}{55.4 \text{ moles}} = \frac{2 \times 10^{-9} \text{ mole } H_3O^+}{\text{mole } H_2O}$$

This result shows that water is about 0.0000002% ionized at 25° C.

It is more useful to express ion concentration as *moles per liter* than as moles per 10,000,000 liters. This change is accomplished by dividing both terms in the expression moles per 10^7 liters by 10^7.

$$\frac{1 \text{ mole } H_3O^+ \div 10^7}{10^7 \text{ liters } H_2O \div 10^7} = \frac{10^{-7} \text{ mole } H_3O^+}{\text{liter } H_2O}$$

Thus, the concentration of H_3O^+ ions (and OH^- ions) in water at 25° C is 10^{-7} mole per liter of H_2O.

Chemists use a standard notation to represent concentration in terms of *moles/liter*. The symbol or formula of the particular ion or molecule is enclosed in brackets, [ ]. *For example,* [H_3O^+] means *hydronium ion concentration in moles per liter.* For the ionic concentrations in water at 25° C, we may write

$$[H_3O^+] = 10^{-7} \text{ mole/liter}$$

$$\text{and } [OH^-] = 10^{-7} \text{ mole/liter}$$

$$\text{or } [H_3O^+] = [OH^-] = 10^{-7} \text{ mole/liter}$$

Because the H_3O^+ ion concentration and the OH^- ion concentration are equal, water is neutral. It is neither acidic nor basic. This neutrality prevails in any solution in which [H_3O^+]= [OH^-].

If the H_3O^+ ion concentration in a solution exceeds 10^{-7} mole/liter, the solution is acidic. For example, a solution containing 10^{-5} mole H_3O^+ ion per liter is acidic. If the OH^- ion concentration exceeds 10^{-7} mole per liter, the solution is basic or alkaline. Thus, a solution containing 10^{-4} mole OH^- ion per liter is basic.

It is also true that the *product* of the [H_3O^+] and [OH^-] remains constant in water and dilute aqueous solutions as long as the temperature does not change. Recall that Le Chatelier's principle tells us that an increase in concentration of either of these ionic species in an aqueous mixture at equilibrium causes a decrease in concentration of the other species. In water and dilute aqueous solutions at 25° C,

$$[H_3O^+] \times [OH^-] = \text{a constant}$$

$$[H_3O^+][OH^-] = (1 \times 10^{-7} \text{ mole/liter})^2$$

$$[H_3O^+][OH^-] = 1 \times 10^{-14} \text{ mole}^2/\text{liter}^2$$

The ionization of water increases as its temperature rises. At 0° C the product [H_3O^+][OH^-] is 0.11×10^{-14} mole² per liter². At 60° C it is 9.6×10^{-14} mole² per liter².

pH

15.5   The pH of a solution

The range of solution concentrations encountered by chemists is great. It varies from about $10\ M$ to perhaps $10^{-15}\ M$. However, concentrations of less than $1\ M$ are most commonly used.

We have stated that the product of [H_3O^+] and [OH^-] is a constant. Therefore, if we know the concentration of either ionic species, we can determine the concentration of the other. For example, the OH^- ion concentration of a 0.01-M NaOH solution is 0.01 or 10^{-2} mole/liter. The H_3O^+ ion concentration of this solution is calculated as follows:

$$[H_3O^+][OH^-] = 1 \times 10^{-14} \text{ mole}^2/\text{liter}^2$$

$$[H_3O^+] = \frac{1 \times 10^{-14} \text{ mole}^2/\text{liter}^2}{[OH^-]}$$

$$[H_3O^+] = \frac{1 \times 10^{-14} \text{ mole}^2/\text{liter}^2}{1 \times 10^{-2} \text{ mole/liter}}$$

$$[H_3O^+] = 1 \times 10^{-12} \text{ mole/liter}$$

See the Sample Problem which follows.

Sample Problem

Nitric acid, HNO_3, is completely ionized in a 0.001-M aqueous solution. (a) What is the H_3O^+ ion concentration in this solution? (b) What is the OH^- concentration?

Solution

(a) HNO_3 is a monoprotic acid giving 1 mole of H_3O^+ ions per mole of HNO_3 when completely ionized in water solution.

For 0.001-M aqueous HNO_3:

$$[H_3O^+] = 0.001 \text{ mole/liter} = 10^{-3} \text{ mole/liter}$$

(b) $[H_3O^+][OH^-] = 10^{-14} \text{ mole}^2/\text{liter}^2$

$$[OH^-] = \frac{10^{-14} \text{ mole}^2/\text{liter}^2}{[H_3O^+]} = \frac{10^{-14} \text{ mole}^2/\text{liter}^2}{10^{-3} \text{ mole/liter}}$$

$$[OH^-] = 10^{-11} \text{ mole/liter}$$

We can express the acidity or alkalinity of a solution in terms of its hydronium ion concentration. An $[H_3O^+]$ *larger* than 10^{-7} mole/liter (a *smaller* negative exponent) indicates an acid solution. An $[H_3O^+]$ *smaller* than 10^{-7} mole/liter (a *larger* negative exponent) indicates an alkaline solution.

Expressing acidity or alkalinity in this way can become cumbersome, especially in dilute solutions, whether decimal or exponential notations are used. Because it is more convenient, chemists use a quantity called pH to indicate the hydronium ion concentration of a solution.

Numerically, the pH of a solution is the common logarithm of the number of liters of solution that contains one mole of H_3O^+ ions. The number of liters of solution is equal to the *reciprocal* of

Table 15–2

APPROXIMATE pH OF SOME COMMON SUBSTANCES

Substance	pH
1.0-N HCl	0.1
1.0-N H_2SO_4	0.3
0.1-N HCl	1.1
0.1-N H_2SO_4	1.2
gastric juice	2.0
0.01-N H_2SO_4	2.1
lemons	2.3
vinegar	2.8
0.1-N $HC_2H_3O_2$	2.9
soft drinks	3.0
apples	3.1
grapefruit	3.1
oranges	3.5
cherries	3.6
tomatoes	4.2
bananas	4.6
bread	5.5
potatoes	5.8
rainwater	6.2
milk	6.5
pure water	7.0
eggs	7.8
0.1-N $NaHCO_3$	8.4
seawater	8.5
milk of magnesia	10.5
0.1-N NH_3	11.1
0.1-N Na_2CO_3	11.6
0.1-N NaOH	13.0
1.0-N NaOH	14.0
1.0-N KOH	14.0

the H_3O^+ ion concentration. This concentration is given in moles of H_3O^+ ions per liter of solution. The reciprocal expression is

$$\frac{1}{[H_3O^+]}$$

*Thus, the **pH** of a solution is defined as the common logarithm of the reciprocal of the hydronium ion concentration. The pH is expressed by the equation:*

$$pH = \log \frac{1}{[H_3O^+]}$$

The common logarithm of a number is the power to which 10 must be raised to give the number. Thus 0.0000001 is 10^{-7} and its reciprocal is 10,000,000, or 10^7. The logarithm of 10^7 is 7.

Pure water is slightly ionized, and at 25° C contains 0.0000001 or 10^{-7} mole of H_3O^+ per liter. The pH of water is therefore

$$pH = \log \frac{1}{0.0000001}$$

$$pH = \log \frac{1}{10^{-7}}$$

$$pH = \log 10^7$$

$$pH = 7$$

Suppose the H_3O^+ ion concentration in a solution is *greater* than that in pure water. Then the number of liters required to provide 1 mole of H_3O^+ ions is *smaller*. Consequently, the pH is a *smaller* number than 7. Such a solution is *acidic*. On the other hand, suppose the H_3O^+ ion concentration is *less than* that in pure water. The pH is then a larger number than 7. Such a solution is *basic*.

The range of pH values usually falls between 0 and 14. The pH system is particularly useful in describing the acidity or alkalinity of solutions that are not far from neutral. This includes many food substances and fluids encountered in physiology. The pH of some common substances is given in Table 15-2.

15.6   pH calculations

There are two basic types of pH problems which concern us. These are

1. the calculation of pH when the $[H_3O^+]$ of a solution is known, and

2. the calculation of $[H_3O^+]$ when the pH of a solution is known.

In the simplest pH problems, the $[H_3O^+]$ of the solution is an integral power of 10 such as 1 M, 0.1 M, or 0.01 M. Such problems can be solved *by inspection*. The pH equation based on the definition stated in Section 15.5 is

$$pH = \log \frac{1}{[H_3O^+]}$$

Since $$\log \frac{1}{[H_3O^+]} = -\log [H_3O^+]$$

we can write the first equation in a more useful form to solve for pH.

$$pH = -\log [H_3O^+]$$

Remember that the base of common logarithms is 10. Thus, this equation can be restated in terms of H_3O^+ as follows:

$$\log [H_3O^+] = -pH$$

and

$$[H_3O^+] = 10^{-pH}$$

In the case of a solution having a $[H_3O^+] = 10^{-6}$ mole/liter, the pH = 6. For a solution in which the pH = 2, $[H_3O^+] = 10^{-2}$ mole/liter. When the pH = 0, $[H_3O^+] = 1$ mole/liter since 10^0 (ten to the zero power) = 1.

Chemical solutions with pH values below 0 and above 14 can be prepared. For example, the pH of 6-M H_2SO_4 is between 0 and −1. The pH of 3-M KOH is near 14.5. However, we will deal only with pH values in the 0-14 range. Observe that the *pH of a solution is the exponent of the hydronium ion concentration with the sign changed.* The following Sample Problems further illustrate this fact.

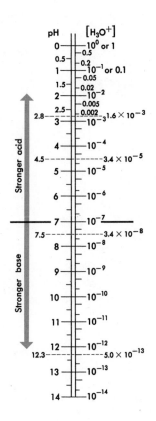

Sample Problem

What is the pH of a 0.001-M HCl solution?

Solution

$$pH = -\log [H_3O^+]$$

$$[H_3O^+] = 0.001 \text{ mole/liter} = 10^{-3} \text{ mole/liter}$$

$$pH = -\log 10^{-3} = -(-3)$$

$$pH = 3$$

(Notice that if the $[H_3O^+] = 10^{-3}$, the pH = 3)

Sample Problem

What is the pH of a 0.001-M NaOH solution?

Solution

$$pH = -\log[H_3O^+]$$

$$[H_3O^+][OH^-] = 10^{-14} \text{ mole}^2/\text{liter}^2$$

$$[H_3O^+] = \frac{10^{-14} \text{ mole}^2/\text{liter}^2}{[OH^-]}$$

$$[OH^-] = 0.001 \text{ mole}/\text{liter} = 10^{-3} \text{ mole}/\text{liter}$$

$$[H_3O^+] = \frac{10^{-14} \text{ mole}^2/\text{liter}^2}{10^{-3} \text{ mole}/\text{liter}} = 10^{-11} \text{ mole}/\text{liter}$$

$$pH = -\log 10^{-11} = -(-11)$$

$$pH = 11$$

Sample Problem

What is the hydronium ion concentration of a sulfuric acid solution which has a pH of 4?

Solution

$$pH = -\log[H_3O^+]$$

$$\log[H_3O^+] = -pH$$

$$[H_3O^+] = \text{antilog}(-pH) = \text{antilog}(-4)$$

$$\text{antilog}(-4) = 10^{-4}$$

$$[H_3O^+] = 10^{-4} \text{ mole}/\text{liter}$$

(Notice that if the pH = 4, the $[H_3O^+] = 10^{-4}$)

The preceding problems have hydronium ion concentrations that are integral powers of ten and pH values that are positive integers. These problems are readily solved by inspection. However, many problems involve hydronium ion concentrations that are not integral powers of ten. Solving such problems requires some basic knowledge of logarithms and exponents.

Suppose the $[H_3O^+]$ of a solution is 3.4×10^{-5} mole/liter. Observe that 3.4×10^{-5} lies between 1×10^{-4} and 1×10^{-5}. Thus, the pH of the solution must be between 4 and 5. Calculations are required to determine a more precise pH value. However, this simple estimate of pH helps prevent errors which otherwise occur quite commonly.

The relationship between the pH and $[H_3O^+]$ is shown on the scale of Figure 15-3. This scale can be used to estimate the pH value described in the preceding paragraph. Calculations for this pH value and for $[H_3O^+]$ from a known pH value are shown in the following Sample Problems.

Sample Problem

What is the pH of a solution if $[H_3O^+]$ is 3.4×10^{-5} mole/liter?

Solution

$$pH = -\log [H_3O^+]$$
$$pH = -\log (3.4 \times 10^{-5})$$

The logarithm of a product is equal to the sum of the logarithms of each of the factors. Thus,

$$pH = -(\log 3.4 + \log 10^{-5})$$

The log of $10^{-5} = -5$ and, from the table of logarithms (Appendix Table 17), the log of 3.4 is found to be 0.53.

$$pH = -(0.53 - 5)$$

Therefore,

$$pH = 4.47$$

Sample Problem

The pH of a solution is found to be 7.52. What is the hydronium ion concentration?

Solution

The $[H_3O^+]$ is the number whose logarithm is -7.52. Therefore the antilog of -7.52 will give the hydronium ion concentration.

$$pH = -\log [H_3O^+]$$

Solving for $[H_3O^+]$

$$log [H_3O^+] = -pH$$
$$[H_3O^+] = antilog (-pH)$$
$$[H_3O^+] = antilog (-7.52)$$

But

$$\text{antilog} \, (-7.52) = \text{antilog} \, (0.48 - 8)$$

Thus

$$[H_3O^+] = \text{antilog} \, (0.48 - 8)$$
$$[H_3O^+] = \text{antilog} \, (0.48) \times \text{antilog} \, (-8)$$

The antilog of $(-8) = 10^{-8}$. The antilog of (0.48) is found from the table of logarithms to be 3.0. Therefore,

$$[H_3O^+] = 3.0 \times 10^{-8} \, \text{mole/liter}$$

Table 15-3 shows the relationship between the hydronium ion and hydroxide ion concentrations, the product of these concentrations, and the pH for several solutions of typical molarities. Since KOH is a soluble ionic compound, its aqueous solutions are completely ionized. The molarity of each KOH solution indicates directly the $[OH^-]$. Note that the product $[H_3O^+][OH^-]$ is constant, 10^{-14} mole^2 per liter^2 at 25° C. Therefore, the $[H_3O^+]$ can be calculated. If we know the $[H_3O^+]$, we can then determine the pH as $-\log [H_3O^+]$.

Any aqueous solution of HCl that has a concentration below 1-M can be considered to be completely ionized. Thus, the molarity of the 0.001-M HCl solution indicates directly the $[H_3O^+]$.

The weakly ionized $HC_2H_3O_2$ solution presents a different problem. We may lack information about the concentrations of $HC_2H_3O_2$ molecules, H_3O^+ ions, and $C_2H_3O_2^-$ ions in the equilibrium mixture in the aqueous solution. However, we can determine the pH of the solution experimentally. If we know the pH, the $[H_3O^+]$ can be computed as antilog $(-pH)$.

15.7 Acid-base titration

In a neutralization reaction, the basic OH^- ion acquires a proton from the H_3O^+ ion and forms a molecule of water.

$$H_3O^+ + OH^- \rightarrow 2H_2O$$

Table 15-3
RELATIONSHIP OF $[H_3O^+]$ TO $[OH^-]$ AND pH

Solution	$[H_3O^+]$	$[OH^-]$	$[H_3O^+][OH^-]$	pH
0.02-M KOH	5.0×10^{-13}	2.0×10^{-2}	1.0×10^{-14}	12.3
0.01-M KOH	1.0×10^{-12}	1.0×10^{-2}	1.0×10^{-14}	12.0
pure H_2O	1.0×10^{-7}	1.0×10^{-7}	1.0×10^{-14}	7.0
0.001-M HCl	1.0×10^{-3}	1.0×10^{-11}	1.0×10^{-14}	3.0
0.1-M $HC_2H_3O_2$	1.3×10^{-3}	7.7×10^{-12}	1.0×10^{-14}	2.9

One mole of H_3O^+ ions (19 g) and 1 mole of OH^- ions (17 g) are chemically equivalent. Neutralization occurs when H_3O^+ ions and OH^- ions are supplied in equal numbers. We know that a liter of water at room temperature has an $[H_3O^+]$ and $[OH^-]$ of 10^{-7} M each. Furthermore, we know that the product $[H_3O^+][OH^-]$ of 10^{-14} mole²/liter² is a constant for water and all dilute aqueous solutions.

If 0.1 mole of a gaseous HCl is dissolved in the liter of water, the H_3O^+ ion concentration rises to 0.1 or 10^{-1} M. Since the product $[H_3O^+][OH^-]$ remains at 10^{-14}, the $[OH^-]$ obviously must decrease from 10^{-7} to 10^{-13} M.

According to the above equation, OH^- ions are removed from the solution when they combine with H_3O^+ ions. Almost 10^{-7} mole of H_3O^+ ions is also removed in this way. However, this is only a small portion (0.0001%) of the 0.1 mole of H_3O^+ ions present in the liter of solution.

Now suppose we add 0.1 mole (4 g) of solid NaOH to the liter of 0.1-M HCl solution. Imagine, also, that the hydroxide and hydronium ions are somehow temporarily prevented from reacting with each other. The NaOH dissolves and supplies 0.1 mole of OH^- ions to the solution. Both $[H_3O^+]$ and $[OH^-]$ are now high and their product is much greater than the constant value 10^{-14} for the dilute aqueous solution.

Now, suppose the chemical reaction is allowed to begin. The ion-removal reaction will be as before except that this time there are as many OH^- ions as H_3O^+ ions to be removed. H_3O^+ and OH^- ions combine until the product $[H_3O^+][OH^-]$ returns to the constant value 10^{-14} and

$$[H_3O^+] = [OH^-] = 10^{-7}\ M$$

The solution is now neither acidic nor basic, but neutral. The process was one in which chemically equivalent quantities of H_3O^+ ions and OH^- ions combined, a neutralization reaction.

These examples should help you understand the nature of the chemical reaction which occurs between acids and bases. The gradual addition of an acid to a base or a base to an acid in order to compare their concentrations is called *titration*. *Titration is the process by which the capacity of a solution of unknown concentration to combine with one of known concentration is quantitatively measured.*

Titration provides a sensitive means of determining the relative volumes of chemically equivalent acidic and basic solutions. If we know the concentration of one, we can calculate the concentration of the other. Titration is an important laboratory procedure and is much used in analytical chemistry.

Suppose we make gradual additions of a base to a measured volume of an acid. Eventually, the acid is neutralized. With continued addition, the solution becomes distinctly basic. The pH has now changed from a low to a high numerical value. The change in pH occurs slowly at first, then rapidly through the

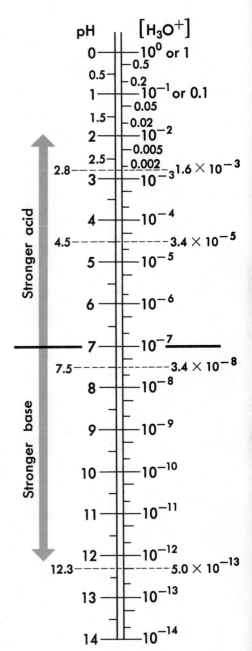

Fig. 15-3. The relationship between the numerical expression for the pH of a solution and its corresponding hydronium ion concentration, $[H_3O^+]$, may be easily compared in this chart.

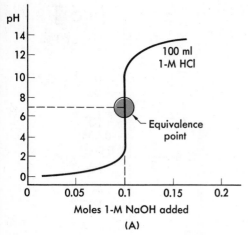

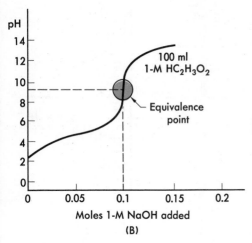

Fig. 15-4. Acid-base titration curves: (A) strong acid-strong base; (B) weak acid-strong base.

neutral point, and slowly again as the solution becomes basic. Typical pH curves for strong acid-strong base and weak acid-strong base titrations are shown in Figure 15-4.

The very rapid change in pH occurs in the region where equivalent quantities of H_3O^+ and OH^- ions are present. Any method which shows this abrupt change in pH can be used to detect the *equivalence point* of the titration.

Many dyes have colors that are sensitive to pH changes. Some change color within the pH range in which an equivalence point occurs. Such dyes may serve as *indicators* in the titration process. Several indicators are listed in Table 15-4.

Burets like those shown in Figure 15-5 are used in titration to measure solution volumes with good precision. Suppose we have an NaOH solution of unknown concentration. We gradually add small amounts of this solution to 10.0 ml of 0.01-*M* HCl solution containing a few drops of a suitable indicator. Finally, the indicator shows that the equivalence point is reached. Careful readings of the base buret show that 20.0 ml of the basic solution has been used. How can these titration data indicate the molarity of the basic solution?

The empirical equation for the neutralization reaction is

$$\text{HCl} + \text{NaOH} \rightarrow \text{NaCl} + \text{H}_2\text{O}$$

We know the volume and molarity of the solution of HCl used. From these data, we can determine the quantity, in moles, of HCl used:

$$\frac{10.0 \text{ ml}}{1000 \text{ ml/liter}} \times \frac{0.01 \text{ mole HCl}}{\text{liter}} = 0.0001 \text{ mole HCl used}$$

The balanced equation shows that *1 mole* of NaOH is used for *1 mole* of HCl. In other words, NaOH and HCl show chemical equivalence in the reaction, mole for mole. Therefore, the quantity of NaOH used in the titration is also 0.0001 mole. This quantity was furnished by 20.0 ml of NaOH solution. The molarity of the NaOH solution is obtained as follows:

$$\frac{0.0001 \text{ mole NaOH}}{20.0 \text{ ml}} \times \frac{1000 \text{ ml}}{\text{liter}} = 0.005 \text{ mole NaOH/liter}$$

or

0.005-*M* NaOH

The accuracy of the titration method is limited by the accuracy with which the concentration of the "known" solution is actually known. For this reason, much care is taken to establish the concentration of a known solution used in titration.

Such a solution is first prepared and adjusted volumetrically to the desired concentration. This concentration is established with maximum precision by titrating the solution against a carefully measured quantity of a highly purified compound known as a *primary standard*. The process is called a *standardization* and the solution is referred to as a standard solution.

Let us return to the titration example above but use a different unknown NaOH solution. Suppose that the diprotic acid H_2SO_4 is used as the standard solution instead of HCl. The same titration data now yield a different answer for the molarity of the NaOH solution. The equation is

$$H_2SO_4 + 2NaOH \rightarrow Na_2SO_4 + 2H_2O$$

$$\frac{10.0 \text{ ml}}{1000 \text{ ml/liter}} \times \frac{0.01 \text{ mole } H_2SO_4}{\text{liter}} = 0.0001 \text{ mole } H_2SO_4 \text{ used}$$

The equation shows that *2 moles* of NaOH are required for *1 mole* of H_2SO_4. Therefore, 0.0002 mole NaOH is used in the titration as the chemical equivalent of 0.0001 mole H_2SO_4. The molarity of the NaOH solution is obtained as follows:

$$\frac{0.0002 \text{ mole NaOH}}{20.0 \text{ ml}} \times \frac{1000 \text{ ml}}{\text{liter}} = 0.01 \text{ mole NaOH/liter}$$

or

$$0.01\text{-}M \text{ NaOH}$$

To summarize, we can determine the molarity of an aqueous base (or acid) of unknown concentration by titrating against an aqueous acid (or base) of known concentration. The following steps are involved:

1. *Determine moles solute of known solution used in the titration.*
2. *Determine ratio—moles unknown solute/moles known solute—from balanced equation.*
3. *Determine moles solute of unknown solution used in the titration.*
4. *Determine molarity of unknown solution.*

The accompanying Sample Problem illustrates the titration process.

From the CHEM Study Film: Acid-Base Indicators

Fig. 15-5. An acid-base titration using an indicator.

Sample Problem

In a titration, 27.4 ml of a standard solution of $Ba(OH)_2$ is added to a 20.0 ml-sample of an HCl solution. The concentration of the standard solution is 0.0154 *M*. What is the molarity of the acid solution?

The equation for this reaction is

Solution

$$2HCl + Ba(OH)_2 \rightarrow BaCl_2 + 2H_2O$$

The quantity, in moles, of $Ba(OH)_2$ used in the reaction can be found from the molarity of the standard solution and the volume used.

$$\frac{27.4 \text{ ml}}{1000 \text{ ml/liter}} \times \frac{0.0154 \text{ mole } Ba(OH)_2}{\text{liter}} = 0.000422 \text{ mole } Ba(OH)_2 \text{ used}$$

The equation shows that *2 moles* of HCl are used for *1 mole* of $Ba(OH)_2$. Therefore, 0.000844 mole of HCl is used since this is the chemical equivalent of 0.000422 mole of $Ba(OH)_2$.

20.0 ml of the unknown solution contains 0.000844 mole of HCl. The concentration is

$$\frac{0.000844 \text{ mole HCl}}{20.0 \text{ ml}} \times \frac{1000 \text{ ml}}{\text{liter}} = 0.0422 \text{ mole/liter}$$

or

0.0422-*M* HCl

Chemists sometimes prefer to express solution concentrations in terms of *normality*. The advantage in doing so is that concentrations are expressed directly in terms of equivalents of solute. Solutions of the same normality are always chemically equivalent, milliliter for milliliter. We have seen that the *molarity* and the *normality* of a given solution may or may not be numerically the same. The relationship between the two depends upon the substance and the reaction in which it is involved.

A very simple relationship exists between volumes and normalities of solutions used in titration. For example, suppose 50.0 ml of a standard solution of 0.100-*N* NaOH reaches an equivalence point with 10.0 ml of vinegar, a water solution of acetic acid. We see that 5.00 times as much standard base solution was used in the titration as vinegar. Clearly, the vinegar is 5.00 times as concentrated as the base. Therefore, the concentration of the vinegar is 0.500 *N*.

The relationship between volumes and normalities in titration is expressed in equation form as follows:

$$V_1N_1 = V_2N_2$$

V_1 and N_1 are the volume and normality, respectively, of the standard solution. V_2 and N_2 are those of the unknown solution.

The acidity of vinegar is due to the presence of acetic acid. A 1.0-*N* acetic acid solution contains 1.0 equivalent per liter of solution. In this case, 1.0 equivalent equals 1.0 mole or $6\bar{0}$ g of $HC_2H_3O_2$ per liter of solution. The 0.50-*N* solution must contain $3\bar{0}$ g of $HC_2H_3O_2$ per liter. A liter of vinegar has a mass of about 1000 g. Thus, the sample of vinegar used contains 3.0% acetic acid.

Aqueous solutions of some salts may be acidic or basic, depending on the composition of the salt. If the anions are sufficiently basic, some protons are removed from water and the [OH⁻] increases. On the other hand, if the cations are slightly acidic, some protons are donated to water and the [H₃O⁺] increases.

NaOH is a strong base and $HC_2H_3O_2$ is a weak acid. The pH curve for this titration, Figure 15-4(B), differs from the curve for a strong acid-strong base titration. The equivalence point occurs at a higher pH because the sodium acetate solution formed in the titration is slightly basic.

15.8 Indicators in titration

Chemists have a wide choice of indicators for use in titration. They are able to choose one which changes color over the correct pH range for any particular reaction. Let us see why it is not always suitable to have an indicator that changes color at a pH of 7.

Solutions of soluble hydroxides and acids mixed in chemically equivalent quantities may not be exactly neutral. They are neutral only if both solutes are ionized to the same degree. The purpose of the indicator is to show that the equivalence point has been reached. That is, it shows when equivalent quantities of the two solutes are together. Table 15-4 gives the color changes of several common indicators used in acid-base titrations. In this table, the pH range over which an indicator color change occurs is referred to as its *transition interval*. Notice the variations in the transition intervals for the different indicators. These variations enable a chemist to choose the best indicator for a given acid-base reaction.

There are four possible types of acid-base combinations. In titration, these combinations may have equivalence points occurring in different pH ranges as follows:

1. Strong acid—strong base: pH is about 7. Litmus is a suitable indicator, but the color change is not sharply defined. Bromthymol blue performs more satisfactorily. See Figure 15-8.

2. Strong acid—weak base: pH is less than 7. Methyl orange is a suitable indicator.

3. Weak acid—strong base: pH is greater than 7. Phenolphthalein is a suitable indicator.

4. Weak acid—weak base: pH may be either greater than or less than 7, depending on which solution is stronger. None of the indicators performs very well.

Table 15-4
INDICATOR COLORS

Indicator	Color			Transition interval (pH)
	acid	*transition*	*base*	
methyl violet	yellow	aqua	blue	0.0— 1.6
methyl yellow	red	orange	yellow	2.9— 4.0
bromphenol blue	yellow	green	blue	3.0— 4.6
methyl orange	red	orange	yellow	3.2— 4.4
methyl red	red	buff	yellow	4.8— 6.0
litmus	red	pink	blue	5.5— 8.0
bromthymol blue	yellow	green	blue	6.0— 7.6
phenol red	yellow	orange	red	6.6— 8.0
phenolphthalein	colorless	pink	red	8.2—10.6
thymolphthalein	colorless	pale blue	blue	9.4—10.6
alizarin yellow	yellow	orange	red	10.0—12.0

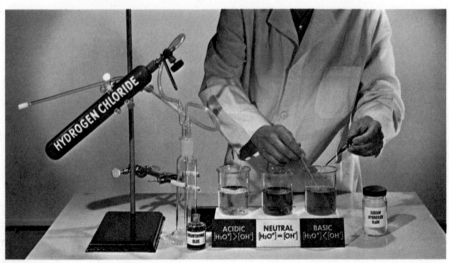

From the CHEM Study Film: Acid-Base Indicators

Fig. 15-6. The acid, base, and transition colors of bromthymol blue.

Fig. 15-7. A modern pH meter in use in the laboratory.

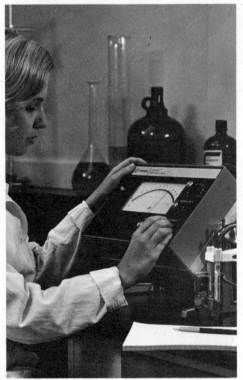

Fisher Scientific Company

15.9   pH measurements

Indicators used to detect equivalence points in neutralization reactions are organic compounds. They possess weak acidic or basic characteristics. When added to a solution in suitable form and concentration, an indicator gives the solution a characteristic color. If the pH of the solution is changed, as in titration, the indicator changes color over a definite range of pH. We have called this range the *transition interval.*

Why does an indicator have different colors at pH values above and below its transition interval? The color of the un-ionized indicator molecule is different from that of the indicator ions. The ratio of indicator-ions to indicator molecules changes with the pH of the solutions. Therefore, the indicator color depends on the pH of the solution and changes as the pH does. The acid, base, and transition colors of several indicators are shown in Figure 15-8.

An indicator added to different solutions may show the same *transition color.* If so, the solutions are considered to have the same pH. This is the basis for the common *colorimetric* determination of pH. A measured volume of a suitable indicator is added to each solution whose pH is to be determined. The color is then compared with that of the same indicator in solutions of known pH. By careful color comparison, the pH of a solution can be estimated to the nearest 0.1 pH unit.

The use of indicators to determine equivalence points in titrations and the pH of solutions involves simple and common techniques in chemistry. However, it is by no means the only way to perform these procedures. Modern instruments enable chemists to make very rapid titrations and pH determinations. These instruments also give much higher precision than is possible with color-comparison methods.

Indicator	Acid color	Transition color	Base color

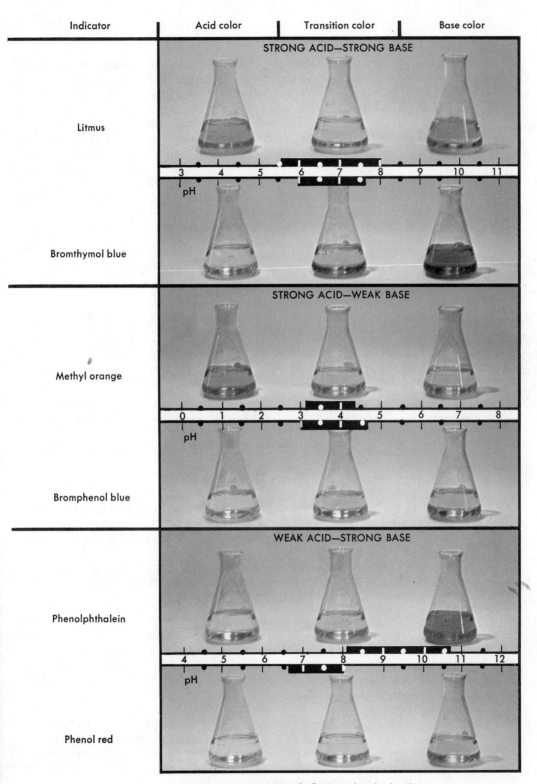

Fig. 15-8 Indicator colors in titration.

A laboratory *pH meter* provides the most convenient method of measuring the pH of a solution. The pH meter measures the voltage difference between a special electrode and a reference (standard) electrode placed in the solution. The special electrode is usually a thin-walled glass electrode. The voltage changes as the H_3O^+ ion concentration of the solution changes. In an acid-base titration, a large change in the voltage occurs at the equivalence point. This change is related to the sharp color change of an indicator near the equivalence point. When properly used, the pH meter provides more accurate pH readings than can be obtained by using color indicators.

QUESTIONS

Group A

1. Distinguish between solution concentrations expressed in terms of molality and molarity.
2. (*a*) What determines the mass of 1 equivalent of an acid? (*b*) of a base?
3. How many grams are in 1 equivalent of each of the following? (*a*) $Ca(NO_3)_2$ (*b*) Zn (*c*) HCO_3^- (*d*) KCl (*e*) Li (*f*) H_3O^+ (*g*) SiO_2 (*h*) OH^- (*i*) $HC_2H_3O_2$ (*j*) $Al_2(SO_4)_3$.
4. Determine the number of equivalents per mole of each of the following: (*a*) H_2O (*b*) $HClO_4$ (*c*) $Sr(NO_3)_2$ (*d*) $AuCl_3$ (*e*) $Mg(OH)_2$ (*f*) HF (*g*) $NaC_2H_3O_2$ (*h*) K_2SO_4 (*i*) HPO_4^{--} (*j*) Bi.
5. Write the equations which show the partial and complete ionization of sulfuric acid.
6. What is the conjugate base for the HCO_3^- ion?
7. Explain the meaning of the notation $[NH_4^+]$.
8. (*a*) Explain the meaning of pH. (*b*) What is the usual range of the pH scale?
9. In a certain aqueous solution, the hydronium ion concentration is 1×10^{-3} mole per liter. (*a*) What is the pH of the solution? (*b*) What is the hydroxide ion concentration?
10. (*a*) Explain why neither bromphenol blue nor methyl orange is a suitable indicator for the titration of 0.02-*N* acetic acid with sodium hydroxide. (*b*) Name two indicators that are suitable for this titration.

Group B

11. Hydrogen chloride, HCl, has 1 equivalent of hydrogen per mole and hydrogen carbonate, H_2CO_3, has 2 equivalents of hydrogen per mole. Yet hydrochloric acid is described as a *strong* acid and carbonic acid as a *weak* acid. Explain.
12. (*a*) How would you test the soil in your lawn or garden to find out whether it is acidic or basic? (*b*) If you find it to be acidic, what can be added to it to remedy the condition?
13. Test your saliva with litmus paper. (*a*) Is the saliva acidic or alkaline? (*b*) Do you think that a tooth paste is likely to be acidic or basic? Test some of them.
14. In a neutralization reaction between hydrochloric acid and potassium hydroxide, the K^+ ion and the Cl^- ion are called *spectator ions*. (*a*) Explain. (*b*) How could the potassium chloride be recovered?

15. What indicator would you use to show the end-point of the neutralization reaction described in Question 14? Justify your selection.
16. How many moles of sodium hydroxide are needed for the complete neutralization of: (*a*) 1 mole of hydrochloric acid? (*b*) 1 mole of sulfuric acid? (*c*) 1 mole of phosphoric acid? (*d*) Write the equation for each reaction.
17. (*a*) What mass of calcium hydroxide is required to prepare 1.0 liter of 0.010-*N* solution? (*b*) to prepare 1.0 liter of 0.010-*M* solution?
18. (*a*) What volume of water contains a mole of H_3O^+ ions? (*b*) How many equivalents of hydronium ions is this? (*c*) How many grams of H_3O^+ ion? (*d*) What is the mole-concentration of OH^- ion in this volume of water? (*e*) How many equivalents of hydroxide ions is this? (*f*) How many grams of OH^- ion?
19. What is the normality of (*a*) a 0.0040-*M* solution of phosphoric acid? (*b*) a 0.15-*M* solution of potassium hydroxide? (*c*) a 2-*M* solution of sulfuric acid?
20. What is the molarity of (*a*) a 0.006-*N* solution of phosphoric acid? (*b*) a 0.0036-*N* solution of aluminum sulfate? (*c*) a 0.030-*N* solution of barium hydroxide?

PROBLEMS

Group A

1. (*a*) How many grams of sodium hydroxide are required to neutralize 54.75 g of hydrogen chloride in water solution? (*b*) How many moles of each reactant are involved in the reaction?
2. What quantity of potassium nitrate would you add to $50\overline{0}$ g of water to prepare a 0.250-*M* solution?
3. How many grams of sugar, $C_{12}H_{22}O_{11}$, are contained in 50.0 ml of an 0.800-*M* solution?
4. What is the molarity of a solution containing 49.0 g of H_2SO_4 in 3.00 liters of solution?
5. What is the molarity of a $CuBr_2$ solution which contains 446 g of solute in 5.00 liters of solution?
6. How many grams of NaCl are required to make $25\overline{0}$ ml of 0.500-*M* solution?
7. How many grams of $Al_2(SO_4)_3 \cdot 18\ H_2O$ are required to make $80\overline{0}$ ml of 0.300-*M* solution?
8. Calculate the mass of one equivalent of (*a*) K; (*b*) Ca; (*c*) NaCl; (*d*) $CuSO_4$; (*e*) $Na_2CO_2 \cdot 10H_2O$; (*f*) $FeCl_3 \cdot 6H_2O$.
9. What is the normality of a solution which contains 4.0 g of Na_2SO_4 per liter of solution?
10. Calculate the normality of a solution containing $71\overline{0}$ g of $Al(NO_3)_3$ in 15.0 liters of solution?
11. How many grams of $CuSO_4 \cdot 5H_2O$ are needed to make up $50\overline{0}$ ml of 0.100-*N* solution?
12. How many grams of $FeCl_3 \cdot 6H_2O$ are needed to prepare $20\overline{0}$ ml of 0.500-*N* solution?
13. (*a*) What is the pH of a 0.01-*M* solution of HCl, assuming complete ionization? (*b*) What is the $[OH^-]$ of a 0.01-*M* solution of sodium hydroxide? (*c*) What is the pH of this solution?

14. How many milliliters of a 0.150-N solution of a metallic hydroxide are required to neutralize 30.0 ml of a 0.500-N solution of an acid?

15. A chemistry student finds that it takes 34 ml of a 0.50-N acid solution to neutralize $10\overline{}$ ml of a sample of household ammonia. What is the normality of the ammonia-water solution?

Group B

16. How many solute molecules are contained in each milliliter of a 0.1-M solution of a nonelectrolyte?

17. An excess of zinc reacts with $400\overline{}$ ml of hydrochloric acid, and 2.55 liters of H_2 gas is collected over water at $20°$ C and 745.0 mm. What is the molarity of the acid?

18. Concentrated hydrochloric acid has a density of 1.19 g/ml and contains 37.2% HCl by weight. How many milliliters of concentrated hydrochloric acid are required to prepare (a) 1.00 liter of 1.00-M HCl solution; (b) 2.00 liters of 3.00-M HCl solution; (c) 5.00 liters of 0.100-N HCl solution; (d) $250\overline{}$ ml of 0.200-N HCl solution?

19. The stockroom supply of concentrated sulfuric acid is 95.0% H_2SO_4 by weight and has a density of 1.84 g/ml. How many milliliters of concentrated sulfuric acid are needed to prepare (a) 2.50 liters of 0.500-M H_2SO_4 solution; (b) $100\overline{}$ ml of 0.250-M H_2SO_4 solution; (c) 1.00 liter of 1.00-N H_2SO_4 solution; (d) 3.00 liters of 0.200-N H_2SO_4 solution?

20. In a laboratory titration, 15.0 ml of 0.275-M H_2SO_4 solution neutralizes 20.0 ml of NaOH solution. What is the molarity of the NaOH solution?

21. Suppose a 10.0 ml sample of vinegar is diluted to $100\overline{}$ ml with distilled water and titrated against 0.100-M sodium hydroxide solution. From the burets, 30.0 ml of the diluted vinegar and 25.0 ml of the solution of the base were withdrawn. What percentage of acetic acid, $HC_2H_3O_2$, does the vinegar contain?

22. A solution is determined experimentally to have a pH of 2.9. (a) Find the $[H_3O^+]$. (b) What is the $[OH^-]$?

23. Find the pH of a 0.02-M LiOH solution.

24. What is the pH of a 0.054-M solution of HCl?

25. Suppose 25.0 ml of 0.150-M NaOH and 50.0 ml of 0.100-M HCl solutions are mixed. What is the pH of the resulting solution?

Chapter **16**

Carbon and Its Oxides

CARBON

16.1 Abundance and importance

Carbon has been known from earliest times in the forms of charcoal and soot. In abundance, carbon ranks seventeenth by weight among the elements in the earth's crust. In importance, it ranks far higher. It is present in the tissues of our bodies and in the foods we eat. It is found in coal, petroleum, natural gas, limestone, and in all living things. In addition, chemists have synthesized hundreds of thousands of carbon compounds in the laboratory. The study of carbon compounds is so important that it forms a separate branch of chemistry called *organic chemistry.* Originally, organic chemistry was defined as the study of materials derived from living organisms. Inorganic chemistry was the study of materials derived from mineral sources. We have known for over a century that this is not a clear distinction. Many substances identical to those produced in living things can also be made from mineral materials. As a result, *organic chemistry today includes the study of carbon compounds whether or not these compounds are produced by living organisms.*

In most substances containing carbon, the carbon is present in the *combined* form. It is usually united with hydrogen, or with hydrogen and oxygen. In this chapter, we shall first describe carbon in its *free* or *uncombined* forms. Then we shall consider carbon dioxide and carbon monoxide.

311

16.2 Characteristics of carbon atoms

Carbon is the element with atomic number 6 and electron configuration $1s^2 2s^2 2p^2$. On the periodic table, it is in the second period, midway between the active metal lithium and the active nonmetal fluorine. The two $1s$ electrons are tightly bound to the nucleus. The two $2s$ electrons and the two $2p$ electrons are the valence electrons. Carbon atoms show a very strong tendency to share electrons and form covalent bonds. This electron sharing usually has the effect of producing a stable outer-shell octet about a carbon atom. Having four valence electrons makes it possible for a carbon atom to form four covalent bonds. In sp^3 hybridization, these bonds are directed in space toward the four vertices of a regular tetrahedron. The nucleus of the atom is at the center of the tetrahedron. See Figure 16-1.

The property of forming covalent bonds is so strong in carbon atoms that they join readily with other elements. They also link together with other carbon atoms in chains, rings, plates, and networks. The variety of ways in which carbon atoms can be linked explains why there are several times as many carbon compounds as noncarbon compounds.

16.3 Allotropic forms of carbon

Carbon and some other nonmetallic elements such as oxygen, sulfur, and phosphorus, exhibit *allotropy*. **Allotropy** *is the existence of an element in two or more forms in the same physical phase.* Allotropy occurs for either of two reasons:

1. An element has two or more kinds of molecules, each with different numbers of atoms.

2. An element has two or more different arrangements of atoms or molecules in a crystal.

Carbon occurs in two solid allotropic forms. *Diamond* is a hard crystalline form. *Graphite* is a soft, grayish-black crystalline form.

When substances which contain combined carbon are decomposed by heat, they leave black residues. These residues are sometimes collectively called *amorphous carbon* because they seem to have no definite crystalline shape. Examples of amorphous carbon are *coke, charcoal, boneblack,* and *carbon black.* Studies of the structures of these substances have been made by X-ray scattering. These studies reveal that the various forms of so-called amorphous carbon actually contain regions in which the carbon atoms are arranged in an orderly way. In carbon black, for example, the carbon atoms are arranged somewhat as they are in a layer of graphite.

16.4 Diamond

The most famous diamond mines in the world are located in South Africa. Diamonds in this region usually occur in the

Hybridization was explained in Section 6.12.

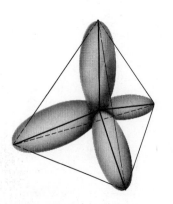

Fig. 16-1. In sp^3 hybridization the four covalent bonds of a carbon atom are directed in space toward the four vertices of a regular tetrahedron. The nucleus of the atom is at the center of the tetrahedron.

shafts of extinct volcanoes. It is believed that they were formed slowly under extreme heat and pressure. Diamonds, as they are mined, do not have the shape or sparkle of gem stones. The art of cutting and polishing gives them their brilliant appearance.

Synthetic diamonds are chemically identical to natural diamonds but are produced in the laboratory. They are prepared by subjecting a carbon-containing compound and a metal catalyst to extremely high pressure and temperature for nearly a day. A catalyst is a substance that increases the rate of a chemical reaction without itself being permanently changed.

Diamond is one of the hardest materials. It is the densest form of carbon, about 3.5 times as dense as water. Both the hardness (resistance to wear) and density are explained by its structure. Figure 16-2 shows that carbon atoms in diamond are covalently bonded in a strong, compact fashion. The distances between the carbon nuclei are 1.54 Å. Note that each carbon atom is tetrahedrally oriented to its four nearest neighbors. This type of structure is strong in all three dimensions.

The rigidity of its structure gives diamond its hardness. The compactness, resulting from the small distances between nuclei, gives diamond its high density. The covalent network structure of diamond accounts for its extremely high melting point, above 3500°C. Since all the valence electrons are used in forming covalent bonds, none is free to migrate. This explains why diamond is a nonconductor of electricity. Besides its use as a gem, diamond is used for cutting, drilling, and grinding because of its extreme hardness. A diamond is used as a long-lasting phonograph needle.

Diamond is insoluble in ordinary solvents. The French chemist Antoine Laurent Lavoisier (1743–1794) burned a clear diamond in pure oxygen and obtained carbon dioxide as a product. This experiment proved to him that diamond contains carbon. The English chemist Sir Humphry Davy (1778–1829) and other scientists repeated the experiment. They found that the mass of carbon dioxide produced was the same as that which would be produced if diamond were pure carbon.

Fig. 16-2. The crystal structure of diamond.

Fig. 16-3. Antoine Laurent Lavoisier was a noted French chemist. His experiments on the nature of burning led him to discover the part that the oxygen of the air plays in that process.

16.5 Graphite

Natural graphite deposits are found throughout the world. The major producers are the Republic of Korea, Austria, North Korea, and the Soviet Union.

More than 70% of the graphite used in the United States is synthetic graphite. Most of this synthetic graphite is produced from petroleum coke. The process involves heating petroleum coke to about 2800°C in special furnaces.

Graphite is nearly as remarkable for its softness as diamond is for its hardness. It is easily crumbled and has a greasy feel. Graphite crystals are hexagonal (six-sided) in cross-section, with

The Bettmann Archive, Inc.

a density of about 2.25 g/cm³. Although graphite is a nonmetal, it is a fairly good conductor of electricity.

The structure of graphite readily explains these properties. The carbon atoms in graphite are arranged in layers of thin hexagonal plates (Figure 16-3). The distance between the centers of adjacent carbon atoms within a layer is 1.42 Å. This distance is less than the distance between adjacent carbon atoms in diamond. However, the distance between the centers of atoms in adjacent layers is 3.35 Å. Each carbon atom in a layer is bonded to only three other carbon atoms in that layer.

Figure 16-4 shows the bonding within a layer of graphite. This bonding consists of single and double covalent bonds between carbon atoms. When represented in this fashion, three *different* equivalent patterns appear. In each of these, some carbon-carbon bonds are single and others are double. There is, however, no experimental evidence that the bonds in a layer of graphite are of these two distinct types. On the contrary, the evidence indicates that the bonds are all the same. The layers of graphite have a resonance structure in which the carbon-carbon bonds are intermediate in character between single and double bonds.

Each layer in graphite is a strongly-bonded covalent network structure. As with diamond, this structure gives graphite a very high melting point, about 3500° C. The layers of carbon atoms in graphite, however, are too far apart for the formation of covalent bonds between them. They are held together by weak dispersion interaction forces. These forces result from electron motion within the layers. The weak attraction between layers accounts for the softness of graphite and its greasy feel as one layer slides over another. On the average, the carbon atoms in graphite are farther apart than they are in diamond, so graphite has a lower density. The mobile electrons in each carbon-atom layer make graphite a fairly good conductor of electricity.

Like diamond, graphite does not dissolve in any ordinary solvent. Similarly, it forms carbon dioxide when burned in oxygen.

16.6   Uses of graphite

The largest single use of natural graphite is for coating the molds used in metal casting. It is also used to increase the carbon content of steel and make clay-graphite crucibles in which steel and other metals are melted. All of these applications take advantage of the very high melting point of graphite. Graphite is a very good lubricant. It is sometimes mixed with petroleum jelly to form a graphite grease. It can be used for lubricating machine parts that operate at temperatures too high for the usual petroleum lubricants. Graphite leaves a gray streak or mark when it is drawn across a sheet of paper. In making "lead" pencils, graphite is powdered, mixed with clay, and then formed

Resonance was explained in Section 6.11.

Fig. 16-4. The crystal structure of graphite. The distance between the layers has been exaggerated in order to show the structure of each layer more clearly.

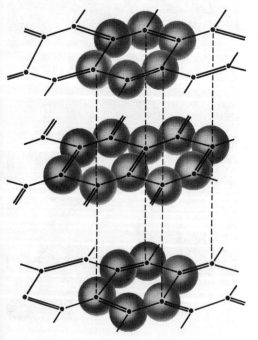

into sticks. The hardness of a pencil depends upon the relative amount of clay that is used.

The most important use of synthetic graphite is in electrodes for electric-arc steelmaking furnaces. Synthetic graphite electrodes are also used in the electrolysis of salt water for making chlorine and sodium hydroxide. Graphite does not react with acids, bases, and organic and inorganic solvents. These properties make it useful for equipment for a variety of processes in the food, chemical, and petroleum industries. Graphite is also used in nuclear reactors.

16.7 Destructive distillation

Suppose a complex material containing compounds of carbon such as wood or bituminous coal is *heated in a closed container without access to air or oxygen. The complex material decomposes into simpler substances.* This process is known as *destructive distillation.* Coke, charcoal, and boneblack are prepared by destructive distillation of coal, wood, and bones, respectively.

16.8 Coke

When bituminous coal is heated in a hard-glass test tube, a gas escapes that is flammable. It burns readily if mixed with air and ignited. Also, a tar-like liquid condenses on the upper walls of the tube. If the heating is continued until all the volatile material is driven off, coke is left as a residue.

Commercially, coke is prepared by destructive distillation of bituminous coal in by-product coke ovens. The volatile (easily vaporized) products are separated into *coal gas, ammonia,* and *coal tar.* Coal gas can be used as a fuel. Ammonia is used in making fertilizers. Coal tar can be separated by distillation into many useful materials. These materials are used to make drugs, dyes, and explosives. The black pitch that remains after distillation of coal tar is used to surface roads.

Nearly 70,000,000 tons of coke are produced each year in the United States. Coke is a gray, porous solid that is harder and denser than charcoal. It burns with little flame, has a high heat content, and is a valuable fuel.

Coke is an excellent reducing agent. It is widely used in obtaining the metals from the ores of iron, tin, copper, and zinc. These ores are either oxides or are converted into oxides. Coke readily reduces the metals in these oxides. It also has unusually high structural strength and is free from volatile impurities.

16.9 Charcoal

Destructive distillation of wood yields several gases that can be burned. It also produces methanol (wood alcohol), acetic

Fig. 16-5. Coke is produced by the destructive distillation of bituminous coal in by-product coke ovens. Here the red-hot coke is being discharged from an oven into a waiting railroad car.

Bethlehem Steel Corporation

acid, and other volatile products. The solid part, or *residue,* that remains is charcoal. Charcoal is prepared commercially by heating wood in *retorts.* These are closed containers in which substances are distilled or decomposed by heat. The burnable gases that result provide supplementary fuel. The other volatile products may be condensed and sold as by-products.

Charcoal is a porous, black, brittle solid. It is odorless and tasteless. It is denser than water, but it often adsorbs enough gas to make it float on water. This ability to *adsorb* a large quantity of gas is the most remarkable physical property of charcoal. **Adsorption** *is the concentration of a gas, liquid, or solid on the surface of a liquid or solid with which it is in contact.* One cubic centimeter of freshly prepared willow charcoal adsorbs about 90 cubic centimeters of ammonia gas.

At ordinary temperatures, charcoal is inactive and insoluble in all ordinary solvents. It is a good reducing agent because it unites with oxygen at a high temperature. Charcoal is also a good fuel, but it is more expensive than other common fuels.

16.10 Boneblack

Animal charcoal, or *boneblack,* is produced by the destructive distillation of bones. The by-products of the process include bone oil and pyridine. These products are used for *denaturing* alcohol (making it unfit for humans to drink). Boneblack usually contains calcium phosphate as an impurity. This can be removed by treating the boneblack with an acid.

16.11 Activated carbon

Activated carbon is a form of carbon which is prepared in a way which gives it a very large internal surface area. This large surface area makes activated carbon useful for the adsorption of liquid or gaseous substances. Activated carbon can be made from a variety of carbon-containing materials. Such a material is first destructively distilled. The carbon produced is treated with steam or carbon dioxide at about 100° C. These two processes produce a very porous form of carbon. This porosity creates a very large internal surface area. The surface area of a portion of activated carbon may be as high as 2000 m²/g, most of the area being internal.

Activated carbon used for adsorption of gases must have a small pore structure. Coconut and other nut shells are the best sources of this type of activated carbon. Gas-adsorbent activated carbon is used in gas masks. It is also used for the recovery of volatile solvent vapors and the removal of impurities from gases in industrial processes. It is also used to remove odors from the air circulated by large air conditioning systems in offices, restaurants, and theaters.

Activated carbon used for adsorption from the liquid phase comes from both animal and vegetable sources. Boneblack was first used for this purpose, but now such activated carbon is also made from coal, peat, and wood. Inorganic impurities are removed from activated carbon which is to be used in processing food or chemical products. Acids such as dilute hydrochloric or sulfuric react with these impurities forming soluble products that are washed away with water. Liquid-adsorbent activated carbon is used in the refining of cane sugar, beet sugar, and corn syrup. It is also used in municipal and industrial water treatment to adsorb impurities which would give the water an objectionable odor and taste.

16.12   Other forms of amorphous carbon

Finely divided particles of carbon are set free when liquid or gaseous fuels composed of carbon and hydrogen are burned in an insufficient supply of air. We commonly call these particles *soot*. Soot is an example of the form of amorphous carbon called *carbon black*. Commercially, the production of carbon black involves making soot under carefully controlled conditions.

The most important method of making carbon black is called the *furnace process*. The furnace is made of materials which have high melting points, such as fire brick. In making carbon black, three materials are introduced into the furnace:

1.   A spray of liquid fuel or the gaseous fuel vapor.

2.   An additional fuel, such as natural gas. *Petroleum-refinery* gas, the fuel gas produced when petroleum is refined, may also be used. So may coal gas, the fuel gas produced by destructive distillation of bituminous coal in by-product ovens.

3.   Air, as a source of oxygen.

The supply of oxygen is so low that the fuels are only partially burned in the furnace. But enough fuel burns to provide the energy needed for decomposing the rest of the fuel. The carbon black is collected from the combustion products.

Over 95% of all carbon black produced is used in natural and synthetic rubber. It adds bulk to the rubber and acts as a reinforcing agent. Most of this rubber is used in tires. Carbon black helps to preserve the rubber and makes the tire wear longer. The second largest use of carbon black is in printer's ink. Other uses are in paints, phonograph records, carbon paper, and in coloring plastics and synthetic fibers.

An oil residue remains after the refining of crude petroleum. When destructively distilled, this residue produces a form of amorphous carbon called *petroleum coke*. Rods of petroleum coke are converted to synthetic graphite for use as electrodes. Such electrodes are used as the positive electrodes in dry cells. They also are used in the production of aluminum by electrolysis.

National Oceanic and Atmospheric Administration

Fig. 16-6. The concentration of carbon dioxide in the air is increasing at the rate of about 0.25% each year. Predictions of the future climate of the earth require global measurements of the components of the atmosphere. The Mauna Loa Observatory shown in the photograph is the main station in the world-wide system being set up to make atmospheric measurements. It is located at an altitude of 11,200 feet above sea level on the island of Hawaii, where it is unaffected by pollution sources. Other stations are planned for Alaska, the southwest Pacific Ocean, and the South Pole.

CARBON DIOXIDE

16.13 Occurrence

Carbon dioxide comprises only about 0.03% of the atmosphere by volume. But it is a very important component of the air. The water of rivers, lakes, and oceans contains about sixty times as much dissolved carbon dioxide as the atmosphere. The decay of organic matter and the burning of fossil fuels both produce carbon dioxide. So do the respiration processes of living things. Carbon dioxide is somewhat denser than air. So it sometimes gathers in relatively high amounts in low-lying areas such as bogs, swamps, and marshes. It may also collect in mines, caves, and caverns. Some natural gases contain significant amounts of carbon dioxide.

16.14 Preparation of carbon dioxide

1. By burning material that contains the element carbon. Carbon dioxide is one of the products of the complete combustion in oxygen or air of any material which contains carbon. If air is used, the carbon dioxide prepared in this way is mixed with other gases. But if these gases do not interfere with the intended use of the carbon dioxide, this method is by far the cheapest and easiest.

$$\text{C (combined)} + O_2 \rightarrow CO_2$$

2. *By reaction of steam and natural gas.* Natural gas is usually a mixture of several gaseous compounds of carbon and hydrogen. The principal component of natural gas is methane, CH_4. Methane undergoes a series of reactions with steam in the presence of metallic oxide catalysts at temperatures between 500° C and 1000° C. The end products of these reactions are carbon dioxide and hydrogen. The equation for the over-all reaction is

$$CH_4 + 2H_2O \rightarrow 4H_2 + CO_2$$

The primary purpose of this reaction is the preparation of hydrogen for making synthetic ammonia. The carbon dioxide is a by-product. The carbon dioxide is separated from the hydrogen by dissolving the carbon dioxide in cold water under high pressure.

3. *By fermentation of molasses.* The enzymes of *zymase* are produced by yeast. They catalyze the fermentation of the sugar, $C_6H_{12}O_6$, in molasses. This fermentation produces ethanol (ethyl alcohol) and carbon dioxide. While the process is complex, the over-all reaction is

$$C_6H_{12}O_6(aq) \rightarrow 2C_2H_5OH(aq) + 2CO_2(g)$$

This equation represents a method by which some industrial alcohol is produced. The process is also an important source of carbon dioxide.

Fig. 16-7. The laboratory preparation of carbon dioxide.

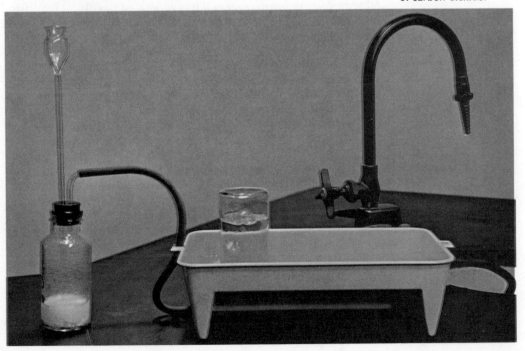

4. *By heating a carbonate.* When calcium carbonate (as lime-stone, marble, or shells) is heated strongly, calcium oxide and carbon dioxide are the products.

$$CaCO_3 \rightarrow CaO + CO_2$$

Calcium oxide, known as *quicklime,* is used for making plaster and mortar. The carbon dioxide is a by-product. It is piped from the kiln (oven) in which the carbonate is heated. It may be compressed and then stored in steel containers.

5. *By the action of an acid on a carbonate.* This is the usual laboratory method for preparing carbon dioxide. The gas-generating bottle in Figure 16-7 contains a few pieces of marble, $CaCO_3$. If dilute hydrochloric acid is poured through the funnel tube, carbon dioxide is given off rapidly. Calcium chloride may be recovered from the solution in the bottle.

This reaction proceeds in two stages. *First,* the marble and hydrochloric acid undergo an exchange reaction:

$$CaCO_3(s) + 2HCl(aq) \rightarrow CaCl_2(aq) + H_2CO_3(aq)$$

Second, carbonic acid is unstable and decomposes:

$$H_2CO_3(aq) \rightarrow H_2O(l) + CO_2(g)$$

The equation which summarizes these two reactions is

$$CaCO_3(s) + 2HCl(aq) \rightarrow CaCl_2(aq) + H_2O(l) + CO_2(g)$$

Even though carbon dioxide is soluble in water, it may be collected by water displacement if it is generated rapidly. It may also be collected by displacement of air. In this case, the receiver must be kept *mouth upward* because carbon dioxide is denser than air.

This reaction is an example of the general reaction of an acid and carbonate. Almost any acid may be used, even a weak one such as the acetic acid in vinegar. Almost any carbonate may also be used, provided its cation does not have an interfering reaction with the anion of the acid. The ionic equation for the reaction is

$$CO_3^{--} + 2H_3O^+ \rightarrow 3H_2O + CO_2(g)$$

6. *By respiration and decay.* This process is a natural method of preparing carbon dioxide. The foods we eat contain compounds of carbon. Oxygen from the air we inhale is used in oxidizing this food. This oxidation supplies us with energy to maintain body temperature, move muscles, synthesize new compounds in the body, and transmit nerve impulses. Carbon dioxide, which we exhale into the air, is one of the products of this oxidation. All living things give off carbon dioxide during respiration.

When plants and animals die, decay begins and carbon dioxide is produced. This gas eventually finds its way into the surrounding air, or becomes dissolved in surface or underground streams.

16.15   Structure of carbon dioxide molecules

Carbon dioxide molecules are linear, with the two oxygen atoms bonded on opposite sides of the carbon atom. See Figure 16-8. The carbon-oxygen bonds in the molecule are somewhat polar. This polarity is explained by the electronegativity difference between carbon and oxygen. However, the arrangement of these bonds, exactly opposite one another, causes the molecule to be nonpolar.

Considering the electron-dot symbols for carbon and oxygen, we might assign carbon dioxide molecules the electron-dot formula

$$:\!\overset{..}{O}::C::\overset{..}{O}\!:$$

However, this formula is not strictly accurate. The carbon-oxygen bond distance predicted by it is larger than that actually found in carbon dioxide molecules. Carbon dioxide molecules are believed to be *resonance hybrids of four electron structures.* Each of these structures contributes about equally to the actual structure.

$$\left\{ \begin{array}{ll} :\!\overset{..}{O}::C::\overset{..}{O}\!: & -:\!\overset{..}{\underset{..}{O}}:C:::O\!:^{+} \\[2ex] :\!\overset{..}{\underset{..}{O}}::C::\underset{..}{O}\!: & ^{+}:\!O:::C:\overset{..}{\underset{..}{O}}\!:^{-} \end{array} \right\}$$

Such a resonance hybrid has the carbon-oxygen bond distance and energy actually observed for carbon dioxide molecules.

16.16   Physical properties of carbon dioxide

Carbon dioxide is a gas at room temperature. This fact supports our theory that it has a simple nonpolar molecular structure. Carbon dioxide is colorless with a faintly irritating odor and a slightly sour taste. The molecular weight of carbon dioxide is 44. Thus, its density is about 1.5 times that of air at the same temperature and pressure. The large, heavy molecules of carbon dioxide gas move more slowly than the smaller, lighter molecules of gaseous oxygen or hydrogen. Because of its high density and slow rate of diffusion, carbon dioxide can be poured from one vessel to another.

At room temperature, a pressure of about 70 atmospheres pushes carbon dioxide molecules very close together. They then attract each other strongly enough to condense to a liquid. If this liquid is permitted to evaporate rapidly under atmospheric pressure, part of it changes into a gas. This process absorbs heat from the remaining liquid, which is thus cooled until it solidifies in the form called *Dry Ice.*

Solid carbon dioxide has a high vapor pressure. Many molecules of solid carbon dioxide possess enough energy to escape from the surface of the solid into the air. The vapor pressure of

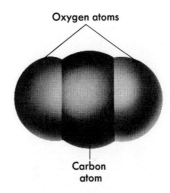

Oxygen atoms

Carbon atom

Fig. 16-8. A carbon dioxide molecule is linear and consists of one carbon atom and two oxygen atoms.

Carbon dioxide has a critical temperature of 31.1° C and a critical pressure of 73.0 atm. (Section 11.7) The liquid carbon dioxide in a fire extinguisher is under a pressure of 60 atm.

solid carbon dioxide equals atmospheric pressure at $-78.5°$ C. As a result, solid carbon dioxide under atmospheric pressure sublimes (changes directly from a solid to a gas) at this temperature. Liquid carbon dioxide does not exist at atmospheric pressure. It can exist only at low temperatures with pressures higher than 5 atmospheres.

16.17 Chemical properties of carbon dioxide

Carbon dioxide is a stable gas. It neither burns nor supports combustion. However, burning magnesium is hot enough to decompose carbon dioxide. A piece of burning magnesium ribbon continues to burn in a bottle of the gas. The magnesium unites vigorously with the oxygen set free by the decomposition. Carbon is produced, as shown by a coating of soot on the inside of the bottle.

$$2Mg(s) + CO_2(g) \rightarrow 2MgO(s) + C(s)$$

Carbon dioxide dissolves readily in cold water. A few of the dissolved molecules also unite with the water and form carbonic acid. Carbon dioxide is therefore the acid anhydride of carbonic acid.

An acid anhydride is the compound formed by removal of water from an acid.

$$H_2O + CO_2 \rightleftarrows H_2CO_3$$

Almost all of the H_2CO_3 molecules ionize. Carbonic acid exists in water solution principally as ions.

$$H_2O + H_2CO_3 \rightleftarrows H_3O^+ + HCO_3^-$$

$$H_2O + HCO_3^- \rightleftarrows H_3O^+ + CO_3^{--}$$

Carbonic acid is a weak acid because of the slight reaction between CO_2 and H_2O, even though the few H_2CO_3 molecules formed ionize extensively. Carbonic acid is easily decomposed by heat since CO_2 is less soluble at higher temperatures. The reduction of the concentration of CO_2 in the water causes all the equilibria to shift to the left. This shift further decreases the H_2CO_3 and H_3O^+ concentrations.

When carbon dioxide is passed into a water solution of a hydroxide, it reacts and forms a carbonate.

$$CO_2 + 2OH^- \rightarrow CO_3^{--} + H_2O$$

If the positive ion of the hydroxide forms an insoluble carbonate, it is precipitated when carbon dioxide passes through the hydroxide solution.

A *test for carbon dioxide* is to bubble the gas through a saturated solution of $Ca(OH)_2$, called limewater. A precipitate of white calcium carbonate indicates the presence of carbon dioxide.

$$Ca^{++} + 2OH^- + CO_2 \rightarrow Ca^{++}CO_3^{--}(s) + H_2O$$

If excess carbon dioxide gas is bubbled through the solution, the precipitate disappears. It does so because the excess carbon dioxide reacts with the precipitate and water and forms soluble calcium hydrogen carbonate.

$$Ca^{++}CO_3^{--} + H_2O + CO_2 \rightarrow Ca^{++} + 2HCO_3^-$$

As stated earlier (Section 16.13), normal air contains about 0.03% carbon dioxide by volume. The air in a crowded, poorly ventilated room may contain as much as 1% carbon dioxide by volume. A concentration of from about 0.1% to 1% brings on a feeling of drowsiness and a headache. Concentrations of 8% to 10% or more cause death from lack of oxygen.

16.18   Uses of carbon dioxide

1. It is necessary for photosynthesis. **Photosynthesis** *means "putting together by means of light."* It is a complex process by which green plants manufacture carbohydrates with the aid of sunlight. *Chlorophyll,* the green coloring matter of plants, acts as a catalyst. Carbon dioxide from the air and water from the soil are the raw materials. Glucose, a simple sugar, $C_6H_{12}O_6$, is one of the products. The following simplified equation gives only the *reactants* and the *final products.*

$$6CO_2 + 12H_2O \rightarrow C_6H_{12}O_6 + 6O_2 + 6H_2O$$

The sugar may then be converted into a great variety of other plant products. The oxygen is given off to the atmosphere. Photosynthesis and the various other natural and artificial methods of producing atmospheric carbon dioxide comprise the *oxygen-carbon dioxide cycle.*

2. Carbon dioxide is used in most fire extinguishers. When the *soda-acid type* of fire extinguisher is inverted, sulfuric acid reacts with sodium hydrogen carbonate solution.

$$2NaHCO_3(aq) + H_2SO_4(aq) \rightarrow Na_2SO_4(aq) + 2H_2O(l) + 2CO_2(g)$$

The pressure of the gas forces a stream of liquid a considerable distance. The carbon dioxide dissolved in the liquid helps put out the fire, but water is the main extinguishing agent.

The *foam type* of fire extinguisher contains a solution of aluminum sulfate, $Al_2(SO_4)_3$. This solution contains hydronium ions because of the reaction of aluminum sulfate with the water in which it is dissolved.

$$2Al^{+++} + 3SO_4^{--} + 4H_2O \rightleftarrows 2Al(OH)^{++} + 2H_3O^+ + 3SO_4^{--}$$

The hydronium ions of the aluminum sulfate solution react with sodium hydrogen carbonate solution and carbon dioxide is given off.

$$Na^+ + HCO_3^- + H_3O^+ \rightarrow Na^+ + 2H_2O + CO_2(g)$$

Walter Kidde and Company, Inc.

Fig. 16-9. A liquid carbon dioxide fire extinguisher is effective in putting out oil fires.

A sticky substance is dissolved in the sodium hydrogen carbonate solution. This substance strengthens the foam bubbles so that the gas does not escape from them. The sprayed foam forms a thick, frothy blanket where it falls. It shuts off the air, smothering the fire. Foam fire extinguishers are particularly effective for putting out oil and gasoline fires.

Liquid carbon dioxide fire extinguishers are widely used and very efficient. When the valve is opened, the nozzle directs a stream of carbon dioxide "snow" against the flame. Such an extinguisher is effective against oil fires. Also, it may be used around electric switchboards where water would be hazardous.

3.   Carbonated beverages contain carbon dioxide in solution. Soft drinks are carbonated by forcing the gas into the beverages under pressure. When the bottles are opened, the excess pressure is released. Bubbles of carbon dioxide then escape rapidly from the liquid.

4.   Leavening agents produce carbon dioxide. Yeast is a common leavening agent. It is mixed with the flour and other ingredients used in making dough for bread. The living yeast plants produce an enzyme which ferments the starches and sugars in the dough. This fermentation reaction produces ethanol and carbon dioxide. The carbon dioxide forms bubbles in the soft dough, causing it to "rise," or decrease in density. The ethanol is vaporized and driven off during the baking process.

Baking powder differs from baking soda, which is the compound sodium hydrogen carbonate. Baking powder is not a compound. Instead, it is a dry mixture of compounds. It contains baking soda, which can yield the carbon dioxide. It also contains some powder that forms an acid when water is added. The acid compound varies with the kind of baking powder used. Cornstarch is used in baking powders to keep them dry until they are used.

5. Carbon dioxide is used as a refrigerant. Dry Ice costs more than ice for refrigeration. But it is superior to ice in two respects. First, it leaves no liquid because it changes directly from a solid to a gas. Also, because of its low temperature, Dry Ice produces a greater cooling effect than an equal weight of ice. The temperature of Dry Ice is so low that it *must never be handled with bare hands,* because serious frostbite may result.

CARBON MONOXIDE

16.19   Carbon monoxide in the air

Carbon monoxide is found in samples of the atmosphere all over the world. The amounts vary from 0.04 ppm over the South Pacific Ocean to 360 ppm at street level in a crowded city on a calm day. (Ppm means parts per million. 1 ppm = 0.0001%.) A safe amount of carbon monoxide is somewhat under 50 ppm.

In congested areas, the carbon monoxide in the air comes mainly from poorly burned fuels. The sources range from the chimney gases of improperly fired coal-burning furnaces to the exhaust gases from automobile engines. In the United States, as much as 90% of the man-caused carbon monoxide in the air may come from gasoline engines. It recently was found that decaying plants and live freshwater algae add significant amounts of carbon monoxide to the air.

Specialists estimate that the carbon monoxide produced on a given day remains in the air for about one to three months. Research is being carried out to determine what happens to carbon monoxide in the air, since no world-wide increase in its concentration has yet been detected. One explanation under study is that certain soil fungi convert carbon monoxide in the air to carbon dioxide. Another possible explanation is that carbon monoxide reacts with OH groups in the lower stratosphere and forms carbon dioxide and hydrogen.

16.20   Preparation of carbon monoxide

1. By reducing carbon dioxide. If carbon dioxide comes into contact with white-hot carbon or coke, it is reduced to carbon monoxide.

$$CO_2(g) + C(s) \rightarrow 2CO(g)$$

2. By action of steam on hot coke. Passing steam over white-hot coke produces a mixture called *water gas*. This mixture

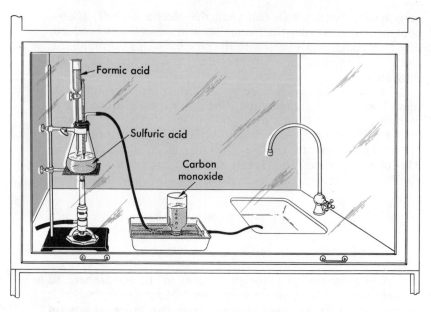

Fig. 16-10. Carbon monoxide can be prepared in the laboratory by decomposing formic acid with hot, concentrated sulfuric acid.

consists mainly of carbon monoxide and hydrogen. This industrial method produces both carbon monoxide and hydrogen for use as fuel gases.

$$C(s) + H_2O(g) \rightarrow CO(g) + H_2(g)$$

The two gases may be separated by cooling and compression. This process liquifies the carbon monoxide but not the hydrogen.

3. By decomposing formic acid. This decomposition reaction is the usual laboratory method for preparing carbon monoxide. Formic acid, HCOOH, is introduced one drop at a time into hot, concentrated sulfuric acid. Carbon monoxide is produced as each drop strikes the hot acid (see Figure 16-10). Concentrated sulfuric acid is an excellent dehydrating agent. It removes a molecule of water from each molecule of the formic acid, leaving only carbon monoxide, CO.

$$HCOOH(l) \xrightarrow{H_2SO_4} H_2O(l) + CO(g)$$

CAUTION: *When using this method, be sure the connections are tight so that the carbon monoxide does not escape.* It is preferable to prepare carbon monoxide in a hood.

16.21 Structure of the carbon monoxide molecule

Fig. 16-11. A carbon monoxide molecule is a slightly polar molecule consisting of one carbon atom and one oxygen atom.

Carbon monoxide molecules consist of one carbon atom and one oxygen atom covalently bonded. See Figure 16-11. The distance between the nuclei is 1.13 Å. The molecule is slightly polar, with *the carbon atom somewhat negative.* In order to account for these properties, the carbon monoxide molecule is believed to be a resonance hybrid of four structures:

$$\left\{ \begin{array}{ll} \textrm{+:C:}\ddot{\textrm{O}}\textrm{:}^- & \textrm{:C::}\ddot{\textrm{O}}\textrm{:} \\ \textrm{:C::}\underset{\cdot\cdot}{\textrm{O}}\textrm{:} & {}^-\textrm{:C:::O:}^+ \end{array} \right\}$$

Unlike carbon dioxide, however, these four structures do not contribute equally. The hybrid is estimated to be 10 percent +:C:$\ddot{\textrm{O}}$:$^-$, 20 percent each :C::$\dot{\textrm{O}}$: and :C::$\underset{\cdot\cdot}{\textrm{O}}$:, and 50 percent $^-$:C:::O:$^+$. The electronegativity difference discussed in Chapter 6 indicates that the oxygen in carbon monoxide would be negative. However, you must remember that those data apply only to *single* bonds between elements. The structure of carbon monoxide is complicated. Carbon monoxide's stability at ordinary temperatures is explained by the effect of the high percentage of triple-bonded structure. It also gives the carbon atom the slight negative charge in the polar molecule.

16.22   Physical properties of carbon monoxide

Carbon monoxide is a colorless, odorless, tasteless gas. It is slightly less dense than air and is only slightly soluble in water. Carbon monoxide has a low critical temperature, $-138.7°$ C, and a high critical pressure, 34.6 atm (atmospheres). These

Mine Safety Appliances Co.

Fig. 16-12. A fireman wearing a self-contained breathing apparatus. This equipment furnishes oxygen from the cylinder worn on the back through a hose to the face mask. With this equipment a fireman can work safely in an atmosphere containing carbon monoxide.

data indicate that the attractive forces between carbon monoxide molecules are low. Consequently, carbon monoxide is not easily liquified. Neither is it readily adsorbed by charcoal. However, charcoal can be treated with certain metallic oxides that oxidize carbon monoxide to carbon dioxide. Gas masks containing treated charcoal protect wearers against carbon monoxide concentrations up to 2%. In atmospheres containing more than 2% carbon monoxide, a self-contained breathing apparatus is needed. This equipment, often used by firemen, furnishes oxygen to the wearer through a mask.

16.23 Chemical properties and uses of carbon monoxide

1. As a reducing agent. Carbon monoxide is used in the production of iron, copper, and other metals from their oxides.

$$Fe_2O_3(s) + 3CO(g) \rightarrow 2Fe(s) + 3CO_2(g)$$

2. As a fuel. Carbon monoxide burns with a blue flame. Many fuel gases contain carbon monoxide mixed with other gases that can be burned. Coal gas and water gas always contain some carbon monoxide.

3. For synthesizing organic compounds. Methanol, CH_3OH, is made from carbon monoxide and hydrogen under pressure. A mixture of oxides of copper, zinc, and chromium is used as a catalyst.

$$CO + 2H_2 \rightarrow CH_3OH$$

Carbon monoxide is also used in the synthesis of many other organic compounds.

16.24 The action of carbon monoxide on the human body

Carbon monoxide is poisonous because it unites very readily with *hemoglobin*. Hemoglobin is the substance in red blood cells that serves as an oxygen carrier in the human body. The attraction of hemoglobin for carbon monoxide is about 300 times greater than for oxygen. If carbon monoxide unites with hemoglobin, the hemoglobin is not available for carrying oxygen. When a person breathes a large enough amount of carbon monoxide, he collapses because of oxygen starvation.

As stated earlier, Section 16.19, the safe level of carbon monoxide in the air is less than 50 ppm (parts per million). A person breathing air with as little as one part of carbon monoxide per thousand parts of air (1000 ppm) experiences nausea and headache in less than one hour. One part of carbon monoxide in one hundred parts of air (10,000 ppm) may kill people in ten minutes.

To repeat: Carbon monoxide is colorless, odorless, tasteless, and induces drowsiness before actual collapse and death. Therefore, *extreme care must be taken to see that it does not con-taminate the air in closed areas.* If a coal-burning furnace is not properly operated, carbon monoxide may escape and mix with the air in living or sleeping rooms. An unvented gas heater, one without a chimney to the outside, is also a potential source of carbon monoxide in a home. Carbon monoxide is a component of some fuel gases. Leaking gas lines are dangerous because of the poisonous nature of the gas as well as the fire hazard. Carbon monoxide is present in the exhaust of internal combustion engines. Therefore, the engine of an automobile should never be left running in a closed garage. Similarly, an automobile should not be kept running to provide heat in a car parked with the windows closed. The smoke from burning tobacco also contains measurable quantities of carbon monoxide.

QUESTIONS

1. (*a*) Why is the study of carbon compounds a separate branch of chemistry? **Group A**
   (*b*) What is this branch of chemistry called?
2. What is the orientation of the four covalent bonds of a carbon atom in *sp*³ hybridization?
3. What property of carbon atoms makes possible the large number of carbon compounds?
4. (*a*) What is *allotropy?* (*b*) What are the allotropic forms of carbon? (*c*) Why is amorphous carbon not considered to be a third allotropic form of carbon?
5. Why are diamonds useful in industry?
6. Using valence-bond structures for graphite layers, show how the structure of graphite illustrates resonance.
7. Give several reasons why graphite is used as a lubricant.
8. (*a*) What is *destructive distillation?* (*b*) Is it really destructive? Explain.
9. Why does a form of carbon such as charcoal or coke remain after the destructive distillation of bituminous coal or wood?
10. What is *adsorption?*
11. Why is boneblack a relatively impure form of carbon?
12. What physical characteristic of activated carbon makes it a useful adsorbent?
13. What are the two successive steps in the preparation of activated carbon?
14. What is the most important use of carbon black?
15. What use is made of petroleum coke?
16. Why is carbon dioxide an important component of the atmosphere even though it occurs to only 0.03% by volume?
17. (*a*) Name the four commercial methods for preparing carbon dioxide. (*b*) What is the usual laboratory method? (*c*) Write balanced chemical equations for these methods.
18. What is the function of an enzyme?
19. What difficulties are experienced when collecting carbon dioxide: (*a*) by water displacement; (*b*) by air displacement?
20. What are the chemical properties of carbon dioxide?
21. (*a*) How is carbonic acid produced? (*b*) Is it a strong or a weak acid? Explain.

22. What is the test for carbon dioxide?
23. What are the two parts of the oxygen-carbon dioxide cycle?
24. How does a liquid carbon-dioxide fire extinguisher put out fires?
25. (a) Write a balanced formula equation for the reaction which occurs in the discharging of a soda-acid fire extinguisher. (b) Write the ionic and net ionic equations.
26. (a) What is the source of carbon dioxide in most leavening agents? (b) How is it released?
27. What are the sources of carbon monoxide contamination in the atmosphere?
28. What is the function of sulfuric acid in the preparation of carbon monoxide from formic acid?
29. By comparing their molecular weights, arrange oxygen, hydrogen, carbon dioxide, and carbon monoxide in order of increasing density.
30. What are three uses of carbon monoxide?

Group B

31. Explain why carbon atoms usually do not form ionic bonds with other elements.
32. Show how the carbon atom illustrates hybridization in the formation of sp^3 orbitals.
33. (a) What are the two reasons for allotropy? (b) Which of these reasons is illustrated by the allotropic forms of carbon?
34. What proof is there that diamond is pure carbon?
35. Diamond is very hard and is a nonconductor of electricity. Graphite is soft and is a conductor of electricity. Diamond is more dense than graphite. Both diamond and graphite withstand very high temperatures without melting. Explain how these properties are related to the similarities and differences in the structures of diamond and graphite.
36. (a) What uses does natural graphite find in metallurgy? (b) What property of graphite makes these uses possible?
37. (a) What is the most important use for synthetic graphite? (b) What property of graphite makes this use possible?
38. When coke is used as a reducing agent, what is oxidized?
39. Powdered charcoal, copper(II) oxide, and manganese dioxide are all black substances. How could you identify each?
40. For what purposes might activated carbon be used in a large dry cleaning plant?
41. (a) What materials are used in producing carbon black? (b) What is the function of each?
42. Why is it so difficult to remove stains made by printer's ink?
43. Write a net ionic equation for the reaction between calcium carbonate and hydrochloric acid which produces carbon dioxide.
44. Write a net ionic equation for the reaction between sodium carbonate and sulfuric acid.
45. What property of a solid determines whether it will sublime or melt when heated?
46. Does magnesium ribbon actually burn in carbon dioxide? Explain.
47. Show by means of ionic equations that the reaction between carbon dioxide and aqueous sodium hydroxide may be considered to be a hydronium ion-hydroxide ion neutralization reaction.
48. Show by means of ionic equations that the reaction which serves as a test for carbon dioxide may be considered to be a neutralization reaction combined with a precipitation.

49. When a bottle of limewater is left unstoppered, a white ring is formed on the inside of the bottle at the surface of the liquid. Explain its cause, and tell how it can be removed.
50. Distinguish between baking soda and baking powder.
51. Explain why carbon dioxide molecules are nonpolar, while carbon monoxide molecules are polar.
52. Why are both carbon dioxide and carbon monoxide gases at room temperature when water, with a lower molecular weight, is a liquid?
53. Both carbon dioxide and carbon monoxide will produce asphyxiation. Explain the difference in their action on the body.

PROBLEMS

Group A

1. What is the percentage composition of formic acid, HCOOH?
2. (a) How many moles of iron(III) oxide can be reduced by the carbon in 2.00 moles of carbon monoxide, according to the equation: $Fe_2O_3 + 3CO \rightarrow 2Fe + 3CO_2$? (b) How many moles of iron are produced? (c) How many moles of carbon dioxide are produced?
3. How many grams of carbon monoxide are needed to react with 12.2 g of zinc oxide and produce elemental zinc? $ZnO + CO \rightarrow Zn + CO_2$
4. In Problem 3 (a) how many grams of zinc are produced? (b) What is the volume in liters at STP of the carbon dioxide produced?
5. How many grams of H_2SO_4 are required for the reaction with 1.00 kg of sodium hydrogen carbonate in a soda-acid fire extinguisher?
$$2NaHCO_3 + H_2SO_4 \rightarrow Na_2SO_4 + 2H_2O + 2CO_2$$
6. Calculate the number of liters of carbon dioxide at STP given off during the discharge of the fire extinguisher of Problem 5.

Group B

7. How many grams of carbon monoxide can be obtained by the dehydration of $23\overline{0}$ g of formic acid by sulfuric acid?
8. How many liters of dry carbon monoxide will be produced in Problem 7 if the temperature is 27° C and the barometer reading is $75\overline{0}$ mm?
9. How many liters of carbon dioxide will be produced by the combustion of the carbon monoxide of Problem 8 if the product is restored to 27° C and $75\overline{0}$ mm pressure?
10. A pupil wishes to prepare 2.50 liters of dry carbon dioxide at 17° C and $74\overline{0}$ mm pressure by the reaction between calcium carbonate and hydrochloric acid. How many grams of calcium carbonate will be required?
11. How many milliliters of concentrated hydrochloric acid must be diluted with water to provide the HCl needed for the reaction of Problem 10? Concentrated hydrochloric acid is 38.0% HCl by weight and has a density of 1.20 g/ml.
12. A gaseous compound contains 52.9% carbon and 47.1% oxygen. One volume of this gas reacts with two volumes of oxygen and yields three volumes of carbon dioxide. Knowing that oxygen molecules are diatomic, determine the molecular formula of this compound.

Chapter 17

Hydrocarbons

17.1 Abundance of carbon compounds

The number of possible carbon compounds seems almost unlimited. Over 3,000,000 are known and about 100,000 new ones are isolated or synthesized each year. In this chapter, we will describe only a few compounds which are basic to an understanding of organic chemistry. In Chapter 18, we will discuss organic compounds important in everyday life.

There are two reasons for the existence of so many carbon compounds:

1. Carbon atoms link together with covalent bonds. In Chapter 16, we described how carbon atoms readily form covalent bonds with other carbon atoms. This makes possible the existence of molecules in which as many as 70 carbon atoms are bonded one after another in a single long chain. The molecules of some organic compounds are principally long carbon-atom chains with carbon-atom groups attached. Other carbon-compound molecules have carbon atoms linked together in rings. Still others may consist of several such rings joined together. Not only are carbon atoms linked by single covalent bonds, but they are sometimes linked by double or triple covalent bonds.

2. The same atoms may be arranged in several different ways. One of the substances in petroleum is a compound called *octane*. Its molecular formula is C_8H_{18}. A molecule of octane consists of 8 carbon atoms and 18 hydrogen atoms. A carbon atom may form four single covalent bonds while a hydrogen atom forms

332

only one single covalent bond. The straight-chain electron-dot structure for an octane molecule is written like this:

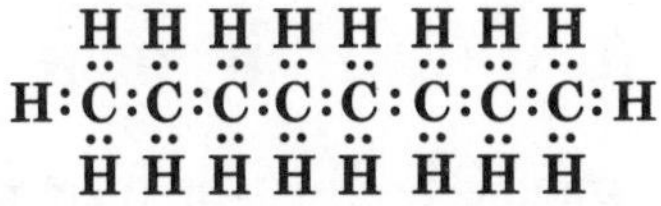

$$\overset{\displaystyle H\ H\ H\ H\ H\ H\ H\ H}{\underset{\displaystyle H\ H\ H\ H\ H\ H\ H\ H}{H:\ddot{C}:\ddot{C}:\ddot{C}:\ddot{C}:\ddot{C}:\ddot{C}:\ddot{C}:\ddot{C}:H}}$$

But there are other ways in which these same atoms can be arranged. For instance, here are three branched-chain formulas:

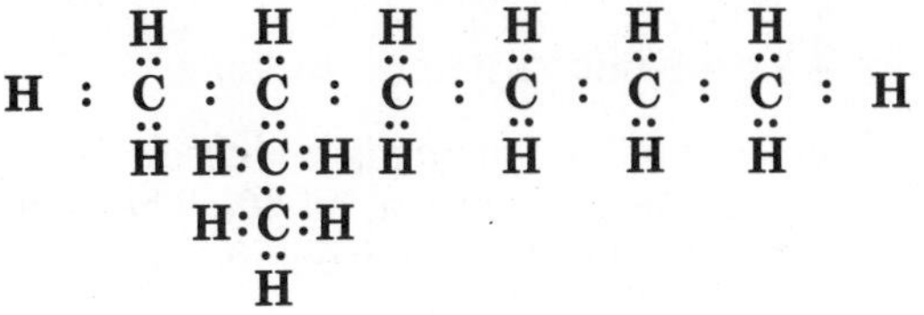

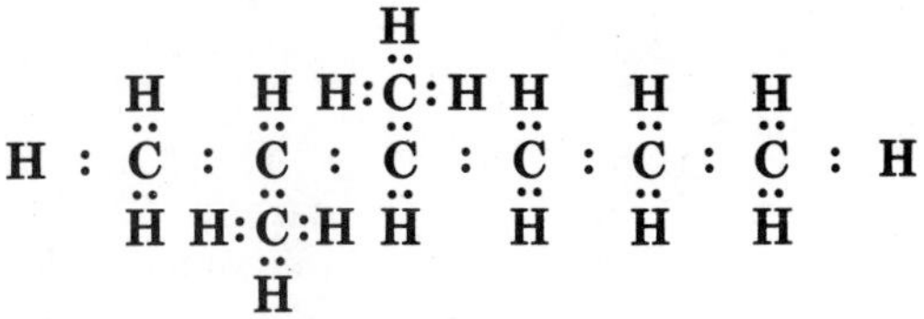

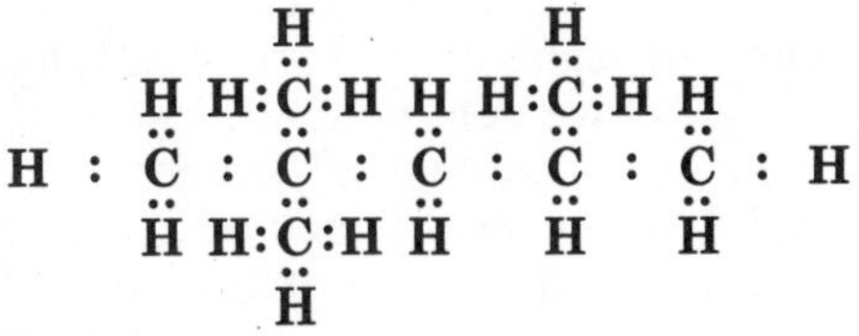

All of these formulas represent arrangements of 8 carbon atoms and 18 hydrogen atoms. Each carbon atom shares four electrons and each hydrogen atom shares one electron. In addition to these four structures for octane, there are 14 others, making a total of 18 possible structures for octane. Each of these 18 structures has the same molecular formula. However, the different arrangements of the atoms in the molecules give each molecule slightly different properties. Thus, each of these molecular arrangements represents a separate chemical compound. *Different compounds which all have the same molecular formula but which have different structures are called* **isomers**.

17.2 Structural formulas for organic compounds

The formula H_2SO_4 for sulfuric acid gives enough information for most purposes in inorganic chemistry. But a molecular formula such as C_8H_{18} is not at all satisfactory in organic chemistry. We have already noted that there are 18 different isomers of this compound. In order to indicate clearly a particular isomer, the organic chemist uses a **structural formula**. *Such a formula not only indicates what kinds of atoms and how many of each, but also shows how they are arranged in the molecule.* Electron-dot formulas have been used to illustrate the isomers of octane. However, such formulas are tedious to draw for routine equation work. Organic chemists often substitute a dash (−) for the pair of shared electrons forming a covalent bond. Using the dash, the straight-chain structural formula for octane can be represented

$$
\begin{array}{ccccccccc}
 & H & H & H & H & H & H & H & H \\
 & | & | & | & | & | & | & | & | \\
H- & C- & C- & C- & C- & C- & C- & C- & C-H \\
 & | & | & | & | & | & | & | & | \\
 & H & H & H & H & H & H & H & H
\end{array}
$$

When structural formulas are written, there must be no dangling bonds. Each dash must represent an electron pair which forms the covalent bond linking two atoms.

17.3   Determination of an organic structural formula

There are two different organic compounds which consist of carbon, 52.2%, hydrogen, 13.0%, and oxygen, 34.8%. They have the same molecular weight, 46, and thus are isomers. One compound is a colorless liquid which boils at 78° C. The other is a colorless gas which condenses to a liquid at −25° C under one atmosphere pressure. Each has its own distinctive odor. How can we determine their structural formulas?

From the percentage composition, we can calculate the empirical formula by the method described in Section 7.12. We find the empirical formula to be C_2H_6O. Since this empirical formula has a formula weight of 46, it must also be the molecular formula of each compound. From what we have already learned about bonding, there are only two ways in which two carbon atoms, six hydrogen atoms, and a single oxygen atom can combine:

$$
\begin{array}{cc}
\begin{array}{ccc}
H & H & \\
| & | & \\
H-C- & C-O-H \\
| & | & \\
H & H &
\end{array}
&
\begin{array}{ccc}
H & & H \\
| & & | \\
H-C- & O- & C-H \\
| & & | \\
H & & H
\end{array}
\\
\textbf{Structure } A & \textbf{Structure } B
\end{array}
$$

Now our problem is to match these structures to the two compounds. If we test each compound for reaction with metallic sodium, only the liquid reacts. In the reaction, hydrogen is given off. The amount of hydrogen given off is equal to one-sixth of the hydrogen which the compound contains. This evidence indicates that in the molecules of the liquid one of the six hydrogen atoms is bonded differently from the others. Structure A is indicated.

Next we discover that the liquid reacts with phosphorus trichloride and gives a product with the molecular formula C_2H_5Cl. In this reaction, chlorine has replaced both a hydrogen atom and an oxygen atom. We can write only one structural formula for C_2H_5Cl:

$$
\begin{array}{ccc}
H & H & \\
| & | & \\
H-C- & C- & Cl \\
| & | & \\
H & H &
\end{array}
$$

We may assume that the chlorine atom occupies the same position as the oxygen and hydrogen atoms which it replaced. Structure *A* is again indicated. We might continue further, because much more evidence can be found to indicate that the liquid does indeed have Structure *A*. This liquid substance is ethanol or ethyl alcohol. The gaseous substance has the other structural formula and is called dimethyl ether.

We can use methods similar to those just described to determine the structural formulas of other simple organic compounds. Complicated molecules are generally broken down into simpler molecules. From the structures of these simpler molecules, we can reason out the structure of the complex molecule. Sometimes simple molecules of known structure are combined to produce a complex molecule. A comparison of chemical and physical properties of compounds of unknown structure with those of known structure is sometimes helpful.

17.4   Differences between organic and inorganic compounds

The basic laws of chemistry are the same for organic and inorganic chemistry. However, the behavior of organic compounds is somewhat different from that of inorganic compounds. Some of the most important differences are:

1.   Most organic compounds do not dissolve in water. The majority of inorganic compounds do dissolve more or less readily in water. Organic compounds generally dissolve in such organic liquids as alcohol, chloroform, ether, carbon disulfide, or carbon tetrachloride.

2.   Organic compounds are decomposed by heat more easily than most inorganic compounds. The decomposition (charring) of sugar when it is heated moderately is familiar. Such charring on heating is often a test for organic substances. But many inorganic compounds, such as common salt (sodium chloride), can be vaporized at a red heat without decomposition.

3.   Organic reactions generally proceed at much slower rates. Such reactions often require hours or even days for completion. However, organic reactions in living cells may take place with great speed. Most inorganic reactions occur almost as soon as solutions of the reactants are brought together.

4.   Organic compounds exist as molecules consisting of atoms joined by covalent bonds. Many inorganic compounds have ionic bonds.

CAUTION:*Many organic compounds are **flammable** and **poisonous**. Some organic reactions are rapid and highly exothermic. A student should not perform any experiments with organic compounds without detailed laboratory directions, and then only under the supervision of an experienced instructor.*

17.5   Classification of hydrocarbons

Compounds composed of only the two elements — hydrogen and carbon — are called **hydrocarbons.** Any study of organic compounds logically begins with a study of the hydrocarbons. The hydrocarbons have the basic structures from which other organic compounds are derived. Hydrocarbons may be grouped into several different series of compounds. These groupings are based mainly on the type of bonding between carbon atoms.

1. The *alkanes* (al-*kaynes*) are straight-chain or branched-chain hydrocarbons. Their carbon atoms are connected by only *single* covalent bonds:

$$\begin{array}{ccc} & H & H \\ & | & | \\ H - & C - C & - H \\ & | & | \\ & H & H \end{array}$$

2. The *alkenes* (al-*keens*) are straight- or branched-chain hydrocarbons in which two carbon atoms in each molecule are connected by a *double* covalent bond:

$$\begin{array}{cc} H & H \\ \diagdown & \diagup \\ C = C \\ \diagup & \diagdown \\ H & H \end{array}$$

3. The *alkynes* (al-*kynes*) are straight- or branched-chain hydrocarbons in which two carbon atoms in each molecule are connected by a *triple* covalent bond:

$$H - C \equiv C - H$$

4. The *alkadienes* (al-kah-*dy*-eens) are straight- or branched-chain hydrocarbons which have *two double* covalent bonds between carbon atoms in each molecule:

$$\begin{array}{ccccc} H & & H & H & & H \\ \diagdown & & | & | & & \diagup \\ C & = C & - C & = C \\ \diagup & & & & \diagdown \\ H & & & & H \end{array}$$

5. The *aromatic hydrocarbons* have resonance structures. These structures sometimes are represented by alternate single and double covalent bonds in six-membered carbon *rings:*

17.6   The alkane series

This series of organic compounds is sometimes called the *paraffin series* because paraffin wax is a mixture of hydrocarbons of this series. The word *paraffin* means *little attraction.* Compared with the other hydrocarbon series, the alkanes have low chemical reactivity. This stability results from their single covalent bonds. Because they have only single covalent bonds in each molecule, the alkanes are known as *saturated hydrocarbons.* Saturated bonding occurs when each carbon atom in the molecule forms four single covalent bonds to other atoms.

Table 17-1 lists a few members of the alkane series. The names of the first four members of this series follow no system. However, beginning with pentane, the first part of each name is a Greek or Latin numerical prefix. This prefix indicates the number of carbon atoms. The name of each member ends in *-ane,* the same as the name of the series. The letter prefix "*n*" for "normal" indicates the straight-chain isomer.

If you examine the formulas for successive alkanes, you will see a clear pattern. Each member of the series differs from the preceding one by the group CH_2,

Table 17–1

SOME MEMBERS OF THE ALKANE SERIES

Name	Formula	Melting point (°C)	Boiling point (°C)
methane	CH_4	−182	−161
ethane	C_2H_6	−183	−89
propane	C_3H_8	−19$\overline{0}$	−44
n–butane	C_4H_{10}	−138	$\overline{0}$
isobutane	C_4H_{10}	−16$\overline{0}$	−12
n–pentane	C_5H_{12}	−13$\overline{0}$	36
isopentane	C_5H_{12}	−16$\overline{0}$	28
neopentane	C_5H_{12}	−2$\overline{0}$	1$\overline{0}$
n–hexane	C_6H_{14}	−95	68
n–heptane	C_7H_{16}	−91	98
n–octane	C_8H_{18}	−56	126
n–nonane	C_9H_{20}	−51	151
n–decane	$C_{10}H_{22}$	−3$\overline{0}$	174
***			
n–eicosane	$C_{20}H_{42}$	37	343
***			
n–hexacontane	$C_{60}H_{122}$	99	

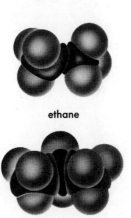

methane

ethane

propane

Fig. 17-1. Models of molecules of the first three members of the alkane series of hydrocarbons.

Compounds which differ in this fashion belong to a *homologous series*. It is not necessary to remember the formulas for all members of a homologous series. A general formula, such as C_nH_{2n+2} for the alkanes, can be derived. Suppose a member of this series has 30 carbon atoms in its molecules. To find the number of hydrogen atoms, multiply 30 by 2, then add 2. The formula is $C_{30}H_{62}$.

17.7 Structures of the lower alkanes

Each of the first three alkanes can have only *one* molecular structure. The formulas for these structures are

methane   **ethane**   **propane**

Butane, the alkane with four carbon atoms and ten hydrogen atoms, has *two* isomers. The straight-chain molecule is named *n*-butane (*n* for *normal*). The branched-chain molecule is named isobutane or 2-methylpropane. Their melting and boiling points are given in Table 17-1.

n-butane   **isobutane or 2-methylpropane**

The name 2-methylpropane is derived directly from the structure of the molecule. The longest continuous carbon chain in the molecule is three carbon atoms long, as in propane. One hydrogen atom attached to the second carbon atom in propane is replaced by the CH_3— group. This is a *substitution group*. It is called the *methyl group*. H—C—H is methane with one of the

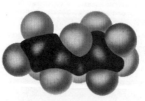

n-butane

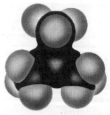

isobutane

Fig. 17-2. Models of molecules of the two isomers of butane.

H H H H H
| | | | |
H—C—C—C—C—C—H
| | | | |
H H H H H

n-pentane

H H H H
| | | |
H—C¹—C²—C³—C⁴—H
| | | |
H—C—H
| H H
H H

**isopentane
2-methylbutane**

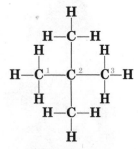

H
|
H—C—H
| H H
| | |
H—C¹—C²—C³—H
| | |
H H H
H—C—H
|
H

**neopentane
2,2-dimethylpropane**

hydrogen atoms removed. The carbon atoms in the main chain of the molecule are numbered. This numbering begins at the end of the molecule that gives the carbon atoms with substitution groups the smallest numbers.

Thus in the name **2-methylpropane**, the *2* refers to the number of the carbon atom on which there is a substitution. *Methyl* is the substituting group. *Propane* is the parent hydrocarbon.

There are *three* possible pentanes (C_5H_{12}): *n*-pentane, isopentane, and neopentane. Their melting and boiling points are given in Table 17-1. Their structural formulas are above.

Isopentane is also called 2-methylbutane. Why would 3-methylbutane be incorrect? Another name for neopentane is **2,2-dimethylpropane**. The *2,2* refers to the position of both substitutions. The prefix *dimethyl* shows that the *two* substitutions are both *methyl* groups. *Propane* is the parent hydrocarbon.

Just as the **CH₃—** group derived from methane is the *methyl* group, **C₂H₅—** derived from ethane is the *ethyl* group. **C₃H₇—** derived from propane is the *propyl* group. **C₄H₉—** derived from butane is the *butyl* group. **C₅H₁₁—** is usually called the *amyl* group rather than the pentyl group. Other groups are given names following the general rule of dropping the *-ane* suffix and adding *-yl*. Any such group derived from an *alkane* is an *alkyl* group. The symbol **R—** is frequently used to represent an *alkyl* group in a formula.

17.8 Bonding in the alkanes

Hydrocarbon molecules contain carbon-hydrogen and carbon-carbon bonds. The electronegativity difference between carbon and hydrogen is slight (2.5 − 2.1 = 0.4). Thus, carbon-hydrogen bonds have about 4% ionic character and are essentially nonpolar bonds. Carbon-carbon bonds, since they are between atoms that are alike, are nonpolar bonds.

In ethane there are one carbon-carbon bond and six carbon-hydrogen bonds. The carbon-carbon bond is an *sp³-sp³* bond. It is formed by electron sharing between two *sp³* hybrid orbitals, one from each of the bonded carbon atoms. The carbon-hydrogen bonds are *sp³-s* bonds. These bonds are formed by electron sharing between a carbon *sp³* orbital and a hydrogen *s* orbital. Remember that *sp³* bonds are directed in space from the center of a regular tetrahedron to each of its four vertices. Rotation can

Fig. 17-3. Bonding in ethane. Each carbon atom has four *sp³* hybrid orbitals. Each hydrogen atom has one *s* orbital. The carbon-carbon bond is an *sp³ − sp³* bond. The carbon-hydrogen bonds are *sp³ − s* bonds.

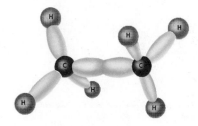

Carolyn Polese

Fig. 17-4. A small quantity of methane can be prepared in the laboratory by heating a mixture of sodium acetate and soda lime.

occur about the sp^3-sp^3 bond. This rotation is somewhat restricted, however, by the interaction of the groups of carbon-hydrogen bonds at the ends of the molecule. Rotation is greatly restricted about an sp^3-sp^3 bond if the groups at the ends of the bond are complex.

17.9   Preparation of the alkanes

The alkanes are generally found in petroleum and natural gas. They are separated from these mixtures by the process of *fractional distillation*. **Fractional distillation** *is a method of separating the components of a mixture on the basis of differences in their boiling points*. It is fairly easy to separate the lower members of the alkane series from petroleum and natural gas by fractional distillation. However, it usually is not possible to separate directly the alkanes with higher boiling points. Instead, such substances are separated as mixtures of compounds having similar boiling points.

Methane is a colorless, nearly odorless gas which forms about 90% of natural gas. Pure methane can be separated from the other components of natural gas. Chemists sometimes prepare small amounts of methane in the laboratory by heating soda lime (which contains sodium hydroxide) with sodium acetate.

$$NaC_2H_3O_2(s) + NaOH(s) \rightarrow CH_4(g) + Na_2CO_3(s)$$

Ethane is a colorless gas which occurs in natural gas and as a product of petroleum refining. It has a higher melting point and boiling point than methane. These properties are to be expected because of ethane's higher molecular weight.

17.10   Reactions of the alkanes

1.   Combustion. The most important reaction of the alkanes is combustion, since they make up a large proportion of our gaseous and liquid fuels. Methane burns with a bluish flame.

$$CH_4 + 2O_2 \rightarrow CO_2 + 2H_2O$$

Ethane and other alkanes also burn in air and form carbon dioxide and water vapor.

$$2C_2H_6 + 7O_2 \rightarrow 4CO_2 + 6H_2O$$

2.   Substitution. The alkanes react with halogens such as chlorine or bromine. In such reactions, one or more atoms of a halogen are substituted for one or more atoms of hydrogen. Therefore, the products are called *substitution products*.

$$\begin{array}{ccc} & H & & & H \\ & | & & & | \\ H-&C&-H + Br_2 \rightarrow H-&C&-Br + HBr \\ & | & & & | \\ & H & & & H \end{array}$$

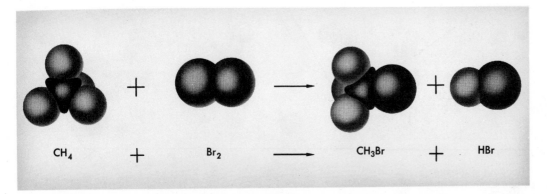

$$CH_4 \quad + \quad Br_2 \quad \longrightarrow \quad CH_3Br \quad + \quad HBr$$

Fig. 17-5. Methane and bromine undergo a substitution reaction.

By supplying additional molecules of the halogen, a halogen atom can be substituted for each of the hydrogen atoms.

   3. *Preparation of hydrogen.* Propane reacts with steam in the presence of a nickel catalyst at a temperature of about 850° C.

$$C_3H_8 + 6H_2O \rightarrow 3CO_2 + 10H_2$$

To separate the carbon dioxide from the hydrogen, the carbon dioxide under pressure may be dissolved in water.

   Hydrogen is also prepared by heating hydrocarbons in the absence of air. The decomposition of methane is shown as:

$$CH_4 \rightarrow C + 2H_2$$

The carbon produced is in the form of carbon black.

17.11 Alkene series

   The alkenes, sometimes called the *olefin series,* are distinguished by a double covalent bond between two carbon atoms. Thus, the simplest alkene must have two carbon atoms. Its structural formula is

$$\begin{array}{c} H \qquad\quad H \\ \diagdown \qquad \diagup \\ C = C \\ \diagup \qquad \diagdown \\ H \qquad\quad H \end{array}$$

Its name is ethene. The name of an alkene comes from the name of the alkane with the same number of carbon atoms. We simply substitute the suffix *-ene* for the suffix *-ane.* Since eth*ane* is the alk*ane* with two carbon atoms, the alk*ene* with two carbon atoms is named eth*ene.* (This substance is also commonly called *ethylene.*) The general formula for the alkenes is C_nH_{2n}.

   In ethene, the bonding mechanism is more complex than in the alkanes. It is believed that the carbon atoms form three sp^2 hybrid orbitals which produce bonds that are 120° apart in a plane. How are these sp^2 orbitals formed? First, a $2s$ electron is promoted to the vacant $2p$ orbital. Then hybridization of one $2s$ and *two* $2p$ orbitals occurs. This arrangement leaves in each

Compare this reaction with the one in Sec. 16.14(2).

Fig. 17-6. The United States will increase its supply of natural gas by importing this valuable chemical raw material. It will be brought in liquid form from foreign sources in tanker ships such as the one shown in the photograph. Each tank is 35 meters in diameter and holds over 20,000 m³ of liquified natural gas.

American Gas Association

(A)

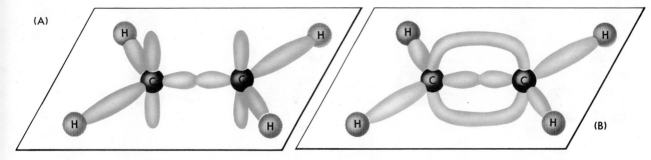

Fig. 17-7. Bonding in ethene.
(A) Each carbon atom has three sp^2 hybrid orbitals in the plane and a $2p$ orbital perpendicular to the plane. Each hydrogen atom has one s orbital. (B) The carbon-carbon double bond is a combination of an $sp^2 - sp^2$ bond with a p-p overlap bond having rounded projections above and below the plane. The carbon-hydrogen bonds are $sp^2 - s$ bonds.

carbon atom one $2p$ orbital with one electron positioned perpendicular to the plane. See Figure 17-7(A). These $2p$ orbitals can overlap and form a new orbital consisting of two rounded projections, one above and one below the plane. See Figure 17-7(B). This combination of an sp^2-sp^2 bond and the p-p overlap bond makes up the double bond in the ethene molecule. No rotation occurs about a carbon-carbon double bond. Hence, the six atoms, the carbon-carbon sp^2-sp^2 bond, and the four carbon-hydrogen sp^2-s bonds all lie in the same plane. The distance between carbon nuclei is shorter in ethene than in ethane. In ethane it is 1.53 Å, almost the same as that found in diamond. In ethene, it is 1.33 Å.

17.12   Preparations of alkenes

1.   Cracking alkanes. One method of producing alkenes is by *cracking* petroleum. ***Cracking** is a process by which complex organic molecules are broken up into simpler molecules. This process involves the action of heat and, usually, a catalyst.* The cracking of ethane at about 600° C produces ethene and hydrogen.

Important reaction conditions are sometimes written near the yields sign.

$$C_2H_6 \xrightarrow{\text{600° C}} C_2H_4 + H_2$$

2.   Dehydration of alcohols. Ethene can be prepared in the laboratory by dehydrating, or removing water from, ethyl alcohol. Hot concentrated sulfuric acid is used as the dehydrating agent.

$$C_2H_5OH \xrightarrow{\text{H}_2\text{SO}_4} C_2H_4 + H_2O$$

17.13   Reactions of alkenes

1.   Addition. An organic compound which has one or more double or triple covalent bonds in each molecule is said to be *unsaturated.* It is chemically possible to add other atoms directly to such molecules and form molecules of a new compound. For example, hydrogen atoms may be added to an alkene in the presence of a finely divided nickel catalyst. This reaction produces the corresponding alkane.

$$\begin{array}{c}H \\ \diagdown \\ C=C \\ \diagup \\ H\end{array}\begin{array}{c}H \\ \diagup \\ \diagdown \\ H\end{array} + H_2 \xrightarrow{\text{Ni}} H-\underset{\underset{H}{|}}{\overset{\overset{H}{|}}{C}}-\underset{\underset{H}{|}}{\overset{\overset{H}{|}}{C}}-H$$

Halogen atoms can be added readily to alkene molecules. For example, two bromine atoms added directly to ethene form 1,2-dibromoethane.

$$\begin{array}{c}H \\ \diagdown \\ C=C \\ \diagup \\ H\end{array}\begin{array}{c}H \\ \diagup \\ \diagdown \\ H\end{array} + Br_2 \rightarrow H-\underset{\underset{H}{|}}{\overset{\overset{Br}{|}}{C}}-\underset{\underset{H}{|}}{\overset{\overset{Br}{|}}{C}}-H$$

As the double bond between the carbon atoms breaks, there is one bond position available for each bromine atom.

The name of the product is 1,2-dibromoethane. The basic part of the name, *ethane,* is that of the related alkane with two carbon atoms. *Dibromo-* refers to the two bromine atoms which have been substituted for hydrogen atoms in ethane. *1,2-* means that one bromine atom is bonded to the first carbon atom and the other is bonded to the second carbon atom. An isomer, 1,1-dibromoethane has the formula

$$Br-\underset{\underset{H}{|}}{\overset{\overset{Br}{|}}{C}}-\underset{\underset{H}{|}}{\overset{\overset{H}{|}}{C}}-H$$

A molecule of a hydrogen halide, such as hydrogen bromide, can be added to an alkene molecule.

$$\begin{array}{c}H \\ \diagdown \\ C=C \\ \diagup \\ H\end{array}\begin{array}{c}H \\ \diagup \\ \diagdown \\ H\end{array} + HBr \rightarrow H-\underset{\underset{H}{|}}{\overset{\overset{H}{|}}{C}}-\underset{\underset{H}{|}}{\overset{\overset{Br}{|}}{C}}-H$$

Fig. 17-8. Ethene and bromine undergo an addition reaction.

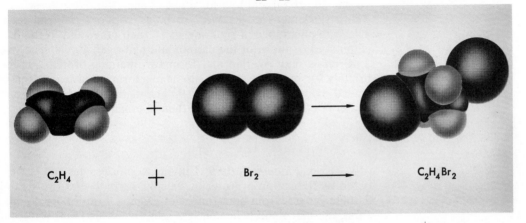

C_2H_4 + Br_2 $\longrightarrow$ $C_2H_4Br_2$

2. *Polymerization.* Molecules of ethene join together, or *polymerize*, at 250° C and 1000 atmospheres pressure. The resulting large molecules have molecular weights of about 30,000. This polymerized material is called *polyethylene.* It is made up of many single units called *monomers.*

$$\begin{array}{c} \quad\ \text{H}\ \ \text{H} \\ \quad\ |\quad | \\ -\text{C}-\text{C}- \\ \quad\ |\quad | \\ \quad\ \text{H}\ \ \text{H} \end{array}$$

Many monomers join together to make the **polymer** (many units). Polyethylene is used in electric insulation, transparent wrappings, and a variety of containers.

3. *Combustion.* The alkenes burn in oxygen. For example,

$$\text{C}_2\text{H}_4 + 3\text{O}_2 \rightarrow 2\text{CO}_2 + 2\text{H}_2\text{O}$$

17.14 Alkyne series

The alkynes are distinguished by a triple covalent bond between two carbon atoms. This series is sometimes called the *acetylene series* because the simplest alkyne has the common name *acetylene.* It has two carbon atoms, with the formula

$$\text{H}-\text{C}\equiv\text{C}-\text{H}$$

The names of the alk*ynes* are derived from the names of the alk*anes* that have the same number of carbon atoms. The suffix *-yne* is substituted for *-ane.* Hence the chemical name for acetylene, the simplest alkyne, is *ethyne.* The general formula for the alkynes is $\text{C}_n\text{H}_{2n-2}$.

In ethyne, C_2H_2, the carbon atoms form two *sp* hybrid orbitals, positioned 180° apart. One *sp* orbital forms a bond with the other carbon atom. The second *sp* orbital forms an *sp-s* bond with a hydrogen atom. Hence, the ethyne molecule is linear. The *sp* hybrid orbitals are formed by promotion of a 2*s* electron to the vacant 2*p* orbital and hybridization of one 2*s* and *one* 2*p* orbital. This arrangement leaves two 2*p* orbitals, with one electron each. They are positioned at right angles to each other and to the line adjoining the nuclei of the carbon and hydrogen atoms. The two 2*p* orbitals may overlap and form two merging orbitals. These orbitals surround the carbon atoms in a form resembling a thick-walled cylinder. See Figure 17-9. The distance between carbon nuclei in ethyne is 1.20 Å, less than in ethane or ethene.

17.15 Preparations of ethyne

1. *From calcium carbide.* Ethyne, a colorless gas can be prepared by the action of water on calcium carbide, CaC_2. Calcium carbide is made from limestone, CaCO_3, in a series of operations. First, the limestone is heated in a kiln (oven). CaO is produced.

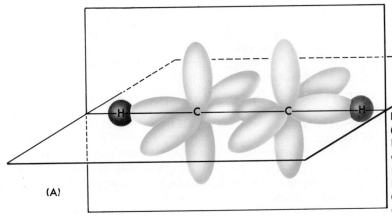

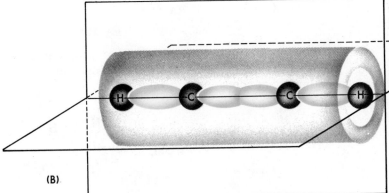

(A)

(B)

Fig. 17-9. Bonding in ethyne. (A) Each carbon atom has two *sp* hybrid orbitals in the line of intersection of the planes and two *2p* orbitals perpendicular to each other in the planes. Each hydrogen atom has one *s* orbital. (B) The carbon-carbon triple bond is a combination of an *sp-sp* bond with two *p-p* overlap bonds which surround the carbon atoms like a thick-walled cylinder. The carbon-hydrogen bonds are *sp-s* bonds.

Fig. 17-10. A convenient method of preparing a small quantity of ethyne (acetylene) in the laboratory by the action of water on calcium carbide.

$$CaCO_3(s) \rightarrow CaO(s) + CO_2(g)$$

The calcium oxide is then heated with coke at 2000° C in an electric resistance furnace.

$$CaO(s) + 3C(s) \rightarrow CaC_2(s) + CO(g)$$

Calcium carbide is an ionic compound with the electron-dot structure

$$Ca^{++}$$
$$^{-} \!\!\times\!\! C \!:\!:\!: C \!\!\times\!\!^{-}$$

When it reacts with water, two hydrogen atoms replace the calcium in the calcium carbide structure.

$$CaC_2(s) + 2H_2O(l) \rightarrow C_2H_2(g) + Ca(OH)_2(aq)$$

2. By cracking alkanes. Ethyne can be produced by passing methane through an electric arc.

$$2CH_4 \rightarrow C_2H_2 + 3H_2$$

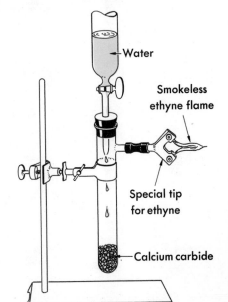

Water

Smokeless ethyne flame

Special tip for ethyne

Calcium carbide

17.16   Reactions of ethyne

1. Combustion. Ethyne burns in air with a very smoky flame. Carbon, carbon dioxide, and water vapor are the products of combustion. With special burners, the combustion to carbon dioxide and water vapor is complete.

$$2C_2H_2 + 5O_2 \rightarrow 4CO_2 + 2H_2O$$

The oxyacetylene welding torch burns ethyne in the presence of oxygen.

2. Halogen addition. Ethyne is more unsaturated than ethene because of the triple bond. It is chemically possible to add to mole of ethyne molecule two moles of bromine and form 1,1,2,2,-tetrabromoethane.

$$H-C{\equiv}C-H + 2Br_2 \rightarrow H-\overset{\displaystyle Br}{\underset{\displaystyle Br}{C}}-\overset{\displaystyle Br}{\underset{\displaystyle Br}{C}}-H$$

3. Water addition. Ethyne reacts with water from dilute sulfuric acid in the presence of mercury(I) sulfate. This reaction yields an important compound, *acetaldehyde.*

$$H-C{\equiv}C-H + H_2O \xrightarrow[\text{Hg}_2\text{SO}_4]{\text{H}_2\text{SO}_4} \quad H-\overset{\displaystyle H}{\underset{\displaystyle H}{C}}-C\overset{\displaystyle H}{\underset{\displaystyle O}{\diagup}}$$

4. Dimerization. Two molecules of ethyne may combine and form the *dimer* (two units), vinylacetylene. This dimerization is brought about by passing ethyne through a water solution of copper(I) chloride and ammonium chloride. This solution acts as a catalyst.

$$2H-C{\equiv}C-H \xrightarrow[\text{NH}_4\text{Cl}]{\text{Cu}_2\text{Cl}_2} \quad \overset{\displaystyle H}{\underset{\displaystyle H}{\diagup}}C{=}\overset{\displaystyle H}{C}-C{\equiv}C-H$$

vinylacetylene

The $CH_2{=}CH-$ group is the *vinyl* group. Vinylacetylene is the basic raw material for producing Neoprene, a synthetic rubber.

17.17   Butadiene: an important alkadiene

Alkadienes have two double covalent bonds in each molecule. The *-ene* suffix indicates a double bond. The *-diene* suffix indicates two double bonds. The names of the alkadienes are derived in much the same way as those of the other hydrocarbon series. Butadiene must, therefore, have four carbon atoms and contain two double bonds in each molecule.

Actually, this structure is 1,3-butadiene, since the double bonds follow the first and third carbon atoms. However, 1,2-butadiene, its isomer, is so uncommon that 1,3-butadiene is usually called simply butadiene.

Butadiene is prepared by cracking petroleum fractions containing butane. It is used in the manufacture of *SBR* rubber, the most common type of synthetic rubber.

17.18 The aromatic hydrocarbons

The aromatic hydrocarbons are generally obtained from coal tar and petroleum. Benzene, the best known aromatic hydrocarbon, has the molecular formula C_6H_6. It may be represented by the following resonance formula, in which the two structures contribute equally.

The bonds in benzene are neither single bonds nor double bonds. Instead, each bond is a *resonance hybrid bond*. All the carbon-carbon bonds in the molecule are the same. As a result, benzene and other aromatic hydrocarbons are not as unsaturated as the alkenes.

The carbon-carbon bonding in the benzene molecule is believed to be sp^2-sp^2 bonding. It is similar to that in the ethene structure. The carbon-hydrogen bonding is sp^2-s bonding. This arrangement results in 120° bond angles, and a molecule whose atoms all lie in the same plane. The singly occupied p orbitals of each carbon atom are perpendicular to the plane of the molecule. These p orbitals above and below the plane overlap and form three orbitals. The principal one of these orbitals consists of two doughnut-shaped rings, one above and one below the plane of the molecule. See Figure 17-11. The other two orbitals also go around the entire molecule, but are difficult to represent in a diagram.

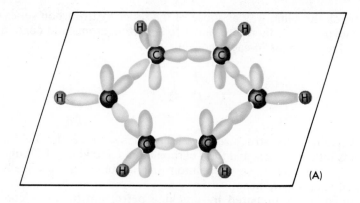

Fig. 17-11. Bonding in benzene. (A) Each carbon atom has three sp^2 hybrid orbitals in the plane and a $2p$ orbital perpendicular to the plane. Each hydrogen atom has one s orbital. (B) The carbon-carbon bonds are combinations of sp^2-sp^2 bonds with p-p overlap bonds which may be partially represented by rings above and below the plane of the molecule. The carbon-hydrogen bonds are sp^2-s bonds.

Because of the resonance structure of benzene, the benzene ring is sometimes abbreviated:

The C_6H_5— group derived from benzene is called the *phenyl* group.

Benzene is obtained commercially by distilling coal tar. It is a flammable liquid that is used as a solvent. Benzene is used in manufacturing many other chemicals, including dyes, drugs, and explosives. Benzene has a strong, yet fairly pleasant, aromatic odor. It is less dense than water and only very slightly soluble in water. *Benzene is poisonous.* The vapors are harmful to breathe and are very flammable. It should be used only where there is adequate ventilation.

17.19   Reactions of benzene

1. Halogenation. Benzene reacts with bromine in the presence of iron and forms the substitution product, bromobenzene, or phenyl bromide.

$$\text{benzene} + Br_2 \xrightarrow{Fe} \text{bromobenzene} + HBr$$

Further treatment causes the successive substitution of other bromine atoms for hydrogen atoms. With complete substitution, hexabromobenzene is produced.

$$\text{hexabromobenzene structure}$$

2. *Nitration.* Nitrobenzene is produced by treating benzene with concentrated nitric and sulfuric acids.

$$\text{benzene} + HNO_3 \xrightarrow{H_2SO_4} \text{nitrobenzene} + H_2O$$

3. *Sulfonation.* Benzenesulfonic acid is produced at room temperature by treating benzene with fuming sulfuric acid. (Fuming sulfuric acid contains an excess of sulfur trioxide.)

$$\text{benzene} + H_2SO_4 \xrightarrow{SO_3} \text{benzenesulfonic acid} + H_2O$$

4. *Friedel-Crafts reaction.* An alkyl group may be introduced into the benzene ring by using an alkyl halide in the presence of anhydrous aluminum chloride.

$$\text{benzene} + RCl \xrightarrow{AlCl_3} \text{alkylbenzene} + HCl$$

17.20 Other aromatic hydrocarbons

Toluene, or methyl benzene, is obtained from coal tar or petroleum.

$$\text{toluene (CH}_3\text{)}$$

benzene

toluene

naphthalene

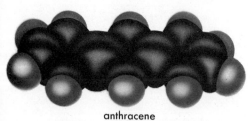

anthracene

Fig. 17-12. Molecular models of common aromatic hydro-carbons.

The xylenes or dimethylbenzenes, $C_6H_4(CH_3)_2$, are a mixture of three liquid isomers. The xylenes are used as starting materials for the production of certain synthetic fibers and films.

Ethylbenzene is produced by the Friedel-Crafts reaction of benzene and ethene in the presence of hydrogen chloride.

$$\bigcirc + C_2H_4 \xrightarrow[\text{HCl}]{\text{AlCl}_3} \bigcirc^{C_2H_5}$$

Ethylbenzene is treated with a catalyst of mixed metallic oxides to eliminate hydrogen and produce styrene, used along with butadiene in making *SBR* synthetic rubber.

$$\bigcirc^{C_2H_5} \xrightarrow[650°]{\text{catalyst}} \bigcirc^{\overset{\text{H} \quad \text{H}}{\underset{\text{H}}{\text{C}=\text{C}}}} + H_2$$

Styrene may be polymerized to polystyrene, a tough, transparent plastic. Polystyrene molecules in this form have molecular weights of about 500,000. Styrofoam, a porous form of polystyrene, is used as a packaging and insulating material.

Naphthalene, $C_{10}H_8$, is a coal-tar product which crystallizes in white shining scales. It is the largest single component of tar. It sometimes occurs in quantities as high as 6%. Naphthalene molecules have a structure made up of two benzene rings joined by a common side.

Naphthalene can be used, either as flakes or balls, to kill larvae of moths that attack woolen garments. Naphthalene is also used as a raw material for the manufacture of some resins (raw materials for plastics) and dyes.

Anthracene, $C_{14}H_{10}$, has a structure made up of three benzene rings joined together.

Like naphthalene, anthracene forms a whole series of hydrocarbons. They differ from the compounds related to benzene in that there is more than one ring. Anthracene, like naphthalene, is obtained commercially from coal tar. It is used in the production of synthetic dyes.

PETROLEUM

17.21 The nature of petroleum

Petroleum, sometimes called crude oil, is obtained from beneath the surface of the ground. Petroleum is mostly a complex
mixture of hydrocarbons. This mixture varies greatly in composition from place to place. The hydrocarbon molecules in
petroleum contain from one to more than 50 carbon atoms. These
hydrocarbons include alkanes, aromatic hydrocarbons, and
naphthenes (saturated ring-type hydrocarbons). Many important
organic chemicals are found in, or derived from, petroleum.

17.22 The refining of petroleum

Petroleum is refined by separating crude oil into portions with
properties suitable for certain uses. The method used is fractional
distillation (see Section 17.9). No attempt is made to separate
the petroleum into individual hydrocarbons. Instead, portions
that distill between certain temperature ranges are collected in
separate receivers. Table 17-2 summarizes the characteristics of
the portions obtained from the fractional distillation of petroleum.
Petroleum refining is carried out in a *pipe still* and a *fractionating tower*. See Figure 17-13. The crude oil is heated to about
370° C in the pipe still. At this temperature, nearly all the components of the crude oil are vaporized. The hot vapors are then

Table 17–2
SUMMARY OF FRACTIONAL DISTILLATION OF PETROLEUM

Portion	No. of C atoms per molecule	Boiling point range (°C)	Uses
gas	C_1 to C_5	−161− 30	fuel; making carbon black, hydrogen, gasoline by polymerization
petroleum ether	C_5 to C_7	20−100	solvent; dry cleaning
gasoline	C_5 to C_{12}	30−200	motor fuel
kerosene	C_{12} to C_{16}	175−275	fuel
fuel oil Diesel oil	C_{15} to C_{18}	250−400	furnace fuel; diesel engine fuel; cracking
lubricating oils greases petroleum jelly	C_{16}	350	lubrication
paraffin wax	C_{20}	melts 52−57	Candles; waterproofing; home canning
pitch tar		residue	road construction
petroleum coke		residue	electrodes

Fig. 17-13. A cross-section of a pipe still and fractionating tower used in refining petroleum.

Fig. 17-14. A petroleum refinery. The buildings with the tall chimneys are the pipe stills. The tower-like structures are fractionating towers.

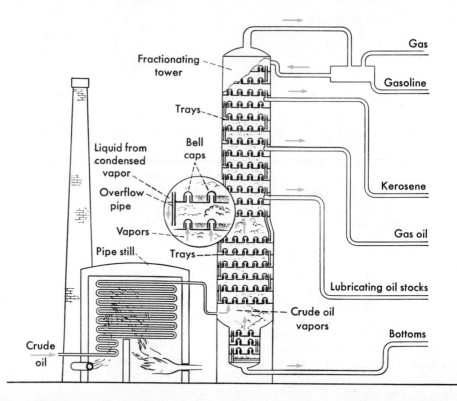

Fractionating tower

Gas

Gasoline

Trays

Bell caps

Liquid from condensed vapor

Overflow pipe

Vapors

Trays

Kerosene

Gas oil

Pipe still

Crude oil vapors

Lubricating oil stocks

Crude oil

Bottoms

discharged into the fractionating tower at a point near its base. Here, the portions with the highest condensation temperatures condense and are drawn off to collecting vessels. Portions with lower condensation temperatures continue to rise in the tower. As they rise, they are gradually cooled. In this way, the various portions reach their condensation temperatures at different levels. As they condense, the liquids collect in shallow troughs which line the inside of the tower. Pipes lead off the overflow of condensed liquids from the troughs. Gasoline, together with the more volatile portions of the petroleum, passes as a gas from the top of the tower. The gasoline is liquefied in separate condensers. The uncondensed gases may be piped to the polymerizer (see Section 17.13), or they may be used as fuel in the refinery.

17.23   Octane number of gasoline

Knocking occurs in an automobile engine when the mixture of gasoline vapor and air in the cylinders explodes spontaneously rather than burning at a uniform rate. Knocking causes a loss of power and may harm the engine. It can be prevented by using a gasoline which resists this tendency to explode spontaneously as the temperature and pressure increase within the cylinder.

Air mixtures of gasoline that consist mostly of straight-chain hydrocarbons tend to knock badly in automobiles. Air mixtures of hydrocarbons with branched-chains and rings resist exploding spontaneously as the temperature and pressure in the cylinder increase. Thus, branched-chain and ring hydrocarbons have less tendency to knock than straight-chain hydrocarbons. To improve the antiknock qualities, refiners produce a gasoline mixture that contains a large proportion of branched-chain and ring hydrocarbon molecules.

Fig. 17-15. A technician determining the octane rating of a sample of gasoline.

Certain compounds, when added to gasoline in small amounts, improve the antiknock properties. The best known of these is lead tetraethyl, $Pb(C_2H_5)_4$. The use of lead tetraethyl in gasoline is currently being reduced because it contributes to air pollution.

The octane rating of a gasoline is a number which indicates the tendency of a gasoline to knock in a high-compression engine. The higher the number, the less the tendency of the gasoline to knock. To determine the octane rating, the gasoline is burned in a standard test engine. Its performance in the test engine is compared with a fuel of known octane rating. The fuels used as standards are *n*-heptane and 2,2,4-trimethylpentane, which is also named iso-octane. Iso-octane has excellent antiknock properties. It has an arbitrary octane rating of 100. Normal heptane knocks very badly and has a rating of zero. A gasoline with the characteristics of a mixture of 90% iso-octane and 10% *n*-heptane has an octane rating of 90.

Straight-chain alkanes have low octane ratings. Naphthenes have intermediate octane ratings. Highly-branched alkanes and aromatic (benzene ring-shaped) hydrocarbons have high octane ratings.

Esso Research and Engineering Co.

17.24 Increasing the yield and octane rating of gasoline from petroleum

Crude oil contains only a small percentage of gasoline, and this is of low octane rating. The yield and octane rating of gasoline are increased by a number of methods.

1. *Thermal cracking.* This method involves heating petroleum portions containing molecules with 15 to 18 carbon atoms to a high temperature under high pressure. The heat and pressure weaken the bonds of the molecules. The molecules can then be "cracked" or broken into simpler molecules. For example, a molecule of $C_{16}H_{34}$ can be cracked to yield a molecule of C_8H_{18}, octane, and a molecule of C_8H_{16}, octene. This process increases the yield of gasoline from a given amount of petroleum.

2. *Catalytic cracking.* This cracking process uses heat, but at atmospheric pressure. A catalyst causes the cracking reactions to produce more molecules of the branched-chain and aromatic types. The catalysts used are mostly oxides of silicon and aluminum. Catalytic cracking produces gasoline of higher octane rating than thermal cracking.

3. *Polymerization.* Polymerization is the opposite of cracking. Simple hydrocarbon molecules containing 3 or 4 carbon atoms are polymerized to make larger molecules required for gasoline. This is accomplished by heating the hydrocarbons under high pressure with a phosphoric acid catalyst. An example of a polymerization reaction is that between two molecules of isobutene, C_4H_8. The isobutene molecules react and form an isomer of octene, C_8H_{16}. This isomer is then hydrogenated to form an isomer of octane. Like the cracking processes, polymerization increases the yield of gasoline from a given amount of petroleum.

4. *Reforming.* Reforming consists of heating the gasoline portion from petroleum distillation with hydrogen in the presence of a platinum catalyst. Aromatic hydrocarbon compounds are formed from naphthenes and alkanes. Reformed gasoline consequently has a high octane rating.

5. *Alkylation.* In alkylation, gaseous alkanes are combined with gaseous alkenes such as ethene, C_2H_4. These gaseous substances are heated in the presence of a sulfuric acid or anhydrous hydrogen fluoride catalyst. The result is a gasoline containing highly-branched alkanes. Alkylation, therefore, produces gasoline of very high octane rating. It also increases the amount of gasoline which can be obtained from a given amount of petroleum.

RUBBER

17.25 Nature of rubber

Rubber is a plastic hydrocarbon obtained from rubber trees. Each tree yields, daily, about one ounce of a milky fluid called *latex*. Latex contains about 35% rubber in colloidal suspension. When acetic acid is added to latex, the rubber separates out as a curd-like mass. After being washed and dried, it is shipped to market as large sheets of crude rubber.

The simplest formula for rubber is $(C_5H_8)_x$. The structural formula for a single C_5H_8 unit is thought to be

$$
\begin{array}{ccccc}
 & & \text{H} & & \\
 & & | & & \\
\text{H} & \text{H}-\text{C}-\text{H} & & \text{H} & \\
 & & & & | \\
-\text{C} & -\text{C} & =\text{C} & -\text{C}- & \\
 & | & | & | & \\
\text{H} & & \text{H} & \text{H} &
\end{array}
$$

The C_5H_8 unit is a monomer of rubber. The "*x*" is believed to be a large number. Thus, rubber is a polymer made up of a large number of C_5H_8 units. The units are joined in a zigzag chain. This arrangement accounts for the elasticity of rubber.

17.26 Compounding of rubber

For commercial processing, raw rubber is mixed with a number of other materials in large batches. The ingredients in these batches vary according to the products to be made. Sulfur,

Fig. 17-16. A testing laboratory where scientists blend crude rubber with various materials (left) and determine the properties of the resulting mixtures (right).

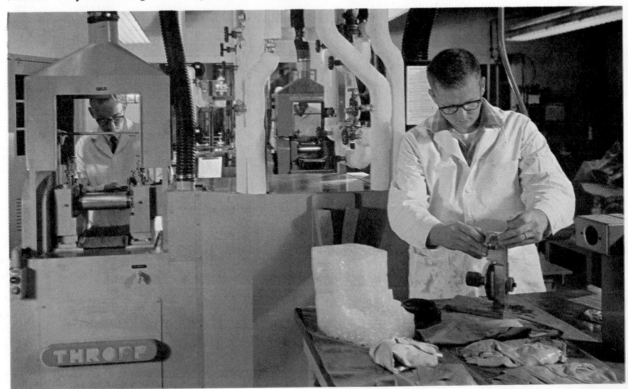

however, is always one of the ingredients. Automobile tires contain considerable amounts of carbon black. This substance adds to the bulk and increases the wearing qualities of the tires.

After mixing, the product is shaped either in a mold or from thin sheets. The whole mass is then vulcanized. *Vulcanization*[1] *involves heating the rubber mixture to a definite temperature for a definite time.* It gives the article a permanent shape, makes the rubber more elastic, and causes it to lose its sticky qualities. The changes which occur during vulcanization are many and complex. It is believed, however, that the sulfur atoms form bonds between adjacent rubber molecules. Organic catalysts are added to speed the process. Other organic chemicals are added to reduce the effect of oxygen from the air. This treatment slows the aging process that makes the rubber become hard and brittle.

17.27 Neoprene, a synthetic rubber

About the year 1910, scientists first produced hydrocarbon synthetic rubber by polymerizing isoprene, C_5H_8. This synthetic product cost too much and was inferior to natural rubber from plantations in the East Indies. In 1931, a successful synthetic rubber called *neoprene* appeared on the market.

Hydrogen chloride adds to vinylacetylene and yields chloroprene:

$$
\begin{array}{cc}
\underset{\substack{|\\ H}}{\overset{\substack{H \ \ H}}{C{=}C}}{-}C{\equiv}C{-}H + HCl \rightarrow &
\underset{\substack{|\ \ \ |\\ H \ \ Cl}}{\overset{\substack{H \ \ H \ \ \ \ \ \ H}}{C{=}C{-}C{=}C}}\underset{H}{}
\end{array}
$$

vinylacetylene   **chloroprene**

The catalytic polymerization of chloroprene yields the neoprene unit:

$$
\underset{\substack{|\ \ \ \ \ \ \ \ \ \ \ |}}{\overset{\substack{H \ \ Cl \ \ H \ \ H}}{{-}C{-}C{=}C{-}C{-}}}
$$

Oils and greases cause natural rubber to swell and rot. They have little effect on neoprene. Hence, neoprene is used in gasoline delivery hoses and in other objects which must be flexible while resisting the action of hydrocarbons.

17.28 *SBR*, a synthetic rubber for tires

SBR, Styrene Butadiene Rubber, is a good all-purpose synthetic rubber. It can replace natural rubber for most purposes. It is used for automobile tire treads because it resists wear better than other synthetic rubbers. It is made by churning *butadiene* (Section 17.17) and *styrene* (Section 17.20) together in soapy water. The churning is carried out at 5° C, using a catalyst. This causes the chemicals to polymerize and form *SBR* rubber. The addition of an acid causes the rubber to separate in curd-like masses, which are washed and dried. A possible structural unit is shown in the following structural formula:

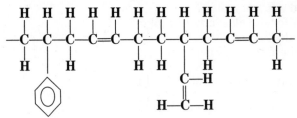

SBR structural unit

QUESTIONS

Group A

1. Give two reasons for the existence of so many carbon compounds.
2. What does a dash (—) represent in a structural formula?
3. What information do you obtain from a properly written structural formula?
4. Give four important differences between organic and inorganic compounds.
5. What are the general formulas for (*a*) the alkane series; (*b*) the alkene series; (*c*) the alkyne series?
6. A hydrocarbon contains 6 carbon atoms. Give its empirical formula if it is: (*a*) an alkane; (*b*) an alkene; (*c*) an alkyne.
7. Beyond the first four members of the alkane series, how are the hydrocarbons of this series named?
8. What does the formula RH represent?
9. (*a*) What is *fractional distillation?* (*b*) How effective is it in separating the alkanes?
10. How is methane produced in the laboratory?
11. Write a balanced formula equation for the complete combustion of: (*a*) methane; (*b*) ethene; (*c*) ethyne; (*d*) butadiene.
12. Write equations for the step-by-step substitution of each of the hydrogen atoms in methane by bromine.
13. Butene reacts with hydrogen in the presence of a nickel catalyst. Write a structural-formula equation for the reaction.
14. (*a*) What is a monomer? (*b*) a dimer? (*c*) a polymer? (*d*) polymerization?
15. What are two uses for ethyne?
16. What do the terms *saturated* and *unsaturated* mean when applied to hydrocarbons?
17. Why is calcium carbide sold in air-tight metal cans?
18. How are naphthalene and anthracene related structurally to benzene?
19. Describe the composition of petroleum.
20. How is petroleum separated into suitable portions having useful properties?

21. (a) What use is made of the petroleum fraction having 5 to 7 carbon atoms per molecule? (b) What use is made of the petroleum fraction which has a boiling point range of 250° C to 400° C?
22. (a) What causes knocking in an automobile engine? (b) How is gasoline formulated to prevent knocking?
23. If a gasoline has an octane rating of 96, what does this mean?
24. How is rubber separated out from latex?
25. What probably accounts for the elasticity of rubber?
26. How is rubber compounded?
27. Why are additives used in making rubber goods?
28. What is vulcanization?
29. What advantage does neoprene have over natural rubber?

Group B

30. Why would you expect organic compounds with covalent bonds to be less stable to heat than inorganic compounds with ionic bonds?
31. Draw structural formulas for the five isomers of hexane.
32. When burned completely, decane, $C_{10}H_{22}$, forms carbon dioxide and water vapor. Write the chemical equation.
33. Draw the structural formula for 2,2-dichloropropane.
34. Draw structural formulas for three isomers of trichloropentane.
35. The element which appears in the greatest number of compounds is hydrogen. The element forming the second greatest number of compounds is carbon. Why are there more hydrogen compounds than carbon compounds?
36. Write structural formula equations for the preparation of (a) acetaldehyde from ethyne; (b) vinylacetylene from ethyne.
37. (a) Is it geometrically possible for the four hydrogen atoms attached to the end carbon atoms in the 1,3-butadiene molecule to lie in the same plane? (b) If carbon-hydrogen bonds on adjacent singly-bonded carbon atoms tend to repel each other, would it be likely that all six hydrogen atoms lie in the same plane? (c) If they do, what is their relation to the plane of the carbon atoms?
38. For the compound propadiene (a) draw the structural formula; (b) write the electron-dot formula; (c) using tetrahedral carbon atoms, draw the molecule, showing the orientation of the valence bonds; (d) from your drawing, decide whether all the hydrogen atoms lie in the same plane or not.
39. The formulas for the first four members of the benzene series are C_6H_6, C_7H_8, C_8H_{10}, C_9H_{12}. What is the general formula for the benzene series?
40. (a) What is *resonance?* (b) Using structural valence-bond formulas, explain resonance in the benzene molecule. (c) Is a double bond in a benzene molecule the same as a double bond in an ethene molecule?
41. Compare the carbon-carbon bonding in ethane, ethene, ethyne, and benzene according to the orbital theory.
42. Write equations for the step-by-step substitution of each of the hydrogen atoms in benzene by bromine.
43. Write a structural-formula equation for the preparation of methyl benzene from benzene and methyl chloride by the Friedel-Crafts reaction.
44. Draw: (a) the three possible valence-bond structural formulas for naphthalene; (b) the four possible valence-bond structural formulas for anthracene.
45. Compare the action shown in Figure 11-6 with that on a single trough in Figure 17-13.

46. For each of the five methods described for increasing the yield and octane rating of gasoline from petroleum, indicate whether the method increases the yield, increases the octane rating, or both.

47. (a) What materials are polymerized to produce *SBR* rubber? (b) What is an important use for *SBR* rubber? (c) Why is it used for this purpose?

PROBLEMS

Group A

1. What is the mass in kilograms of 15.0 gallons of gasoline? Assume the gasoline is iso-octane which has a density of 0.692 g/ml.
2. Calculate the percentage composition of butane.
3. What volume of carbon dioxide is produced by the complete combustion of 25.0 liters of propane? The volumes of carbon dioxide and of propane are measured under the same conditions.
4. How many grams of calcium carbide are required for the production of 2.0 liters of ethyne at STP?

Group B

5. A compound consists of 60.0% carbon, 26.7% oxygen, and 13.3% hydrogen. Its molecular weight is 60. What are the possible structures for molecules of this compound?
6. Calculate the energy change of the substitution reaction between one mole of methane and one mole of bromine molecules. Use the bond energies given in Table 6-4.
7. A volume of ethene (135 ml) is collected by water displacement at 22° C and 738 mm pressure. What is the volume of the dry ethene at STP?
8. A compound consists of 93.75% carbon and 6.25% hydrogen. The substance dissolves in benzene and 6.40 g of it lowers the freezing point of 100 g of benzene 2.55 C°. (a) What is the empirical formula of the compound? (b) What is its molecular weight? (c) What is its molecular formula? See Table 12-5 for necessary data.

Chapter 18

Hydrocarbon Substitution Products

18.1 Preparation of alkyl halides

*An **alkyl halide** is an alkane in which a halogen atom*—fluorine, chlorine, bromine, or iodine—*is substituted for a hydrogen atom.* Since **R** often is used to represent an alkyl group and **X** may represent any halogen, we may represent an alkyl halide as **RX**.

1. Direct halogenation. In Section 17.10, we noted that the halogens react with alkanes and form substitution products. Under suitable conditions, for example, halogen atoms can be substituted for each of the four hydrogen atoms in methane. This reaction occurs in four steps.

$$CH_4 + X_2 \rightarrow CH_3X + HX$$
$$CH_3X + X_2 \rightarrow CH_2X_2 + HX$$
$$CH_2X_2 + X_2 \rightarrow CHX_3 + HX$$
$$CHX_3 + X_2 \rightarrow CX_4 + HX$$

2. From alkenes and alkynes. We recognized in Sections 17.13 and 17.16 that alkenes and alkynes react with halogens or hydrogen halides and form alkyl halides.

3. From alcohols. Alcohols are alkanes in which the hydroxyl group, **—OH,** has been substituted for hydrogen. Hence, an alcohol has the type formula **ROH.** The reaction of an alcohol with a hydrogen halide, HCl, HBr, or HI, yields the corresponding alkyl halide.

$$ROH + HX \rightarrow RX + H_2O$$

18.2 Reactions of the alkyl halides

1. Grignard reagent formation. When an alkyl halide is slowly added to dry ether containing magnesium, a vigorous exothermic reaction occurs. One product of this reaction is a compound in which the alkyl group and a halogen atom are combined with an atom of magnesium.

$$RX + Mg \rightarrow RMgX$$

Compounds of the **RMgX** type are called *Grignard reagents* after the French chemist Victor Grignard (1871–1935).

2. With hydroxide ion. Alkyl halides react with water solutions of strong hydroxides and yield alcohols and the halide ion.

$$RX + OH^- \rightarrow ROH + X^-$$

18.3 Specific alkyl halides

Tetrachloromethane, CCl_4, is commonly called carbon tetrachloride. It is a colorless, volatile, nonflammable liquid. It is an excellent solvent. Carbon tetrachloride is sometimes used for dry cleaning fabrics, removing grease from metals, and extracting oils from seeds. Its vapors are poisonous. Therefore, *there must be good ventilation whenever carbon tetrachloride is used.* Its most important use is in the preparation of Freon refrigerants and spray can propellants. Carbon tetrachloride is prepared commercially by the direct chlorination of methane.

$$CH_4 + 4Cl_2 \longrightarrow CCl_4 + 4HCl$$

Trichloromethane, $CHCl_3$, commonly named chloroform, is a sweet-smelling, colorless liquid. It is used as a solvent and also in medicinal preparations. Chloroform is manufactured by reducing carbon tetrachloride with moist iron.

Dichlorodifluoromethane, CCl_2F_2, is the most important member of a family of compounds named Freon. It is used as a refrigerant in mechanical refrigerators and air conditioners. It is also the propellant in spray cans of various kinds. This particular Freon is an odorless, nontoxic, nonflammable, easily liquefied gas. It is prepared from carbon tetrachloride and hydrofluoric acid with antimony compounds as catalysts.

$$CCl_4 + 2HF \xrightarrow{\text{catalyst}} CCl_2F_2 + 2HCl$$

Tetrafluoroethene, C_2F_4, can be polymerized. The product has a structure in which the following unit occurs again and again:

$$-\underset{\underset{F}{|}}{\overset{\overset{F}{|}}{C}}-\underset{\underset{F}{|}}{\overset{\overset{F}{|}}{C}}-$$

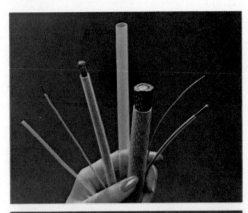

Fig. 18-1. Teflon is used to make tubing, wire insulation, a variety of molded containers, and a nonstick coating on cooking utensils.

E.I. DuPont De Nemours & Company

This material is called Teflon. Teflon is a very inactive, flexible substance which is stable up to about 325° C. It is made into fibers for weaving chemical-resistant fabrics, or into rods from which small parts may be formed. Teflon has a very low co-efficient of friction. It is useful where heat-resistant, nonlubricated moving parts are needed. It is also used to coat metals and give them a "non-sticking" surface.

ALCOHOLS

18.4 Preparations of alcohols

Alcohols are alkanes in which one or more *hydroxyl* groups, −OH, have been substituted for a like number of hydrogen atoms. (The covalent bonded hydroxyl group must not be confused with the ionic bonded hydroxide ion.)

1. Hydration of alkenes. Ethene reacts exothermically with concentrated sulfuric acid at room temperature. The sulfuric acid molecule adds to the double bond. One hydrogen atom of the sulfuric acid molecule adds to one carbon. The remainder of the sulfuric acid molecule adds to the other carbon.

$$H_2C{=}CH_2 + \underset{H-O}{\overset{H-O}{}}S\underset{O}{\overset{O}{}} \rightarrow H-\overset{H}{\underset{H}{C}}-\overset{H}{\underset{H}{C}}-O-\overset{O}{\underset{O}{S}}-O-H$$

If this mixture is diluted with water, the ethene-sulfuric acid-addition compound reacts and produces C_2H_5OH, called ethanol or ethyl alcohol.

$$H-\overset{H}{\underset{H}{C}}-\overset{H}{\underset{H}{C}}-O-\overset{O}{\underset{O}{S}}-O-H + H-O-H \rightarrow H-\overset{H}{\underset{H}{C}}-\overset{H}{\underset{H}{C}}-O-H + \underset{H-O}{\overset{H-O}{}}S\underset{O}{\overset{O}{}}$$

The over-all effect of these two reactions is the addition of water across the ethene double bond.

2. From alkyl halides. We mentioned in Section 18.2 that alkyl halides react with water solutions of strong hydroxides and yield alcohols.

3. Methanol. Methanol is prepared from carbon monoxide and hydrogen under pressure, using a catalyst. See Section 16.23. Methanol is a colorless liquid with a rather pleasant odor. It has a low density, and boils at 64.7° C. *It is very poisonous, even when used externally.* If taken internally in small quantities, it causes blindness by destroying the cells of the nerve that connects the eyes to the brain. Larger quantities may cause death. Methanol is a good fuel, burning with a hot, smokeless flame. It is used as a solvent and in denaturing alcohol. It serves as a starting material for preparing other organic compounds such as formaldehyde, HCHO.

4. Ethanol. Large quantities of ethanol are produced by hydrating ethene. Another method is by fermentation. If we add yeast to a dilute solution of sugar or molasses at room temperature, chemical action soon occurs. The yeast plants secrete the enzymes sucrase and zymase. These enzymes act as catalysts in changing the sugar into alcohol and carbon dioxide.

$$C_{12}H_{22}O_{11} + H_2O \rightarrow 4CO_2 + 4C_2H_5OH$$

Both processes are used in producing industrial ethanol. However, hydration of ethene is a less expensive method and is replacing the fermentation process.

Ethanol is a colorless liquid. It has a characteristic odor and a sharp, biting taste. It boils at 78° C, freezes at −115°´C, and burns with a nearly colorless blue flame. Ethanol is a good solvent for many organic compounds which are insoluble in water. Accordingly, it is used for making a variety of solutions for medicinal use. Ethanol is also used for making ether and acetaldehyde.

Denatured alcohol is a mixture composed principally of ethanol. But it contains added poisonous and nauseating materials which make it unfit for beverage purposes.

5. Ethylene glycol. The compound ethylene glycol, $C_2H_4(OH)_2$, has the structural formula

$$
\begin{array}{c}
\text{H} \quad \text{H} \\
| \quad\; | \\
\text{H}-\text{C}-\text{C}-\text{H} \\
| \quad\; | \\
\text{O} \quad \text{O} \\
| \quad\; | \\
\text{H} \quad \text{H}
\end{array}
$$

Ethylene glycol is an alcohol containing two hydroxyl groups. It is used extensively as a "permanent" antifreeze in automobile radiators. Its boiling point is so much higher than that of water that it does not readily evaporate or boil away. Ethylene glycol is poisonous.

6. Glycerol. Glycerol, or glycerin, $C_3H_5(OH)_3$, has the structural formula

$$
\begin{array}{c}
\text{H} \\
| \\
\text{H}-\text{C}-\text{O}-\text{H} \\
| \\
\text{H}-\text{C}-\text{O}-\text{H} \\
| \\
\text{H}-\text{C}-\text{O}-\text{H} \\
| \\
\text{H}
\end{array}
$$

It is a colorless, odorless, slow-flowing liquid with a sweet taste. It has a low vapor pressure and is hygroscopic (absorbs water from the air). It is used in making synthetic resins for paints and

Mario Menesini

Fig. 18-2. In this plant ethanol is produced by hydrating ethene.

in cigarettes to keep the tobacco moist. It is also used in the manufacture of cellophane, in making nitroglycerin, and in some toilet soaps. Glycerol is an important ingredient of cosmetics and drugs and is used in many foods and beverages. It is a byproduct of soap manufacture. Large quantities of glycerol are synthesized from propene, a product of petroleum cracking.

18.5 Reactions of alcohols

1. With sodium. Sodium reacts vigorously with ethanol, releasing hydrogen. A second product of the reaction is sodium ethoxide, C_2H_5ONa. This compound is recovered as a white solid after the excess ethanol is evaporated. This reaction is similar to the reaction of sodium with water.

$$2C_2H_5OH + 2Na \rightarrow 2C_2H_5ONa + H_2$$

2. With HX and PX$_3$. Alcohols react with concentrated water solutions of hydrogen halides, particularly hydrobromic, HBr, and hydriodic, HI, acids. These reactions produce alkyl halides. Sulfuric acid is used as a dehydrating agent.

$$ROH + HBr \rightarrow RBr + H_2O$$

Alcohols also react with phosphorus trihalides and yield alkyl halides. Using phosphorus tribromide,

$$3ROH + PBr_3 \rightarrow 3RBr + H_3PO_3$$

H_3PO_3 is known as phosphorous acid.

3. Dehydration. Depending on reaction conditions, ethanol dehydrated by hot concentrated sulfuric acid yields either diethyl ether, $C_2H_5OC_2H_5$, or ethene, C_2H_4.

$$2C_2H_5OH \rightarrow C_2H_5OC_2H_5 + H_2O$$

$$C_2H_5OH \rightarrow C_2H_4 + H_2O$$

4. Oxidation. Alcohols which have the hydroxyl group attached to the end carbon may be oxidized by hot copper(II) oxide. The product of such an oxidation is an aldehyde, RCHO.

$$RCH_2OH + CuO \rightarrow RCHO + H_2O + Cu$$

Low-molecular-weight alcohols are flammable, and burn readily in air.

$$2CH_3OH + 3O_2 \rightarrow 2CO_2 + 4H_2O$$

5. Sulfation of long-chain alcohols. 1-dodecanol, $C_{12}H_{25}OH$, is commonly called lauryl alcohol. It is obtained from coconut oil by hydrogenation and partial decomposition. Lauryl alcohol may be *sulfated* by treatment with sulfuric acid and then neutralized with sodium hydroxide. This process yields sodium lauryl sulfate, $C_{12}H_{25}OSO_2ONa$, a very effective cleaning agent.

$$C_{12}H_{25}OH + H_2SO_4 \rightarrow C_{12}H_{25}OSO_2OH + H_2O$$

$$C_{12}H_{25}OSO_2OH + NaOH \rightarrow C_{12}H_{25}OSO_2ONa + H_2O$$

ETHERS

18.6 Ethers: organic oxides

Ethers have the general formula **ROR′. R** and **R′** represent the same or different alkyl groups. Ethers may be thought of as being structurally similar to water. But both hydrogen atoms have been replaced by alkyl groups. Ethers can be prepared by dehydrating alcohols as described in Section 18.5. Diethyl ether is commonly known as *ether*. It is a volatile, very flammable, colorless liquid of characteristic odor. It can be made by heating ethanol and sulfuric acid to 140° C.

$$2C_2H_5OH \xrightarrow{H_2SO_4} C_2H_5OC_2H_5 + H_2O$$

Fig. 18-3. In an operating room of Massachusetts General Hospital in 1846, W.T.G. Morton, a Boston dentist, demonstrated the use of ether as an anesthetic. Because of Morton's demonstrations, the use of ether as an anesthetic became world-wide within a year.

Besides its use as an anesthetic, ether is employed as a solvent for fats and oils.

Ethers may be synthesized by the action of a sodium alkoxide, such as sodium ethoxide, on an alkyle halide, such as methyl bromide. The ether and a sodium halide are products.

$$RONa + R'X \rightarrow ROR' + NaX$$

$$C_2H_5ONa + CH_3Br \rightarrow C_2H_5OCH_3 + NaBr$$

Depending on the alkyl group in the alkoxide and in the alkyl halide, ethers with different alkyl groups attached to the oxygen may be produced. The equation above shows the preparation of methyl ethyl ether. This method is known as the *Williamson synthesis*. It is named after the English chemist, Alexander W. Williamson (1824–1904).

ALDEHYDES

18.7 Preparations of aldehydes

An aldehyde is a compound which has a hydrocarbon group and one or more *formyl* groups, $-C\!\!\begin{array}{c} {}^{\displaystyle O} \\ {}_{\displaystyle H} \end{array}$ The general formula for an *aldehyde* is **RCHO**.

1. From alcohols. This method of preparing aldehydes was mentioned in Section 18.5. A common process of this type involves passing methanol vapor and a regulated amount of air over heated copper. Formaldehyde, HCHO, is produced.

$$2Cu + O_2 \rightarrow 2CuO$$

$$CH_3OH + CuO \rightarrow HCHO + H_2O + Cu$$

The commercial preparation of formaldehyde involves a silver or an iron-molybdenum oxide catalyst. At room temperature, formaldehyde is a gas with a strangling odor. Dissolved in water, it makes an excellent disinfectant. It is also used to preserve biological or medical specimens. By far the largest use of formaldehyde is in making certain types of plastics.

2. Acetaldehyde from ethyne. Acetaldehyde is manufactured commercially by the addition of water to ethyne. See Section 17.16. Acetaldehyde is a stable liquid used in preparing other organic compounds.

18.8 Reactions of aldehydes

1. Oxidation. The mild oxidation of an aldehyde produces the organic acid having the same number of carbon atoms. The oxidation of acetaldehyde to acetic acid is typical.

$$CH_3CHO + O \text{ (from oxidizing agent)} \rightarrow CH_3COOH$$

2. Fehling's test. Fehling's solution A is copper(II) sulfate solution. Fehling's solution B is sodium hydroxide and sodium tartrate solution. If these are mixed with an aldehyde and heated, the aldehyde is oxidized. The copper(II) ion is reduced to copper(I) and precipitated as brick-red copper(I) oxide.

$$RCHO + 2CuSO_4 + 5NaOH \rightarrow RCOONa + Cu_2O + 2Na_2SO_4 + 3H_2O$$

3. Hydrogen addition. Adding hydrogen to aldehydes in the presence of finely divided nickel or platinum produces alcohols.

$$RCHO + H_2 \xrightarrow{\text{Ni}} RCH_2OH$$

This reaction is the reverse of the oxidation of alcohols to aldehydes.

4. Grignard reagent. Grignard reagents add to aldehydes. Then *hydrolysis* with dilute acid produces an alcohol. Here, *hydrolysis is a chemical reaction which involves bond splitting. Then hydrogen and oxygen atoms add to the free bond ends. They add in the two-to-one proportion in which they are found in water.*

Fig. 18-4. A brick-red precipitate of copper (I) oxide is evidence of a positive Fehling's test.

$$RCHO + R'MgX \rightarrow R-\overset{\overset{\displaystyle R'}{|}}{\underset{\underset{\displaystyle H}{|}}{C}}-O-Mg-X$$

$$R-\overset{\overset{\displaystyle R'}{|}}{\underset{\underset{\displaystyle H}{|}}{C}}-O-Mg-X + H_2O \rightarrow R-\overset{\overset{\displaystyle R'}{|}}{\underset{\underset{\displaystyle H}{|}}{C}}-O-H + H-O-Mg-X$$

5. Aldol condensation. Under certain conditions, one molecule of an aldehyde adds to the $\diagdown$C=O, *carbonyl,* group of a second aldehyde molecule. For example, two molecules of acetaldehyde combine and form *aldol,* from which the name of this type of reaction is derived.

acetaldehyde   acetaldehyde   aldol

Carolyn Polese

With higher aldehydes, the bonding occurs in a definite pattern. Only a hydrogen atom on the carbon atom next to the carbonyl group adds to the other aldehyde molecule.

propionaldehyde   propionaldehyde

propionaldol

KETONES

18.9 Preparation of ketones

Organic compounds containing the carbonyl group and having the general formula **RCOR'** are *ketones*.

Ketones may be prepared from alcohols which do *not* have the hydroxyl group attached to an end-carbon atom. For example, acetone, CH_3COCH_3, is prepared by the mild oxidation of 2-propanol, $CH_3CHOHCH_3$.

2-propanol   acetone

Acetone is a colorless, volatile liquid. It is widely used as a solvent in the manufacture of acetate rayon. Storage tanks for ethyne gas are loosely filled with asbestos saturated with acetone. The ethyne dissolves in the acetone and by doing so occupies less volume. This procedure increases the amount of ethyne which can safely be compressed into the tank. Acetone and other ketones are used for cleaning metals, removing stains, and for preparing synthetic organic chemicals. Acetone is a digestive product of untreated diabetics.

18.10 Reactions of ketones

1. Hydrogen addition. Hydrogen may be added to a ketone in the presence of finely divided metal catalysts. This reaction produces an alcohol with the hydroxyl group attached to the carbonyl carbon of the original ketone.

Weil

Fig. 18-5. Welding, using ethyne (acetylene) gas. The tank in which the ethyne is stored is loosely filled with asbestos saturated with acetone. The ethyne dissolves in the acetone. Thus the amount of ethyne which may be safely stored in the tank under pressure is increased.

2. *Grignard reagent.* A Grignard reagent adds to the oxygen of the carbonyl group of a ketone. Hydrolysis produces an alcohol. In this alcohol the hydroxyl group is attached to a carbon atom to which three different alkyl groups may also be bonded. This potential for bonding makes it possible to prepare a large variety of alcohols.

3. *Aldol condensation.* Two molecules of acetone react in an aldol condensation in the presence of a barium hydroxide catalyst. The product is called diacetone alcohol. It is used as a solvent in the preparation of other compounds.

acetone   acetone   diacetone alcohol

CARBOXYLIC ACIDS
AND ESTERS

18.11 Preparations of carboxylic acids

Many organic acids and their salts occur naturally. They are found in sour milk, unripe fruits, rhubarb, sorrel, and other plants. All organic acids contain the *carboxyl* group,

$$-C{\displaystyle {\stackrel{\displaystyle O}{\diagdown}}\atop{\displaystyle O-H}}$$

The general formula for a *carboxylic acid* is **RCOOH.**

1. Oxidation of alcohols or aldehydes. The oxidation of alcohols to aldehydes and of aldehydes to carboxylic acids was described in Sections 18.5 and 18.8. Pure acetic acid is produced by the catalytic oxidation of acetaldehyde. Concentrated acetic acid is a colorless liquid that is a good solvent for some organic chemicals. It is used for making cellulose acetate, a basic material of many fibers and films.

Cider vinegar is made from apple cider which has fermented to hard cider. The ethanol in hard cider is slowly oxidized by the oxygen of the air. This oxidation produces acetic acid. The reaction is catalyzed by enzymes from certain bacteria.

$$C_2H_5OH + O_2 \rightarrow CH_3COOH + H_2O$$

Vinegar contains from 4% to 6% acetic acid.

2. Formic acid. Formic acid, HCOOH, is prepared from sodium hydroxide solution and carbon monoxide under pressure. This reaction yields sodium formate, HCOONa.

$$NaOH + CO \rightarrow HCOONa$$

If sodium formate is carefully heated with sulfuric acid, formic acid distills off.

$$HCOONa + H_2SO_4 \rightarrow HCOOH + NaHSO_4$$

Formic acid is found in nature in stinging nettle plants, in the sting of bees, wasps, and hornets, and in red ants. Formic acid is used as an acidifying agent in the textile industry.

18.12 Reactions of carboxylic acids

1. Ionization. This reaction involves the one hydrogen atom bonded to an oxygen atom in the carboxyl group. This hydrogen atom ionizes in water solution, giving carboxylic acids their acid properties. The hydrogen atoms bonded to carbon atoms in these acids *never* ionize in water solution.

$$HCOOH + H_2O \rightleftharpoons H_3O^+ + HCOO^-$$

$$CH_3COOH + H_2O \rightleftharpoons H_3O^+ + CH_3COO^-$$

These equilibria yield low H_3O^+ ion concentrations. Therefore, carboxylic acids are generally weak acids.

2. *Neutralization.* An organic acid may be neutralized by a hydroxide. A salt is formed in a reaction similar to those of inorganic acids.

$$CH_3COOH + NaOH \rightarrow CH_3COONa + H_2O$$

3. *Esterification. An **ester** is produced when an acid reacts with an alcohol.* Such reactions are called *esterification reactions.* For example, ethyl acetate is the ester formed when ethanol and acetic acid react.

$$CH_3COOH + C_2H_5OH \xrightarrow{H_2SO_4} CH_3COOC_2H_5 + H_2O$$

All such reactions between acids and alcohols are reversible. Achievement of equilibrium is slow and a small amount of sulfuric acid is used as a catalyst. Experiments with alcohols containing oxygen-18 show that the oxygen of the water product comes from the acid.

18.13 Esters

It is also possible to prepare esters by the reaction of alcohols with inorganic acids. Glyceryl trinitrate, known as nitroglycerin, is an example.

$$C_3H_5(OH)_3 + 3HNO_3 \xrightarrow{H_2SO_4} C_3H_5(NO_3)_3 + 3H_2O$$

Esters give fruits their characteristic flavors and odors. Amyl acetate, $CH_3COOC_5H_{11}$, has an odor somewhat resembling bananas. As "banana oil," this ester is used as the carrier for some aluminum paints. Ethyl butyrate has an odor and flavor that resembles pineapples. Ripe pineapples contain some of this ester and smaller amounts of other esters.

Esters can be decomposed by hydrolysis into the alcohol and acid from which they were derived. This hydrolysis may occur in the presence of dilute acid or metallic hydroxide solutions.

18.14   Saponification

Fats and oils are esters of glycerol and long-carbon-chain acids. The carbon chains of the acids usually contain from 12 to 20 carbon atoms. The structure of a fat or oil may be represented as

$$RCOOCH_2$$
$$R'COOCH$$
$$R''COOCH_2$$

R, R', and R'' are saturated or unsaturated long-chain-hydrocarbon groups.

The only difference between a fat and an oil is the physical phase of each at room temperature. Oils are liquids at room temperature, while fats are solids. Long-carbon-chain acids with double bonds produce esters having lower melting points. Hence, oils usually contain more unsaturated hydrocarbon chains than those found in fats.

Saponification is the hydrolysis of a fat using a solution of a strong hydroxide. Alkaline hydrolysis produces the sodium salt of the long-chain carboxylic acid instead of the acid itself.

$$RCOOCH_2$$
$$R'COOCH + 3NaOH \rightarrow RCOONa + R'COONa + R''COONa + C_3H_5(OH)_3$$
$$R''COOCH_2$$

Soaps are generally made by hydrolyzing fats and oils with water heated to about 250° C. The water is under a pressure of about 50 atmospheres so it does not boil. The long-chain carboxylic acids thus produced are neutralized with sodium hydroxide. This neutralization yields a mixture of sodium salts which makes up soap.

If the acid chains are unsaturated, a soft soap results. Soaps with hydrocarbon chains of 10 to 12 carbon atoms are soluble in water and produce a large-bubble lather. Soaps containing hydrocarbon chains of 16 to 18 carbon atoms are less soluble in water and give a longer-lasting small-bubble lather. Soap which is a mixture of potassium salts, rather than of sodium salts, is generally more soluble in water.

QUESTIONS

Group A

1. What are the type formulas for (*a*) alkyl halides; (*b*) alcohols; (*c*) ethers; (*d*) aldehydes; (*e*) ketones; (*f*) carboxylic acids; (*g*) esters?
2. (*a*) What are the uses of carbon tetrachloride? (*b*) What precautions must be exercised in its use?
3. How do alcohols differ from inorganic hydroxides?
4. What is the effect of methanol on the human body?
5. What property of glycerol makes it useful for keeping tobacco moist?
6. Compare the action of sodium with water and with methanol.
7. How many molecules of oxygen are required for the complete combustion of one molecule of butanol?
8. How is formaldehyde used in a biology laboratory?
9. (*a*) What is Fehling's test? (*b*) What organic group gives a positive Fehling's test?
10. For what purposes is acetone used?
11. (*a*) What is cider vinegar? (*b*) How may it be prepared?
12. (*a*) Oxalic acid is a dicarboxylic acid with the structural formula

    Write equations for the step-by-step complete ionization of oxalic acid. (*b*) How many moles of potassium hydroxide are required for the complete neutralization of four moles of oxalic acid?
13. What is the source of the hydrogen and oxygen atoms of the water eliminated during an esterification reaction?
14. In what types of reactions mentioned in this chapter is sulfuric acid used as a dehydrating agent?
15. (*a*) How are fats and oils alike? (*b*) How do they differ? (*c*) Why do they differ?
16. What is *saponification?*

Group B

17. Draw structural formulas for (*a*) dichloromethane; (*b*) 1,2,3-trihydroxypropane; (*c*) diethyl ether; (*d*) formaldehyde; (*e*) diethylketone; (*f*) acetic acid; (*g*) methyl formate.
18. Write the equations for the preparation of ethyl chloride starting with (*a*) ethane; (*b*) ethene; (*c*) ethanol.
19. (*a*) How are Grignard reagents prepared? (*b*) What type of compound is prepared when a Grignard reagent reacts with an aldehyde and the intermediate product is hydrolyzed? (*c*) What type of compound is prepared when a Grignard reagent reacts with a ketone and the intermediate product is hydrolyzed?
20. Starting with methane, chlorine, and hydrogen fluoride, show how dichlorodifluoromethane is prepared.
21. Using structural formula equations, show how ethanol may be prepared from (*a*) ethene; (*b*) ethyl chloride; (*c*) sugar ($C_{12}H_{22}O_{11}$).

22. On the basis of molecular weight and boiling point, what are the comparative advantages of methanol, ethanol, and ethylene glycol as automobile antifreezes?
23. Write equations for two different methods of preparing propyl iodide starting with propyl alcohol.
24. Describe two methods by which dipropyl ether may be prepared.
25. Starting with ethyne, show how acetic acid may be prepared.
26. What ketone is prepared by the mild oxidation of 2-butanol?
27. Write a structural formula equation showing the reaction which occurs when hydrogen is catalytically added to diethyl ketone.
28. What shift in atomic arrangement occurs during an aldol condensation?
29. Write an equation showing the formation of the ester n-butyl acetate.
30. A fat has the formula $(C_{17}H_{35}COO)_3C_3H_5$. Write a balanced formula equation for its saponification with NaOH.

PROBLEMS

Group A

1. Calculate the molecular weight of dichlorodifluoromethane.
2. Sodium hydroxide solution (40.0 ml) exactly neutralizes 35.0 ml of 0.150-N formic acid solution. What is the normality of the sodium hydroxide solution?
3. How many grams of glycerol must be dissolved in 0.300 kg of water to prepare a 0.400-m solution?
4. How many grams of diprotic oxalic acid, $(COOH)_2$, are required for 1.50 liters of 0.200-N acid?

Group B

5. What is the percentage composition of sodium lauryl sulfate, $C_{12}H_{25}OSO_2ONa$?
6. A compound is analyzed and is found to contain 62.1% carbon, 10.3% hydrogen and 27.6% oxygen. (*a*) Determine the empirical formula. (*b*) If the molecular weight is 116, what is the molecular formula?
7. The hydronium ion concentration in 0.05-M acetic acid is 9.4×10^{-4} mole/liter. What is the pH of this solution?
8. What volume of ethanol must be diluted with water to prepare $50\overline{0}$ ml of 0.750-M solution? The density of ethanol is 0.789 g/ml.

19

Reaction Energy and Reaction Kinetics

19.1 Introduction

Chemists have recently developed many new analytical processes and synthesis techniques. These advances became possible because related problems in *chemical kinetics* had been solved. Chemical kinetics is a branch of chemistry that deals with

1. the sequence of steps or the pathways by which chemical reactions occur and
2. the rates at which they proceed.

Reacting particles undergo step-by-step changes as they are changed to products. These changes are known collectively as the *reaction mechanism*. Reaction rates are also called *reaction velocities*.

When chemists investigate reaction systems they seek to learn the role of energy in these processes. Every substance has a characteristic internal energy because of its structure and its physical state. Evidence of this fact comes from the knowledge that definite amounts of energy are released or absorbed when new substances are formed from reacting substances. These energy changes occur even when products and reactants are both at the same temperature. The energy change is related directly to the change in number and strengths of bonds as the reactants form products.

In the first division of this chapter we will study changes in heat energy that accompany chemical reactions. This field of study is called *thermochemistry*. Later in the chapter, we will study the modern theories of reaction pathways and reaction rates.

ENERGY OF REACTION

19.2 Heat of reaction

In most chemical reactions the energy change can be measured in terms of the heat released or absorbed during the reaction. That is, the energy change can be measured in terms of the *change in heat content* of the substances involved. Chemical reactions are usually carried out in open vessels. Volumes may change in such vessels, but pressures remain constant. The heat content of a substance under constant pressure is often called the *enthalpy* of the substance. The symbol for enthalpy (and for heat content at constant pressure) is H.

If a process is *exothermic,* the *total heat content* of the products is *lower* than that of the reactants. The products of an *endothermic* reaction must have a *higher* heat content than the reactants.

One mole of a substance has a characteristic heat content just as it has a characteristic mass. The heat content is a measure of the internal energy stored in the substance during its formation. This stored heat content cannot be measured directly. However, the *change* in heat content that occurs during chemical reaction *can* be measured. This quantity is the heat released during an exothermic change or the heat absorbed during an endothermic change. It is called *heat of reaction. The* **heat of reaction** *is the quantity of heat released or absorbed during a chemical reaction.*

The heat of reaction is measured when the final state of a system is brought to the same temperature as that of the initial state. Unless otherwise stated, the reaction is assumed to be at 25° C under standard atmospheric pressure. Further, each substance is assumed to be in its usual (standard) state at these conditions. For this reason, the phases of reactants and products should be shown along with their formulas in thermochemical equations. (A *thermochemical equation* is one which includes heat of reaction information.)

If a mixture of hydrogen and oxygen is ignited, water is formed and heat energy is released. By experiment we find the quantity of heat given up to be proportional to the quantity of water produced. No heat was supplied externally, except to ignite the mixture. Therefore, the heat content of the product water must be less than that of the reactants before ignition. The equation for this reaction is ordinarily written

$$2H_2 + O_2 \rightarrow 2H_2O$$

From this equation we may state: when 2 moles of hydrogen gas at room temperature are burned, 1 mole of oxygen gas is used and 2 moles of water vapor are formed.

Suppose the product water is brought back to room temperature (the temperature of the initial state). The reaction heat given up by the system is found to be 136.64 kcal. The thermochemical equation is then written

$$2H_2(g) + O_2(g) \rightarrow 2H_2O(l) + 136.64 \text{ kcal}$$

Here, (g) and (l) indicate gas and liquid phases respectively. When a solid phase is indicated, (s) is used.

Heats of reaction are usually expressed in terms of *kilocalories per mole* of substance. From the previous equation, the following equality can be stated:

**heat content   heat content   heat content
of 1 mole of + of ½ mole of = of 1 mole of + 68.32 kcal
hydrogen gas   oxygen gas   liquid water**

We can now write the thermochemical equation to indicate the heat of reaction in kcal/mole of product:

$$H_2(g) + \tfrac{1}{2}O_2(g) \rightarrow H_2O(l) + 68.32 \text{ kcal}$$

This equation tells us that one mole of the product (liquid) water has a heat content 68.32 kcal *lower* than that of the gaseous reactants. To decompose one mole of water and produce hydrogen and oxygen, this much energy must be supplied from an external source. The reaction is written

$$H_2O(l) + 68.32 \text{ kcal} \rightarrow H_2(g) + \tfrac{1}{2}O_2(g)$$

Here the products are 1 mole of hydrogen plus ½ mole of oxygen. Together, they have a heat content *higher* by 68.32 kcal than the 1 mole of water which is decomposed. The two reactions can be shown by a reversible equation:

$$H_2(g) + \tfrac{1}{2}O_2(g) \rightleftharpoons H_2O(l) + 68.32 \text{ kcal}$$

As stated, we symbolize the heat content of a substance by the letter H. We can represent a *change* in heat content by ΔH. The Greek letter Δ (delta) signifies "change in." The change in heat content, ΔH, during a reaction is the difference between the heat content of the products and the heat content of the reactants.

ΔH = heat content of products − heat content of reactants

In this notation scheme, the ΔH for an exothermic reaction has a *negative* sign. Thus, in the above reaction

$$\Delta H = -68.32 \text{ kcal/mole}$$

The thermochemical equation

$$H_2(g) + \tfrac{1}{2}O_2(g) \rightarrow H_2O(l) \qquad \Delta H = -68.32 \text{ kcal}$$

can also be written

$$H_2(g) + \tfrac{1}{2}O_2(g) \rightarrow H_2O(l) + 68.32 \text{ kcal}$$

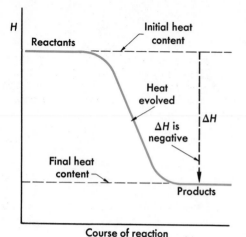

(A) Exothermic change

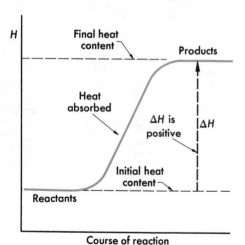

(B) Endothermic change

Fig. 19-1. Change in heat content during chemical action.

The ΔH for an endothermic reaction is signified by using a *positive* sign. This sign convention is an arbitrary one, but it is logical since the heat of reaction is said to be *negative* when the heat content of the system is *decreasing* (exothermic reaction). It is said to be *positive* when the heat content of the system is *increasing* (endothermic reaction). See Figure 19-1.

19.3 Heat of formation

Chemical reactions in which elements combine and form compounds are generally exothermic. In these composition reactions the product compounds have lower heat contents than their separate elements, the reactants. The products are also more stable than the uncombined reactants. The formation of water from hydrogen and oxygen illustrates this change in stability.

Elementary hydrogen and oxygen exist as nonpolar diatomic molecules. Water molecules are covalent structures. They are polar because they are bent molecules with an electronegativity difference between the hydrogen and oxygen atoms.

Energy was given up when the single covalent bonds of the diatomic hydrogen and oxygen molecules were formed originally. Therefore, energy is required to break these bonds if the hydrogen and oxygen atoms are to combine. On the other hand, a great deal of energy is released when the two polar bonds of the water molecule are formed. Consequently, heat is given off during the composition reaction. The heat of reaction is quite high ($\Delta H = -68.3$ kcal/mole of water formed). This high heat of reaction suggests that water molecules are more stable than hydrogen and oxygen molecules.

The heat released or absorbed in a composition reaction is a useful indicator of product stability. It is referred to as the *heat of formation* of the compound. *The heat of reaction released or absorbed when 1 mole of a compound is formed from its elements is called the* **molar heat of formation** *of the compound.* Table 19-1 gives the heats of formation of some common compounds. A more complete list is given in Table 14 of the Appendix.

The sign convention and ΔH notation we adopted for heat of reaction apply to heat of formation as well. Heat of formation is merely one category of reaction heats. To distinguish a particular reaction heat as a heat of formation, we may use the more specific notation ΔH_f. Heats of formation have negative values for exothermic composition reactions. They have positive values for endothermic composition reactions.

Observe that most of the heats of formation given in Appendix Table 14 are negative. Only a few compounds, such as hydrogen iodide and carbon disulfide, have positive heats of formation.

19.4 Stability and heat of formation

A large amount of energy is released when a compound with a high negative heat of formation is formed. The same amount of energy is required to decompose such a compound into its separate elements. This energy must be supplied to the reaction from an external source. *Such compounds are very stable.* The reactions forming them proceed spontaneously, once they start, and are usually vigorous. Carbon dioxide has a high heat of formation. The ΔH_f of carbon dioxide is -94.05 kcal per mole of gas produced.

Compounds with low positive and negative values of heats of formation are generally unstable. Hydrogen sulfide, H_2S has a heat of formation of -4.82 kcal per mole. It is not very stable and decomposes when heated. Hydrogen iodide, HI, has a low positive heat of formation, $+6.20$ kcal/mole. It is a colorless gas which decomposes somewhat when stored at room temperature. As it does, violet iodine vapor becomes visible throughout the container of the gas.

A compound with a high positive heat of formation may react or decompose explosively. For example, ethyne reacts explosively with oxygen. Nitrogen tri-iodide and mercury fulminate decompose explosively. The formation reactions of such compounds store a great deal of energy within them. Mercury fulminate, $HgC_2N_2O_3$, has a heat of formation of $+64$ kcal/mole. It is used as a detonator for explosives because of its instability.

19.5 The heat of combustion

Fuels, whether for the furnace, automobile, or rocket, are energy-rich substances. The products of their combustion are energy-poor substances. In these combustion reactions the energy yield may be very high. The products of the chemical action may be of little importance compared to the quantity of heat energy given off.

The combustion of 1 mole of pure carbon (graphite) yields 94.05 kcal of heat energy.

$$C(s) + O_2(g) \rightarrow CO_2(g) \qquad \Delta H = -94.05 \text{ kcal}$$

The heat of reaction released by the complete combustion of 1 mole of a substance is called the **heat of combustion** *of the substance.* Observe that we define the heat of combustion in terms of *1 mole of reactant.* The heat of formation on the other hand, is defined in terms of *1 mole of product.* The general ΔH notation applies to heats of combustion. However, the more specific ΔH_c notation may be used to distinguish a particular reaction heat as a heat of combustion. See Table 19-2.

In some cases, a substance cannot be formed in a rapid composition reaction directly from its elements. If so, heat of

Table 19-1

HEAT OF FORMATION

ΔH_f = heat of formation of the substance from its elements. All values of ΔH_f are expressed as kcal/mole at 25° C. Negative values of ΔH_f indicate exothermic reactions. (s) = solid, (l) = liquid, (g) = gas.

Substance	Formula	ΔH_f
ammonia (g)	NH_3	-11.04
barium nitrate (s)	$Ba(NO_3)_2$	-237.06
benzene (l)	C_6H_6	$+11.72$
calcium chloride (s)	$CaCl_2$	-190.00
carbon (diamond) (s)	C	$+0.45$
carbon (graphite) (s)	C	0.00
copper (II) sulfate (s)	$CuSO_4$	-184.00
ethyne (acetylene) (g)	C_2H_2	$+54.19$
hydrogen chloride (g)	HCl	-22.06
hydrogen oxide (water) (l)	H_2O	-68.32
mercury (II) fulminate (s)	$HgC_2N_2O_3$	$+64$
nitrogen dioxide (g)	NO_2	$+8.09$
ozone (g)	O_3	$+34.00$
sodium chloride (s)	NaCl	-98.23
sulfur dioxide (g)	SO_2	-70.96
zinc sulfate (s)	$ZnSO_4$	-233.88

formation is calculated by using the heats of reaction of a series of related reactions as illustrated below. Heats of combustion of such substances are sometimes useful in these calculations.

The products of complete combustion of many organic compounds are CO_2 and H_2O. The heats of formation of these two substances are known. Thus, the heats of formation of the organic compounds can be calculated from the following equality:

$$\begin{array}{c}\text{heat of formation}\\\text{of compound X}\end{array}=\begin{array}{c}\textbf{sum of heats of formation}\\\textbf{of products of combustion}\\\text{of compound X}\end{array}-\begin{array}{c}\text{heat of combustion}\\\text{of compound X}\end{array}$$

When carbon is burned in a limited supply of oxygen, carbon monoxide is produced. In this reaction carbon is probably first oxidized to CO_2. Some of the CO_2 may be reduced in turn to CO by hot carbon. The result is an uncertain mixture of the two gases.

$$C(s) + O_2(g) \rightarrow CO_2(g)$$

$$C(s) + CO_2(g) \rightarrow 2CO(g)$$

Because of this uncertainty, we cannot determine the heat of formation of CO by measuring directly the heat given off during the reaction. However, both carbon and carbon monoxide can be burned completely to carbon dioxide. The heat of formation of CO_2 and the heat of combustion of CO are then known (Tables 19-1 and 19-2). From these reaction heats, we can find the heat of formation of CO by using the equality stated earlier in this section.

For the combustion of carbon:

$$C(s) + O_2(g) \rightarrow CO_2(g) + 94.05 \text{ kcal}$$

Thus

$$\Delta H_f \text{ of } CO_2 = -94.05 \text{ kcal/mole}$$

For the combustion of carbon monoxide:

$$2CO(g) + O_2(g) \rightarrow 2CO_2(g) + 135.28 \text{ kcal}$$

Rewriting this equation in the form which yields 1 mole of CO_2:

$$CO(g) + \tfrac{1}{2}O_2(g) \rightarrow CO_2(g) + 67.64 \text{ kcal}$$

Thus

$$\Delta H_c \text{ of } CO = -67.64 \text{ kcal/mole}$$

But

$$\Delta H_f(CO) = \Delta H_f(CO_2) - \Delta H_c(CO)$$

Then, by substitution,

$$\Delta H_f(CO) = -94.05 \text{ kcal/mole} - (-67.64 \text{ kcal/mole})$$

$$\Delta H_f(CO) = -26.41 \text{ kcal/mole}$$

Table 19-2

HEAT OF COMBUSTION

ΔH_c = heat of combustion of the given substance. All values of ΔH_c are expressed as kcal/mole of substance oxidized to H_2O (l) and/or CO_2 (g) at constant pressure and $25°$ C. (s) = solid, (l) = liquid, (g) = gas.

Substance	Formula	ΔH_f
hydrogen (g)	H_2	−68.32
carbon (graphite) (s)	C	−94.05
carbon monoxide (g)	CO	−67.64
methane (g)	CH_4	−212.80
ethane (g)	C_2H_6	−372.82
propane (g)	C_3H_8	−530.60
butane (g)	C_4H_{10}	−687.98
pentane (g)	C_5H_{12}	−845.16
hexane (l)	C_6H_{14}	−995.01
heptane (l)	C_7H_{16}	−1151.27
octane (l)	C_8H_{18}	−1307.53
ethene (ethylene) (g)	C_2H_4	−337.23
propene (propylene) (g)	C_3H_6	−491.99
ethyne (acetylene) (g)	C_2H_2	−310.62
benzene (l)	C_6H_6	−780.98
toluene (l)	C_7H_8	−934.50

Now we know the heat of formation of CO. We can add this to the heat of combustion of CO and find the heat of formation of CO_2 as follows:

$$C(s) + \tfrac{1}{2}O_2(g) \rightarrow \cancel{CO(g)} \qquad \Delta H_f = -26.41 \text{ kcal}$$

$$\cancel{CO(g)} + \tfrac{1}{2}O_2(g) \rightarrow CO_2(g) \qquad \Delta H_c = -67.64 \text{ kcal}$$

$$C(s) + O_2(g) \rightarrow CO_2(g) \qquad \Delta H_f = -94.05 \text{ kcal}$$

We can now derive a thermochemical equation for the formation of CO directly from its elements. To do so, we employ the equations for the oxidation of carbon and the reduction of carbon dioxide as follows:

$$C(s) + O_2(g) \rightarrow \cancel{CO_2(g)} \qquad \textbf{(oxidation of C)}$$

$$C(s) + \cancel{CO_2(g)} \rightarrow 2CO(g) \qquad \textbf{(reduction of } CO_2\textbf{)}$$

$$2C(s) + O_2(g) \rightarrow 2CO(g) \qquad \textbf{(net reaction)}$$

Energy is conserved during a chemical reaction; the heat absorbed in decomposing a compound must be equal to the heat released in its formation under the same conditions. Thus, if we have reason to write the equation for a reaction in reverse form, we must reverse the sign of ΔH for the reaction.

Let us apply these principles to the thermochemical equation for the combustion of carbon monoxide:

$$CO(g) + \tfrac{1}{2}O_2(g) \rightarrow CO_2(g) \quad \Delta H_c = -67.64 \text{ kcal}$$

Writing the reverse of this reaction:

$$CO_2(g) \rightarrow CO(g) + \tfrac{1}{2}O_2(g) \quad \Delta H_c = +67.64 \text{ kcal}$$

Here we have applied the principle of reversing the sign of ΔH to express the change in heat content for a reverse action. This principle is actually part of a more general one: *The heat of a given over-all reaction is the same regardless of the intermediate steps involved.* The heat of formation of CO calculated from the following equations illustrates this additivity principle.

$$C(s) + O_2(g) \rightarrow CO_2(g) \qquad \Delta H_f = -94.05 \text{ kcal}$$

$$CO_2(g) \rightarrow CO(g) + \tfrac{1}{2}O_2(g) \qquad \Delta H_c = +67.64 \text{ kcal}$$

$$C(s) + \tfrac{1}{2}O_2(g) \rightarrow CO(g) \qquad \Delta H_f = -26.41 \text{ kcal}$$

In Section 2.15 we mentioned an endothermic reaction between carbon and steam. This "water-gas" reaction occurs spontaneously at the temperature of white-hot carbon. It produces a mixture of CO and H_2 that can be used as a gaseous fuel. What is the thermochemistry of this fuel?

The heat of formation of water is normally expressed in terms of the change in heat content between liquid water at 25° C and its separate elements at the same temperature. Water vapor

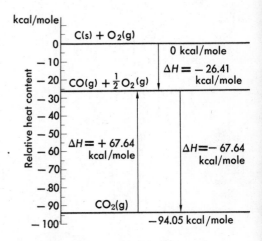

Fig. 19-2. Heat of formation diagram for carbon dioxide and carbon monoxide.

must give up 10.52 kcal/mole in order to condense to its liquid phase at 25° C. This condensation is a physical change.

$$H_2O(g) \rightarrow H_2O(l) + 10.52 \text{ kcal}$$

Thus, the steam in the reaction has a higher heat content (and a lower heat of formation) by 10.52 kcal than liquid water.

The following thermochemical equation shows the heat of formation of the product water as a gas from its composition reaction.

$$H_2(g) + \tfrac{1}{2}O_2(g) \rightarrow H_2O(g) + 57.80 \text{ kcal}$$

The complete relationship is shown by the following series of equations.

$$H_2(g) + \tfrac{1}{2}O_2(g) \rightarrow H_2O(g) \qquad \Delta H = -57.80 \text{ kcal}$$
$$\underline{H_2O(g) \rightarrow H_2O(l) \qquad \Delta H = -10.52 \text{ kcal}}$$
$$H_2(g) + \tfrac{1}{2}O_2(g) \rightarrow H_2O(l) \qquad \Delta H = -68.32 \text{ kcal}$$

Experiments have established the quantity of heat absorbed in the water-gas reaction as 31.39 kcal per mole of carbon used. The thermochemical equation is

$$H_2O(g) + C(s) + 31.39 \text{ kcal} \rightarrow CO(g) + H_2(g)$$

The heat of reaction is absorbed; the heat content of the products CO and H_2 is greater than the heat content of the reactants C and H_2O.

When the product gases are burned as fuel, two combustion reactions occur. Carbon dioxide is the product of one and water vapor is the product of the other. Both are familiar reactions shown earlier in this section.

$$CO(g) + \tfrac{1}{2}O_2(g) \rightarrow CO_2(g) + 67.64 \text{ kcal}$$

$$H_2(g) + \tfrac{1}{2}O_2(g) \rightarrow H_2O(g) + 57.80 \text{ kcal}$$

These reactions are exothermic and the heats of combustion have negative values.

We now have three thermochemical equations representing the formation of the water gas and its combustion as a fuel. Suppose we arrange these equations in a series. The net additive result is shown below.

$$H_2O(g) + C(s) \rightarrow CO(g) + H_2(g) \qquad \Delta H = +31.39 \text{ kcal}$$
$$CO(g) + \tfrac{1}{2}O_2(g) \rightarrow CO_2(g) \qquad \Delta H = -67.64 \text{ kcal}$$
$$\underline{H_2(g) + \tfrac{1}{2}O_2(g) \rightarrow H_2O(g) \qquad \Delta H = -57.80 \text{ kcal}}$$
$$C(s) + O_2(g) \rightarrow CO_2(g) \qquad \Delta H = -94.05 \text{ kcal}$$

The combined heat of combustion of CO and H_2 is -125.44 kcal. Observe that this value is higher than that of carbon (-94.05 kcal). However, it is higher only by the amount of heat energy put into the first reaction ($+31.39$ kcal).

19.6   Bond energy and reaction heat

In Section 19.1 we stated that the change in heat content of a reaction system is related to the *change in the number and strength of bonds as the system is transformed from reactants to products*. We can use the reaction for the formation of water gas to test this relationship.

The two oxygen-to-hydrogen bonds of each steam molecule must be broken. So must the carbon-to-carbon bonds of the graphite. Carbon-to-oxygen and hydrogen-to-hydrogen bonds must be formed. Energy is absorbed when bonds are broken and energy is released when bonds are formed.

Let us assume a possible reaction mechanism in which there is an intermediate stage of free atoms. This reaction mechanism is illustrated in Figure 19-3. Notice that a heat input of 390 kcal

Fig. 19-3.   A possible mechanism for the water-gas reaction.

$$C(s) + H_2O(g) + 31.4\ kcal \longrightarrow CO(g) + H_2(g)$$

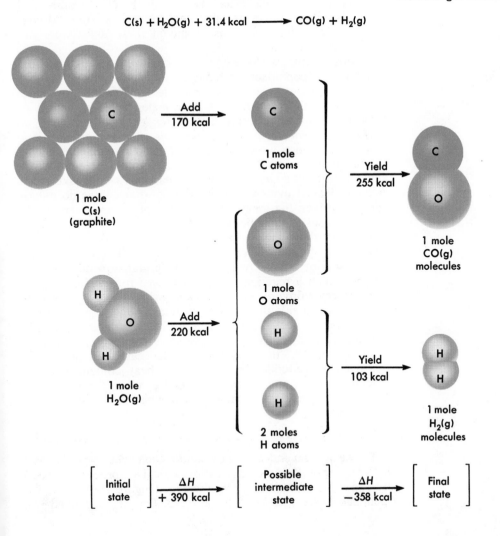

is required to break the bonds of 1 mole of graphite and 1 mole of steam. The formation of bonds in the final state releases 358 kcal of heat energy. The net effect is that 32 kcal of heat must be supplied to the system from an external source. This quantity agrees closely with the experimental value of 31.39 kcal of heat input per mole of carbon used.

19.7 The driving force of reactions

"Whether a reaction will occur" and "why a reaction does occur" are questions that have always concerned chemists. We can find complete answers to these questions only through a thorough quantitative study of reaction mechanisms and reaction kinetics. This study must be conducted within the framework of the laws of thermodynamics. Such work is in the realm of *physical chemistry*. What we can do here is examine the concepts which chemists label collectively as the "driving force" of chemical reactions. Some of these ideas were discussed briefly in Section 2.15.

By observation, we have come to recognize that most reactions which occur spontaneously in nature are exothermic. These exothermic processes give off energy and lead to lower energy states and more stable configurations. One major factor in the driving force of chemical reactions is this *tendency for processes to occur which lead to the lowest possible energy state*.

If this tendency were the only factor, no spontaneous chemical reaction could take place with absorption of energy. We could predict that only exothermic reactions would take place. A great deal of evidence shows that most reactions do release energy. In fact, the greater the quantity of energy given up, the more vigorous the reactions tend to be.

The disturbing fact is that chemical reactions *do* take place spontaneously with absorption of energy. They occur simply as a result of mixing reactants. The production of water gas involves such a reaction. Steam is passed into white-hot coke and the reaction proceeds spontaneously. It is not driven by any activity outside the reacting system. The absorption of heat has a cooling effect. Therefore, more heat must be supplied by blowing air into the coke to cause some combustion. We know from Section 19.5 that the product gases, carbon monoxide and hydrogen, have collectively a higher heat content than the reactants, steam and carbon. The energy change is positive so this unfavorable energy change cannot be the driving force of the reaction.

$$H_2O(g) + C(s) \rightarrow CO(g) + H_2(g) \qquad \Delta H = +31.39 \text{ kcal}$$

To see how an endothermic reaction can occur spontaneously, let us observe a simple physical process. This process proceeds by and of itself *with no energy change*. Figure 19-4 shows two identical flasks connected by a valve. One flask is filled with ideal gas **A** and the other with ideal gas **B**. The entire system is at room temperature.

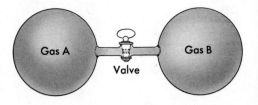

Fig. 19-4. The mixing of the gases may occur without an energy change.

When the valve is opened, the two gases mix until they are distributed evenly throughout the two containers. The gases will remain in this state indefinitely, with no tendency to separate or become unmixed. The temperature remains constant throughout the process. Thus the total heat content cannot have changed to a lower level. Clearly, the self-mixing process must be caused by a driving force other than the energy-change tendency. What, then, is the driving force for this process?

In Section 2.15, we identified *a tendency for processes to occur which lead to the highest possible state of disorder.* In general, a system that can go from one state to another without an energy change will adopt the more disordered state. The property which describes the state of disorder of a system is called *entropy.* In our example above, the final mixed system of gases represents a more disordered state than the initial pure-gas system. In other words, an entropy change has occurred. The driving force in this case was the tendency for the entropy of the system to *increase.*

Thus, the property of a system that makes the reaction go consists of two driving forces. One is a tendency toward the *lowest* energy; the other is a tendency toward the *highest* entropy. The net driving force is called the *free-energy change* of the system. Where the energy change and the entropy change oppose each other, the direction of the net driving force is determined by the larger of them.

For reactions carried out at a constant pressure and temperature, the free-energy change is

$$\Delta G = \Delta H - T\Delta S$$

Here ΔG is the change in free energy of the system, ΔH is the change in heat content, T is the temperature in °K, and ΔS is the change in entropy. (ΔG, ΔH, and the product $T\Delta S$ all have the same dimensions, usually kilocalories per mole. What are the dimensions of ΔS?)

A chemical reaction proceeds spontaneously if it is accompanied by a decrease in free energy. That is, it proceeds spontaneously if the free energy of the products is less than that of the reactants. In such a case, the *free energy change*, ΔG, in the system is *negative.*

In exothermic reactions ΔH has a negative value. In endothermic reactions its value is positive. The entropy change ΔS is positive in any change that increases entropy. It is negative for a decrease in entropy. Thus an endothermic reaction will proceed only if it involves an increase in entropy such that $T\Delta S$ is positive and larger than ΔH. Then the expression for ΔG, which is $H - T\Delta S$, will have a negative value. This is the foremost fundamental principle of chemical spontaneity: *A chemical reaction tends to proceed spontaneously in the direction of* *diminished free-energy content. This means that when the free-energy change ΔG for the reaction is negative, the reaction can occur spontaneously.*

Let us return to the water-gas reaction:

$$H_2O(g) + C(s) \rightarrow CO(g) + H_2(g)\ \Delta H = +31.39\ kcal$$

Here, a negative free-energy change would require that $T\Delta S$ be positive and greater than 31.39 kcal. This can be so if T is large, or if ΔS is large and positive, or both. Let us first look at the sign and size of ΔS.

Recall that the solid phase is well ordered and the gaseous phase is random. One of the reactants, carbon, is a solid and the other, steam, is a gas. However, both products are gases. The change from the orderly solid phase to the random gaseous phase involves an *increase* in entropy.

In general, a change from a solid to a gas will proceed with an increase in entropy. If all reactants and products are gases, an increase in the number of product particles increases entropy.

At low temperatures, whether ΔS is positive or negative, the product $T\Delta S$ may be small compared to ΔH. In such cases the reaction proceeds as the energy change predicts.

Careful measurements show that ΔS for the water-gas reaction is +0.0320 kcal/mole °K at 25° C (298° K). Thus

$$T\Delta S = 298°\ K \times 0.0320\ \frac{kcal}{mole\ °K} = 9.54\ \frac{kcal}{mole}$$

$$\Delta G = \Delta H - T\Delta S = +31.39\ \frac{kcal}{mole} - 9.54\ \frac{kcal}{mole}$$

and

$$\Delta G = +21.85\ \frac{kcal}{mole}$$

Since ΔG has a positive value, the reaction is not spontaneous at 25° C.

Increases in temperature tend to favor increases in entropy. When ΔS is positive, a high temperature gives $T\Delta S$ a large positive value. We can expect that at a high enough temperature $T\Delta S$ will be larger than ΔH and ΔG will be negative. Then the water-gas reaction will proceed spontaneously.

REACTION MECHANISMS

19.8   Reaction pathways

Chemical reactions involve breaking existing chemical bonds and forming new ones. The relationships and arrangements of atoms in the products of a reaction are different from those in the reactants. Colorless hydrogen gas consists of pairs of hydrogen atoms bonded together as diatomic molecules, H_2. Violet-colored iodine vapor is also diatomic, consisting of pairs of iodine atoms bonded together as I_2 molecules. A chemical reaction between these two gases produces hydrogen iodide, HI, a colorless gas. Hydrogen iodide molecules, in turn, tend to decompose, reforming hydrogen and iodine molecules. We may write the equations for the reactions as follows:

$$H_2(g) + I_2(g) \rightarrow 2HI(g)$$

and

$$2HI(g) \rightarrow H_2(g) + I_2(g)$$

These equations indicate only what molecular species disappear as a result of the reactions and what species are produced. They do not show the pathway along which either reaction proceeds. That is, they do not show the step-by-step sequence of reactions by which the over-all chemical change may occur. Such a sequence, when known, is called the *reaction pathway* or *reaction mechanism*.

We usually can examine a chemical system before reaction occurs or after the reaction is over. However, such an examination reveals nothing about the pathway along which the action proceeded. See Figure 19-5. For most chemical reactions, only the reactants which disappear and the final products which appear are known. In other words, only the net chemical change is directly observable.

Sometimes the chemist is able to devise experiments which reveal a sequence of steps in a reaction pathway. He attempts to learn how the speed of a reaction is affected by various factors. Such factors may include temperature, concentrations of reactants and products, and the effects of catalysts. Radioactive tracer techniques are sometimes helpful.

Very fast reactions require special methods which have been developed only recently. Among these, *flash photolysis* techniques are perhaps the most dramatic. An intense flash of light first causes a photochemical reaction in a reaction cell. A monitoring flash of light is triggered a very short time interval later. This flash produces spectra characteristic of short-lived species existing in the reaction cell at that instant. By varying the time interval of the delayed flash, the separate events that occur during the very brief time of a fast reaction can be recorded. This technique has been used to study very fast reactions in solution and in the gas phase.

A chemical reaction might occur in a single step or in a sequence of steps. Each reaction step is usually a relatively simple process. Complicated chemical reactions take place in a sequence of simple steps. Even a reaction which appears from its balanced equation to be a simple process may actually occur in a sequence of steps. As stated earlier, a balanced chemical equation reveals nothing about the reaction mechanism.

Fig. 19-5. The initial and final states of a mixture of hydrogen gas and iodine vapor which react to form hydrogen iodide gas.

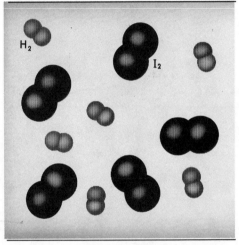

Initial state

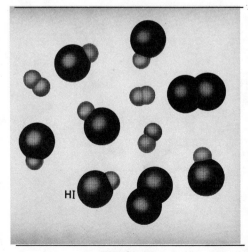

Final state

The reaction between hydrogen gas and bromine vapor which produces hydrogen bromide gas is an example of a *homogeneous reaction*. The chemical change takes place in one phase—the gas phase. This reaction system is also an example of a *homogeneous chemical system*. In such a system, all reactants and products are in the same phase. The net chemical equation for this reaction is

$$H_2(g) + Br_2(g) \rightleftarrows 2HBr(g)$$

It might appear that one hydrogen molecule reacts with one bromine molecule (a *bimolecular* reaction) and forms the product in a simple, one-step process. However, chemists have found through kinetic studies that the reaction follows a more complex pathway. The initial forward reaction (and the terminating reverse reaction) is

$$Br_2 \rightleftarrows 2Br \qquad (1)$$

This initial step provides bromine atoms. These atoms initiate a sequence of two steps which can repeat themselves.

$$Br + H_2 \rightleftarrows HBr + H \qquad (2)$$
$$H + Br_2 \rightleftarrows HBr + Br \qquad (3)$$

Observe that the sum of steps 2 and 3 gives the net reaction.
  The equation

$$H_2(g) + I_2(g) \rightleftarrows 2HI(g)$$

represents another homogeneous chemical system. For many years chemists thought that this reaction was a simple, one-step process. They assumed it involved two molecules, $H_2 + I_2$, in the forward direction and two molecules, $HI + HI$, in the reverse reaction.

  Recent experiments using flash photolysis techniques have disproved this assumption. The bimolecular reaction, $H_2 + I_2$, does not take place. Instead, two possible mechanisms have been proposed. The first has a two-step pathway:

$$I_2 \rightleftarrows 2I \qquad (1)$$
$$2I + H_2 \rightleftarrows 2HI \qquad (2)$$

The second possible mechanism has a three-step pathway:

$$I_2 \rightleftarrows 2I \qquad (1)$$
$$I + H_2 \rightleftarrows H_2I \qquad (2)$$
$$H_2I + I \rightleftarrows 2HI \qquad (3)$$

It appears that, no matter how simple the balanced equation, the reaction pathway may be complicated and difficult to determine. Some chemists feel that simple, one-step reaction mechanisms are unlikely. They suggest that the only simple reactions are those which have not been thoroughly studied.

19.9 Collision theory

In order for reactions to occur between substances, their particles (molecules, atoms, or ions) must collide. Further, these collisions must result in interactions. Chemists use this *collision theory* to interpret many facts they observe about chemical reactions.

From the kinetic theory we know that the molecules of gases are continuously in random motion. The molecules have kinetic energies ranging from very low to very high values. The energies of the greatest portion are near the average for all the molecules in the system. When the temperature of a gas is raised, the average kinetic energy of the molecules is increased. Therefore, their speed is increased. This relationship is shown in Figure 19-6.

Let us consider what happens on a molecular scale in one step of a homogeneous reaction system. A good example is the decomposition of hydrogen iodide. The reaction for the first step in the decomposition pathway is

$$HI + HI \rightarrow H_2 + 2I$$

According to the collision theory, for the two gas molecules to react, they must collide. Further, they must collide while favorably oriented and with enough energy to disrupt the bonds of the molecules. If they do so, a re-shuffling of bonds leads to the formation of the new particle species of the products.

A collision may be too gentle. Here, the distance between the colliding molecules is never small enough to disrupt old bonds or form new ones. The two molecules simply rebound from each other unchanged. This effect is illustrated in Figure 19-7(A).

Similarly, a collision in which the reactant molecules are poorly oriented has little effect. The distance between certain of the atoms is never small enough for new bonds to form. The colliding molecules rebound without changing. A poorly oriented collision is shown in Figure 19-7(B).

However, a collision may be suitably oriented and violent enough to cause an interpenetration of the electron clouds of the colliding molecules. Then the distance between the reactant particles *does* become small enough for new bonds to form. See Figure 19-7(C). The minimum energy required to produce this effective collision is called the *activation energy* for the reaction.

Thus, collision theory provides two reasons why a collision between reactant molecules may fail to produce new chemical species. (1) *The collision is not energetic enough to supply the required activation energy.* (2) *The colliding molecules are not oriented in a way that enables them to react with each other.* What then is the reaction pathway of an effective collision which produces new chemical species?

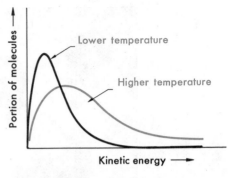

Fig. 19-6. Energy distribution among gas molecules at two different temperatures.

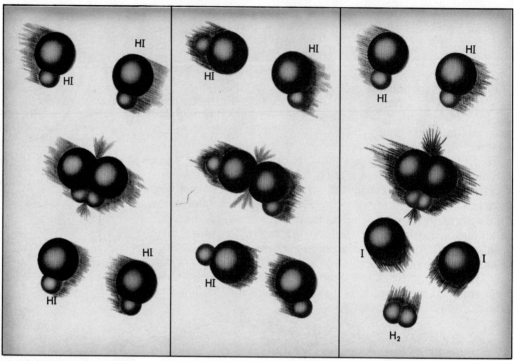

(A) Collision too gentle   (B) Collision in poor orientation   (C) Effective collision

Fig. 19-7. Possible collision patterns for HI molecules.

Fig. 19-8. A mixture of hydrogen and oxygen molecules will form very stable water molecules when properly activated.

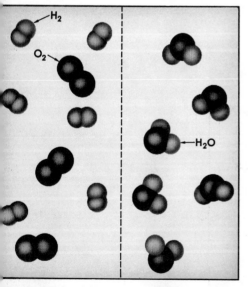

19.10 Activation energy

Let us consider the reaction for the formation of water from the diatomic gases, oxygen and hydrogen. The heat of formation is quite high; $\Delta H = -68.3$ kcal/mole at $25°$C. The free energy change is also large, ΔG_f being -56.7 kcal/mole. Why then, when hydrogen and oxygen are mixed at room temperature, do they not combine spontaneously and form water?

Hydrogen and oxygen gases exist as diatomic molecules. By some reaction mechanism, the bonds of these molecular species must be broken. Then new bonds between oxygen and hydrogen atoms must be formed. Bond-breaking is an endothermic process and bond-forming is exothermic. Even though the net process is exothermic, it appears that an initial energy "kick" is needed to start the action.

It might help to think of the reactants as lying in an energy "trough." They must be lifted from this trough before they can react and form water, even though the energy content of the product is lower than that of the reactants. Once the reaction is started, the energy released is enough to sustain the reaction by activating other molecules. Thus, the reaction rate keeps increasing. It is finally limited only by the time required for reactant particles to acquire the energy and make contact.

The energy needed to lift the reactants from the energy trough is called *activation energy*. It is the energy required to loosen bonds in molecules so they can become reactive. Energy from a flame, a spark discharge, or the energy associated with high temperatures or radiations may start reactants along the pathway of reaction. See Figure 19-9.

The reverse reaction is the decomposition of water molecules. The product water lies in an energy trough deeper than the one from which the reactants were lifted. The water molecules must be lifted from this deeper energy trough before they can decompose and form oxygen and hydrogen. The activation energy needed to start this endothermic reaction is greater than that required for the original exothermic change. The difference equals the amount of energy of reaction ΔE released in the original reaction. See Figure 19-10.

We could compare this situation to two mountain valleys separated by a high mountain pass. One valley is lower than the other. Still, to get to it from the upper valley, one must climb over the high pass. The return trip to the upper valley can be made only by climbing over the same high pass again. However, for this trip, one must climb up a greater height since the starting point is lower.

In Figure 19-11, we can compare the difference in height of the two valley floors with the energy of reaction, ΔE. Energies E_a and E_a' represent the activation energies of the forward and reverse reactions respectively. We can compare these quantities to the heights of the pass above the high and low valleys.

19.11 The activated complex

The possession of high motion (kinetic) energy does not make molecules unstable. However, when molecules collide, some of this energy is converted into internal (potential) energy within the colliding molecules. If enough energy is converted, the molecules may be activated.

When particles collide with energy at least equal to the activation energy for the species involved, their interpenetration disrupts existing bonds. New bonds can then form. In the brief interval of bond disruption and bond formation, the *collision complex* is said to be in a *transition state*. Some sort of partial bonding exists in this state. *A transitional structure results from an effective collision. This structure persists while old bonds are breaking and new bonds are forming. It is called the* **activated complex.**

An activated complex is formed when an effective collision raises the internal energies of the reactants to their *minimum-energy-for-reaction level*. See Figure 19-11. Both forward and reverse reactions go through the same activated complex. Suppose a bond is in the process of being broken in the activated complex for the forward reaction. The same bond is in the

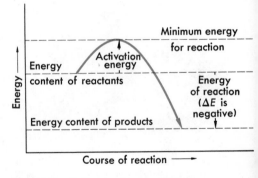

Fig. 19-9. Pathway of an exothermic reaction.

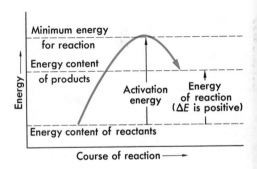

Fig. 19-10. Pathway of an endothermic reaction.

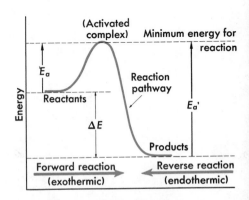

Fig. 19-11. Activation energies for the forward reaction E_a and the reverse reaction E_a', and the change in internal energy ΔE in a reversible reaction.

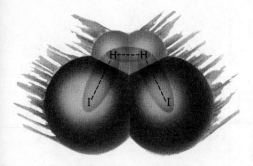

Fig. 19-12. Possible activated complex configuration which could form either 2HI or $H_2 + 2I$.

Fig. 19-13. An energy profile: experimental results of kinetic studies of hydrogen iodide decomposition.

process of being formed in the activated complex for the reverse reaction. Observe that the activated complex occurs at the maximum energy position along the reaction pathway. In this sense the activated complex defines the activation energy for the system. *Activation energy is the energy required to transform the reactants into the activated complex.*

In its brief existence, the activated complex has partial bonding of both reactant and product. In this state, it may respond to either of two possibilities. (1) It may re-form the original bonds and separate into the reactant particles. (2) It may form new bonds and separate into product particles. Usually the formation of products is just as likely as the formation of reactants. Do not confuse the activated complex with the intermediate compounds produced at different steps of a reaction mechanism. It is a molecular complex in which bonds are in the process of being broken or formed.

A possible configuration of the activated complex in the hydrogen iodide reaction is shown in Figure 19-12. The broken lines represent some sort of partial bonding in the particle. This transitional structure may produce two HI molecules or an H_2 molecule and two I atoms.

Figure 19-13 shows the energy profile for the HI decomposition. Of the 43.8 kcal activation energy, 40.8 kcal is available for excitation of the H_2 and I_2 molecules. Of this amount, 35.5 kcal is used in producing I atoms.

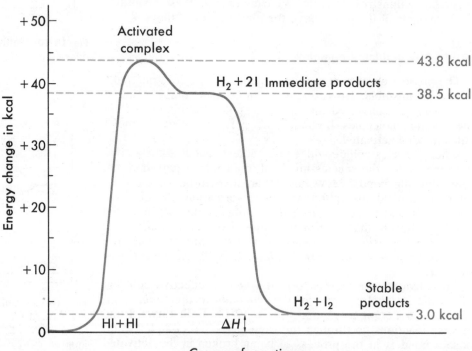

REACTION RATES

19.12 Rate influencing factors

The rates of chemical reactions vary widely. Some reactions are over in an instant, while others take months or years to complete. *The rate of reaction is measured by the amount of reactants converted to products in a unit of time.* We have seen that two conditions are necessary for reactions (other than simple decompositions) to occur at all. First, particles must come in contact. Second, this contact must result in interaction. Thus, the *rate* of a reaction depends on the *collision frequency* of the reactants and on the *collision efficiency*. (An efficient collision is one with enough energy for activation and in which the reactant molecules are favorably oriented.)

Changing conditions may affect either the frequency of collisions or the collision efficiency. Any such change influences the reaction rate. Let us consider five important factors which influence the rate of chemical reaction.

1. Nature of the reactants. Hydrogen combines vigorously with chlorine under certain conditions. Under the same conditions it may react only feebly with nitrogen. Sodium and oxygen combine much more rapidly than iron and oxygen under similar conditions. Platinum and oxygen do not combine directly. Atoms,

Fig. 19-14. Carbon burns faster in oxygen than in air because of the higher concentration of oxygen molecules.

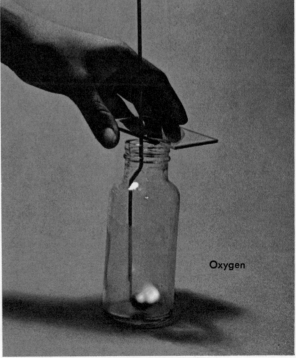

ions, and molecules are the particles of substances that react. Bonds are broken and other bonds are formed in chemical reactions. The rate of reaction depends on the particular bonds involved.

2. Amount of surface. We know that the solution rate for a crystalline solid in water is increased if the crystals are first broken down into small pieces. A cube of solute measuring 1 cm on each edge presents only 6 cm² of contact area to the solvent. This same cube when ground to a fine powder might provide a contact area 10^4 times the original area. Consequently, the solution rate of the powdered solid is greatly increased.

A lump of coal burns slowly when kindled in air. The rate of burning can be increased by breaking the lump into smaller pieces, exposing new surfaces. If the piece of coal is powdered and ignited while suspended in air, it burns explosively. Nickel in large pieces shows no noticeable oxidation in air, but finely powdered nickel reacts vigorously and spectacularly.

These reactions between solids and gases are examples of *heterogeneous reactions. Heterogeneous reactions involve reactants in two different phases or states.* Such reactions can occur only where the two phases are in contact. Thus, the amount of surface of a solid (or liquid) reactant is an important *rate* consideration. *Gases* and *dissolved* particles do not have surfaces in the sense just described. *In heterogeneous reactions the reaction rate is proportional to the area of contact of the reacting substances.*

Some chemical reactions between gases actually take place at the walls of the container. Others occur at the surface of a solid or liquid catalyst. If the products are also gases, such a reaction system presents a problem of language. It is a *heterogeneous* reaction because it takes place between two phases. On the other hand, it is a *homogeneous* chemical system because all of the reactants and all of the products are in one phase.

3. Effect of concentration. Suppose a small lump of charcoal is heated in air until combustion begins. If it is then lowered into a bottle of pure oxygen, the reaction proceeds at a much faster rate. A substance which oxidizes in air reacts more vigorously in pure oxygen. See Figure 19-14. The partial pressure of oxygen in air is approximately one-fifth of the total pressure. Pure oxygen at the same pressure as the air has five times the *concentration* of oxygen molecules.

This charcoal oxidation is a heterogeneous reaction system in which one reactant is a gas. Not only does the reaction rate depend on the amount of exposed charcoal surface; *it depends on the concentration of the gas as well.*

Homogeneous reactions may involve reactants in liquid or gaseous solutions. The concentration of gases changes with pressure according to Boyle's law. In liquid solutions, the concentration of reactants changes if either the quantity of solute or the quantity of solvent is changed. Solids and liquids are practically incompressible. Thus, it is not possible to change the concentration of pure solids and pure liquids to any measurable extent.

In homogeneous reaction systems, reaction rates depend on the concentration of the reactants. From collision theory, we might expect a rate increase if the concentration of one or more of the reactants is increased. Lowering the concentration should have the opposite effect. However, the specific effect of concentration changes in a reaction system *must be determined experimentally*.

Increasing the concentration of substance **A** in reaction with substance **B** could increase the reaction rate, decrease it, or have no effect on it. The effect depends on the particular reaction. *One cannot tell from the balanced equation for the net reaction how the reaction rate is affected by a change in concentration of reactants.* Chemists account for these differences in behavior in terms of the reaction mechanisms.

Complex chemical reactions may take place in a *series* of simple steps. Instead of a single activated complex, there may be several activated complexes in sequence along the reaction pathway. Of these steps, the one which proceeds at the slowest rate will determine the overall reaction rate. When this slowest-rate step can be identified, it is called the *rate-determining step* for the reaction.

4. Effect of temperature. The average kinetic energy of the particles of a substance is proportional to the temperature of the substance. Collision theory explains why a rise in temperature increases the rate of chemical reaction. According to this theory, a decrease in temperature lowers the reaction rate for both exothermic and endothermic reactions.

At room temperature, the rates of many reactions roughly double or triple with a 10° C rise in temperature. However, this rule must be used with caution. The actual increase in reaction rate with a given rise in temperature must be determined experimentally.

Large increases in reaction rate are caused partly by the increase in collision frequency of reactant particles. However, for chemical reaction to occur, the particles must also collide with enough energy to cause them to react. At higher temperatures more particles possess enough energy to form the activated complex when collisions occur. In other words, more particles have the necessary activation energy. Thus, a rise in temperature produces an increase in collision energy as well as collision frequency.

5. Action of catalysts. Some reactions proceed quite slowly. Frequently, the rate of such reactions can be increased greatly by the presence of *catalysts*. Catalysts are foreign substances, sometimes present in trace quantities. They do not themselves appear in the final products of the reaction.

A catalyst which is in the same phase as all the reactants and products in a reaction system is called a *homogeneous catalyst*.

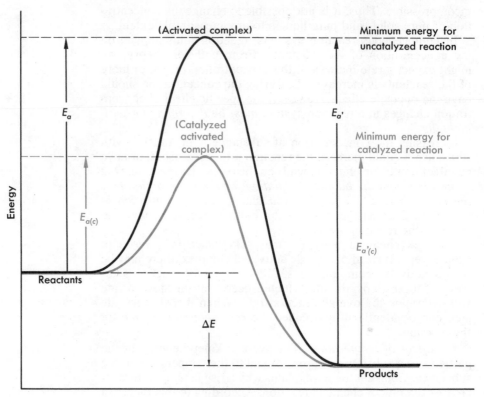

Fig. 19-15. Possible difference in potential-energy change along alternate reaction pathways, one catalyzed and the other uncatalyzed.

When the phase is different from that of the reactants, it is called a *heterogeneous catalyst*. Metals are often used in this category.

Catalytic action may be hindered by the presence of substances called *inhibitors*. Trace quantities of certain other substances may increase the activity of catalysts. These substances are called *promoters*. A catalyst that promotes one reaction may be worthless in another reaction. Catalysis plays an important role in many modern chemical processes. Nonetheless the catalytic mechanism is little understood and remains one of the challenging problems in chemistry.

It is believed that a catalyst somehow provides an alternate pathway or reaction mechanism. On this pathway, the potential energy barrier between reactants and products is lowered. It is thought that the catalyst may help to form an alternate activated complex requiring a lower activation energy. See Figure 19-15.

19.13 Reaction rate law

We have mentioned the influence of reactant concentrations on reaction rate in a given chemical system. Measuring this influence is a challenging part of kinetics. How do chemists determine the relationship between the rate of a reaction and the concentration of one reactant? First, the concentrations of other reactants and the temperature of the system are kept constant. Then the reaction rate is measured for various concentrations of the reactant in question. A series of such experiments reveals how the concentration of each reactant affects the reaction rate.

We will use the following homogeneous reaction as an illustration. It is carried out in a vessel of constant volume and at an elevated *constant* temperature.

$$2H_2(g) + 2NO(g) \rightarrow N_2(g) + 2H_2O(g)$$

Here, four moles of reactant gases produce three moles of product gases. Thus, the pressure of the system will diminish as the reaction proceeds. We can measure the rate of the reaction by measuring the change with time of the pressure in the vessel.

Suppose we conduct a series of experiments. We use the same initial concentration of nitrogen monoxide but vary the initial concentrations of hydrogen. The initial reaction rate is found to vary directly with the hydrogen concentration. That is, doubling the concentration of H_2 doubles the rate and tripling the concentration of H_2 triples the rate. Therefore,

$$R \propto [H_2]$$

Here, R is the reaction rate and $[H_2]$ is the molecular concentration of hydrogen in moles per liter. The $\propto$ is a proportionality symbol meaning "is proportional to" or "varies directly with."

Suppose we now use the same initial concentration of hydrogen but vary the initial concentrations of nitrogen monoxide. We find that the initial reaction rate increases four times when the NO concentration is doubled. It increases *nine* times when the concentration of NO is tripled. Thus, the reaction rate varies directly with the *square* of the nitrogen monoxide concentration.

$$R \propto [NO]^2$$

Since R is proportional to $[H_2]$ and to $[NO]^2$, it is proportional to their product.

$$R \propto [H_2][NO]^2$$

By introducing an appropriate proportionality constant, k, the expression becomes an equality.

$$R = k[H_2][NO]^2$$

This equation is called the *rate law* for the reaction. The proportionality constant k is the *specific rate constant*. It is constant for a specific reaction at a given temperature. A rise in temperature causes an increase in the rate of nearly all reactions. Thus, the value of k usually increases as the temperature increases.

Collision theory indicates that the number of collisions between particles increases as the concentration of these particles is raised. The reaction rate for any step in a reaction pathway is directly proportional to the frequency of collisions between the

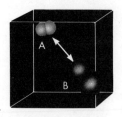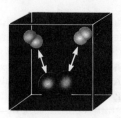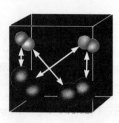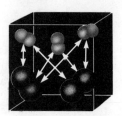

Fig. 19-16. Under constant condition, the collision frequency increases with the concentration of each reactant.

particles involved. It is also directly proportional to the collision efficiency.

Let us consider a single step in a reaction pathway. Suppose one molecule of gas **A** collides with one molecule of gas **B** and forms two molecules of substance **C**. The equation for the step is

$$A + B \rightarrow 2C$$

One particle of each reactant is involved in each collision. Thus, doubling the concentration of either reactant will double the collision frequency. It also will double the reaction rate *for this step*. Therefore, the rate is directly proportional to the concentration of **A** and of **B**. The rate law for the step becomes

$$R = k[A][B]$$

Now, suppose the reaction is reversible. In this reverse step, two molecules of **C** must collide and form one molecule of **A** and one of **B**.

$$2C \rightarrow A + B$$

Thus, the reaction rate *for this reverse step* is directly proportional to $[C] \times [C]$. The rate law for the step becomes

$$R = k[C]^2$$

A simple relationship generally exists between the chemical equation *for a step in a reaction pathway* and *the rate law for that step*. Note the *power* to which the molar concentration of each reactant or product is raised in the rate laws above. *This exponent is the same as the coefficient for the reactant or product in the balanced equation.*

Consider the reversible reaction

$$nA + mB \rightleftharpoons xC + yD$$

The *n, m, x,* and *y* are numerical coefficients in the balanced equation. By the relationship just described, the rate law for the forward step becomes

$$R_f = k_f[A]^n[B]^m$$

Similarly, the rate law for the reverse step is

$$R_r = k_r[C]^x[D]^y$$

This relationship does not *always* hold. It holds if the reaction follows a simple one-step pathway. Remember that many reactions proceed in a series of steps. In such reactions, the rate law is simply the rate law for the slowest (rate determining) step. Thus, the rate law for a reaction must be determined experimentally. It cannot be written from the balanced equation for the net reaction.

Let us return to the hydrogen-nitrogen monoxide reaction. The balanced equation for the net reaction is

$$2H_2(g) + 2NO(g) \rightarrow N_2(g) + 2H_2O(g)$$

Suppose we assume that this reaction occurs in a single step involving a collision between two H_2 molecules and two NO molecules. Doubling the concentration of either reactant would quadruple the collision frequency and the rate. The rate law would be proportional to $[H_2]^2$ as well as $[NO]^2$. It would take the form

$$R = k[H_2]^2[NO]^2$$

This equation is not in agreement with experimental results. Thus, our assumed reaction mechanism cannot be correct.

The experimental rate law for the net reaction is actually

$$R = k[H_2][NO]^2$$

Therefore, the reaction pathway must consist of more than one step. The slowest step is rate-determining. The rate law found experimentally for the net reaction is the rate expression of this step.

The general form for a rate law is

$$R = k[A]^n[B]^m\text{-----}$$

Here R is the reaction rate, k is the rate constant, and $[A]$ and $[B]$----- represent the molar concentrations of reactants. The n and m are the respective powers to which the concentrations must be raised, *based on experimental data*. Again it should be emphasized: one *cannot* assume that the coefficients in the balanced equation for a net reaction are the exponents in the rate law for the reaction.

The dependence of reaction rate on concentration of reactants was first recognized as a general principle by two Norwegian chemists, Guldberg and Waage, in 1867. It was stated as the *law of mass action: the rate of a chemical reaction is directly proportional to the product of the concentrations of reacting substances, each raised to the appropriate power.* This principle is interpreted in terms of the rate law for a chemical system in modern reaction kinetics.

QUESTIONS

Group A

1. What evidence can be cited to show that a substance has a characteristic internal energy?
2. How does the heat content of the products of a reaction system compare with the heat content of the reactants when the reaction is (a) exothermic? (b) endothermic?
3. Define the molar heat of formation of a compound.
4. Name two factors that can be identified in the driving force of chemical reactions.
5. What is the basis for assigning a negative value to the change in heat content, ΔH, in an exothermic system?
6. Changes of state in the direction of the solid state favor what kind of an entropy change?
7. What is the effect on the entropy of a system when temperature is raised?
8. Define activation energy in terms of the activated complex.
9. In a reversible reaction, how does the activation energy required for the exothermic change compare with the activation energy for the endothermic change?
10. Give two reasons why a collision between reactant molecules may not be effective in producing new chemical species.
11. To what does the term "activated complex" refer?

Group B

12. Considering the structure and physical phase of substances in a reacting system, to what is the energy change in the reaction related?
13. Using the energy profile of Figure 19-13, what is the activation energy for the reaction which produces hydrogen iodide?
14. A compound is found to have a heat of formation H_f of -87.3 kcal/mole. What is the implication regarding its stability? Explain.
15. Suppose flasks containing two different gases at room temperature are connected so that the gases mix. What kind of evidence would show that they experienced no change in energy content during the mixing?
16. How can the mixing tendency of Question 15 be explained?
17. Explain the circumstances under which an exothermic reaction does not proceed spontaneously.
18. Explain the circumstances under which an endothermic reaction is spontaneous.
19. Referring to Figure 19-11, (a) how could you justify calling the reaction pathway the minimum energy pathway for reaction? (b) What significance is associated with the maximum energy region of this minimum energy pathway?
20. The balanced equation for a homogeneous reaction between two gases shows that 4 molecules of A react with 1 molecule of B and form 2 molecules of C and 2 molecules of D. $4A + B \rightarrow 2C + 2D$. The simultaneous collision of 4 molecules of one reactant with 1 molecule of the other reactant is extremely improbable. Recognizing this, what would you assume about the nature of the reaction mechanism for this reaction system?
21. Suppose 2 moles of hydrogen gas and 1 mole of iodine vapor are passed simultaneously into a 1-liter flask. The rate law for the forward reaction is $R = k[I]^2[H_2] = k[I_2][H_2]$. What is the effect on the rate of the forward reaction if: (a) the temperature is increased; (b) 1 mole of iodine vapor is added; (c) 1 mole of hydrogen is removed; (d) the volume of the flask is reduced (assume this is possible); (e) a catalyst is introduced into the flask?

22. The decomposition of nitrogen dioxide

$$2NO_2 \rightarrow 2NO + O_2$$

occurs in a two-step sequence at elevated temperatures. The first step is

$$NO_2 \rightarrow NO + O$$

Predict a possible second step which, when combined with the first step, gives the complete reaction.

23. For each of the following reactions, predict whether the reaction, once started, is likely to proceed rapidly or slowly. State the reason for each prediction.

(a) $H_2(g) + Cl_2(g) \rightarrow 2HCl(g)$

(b) $Ag^+(aq) + Cl^-(aq) \rightarrow AgCl(s)$

(c) $Fe(chunk) + S(l) \rightarrow FeS(s)$

24. What property would you measure in order to determine the reaction rate for the following reaction? Justify your choice.

$$2NO_2(g) \rightarrow N_2O_4(g)$$

25. Ozone decomposes according to the following equation.

$$2O_3 \rightarrow 3O_2$$

The reaction proceeds in two steps. Propose a possible 2-step mechanism.

PROBLEMS

(Consult Appendix tables for essential thermochemical data.)

1. Write the thermochemical equation for the complete combustion of 1 mole of methane gas. Then calculate its heat of formation from the heat of reaction and product heats of formation data.

Group A

2. Write the thermochemical equation for the complete combustion of 1 mole of ethyne (acetylene) and calculate its heat of formation.

3. Write the thermochemical equation for the complete combustion of 1 mole of benzene and calculate its heat of formation.

4. Using heats of formation data, calculate the heat of combustion of 1 mole of hydrogen gas.

5. The concentration of reactant A changes from 0.0375 M to 0.0268 M in the reaction time interval 0.0 min − 18.0 min. What is the reaction rate during this time interval (a) per minute? (b) per second?

Group B   6. Calculate the heat of formation of $H_2SO_4(1)$ from the ΔH for the combustion of sulfur to $SO_2(g)$, the oxidation of SO_2 to $SO_3(g)$, and the solution of SO_3 in $H_2O(1)$ to give $H_2SO_4(1)$ at $25°C$.

7. Suppose the following reactants could be used to provide thrust for a rocket engine:

$$(1) \quad H_2(g) + \tfrac{1}{2}O_2(g) \rightarrow H_2O(g)$$

$$(2) \quad H_2(g) + \quad F_2(g) \rightarrow 2HF(g)$$

(a) Calculate the heat of reaction ΔH at $25°C$ for each reaction per kilogram of reactants carried aloft.

(b) Since the thrust is greater when the molecular weight of the exhaust gas is lower, which reaction would be preferred on the basis of thrust?

8. A chemical reaction is expressed by the balanced chemical equation

$$A + B \rightarrow C$$

and three reaction rate experiments yielded the following data:

Experiment number	Initial [A]	Initial [B]	Initial rate of formation of C
1	0.20 M	0.20 M	2.0×10^{-4} M/min
2	0.20 M	0.40 M	8.0×10^{-4} M/min
3	0.40 M	0.40 M	1.6×10^{-3} M/min

(a) Determine the rate law for the reaction.

(b) Calculate the value of the specific rate constant.

(c) If the initial concentrations of both A and B are 0.30 M, at what initial rate is C formed?

Chapter 20

Chemical Equilibrium

20.1 Reversible reactions

Chemists recognize that most chemical reactions may be reversible. That is, the products re-form the original reactants if conditions are suitable. Some reverse reactions occur less easily than others. For example, it requires a temperature near 3000°C to decompose water vapor into hydrogen and oxygen in measurable amounts. In some cases the conditions for the reverse reactions are not known. An example is the reaction in which potassium chlorate decomposes to oxygen and potassium chloride. Chemists do not know how to reverse this reaction in a single process.

We have seen that mercury(II) oxide decomposes when heated strongly.

$$2HgO(s) \rightarrow 2Hg(l) + O_2(g)$$

Fig. 20-1. A reversible reaction. Water vapor passed over the hot iron is reduced to hydrogen while the iron is oxidized to iron (II,III) oxide. Hydrogen passed over the hot iron oxide is oxidized to water vapor and the iron oxide is reduced to iron.

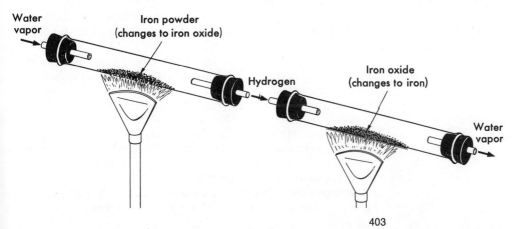

Water vapor

Iron powder
(changes to iron oxide)

Hydrogen

Iron oxide
(changes to iron)

Water vapor

However, mercury and oxygen combine and form mercury(II) oxide when heated gently.

$$2Hg(l) + O_2(g) \rightarrow 2HgO(s)$$

Suppose mercury(II) oxide is heated in a closed container from which neither the mercury nor the oxygen can escape. Once decomposition has begun, the mercury and oxygen released can recombine, forming mercury(II) oxide again. Thus both reactions proceed at the same time. Under these conditions, the rate of the composition reaction will eventually equal that of the decomposition reaction. Mercury and oxygen combine and form mercury(II) oxide just as fast as mercury(II) oxide decomposes to mercury and oxygen. We can expect the amount of mercury(II) oxide, mercury, and oxygen to remain constant as long as these conditions persist. A state of *equilibrium* has been reached between the two chemical reactions. *Both reactions continue, but there is no net change in the composition of the system.* The equilibrium may be written as

$$2HgO(s) \rightleftarrows 2Hg(l) + O_2(g)$$

Chemical equilibrium is a state of balance in which the rates of opposing reactions are exactly equal.

A reaction system in equilibrium shows equal tendencies to proceed in the forward and reverse directions. In Section 19.7 we distinguished two factors that make up the driving force for reactions. These factors were the tendency toward lower energy and the tendency toward higher entropy. At equilibrium, the driving force of the energy change is balanced by the driving force of the entropy change.

20.2 Equilibrium, a dynamic state

We have already discussed several examples of opposing processes occurring simultaneously at the same rate. The evaporation of a liquid in a closed vessel and the condensation of its saturated vapor proceed at equal rates. The equilibrium vapor pressure established is characteristic of the liquid at the prevailing temperature.

If an excess of sugar is placed in water, sugar molecules go into solution. Some of these molecules in turn separate from solution and rejoin the crystals. At saturation, molecules of sugar are crystallizing at the same rate that crystal molecules are dissolving.

The above are examples of *physical equilibria*. The opposing physical processes occur at exactly the same rate. Equilibrium is a *dynamic* state in which two opposing processes proceed simultaneously at the same rate.

Electrovalent compounds, such as sodium chloride, are completely ionized in water solution. When an excess of sodium

chloride is placed in water, a saturated solution eventually results. The saturated solution is at equilibrium. The rate of association of ions re-forming the crystal equals the rate of dissociation of ions from the crystal. This equilibrium is shown in the
ionic equation

$$Na^+Cl^-(s) \rightleftarrows Na^+(aq) + Cl^-(aq)$$

The dynamic character of this equilibrium system is easily
demonstrated. Suppose we place an irregularly shaped crystal of
sodium chloride in a saturated solution of the salt. The *shape* of
the crystal gradually changes, becoming more regular as time
passes. However, the *mass* of the crystal does not change.

Polar compounds, such as acetic acid, are very soluble in
water. Molecules of acetic acid in water solution ionize, forming
H_3O^+ and $C_2H_3O_2^-$ ions. Pairs of these ions tend to rejoin, forming acetic acid molecules in the solution. This tendency is very
strong. Even in fairly dilute solutions, equilibrium is quickly
established between un-ionized molecules in solution and their
hydrated ions. This system is an example of *ionic equilibrium*.
The ionic equilibrium of acetic acid in water solution is represented by the equation

$$HC_2H_3O_2(aq) + H_2O(l) \rightleftarrows H_3O^+(aq) + C_2H_3O_2^-(aq)$$

Many chemical reactions are reversible under ordinary conditions of temperature and concentration. They may reach a state
of equilibrium unless at least one of the substances involved
escapes or is removed. In some cases, however, the forward
reaction is nearly completed before the reverse reaction rate
becomes high enough to establish equilibrium. *Here the products of the forward reaction ($\rightarrow$) are favored.* This kind of reaction is referred to as the *reaction to the right* because the
convention for writing chemical reactions is that *left-to-right* is
forward and *right-to-left* is reverse. In other cases the forward
reaction is barely under way when the rate of the reverse reaction becomes equal to that of the forward reaction and equilibrium is established. *In these cases the products of the reverse
reaction ($\leftarrow$), the original reactants, are favored.* This kind of
reaction is referred to as the *reaction to the left.* In still other
cases, both the forward and reverse reactions occur to nearly
the same extent before chemical equilibrium is established.
*Neither reaction is favored; considerable concentrations of
both reactants and products are present at equilibrium.*

Chemical reactions are employed ordinarily to convert available reactants into more desirable products. Chemists try to
produce as much of these products as possible from the reactants used. Chemical equilibrium may seriously limit the possibilities of a seemingly useful reaction. In dealing with equilibrium systems, it is important to recognize the conditions which
influence reaction rates. Factors which determine the rate of
chemical action were discussed in Section 19.12. These are:

(1) the nature of the reactants, (2) the temperature, (3) the presence of a catalyst, (4) the surface area, and (5) the concentration of reactants.

In heterogeneous reactions, the chemical reaction takes place at the surfaces where the reactants in different phases meet. Thus, the surface area presented by solid and liquid reactants is important in rate considerations. Homogeneous reactions occur between gases and between substances dissolved in liquid solvents. Here, the concentration of each reactant is an important rate factor.

20.3   The equilibrium constant

Many chemical reactions seem likely to yield useful products. After they are started, however, they *appear* to slow down and finally stop without having run to completion. Such reactions are reversible and happen to *reach a state of equilibrium* before the reactants are completely changed into products. Both forward and reverse processes continue at the same rate. However, the concentrations of products and reactants remain constant.

The time required for reaction systems to reach equilibrium varies widely. It may be a fraction of a second or a great many years, depending on the system and the conditions. Ionic reactions in solution usually reach equilibrium very quickly.

Suppose two substances, A and B, react and form products C and D. In turn, C and D react and produce A and B. Under certain conditions equilibrium occurs in this reversible reaction. See Figure 20-2. This hypothetical equilibrium reaction is represented by the equation

$$A + B \rightleftarrows C + D$$

Initially, the concentrations of C and D are zero and those of A and B are maximum. With time, the rate of the forward reaction *decreases* as A and B are used up. Meanwhile, the rate of the reverse reaction increases as C and D are formed. As these two reaction rates become equal, equilibrium is established. The individual concentrations of A, B, C, and D undergo no further change if conditions remain the same.

At equilibrium, the ratio of the product [C] × [D] *to the product* [A] × [B] *has a definite numerical value at a given temperature.* It is known as the **equilibrium constant** of the reaction and is designated by the letter **K**. Thus,

$$\frac{[C] \times [D]}{[A] \times [B]} = K$$

Notice that the concentrations of substances on the right side of the chemical equation are given in the numerator. These substances are the *products* of the forward reaction. The concentrations of substances on the left side of the chemical equa-

Fig. 20-2. Reaction rates for the hypothetical reaction system **A + B** ⇌ **C + D.** The rate of the forward reaction is represented by curve **A + B.** Curve **C + D** represents the rate of the reverse reaction. At equilibrium the two rates are equal.

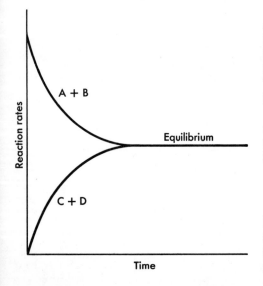

A + B

Equilibrium

C + D

Reaction rates

Time

tion are in the denominator. These substances are the *reactants* of the forward reaction. Concentrations of reactants and products are given in *moles per liter*. The constant, *K,* is independent of the initial concentrations. It is, however, dependent on the fixed temperature of the system.

The value of *K* for a given equilibrium reaction is important to the chemist. It shows him the extent to which the reactants are converted into the products of the reaction. If *K* is equal to 1, the products of the concentrations in the numerator and denominator have the same value. If the value of *K* is very small, the forward reaction occurs only very slightly before equilibrium is established. A large value of *K* indicates an equilibrium in which the original reactants are largely converted to products. The numerical value of *K* for a particular equilibrium system is obtained experimentally. The chemist must analyze the equilibrium mixture and determine the concentrations of all substances present.

Suppose the balanced equation for an equilibrium system has the general form

$$n\text{A} + m\text{B} + \text{-----} \rightleftarrows x\text{C} + y\text{D} + \text{-----}$$

The constant relationship at equilibrium (*K* for this generalized reaction system) becomes

$$K = \frac{[\text{C}]^x[\text{D}]^{y}\text{-----}}{[\text{A}]^n[\text{B}]^m\text{-----}}$$

The equilibrium constant is the ratio of the product of the concentrations of substances produced at equilibrium to the product of the concentrations of reacting substances. Each concentration is raised to the power which is the coefficient of that substance in the chemical equation. This equation for *K* is sometimes referred to as the *chemical equilibrium law* or as the *mass action expression.*

To illustrate, suppose a reaction system at equilibrium is shown by the equation

$$3\text{A} + \text{B} \rightleftarrows 2\text{C} + 3\text{D}$$

The equilibrium constant *K* is given by the expression

$$K = \frac{[\text{C}]^2[\text{D}]^3}{[\text{A}]^3[\text{B}]}$$

The reaction between H_2 and I_2 in a closed flask at elevated temperatures is easy to follow. We simply observe the rate at which the violet color of the iodine vapor diminishes. Suppose this reaction ran to completion with respect to iodine. If so, the color would disappear entirely since the product, hydrogen iodide, is a colorless gas.

However, the reaction is reversible and hydrogen iodide decomposes and re-forms hydrogen and iodine. The rate of this reverse reaction increases as the concentration of hydrogen iodide builds up. Meanwhile, the concentrations of hydrogen and iodine decrease as they are used up. The rate of the forward reaction decreases accordingly.

As the rates of the opposing reactions become equal, an equilibrium is established. A constant intensity of the violet color indicates that equilibrium has been reached among hydrogen, iodine, and hydrogen iodide. Similarly, the equilibrium state would be reached if the flask had initially contained hydrogen iodide. The net chemical equation for the system at equilibrium is

$$H_2(g) + I_2(g) \rightleftarrows 2HI(g)$$

Thus,

$$K = \frac{[HI]^2}{[H_2][I_2]}$$

Chemists have carefully measured the concentrations of H_2, I_2, and HI in equilibrium mixtures at various temperatures. In some experiments, the flasks were filled with hydrogen iodide at known pressure. The flasks were held at fixed temperatures until equilibrium was established. In other experiments, hydrogen and iodine were the substances introduced.

Experimental data together with the calculated values for K are listed in Table 20-1. Experiments 1 and 2 began with hydrogen iodide. Experiments 3 and 4 began with hydrogen and iodine. Note the close agreement obtained for numerical values of the equilibrium constant.

The equilibrium constant K for the H_2, I_2, and HI equilibrium at 425° C was established experimentally as 54.34 from the data given. This value for K should hold for any system of H_2, I_2, and HI at equilibrium *at this temperature*. If the calculation for K yields a different result, there must be a reason. Either the H_2, I_2, and HI system has not reached equilibrium or the temperature of the system is not 425° C. See the following Sample Problem.

Table 20-1

TYPICAL EQUILIBRIUM CONCENTRATIONS OF H_2, I_2, AND HI IN MOLE/LITER AT 425° C

Exp.	$[H_2]$	$[I_2]$	$[HI]$	$K = \dfrac{[HI]^2}{[H_2][I_2]}$
(1)	0.4953 X 10^{-3}	0.4953 X 10^{-3}	3.655 X 10^{-3}	54.56
(2)	1.141 X 10^{-3}	1.141 X 10^{-3}	8.410 X 10^{-3}	54.33
(3)	3.560 X 10^{-3}	1.250 X 10^{-3}	15.59 X 10^{-3}	54.62
(4)	2.252 X 10^{-3}	2.336 X 10^{-3}	16.85 X 10^{-3}	53.97
			Average	54.34

An equilibrium mixture of H_2, I_2, and HI gases at 425° C is determined to consist of 4.5647 × 10⁻³ mole/liter of H_2, 0.7378 × 10⁻³ mole/liter of I_2, and 13.544 × 10⁻³ mole/liter of HI. What is the equilibrium constant for the system at this temperature?

The balanced equation for the equilibrium system is

$$H_2(g) + I_2(g) \rightleftarrows 2HI(g)$$

$$K = \frac{[HI]^2}{[H_2][I_2]}$$

$$K = \frac{[13.544 \times 10^{-3}]^2}{[4.5647 \times 10^{-3}][0.7378 \times 10^{-3}]} = 54.46$$

This value is in close agreement with the average of the four experimental values given in Table 20-1.

The balanced chemical equation for the equilibrium system yields the expression for the equilibrium constant. The data in Table 20-1 show that this expression is an experimental fact. The equilibrium concentrations of reactants and product are determined experimentally. The values of K are calculated from these concentrations. No information concerning the kinetics of the reacting systems is required.

However, we know that an equilibrium system involves forward and reverse reactions proceeding at equal rates. Thus, the rate laws for the forward and reverse reactions should yield the same equilibrium constant as does the balanced chemical equation.

Suppose we have an equilibrium system expressed by the chemical equation

$$A_2 + B_2 \rightleftarrows 2C$$

We will assume that both forward and reverse reactions are simple, one-step processes. The rate law for the forward reaction becomes

$$R_f = k_f[A_2][B_2]$$

The rate law for the reverse reaction becomes

$$R_r = k_r[C]^2$$

At equilibrium,

$$R_f = R_r$$

Therefore,

$$k_f[A_2][B_2] = k_r[C]^2$$

Rearranging terms,

$$\frac{k_f}{k_r} = \frac{[C]^2}{[A_2][B_2]} = K$$

The expression is the same as the mass action equation derived from the balanced chemical equation (Section 20.3).

Most reaction mechanisms are complex and proceed by way of a sequence of simple steps. We know that the exponents in the rate equation for such a reaction cannot be taken from the balanced equation. They must be determined experimentally.

Let us consider an equilibrium system given by the following equation:

$$2A_2 + 2BC \rightleftarrows B_2 + 2A_2C$$

The reaction may take place in two elementary steps:

$$A_2 + 2BC \rightleftarrows B_2 + A_2C_2 \quad \text{(slow)} \quad \text{(1)}$$

$$A_2 + A_2C_2 \rightleftarrows 2A_2C \qquad\quad \text{(fast)} \quad \text{(2)}$$

Since both simple steps are reversible, each of them and the overall chemical reaction reach equilibrium at the same time. Thus, the forward and reverse reaction rates in each step are equal.

For Step 1: $R_f = k_f[A_2][BC]^2$

and $R_r = k_r[B_2][A_2C_2]$

Since $R_f = R_r$,

$$k_f[A_2][BC]^2 = k_r[B_2][A_2C_2]$$

then $K_1 = \dfrac{[B_2][A_2C_2]}{[A_2][BC]^2}$

For Step 2: $R_f = k_f[A_2][A_2C_2]$

and $R_r = k_r[A_2C]^2$

Since $R_f = R_r$,

$$k_f[A_2][A_2C_2] = k_r[A_2C]^2$$

then $K_2 = \dfrac{[A_2C]^2}{[A_2][A_2C_2]}$

Multiplying K_1 by K_2:

$$K_1 \times K_2 = \frac{[B_2][A_2C_2][A_2C]^2}{[A_2]^2[BC]^2[A_2C_2]} = K$$

Therefore, $K = \dfrac{[B_2][A_2C]^2}{[A_2]^2[BC]^2}$

This is the same expression we get by writing the mass action equation directly from the balanced chemical equation.

20.4   Factors that disturb equilibrium

In systems that have attained chemical equilibrium, opposing reactions occur at equal rates. Any change which alters the rate of either reaction *disturbs the original equilibrium*. The system then seeks a new equilibrium state. By displacing an equilibrium in the desired direction, chemists can often increase production of important industrial chemicals.

Le Chatelier's principle provides a means of predicting the influence of disturbing factors on equilibrium systems. We have already made use of this important principle on several occasions. It may be helpful at this point to re-state Le Chatelier's principle: *If a system at equilibrium is subjected to a stress, the equilibrium is displaced in the direction that relieves the stress.* This principle holds for all kinds of dynamic equilibria, physical and ionic as well as chemical. In applying Le Chatelier's principle to chemical equilibrium, we will consider three important stresses.

1. Change in concentration. From collision theory, we know that an increase in the concentration of a reactant causes an increase in collision frequency. We also know that a reaction resulting from these collisions should then proceed at a faster rate. Consider the hypothetical reaction

$$A + B \rightleftarrows C + D$$

An increase in the concentration of A will displace the equilibrium to the *right*. Both A and B will be used up faster and more of C and D will be formed. The equilibrium will be reestablished with a lower concentration of B. *The equilibrium has shifted in such direction as to reduce the stress caused by the increase in concentration.*

Similarly, an increase in the concentration of B drives the reaction to the *right*. An increase in either C or D displaces the equilibrium to the *left*. A *decrease* in the concentration of either C or D has the same effect as an *increase* in the concentration of A or B. That is, it will displace the equilibrium to the *right*.

Changes in concentration have no effect on the value of the equilibrium constant. All concentrations still give the same numerical ratio for the equilibrium constant when equilibrium is reestablished. Thus, Le Chatelier's principle leads us to the same predictions for changes in concentration as does the equilibrium constant.

2. Change in pressure. A change in pressure can affect only equilibrium systems in which *gases* are involved. According to Le Chatelier's principle, *if the pressure on an equilibrium system is increased, the reaction is driven in the direction which relieves the pressure.*

The Haber process for catalytic synthesis of ammonia from its elements illustrates the influence of pressure on an equilibrium system.

$$N_2(g) + 3H_2(g) \rightleftarrows 2NH_3(g)$$

The equation indicates that 4 molecules of the reactant gases form 2 molecules of ammonia gas. Suppose the equilibrium mixture is subjected to an increase in pressure. This pressure can be relieved by the reaction that produces fewer gas molecules and therefore a smaller volume. Thus, the stress is *lessened* by the formation of ammonia. Equilibrium is displaced toward the right. *High* pressure is desirable in this industrial process. Figure 20-3 shows the effect of pressure on this equilibrium system.

In the Haber process, the ammonia produced is continuously removed by condensation to a liquid. This condensation removes most of the product from the phase in which the reaction occurs. This change in concentration also tends to displace the equilibrium to the right.

Many chemical processes involve heterogeneous reactions in which the reactants and products are in different phases. The *concentrations* in equilibrium systems of pure substances in solid and liquid phases are not changed by adding or removing quantities of such substances. The equilibrium constant expresses a relationship between *relative* concentrations of reactants and products. Therefore, a pure substance in a condensed phase can be removed from the expression for the equilibrium constant; we simply substitute the number "1" for its concentration (which remains at unity value in the equilibrium system).

Consider the equilibrium system represented by the equation

$$CaCO_3(s) \rightleftarrows CaO(s) + CO_2(g)$$

Carbon dioxide is the only substance in the system subject to changes in concentration. Since it is a gas, the forward (decomposition) reaction is favored by a *low* pressure.

The expression for the equilibrium constant is

$$K = \frac{[CaO][CO_2]}{[CaCO_3]} = \frac{[1][CO_2]}{[1]} = [CO_2]$$

In the reaction,

$$CO(g) + H_2O(g) \rightleftarrows CO_2(g) + H_2(g)$$

there are equal numbers of molecules of gaseous reactants and gaseous products. Pressure change could not produce a shift in equilibrium. Thus, *pressure change has no effect* on this equilibrium reaction.

Obviously, an increase in pressure on confined gases has the same effect as an increase in the concentrations of these gases. We stated earlier that changes in concentration have no effect on the value of the equilibrium constant. Thus, *changes in pressure do not affect the value of the equilibrium constant.*

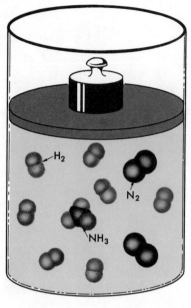

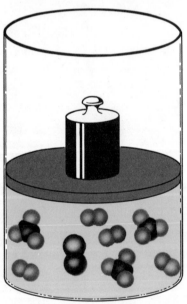

Fig. 20-3. Increased pressure results in a higher yield of ammonia since the equilibrium shifts in the direction which produces fewer molecules.

3. *Change in temperature.* Chemical reactions are either exothermic or endothermic. Reversible reactions are exothermic in one direction and endothermic in the other. The effect of changing the temperature of an equilibrium mixture depends on which of the opposing reactions is endothermic.

According to Le Chatelier's principle, *addition* of heat displaces the equilibrium so that heat is absorbed. This favors the *endothermic* reaction. The *removal* of heat favors the *exothermic* reaction. A rise in temperature increases the rate of any reaction. In an equilibrium, the rates of the opposing reactions are raised *unequally.* Thus, *the value of the equilibrium constant for a given system is affected by the temperature.*

The synthesis of ammonia is *exothermic.*

$$N_2(g) + 3H_2(g) \rightleftarrows 2NH_3(g) + 22 \text{ kcal}$$

A high temperature is not desirable as it favors the decomposition of ammonia, the *endothermic* reaction. However, at ordinary temperatures, the forward reaction is too slow to be commercially useful. The temperature used represents a compromise between kinetic and equilibrium requirements. It is high enough that equilibrium is established rapidly, but low enough that the equilibrium concentration of ammonia is significant. The reactions of the system are also accelerated by the use of a suitable catalyst. Moderate temperatures (about 500° C) and very high pressure (700-1000 atmospheres) produce satisfactory yields of ammonia.

The numerical values of equilibrium constants range from very large to very small numbers. We have found that they are independent of changes in concentrations but not of changes in

Table 20–2

EQUILIBRIUM CONSTANTS

Equilibrium system	Value of K	Temp. (°C)
$N_2(g) + 3H_2(g) \rightleftarrows 2NH_3(g)$	2.66×10^{-2}	350°
$N_2(g) + 3H_2(g) \rightleftarrows 2NH_3(g)$	6.59×10^{-3}	450°
$N_2(g) + 3H_2(g) \rightleftarrows 2NH_3(g)$	2.37×10^{-3}	727°
$2H_2(g) + S_2(g) \rightleftarrows 2H_2S(g)$	9.39×10^{-5}	477°
$H_2(g) + CO_2(g) \rightleftarrows H_2O(g) + CO(g)$	4.40	1727°
$2H_2O(g) \rightleftarrows 2H_2(g) + O_2(g)$	5.31×10^{-10}	1727°
$2CO(g) + O_2(g) \rightleftarrows 2CO_2(g)$	2.24×10^{22}	727°
$H_2(g) + I_2(g) \rightleftarrows 2HI(g)$	66.9	350°
$H_2(g) + I_2(g) \rightleftarrows 2HI(g)$	54.4	425°
$H_2(g) + I_2(g) \rightleftarrows 2HI(g)$	45.9	490°
$C(s) + CO_2(g) \rightleftarrows 2CO(g)$	14.1	1123°
$Cu(s) + 2Ag^+(aq) \rightleftarrows Cu^{++}(aq) + 2Ag(s)$	2×10^{15}	25°
$I_2(g) \rightleftarrows 2I(g)$	3.76×10^{-5}	727°
$2O_3(g) \rightleftarrows 3O_2(g)$	2.54×10^{12}	1727°
$N_2(g) \rightleftarrows 2N(g)$	1.31×10^{-31}	1000°

temperature. The addition of a catalyst accelerates both forward and reverse reactions equally. Therefore, it does not affect the value of *K*. The time required for a system to reach equilibrium may be reduced dramatically when the system is catalyzed.

Several equilibrium systems are listed in Table 20-2. The table also gives numerical values of the equilibrium constants at various temperatures. A very small *K* value means that the equilibrium mixture consists mainly of the substances on the left of the equation. If the value of *K* is large, the equilibrium mixture consists mainly of the substances on the right of the equation.

20.5   Reactions that run to completion

Many reactions are easily reversible under suitable conditions. A state of equilibrium may be established unless one or more of the products escapes or is removed. An equilibrium reaction may be driven in the preferred direction by applying Le Chatelier's principle.

Some reactions appear to go to completion in the forward direction. No one has found a method of recombining potassium chloride and oxygen directly once potassium chlorate decomposes. Sugar is decomposed into carbon and water by the application of heat. Yet no single-step method of recombining these products is known.

Many compounds are formed by the interaction of ions in solutions. If solutions of two electrolytes are mixed, two pairings of ions are possible. These pairings may or may not occur. If dilute solutions of sodium chloride and potassium bromide are mixed, no reaction occurs. The resulting solution merely contains a mixture of Na^+, K^+, Cl^-, and Br^- ions. Association of ions occurs only if enough water is evaporated to cause crystals to separate from solution. The yield is then a mixture of NaCl, KCl, NaBr, and KBr.

With some combinations of ions, reactions do occur. *Such reactions may run to completion in the sense that the ions are almost completely removed from solution.* Chemists can predict that certain ion reactions will run to completion. The extent to which the reacting ions are removed from solution depends on: (*1*) *the solubility of the compound formed* and (*2*) *the degree of ionization, if the compound is soluble.* Thus, a product which *escapes as a gas or is precipitated as a solid, or is only slightly ionized,* effectively removes the reacting ions from solution. Let us consider some specific examples of the different types of reactions that run to completion.

1.   Formation of a gas. Unstable substances formed as products of ionic reactions decompose spontaneously. An example is carbonic acid, which yields a gas as a decomposition product.

$$H_2CO_3 \rightarrow H_2O + CO_2(g)$$

Carbonic acid is produced in the reaction between sodium hydrogen carbonate and hydrochloric acid as shown by the equation

$$NaHCO_3 + HCl \rightarrow NaCl + H_2CO_3$$

The water solution of HCl contains H_3O^+ and Cl^- ions. Thus, a closer examination of the reaction mechanism suggests that the HCO_3^- ion acts as a base and acquires a proton from the H_3O^+ acid. The Na^+ and Cl^- ions are merely spectator ions in the water solution. Thus, the following equations may be more appropriate for this reaction.

$$H_3O^+ + HCO_3^- \rightarrow H_2O + H_2CO_3$$

$$H_2CO_3 \rightarrow H_2O + CO_2(g)$$

or, simply,

$$H_3O^+ + HCO_3^- \rightarrow 2H_2O + CO_2(g)$$

The reaction runs to completion because one of the products escapes as a gas. Of course, the sodium ions and chloride ions produce sodium chloride crystals when the water is evaporated.

The reaction between iron(II) sulfide and hydrochloric acid goes to completion because a gaseous product escapes. The reaction equation is

$$FeS + 2HCl \rightarrow FeCl_2 + H_2S(g)$$

The net ionic equation is

$$FeS(s) + 2H_3O^+(aq) \rightarrow Fe^{++}(aq) + H_2S(g) + 2H_2O(l)$$

The hydrogen sulfide formed is only moderately soluble and is given off as a gas. The iron(II) chloride is formed on evaporation of the water.

2. *Formation of a precipitate.* When solutions of sodium chloride and silver nitrate are mixed, a white precipitate of silver chloride immediately forms.

$$Na^+ + Cl^- + Ag^+ + NO_3^- \rightarrow Na^+ + NO_3^- + Ag^+Cl^-(s)$$

If chemically equivalent amounts of the two solutes are used, only sodium ions and nitrate ions remain in solution in appreciable amounts. The silver ions and chloride ions combine quantitatively and form a precipitate of that salt. Silver chloride is only very slightly soluble. *The reaction runs to completion because an insoluble product is formed.*

The only reaction that occurs is between the silver ions and chloride ions. Omitting the spectator ions, Na^+ and NO_3^-, the equation is rewritten simply as

$$Ag^+(aq) + Cl^-(aq) \rightarrow Ag^+Cl^-(s)$$

Crystalline sodium nitrate is recovered by evaporation of the water.

3. *Formation of a slightly ionized product.* Neutralization reactions occur between H_3O^+ ions from acids ionized in water and OH^- ions from basic solutions. Water molecules are formed in the neutralization process. A reaction between HCl and NaOH illustrates this. The water solution of HCl provides H_3O^+ ions and Cl^- ions. The water solution of NaOH supplies Na^+ ions and OH^- ions. The ionic equation is

$$H_3O^+ + Cl^- + Na^+ + OH^- \rightarrow Na^+ + Cl^- + 2H_2O$$

Neglecting the spectator ions, the net ionic equation is simply

$$H_3O^+(aq) + OH^-(aq) \rightarrow 2H_2O(l)$$

Water is only slightly ionized and exists almost entirely as covalent molecules. Thus, hydronium ions and hydroxide ions are effectively removed from the solution. *The reaction runs to completion because the product is only slightly ionized.* After the reaction between hydrochloric acid and sodium hydroxide, sodium chloride crystallizes on evaporation of the water.

20.6 Common ion effect

Suppose hydrogen chloride gas is bubbled into a saturated solution of sodium chloride. As the hydrogen chloride dissolves, sodium chloride separates as a precipitate. The mass action principle applies to this example, since chloride ions are *common* to both solutes. The concentration of chloride ions is increased, while that of sodium ions is not. As sodium chloride crystals form, the concentration of sodium ions in the solution is lowered. Thus, increasing the concentration of chloride ions has the effect of decreasing the concentration of sodium ions. *This phenomenon is known as the common ion effect.* Eventually, the rate of dissociation of sodium chloride crystals equals the rate of association of sodium and chloride ions. An equilibrium then exists:

$$Na^+Cl^-(s) \rightleftarrows Na^+(aq) + Cl^-(aq)$$

Further additions of hydrogen chloride disturb this equilibrium and drive the reaction to the *left. By forcing the reaction to the left,* more sodium chloride separates. This further reduces the concentration of the sodium ions in solution.

The common ion effect is also observed when *one* ion species of a weak electrolyte is added in excess to a solution. Acetic acid is such an electrolyte. A 0.1-M $HC_2H_3O_2$ solution is about 1.4% ionized. The ionic equilibrium is shown by the equation

$$HC_2H_3O_2 + H_2O \rightleftarrows H_3O^+ + C_2H_3O_2^-$$

Sodium acetate, an ionic salt, is completely dissociated in water solution. Small additions of sodium acetate to a solution containing acetic acid greatly increase the acetate ion concentration. The equilibrium shifts in the direction which uses acetate ions. More molecules of acetic acid are formed and the concentration of hydronium ions is reduced. In general, *the addition of a salt with an ion common to the solution of a weak electrolyte reduces the ionization of the electrolyte.* A 0.1-*M* $HC_2H_3O_2$ solution has a pH of 2.9. A solution containing 0.1-*M* concentrations of both acetic acid and sodium acetate has a pH of 4.6.

20.7 Ionization constant of a weak acid

About 1.4% of the solute molecules in a 0.1-*M* acetic acid solution are ionized at room temperature. The remaining 98.6% of the $HC_2H_3O_2$ molecules are un-ionized. Thus, the water solution contains three species of particles in equilibrium. These species are $HC_2H_3O_2$ molecules, H_3O^+ ions, and $C_2H_3O_2^-$ ions.

At equilibrium, the *rate* of the forward reaction

$$HC_2H_3O_2 + H_2O \rightarrow H_3O^+ + C_2H_3O_2^-$$

is equal to the *rate* of the reverse reaction

$$HC_2H_3O_2 + H_2O \leftarrow H_3O^+ + C_2H_3O_2^-$$

The equilibrium equation is

$$HC_2H_3O_2 + H_2O \rightleftarrows H_3O^+ + C_2H_3O_2^-$$

The equilibrium constant for this system expresses the *equilibrium ratio of ions to molecules.*

From the equilibrium equation for the ionization of acetic acid,

$$K = \frac{[H_3O^+][C_2H_3O_2^-]}{[HC_2H_3O_2][H_2O]}$$

Water molecules are greatly in excess of acetic acid molecules at the 0.1-*M* concentration. Without introducing a measurable error, we can assume that the mole concentration of H_2O molecules remains constant in such a solution. Thus, the product $K[H_2O]$ is constant.

$$K[H_2O] = \frac{[H_3O^+][C_2H_3O_2^-]}{[HC_2H_3O_2]}$$

By setting $K[H_2O] = K_a$,

$$K_a = \frac{[H_3O^+][C_2H_3O_2^-]}{[HC_2H_3O_2]}$$

In this expression, K_a is called the *ionization constant* of the weak acid. The concentration of water molecules in pure water and in dilute solutions is about 55 moles per liter. (See Section 20.8.) Therefore, the ionization constant of a weak acid, K_a, is about 55 times larger than the equilibrium constant K.

The equilibrium equation for the typical weak acid **HB** is

$$HB(aq) + H_2O(l) \rightleftharpoons H_3O^+(aq) + B^-(aq)$$

From this equation, we can write the expression for K_a in the general form

$$K_a = \frac{[H_3O^+][B^-]}{[HB]}$$

How can we determine the numerical value of the ionization constant K_a for acetic acid at a specific temperature? First we must know the equilibrium concentrations of H_3O^+ ions, $C_2H_3O_2^-$ ions, and $HC_2H_3O_2$ molecules. The ionization of a molecule of $HC_2H_3O_2$ in water yields one H_3O^+ ion and one $C_2H_3O_2^-$ ion. Therefore, these concentrations can be found experimentally by measuring the pH of the solution.

Suppose that precise measurements in an experiment show the pH of a 0.1000-M solution of acetic acid to be 2.876 at 25° C. We can determine the numerical value of K_a for $HC_2H_3O_2$ at 25° C as follows:

$$[H_3O^+] = [C_2H_3O_2^-] = 10^{-2.876} \frac{mole}{liter}$$

$$\textbf{antilog}\,(-2.876) = \textbf{antilog}\,(0.124 - 3) = 1.33 \times 10^{-3}$$

$$[H_3O^+] = [C_2H_3O_2^-] = 1.33 \times 10^{-3}$$

$$[HC_2H_3O_2] = 0.1000 - 0.00133 = 0.0987$$

$$K_a = \frac{[H_3O^+][C_2H_3O_2^-]}{[HC_2H_3O_2]}$$

$$K_a = \frac{(1.33 \times 10^{-3})^2}{9.87 \times 10^{-2}} = 1.79 \times 10^{-5}$$

Ionization data and constants for some dilute acetic acid solutions at room temperature are given in Table 20-3.

An increase in temperature causes the equilibrium to shift according to Le Chatelier's principle. Thus, K_a has a new value for each temperature. An increase in the concentration of $C_2H_3O_2^-$ ions, through the addition of $NaC_2H_3O_2$, also disturbs

Table 20-3

IONIZATION CONSTANT OF ACETIC ACID
(25° C)

Molarity	% ionized	$[H_3O^+]$	$[HC_2H_3O_2]$	K_a
0.1000	1.35	0.00135	0.09865	1.85×10^{-5}
0.0500	1.90	0.000950	0.04905	1.84×10^{-5}
0.0100	4.16	0.000416	0.009584	1.81×10^{-5}
0.0050	5.84	0.000292	0.004708	1.81×10^{-5}
0.0010	12.48	0.000125	0.000875	1.78×10^{-5}

the equilibrium. This disturbance causes a decrease in $[H_3O^+]$ and an increase in $[HC_2H_3O_2]$. Eventually the equilibrium is reestablished with the same value of K_a. However, there is a higher concentration of un-ionized acetic acid molecules and a lower concentration of H_3O^+ ions. Changes in the hydronium ion concentration and changes in pH go together. In this example, the reduction in $[H_3O^+]$ means an increase in the pH of the solution.

If the proper ions are present, the pH of a weakly acidic or alkaline solution tends to remain practically constant. It does so regardless of the addition of other ions. The concentration of hydronium ions will hardly vary in a solution of acetic acid containing a high concentration of sodium acetate. Similarly, the hydroxide ion concentration in an ammonia-water solution will remain almost constant if the solution contains a high concentration of ammonium chloride. Salts used in this way are called *buffer salts*. The solutions are said to be *buffered* against changes in pH. Such changes would otherwise occur as small quantities of acids or bases were added or removed.

Buffer action has many important applications in chemistry and physiology. Human blood is naturally buffered to maintain a pH of about 7.3. Certain physiological functions require slight variations in pH. However, large changes would lead to serious disturbances of normal body functions, or even death.

20.8 Ionization constant of water

Pure water is a very poor conductor of electricity because it is very slightly ionized. According to the modern concept of acids and bases, some water molecules donate protons, acting as an acid. Other water molecules, which accept these protons, act as a base.

$$H_2O + H_2O \rightleftharpoons H_3O^+ + OH^-$$

The degree of ionization is slight. Equilibrium is quickly established with a very low concentration of H_3O^+ and OH^- ions.

Conductivity experiments with very pure water at 25° C show that the concentrations of H_3O^+ and OH^- ions are both 10^{-7} mole per liter. The expression for the equilibrium constant is

$$K = \frac{[H_3O^+][OH^-]}{[H_2O]^2}$$

A liter of water at 25° C (see Table 11-4) contains

$$\frac{998 \text{ g}}{18.0 \text{ g/mole}} = 55.4 \text{ moles}$$

This concentration of water molecules remains practically the same in all dilute solutions.

Thus, both $[H_2O]^2$ and K in the above equilibrium expression are constants. Their product is the constant K_w, *the ion-product constant for water.* It is equal to the product of the molar concentrations of the H_3O^+ and OH^- ions.

$$K_w = [H_3O^+][OH^-]$$

At 25° C,

$$K_w = 10^{-7} \times 10^{-7} = 10^{-14}$$

The product (K_w) of the molar concentrations of H_3O^+ and OH^- has this constant value not only in pure water, but in all water solutions at 25° C. An acid solution with a pH of 4 has a $[H_3O]$ of 10^{-4} mole per liter and a $[OH^-]$ of 10^{-10} mole per liter. An alkaline solution with a pH of 8 has a $[H_3O^+]$ of 10^{-8} mole per liter and a $[OH^-]$ of 10^{-6} mole per liter.

20.9 Hydrolysis of salts

When a salt is dissolved in water, we might expect the solution to be neutral. The aqueous solutions of many salts, such as $NaCl$ and KNO_3, are neutral. *These salts are formed from strong acids and strong hydroxides;* their solutions have a pH of 7.

When other salts are dissolved in water, solutions may be produced that are not neutral; they may be either acidic or alkaline. Such salts are said to *hydrolyze* in water solution. *Hydrolysis is a reaction between water and ions of a dissolved salt.*

These are two general types of hydrolysis reactions:

1. Reactions between an anion (negative ion) base and water. Some anions, such as CO_3^{--} and $C_2H_3O_2^-$ ions, are the conjugate bases of weak acids. These anions may act as proton acceptors in water solution. Water molecules are the proton donors. The net effect is an increase in the hydroxide-ion concentration of the solution.

2. Reactions between a cation (positive ion) acid and water. Some cations contain hydrogen. Examples are the NH_4^+ ion and hydrated cations like the $Cu(H_2O)_4^{++}$ ion. Such cations may act as proton donors in water solution. Water molecules are the proton acceptors. The net effect is an increase in the hydronium-ion concentration of the solution.

20.10 Basic anion hydrolysis

This type of hydrolysis involves a salt whose cation is not an acid, but whose anion is a base. Such salts form basic solutions in water. The net reaction pattern for the basic anion B^- in water is:

$$B^-(aq) + H_2O(l) \rightleftarrows HB(aq) + OH^-(aq)$$

A basic B^- ion accepts a proton from a water molecule and forms the weak acid HB and the basic OH^- ion. This *anion hydrolysis* increases the hydroxide ion concentration $[OH^-]$ of the solution.

The equilibrium constant of a hydrolysis reaction is called the *hydrolysis constant* (K_h). From the general hydrolysis equation above, we can write the expression for K_h as

$$K_h = \frac{[HB][OH^-]}{[B^-]}$$

This hydrolysis constant K_h may be expressed in terms of the ion-product constant K_w for water and the ionization constant K_a for the weak acid.

$$K_h = \frac{K_w}{K_a}$$

We can demonstrate the validity of this expression in the following way. From Sections 20.7 and 20.8,

$$K_w = [H_3O^+][OH^-] \quad \text{and} \quad K_a = \frac{[H_3O^+][B^-]}{[HB]}$$

Thus, $\quad K_h = \dfrac{K_w}{K_a} = \dfrac{[H_3O^+][OH^-]}{\dfrac{[H_3O^+][B^-]}{[HB]}} = \dfrac{[HB][OH^-]}{[B^-]}$

Suppose we dissolve sodium carbonate in water and test the solution with litmus papers. We find that the solution turns red litmus blue. The solution contains more OH^- ions than pure water and is alkaline or basic.

Sodium ions do not react noticeably with water. Carbonate ions, CO_3^{--}, react as a base. Each accepts a proton from a water molecule and forms the slightly ionized hydrogen carbonate ion, HCO_3^-, and the OH^- ion.

$$CO_3^{--} + H_2O \rightleftarrows HCO_3^- + OH^-$$

The OH^- ion concentration builds up until equilibrium is reached. The H_3O^+ ion concentration decreases since the product $[H_3O^+][OH^-]$ remains equal to the ionization constant of water, 10^{-14}. Thus the pH is *greater* than 7 and the solution is *alkaline*. In general, *salts formed from weak acids and strong hydroxides hydrolyze in water and form alkaline solutions.*

20.11 Acid cation hydrolysis

A water solution of ammonium chloride, NH_4Cl, turns blue litmus paper red. This shows that hydrolysis occurs and the solution contains more H_3O^+ ions than does pure water. Chloride ions show no noticeable tendency to react with water in solution. The ammonium ions donate protons to water molecules.

$$NH_4^+ + H_2O \rightleftarrows H_3O^+ + NH_3$$

Equilibrium is established with an increased H_3O^+ concentration. The pH is *less* than 7 and the solution is thus *acidic*.

The metallic ions of many salts are hydrated in water solution. Such hydrated ions may donate protons to water molecules. The solution then becomes acidic. For example, aluminum chloride produces the hydrated cations

$$Al(H_2O)_6^{+++}$$

Copper(II) sulfate in water solution yields the light-blue hydrated cations

$$Cu(H_2O)_4^{++}$$

These ions react with water and produce hydronium ions as follows:

$$Al(H_2O)_6^{+++} + H_2O \rightleftarrows Al(H_2O)_5OH^{++} + H_3O^+$$

$$Cu(H_2O)_4^{++} + H_2O \rightleftarrows Cu(H_2O)_3OH^+ + H_3O^+$$

Hydrated copper(II) hydroxide is not very soluble. The scummy appearance of reagent bottles in which copper(II) salt solutions are stored for a long time is caused by the slight secondary hydrolysis of $Cu(H_2O)_3OH^+$ cations. This hydrolysis is aided by the formation of a slightly soluble product.

Cations such as $Cu(H_2O)_3OH^+$ ions may experience a secondary hydrolysis to a slight extent:

$$Cu(H_2O)_3OH^+ + H_2O \rightleftarrows Cu(H_2O)_2(OH)_2 + H_3O^+$$

Expressions for the hydrolysis constant K_h for cation acids are similar to those for anion bases. In general, *salts formed from strong acids and weak hydroxides hydrolyze in water and form acidic solutions.*

Both ions of a salt formed from a *weak acid* and a *weak base* hydrolyze extensively in water. If both ions hydrolyze equally, the solution remains neutral. Ammonium acetate is such a salt. In extreme cases, both the acid and the base are very weak indeed. In these cases, the salt may undergo complete decomposition to hydrolysis products.

When aluminum sulfide is placed in water, both a precipitate and a gas form as hydrolysis products. The reaction is

$$Al_2S_3 + 6H_2O \rightarrow 2Al(OH)_3(s) + 3H_2S(g)$$

Both products are removed from the solution and the hydrolysis therefore runs to completion.

Hydrolysis often has important effects on the properties of solutions. Sodium carbonate, washing soda, is widely used as a cleaning agent because of the alkaline properties of its water solution. Sodium hydrogen carbonate, baking soda, forms a mildly alkaline solution in water and has many practical uses. Through the study of hydrolysis we can understand why the equivalence point of a neutralization reaction (Section 15.8) may occur at a pH other than 7.

20.12 Solubility product

A *saturated* solution contains the maximum amount of solute possible at a given temperature. This solute usually exists in equilibrium with an undissolved excess of the substance. A saturated solution is *not necessarily* a concentrated solution. The concentration may be large or small, depending on solubility of the solute.

A rough rule is often used to express solubilities qualitatively. By this rule, a substance is said to be *soluble* if the solubility is greater than 1 g per 100 g of water. It is said to be *insoluble* if the solubility is less than 0.1 g per 100 g of water. Solubilities that fall between these limits are described as *slightly soluble*.

Substances usually referred to as insoluble are, in fact, very *sparingly soluble*. An extremely small quantity of such a solute saturates the solution. Equilibrium is established with the undissolved excess remaining in contact with the solution. Equilibria between sparingly soluble solids and their saturated solutions are especially important in analytical chemistry.

We have observed that silver chloride precipitates when Ag^+ and Cl^- ions are placed in the same solution. Silver chloride is so sparingly soluble in water that it is described as insoluble. The solution reaches saturation at a very small concentration of its ions. All Ag^+ and Cl^- ions in excess of this concentration eventually separate as solid AgCl.

The equilibrium principles developed in this chapter apply to all saturated solutions of sparingly soluble salts. Suppose we consider the equilibrium system in a saturated solution of silver chloride. The system contains an excess of the solid salt. The equilibrium equation is

$$AgCl(s) \rightleftarrows Ag^+(aq) + Cl^-(aq)$$

The equilibrium constant is expressed as follows:

$$K = \frac{[Ag^+][Cl^-]}{[AgCl]}$$

In Section 20.4, we stated that the concentration of a *pure* substance in the solid or liquid phase remains constant. In this equilibrium system, adding more solid AgCl would not change the *concentration* of the undissolved AgCl present. Thus, [AgCl] in the above equation is a constant. By combining the two constants we can write

$$K[AgCl] = [Ag^+][Cl^-]$$

The product, $K[AgCl]$, is also a constant. It is called the *solubility-product constant* K_{sp}.

$$K_{sp} = K[AgCl]$$

Therefore,

$$K_{sp} = [Ag^+][Cl^-]$$

Thus, the solubility-product constant K_{sp} of AgCl *is the product of the molar concentrations of its ions in a saturated solution.*

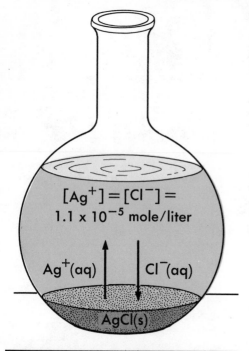

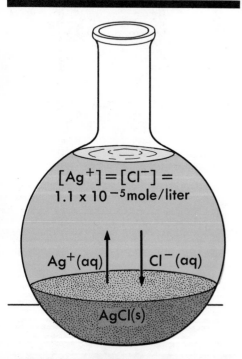

Fig. 20-4. The heterogeneous equilibrium in a saturated solution is not disturbed by the addition of more of the solid phase.

Calcium fluoride is another sparingly soluble salt. The equilibrium system in a saturated CaF_2 solution is given by the equation

$$CaF_2(s) \rightleftharpoons Ca^{++}(aq) + 2F^-(aq)$$

The solubility-product constant is given by

$$K_{sp} = [Ca^{++}][F^-]^2$$

Note how this constant differs from the solubility-product constant for AgCl. For CaF_2, K_{sp} is the product of the molar concentration of Ca^{++} ions and the molar concentration *squared* of F^- ions.

Similar equations apply to any sparingly soluble salt having the general formula M_aX_b. The equilibrium system in a saturated solution is shown by

$$M_aX_b \rightleftharpoons aM^{+b} + bX^{-a}$$

The solubility-product constant is expressed by

$$K_{sp} = [M^{+b}]^a[X^{-a}]^b$$

*The **solubility-product constant** of a substance is the product of the molar concentrations of its ions in a saturated solution, each raised to the appropriate power.*

From solubility data, Appendix Table 13, we find that 1.5×10^{-4} g of AgCl saturates 100 g of water at 20° C. We know that 1 mole of AgCl has a mass of 143.4 g. Thus, we can express the saturation concentration (solubility) of AgCl in moles per liter:

$$\frac{1.5 \times 10^{-4}\text{ g}}{10^2\text{ g}} \times \frac{10^3\text{ g}}{\text{liter}} \times \frac{\text{mole}}{1.434 \times 10^2\text{ g}} = 1.0 \times 10^{-5}\text{ mole/liter}$$

The equilibrium equation is

$$AgCl \rightleftharpoons Ag^+ + Cl^-$$

Silver chloride dissociates in solution and yields equal numbers of Ag^+ ions and Cl^- ions. Therefore, the ion concentrations in the saturated solution are

$$[Ag^+] = 1.0 \times 10^{-5}$$
$$[Cl^-] = 1.0 \times 10^{-5}$$

and

$$K_{sp} = [Ag^+][Cl^-]$$
$$K_{sp} = (1.0 \times 10^{-5})(1.0 \times 10^{-5})$$
$$K_{sp} = (1.0 \times 10^{-5})^2 = 1.0 \times 10^{-10}$$

This is the solubility-product constant of AgCl at 20° C.

The solubility of CaF_2 at 25° C is 1.7×10^{-3} g/100 g H_2O (see Appendix Table 13). Expressed in moles per liter as above, this concentration becomes 2.2×10^{-4} mole/liter.

The equilibrium equation for a saturated solution of CaF_2 is

$$CaF_2 \rightleftarrows Ca^{++} + 2F^-$$

Thus, CaF_2 dissociates in solution and yields *twice as many* F^- ions as Ca^{++} ions. The ion concentrations in the saturated solution are

$$[Ca^{++}] = 2.2 \times 10^{-4}$$
$$[F^-] = 2(2.2 \times 10^{-4})$$

and

$$K_{sp} = [Ca^{++}][F^-]^2$$
$$K_{sp} = (2.2 \times 10^{-4})(4.4 \times 10^{-4})^2$$
$$K_{sp} = (2.2 \times 10^{-4})(1.9 \times 10^{-7})$$
$$K_{sp} = 4.2 \times 10^{-11}$$

Thus, the solubility-product constant of CaF_2 is 4.2×10^{-11} at 25° C.

If the product $[Ca^{++}][F^-]^2$ is *less* than the value for K_{sp}, the solution is *unsaturated*. If the ion product is *greater* than the value for K_{sp}, CaF_2 precipitates. This precipitation reduces the concentrations of Ca^{++} and F^- ions until equilibrium is established. The solubility equilibrium is then

$$CaF_2(s) \rightleftarrows Ca^{++}(aq) + 2F^-(aq)$$

It is difficult to measure very small concentrations of a solute with precision. For this reason, solubility data from different sources may result in slightly different values of K_{sp} for a substance. Thus, calculations of K_{sp} ordinarily should be limited to two significant figures. The values of K_{sp} at 25° C for some sparingly soluble compounds are listed in Table 20-4.

20.13 Calculating solubilities

Solubility-product constants are computed from very careful measurements of solubilities and other solution properties. Once known, the solubility product is very helpful in determining the solubility of a sparingly soluble salt.

Suppose we wish to know how much barium carbonate, $BaCO_3$, can be dissolved in one liter of water at 25° C. From Table 20-4 we find that K_{sp} for $BaCO_3$ has the numerical value 4.9×10^{-9}. The solubility equation is written as follows:

$$BaCO_3(s) \rightleftarrows Ba^{++}(aq) + CO_3^{--}(aq)$$

Knowing the value for K_{sp}, we can write

$$K_{sp} = [Ba^{++}][CO_3^{--}] = 4.9 \times 10^{-9}$$

We see that $BaCO_3$ dissolves until the product of the molar concentrations of Ba^{++} and CO_3^{--} equals 4.9×10^{-9}.

Table 20–4

SOLUBILITY-PRODUCT CONSTANTS K_{sp} at 25° C

Salt	Ion product	K_{sp}
$AgC_2H_3O_2$	$[Ag^+]\,[C_2H_3O_2^-]$	2.5×10^{-3}
$AgBr$	$[Ag^+]\,[Br^-]$	4.8×10^{-13}
Ag_2CO_3	$[Ag^+]_2\,[CO_3^{--}]$	8.2×10^{-12}
$AgCl$	$[Ag^+]\,[Cl^-]$	1.2×10^{-10}
AgI	$[Ag^+]\,[I^-]$	1.5×10^{-16}
Ag_2S	$[Ag^+]^2\,[S^{--}]$	1.1×10^{-49}
$Al(OH)_3$	$[Al^{+3}]\,[OH^-]^3$	$5 \;\;\times 10^{-33}$
$BaCO_3$	$[Ba^{++}]\,[CO_3^{--}]$	4.9×10^{-9}
$BaSO_4$	$[Ba^{++}]\,[SO_4^{--}]$	1.1×10^{-10}
Bi_2S_3	$[Bi^{+++}]^2\,[S^{--}]^3$	6.8×10^{-97}
CdS	$[Cd^{++}]\,[S^{--}]$	7.8×10^{-27}
$CaCO_3$	$[Ca^{++}]\,[CO_3^{--}]$	4.8×10^{-9}
CaF_2	$[Ca^{++}]\,[F^-]^2$	4.2×10^{-11}
$Ca(OH)_2$	$[Ca^{++}]\,[OH^-]^2$	1.3×10^{-6}
$CaSO_4$	$[Ca^{++}]\,[SO_4^{--}]$	6.1×10^{-5}
CoS	$[Co^{++}]\,[S^{--}]$	8.7×10^{-23}
Co_2S_3	$[Co^{+++}]^2\,[S^{--}]^3$	2.6×10^{-124}
$CuCl$	$[Cu^+]\,[Cl^-]$	3.2×10^{-7}
Cu_2S	$[Cu^+]^2\,[S^{--}]$	1.6×10^{-48}
CuS	$[Cu^{++}]\,[S^{--}]$	8.7×10^{-36}
FeS	$[Fe^{++}]\,[S^{--}]$	4.9×10^{-18}
Fe_2S_3	$[Fe^{+++}]^2\,[S^{--}]^3$	1.4×10^{-85}
$Fe(OH)_3$	$[Fe^{+3}]\,[OH^-]^3$	1.5×10^{-36}
HgS	$[Hg^{++}]\,[S^{--}]$	$3 \;\;\times 10^{-52}$
$MgCO_3$	$[Mg^{++}]\,[CO_3^{--}]$	2.5×10^{-5}
$Mg(OH)_2$	$[Mg^{++}]\,[OH^-]^2$	1.2×10^{-11}
MnS	$[Mn^{++}]\,[S^{--}]$	5.1×10^{-15}
NiS	$[Ni^{++}]\,[S^{--}]$	1.8×10^{-21}
$PbCl_2$	$[Pb^{++}]\,[Cl^-]^2$	1.0×10^{-4}
$PbCrO_4$	$[Pb^{++}]\,[CrO_4^{--}]$	1.8×10^{-14}
$PbSO_4$	$[Pb^{++}]\,[SO_4^{--}]$	1.9×10^{-8}
PbS	$[Pb^{++}]\,[S^{--}]$	8.4×10^{-28}
SnS	$[Sn^{++}]\,[S^{--}]$	1.2×10^{-25}
$SrSO_4$	$[Sr^{++}]\,[SO_4^{--}]$	1.8×10^{-7}
ZnS	$[Zn^{++}]\,[S^{--}]$	1.1×10^{-21}

The solubility equilibrium equation shows that Ba^{++} ions and CO_3^{--} ions enter the solution in equal numbers as the salt dissolves. Thus,

$$[Ba^{++}] = [CO_3^{--}] = [BaCO_3] \text{ dissolved}$$

$$K_{sp} = 4.9 \times 10^{-9} = [BaCO_3]^2$$

$$[BaCO_3] = \sqrt{4.9 \times 10^{-9}} = \sqrt{49 \times 10^{-10}}$$

$$[BaCO_3] = 7.0 \times 10^{-5} \text{ mole/liter}$$

The solubility of $BaCO_3$ is 7.0×10^{-5} mole/liter. Thus, the solution concentration is 7.0×10^{-5} M for Ba^{++} ions and 7.0×10^{-5} M for CO_3^{--} ions.

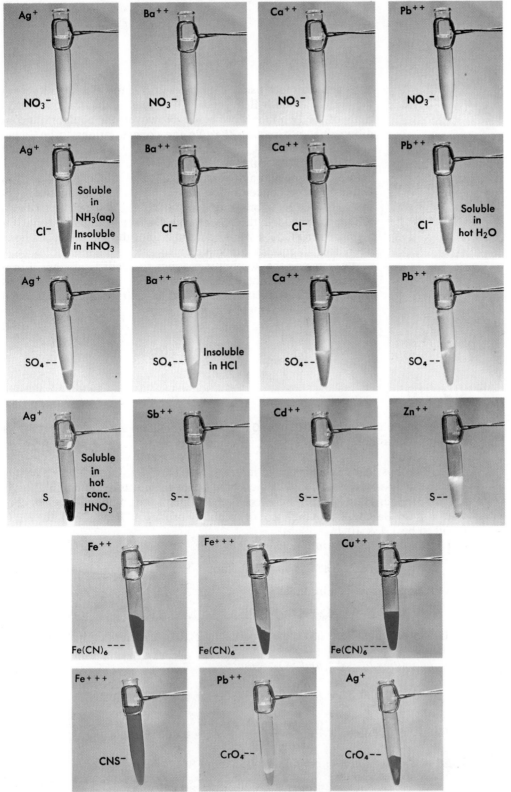

Fig. 20-5 The behavior of some negative ions in the presence of certain metallic ions.

20.14   Precipitation calculations

In the example used in Section 20.13, the $BaCO_3$ served as the source of both Ba^{++} and CO_3^{--} ions. Thus, the concentrations of the two ions were equal. However, the equilibrium condition does not require the two ion concentrations to be equal. It requires only that the *ion product* $[Ba^{++}][CO_3^{--}]$ *not* exceed the value of K_{sp} for the system.

Suppose unequal amounts of $BaCl_2$ and $CaCO_3$ are added to water. A large concentration of Ba^{++} ions and a small concentration of CO_3^{--} ions might result. If the ion product $[Ba^{++}]$ $[CO_3^{--}]$ exceeded the K_{sp} of $BaCO_3$, a precipitate of $BaCO_3$ forms. Precipitation would continue until the ion concentrations decreased to equilibrium values.

We can use the solubility product to predict whether a precipitate forms or not when two solutions are mixed. An illustration of the calculations involved in such a prediction is given in the following Sample Problem.

Sample Problem

Will a precipitate form if 20.0 ml of 0.010-M $BaCl_2$ solution are mixed with 20.0 ml of 0.0050-M Na_2SO_4 solution?

Solution

The two possible new pairings of ions are $NaCl$ and $BaSO_4$. Of these, $BaSO_4$ is a sparingly soluble salt. It will then precipitate from the resulting solution if the ion product $[Ba^{++}][SO_4^{--}]$ exceeds the value of the solubility-product constant K_{sp} for $BaSO_4$. From the table of solubility products (Table 20-4), the K_{sp} is found to be 1.1×10^{-10}.

The solubility equilibrium equation is

$$BaSO_4(s) \rightleftarrows Ba^{++}(aq) + SO_4^{--}(aq)$$

and the equilibrium condition is

$$K_{sp} = [Ba^{++}][SO_4^{--}] = 1.1 \times 10^{-10}$$

If the ion product $[Ba^{++}][SO_4^{--}]$ exceeds 1.1×10^{-10}, precipitation of $BaSO_4$ is predicted.

Mole quantities of Ba^{++} *and* SO_4^{--} *ions:*

$$0.020 \text{ liter} \times \frac{0.010 \text{ mole } Ba^{++}}{\text{liter}} = 0.00020 \text{ mole } Ba^{++}$$

$$0.020 \text{ liter} \times \frac{0.0050 \text{ mole } SO_4^{--}}{\text{liter}} = 0.00010 \text{ mole } SO_4^{--}$$

Total volume of solution containing Ba^{++} *and* SO_4^{--} *ions:*

$$0.020 \text{ liter} + 0.020 \text{ liter} = 0.040 \text{ liter}$$

Ba^{++} *and* SO$_4$$^{--}$ *ion concentrations:*

$$\frac{0.00020 \text{ mole Ba}^{++}}{0.040 \text{ liter}} = 5.0 \times 10^{-3} \text{ mole Ba}^{++}/\text{liter}$$

$$\frac{0.00010 \text{ mole SO}_4^{--}}{0.040 \text{ liter}} = 2.5 \times 10^{-3} \text{ mole SO}_4^{--}/\text{liter}$$

Trial value of ion product:

$$[\text{Ba}^{++}][\text{SO}_4^{--}] = (5.0 \times 10^{-3})(2.5 \times 10^{-3}) = 1.2 \times 10^{-5}$$

The ion product is much greater than K_{sp} ($K_{sp} = 1.1 \times 10^{-10}$), so precipitation occurs.

The solubility-product principle can be very useful when applied to solutions of sparingly soluble substances. It *cannot* be applied to solutions of moderately soluble or very soluble substances. Many solubility-product constants are known only roughly because of difficulties involved in solubility measurements. Sometimes, as with the hydrolysis of an ion in solution, it is necessary to consider two equilibria simultaneously. Finally, the solubility product is sensitive to changes in solution temperature to the extent that the solubility of the dissolved substance is affected by such changes.

QUESTIONS

Group A

1. State three examples of physical equilibrium.
2. Write the ionic equations for three examples of ionic equilibrium.
3. What is wrong with this statement? When equilibrium is reached, the opposing reactions stop.
4. State the law of mass action.
5. A combustion reaction proceeding in air under standard pressure is transferred to an atmosphere of pure oxygen under the same pressure. (*a*) What effect would you observe? (*b*) How can you account for this effect?
6. (*a*) State the principle of Le Chatelier. (*b*) To what kinds of equilibria does it apply?
7. (*a*) Name three factors which may disturb, or shift, an equilibrium. (*b*) Which of these affects the value of the equilibrium constant?
8. What are the three conditions under which ionic reactions involving ionic substances may run to completion? Write an equation for each.
9. What are the solubility characteristics of substances involved in solubility equilibrium systems?
10. Define the solubility-product constant.

Group B

11. The reaction between steam and iron is reversible. Steam passed over hot iron produces magnetic iron oxide (Fe$_3$O$_4$) and hydrogen. Hydrogen passed over hot magnetic iron oxide reduces it to iron and forms steam. Suggest a method by which this reversible reaction may be brought to a state of equilibrium.

12. What is the meaning of the term *dynamic* as applied to an equilibrium state?
13. Methanol is produced synthetically as a gas by the reaction between carbon monoxide and hydrogen, in the presence of a catalyst, according to the equilibrium reaction: $CO + 2H_2 \rightleftarrows CH_3OH + 24$ kcal. Write the expression for the equilibrium constant of this reaction.
14. How would you propose to regulate the temperature of the equilibrium mixture of CO, H_2, and CH_3OH of Question 13 in order to increase the yield of methanol? Explain.
15. How would you propose to regulate the pressure on the equilibrium mixture of Question 13 in order to increase the yield of methanol? Explain.
16. In the reaction, $A + B \rightleftarrows C$, the concentration of A, B, and C in the equilibrium mixture were found to be 2.0, 3.0, and 1.0 moles per liter respectively. What is the equilibrium constant of this reaction?
17. Write the balanced ionic equations for the following reactions in water solution. If no visible reaction takes place, write NO REACTION. Omit all *spectator* ions. Show precipitates by (s) and gases by (g). Use solubility data in the Appendix as needed. Use a separate sheet of paper. (*Do not write in this book.*)

   (a) $BaCO_3 + HNO_3 \rightarrow$ (f) $FeS + NaCl \rightarrow$
   (b) $Pb(NO_3)_2 + NaCl \rightarrow$ (g) $AgC_2H_3O_2 + HCl \rightarrow$
   (c) $CuSO_4 + HCl \rightarrow$ (h) $Na_3PO_4 + CuSO_4 \rightarrow$
   (d) $Ca_3(PO_4)_2 + NaNO_3 \rightarrow$ (i) $BaCl_2 + Na_2SO_4 \rightarrow$
   (e) $Ba(NO_3)_2 + H_2SO_4 \rightarrow$ (j) $CuO + H_2SO_4 \rightarrow$

18. Explain why the pH of a solution containing both acetic acid and sodium acetate is higher than that of a solution containing the same concentration of acetic acid alone.
19. Complete the following table, using a separate sheet of paper. *Do not write in this book.*

pH	$[H_3O^+]$ (*mole/liter*)	$[OH^-]$ (*mole/liter*)	$[H_3O^+][OH^-]$	*Property*
0				
1				
3				
5				
7	$10^{-7} = 0.0000001$	$10^{-7} = 0.0000001$	10^{-14}	Neutral
9				
11				
13				
14				

20. Referring to Table 20-2, write the expression for the equilibrium constant for each equilibrium system listed.
21. Referring to Table 20-1, explain why $[H_2] = [I_2]$ in the first two experiments.
22. What is the effect of changes in pressure on the $H_2 + I_2 \rightleftarrows 2HI$ equilibrium? Explain.

23. (a) From the development of K_a in Section 20.7, show how you would express an ionization constant K_b for the weak base NH_3. (b) In this case $K_b = 1.8 \times 10^{-5}$. What is the meaning of this numerical value?
24. Given the hydrolysis reaction $B^- + H_2O \rightleftarrows HB + OH^-$, demonstrate that $K_h = K_w/K_a$.
25. The ionization constant K_a for acetic acid is 1.8×10^{-5} at 25° C. Explain the meaning of this value.

PROBLEMS

Group A

1. The H_3O^+ ion concentration of a solution is 0.00040 mole per liter. This may be expressed as $H_3O^+ = 4.0 \times 10^{-4}$ mole per liter. What is the pH of the solution?
2. What is the pH of a 0.002-M solution of HCl? (At this concentration HCl is completely ionized.)
3. Find the pH of a 0.02-M solution of KOH.
4. Given a 250 ml volumetric flask, distilled water, and NaOH, (a) state how you would prepare 250 ml of 0.50-M NaOH solution. (b) What is the normality of the solution?
5. What quantity of copper(II) sulfate pentahydrate is required to prepare $75\overline{0}$ ml of 2.00-M solution?

Group B

6. A 0.01000-N solution of acetic acid is found to have a pH of 3.3799 at 18° C. What is the ionization constant of this weak acid?
7. Ammonia is a weak base and its water solution is slightly basic. The ionization constant for the equilibrium reaction $NH_3 + H_2O \leftrightarrows NH_4^+ + OH^-$ is $K_b = 1.8 \times 10^{-5}$. What is the pH of a 0.50-M NH_3 solution? (Note: Assume that the change in mole concentration of NH_3 at equilibrium is insignificant.)
8. It is found by experiment that 1.3×10^{-4} g AgBr dissolves in 1 liter of water and forms a saturated solution. Find K_{sp} for AgBr.
9. How many grams of $AgC_2H_3O_2$ can be dissolved in 10.0 liters of water at 25° C? (Note: The value of K_{sp} for $AgC_2H_3O_2$ can be found in Table 20-4.)
10. If 0.0015 mole of solid $Pb(NO_3)_2$ is added to one liter of 0.0015-M H_2SO_4, (a) what substance might precipitate? (b) Will the precipitate form?

Chapter 21

Oxidation-Reduction Reactions

In Section 6.5, we defined reactions which involve the loss of electrons by an atom or ion as oxidation processes. The particles that lose the electrons are said to be *oxidized*. The combustion of sodium in an atmosphere of chlorine illustrates an electron-transfer process. In this reaction, a sodium atom loses an electron to a chlorine atom and becomes a sodium ion.

The loss of an electron by a sodium atom was shown in Section 6.5 as

$$Na - e^- \rightarrow Na^+$$

This electronic equation is equivalent to

$$Na \rightarrow Na^+ + e^-$$

We will use this second form of the equation to represent oxidation processes in our study of oxidation-reduction reactions. This form is more familiar because the "$+e^-$" notation is similar to that employed for reactants and products in ordinary chemical equations.

The oxidation state of sodium has changed from the 0 state of the atom to the $+1$ state of the ion. This change in oxidation state is indicated by the oxidation numbers assigned to the atom and the ion.

$$\overset{0}{Na} \rightarrow \overset{+1}{Na^+} + e^-$$

An equally definite but less obvious oxidation process occurs when hydrogen burns in chlorine and forms hydrogen chloride. The hydrogen-chlorine bond is covalent. We may think of this

432

reaction as a process in which the hydrogen atom *merely changes the way it shares electrons* with another atom. Originally, it shared electrons with another hydrogen atom in the hydrogen molecule. Now it shares electrons with a chlorine atom in a molecule of the hydrogen chloride product.

We presented detailed rules for assigning oxidation numbers in Chapter 6. By these rules, the oxidation state of the hydrogen atom in the hydrogen molecule is zero. This zero oxidation state is true for both hydrogen atoms in the molecule. In the hydrogen chloride product, a hydrogen atom shares a pair of electrons with a chlorine atom. Chlorine atoms are more electro-negative than hydrogen atoms. Thus, the electron pair in this molecule is less attracted to the hydrogen atom than to the chlorine atom. This unequal sharing amounts to a partial transfer of electrons; it constitutes a polar covalent bond. The hydrogen atom is considered to have changed from the 0 to the +1 oxidation state. This change is an oxidation process.

How shall we regard the behavior of chlorine in these reactions with sodium and hydrogen? With sodium, the result is clear. Each chlorine atom acquires an electron from a sodium atom and becomes a chloride ion. Reactions which involve a *gain* of electrons have been defined as *reduction* processes. The particles that gain the electrons are said to be *reduced*. The oxidation state of chlorine changes from the 0 state of the chlorine atom to the -1 state of the chloride ion. For the chlorine molecule:

$$\overset{0}{Cl_2} + 2e^- \rightarrow \overset{-1}{2Cl^-}$$

The hydrogen-chlorine reaction is more obscure. The pair of electrons shared by the hydrogen and chlorine atoms is not shared equally. The electrons are more strongly attracted to the chlorine atom because of its higher electronegativity. In this sense, the chlorine atom changes from the 0 to the -1 oxidation state, a reduction process.

In this way oxidation numbers are assigned to the atoms of covalent molecular species to indicate their oxidation states. In the hydrogen chloride molecule, the oxidation number of the hydrogen atom is +1 and that of the chlorine atom is -1. The rules for assigning oxidation numbers are restated in summary form in Table 21-1.

21.2 Oxidation and reduction occur simultaneously

Clearly, one particle cannot gain electrons unless another particle loses electrons. If *oxidation* occurs during a chemical reaction, then *reduction* must occur simultaneously. Furthermore, the *amount of oxidation* that occurs must match the *amount of reduction* that occurs. For example, suppose we devise a scheme in which sodium metal is oxidized to Na^+ ions while Mg^{++} ions are reduced to magnesium metal. For the *amounts* of oxidation

---

Table 21-1

RULES FOR ASSIGNING OXIDATION NUMBERS

1. The oxidation number of an atom of a free element is zero.

2. The oxidation number of a monatomic ion is equal to its charge.

3. The algebraic sum of the oxidation numbers of the atoms in the formula of a compound is zero.

4. The oxidation number of hydrogen is +1, except in metallic hydrides where it is -1.

5. The oxidation number of oxygen is -2. A common exception is in peroxides where it is -1. (In compounds with fluorine, the oxidation number of oxygen is +2.)

6. In combinations of nonmetals, the oxidation number of the less electronegative element is positive and of the more electronegative element is negative.

7. The algebraic sum of the oxidation numbers of the atoms in the formula of a polyatomic ion is equal to its charge.

Fig. 21-1. The combustion of antimony in chlorine is an oxidation-reduction reaction.

and reduction to match, two Na^+ ions must be produced for each Mg^{++} ion that disappears.

Any chemical process in which there is a transfer of electrons, either partial or complete, is an **oxidation-reduction reaction.** This name is often shortened to *"redox" reaction.* Many of the reactions studied in elementary chemistry are oxidation-reduction reactions. In composition reactions having ionic products and in replacement reactions, the electron transfer is complete. In reactions which form polar covalent bonds, the electron transfer is not complete. In these reactions, however, we consider the *less* electronegative substance to be oxidized. The *more* electronegative substance is considered to be reduced. Few covalent bonds are completely nonpolar.

Reactions which undergo no change in oxidation state do not involve oxidation-reduction. If sodium chloride is added to a solution of silver nitrate, silver chloride precipitates.

$$Na^+ + Cl^- + Ag^+ + NO_3^- \rightarrow Na^+ + NO_3^- + Ag^+Cl^-(s)$$

Or more simply,

$$Ag^+(aq) + Cl^-(aq) \rightarrow Ag^+Cl^-(s)$$

Silver chloride is an ionic compound. Note that the charge of each ion remains the same; no electrons have been transferred. This is *not* an oxidation-reduction reaction.

Oxidation-reduction reactions sometimes involve electron transfers that are difficult to interpret. An example is the *permanganate ion* in a solution of potassium permanganate. It is a polyatomic ion with an ionic charge of -1, MnO_4^-. Under proper conditions this ion can be reduced to the *manganese(II) ion,* Mn^{++}. Under other conditions, the MnO_4^- ions can be reduced to the *manganate ion,* MnO_4^{--}.

In writing the equation for either of these reactions, we must know the number of electrons transferred. The ionic charge alone is of little help if the ion consists of two or more different elements. Assigning the proper oxidation number to each atom present simplifies the task of balancing oxidation-reduction equations. Suppose we review the assignment of oxidation numbers and their implications in the oxidation-reduction process.

Loss of electrons produces a more *positive* oxidation state, and gain of electrons produces a more *negative* oxidation state. The oxidation state of an atom of an element is 0. This statement holds true whether the atom exists as a free single atom or as one of several in a molecule of the element. We have already seen that the oxidation state is 0 for hydrogen in the molecule H_2. It is also 0 for hydrogen in the gaseous atom H. In the same way, the oxidation state of sulfur is 0 in S, S_2, S_4, S_6, and S_8, all of which exist. All atoms in their elemental form have oxidation numbers of 0. These may be written as: $\overset{0}{Na}$, $\overset{0}{K}$, $\overset{0}{Cu}$, $\overset{0}{H_2}$, and $\overset{0}{N_2}$.

In the following electronic equations, the substances on the left are oxidized.

$$\overset{0}{Na} \rightarrow \overset{+1}{Na^+} + e^-$$
$$\overset{0}{Fe} \rightarrow \overset{+2}{Fe^{++}} + 2e^-$$
$$\overset{+2}{Fe^{++}} \rightarrow \overset{+3}{Fe^{+++}} + e^-$$
$$2\overset{-1}{Cl^-} \rightarrow \overset{0}{Cl_2} + 2e^-$$

The number above each symbol is the oxidation number of that particle. (Ionic charges are shown as right superscripts where appropriate.) The difference between oxidation numbers indicates the number of electrons lost by each atom or ion. Observe that the chloride ion has the oxidation number −1. This is a *negative* oxidation state. *Oxidation results in an algebraic increase in the oxidation number of a substance.* A change from −1 to 0 is an algebraic increase in oxidation number; so is a change from 0 to +1, or +1 to +2. Each of these changes accompanies the loss of 1 electron.

In the electronic equations which follow, the substances on the left are reduced.

$$\overset{+1}{Na^+} + e^- \rightarrow \overset{0}{Na}$$
$$\overset{0}{Cl_2} + 2e^- \rightarrow 2\overset{-1}{Cl^-}$$
$$\overset{+3}{Fe^{+++}} + e^- \rightarrow \overset{+2}{Fe^{++}}$$
$$\overset{+2}{Cu^{++}} + 2e^- \rightarrow \overset{0}{Cu}$$
$$\overset{0}{Br_2} + 2e^- \rightarrow 2\overset{-1}{Br^-}$$

The third equation represents the reduction of the iron(III) ion, oxidation number +3. It is reduced to the iron(II) state, oxidation number +2. Two more electrons would be needed to complete the reduction of the iron(II) ion to the iron atom with oxidation number 0. *Reduction results in an algebraic decrease in the oxidation number of a substance.*

The oxidation state of each monatomic ion in a binary salt is the same as the ionic charge. In binary covalent compounds, shared electrons are arbitrarily assigned to the more electronegative element.

In the two compounds, H_2SO_4 and H_2SO_3, oxygen is given the oxidation number −2 and hydrogen +1. In the H_2SO_4 molecule the total contribution of the 4 atoms of oxygen is 4 times −2, or −8. The total contribution of the 2 atoms of hydrogen is $2(+1) = +2$. The H_2SO_4 molecule is neutral. Therefore, the oxidation number of the single sulfur atom is +6. We can now write the proper oxidation number near each symbol in the formula. (The numbers are usually placed *above* the symbols. In this way, they are not mistaken for ionic charges. This prac-

Fig. 21-2. The displacement of the copper(II) ion by zinc, which happens when a clean strip of zinc is placed in a solution of copper(II) sulfate, is a good example of a spontaneous oxidation-reduction reaction.

Zinc

Layer of copper

$CuSO_4$ solution

tice also prevents undue spreading of the formula in a long equation.)

$$\overset{+1\ +6\ -2}{H_2S\ O_4}$$

$$2(+1) + 1(+6) + 4(-2) = 0$$

In the sulfurous acid molecule, H_2SO_3, the total contribution of oxygen is $3(-2) = -6$. For the hydrogen, it is $2(+1) = +2$. Thus, the oxidation number of the single atom of sulfur must be $+4$.

$$\overset{+1\ +4\ -2}{H_2S\ O_3}$$

$$2(+1) + 1(+4) + 3(-2) = 0$$

This assignment of oxidation numbers is consistent with the electron structures of these two molecules. The electron-dot formula for sulfuric acid is

$$
\begin{array}{c}
: \overset{\cdot\cdot}{O} : \\
\overset{\cdot\cdot}{} \overset{\cdot\cdot}{} \overset{\cdot\cdot}{} \\
H \overset{\cdot\cdot}{:} \overset{\cdot\cdot}{O} \overset{\times\times}{\times} \overset{}{S} \overset{}{\times} \overset{\cdot\cdot}{O} \overset{\cdot\cdot}{:} H \\
: \overset{\cdot\cdot}{O} : \\
\end{array}
$$

Oxygen is the most electronegative element present. Therefore, *we assign to oxygen all electrons shared with oxygen.* The sulfur atom must contribute all of its electrons. Hence, the oxidation number of sulfur is $+6$.

The electron-dot formula for sulfurous acid is

$$
\begin{array}{c}
\overset{\cdot\cdot}{} \overset{\times\times}{} \overset{\cdot\cdot}{} \\
H \overset{\cdot\cdot}{:} \overset{\cdot\cdot}{O} \overset{\times}{} \overset{}{S} \overset{\times}{} \overset{\cdot\cdot}{O} \overset{\cdot\cdot}{:} H \\
: \overset{\cdot\cdot}{O} : \\
\end{array}
$$

Observe that one pair of electrons belonging to sulfur is unshared. The atom of sulfur contributes *four* electrons, hence the oxidation number is $+4$.

Suppose we apply these rules to a salt containing a polyatomic ion. Potassium permanganate is made up of potassium ions, K^+, and polyatomic permanganate ions, MnO_4^-. The empirical formula is $KMnO_4$. Oxygen has the oxidation number -2 as before. The total contribution of the 4 oxygen atoms is $4(-2) = -8$. The K^+ ion is assigned the oxidation number that equals its ionic charge, $+1$. The oxidation number of the manganese atom in the polyatomic ion must then be $+7$. The formula showing these oxidation states of the elements can be written

$$\overset{+1\qquad+7\ -2}{K^+[Mn(O)_4]^-}$$

or more simply,

$$\overset{+1\ +7\ -2}{KMnO_4}$$

Manganese has several important oxidation states. This oxidation number, $+7$, represents its highest oxidation state.

21.3 Balancing oxidation-reduction equations

The principle use of oxidation numbers is in balancing equations for oxidation-reduction reactions. It is very important to follow an orderly procedure in equation writing. First, we must know the *facts:* what the reactants are and what the products are. We must then represent the reactants and products by their *correct formulas.* Finally we must adjust the coefficients of all reactants and products to agree with the *conservation of atoms.*

Oxidation-reduction (redox) reactions are those in which changes in oxidation numbers occur. In writing redox equations, we must provide for *conservation of electrons* as well as for conservation of atoms. In all but the simplest equations, first *balance the electron shift* between the particles oxidized and the particles reduced. Then *adjust the coefficients* for the rest of the equation. The procedure for writing oxidation-reduction equations includes the following steps:

Step 1: Write the skeleton equation for the reaction. To do this we must know the reactants and products and represent each by the correct formula.
Step 2: Assign oxidation numbers to all elements and determine what is oxidized and what is reduced.
Step 3: Write the electronic equation for the oxidation process and the electronic equation for the reduction process.
Step 4: Adjust the coefficients in both electronic equations so that the number of electrons lost equals the number gained.
Step 5: Place these coefficients in the skeleton equation.
Step 6: Supply the proper coefficients for the rest of the equation to satisfy the conservation of atoms.

Let us apply these steps to a very simple oxidation-reduction reaction. Hydrogen sulfide gas burns in air and forms sulfur dioxide and water. These facts enable us to write the skeleton equation.

Step 1:

$$H_2S + O_2 \rightarrow SO_2 + H_2O$$

We now assign oxidation numbers. Changes in oxidation numbers indicate that sulfur is oxidized from the -2 state to the $+4$ state; oxygen is reduced from the 0 state to the -2 state. The oxidation number of hydrogen remains the same; it plays no part in the primary action of oxidation-reduction.

Step 2:

$$\overset{+1\,-2}{H_2S} + \overset{0}{O_2} \rightarrow \overset{+4\,-2}{S\,O_2} + \overset{+1\,-2}{H_2O}$$

The change in oxidation state of sulfur requires the loss of 6 electrons: $(-2) - (+4) = -6$. The change in oxidation state of oxygen requires the gain of 2 electrons: $(0) - (-2) = +2$. The electronic equations for these two reactions are:

Step 3:

$$\overset{+2}{S} \rightarrow \overset{+4}{S} + 6e^- \quad \textbf{(oxidation)}$$

$$\overset{0}{O} + 2e^- \rightarrow \overset{-2}{O} \quad \textbf{(reduction)}$$

Free oxygen is diatomic. Thus, 4 electrons must be gained during the reduction of a molecule of free oxygen.

$$\overset{0}{O_2} + 4e^- \rightarrow 2\overset{-2}{O}$$

We now adjust the coefficients of the two electronic equations. The number of electrons lost in the oxidation of sulfur must equal the number gained in the reduction of oxygen. The smallest number of electrons common to both equations is 12. To show the gain and loss of 12 electrons in the two equations, we multiply the oxidation equation by 2, and multiply the reduction equation by 3.

Step 4:

$$2\overset{-2}{S} \rightarrow 2\overset{+4}{S} + 12e^-$$

$$3\overset{0}{O_2} + 12e^- \rightarrow 6\overset{-2}{O}$$

Hence, the coefficients of H_2S and SO_2 are both 2, and the coefficient of O_2 is 3. Notice that the $6\overset{-2}{O}$ is divided between the two products SO_2 and H_2O. The coefficient 6 is accounted for by the coefficient 2 in front of each formula. These coefficients are transferred to the skeleton equation.

Step 5:

$$\textbf{2H}_2\textbf{S} + \textbf{3O}_2 \rightarrow \textbf{2SO}_2 + \textbf{2H}_2\textbf{O}$$

We can now adjust the coefficients of the equation in the usual way to satisfy the law of conservation of atoms. In this case, no further adjustments are needed; the equation is balanced.

Step 6:

$$\textbf{2H}_2\textbf{S} + \textbf{3O}_2 \rightarrow \textbf{2SO}_2 + \textbf{2H}_2\textbf{O}$$

As a second example, we will use an oxidation-reduction equation that is slightly more difficult to balance. This reaction occurs between manganese dioxide and hydrochloric acid. Water, manganese(II) chloride, and chlorine gas are formed. The skeleton equation is

$$\overset{+4\ -2}{MnO_2} + \overset{+1-1}{HCl} \rightarrow \overset{+1\ -2}{H_2O} + \overset{+2\ -1}{MnCl_2} + \overset{0}{Cl_2}$$

We assign oxidation numbers to the elements in the reaction and see that $\overset{+4}{Mn}$ is reduced to $\overset{+2}{Mn^{++}}$. Also, some of the $\overset{-1}{Cl^-}$ is oxidized to $\overset{0}{Cl}$. Hydrogen and oxygen do not take part in the oxidation-reduction reaction. The electronic equations are

$$\overset{-1}{2Cl^-} \rightarrow \overset{0}{Cl_2} + 2e^-$$
$$\overset{+4}{Mn} + 2e^- \rightarrow \overset{+2}{Mn^{++}}$$

The number of electrons lost and gained is the same. We now transfer the coefficients to the skeleton equation, which becomes

$$MnO_2 + 2HCl \rightarrow H_2O + MnCl_2 + Cl_2$$

The complete equation can now be balanced by inspection. Two additional molecules of HCl are needed to supply the two Cl$^-$ ions of the MnCl$_2$. This balancing requires 2 molecules of water. These water molecules also account for the 2 oxygen atoms of the MnO$_2$. The final equation reads

$$MnO_2 + 4HCl \rightarrow 2H_2O + MnCl_2 + Cl_2$$

The equations for both of these examples can be balanced easily without using electronic equations to balance electron shifts. Let us now apply the step process to a more complicated oxidation-reduction reaction. See the following Sample Problem.

Sample Problem

The oxidation-reduction reaction between hydrochloric acid and potassium permanganate yields water, potassium chloride, manganese(II) chloride, and chlorine gas. Write the balanced equation.

Solution

First, write the skeleton equation. Be careful to show the correct formula of each reactant and each product. Appropriate oxidation numbers are placed above the symbols of the elements.

$$\overset{+1-1}{HCl} + \overset{+1,+7\ -2}{KMnO_4} \rightarrow \overset{+1\ -2}{H_2O} + \overset{+1-1}{KCl} + \overset{+2\ -1}{MnCl_2} + \overset{0}{Cl_2}$$

Some chloride ions are oxidized to chlorine atoms. The manganese of the permanganate ions is reduced to manganese(II) ions. Electronic equations for these two reactions are

$$\overset{-1}{2Cl^-} \rightarrow \overset{0}{Cl_2} + 2e^-$$
$$\overset{+7}{Mn} + 5e^- \rightarrow \overset{+2}{Mn^{++}}$$

The electron shift must involve an equal number of electrons in these two equations. This number is 10. The first equation is multiplied by 5 and the second by 2. We now have

$$\overset{-1}{10Cl^-} \rightarrow \overset{0}{5Cl_2} + 10e^-$$
$$\overset{+7}{2Mn} + 10e^- \rightarrow \overset{+2}{2Mn^{++}}$$

These coefficients are transferred to the skeleton equation, which becomes

$$10HCl + 2KMnO_4 \rightarrow H_2O + KCl + 2MnCl_2 + 5Cl_2$$

By inspection, $2KMnO_4$ produces $2KCl$ and $8H_2O$. Now $2KCl$ and $2MnCl_2$ call for 6 additional molecules of HCl. The balanced equation then becomes

$$16HCl + 2KMnO_4 \rightarrow 8H_2O + 2KCl + 2MnCl_2 + 5Cl_2$$

The method we have used to balance oxidation-reduction reactions has several names. It is called the *electron-shift, electron-transfer,* and *oxidation-state method.* The use of oxidation numbers to represent the oxidation state of an element does not necessarily imply that the element exists as ions. In different compounds, the transfer of electrons may be partial, as in polar covalent bonds, or complete, as in ionic bonds. Oxidation numbers are assigned in either case.

21.4 Oxidizing and reducing agents

An *oxidizing agent* acquires electrons during an oxidation-reduction reaction. A *reducing agent* loses the electrons. It follows that the substance oxidized is also the reducing agent, and the substance reduced is the oxidizing agent. An oxidized substance becomes a potential oxidizing agent. Similarly, a reduced substance is a potential reducing agent. If this seems confusing, study the oxidation-reduction terms presented in Table 21-2.

The relatively large atoms of the sodium family of metals make up Group 1 of the periodic table. These atoms have weak attraction for their valence electrons and form positive ions readily. They are *very active reducing agents.* According to electrochemical measurements, the lithium atom is the most active reducing agent of all the common elements. The lithium ion, on the other hand, is the weakest oxidizing agent of the common ions. The electronegativity scale suggests that Group I metals starting with lithium should become progressively more

A strong oxidizing agent reacts and becomes a weak reducing agent.
A weak oxidizing agent reacts and becomes a strong reducing agent.
A strong reducing agent reacts and becomes a weak oxidizing agent.

Table 21–2
OXIDATION-REDUCTION TERMINOLOGY

Term	Change in oxidation number	Change in electron population
oxidation	increase	loss of electrons
reduction	decrease	gain of electrons
oxidizing agent	decrease	acquires electrons
reducing agent	increase	supplies electrons
substance oxidized	increase	loses electrons
substance reduced	decrease	gains electrons

active reducing agents. With the exception of lithium, this is the case. A possible basis for the unusual activity of lithium is discussed in Chapter 23.

Atoms of the halogen family, Group VII of the periodic table, have strong attraction for electrons. They form negative ions readily and are *very active oxidizing agents*. The fluorine atom is the most highly electronegative atom. It is also the most active oxidizing agent among the elements. Because of its strong attraction for electrons, the fluoride ion is the weakest reducing agent.

It is possible to arrange the elements according to their activity as oxidizing and reducing agents. See Table 21-3. The left column shows the relative abilities of some metals to displace other metals from their compounds. Such displacement is an oxidation-reduction process. Zinc, for example, appears above copper. Thus, zinc is the more active reducing agent and displaces copper ions from solutions of copper compounds.

$$\mathbf{Zn(s) + Cu^{++}(aq) \rightarrow Zn^{++}(aq) + Cu(s)}$$

$$\overset{0}{\mathbf{Zn}} \rightarrow \overset{+2}{\mathbf{Zn^{++}}} + 2e^- \quad \textbf{(oxidation)}$$

$$\overset{+2}{\mathbf{Cu^{++}}} + 2e^- \rightarrow \overset{0}{\mathbf{Cu}} \qquad \textbf{(reduction)}$$

The copper(II) ion, on the other hand, is a more active oxidizing agent than the zinc ion.

Nonmetals and some important ions are included in the series. Any reducing agent is oxidized by the oxidizing agents below it. Observe that F_2 displaces Cl^-, Br^-, and I^- ions from their solutions. Cl_2 displaces Br^- and I^- ions and Br_2 displaces I^- ions.

$$\mathbf{Cl_2 + 2Br^-(aq) \rightarrow 2Cl^-(aq) + Br_2}$$

$$\overset{-1}{\mathbf{2Br^-}} \rightarrow \overset{0}{\mathbf{Br_2}} + 2e^- \quad \textbf{(oxidation)}$$

$$\overset{0}{\mathbf{Cl_2}} + 2e^- \rightarrow \overset{-1}{\mathbf{2Cl^-}} \quad \textbf{(reduction)}$$

Permanganate ions, MnO_4^-, and dichromate ions, $Cr_2O_7^{--}$, are very useful oxidizing agents. They are used mainly in the form of their potassium salts. In neutral or mildly basic solutions, permanganate ions are reduced to MnO_2. If a solution is strongly basic, manganate ions, MnO_4^{--} are formed. In acid solutions, permanganate ions are reduced to manganese(II) ions, Mn^{++}. Dichromate ions, in acid solution, are reduced to chromium(III) ions, Cr^{+++}.

Peroxide ions, O_2^{--}, have a single covalent bond between the two oxygen atoms. The electron-dot formula is

$$\left[\overset{\times\;\;\times}{\underset{\times\bullet\;\;\times\bullet}{:\!\overset{..}{O}\!:\!\overset{..}{O}\!:}} \right]^{--}$$

This structure represents an intermediate state of oxidation between free oxygen and oxides. The oxidation number of oxygen in the peroxide form is -1.

A weak reducing agent reacts and becomes a strong oxidizing agent.

Table 21-3
RELATIVE STRENGTH OF OXIDIZING AND REDUCING AGENTS

	Reducing agents	Oxidizing agents	
Strong	Li	Li$^+$	Weak
	K	K$^+$	
	Ca	Ca^{++}	
	Na	Na$^+$	
	Mg	Mg^{++}	
	Al	Al^{+++}	
	Zn	Zn^{++}	
	Cr	Cr^{+++}	
	Fe	Fe^{++}	
	Ni	Ni^{++}	
	Sn	Sn^{++}	
	Pb	Pb^{++}	
	H$_2$	H$_3$O$^+$	
	H$_2$S	S	
	Cu	Cu^{++}	
	I$^-$	I$_2$	
	MnO$_4$$^{--}$	MnO$_4$$^-$	
	Fe^{++}	Fe^{+++}	
	Hg	Hg$_2$$^{++}$	
	Ag	Ag$^+$	
	NO$_2$$^-$	NO$_3$$^-$	
	Br$^-$	Br$_2$	
	Mn^{++}	MnO$_2$	
	SO$_2$	H$_2$SO$_4$ (conc)	
	Cr^{+++}	Cr$_2$O$_7$$^{--}$	
	Cl$^-$	Cl$_2$	
Weak	Mn^{++}	MnO$_4$$^-$	
	F$^-$	F$_2$	Strong

Hydrogen peroxide, H_2O_2, can act as *both* an oxidizing agent and a reducing agent. As an oxidizing agent, the oxidation number of the oxygen changes from -1 to -2. As a reducing agent, the oxidation number of the oxygen changes from -1 to 0.

In the decomposition of hydrogen peroxide, both water and molecular oxygen are formed.

$$\overset{-1}{H_2O_2} + \overset{-1}{H_2O_2} \rightarrow \overset{-2}{H_2O} + \overset{0}{O_2}(g)$$

Here, the peroxide acts both as an oxidizing agent and as a reducing agent. Such a process is called *auto-oxidation*. Half of the oxygen is reduced to the oxide, forming water. The other half is oxidized to free oxygen. Impurities in a water solution of H_2O_2 act as catalysts and speed up this process.

21.5 Chemical equivalents of oxidizing and reducing agents

In Section 15.2, we recognized the chemical equivalent (equiv) of a reactant as the *mass of the reactant that loses or acquires the Avogadro number of electrons* in a chemical reaction. If a reactant is oxidized, the mass that loses the Avogadro number of electrons is one equivalent (1 equiv) of that reactant. If a reactant is reduced, the mass that acquires the Avogadro number of electrons is one equivalent of the reactant. Thus, 1 equiv of any reducing agent will always react with 1 equiv of any oxidizing agent.

We often express the quantities of reactants in terms of chemical equivalents. To do so for oxidizing and reducing agents, *the particular oxidation-reduction reaction must be known.* For example, one atom of iron loses 2 electrons when oxidized to iron(II), Fe^{++}.

$$Fe \rightarrow Fe^{++} + \overset{.}{2}e^-$$

One mole of iron, 55.8 g, gives up 2 times the Avogadro number of electrons when oxidized to the $+2$ oxidation state. Thus, the mass of iron that releases the Avogadro number of electrons in such a reaction is one-half mole. It follows that one equivalent is 55.8 g Fe $\div$ 2 $=$ 27.9 g Fe.

One atom of iron loses 3 electrons when oxidized to iron(III), Fe^{+++}. One mole of iron oxidized to the $+3$ oxidation state gives up 3 times the Avogadro number of electrons. Therefore, one equivalent of iron oxidized to the $+3$ oxidation state is 55.8 g Fe $\div$ 3 $=$ 18.6 g Fe.

Fe^{+++} ions in an iron(III) chloride solution are reduced to the $+2$ oxidation state by the addition of a tin(II) chloride solution. The Sn^{++} ions are the reducing agent. Here, one mole of Fe^{+++} ions acquires one Avogadro number of electrons and is reduced to Fe^{++} ions. One equivalent of iron in this reaction is 55.8 g $\div$ 1 $=$ 55.8 g. One mole of the reducing agent, Sn^{++} ions, loses 2 times the Avogadro number of electrons. One equivalent of tin in this reaction is 118.7 g ÷ 2 = 59.35 g. These relationships are shown clearly in the electronic equations for this oxidation-reduction reaction:

$$2Fe^{+++} + 2e^- \rightarrow 2Fe^{++}$$

$$Sn^{++} \rightarrow Sn^{++++} + 2e^-$$

$$1 \text{ equiv } Fe^{+++} = \frac{2Fe^{+++}}{e^- \text{ gained}} = \frac{2 \times 55.8 \text{ g}}{2} = 55.8 \text{ g}$$

$$1 \text{ equiv } Sn^{++} = \frac{Sn^{++}}{e^- \text{ lost}} = \frac{118.7 \text{ g}}{2} = 59.35 \text{ g}$$

21.6   Electrochemical reactions

1. Electrolytic cells. Some oxidation-reduction reactions *are not spontaneous.* However, such reactions can be forced to occur by means of electric energy supplied externally. Basically, the **electrolytic cell** consists of a pair of electrodes and an electrolyte solution in a suitable container. An electric current supplied by a battery or other direct-current source is connected across the cell. One electrode (the cathode) then becomes negatively charged and the other (the anode) becomes positively charged.

Ion *migration* in the cell is responsible for the transfer of electric charge. Positively charged ions (cations) *migrate* toward the cathode. Negatively charged ions (anions) migrate toward the anode. This + and − ion migration is shown in Figure 21-3.

In an electrolytic cell, reduction occurs at the cathode. Electrons are removed from the cathode in this process. Oxidation takes place at the anode, which acquires electrons in the process.

In electrolytic cells, reduction occurs at the cathode and oxidation occurs at the anode.

Fig. 21-3. Positively charged copper ions (blue) and negatively charged chromate ions (yellow) in (A) are shown migrating through a gel toward oppositely charged electrodes in (B).

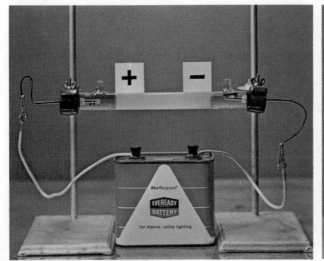

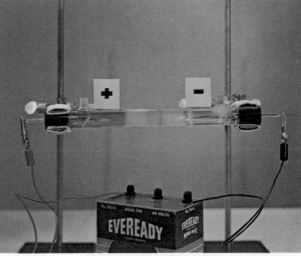

From the CHEM Study Film: *Electric Interactions*

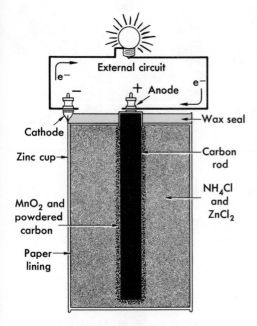

Fig. 21-4. In dry cells, zinc is oxidized at the cathode and manganese(IV) is reduced to manganese (III) at the anode.

The cathode may be defined as an electron-rich electrode.

The anode may be defined as an electron-poor electrode.

In electrochemical cells, oxidation occurs at the cathode (if the electron-rich electrode is called the cathode), and reduction occurs at the anode (which is then the electron-poor electrode).

The chemical reactions at the electrodes complete the electric circuit between the battery and the cell. The closed-loop path for electric current allows energy to be transferred from the battery to the electrolytic cell. This energy drives the electrode reactions in the cell.

2.   *Electrochemical cells.* Oxidation-reduction reactions involve a transfer of electrons from the substance oxidized to the substance reduced. If such reactions occur *spontaneously,* they can be used as sources of electric energy. If the reactants are in contact, the energy released during the electron transfer is in the form of heat. However, suppose we place the reactants separately in an electrolytic solution with a conducting wire joining them. The transfer of electrons then takes place through the wire. Such an arrangement is known as an ***electrochemical cell.*** The flow of electrons through the wire is an electric current. Under these conditions, only part of the energy released during the electron transfer appears as heat; the rest is available as electric energy.

The dry cell is a common source of electric energy in the laboratory. Small dry cells are familiar as flashlight batteries. A zinc container serves as the negative electrode or *cathode.* A carbon rod serves as the positive electrode or *anode.* The carbon rod is surrounded by a mixture of manganese dioxide and powdered carbon. The electrolyte is a moist paste of ammonium chloride containing some zinc chloride. Figure 21-4 shows these parts of the dry cell in a schematic diagram.

When the external circuit is closed, *zinc atoms are oxidized at the cathode.*

$$Zn \rightarrow Zn^{++} + 2e^-$$

Electrons flow through the external circuit to the carbon anode. There, if manganese dioxide were not present, hydrogen gas would be formed.

$$2NH_4^+ + 2e^- \rightarrow 2NH_3 + H_2(g)$$

However, hydrogen gas is oxidized to water by the manganese dioxide. This explains why *manganese* rather than hydrogen *is actually reduced at the anode.*

$$2MnO_2 + 2NH_4^+ + 2e^- \rightarrow Mn_2O_3 + 2NH_3 + H_2O$$

The ammonia is taken up by Zn^{++} ions, forming complex $Zn(NH_3)_4^{++}$ ions.

21.7   Electrolysis of water

In the decomposition of water by electrolysis, energy is transferred from the energy source to the decomposition products. The overall reaction is

$$2H_2O(l) + E \rightarrow 2H_2(g) + O_2(g)$$

A suitable cell arrangement is shown in Figure 21-5. It consists of two electrodes made of platinum immersed in water. A very small amount of an electrolyte, such as H_2SO_4, is added to provide adequate conductivity. The electrodes are connected to a battery. The electric energy supplied drives the decomposition reaction forward.

The electric current provided by the battery consists of a stream of electrons. They flow from the negative electrode of the battery, through the external circuit, and back to the positive electrode of the source. The electrode connected to the cathode of the battery acquires an excess of electrons. This electrode becomes the *cathode* of the electrolytic cell. The other electrode is connected to the anode of the battery. This electrode loses electrons to the battery and becomes the *anode* of the electrolytic cell.

Reduction occurs at the *cathode;* hydrogen gas is the product. If the amount of H_2SO_4 added to improve conductivity is small, its contribution of hydronium ions to the water is also small. At very low hydronium ion concentrations, it is believed that water molecules are reduced by acquiring electrons directly from the cathode.

cathode reaction: (reduction)

$$2H_2O + 2e^- \rightarrow 2OH^- + H_2(g)$$

Larger amounts of H_2SO_4 raise the H_3O^+ ion concentration. If this concentration is high enough, the H_3O^+ ions are reduced at the cathode. However, according to Le Chatelier's principle, additional water molecules also ionize. Thus, the net effect is the same.

$$2H_3O^+ + 2e^- \rightarrow 2H_2O + H_2(g)$$

$$4H_2O \rightarrow 2H_3O^+ + 2OH^-$$

$$\text{net:} \quad 2H_2O + 2e^- \rightarrow 2OH^- + H_2(g)$$

In either case, the OH^- ion concentration in the solution around the cathode rises.

Oxidation occurs at the *anode,* and oxygen gas is the product. There are SO_4^{--} ions, OH^- ions, and water molecules in the region about the anode. The OH^- ion concentration is quite low. With pure water in the cell, $[OH^-] = 10^{-7}$ mole/liter. With H_2SO_4 added to the water, $[H_3O^+] > 10^{-7}$ mole/liter and so $[OH^-] < 10^{-7}$ mole/liter. At this slight concentration, OH^- ions are not likely to appear in the anode reaction. The SO_4^{--} ions are more difficult to oxidize than water molecules. For these reasons, chemists believe that water molecules are oxidized by giving up electrons directly to the anode.

anode reaction: (oxidation)

$$6H_2O \rightarrow 4H_3O^+ + O_2(g) + 4e^-$$

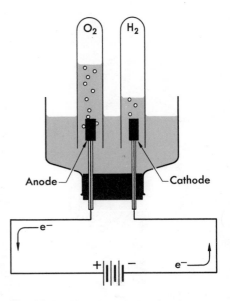

Fig. 21-5. The electrolysis of water. In electrolytic cells, reduction occurs at the cathode, and oxidation occurs at the anode.

Even under conditions favoring the oxidation of OH^- ions at the anode, the net effect remains the same. According to Le Chatelier's principle, additional water molecules ionize and off-set the decrease in OH^- ion concentration at the anode.

$$4OH^- \rightarrow 2H_2O + O_2(g) + 4e^-$$

$$8H_2O \rightarrow 4H_3O^+ + 4OH^-$$

$$\text{net:} \quad 6H_2O \rightarrow 4H_3O^+ + O_2(g) + 4e^-$$

In either case, the H_3O^+ ion concentration in the solution around the anode rises. Also, the OH^- ion concentration around the cathode rises. These ions are repelled from their electrodes because the ion and electrode charges are similar. This effect, and the ordinary mixing tendency in the solution, insures the neutralization of these ions. The neutralization equation is

$$4H_3O^+ + 4OH^- \rightarrow 8H_2O$$

The overall cell reaction is the sum of the net cathode and anode reactions. (The cathode reaction must be doubled to achieve electron balance across the cell.)

cathode: $\quad\quad 4H_2O + 4e^- \rightarrow 4OH^- + 2H_2(g)$

anode: $\quad\quad\quad\quad 6H_2O \rightarrow 4H_3O^+ + O_2(g) + 4e^-$

$$4H_3O^+ + 4OH^- \rightarrow 8H_2O$$

net for cell: $\quad\quad 2H_2O \rightarrow 2H_2(g) + O_2(g)$

Reduction at the cathode lowers the oxidation state of hydrogen from $+1$ to 0; the oxidation state of oxygen at the cathode remains -2. At the anode, oxidation raises the oxidation state of oxygen from -2 to 0; the oxidation state of hydrogen at the anode remains $+1$.

21.8 Electrolysis of aqueous salt solutions

The electrode products from the electrolysis of aqueous salt solutions are determined by the relative ease with which the different particles present can be oxidized or reduced. In the case of aqueous NaCl, for example, Na^+ ions are more difficult to reduce at the cathode than H_2O molecules or H_3O^+ ions. Since the solution of NaCl is neutral, the H_3O^+ ion concentration remains very low (10^{-7} mole/liter). Therefore, H_2O molecules are the particles reduced at the cathode.

cathode reaction: (reduction)

$$2H_2O + 2e^- \rightarrow 2OH^- + H_2(g)$$

Thus, Na^+ ions remain in solution and hydrogen gas is released.

In general, metals which are easily oxidized form ions that are difficult to reduce. That is why hydrogen gas, not sodium metal, is the cathode product above. On the other hand, metals such as copper, silver, and gold are difficult to oxidize and form ions which are easily reduced. Aqueous solutions of their salts give up the metal at the cathode.

The choice for anode reaction in the aqueous NaCl electrolysis lies between Cl^- ions and H_2O molecules. The Cl^- ions are more easily oxidized, so Cl_2 gas is produced at the anode.

anode reaction: (oxidation)

$$2Cl^- \rightarrow Cl_2(g) + 2e^-$$

Adding the cathode and anode equations gives the net reaction for the cell.

net: $2H_2O + 2Cl^- \rightarrow 2OH^- + H_2(g) + Cl_2(g)$

The electrolytic solution gradually changes from aqueous NaCl to aqueous NaOH as the electrolysis continues.

Anions such as NO_3^-, SO_4^{--}, and PO_4^{---} each contain a non-metal in its highest oxidation state. Such anions do not participate in the oxidation reaction at the anode. When aqueous solutions containing these anions are electrolyzed, O_2 gas is the anode product. On the other hand, aqueous solutions of Br^- or I^- ions are electrolyzed like Cl^- ions. Such solutions give the free halogen at the anode rather than oxygen.

21.9 Electroplating

We have noted inactive metals form ions which are more easily reduced than hydrogen. This fact makes possible an electrolytic process called *electroplating*.

An electroplating cell contains a solution of a salt of the plating metal. It has an object to be plated (the cathode) and a piece of the plating metal (the anode). A silverplating cell, for example, contains a solution of a soluble silver salt and a silver anode. The cathode is the object to be plated. See Figure 21-6. The silver anode is connected to the positive electrode of a battery or other source of direct current. The object to be plated is connected to the negative electrode. *Silver ions are reduced at the cathode* of the cell when electrons flow through the circuit.

$$Ag^+ + e^- \rightarrow Ag$$

Silver atoms are oxidized at the anode.

$$Ag \rightarrow Ag^+ + e^-$$

Silver ions are removed from the solution at the cathode and deposited as metallic silver. Meanwhile, metallic silver is removed from the anode as ions. This maintains the Ag^+ ion concentration of the solution. Thus, in effect, silver is transferred from the anode to the cathode of the cell.

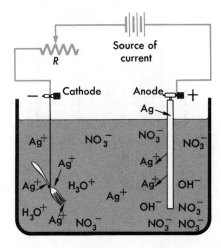

Fig. 21-6. An electrolytic cell used for silver plating.

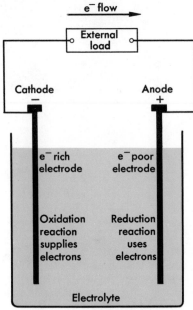

Spontaneous oxidation-reduction
reaction — a source of energy

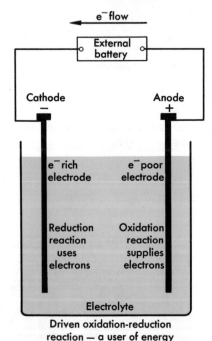

Driven oxidation-reduction
reaction — a user of energy

Fig. 21-7. A comparison of electrochemical and electrolytic cells.

In discussing electrochemical and electrolytic cells we have identified electrodes according to their *state of charge*. We refer to the negative electrode as the cathode and the positive electrode as the anode. These terms agree with modern definitions of such electrodes in physics and electronics. The *electron-rich electrode is the* **cathode** *and the electron-poor electrode is the* **anode** in any system of which they are part.

An older scheme for naming electrodes still is used widely in electrochemistry. This scheme defines the electrode at which oxidation occurs as the anode; the electrode at which reduction occurs is the cathode. One flaw in this system is that we must reverse the names of the electrodes, with respect to their electric charge for electrochemical and electrolytic cell reactions.

This older naming system becomes even more confusing when applied to reversible cells such as the automobile storage battery. It is useless in such a case, since each electrode of a reversible cell would have to be both an anode and a cathode. See Figure 21-7 for some of the terms used to describe electrochemical and electrolytic cells.

In defining the cathode as negative and the anode as positive, we must recognize certain differences. The chemical action at the cathode *is one of oxidation in electrochemical (spontaneous) cells* and *one of reduction in electrolytic (driven) cells*. Similarly, the chemical action at the anode *is one of reduction in electrochemical cells and one of oxidation in electrolytic cells*.

21.10   Lead storage battery

The basic unit of the lead storage battery is a lead(IV) oxide-lead-sulfuric acid cell. The standard twelve-volt automobile battery consists of six of these cells connected in series. As the name implies, the *storage* battery is a *storehouse* of energy. The battery is charged by electric energy from an external source. This electric energy is converted to chemical energy by an oxidation-reduction reaction in which each cell acts as an *electrolytic* cell. While the battery is being discharged, the reverse oxidation-reduction reaction occurs. Chemical energy in the battery is converted to electric energy and the cells act as *electrochemical* cells.

A fully-charged lead storage cell contains an anode of lead(IV) oxide and a cathode of spongy lead. The electrolyte is moderately dilute sulfuric acid. During the *discharging cycle,* the lead at the cathode is oxidized to Pb^{++} ions. Lead(II) sulfate, $PbSO_4$, is formed as a precipitate on the cathode. This oxidation can be summarized as follows:

cathode reaction: (on discharge)

$$Pb(s) + H_2O + HSO_4^- \rightarrow PbSO_4(s) + H_3O^+ + 2e^-$$

At the anode, H_3O^+ ions may be reduced. In turn, they may reduce the PbO_2 to PbO, forming water in the process. Reaction with sulfuric acid then produces lead(II) sulfate and water. Lead(II) sulfate precipitates on the anode. The anode reduction is not fully understood, and the above reactions may oversimplify the actual reaction mechanism. However, we can summarize this reduction as follows:

anode reaction: (on discharge)

$$PbO_2(s) + HSO_4^- + 3H_3O^+ + 2e^- \rightarrow PbSO_4(s) + 5H_2O$$

The net oxidation-reduction reaction of the cell during discharge is the sum of the two electrode reactions.

Exide

Fig. 21-8. A cutaway view of an automobile storage battery. (1) Cover, (2) Intercell connector, (3) Vent plugs, (4) Plates, (5) Insulation, (6) Container.

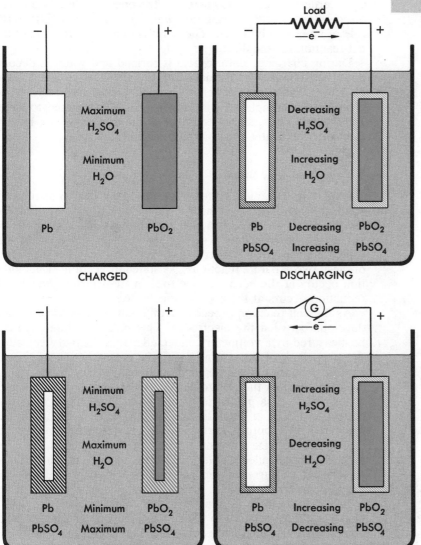

Fig. 21-9. Diagrams illustrating the essential action in a storage cell.

cell reaction: (on discharge)

$$\text{Pb(s)} + \text{PbO}_2(\text{s}) + 2\text{HSO}_4^- + 2\text{H}_3\text{O}^+ \rightarrow 2\text{PbSO}_4(\text{s}) + 4\text{H}_2\text{O}$$

Electrons released by oxidation at the cathode flow through the external circuit to the anode. There, the reduction occurs. This flow of electrons is the electric current. It is capable of delivering energy to devices in the external circuit.

When the battery is completely discharged, both electrodes consist of lead(II) sulfate. The electrolyte, aqueous sulfuric acid, is diluted further by the product water. The cell can be made electrochemically active again by reversing the reaction at each electrode. To recharge the cell, a direct current is supplied from an external source. This current is the opposite direction to the discharging current. During the *charging cycle,* the cell is in the role of an electrolytic cell. The net reaction is the reverse of the net reaction for the discharge cycle.

During charging, sulfuric acid is formed and water is decomposed. The density of the acid solution increases to about 1.300 g/ml for a fully-charged cell. The density decreases during discharge. In a completely discharged cell, it is lowered to about 1.100 g/ml. Thus, a measurement of the density of the battery electrolyte indicates the condition of charge.

21.11 Electrode potentials

Oxidation-reduction systems are the result of two distinct reactions: *1. oxidation,* in which electrons are supplied to the system, and *2. reduction,* in which electrons are acquired from the system. In electrochemical cells, these reactions take place at the separate electrodes. The oxidation-reduction reaction is the sum of these two separate reactions. As stated in Section 21.6, oxidation occurs at the negative electrode in an electrochemical cell; reduction occurs at the positive electrode.

As the cell reaction proceeds, a difference in *electric potential* develops between the electrodes. This potential difference can be measured by a voltmeter connected across the two electrodes. We may think of the potential difference as the *sum of the potentials* produced at the negative and positive electrodes.

Let us consider the electrochemical cell shown in Figure 21-10. A strip of zinc is placed in a solution of ZnSO_4 and a strip of copper is placed in a solution of CuSO_4. The two solutions are separated by a porous partition. This partition permits ions to pass but otherwise prevents mixing of the solutions. Such an arrangement is called a *voltaic cell.* It is capable of generating a small electron current in an external circuit connected between the electrodes.

In the two electrode reactions, the zinc electrode acquires a negative charge relative to the copper. The copper electrode becomes positively charged relative to the zinc. This reaction shows

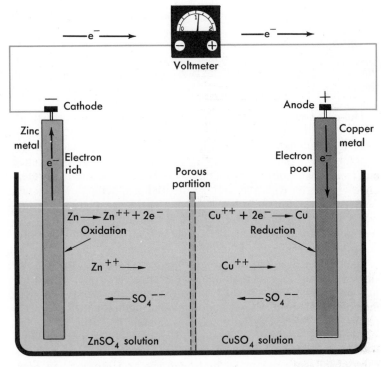

Fig. 21-10. A Zn-Cu voltaic cell.

that zinc atoms have a stronger tendency to enter the solution as ions than do copper atoms. Zinc is said to be more active, or more easily oxidized, than copper.

The reaction at the surface of the zinc electrode is an oxidation. It is shown by the following equation:

$$Zn(s) \rightarrow Zn^{++}(aq) + 2e^-$$

The reaction at the surface of the copper electrode is a reduction:

$$Cu^{++}(aq) + 2e^- \rightarrow Cu(s)$$

As Zn^{++} ions form, electrons accumulate on the zinc electrode, giving it a negative charge. Electrons also migrate through the external circuit toward the copper electrode. Here they replace the electrons removed as Cu^{++} ions undergo reduction to Cu atoms. Thus, in effect, electrons are transferred from Zn atoms through the external circuit to Cu^{++} ions. The overall reaction can be written as

$$Zn + Cu^{++} \rightarrow Zn^{++} + Cu$$

A voltmeter connected across the Cu-Zn voltaic cell measures the potential difference. This difference is about 1.1 volts when the solution concentrations of Zn^{++} and Cu^{++} are each 1 m.

A voltaic cell consists of two metal electrodes, each in contact with a solution of its ions. Each of these portions is called a *half-cell.* The reaction taking place at each electrode is called a *half-reaction.*

*The potential difference between an electrode and its solution in a half-reaction is known as its **electrode potential.*** The sum of the electrode potentials for the two half-reactions roughly equals the potential difference measured across the complete voltaic cell.

The potential difference across a voltaic cell is easily measured. However, there is no way to measure an individual electrode potential. The electrode potential of a half-reaction can be determined by using a *standard half-cell* along with it as a reference electrode. An arbitrary potential is assigned to the standard reference electrode. Relative to this potential, a specific potential can be determined for the other electrode of the complete cell. Electrode potentials are expressed as reduction (or oxidation) potentials. They provide a reliable indication of the tendency of a substance to undergo reduction (or oxidation).

Chemists use a *hydrogen electrode* immersed in a molal solution of $H^+(aq)$ ions as a standard reference electrode. This practice provides a convenient way to examine the relative tendencies of metals to react with aqueous hydrogen ions (H_3O^+). It is responsible for the activity series of metals listed in Table 8-1. A hydrogen electrode is shown in Figure 21-11. It consists of a platinum electrode dipping into an acid solution of $1\text{-}m$ concentration and surrounded by hydrogen gas at 1 atmosphere pressure. This *standard hydrogen electrode is assigned a potential of zero volt.* The half-cell reaction is

$$H_2(g) \rightleftarrows 2H^+(aq) + 2e^-$$

To repeat, the potential of the hydrogen electrode is arbitrarily set at zero volt. Therefore, the potential difference across the complete cell is attributed entirely to the electrode of the other half-cell.

Suppose we construct a complete cell consisting of a zinc half-cell and a standard hydrogen half-cell. See Figure 21-12. The potential difference across the cell measures the electrode potential of the zinc electrode relative to the hydrogen electrode (the zero reference electrode). It is found to be -0.76 volt. *The standard electrode potential, E^0, of an electrode is given a negative value if this electrode has a negative charge relative to the standard hydrogen electrode.* Electrons flow through the external circuit from the zinc electrode to the hydrogen electrode. There, $H^+(aq)$ ions are reduced to H_2 gas.

This reaction means that the tendency for Zn^{++} ions to be reduced to Zn atoms is 0.76 volt less than the tendency for $H^+(aq)$ ions to be reduced to H_2. The half-reaction (as a reduction) is

$$Zn^{++} + 2e^- \rightarrow Zn \qquad E^0 = -0.76 \text{ v}$$

Fig. 21-11. Hydrogen electrode, the standard reference electrode for measuring standard electrode potentials.

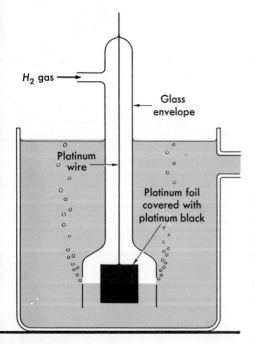

H_2 gas →

Glass envelope

Platinum wire →

Platinum foil covered with platinum black

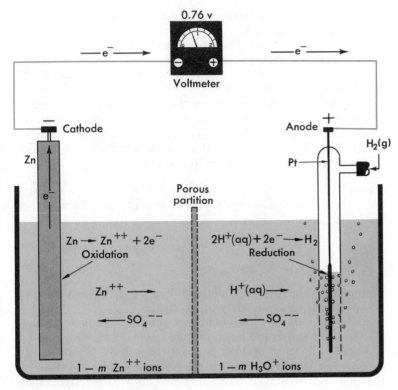

Fig. 21-12. The electrode potential of the zinc half-cell is measured by coupling it with a standard hydrogen electrode.

This reaction has less tendency to occur than

$$2H^+(aq) + 2e^- \rightarrow H_2(g)$$

by 0.76 volt. This statement also means that the half-reaction (as an oxidation)

$$Zn \rightarrow Zn^{++} + 2e^- \qquad E^0 = +0.76 \text{ v}$$

has a greater tendency to occur by 0.76 volt than

$$H_2(g) \rightarrow 2H^+(aq) + 2e^-$$

Observe that the sign of the electrode potential is reversed when the Zn half-cell reaction is written as an oxidation.

A copper half-cell coupled with the standard hydrogen electrode gives a potential difference measurement of +0.34 volt. This measurement indicates that $Cu^{++}(aq)$ ions are more readily reduced than $H^+(aq)$ ions. *The standard electrode potential, E^0, of an electrode is given a positive value if this electrode has a positive charge relative to the standard hydrogen electrode.* The half-reaction for copper (as a reduction) is

$$Cu^{++} + 2e^- \rightarrow Cu \qquad E^0 = +0.34 \text{ v}$$

This reaction has a greater tendency to occur than

$$2H^+(aq) + 2e^- \rightarrow H_2(g)$$

by 0.34 volt.

Table 21–4
STANDARD ELECTRODE POTENTIALS
(as reduction potentials)

Half-reaction	Electrode potential ($E°$)
$Li^+ + e^- \rightleftharpoons Li$	–3.04 v
$K^+ + e^- \rightleftharpoons K$	–2.92 v
$Ba^{++} + 2e^- \rightleftharpoons Ba$	–2.90 v
$Ca^{++} + 2e^- \rightleftharpoons Ca$	–2.76 v
$Na^+ + e^- \rightleftharpoons Na$	–2.71 v
$Mg^{++} + 2e^- \rightleftharpoons Mg$	–2.38 v
$Al^{+++} + 3e^- \rightleftharpoons Al$	–1.71 v
$Zn^{++} + 2e^- \rightleftharpoons Zn$	–0.76 v
$Cr^{+++} + 3e^- \rightleftharpoons Cr$	–0.74 v
$S + 2e^- \rightleftharpoons S^{--}$	–0.51 v
$Fe^{++} + 2e^- \rightleftharpoons Fe$	–0.41 v
$Cd^{++} + 2e^- \rightleftharpoons Cd$	–0.40 v
$Co^{++} + 2e^- \rightleftharpoons Co$	–0.28 v
$Ni^{++} + 2e^- \rightleftharpoons Ni$	–0.23 v
$Sn^{++} + 2e^- \rightleftharpoons Sn$	–0.14 v
$Pb^{++} + 2e^- \rightleftharpoons Pb$	–0.13 v
$Fe^{+++} + 3e^- \rightleftharpoons Fe$	–0.04 v
$2H^+(aq) + 2e^- \rightleftharpoons H_2$	0.00 v
$S + 2H^+(aq) + 2e^- \rightleftharpoons H_2S(aq)$	+0.14 v
$Cu^{++} + e^- \rightleftharpoons Cu^+$	+0.16 v
$Cu^{++} + 2e^- \rightleftharpoons Cu$	+0.34 v
$I_2 + 2e^- \rightleftharpoons 2I^-$	+0.54 v
$MnO_4^- + e^- \rightleftharpoons MnO_4^{--}$	+0.56 v
$Fe^{+++} + e^- \rightleftharpoons Fe^{++}$	+0.77 v
$Hg_2^{++} + 2e^- \rightleftharpoons 2Hg$	+0.80 v
$Ag^+ + e^- \rightleftharpoons Ag$	+0.80 v
$Hg^{++} + 2e^- \rightleftharpoons Hg$	+0.85 v
$Br_2 + 2e^- \rightleftharpoons 2Br^-$	+1.06 v
$MnO_2 + 4H^+(aq) + 2e^- \rightleftharpoons Mn^{++} + 2H_2O$	+1.21 v
$Cr_2O_7^{--} + 14H^+(aq) + 6e^- \rightleftharpoons 2Cr^{+++} + 7H_2O$	+1.33 v
$Cl_2 + 2e^- \rightleftharpoons 2Cl^-$	+1.36 v
$Au^{+++} + 3e^- \rightleftharpoons Au$	+1.42 v
$MnO_4^- + 8H^+(aq) + 5e^- \rightleftharpoons Mn^{++} + 4H_2O$	+1.49 v
$F_2 + 2e^- \rightleftharpoons 2F^-$	+2.87 v

From these measurements, we make two observations. *1.* Zinc has a greater tendency to yield electrons than hydrogen by 0.76 volt. *2.* Hydrogen has a greater tendency to yield electrons than copper by 0.34 volt. Taken together, these potentials indicate that zinc has a greater tendency toward oxidation than copper by 1.10 volts (0.76 v + 0.34 v).

How do these electrode potentials apply to the Zn/Cu voltaic cell of Figure 21-10? First, we obtain the potential difference across the complete cell. This is done by adding the electrode potentials of the two half-reactions, writing the Zn half-reaction as an oxidation and the Cu half-reaction as a reduction.

$$Zn \rightarrow Zn^{++} + 2e^- \qquad E^0 = +0.76 \text{ v}$$
$$\underline{Cu^{++} + 2e^- \rightarrow Cu \qquad E^0 = +0.34 \text{ v}}$$
$$Zn + Cu^{++} \rightarrow Zn^{++} + Cu \qquad E^0 = +1.10 \text{ v}$$

The positive sign of the potential difference shows that the reaction proceeds spontaneously to the right.

Half-reactions for some common electrodes and their standard electrode potentials are listed in Table 21-4. These reactions are arranged according to their standard electrode potentials, E^0, relative to a standard hydrogen reference electrode. All electrode reactions are written as *reduction reactions* to the right. Electrode potentials are given as *reduction potentials*. Half-reactions with *positive* reduction potentials occur spontaneously to the right as *reduction reactions*. Half-reactions with *negative* reduction potentials occur spontaneously to the left as *oxidation reactions*. When a half-reaction is written as an oxidation reaction, the sign of the electrode potential is changed. The potential then becomes an *oxidation potential*.

The magnitude of the electrode potential measures the tendency of the *reduction half-reaction* to occur as written in the table. The half-reaction at the top of the column has the *least* tendency toward reduction (adding electrons). Stated in another way, it has the *greatest* tendency to occur as an oxidation (yielding electrons). The half-reaction at the bottom of the column has the *greatest* tendency to occur as a reduction. Thus, it has the *least* tendency to occur as an oxidation.

The *lower* a half-reaction is in the column, the *greater* is the tendency for its *reduction reaction* to occur. The *higher* a half-reaction is in the column, the *greater* is the tendency for the *oxidation reaction* to occur. For example, potassium has a large negative electrode potential and a strong tendency to form K^+ ions. Thus, potassium is a strong reducing agent. Fluorine has a large positive electrode potential and a strong tendency to form F^- ions. Fluorine, then, is a strong oxidizing agent. Compare the listings in Table 21-3 with those in Table 21-4.

QUESTIONS

Group A

1. Describe the differences between the processes of oxidation and reduction.
2. Why do oxidation and reduction occur simultaneously?
3. What change in oxidation state do particles undergo which acquire electrons during a chemical action?
4. Which of the following are oxidation-reduction reactions?
   (a) $2Na + Cl_2 \rightarrow 2NaCl$
   (b) $C + O_2 \rightarrow CO_2$
   (c) $2H_2O \rightleftarrows 2H_2 + O_2$
   (d) $NaCl + AgNO_3 \rightarrow AgCl + NaNO_3$
   (e) $NH_3 + HCl \rightarrow NH_4 + Cl^-$
   (f) $2KClO_3 \rightarrow 2KCl + 3O_2$
   (g) $H_2 + Cl_2 \rightarrow 2HCl$
   (h) $2H_2 + O_2 + 2H_2O$
   (i) $H_2SO_4 + 2KOH \rightarrow K_2SO_4 + 2H_2O$
   (j) $Zn + CuSO_4 \rightarrow ZnSO_4 + Cu$
5. For each oxidation-reduction reaction in Question 4 identify: (a) the substance oxidized; (b) the substance reduced; (c) the oxidizing agent; and (d) the reducing agent.
6. What is the oxidation number of each element in the following compounds? (a) $CaClO_3$; (b) Na_2HPO_4; (c) K_2SiO_3; (d) H_3PO_3; (e) $Fe(OH)_3$.
7. Assign oxidation numbers to each element in the following compounds: (a) $PbSO_4$; (b) H_2O_2; (c) $K_2Cr_2O_7$; (d) H_2SO_3; (e) $HClO_4$.
8. What constitutes the anode, cathode, and electrolyte of a fully-charged lead storage cell?
9. Define (a) electrode potential; (b) half-reaction; (c) half-cell.
10. Why is the standard hydrogen electrode assigned an electrode potential of 0.00 volt?

Group B

11. What are the six steps involved in balancing oxidation-reduction equations? List them in the proper sequence.
12. Carry out the first four steps called for in Question 11 for the following:
    (a) zinc + hydrochloric acid → zinc chloride + hydrogen.
    (b) iron + copper(II) sulfate → iron(II) sulfate + copper.
    (c) copper + sulfuric acid → copper(II) sulfate + sulfur dioxide + water.
    (d) potassium dichromate + sulfur + water → sulfur dioxide + potassium hydroxide + chromium(II) oxide.
    (e) bromine + water → hydrobromic acid + hypobromous acid.
13. The oxidation-reduction reaction between copper and *concentrated* nitric acid yields the following products: copper(II) nitrate, water and nitrogen dioxide. Write the balanced equation.
14. The reaction between copper and *dilute* nitric acid yields the following products: copper(II) nitrate, water, and nitrogen monoxide. Write the balanced equation.
15. Referring to Table 21-3, the active metals down to magnesium replace hydrogen from water. Magnesium and succeeding metals replace hydrogen from steam. Metals near the bottom of the list will not replace hydrogen from steam. How does this table help to explain this behavior?

16. Balance the oxidation-reduction equation:
    $K_2Cr_2O_7 + HCl \rightarrow KCl + CrCl_3 + H_2O + Cl_2$.
17. Using information from Table 21-4, write the equations for the half-reactions of a voltaic cell having Cu and Ag electrodes.
18. (*a*) Determine the potential difference across the voltaic cell of Question 17. (*b*) Write the equation for the overall reaction of the cell in the direction that it proceeds spontaneously.

Chapter 22

Elements of Period Three

22.1 General appearance

In Chapter 5 we saw that the chemical elements could be arranged by atomic number in a periodic table. In such a table, elements in a given column have similar chemical properties because of their similar outer electron arrangements. In going across a row of the periodic table, the properties of the elements vary widely. The first element is a highly reactive metal. Then come other metals of decreasing activity. These are followed by metalloids, and then by nonmetals of increasing activity. The last element in a row is a noble gas.

In this chapter we shall consider the elements in Period Three. These elements illustrate the variation in properties which occurs within a period. In later chapters, we shall consider elements mainly within their family relationships.

Period Three is a short period containing eight elements. The first three elements are sodium, magnesium, and aluminum. All are silvery metals with characteristic metallic luster. Sodium is soft enough to be cut easily. Magnesium and aluminum are somewhat harder, but can be scratched readily with a knife. Silicon, the fourth element, is still harder. It is gray with a metallic luster. Because silicon has properties between those of metals and nonmetals, it is classed as a *metalloid*. Phosphorus is the fifth element. It commonly exists either as an active, pale, waxy solid, or as a more stable red powder. Phosphorus is a nonmetal. The next two elements, sulfur and chlorine, are also nonmetals. Sulfur is a brittle yellow solid, and chlorine is a yellow-green gas. Argon, the noble gas of this period, is colorless. (See Figure 5-3 on pages 80 and 81 for photographs of samples of the elements of Period Three.)

Table 22-1

PHYSICAL PROPERTIES OF ELEMENTS OF PERIOD THREE

Element	Melting point (°C)	Boiling point (°C)	Density (g/cm³)	Color
sodium	97.8	892	0.97	silver
magnesium	651	1107	1.74	silver
aluminum	660.2	2467	2.70	silver
silicon	1410	2355	2.33	silver-gray
phosphorus	44.1 (white)	280	1.82	waxy-white
sulfur	119 (monoclinic)	444.6	2.07	yellow
chlorine	−101.0	−34.6	3.21 g/liter	yellow-green
argon	−189.2	−185.7	1.78 g/liter	colorless

22.2 Structure and physical properties

Table 22-1 gives melting point, boiling point, density, and color data for the elements of Period Three.

Because sodium, magnesium, and aluminum are metals, they have certain physical properties in common. Each is a good conductor of heat and electricity, has a silvery luster, and is ductile and malleable. Sodium and aluminum form cubic crystals, while those of magnesium are hexagonal. In each, the crystal lattice is made up of metallic ions in an electron "gas" of valence electrons. The good conductivity of these metals is explained by the highly mobile character of their free electrons. Their silvery luster results from free electrons at the crystal surfaces. When light strikes these surfaces, the valence electrons absorb energy and begin to vibrate. These vibrations re-radiate the energy in all directions as light.

The binding force in metallic crystals is the attraction between positive ions and the negative electron gas that fills the lattice. This force is exerted equally in all directions. Its magnitude determines the degree of hardness, ductility, and malleability of these metals. This magnitude is further indicated by the melting and boiling points of the metals. Sodium is softer and has a lower melting point than magnesium and aluminum. These properties indicate that the forces holding sodium ions in fixed positions in the crystal lattice are weaker than those of magnesium and aluminum. The forces holding the mobile ions together in the liquid phases of these metals are quite strong. Evidence for this fact is the rather wide temperature range over which the metals are liquids.

Magnesium is denser than sodium, and aluminum is denser than magnesium. The denser elements have heavier, though smaller, atoms respectively than the less dense ones. Besides being heavier, the smaller atoms tend to pack more closely together.

Silicon exists as a covalent network of atoms with a cubic crystal structure. The pattern of atomic arrangement in the crystal is identical with diamond (see Figure 16-2). However, the distance between nuclei is greater in silicon, 2.35 Å compared to 1.54 Å in diamond. Carbon atoms form four equivalent covalent bonds in the diamond structure. The electron configuration of carbon is $1s^2 2s^2 2p^2$ and hybridization produces four equivalent sp^3 orbitals. Silicon, like diamond, has four equivalent covalent bonds. These four equivalent covalent bonds are explained by hybridization. The electron configuration of silicon is similar to carbon, $1s^2 2s^2 2p^6 3s^2 3p^2$. Silicon also undergoes hybridization in the third energy level, forming four equivalent sp^3 orbitals. Aluminum has a metallic structure, while silicon has a covalent network structure. This change accounts for the great difference in melting points between these two consecutive elements. The silicon structure is less compact than that of aluminum. Thus, silicon is less dense than aluminum, even though silicon atoms are smaller and heavier than aluminum atoms. Some of the valence electrons in silicon crystals are free to move. Thus, unlike diamond, that is practically a nonconductor, silicon has a low electric conductivity.

Phosphorus has the electron configuration $1s^2 2s^2 2p^6 3s^2 3p^3$. With its three half-filled $3p$ orbitals, a phosphorus atom can form three covalent bonds. Elemental white phosphorus exists as separate P_4 molecules, each atom of which forms three covalent bonds. See Figure 22-1. White phosphorus has low melting and boiling points and is quite soft. These properties indicate that only weak dispersion interaction forces exist among the P_4 molecules. White phosphorus has no luster. It is a poor conductor of heat and a nonconductor of electricity. These typical properties of nonmetals are explained by their lack of free electrons.

The electron configuration of sulfur is $1s^2 2s^2 2p^6 3s^2 3p^4$. Hence, sulfur atoms have two half-filled $3p$ orbitals and should form two covalent bonds. They do so in elemental sulfur, but the molecule consists of eight atoms joined together in a puckered ring. See Figure 22-2. The relatively low melting point and brittleness of sulfur are explained by the weak dispersion interaction forces between S_8 molecules. Sulfur has the common nonmetallic properties: no silvery luster, poor thermal conductivity, and nonconduction of electricity.

We have already seen (Section 6.9) that chlorine exists as diatomic molecules, Cl_2. A single covalent bond joins the two atoms. The dispersion interaction forces between chlorine molecules are very weak. Evidence of this fact is that chlorine is a gas at room temperature.

Argon exists as single atoms since it has no half-filled orbitals to use in bond formation. The dispersion interaction forces

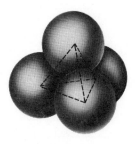

Fig. 22-1. The structure of P_4 molecules of phosphorus.

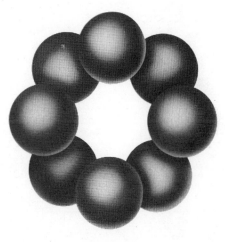

Fig. 22-2. The structure of S_8 molecules of sulfur.

between argon atoms are very weak indeed. This weakness is evident from the very low boiling point of argon.

22.3 Electron configurations, ionization energies, and oxidation states

Table 22-2 lists the electron configuration, ionization energy, oxidation states, and atomic radius for each of the Period Three elements.

We first discussed ionization energy in Section 5.6. There, we pointed out that ionization energy generally increases across a period because of the increasing nuclear charge. But *decreases* in ionization energy do occur in Period Three at aluminum and at sulfur. These decreases are to be expected. The decrease between magnesium and aluminum results from their outer electron arrangements. The outermost electron of aluminum is the first electron in the $3p$ sublevel. The outermost electrons of magnesium occupy the $3s$ sublevel. Less energy is required to remove the $3p$ electron because the $3p$ sublevel has higher energy than the outer $3s$ sublevel of magnesium. A decrease in ionization energy also occurs between phosphorus and sulfur. It results from the beginning of pairing of electrons in the $3p$ sublevel in sulfur. The half-filled $3p$ sublevel of phosphorus has three singly occupied orbitals. This configuration is *more stable* than the $3p$ sublevel with one filled and two singly occupied orbitals in sulfur. (That is, the phosphorus configuration has lower energy.) As a result, more energy is required to remove an electron from a phosphorus atom than from a sulfur atom.

The atomic radii decrease gradually across the period. This general decrease is easily explained. Successive electrons enter the same energy level, while the nuclear charge becomes successively greater and pulls the electrons closer to the nucleus. The relationship between atomic radius and ionic radius for

Table 22-2

ATOMIC STRUCTURE AND RELATED PROPERTIES OF ELEMENTS OF PERIOD THREE

Element	Electron configuration	Ionization energy (kcal/mole atoms)	Principal oxidation states	Atomic radius (Å)
sodium	$1s^2\,2s^2\,2p^6\,3s^1$	119	+1	1.54
magnesium	$1s^2\,2s^2\,2p^6\,3s^2$	176	+2	1.36
aluminum	$1s^2\,2s^2\,2p^6\,3s^2\,3p^1$	138	+3	1.18
silicon	$1s^2\,2s^2\,2p^6\,3s^2\,3p^2$	188	+4	1.11
phosphorus	$1s^2\,2s^2\,2p^6\,3s^2\,3p^3$	254	+3, +5	1.06
sulfur	$1s^2\,2s^2\,2p^6\,3s^2\,3p^4$	239	−2, +4, +6	1.02
chlorine	$1s^2\,2s^2\,2p^6\,3s^2\,3p^5$	$30\overline{0}$	−1, +5, +7	0.99
argon	$1s^2\,2s^2\,2p^6\,3s^2\,3p^6$	363	0	0.98

sodium, magnesium, aluminum, sulfur, and chlorine was described in Section 6.8.

The oxidation states of sodium, $+1$, magnesium, $+2$, and aluminum, $+3$, have been explained already. Sodium has one electron which can be removed at low energy. Magnesium has two, and aluminum three such electrons. (See Section 5.7.) The $+4$ oxidation state of silicon results from its formation of four covalent bonds with sp^3 hybridization. Phosphorus (electron-dot symbol $\cdot \overset{\cdot}{P}:$) may add three electrons to each atom, forming P^{---} ions, as in the compounds of phosphorus known as phosphides. It is also possible for phosphorus atoms to share three or five electrons in forming covalent bonds. Such sharing gives oxidation numbers of $+3$ or $+5$.

Sulfur, electron-dot symbol, S, may add two electrons to each atom, forming sulfide ions, S^{--}, oxidation number -2. Sulfur may also share two, four, or six electrons, giving oxidation states of $+2$, $+4$, or $+6$.

Chlorine, with the electron-dot symbol $:\overset{\cdot\cdot}{Cl}:$, commonly adds one electron to each atom, forming chloride ions. Here, chlorine has the oxidation number -1. However, it is also possible for chlorine to share 1, 3, 5, or even all 7 electrons in covalent bonding. In such cases the oxidation numbers are $+1$, $+3$, $+5$, or $+7$.

Since argon is not yet known to form compounds, it has an oxidation number of zero.

22.4 Properties of oxides of Period Three elements

The elements of Period Three form a great variety of compounds with oxygen. Sodium, phosphorus, sulfur, and chlorine form two or more oxides. For our purpose we need describe only one oxide per element. See Table 22-3.

Table 22-3
OXIDES OF PERIOD THREE ELEMENTS

Oxide	Melting point ($^{\circ}$C)	Boiling point ($^{\circ}$C)	Type of compound	Nature of reaction with water
Na_2O	subl. 1275		ionic	forms OH^-
MgO	2800	3600	ionic	forms OH^-
Al_2O_3	2045	2980	ionic	none; hydroxide is amphiprotic
SiO_2	1710	2230	covalent network	none
P_4O_{10}	subl. 300		molecular	forms H^+(aq)
SO_2	-73	$-1\overline{0}$	molecular	forms H^+(aq)
Cl_2O	$-2\overline{0}$	4	molecular	forms H^+(aq)

Sodium oxide, Na_2O, and magnesium oxide, MgO, are white solids. The reaction of sodium with oxygen usually yields sodium peroxide, Na_2O_2. However, some sodium oxide can be prepared by heating sodium at about $180°$ C in a limited amount of dry oxygen. Magnesium oxide is produced by burning magnesium in pure oxygen. Both sodium oxide and magnesium oxide are ionic compounds. Sodium oxide readily dissolves in water, forming a basic solution which contains Na^+ and OH^- ions.

$$Na_2O + H_2O \rightarrow 2Na^+ + 2OH^-$$

Magnesium oxide is only slightly soluble in water; but it, too, forms a basic solution.

$$MgO + H_2O \rightarrow Mg^{++} + 2OH^-$$

Aluminum oxide, Al_2O_3, is a white ionic compound. It can be produced by burning aluminum in pure oxygen. More commonly, it is prepared by heating aluminum hydroxide or the hydrated oxides of aluminum. Because aluminum oxide is virtually insoluble in water, the dehydration reaction is not reversible. Aluminum hydroxide is a white, insoluble, jelly-like substance. It must be prepared indirectly from aluminum oxide. Aluminum hydroxide is amphiprotic; it reacts as a base in the presence of hydronium ions, and as an acid in the presence of hydroxide ions.

$$Al(OH)_3 + 3H_3O^+ \rightarrow Al(H_2O)_6^{+++}$$
$$Al(OH)_3 + OH^- \rightarrow AlO_2^- + 2H_2O$$

Silicon dioxide, SiO_2, exists widely in nature as quartz. White sand is mostly silicon dioxide. Silicon dioxide has a covalent network structure. It consists of silicon atoms tetrahedrally bonded to four oxygen atoms. Each oxygen atom, in turn, is bonded to another silicon atom tetrahedrally bonded to four oxygen atoms. This structure extends indefinitely. All the silicon-oxygen bond distances are equal in length. The silicon-oxygen bonds are covalent, but with some degree of ionic character.

Silicon dioxide is practically insoluble in water. It acts as an acid in hot, concentrated solutions containing hydroxide ions.

$$SiO_2 + 4OH^- \rightarrow SiO_4^{----} + 2H_2O$$

Silicon dioxide does not react with common acids, but does react with hydrofluoric acid.

$$SiO_2 + 4HF \rightarrow SiF_4(g) + 2H_2O$$

In an abundant supply of oxygen, phosphorus burns and forms diphosphorus pentoxide, P_4O_{10}. (This formula is the correct molecular formula. The name is taken from the corresponding empirical formula P_2O_5.) P_4O_{10} is a white molecular solid. It reacts rapidly with water, forming a solution containing phosphoric acid, H_3PO_4.

$$P_4O_{10} + 6H_2O \rightarrow 4H^+(aq) + 4H_2PO_4^-$$

Phosphoric acid is a moderately strong acid. The equilibrium constant for its first ionization is of the order of 10^{-2}.

Sulfur burns in air or oxygen and forms sulfur dioxide, SO_2. This compound is molecular. At room temperature it is a colorless gas with a choking odor. Sulfur dioxide readily dissolves in and reacts with water. This reaction forms a solution containing sulfurous acid, H_2SO_3.

$$SO_2 + H_2O \rightarrow H^+(aq) + HSO_3^-$$

This acid is also moderately strong. The equilibrium constant for its first ionization is of the order of 10^{-2}.

Dichlorine monoxide, Cl_2O, is prepared by the moderate oxidation of chlorine with mercury(II) oxide.

$$2Cl_2 + HgO \rightarrow HgCl_2 + Cl_2O$$

This compound is an unstable yellow gas. It reacts with water and gives a solution containing hypochlorous acid, $HClO$.

$$Cl_2O + H_2O \rightarrow 2HClO$$
$$2HClO \rightleftharpoons 2H^+(aq) + 2ClO^-$$

Hypochlorous acid is a very weak acid which exists only in water solution. Its ionization constant is of the order of 10^{-8}.

22.5 Properties of the binary hydrogen compounds of Period Three elements

Each of the elements of Period Three forms at least one binary compound with hydrogen. Silicon, phosphorus, and sulfur each form two or more binary hydrogen compounds. As with the oxides, we shall describe only one binary hydrogen compound of each Period Three element. See Table 22-4.

Sodium hydride, NaH, is formed from sodium and hydrogen at moderately high temperatures. It is an ionic compound, and

Table 22-4

BINARY HYDROGEN COMPOUNDS OF PERIOD THREE ELEMENTS

Compound	Melting point (°C)	Boiling point (°C)	Type of compound	Nature of reaction with water
NaH	d. 800		ionic	forms $OH^- + H_2$
$(MgH_2)_x$	d. 280		polymeric	forms $OH^- + H_2$
$(AlH_3)_x$	d. 1$\overline{0}$0		polymeric	forms $OH^- + H_2$
SiH_4	−185	−112	molecular	forms $SiO_2 + H_2$
PH_3	−133	−88	molecular	none
H_2S	−86	−61	molecular	forms $H^+(aq)$
HCl	−115	−85	molecular	forms $H^+(aq)$

crystallizes in a cubic system like sodium chloride. The negative ion here, however, is the hydride ion, H^-. Sodium hydride reacts vigorously with water, yielding hydrogen gas and hydroxide ions.

$$NaH + H_2O \rightarrow H_2 + Na^+ + OH^-$$

Magnesium hydride, MgH_2, is a less stable compound than sodium hydride. It was first prepared about 1950. It can be made directly by heating the elements under high pressure in the presence of magnesium iodide. Complex indirect methods are more satisfactory, however. Magnesium hydride is a non-volatile, colorless solid which reacts violently with water.

$$MgH_2 + 2H_2O \rightarrow Mg(OH)_2 + 2H_2$$

In a vacuum, magnesium hydride is stable to about 300° C. Above this temperature, it decomposes into its elements. The structure of magnesium hydride is believed to be like that of a polymer. The MgH_2 units are bonded together as $(MgH_2)_x$, in which x is indefinite.

Aluminum hydride has been known only since the 1940's. It can be made by the action of lithium hydride on aluminum chloride in ether solution.

$$3LiH + AlCl_3 \xrightarrow[\text{solution}]{\text{(ether)}} AlH_3 + 3LiCl$$

Aluminum hydride is a white amorphous solid. Its structure is unknown but is probably a polymer $(AlH_3)_x$. It reacts vigorously with water. It is stable in a vacuum up to about 100° C. At higher temperatures it decomposes to aluminum and hydrogen.

Monosilane, SiH_4, is a colorless, stable, but readily flammable gas. It consists of nonpolar covalent molecules. Along with other silicon hydrides, it is produced when magnesium silicide is treated with dilute hydrochloric acid.

$$Mg_2Si + 4H^+(aq) \rightarrow 2Mg^{++} + SiH_4$$

Monosilane reacts very readily with water and yields hydrogen and silicon dioxide.

$$SiH_4 + 2H_2O \rightarrow SiO_2 + 4H_2$$

Other known silicon hydrides are: Si_2H_6, Si_3H_8, Si_4H_{10}, Si_5H_{12}, and Si_6H_{14}. Notice the similarity of these formulas to those of the alkanes. However, these compounds are much more reactive than the alkanes. The reason is that silicon-silicon bonds and silicon-hydrogen bonds are weaker than the carbon-carbon and carbon-hydrogen bonds in the alkanes.

Phosphine, PH_3, is one of two or three known binary phosphorus-hydrogen compounds. It is a molecular substance in which the atoms are covalently bonded in an ammonia-type structure. At room temperature it is a colorless gas with an unpleasant odor like that of decayed fish. Phosphine is very poison-

ous and flammable. The simplest method of preparing phosphine is by treating calcium phosphide with water. Phosphine prepared by this method is spontaneously flammable in air because of impurities.

$$Ca_3P_2 + 6H_2O \rightarrow 3Ca(OH)_2 + 2PH_3$$

Phosphine dissolves in water, producing a nearly neutral solution.

Hydrogen sulfide, H_2S, is a colorless, foul-smelling, and very poisonous gas. Its odor resembles that of decayed eggs. It is a molecular compound, with slightly polar covalent bonding within the molecule. Hydrogen sulfide is usually prepared in the laboratory by the action of dilute hydrochloric acid on iron(II) sulfide.

$$FeS + 2H^+(aq) \rightarrow Fe^{++} + H_2S$$

Hydrogen sulfide is flammable. The products of combustion are water vapor and sulfur or sulfur dioxide, depending on combustion conditions.

Hydrogen sulfide dissolves in and reacts with water, forming a weakly acid solution of hydrosulfuric acid. The first ionization constant of hydrosulfuric acid is of the order of 10^{-7}.

$$H_2S \rightleftarrows H^+(aq) + HS^-$$

The binary hydrogen compound of chlorine is hydrogen chloride, HCl. This is a colorless, sharp-odored, poisonous gas. Hydrogen chloride consists of highly polar covalent molecules. It can be prepared by direct combination of its elements or by heating sodium chloride with moderately concentrated sulfuric acid.

$$H_2 + Cl_2 \rightarrow 2HCl$$

$$NaCl + H_2SO_4 \rightarrow NaHSO_4 + HCl$$

Hydrogen chloride is very soluble in water. It is almost completely ionized by the water, yielding hydronium ions and chloride ions.

$$HCl \rightleftarrows H^+(aq) + Cl^-$$

This solution, called hydrochloric acid, is a strong acid.

QUESTIONS

1. (a) Describe the variation in metallic-nonmetallic properties across Period Three. **Group A**
   (b) Relate this to the variation in number of outer-shell electrons.
2. (a) What physical properties do metals have in common? (b) What physical properties do nonmetals have in common?
3. Describe the nature of the binding force between (a) atoms of sodium; (b) atoms of silicon; (c) atoms of chlorine; (d) molecules of chlorine; (e) atoms of argon.
4. Even though they are consecutive elements, why is the melting point of silicon so much higher than the melting point of aluminum?

5. What difference is there in the interatomic forces of elements which are malleable and of those which are brittle?
6. Why is the sodium ion so much smaller than the sodium atom?
7. Why is the chloride ion somewhat larger than the chlorine atom?
8. Compare the reactions of Na_2O, SiO_2, and Cl_2O with water.
9. Compare the reactions of NaH, SiH_4, and HCl with water.
10. Why are the silicon hydrides much more reactive than the alkanes?

Group B
11. What accounts for the silvery luster of metals?
12. Why is the density increase between sodium and aluminum proportionally greater than the atomic weight increase?
13. Compare the magnitude of the binding force between atoms of liquid argon and atoms of liquid aluminum.
14. Explain why diamond does not conduct electricity and silicon has a low electric conductivity, when both have the same crystal structure and type of bonding.
15. Phosphorus atoms form three covalent bonds, sulfur atoms form two covalent bonds, and chlorine atoms form one covalent bond; yet phosphorus molecules are tetratomic, sulfur molecules are octatomic, and chlorine molecules are diatomic. Explain.
16. Explain the observed decrease in ionization energy between magnesium and aluminum and between phosphorus and sulfur.
17. (a) Draw electron-dot symbols for the elements of Period Three. (b) Using these symbols explain how the common oxidation states for each element are attained.
18. Relate electronegativity differences to the type of bonding observed in the (a) oxides of the elements of Period Three; (b) binary hydrogen compounds of the elements of Period Three.
19. Compare the structure of silicon dioxide with that of elemental silicon.
20. Compare the structures of (a) NH_3 and PH_3; (b) H_2S and H_2O. In your comparison include molecular shape and size, and type of bonding.
21. Write the balanced formula equation for the reaction of aluminum hydride and water.

PROBLEMS

Group A
1. What is the mass in grams of a block of aluminum 5.0 cm long, 2.0 cm wide, and 1.5 cm high?
2. How many magnesium atoms are there in a length of magnesium ribbon which has a mass of 0.472 g?
3. What is the percentage of phosphorus in P_4O_{10}?
4. What volume of hydrogen at STP is formed by the reaction of $16\overline{0}$ ml of monosilane with water?
5. How many grams of calcium phosphide must react with water to prepare 5.0 g of phosphine?
6. How many liters of SiF_4 at STP can be obtained from 12 g of SiO_2 by reaction with hydrofluoric acid?

7. A solution of 0.14 g of white phosphorus in 10.0 g of benzene lowers the freezing   **Group B**
    point of the benzene 0.58 C°. (*a*) Calculate the molecular weight of white phos-
    phorus from these data. (*b*) What is the corresponding molecular formula? See
    Table 12-5 for additional data.
8. A saturated solution of $Mg(OH)_2$ is approximately 0.000031 N. What is the pH of
    this solution?

Chapter 23

The Metals of Group I

23.1 Structure and properties

The first group of elements at the left of the periodic table includes lithium, sodium, potassium, rubidium, cesium, and francium. These are all chemically active metals. They are known as the *alkali metals* and also as the *Sodium Family* of elements. These metals occur in nature only as ions with a +1 charge. Sodium and potassium are quite abundant, lithium is fairly rare, and rubidium and cesium are rare. Francium does not exist as a stable element. Only trace quantities have been produced in certain nuclear reactions. Table 23-1 lists some representative physical properties of these metals.

The Group I elements form hydroxides that are strongly basic. Their aqueous hydroxide solutions are extremely alkaline, giving rise to the name "alkali" metals. They possess certain metallic characteristics to a high degree. Each has a silvery luster, is a good conductor of electricity and heat, and is ductile and malleable. These metals are relatively soft and can be cut with a knife. The properties of the Group I metals are related to their characteristic crystalline lattice structures.

This crystal lattice is built around a body-centered cubic unit cell made up of metallic ions with a +1 charge. The valence electrons form an electron "gas" that exists throughout the lattice structure. The mobility of these "free" electrons gives Group I metals their high thermal and electric conductivity.

The silvery luster of the metals also results from these free electrons. When light strikes electrons at the metal surface, they absorb energy and begin to vibrate. This vibration re-radiates the energy in all directions as light.

Table 23-1
PROPERTIES OF GROUP I ATOMS

Element	Atomic number	Atomic weight	Electron configuration	Oxidation number	Melting point (°C)	Boiling point (°C)	Density (g/cm³)	Metallic radius (Å)	Ionic radius (Å)
lithium	3	6.939	2,1	+1	179	1317	0.53	1.55	0.68
sodium	11	22.9898	2,8,1	+1	97.8	892	0.97	1.90	0.97
potassium	19	39.102	2,8,8,1	+1	63.6	774	0.86	2.35	1.33
rubidium	37	85.47	2,8,18,8,1	+1	38.8	701	1.53	2.48	1.47
cesium	55	132.905	2,8,18,18,8,1	+1	28.7	685	1.87	2.67	1.67
francium	87	[223]	2,8,18,32,18,8,1	+1	(27)	(677)	–	–	1.80

The binding force in the metallic crystal lattice is the attraction between the positive ions and the negative electron gas. This force is virtually uniform in all directions, explaining the softness, ductility, and malleability of the alkali metals. Little energy is required to cut these metals or change their shape.

The atoms of each element in Group I have a single electron in their outermost shell. Lithium atoms have the electron configuration $1s^2 2s^1$. All other Group I elements have next-to-outermost shells consisting of eight electrons. An outer octet is easily attained by removing a single electron. Thus, an ion formed in this way has the stable electron configuration of the preceding noble gas. For example, the sodium ion has the electron configuration $1s^2 2s^2 2p^6$. This matches the configuration of the neon atom. The electron configuration of the potassium ion, $1s^2 2s^2 2p^6 3s^2 3p^6$, matches that of the argon atom.

23.2 Chemical activity

The Group I metals are vigorous reducing agents. They have a weak attraction for their valence electrons. Ionization energy decreases as the atom size increases going down the group. However, the lithium atom is the strongest reducing agent. This seeming contradiction may result from the very strong hydration tendency of the lithium ion. Thus, the electrode potential for lithium is also unusually high. *Ionization energy* measures the tendency of an isolated atom to hold a valence electron. *Electrode potential* measures the tendency of the metal to form ions in aqueous solution. The first ionization energies and electrode potentials for Group I metals are given in Table 23-2. Electrode potentials are listed as oxidation potentials for the electrode reaction

$$M(s) \rightarrow M^+(aq) + e^-$$

Here, the solid metal $M(s)$ loses electrons and forms ions $M^+(aq)$ in aqueous solution. This reaction was discussed in Section 21.11. See Section 5.7 for a review of ionization energies.

Table 23-2
GROUP I METALS AS REDUCING AGENTS

Element	Oxidation potential (volts)	Ionization energy (kcal/mole)
Li	+3.045	124.3
Na	+2.714	118.5
K	+2.925	100.1
Rb	+2.925	96.34
Cs	+2.923	89.81
Fr	–	–

Electrons which acquire enough energy are elevated to higher energy levels. An atom containing such electrons is said to be *excited*. These electrons eventually fall back to the lower energy levels available to them in the atom structure. The extra energy is then radiated, sometimes as visible light. This radiated energy (light) will be of frequencies characteristic of that atom. Atoms of the Group I metals are quite easily excited to higher energy states. The energy supplied by a Bunsen flame is sufficient. Compounds of these metals give characteristic colors to flames. The flame colors serve as simple identification tests (known as *flame tests*) for the metallic elements. Lithium compounds produce a carmine (red) flame; sodium, yellow; potassium, violet; rubidium and cesium, reddish violet (magenta).

Handling and storing the alkali metals is difficult because of their chemical activity. They usually are stored under kerosene or some other liquid hydrocarbon because they react vigorously with water. See Figure 23-1. In reaction with water, they release hydrogen and form strongly basic solutions. The metals do not exist free in nature, but are found only in combined form.

All of the ordinary compounds of the alkali metals are ionic, including their hydrides. Only lithium forms the oxide directly with oxygen. Sodium forms the peroxide instead, and rubidium and cesium form "superoxides" of the form $M^+O_2^-$. However, the ordinary oxides can be prepared indirectly. These oxides are basic anhydrides. They react with water and form the hydroxides.

Nearly all of the compounds of the alkali metals are quite soluble in water. The alkali-metal ions are colorless. They have little tendency to hydrolyze in water solution or to form polyatomic ions.

LITHIUM

23.3   Lithium and its compounds

Lithium is a fairly common element. It occurs in nature as Li^+ ions in several types of rocks of very complex composition. It was discovered in 1817 by Johan Arfvedson (1792–1841), a student of Berzelius. It was not until 1855 that Robert W. Bunsen and Augustus Matthiessen succeeded in isolating the metal. Lithium has the lowest density of any metal. It is prepared by electrolysis of fused (molten) lithium chloride.

Lithium has many uses in metallurgical processes. Its compounds are used in ceramics, welding, drugs, the manufacture of chemicals, and the synthesis of organic compounds. It dissolves in liquid ammonia, as do the other alkali metals.

In alloys, lithium loses most of its reactivity. Lithium-magnesium alloys have the highest strength-to-weight ratio of all structural materials. Such alloys are important in aircraft and spacecraft design.

T.P. Schmitter

Fig. 23-1. Potassium, a Group I metal, like other members of this group, reacts vigorously with water. The light for this photograph was produced by dropping a small amount of potassium into a beaker of water.

Lithium consists of a mixture of two isotopes, lithium-6 and lithium-7. The mixture ratio is about 7.4 parts lithium-6 to 92.6 parts lithium-7. In Section 30.21 you will learn how lithium-6 plays a key role in thermonuclear (hydrogen bomb) technology. With hydrogen-2 (deuterium), it forms the hydride lithium-6 deuteride.

Lithium reacts with oxygen, the halogens, hydrogen, and water, forming ionic compounds. Its chemical activity results from its electron structure and "density" of the positive charge on its nucleus. When the valence electron is removed, the positive charge on the ion is shielded by only a single electron shell. By comparison, there are two and three electron shells shielding the nuclear charges of sodium and potassium ions.

Lithium chloride demonstrates the high-charge density of the Li^+ ion and its strong hydration tendency. Crystalline LiCl is a vigorous dehydrating agent. It takes water vapor from the air and quickly dissolves in the water it removes. On the other hand, pure sodium chloride is not deliquescent even in damp weather.

Organometallic compounds formed with lithium metal have properties typical of molecules rather than ions. In these cases, lithium behaves quite differently from other alkali metals.

Ethyl-lithium, C_2H_5Li, has a low melting point and low electric conductivity. It dissolves readily in organic solvents. These properties suggest molecules rather than ions. The lithium atom is assumed to be covalently bonded to a carbon atom as shown in Figure 23-2.

On the other hand, the organometal compound ethyl-sodium, C_2H_5Na, resembles NaCl. It has a high melting point, high electric conductivity, and low solubility in organic solvents. These are the properties of an ionically bonded salt and suggest the structure $Na^+C_2H_5^-$.

A flame test of lithium salts reveals the characteristic carmine-red color. This flame color serves as an identification test for lithium. See Figure 23-3. Strontium salts produce a scarlet-red flame and calcium salts give a yellowish-red flame.

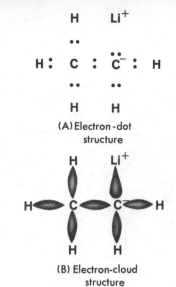

Fig. 23-2. The carbon-lithium bond in C_2H_5Li. (A) Shared pair of electrons shown nearer carbon giving it a slight negative charge. (B) Shared electrons shown spending most time near carbon (where the cloud is thickest).

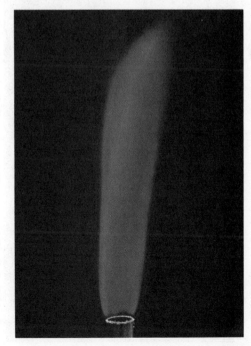

Fig. 23-3. Lithium salts impart a carmine (red) color to the Bunsen flame. The lithium flame appears violet through cobalt-blue glass.

SODIUM

23.4 Occurrence of sodium

Metallic sodium is never found free in nature. However, compounds containing the Na^+ ion and sodium complexes exist widely in soil, natural waters, and in plants and animals. Sodium is such an abundant element that it is difficult to find an absolutely sodium-free material. Vast quantities of sodium chloride are present in sea water and rock salt deposits. There are important deposits of sodium nitrate in Chile and Peru. The carbonates, sulfates, and borates of sodium are found in dry lake beds.

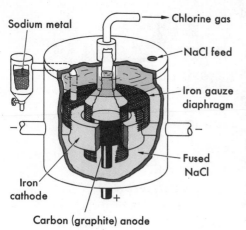

Fig. 23-4. Elementary sodium is produced by the electrolysis of fused sodium chloride in a Downs cell. Chlorine is a valuable by-product.

Fig. 23-5. Sodium salts impart a strong yellow color to the Bunsen flame. The sodium flame is obscured by cobalt-blue glass.

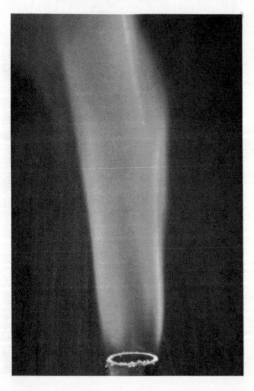

23.5 The preparation of sodium

Sir Humphry Davy first prepared metallic sodium in 1807, by the electrolysis of fused sodium hydroxide. Today, sodium is prepared by the electrolysis of fused sodium chloride. An apparatus called the *Downs cell* (see Figure 23-4) is used in this process. Sodium chloride has a high melting point (801° C). Calcium chloride is mixed with it to lower the melting point to 580° C. Liquid sodium is collected under oil. Chlorine gas is produced simultaneously. This gas is kept separate from the metallic sodium by an iron-gauze diaphragm.

The sodium is recovered by reducing Na^+ ions. This occurs at the cathode of the Downs cell. Each sodium ion acquires an electron from the cathode and forms a neutral sodium atom.

$$Na^+ + e^- \rightarrow Na(l)$$

Chloride ions are oxidized at the anode. Each chloride ion loses an electron to the anode and forms a neutral chlorine atom.

$$Cl^- \rightarrow Cl + e^-$$

Two chlorine atoms, however, form the diatomic molecule of elemental chlorine gas. The net anode reaction is

$$2Cl^- \rightarrow Cl_2(g) + 2e^-$$

In the overall cell reaction, electron-transfer balance is maintained between the electrodes. Two Na^+ ions are reduced for each Cl_2 molecule formed. The cell reaction can be written

cathode:	$2Na^+ + 2e^- \rightarrow 2Na(l)$
anode:	$2Cl^- \rightarrow Cl_2(g) + 2e^-$
cell:	$2Na^+ + 2Cl^- \rightarrow 2Na(l) + Cl_2(g)$

Chemical reduction of sodium ions and of other alkali-metal ions is not generally practical. The reason for this is that the alkali metals themselves are the strongest reducing agents. However, some of the rarer alkali metal ions can be chemically reduced under suitable temperature conditions. See Section 23.16.

23.6 Properties of sodium

Sodium is a silvery-white, lustrous metal that tarnishes rapidly when exposed to air. It is very soft, has a lower density than water, and a low melting point. A pellet of sodium dropped into water melts from the heat of the vigorous exothermic reaction which occurs. This reaction yields hydrogen gas and a strongly basic solution.

$$2Na(s) + 2H_2O \rightarrow 2Na^+(aq) + 2OH^-(aq) + H_2(g)$$

When exposed to air, sodium unites with the oxygen and forms sodium peroxide, Na_2O_2. By supplying sodium in excess, some Na_2O can be produced along with the bulk product Na_2O_2. The Na_2O production may result from the strong reducing character of the sodium atoms. Of the alkali metals, only lithium reacts directly with oxygen and forms the normal oxide. The normal oxide of sodium, Na_2O, can be formed by heating NaOH with sodium.

$$2NaOH + 2Na \rightarrow 2Na_2O + H_2(g)$$

The remaining alkali metals react directly with oxygen and form superoxides of the type $M^+O_2^-$. The oxygen atoms of these superoxides are considered to have an oxidation number of $-\frac{1}{2}$. The superoxide of sodium, NaO_2, can be prepared indirectly.

Sodium reacts with all aqueous acids. It burns in an atmosphere of chlorine gas, uniting directly with the chlorine and forming sodium chloride.

A flame test of sodium compounds reveals a strong yellow color characteristic of vaporized sodium atoms. This yellow flame is a common identification test for sodium. See Figure 23-5.

23.7 Uses of sodium

Most of the sodium produced in the United States is used in making tetraethyl lead, an antiknock additive for gasoline. Sodium is used as a heat-transfer agent and in making dyes and other organic compounds. Another use is in sodium vapor lamps.

Important new uses of sodium are constantly being developed. For example, it is used as a chemical reducing agent in producing titanium, zirconium, niobium, and tantalum from their fused salts.

23.8 Sodium chloride

Sodium chloride is found in sea water, in salt wells, and in deposits of rock salt. Rock salt is mined in many places in the world.

Pure sodium chloride is not deliquescent. Magnesium chloride is very deliquescent, however, and is usually present in sodium salt as an impurity. This explains why table salt becomes wet and sticky in damp weather. Sodium chloride crystallizes in a cubic pattern. See Figure 23-6.

Sodium chloride is essential in the diet of man and animals and is present in certain body fluids. Perspiration contains considerable amounts of it. People who perspire freely in hot weather often need to increase their salt intake by the use of salt tablets.

Fig. 23-6. Native crystals of sodium chloride, known as halite, recovered from the Mojave Desert in California.

B.M. Shaub

Since sodium chloride is the cheapest compound of sodium, it is used as a starting material in making many other sodium compounds. Some sodium compounds are most easily prepared directly from metallic sodium, however. Practically all sodium metal production utilizes sodium chloride as the raw material.

Fused-salt mixtures containing sodium chloride are used in many processes involving atomic fuels. For example, a molten mixture of sodium chloride, potassium chloride, and zinc chloride is used to produce electrolytically refined thorium from spent atomic fuel. The fused-salt mixture acts as the electrolyte and the spent-fuel alloy acts as the anode. The operating voltage of the cell is adjusted to deposit thorium at the cathode. Anode elements less positive than thorium settle out as an insoluble anode sludge. Those more positive than thorium remain in solution.

23.9   Sodium hydroxide

Most commercial sodium hydroxide is produced by electrolysis of an aqueous sodium chloride solution. This electrolysis of aqueous NaCl is somewhat different from that of fused NaCl in the Downs cell. Chlorine gas is produced at the anode, but hydrogen gas (instead of metallic sodium) is produced at the cathode. The solution, meanwhile, becomes aqueous NaOH. Evidence indicates that water molecules acquire electrons from the cathode and are reduced to H_2 gas and OH^- ions.

The cell reaction for the electrolysis of an aqueous NaCl solution is

cathode:	$2H_2O + 2e^- \rightarrow H_2(g) + 2OH^-(aq)$
anode:	$2Cl^- \rightarrow Cl_2(g) + 2e^-$
cell:	$2H_2O + 2Cl^- \rightarrow H_2(g) + Cl_2(g) + 2OH^-(aq)$

As the Cl^- ion concentration diminishes, the OH^- ion concentration increases. The Na^+ ion concentration remains unchanged during the electrolysis. Thus, the solution is converted from aqueous NaCl to aqueous NaOH.

Large amounts of sodium hydroxide are also made by adding calcium hydroxide (slaked lime) to sodium carbonate solution.

$$Na_2CO_3 + Ca(OH)_2 \rightarrow 2NaOH + CaCO_3(s)$$

The precipitated calcium carbonate is filtered off. The remaining solution of sodium hydroxide is concentrated by evaporation.

Sodium hydroxide converts some types of animal and vegetable matter into soluble materials by chemical action. It is a very *caustic* substance and has destructive effects on skin, hair, and wool.

Sodium hydroxide is a white crystalline solid. It is marketed in the form of flakes, pellets, and sticks. It is very deliquescent and dissolves in the water that it removes from the air. It reacts with carbon dioxide from the air, producing sodium carbonate. Its water solution is strongly basic.

Sodium hydroxide reacts with fats, forming soap and glycerol. One of its important uses, therefore, is in making soap. It is also used in the production of rayon, cellulose film, paper pulp, and in petroleum refining. A commercial grade of sodium hydroxide is sold as lye, or caustic soda.

23.10 The Solvay process

Almost all of the sodium carbonate and sodium hydrogen carbonate produced in the world is manufactured by the Solvay process. It was developed in 1864 by Ernest Solvay (1838–1922), a Belgian. The process is a classic example of efficiency in chemical production.

The raw materials for the Solvay process are common salt, limestone, and coal. The salt is pumped as brine from salt wells. The thermal decomposition of limestone yields the carbon dioxide and calcium oxide needed in the process.

$$CaCO_3(s) \rightarrow CaO(s) + CO_2(g)$$

Coal is converted into coke, gas, coal tar, and ammonia by destructive distillation. The coke and gas are used as fuel in the plant. The ammonia is also used in the process, while the coal tar is sold as a useful by-product.

To begin the process, a cold saturated solution of sodium chloride is further saturated with ammonia and carbon dioxide. The following reactions occur:

$$CO_2(g) + H_2O \rightarrow H_2CO_3$$

$$H_2CO_3 + NH_3(g) \rightarrow NH_4^+(aq) + HCO_3^-(aq)$$

net: $CO_2(g) + NH_3(g) + H_2O \rightarrow NH_4^+(aq) + HCO_3^-(aq)$

The HCO_3^- ions form in a solution which has a high concentration of Na^+ ions. Since sodium hydrogen carbonate is only slightly soluble in this cold solution, it precipitates.

$$Na^+(aq) + HCO_3^-(aq) \rightarrow NaHCO_3(s)$$

The solution which remains contains NH_4^+ ions and Cl^- ions. The precipitated sodium hydrogen carbonate is filtered and dried. It is either sold as *baking soda* or converted into sodium carbonate by thermal decomposition.

$$2NaHCO_3(s) \rightarrow Na_2CO_3(s) + H_2O(g) + CO_2(g)$$

The dried sodium carbonate is an important industrial chemical called soda ash.

The ammonia used in the process is more valuable than the sodium carbonate or sodium hydrogen carbonate. Hence, it must be recovered and used over again if the process is to be

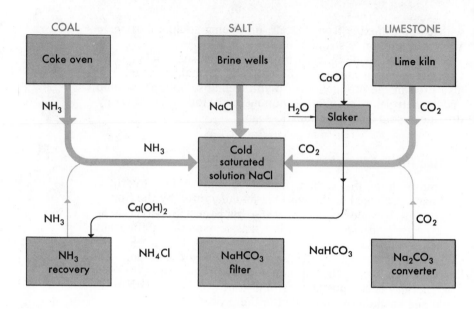

Fig. 23-7. A flow diagram of the Solvay process.

profitable. The calcium oxide from the first reaction is slaked by adding water. Calcium hydroxide is formed in this reaction.

$$CaO(s) + H_2O(l) \rightarrow Ca(OH)_2(s)$$

The calcium hydroxide is added to the solution to release the ammonia from the ammonium ion.

$$NH_4^+(aq) + OH^-(aq) \rightarrow NH_3(g) + H_2O$$

The solution now contains mainly Ca^{++} ions and Cl^- ions. Neither of these ions is recycled into the process. As a by-product, calcium chloride has some use as an inexpensive hygroscopic agent. The supply generally exceeds the demand, however.

Sodium hydrogen carbonate, as baking soda, is the main ingredient of baking powders. One important industrial use of sodium carbonate is in the production of glass. When converted to sodium hydroxide (see Section 23.9), it is used in making soap and in many other industrial processes.

The water solution of sodium carbonate is mildly basic because of hydrolysis of CO_3^{--} ions.

$$CO_3^{--} + H_2O \rightleftharpoons HCO_3^- + OH^-$$

The decahydrate, $Na_2CO_3 \cdot 10H_2O$ is commonly called washing soda. It is formed when sodium carbonate is recrystallized from water solution.

23.11 Other compounds of sodium

If sodium hydroxide is added to a solution of phosphoric acid, a sodium salt of phosphoric acid forms. This salt can be recovered by evaporation of water. Phosphoric acid, H_3PO_4, is triprotic. Thus, the salt product of the reaction depends on the amount of sodium hydroxide used.

$$NaOH + H_3PO_4 \rightarrow NaH_2PO_4 + H_2O$$
sodium
dihydrogen
phosphate

$$2NaOH + H_3PO_4 \rightarrow Na_2HPO_4 + 2H_2O$$
sodium
hydrogen
phosphate

$$3NaOH + H_3PO_4 \rightarrow Na_3PO_4 + 3H_2O$$
sodium
phosphate

When 1 mole of base is used with 1 mole of phosphoric acid, dihydrogen phosphate ions, $H_2PO_4^-$, are formed. The salt product is sodium dihydrogen phosphate. Two moles of NaOH per mole of H_3PO_4 form hydrogen phosphate ions, HPO_4^{--}; the salt is sodium hydrogen phosphate. Three moles of NaOH per mole of H_3PO_4 give the phosphate ion, PO_4^{--}. The salt here is sodium phosphate (also called trisodium phosphate, or TSP).

Sodium phosphate, Na_3PO_4, hydrolyzes in water and the solution is basic. The phosphate ion is a strong enough base to remove a proton from a water molecule. This basic anion hydrolysis increases the OH^- ion concentration of the solution. (See Section 20.10.)

$$PO_4^{---} + H_2O \rightarrow HPO_4^{--} + OH^-$$

Because of the HPO_4^{--} anion hydrolysis, Na_3PO_4 lowers the surface tension of water and increases its "wetting" action.

Many laundry detergents contain phosphates as additives or "builders." These additives are generally in the form of sodium triphosphate, $Na_5P_3O_{10}$. They are important for good cleaning action because they

1.   soften water,
2.   scatter and hold dirt particles in a stable colloidal suspension, and
3.   give a buffered alkaline solution in which acidic perspiration and food residues are effectively removed from fabrics by detergent action.

The synthetic detergents in these laundry products are biodegradable. That is, they can be oxidized by the action of microorganisms after their disposal. However, the phosphates present encourage the growth of organisms in inland lakes and streams that deplete oxygen needed by fish. This action is a matter of great ecological concern. In some inland areas the use of phosphate-containing washing products is forbidden.

Sodium compounds are widely used because they are usually abundant and inexpensive. Common sodium compounds are also soluble in water. Some useful data on well-known compounds of sodium are given in Table 23-3.

Table 23–3

REPRESENTATIVE SODIUM COMPOUNDS

Chemical name	Common name	Formula	Color	Uses
sodium tetraborate, decahydrate	borax	$Na_2B_4O_7 \cdot 10H_2O$	white	as a water softener; in making glass; as a flux
sodium carbonate, decahydrate	washing soda	$Na_2CO_3 \cdot 10H_2O$	white	as a water softener; in glass making
sodium hydrogen carbonate	baking soda	$NaHCO_3$	white	as a leavening agent in baking
sodium cyanide	prussiate of soda	$NaCN$	white	to destroy vermin; to extract gold from ores; in silver and gold plating; in case-hardening steel
sodium hydride	(none)	NaH	white	in cleaning scale and rust from steel forgings and castings
sodium nitrate	Chile saltpeter	$NaNO_3$	white, or colorless	as a fertilizer
sodium peroxide	(none)	Na_2O_2	yellowish white	as an oxidizing and bleaching agent; as a source of oxygen
sodium phosphate, decahydrate	TSP	$Na_3PO_4 \cdot 10H_2O$	white	as a cleaning agent; as a water softener
sodium sulfate, decahydrate	Glauber's salt	$Na_2SO_4 \cdot 10H_2O$	white, or colorless	in making glass; as a cathartic in medicine
sodium thiosulfate, pentahydrate	hypo	$Na_2S_2O_3 \cdot 5H_2O$	white, or colorless	as a fixer in photography; as an antichlor
sodium sulfide	(none)	Na_2S	colorless	in the preparation of sulfur dyes; for dyeing cotton; to remove hair from hides

POTASSIUM

23.12 Occurrence of potassium

Potassium is abundant in nature and is widely distributed, but only in combined form. Great deposits of combined potassium occur in the form of feldspar, a potassium aluminosilicate mineral. This mineral is part of all granitic rocks. It is insoluble and weathers very slowly. Large deposits of potassium chloride, crystallized with magnesium and calcium compounds, are found in Texas and New Mexico. Some potassium compounds are taken from Searles Lake in California.

23.13 Preparation of potassium

Potassium was first prepared by Sir Humphry Davy in 1807. His method involved the electrolysis of fused potassium hydroxide. The small annual production of potassium today is by the reaction

$$KCl + Na \rightarrow NaCl + K$$

The reaction proceeds to the right and equilibrium is prevented by removing the potassium.

23.14 Properties of potassium

Potassium metal is soft and of low density. It has a silvery luster that quickly tarnishes bluish-gray when exposed to air. Potassium is more active than sodium. It floats on water, and reacts with the water so rapidly that the hydrogen gas given off usually ignites.

Potassium imparts a fleeting violet color to a Bunsen flame. The color comes from vaporizing potassium atoms. The presence of sodium, however, masks the violet color of potassium in the flame. Potassium is detected in a mixture of sodium and potassium compounds by observing the colored flame through cobalt-blue glass. This glass filters out the yellow sodium flame color. The violet potassium flame color then shows clearly. A typical potassium flame is shown in Figure 23-9.

23.15 Compounds of potassium

All common potassium compounds are soluble in water. Potassium hydroxide is prepared by the electrolysis of a solution of potassium chloride. It has the typical properties of a strong alkali. Potassium nitrate is made by mixing hot, concentrated solutions of potassium chloride and sodium nitrate.

$$KCl + NaNO_3 \rightarrow KNO_3 + NaCl(s)$$

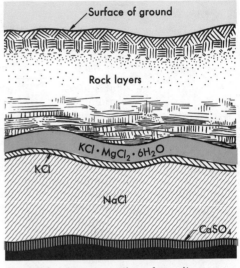

Fig. 23-8. A cross-section of a salt deposit, showing how the different minerals were deposited as the sea water evaporated.

Fig. 23-9. Potassium salts color the Bunsen flame violet. The potassium flame is masked by the presence of sodium salts and is purple through cobalt-blue glass.

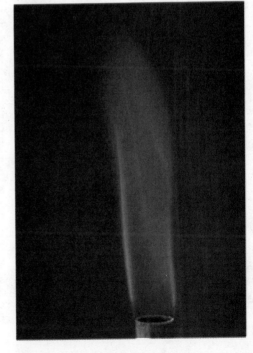

Table 23-4

REPRESENTATIVE POTASSIUM COMPOUNDS

Chemical name	Common name	Formula	Color	Uses
potassium bromide	(none)	KBr	white	as a sedative; in photography
potassium carbonate	potash	K_2CO_3	white	in making glass; in making soap
potassium chlorate	(none)	$KClO_3$	white	as an oxidizing agent; in fire-works; in explosives
potassium chloride	(none)	KCl	white	as a source of potassium; as a fertilizer
potassium hydroxide	caustic potash	KOH	white	in making soft soap; as a battery electrolyte
potassium iodide	(none)	KI	white	in medicine; in iodized salt; in photography
potassium nitrate	saltpeter	KNO_3	white	in black gunpowder; in fire-works; in curing meats
potassium permanganate	(none)	$KMnO_4$	purple	as a germicide; as an oxidizing agent

Sodium chloride is the least soluble of the four salts. When the solutions are mixed, it precipitates and is removed. Then, as the solution cools, the potassium nitrate crystallizes from the saturated sodium chloride solution. Some useful data on well-known potassium compounds are given in Table 23-4.

Sodium compounds are often used instead of potassium compounds because they usually are less expensive. Sodium chlorate can replace potassium chlorate for many uses. Sodium hydroxide is as useful for most purposes as potassium hydroxide. It is not only cheaper, but also supplies more hydroxide ions per gram. Potassium has an atomic weight of 39. Thus, 56 grams of KOH are needed to supply 1 mole (17 g) of hydroxide ions. Sodium, on the other hand, has an atomic weight of 23. Thus, only 40 grams of NaOH are needed to give 1 mole of hydroxide ions.

Most glass is made with sodium carbonate, but potassium carbonate yields a more lustrous glass that is preferred for optical uses. Potassium nitrate is not hygroscopic. For this reason, it is used instead of sodium nitrate in making black gunpowder.

There is one very important use for potassium compounds for which there is no substitution. Green plants must have these compounds to grow properly. Therefore, complete chemical fertilizers always contain an appropriate amount of potassium.

RUBIDIUM, CESIUM, AND FRANCIUM

23.16 Rubidium and cesium

Rubidium and cesium were discovered in 1860 by Bunsen, who examined their spectra with the newly invented spectroscope. These alkali metals have great chemical activity. Therefore, chemical reduction of the Rb^+ and Cs^+ ions would seem impossible. However, the Rb^+ ion can be reduced at a high temperature in fused $RbCl$ with calcium. Here, reduction is possible because rubidium escapes from the reaction environment as a gas.

$$Ca + 2RbCl \rightarrow CaCl_2 + 2Rb(g)$$

Of course, these metals can be produced by the electrolysis of their fused chlorides or hydroxides.

Rubidium and cesium are used as sources of electrons in photoelectric cells. Electrons escape more easily from cesium than from any other metal when light strikes its surface. The ejection of electrons from a metal by light is called the *photoelectric effect*. The metal is said to be photosensitive, that is, sensitive to light. Rubidium and cesium are photosensitive over the full spectrum of *visible* light. For this reason, they are used in photoelectric cells intended for use with such light. These metals are also used for removing the last traces of oxygen from vacuum tubes.

23.17 Francium

Francium was discovered by Marguerita Perey in 1939. She named the metal for her native country, France. It is a radioactive element formed by the disintegration of an isotope of actinium. Francium has been produced only in trace quantities. Little is known of its properties except as they are indicated by its position in the periodic table.

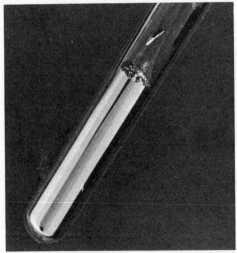

B.M. Shaub

Fig. 23-10. Rubidium, shown here in a sealed ampule, is very slightly radioactive.

Fig. 23-11. Cesium, an extremely active member of the Sodium Family, is sealed in a glass ampule.

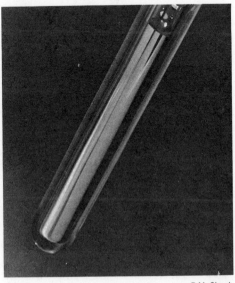

B.M. Shaub

SPECTROSCOPY

23.18 Use of a spectroscope

One type of *spectroscope* consists of a glass prism and a *collimator tube* to focus a narrow beam of light rays upon the prism. It also has a small telescope for examining the light which passes through the prism. When white light passes through a triangular prism, a band of colors called a *continuous spectrum* appears. This effect is caused by the unequal bending of light of different wavelengths.

Examination of a sodium flame by spectroscope reveals a characteristic bright-yellow line. Since this yellow line is always in the same relative place in the spectrum, it identifies sodium. Potassium produces both red and violet spectral lines. The spectrum chart, Figure 23-12, shows the characteristic color lines of several chemical elements. It also shows the continuous spectrum of white light produced by an *incandescent* (white hot) solid.

23.19 Origin of spectral lines

A platinum wire held in a Bunsen flame becomes incandescent and emits (gives off) white light. When the incandescent wire is viewed through a spectroscope, a continuous spectrum of colors is observed. The energy of the white light is distributed over a continuous range of light frequencies. This range includes the entire visible spectrum. Light energy of the shortest wavelength (highest frequency) is bent most; it yields the deep violet color seen at one end of the visible spectrum. Light energy of the longest wavelength (lowest frequency) is bent least; this light yields the deep red color characteristic of the other end of the visible spectrum. Between these two extremes, there is a gradual blending from one color to the next. It is possible to recognize six elementary colors: *red, orange, yellow, green, blue,* and *violet.* In general, incandescent solids and gases under high pressure give continuous spectra.

Luminous (glowing) gases and vapors under low pressure give discontinuous spectra called *bright-line spectra.* These spectra consist of narrow lines of color which correspond to the light energy of certain wavelengths. The atoms of each element produce its own characteristic line spectra.

Electrons in atoms are restricted to energies of only certain values. In unexcited atoms, electrons occupy the lowest energy levels available to them. The energy of an electron can change only as it moves from one energy level to another. A certain amount of energy is absorbed with each jump to a higher energy level; a certain amount is released with each jump to a lower level. The quantity of energy in each change is equal to the difference between the separate energy levels involved.

When substances are vaporized in a flame, electrons are raised to higher energy levels by heat energy. When these electrons fall back into the lower energy levels available to them, energy is released. The energy released by any substance has wavelengths characteristic of that substance. Different wavelengths produce different spectral lines in the spectroscope. Thus, vaporized sodium atoms produce a spectrum consisting of two narrow yellow lines very close together (seen in the ordinary spectroscope as a single yellow line). Potassium atoms produce two red lines and a violet line. Lithium atoms yield intense red and yellow lines and weak blue and violet lines.

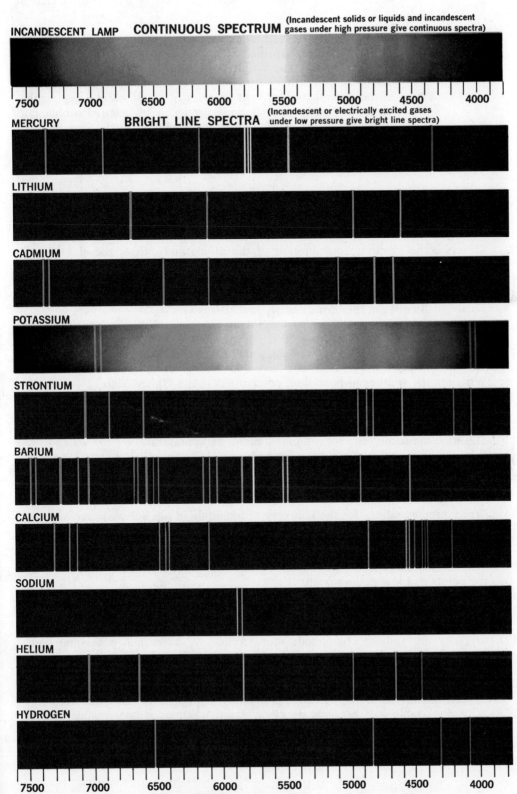

Fig. 23-12. Emission spectra.

The spectra produced by excited atoms of different elements are as distinct as fingerprints.

Bright lines in the visible portion of the spectrum account for the flame coloration produced by certain metals. The color seen is the combination of light energies of the different wavelengths emitted. Some spectral lines produced by excited atoms fall outside the range of visible wavelenghts. Such lines can be photographed even though they cannot be seen with the unaided eye.

QUESTIONS

Group A

1. Describe the electron configuration of the atoms and ions of the elements in Group I.
2. Compare the methods of preparing lithium, sodium, and potassium.
3. List three uses for metallic sodium.
4. Distinguish between the terms *caustic* and *corrosive*.
5. (*a*) What are the raw materials for the Solvay process? (*b*) What are the products and by-products?
6. (*a*) What is caustic soda? (*b*) washing soda? (*c*) baking soda?
7. Why do molasses and baking soda have a leavening action in cookies?
8. What are the sources of potassium compounds in the United States?
9. (*a*) How are sodium and potassium stored in the laboratory stockroom? (*b*) Why must they be stored in this fashion?
10. Write the ionic equation for the reaction of potassium and water.
11. Describe the flame tests for lithium, sodium, and potassium.
12. Why are rubidium and cesium preferred over the other alkali metals for use in ordinary photoelectric cells?
13. Write three equations to show how sodium carbonate can be produced in the Solvay process.
14. Write three equations for the recovery of ammonia in the Solvay process.
15. For what purposes are spectroscopes used in chemical analysis?

Group B

16. Why are the members of the Sodium Family soft, malleable metals with low melting points and low boiling points?
17. Why is NaCl necessary in the diet of many animals and man?
18. Why is sodium chloride used as a starting material for preparing metallic sodium and other compounds of sodium?
19. (*a*) Why are sodium compounds more frequently used than potassium compounds? (*b*) What are the purposes for which sodium compounds cannot be substituted for potassium compounds?
20. What by-product of the Solvay process has such limited use and yet is produced in such quantity that disposal of it is actually a problem to the manufacturers?
21. Why does table salt become sticky in damp weather, although pure sodium chloride is not deliquescent?
22. Explain why potassium has a lower density than sodium, although it consists of heavier atoms.

23. Write the equation for the net reaction which occurs when sodium hydroxide is exposed to the air.
24. In the Solvay process, why does the reaction between sodium chloride and ammonium hydrogen carbonate run to completion?
25. Why does a solution of sodium carbonate in water turn red litmus paper blue?
26. Suppose you had a tremendous quantity of acid that had to be neutralized, and that NaOH, KOH, and LiOH were all available at the same price per pound. Which of these three would you use? Why?
27. A 0.1-M solution of $HC_2H_3O_2$ is found to have a pH of 2.9. A solution of 0.1-M $NaC_2H_3O_2$ is added to the acetic acid solution and the pH rises. Explain.

PROBLEMS

Group A

1. (a) How many grams of sulfuric acid in water solution can be neutralized by 10.0 g of sodium hydroxide? (b) 10.0 g of potassium hydroxide?
2. If you have 1.00 kg of sodium nitrate and 1.00 kg of potassium chloride, how many kilograms of potassium nitrate can you make by reacting these two substances, assuming that all the potassium nitrate can be recovered?
3. If crystallized sodium carbonate, $Na_2CO_3 \cdot 10H_2O$, sells for 12.5 cents per kilogram, what is anhydrous sodium carbonate worth per kilogram?
4. How many liters of carbon dioxide can be liberated from 50.0 g of each of the following? (a) Na_2CO_3; (b) $NaHCO_3$; (c) K_2CO_3; (d) $KHCO_3$

Group B

5. How many kilograms of sodium chloride are required to produce 1.00 metric ton of anhydrous sodium carbonate?
6. How many cubic meters of carbon dioxide (at STP) are needed in Problem 5?
7. How many cubic meters of carbon dioxide gas must be produced at 150° C and 745 mm pressure to supply that needed in Problem 6?
8. A load of limestone, analyzed as 92.0% $CaCO_3$, measured 2.72 metric tons. When decomposed by heat in a lime kiln, how many kilograms of calcium oxide are produced?
9. From the reaction of Problem 8, how many liters of carbon dioxide can be stored at 25° C and 855 mm pressure?
10. A solution is prepared by dissolving 1.1 g NaOH in water and diluting to 500 ml. What is the pH of the solution?

Chapter 24

The Metals of Group II

24.1 Calcium Family

The elements of Group II of the periodic table are members of the Calcium Family. They are the metals beryllium, magnesium, calcium, strontium, barium, and radium. These elements are often called the *alkaline-earth metals*.

Beryllium and magnesium are commercially important light metals. In their chemical behavior, they resemble the corresponding alkali metals, lithium and sodium. Radium is important because it is radioactive. Radioactivity and other properties of radium are discussed in Chapter 30. The remaining three elements of Group II are calcium, strontium, and barium. They have similar properties and are considered "typical" members of the Calcium Family.

Each alkaline-earth element has two outer-shell electrons and forms doubly charged ions of the M^{++} type. The attraction between the metal ions and the electron gas of the metallic crystals is stronger than in the alkali metals. Therefore, these metals are denser, harder, and have higher melting and boiling points than the corresponding Sodium Family metals.

The atoms and ions of the alkaline-earth metals are smaller than those of the corresponding alkali metals because of their higher nuclear charge. For example, the magnesium ion, Mg^{++}, has the same electron configuration as the sodium ion, Na^+. This configuration is $1s^2 2s^2 2p^6$. However, Mg^{++} has a nuclear charge of $+12$, while Na^+ has a nuclear charge of $+11$. The higher nuclear charge of the Mg^{++} ion attracts electrons more strongly and results in smaller K and L shells. Some properties of Group II metals are listed in Table 24-1.

486

Table 24–1
PROPERTIES OF GROUP II ATOMS

Element	Atomic number	Atomic weight	Electron configuration	Oxidation number	Melting point (°C)	Boiling point (°C)	Density (g/cm³)	Metallic radius (Å)	Ionic radius (Å)
beryllium	4	9.0128	2,2	+2	1278	2970	1.85	1.12	0.35
magnesium	12	24.305	2,8,2	+2	651	1107	1.74	1.60	0.66
calcium	20	40.08	2,8,8,2	+2	842	1487	1.54	1.97	0.99
strontium	38	87.62	2,8,18,8,2	+2	769	1384	2.60	2.15	1.12
barium	56	137.34	2,8,18,18,8,2	+2	725	1140	3.50	2.22	1.34
radium	88	226.0254	2,8,18,32,18,8,2	+2	700	<1737	5(?)	–	1.43

The alkaline-earth metals form hydrides, oxides or peroxides, and halides similar to those of the alkali metals. Almost all hydrides of the alkaline-earth metals are ionic and contain H^- ions. (The exception is BeH_2, since binary compounds of beryllium have fairly strong covalent bond character.) They react with water, releasing hydrogen gas and forming basic hydroxide solutions. Calcium hydride is often used as a convenient source of hydrogen in the laboratory.

The oxides of beryllium, magnesium, and calcium have very high melting points. CaO and MgO are used as heat resistant (refractory) materials. Beryllium oxide is amphiprotic and both BeO and MgO are polymeric. All alkaline-earth oxides are more covalent than alkali-metal oxides. Strontium and barium form peroxides with oxygen, probably because of the large size of their ions.

The hydroxides are formed by adding water to the oxides. Except for $Be(OH)_2$ which is amphiprotic, the hydroxides dissociate completely in water solution and yield OH^- ions. Hydroxides above barium are only slightly soluble in water, the solubility increasing with the size of the metallic ions. Solutions of these hydroxides have low concentrations of OH^- ions; they are weakly basic because of the slight solubility in water.

Fig. 24-1. Fused pellets of beryllium. This metal produces alloys that are extremely elastic.

BERYLLIUM

24.2 Preparation and properties

Beryllium is not a common element. It occurs in the mineral *beryl*, $Be_3Al_2Si_6O_{18}$. *Aquamarine* and *emerald* are varieties of beryl which are prized as gems. Beryllium can be isolated by electrolyzing a fused mixture of sodium and beryllium chlorides. It is a very hard, silvery-white metal with a density of 1.85 g/cm³.

Beryllium is used for making windows for X-ray tubes because its atoms are light and absorb very little radiation. This property also makes beryllium useful in a nuclear reactor.

B.M. Shaub

Copper containing as much as 2% beryllium has greatly increased hardness and resistance to fatigue and wear. Beryllium-copper springs are practically unbreakable. This alloy is also non-sparking. Electric switches and tools made of beryllium copper can be used safely where sparks could cause explosions. The addition of beryllium to light-metal alloys makes them easier to form into useful products.

Beryllium compounds are more covalent than those of the other alkaline-earth metals. Its salts are extensively hydrolyzed in water. From these facts, we see that nonmetallic properties in Period 2 begin to appear with beryllium.

MAGNESIUM

24.3 Occurrence of magnesium

Magnesium compounds are widely distributed on land and in the sea. Magnesium sulfate is found in the ground in many places. Important deposits occur in the state of Washington and in British Columbia, Canada. A double chloride of potassium and magnesium is mined from the potash deposits of Texas and New Mexico. Sea water contains significant amounts of magnesium compounds.

Dolomite, $CaCO_3 \cdot MgCO_3$, is a double carbonate of magnesium and calcium which appears widely in the United States and Europe. It is an excellent building stone, and is useful for lining steel furnaces. Pulverized dolomite neutralizes soil acids and also supplies magnesium for the growth of plants.

Talc and asbestos are silicates of magnesium. Asbestos, which is mined in Ontario and Quebec, Canada, is a remarkable mineral. It has a high melting point, is nonflammable, and is a good heat insulator. It is mixed with cement for making asbestos shingles. With magnesium oxide, it is used for covering steam pipes and furnaces. Its structure, consisting of fibers, permits the mineral to be spun into threads and woven into cloth. Asbestos is also used for making automobile brake linings, fireproof curtains and clothing, and as an electric insulator.

Elemental magnesium, shown in Figure 24-2, was first prepared by Davy in 1807. This same series of experiments resulted in the isolation of sodium, calcium, and similar active metals.

24.4 Extraction of magnesium

1. From magnesium chloride. Most commercial magnesium is produced by electrolytic reduction of molten magnesium chloride. The $MgCl_2$ may be obtained from sea water, brine, or minerals. Sea water is the most economical source.

About three kilograms of magnesium are recovered from each metric ton of sea water processed. The water is first treated with

Fig. 24-2. Feathery crystals shown here are composed of magnesium, the eighth most abundant element.

B.M. Shaub

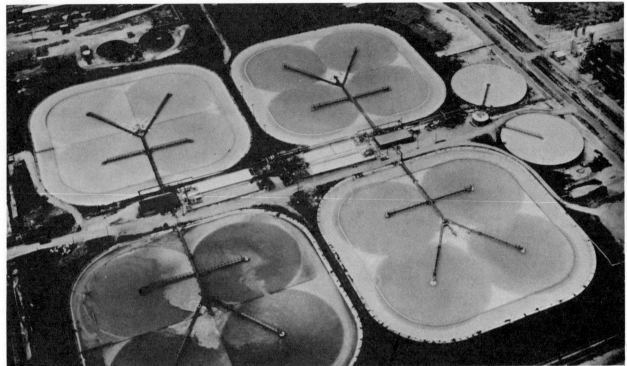

Dow Chemical

lime made from oyster shells, which are cheap and readily available. This treatment causes magnesium ions to precipitate as magnesium hydroxide. The reactions are shown by the following equations.

Fig. 24-3. Large settling tanks in which magnesium is being recovered from sea water as a magnesium hydroxide precipitate.

$$\text{CaO(s)} + \text{H}_2\text{O(l)} \rightarrow \text{Ca(OH)}_2\text{(s)}$$

$$\text{Ca(OH)}_2\text{(s)} \rightleftharpoons \text{Ca}^{++}\text{(aq)} + 2\text{OH}^-\text{(aq)} \qquad K_{sp} = 1.3 \times 10^{-6}$$

$$\text{Mg}^{++}\text{(aq)} + 2\text{OH}^-\text{(aq)} \rightleftharpoons \text{Mg(OH)}_2\text{(s)} \qquad K_{sp} = 1.2 \times 10^{-11}$$

The two values for K_{sp} show that Mg(OH)_2 is less soluble than Ca(OH)_2. The precipitation of Mg(OH)_2 lowers the concentration of OH^- ions in equilibrium with Ca(OH)_2.

Magnesium hydroxide is separated from the water by filtration. The addition of hydrochloric acid converts the magnesium hydroxide to magnesium chloride.

$$\text{Mg(OH)}_2 + 2\text{HCl} \rightarrow \text{MgCl}_2 + 2\text{H}_2\text{O}$$

Calcium chloride and sodium chloride are added to increase the conductivity and lower the melting point of the magnesium chloride. Magnesium metal is then recovered from the fused MgCl_2 by electrolysis.

$$\text{Mg}^{++} + 2\text{Cl}^- \rightarrow \text{Mg(l)} + \text{Cl}_2\text{(g)}$$

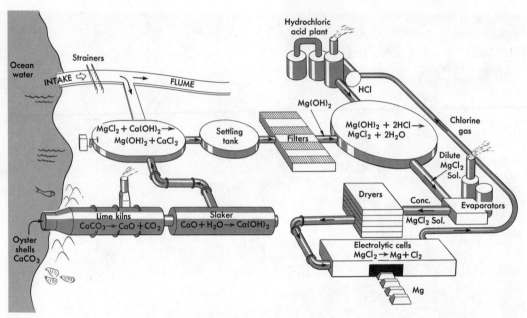

Fig. 24-4. Diagram of a plant for the production of magnesium from sea water.

Chlorine gas collected at the anode is used to produce the hydrochloric acid required in the process. The Ca^{++} and Na$^+$ ions have higher reduction (electrode) potentials than Mg^{++} ions. Thus, they are not reduced under the electrolysis conditions used. A flow diagram for this magnesium extraction process is shown in Figure 24-4.

2. From magnesium oxide. Magnesium of high purity can be prepared from magnesium oxide by reduction with ferrosilicon, an alloy of iron and silicon. The reduction is carried out at a temperature of about 1150° C in a vacuum. At this high temperature and low pressure, the magnesium evaporates. It is then condensed as crystals, melted, and cast into molds. Because of costs, this process is rarely used today.

24.5 Properties of magnesium

Magnesium is a silver-white metal with a density of 1.74 g/cm³. When heated, it becomes ductile and malleable. Its tensile strength (resistance to being pulled apart) is not quite as great as that of aluminum.

Dry air does not affect magnesium. In moist air, however, a coating of basic magnesium carbonate forms on its surface. Because this coating is not porous, it protects the metal underneath from tarnishing. *A metal which forms a nonporous, nonscaling coat of tarnish is said to be a **self-protective metal.***

When heated in air to the kindling point, magnesium burns with an intensely hot flame and gives off a dazzling white light. (See Figure 8-1.) The combustion produces magnesium oxide, MgO, and magnesium nitride, Mg$_3$N$_2$. Magnesium is one of the few metals which combines directly with nitrogen. Boiling water reacts slowly with magnesium and forms the hydroxide and hydrogen. Common acids react with magnesium.

Once ignited, magnesium burns in water, in carbon dioxide, and in nitrogen. These reactions are shown by the equations:

$$Mg + H_2O \rightarrow MgO + H_2$$

$$2Mg + CO_2 \rightarrow 2MgO + C$$

$$3Mg + N_2 \rightarrow Mg_3N_2$$

At about 800° C, magnesium carbonate decomposes to *light* magnesium oxide and carbon dioxide. Further heating to above 1400° C converts the light oxide to *dense* MgO. This dense oxide is a refractory material having a melting point above 2800° C.

24.6   Uses of magnesium

The brilliant white light of burning magnesium makes it useful for flares and fireworks. Magnesium forms light, strong alloys with aluminum. Examples are *magnalium* and *Dowmetal*. Other alloying metals are lithium, thorium, zinc, and manganese. Magnesium alloys are used for making tools and fixtures, for the beams of chemical balances, and for automobile and airplane parts. The growth of the aircraft and aerospace industries has produced a much greater demand for magnesium. Table 24-2 lists some common magnesium compounds.

Halibrand Engineering Co.

Fig. 24-5. A wheel made of a magnesium alloy being machined to precise specification for a racing car.

Table 24–2
COMMON MAGNESIUM COMPOUNDS

Chemical name	Common name	Formula	Appearance	Uses
magnesium carbonate	(none)	$MgCO_3$	white, usually fluffy	for lining furnaces; in making the oxide
basic magnesium carbonate	magnesia alba	$Mg_4(OH)_2(CO_3)_3 \cdot 3H_2O$	soft, white powder	in tooth cleansers; for pipe coverings
magnesium chloride	(none)	$MgCl_2$	white, crystalline solid	with asbestos for stone flooring
magnesium hydroxide	milk of magnesia	$Mg(OH)_2$	white, milky suspension	as antacid; in laxatives
magnesium oxide	magnesia	MgO	white powder	as refractory; for lining furnaces
magnesium sulfate, heptahydrate	Epsom salts	$MgSO_4 \cdot 7H_2O$	white, crystalline solid	in laxatives, cathartics; in dye industry

CALCIUM

24.7   Distribution of calcium

Calcium ranks fifth in abundance by weight among the elements in the earth's crust, atmosphere, and surface waters. It is widely distributed in many rock and mineral forms.

The best known of these mineral forms are the carbonate and the sulfate. Calcium carbonate occurs mainly as limestone, marble, and calcite. Other forms are coral, pearls, and oyster shells. Calcium sulfate occurs as gypsum, $CaSO_4 \cdot 2H_2O$, and the anhydride, $CaSO_4$.

Calcium was first isolated by Davy in 1808. Davy began by electrolyzing a moist mixture of calcium oxide and mercury (II) oxide. He then distilled off the mercury from the resulting calcium-mercury alloy.

24.8   Preparation of calcium

Since calcium occurs as combined Ca^{++} ions, the metal must be recovered by reduction. Electrolytic reduction involves fused calcium chloride.

$$Ca^{++} + 2Cl^- \rightarrow Ca + Cl_2(g)$$

A graphite crucible, which also serves as the anode, holds the fused chloride. An iron cathode dips into the fused salt. As metallic calcium forms on the end of the cathode, the cathode is slowly raised from the mass. In this way an irregular-shaped rod of metallic calcium is produced.

Chemical reduction is generally employed today for recovering calcium. Calcium oxide is heated with aluminum in a vacuum retort.

$$3CaO + 2Al \rightarrow Al_2O_3 + 3Ca(g)$$

The reaction proceeds because the calcium metal is distilled off as a gas at the reaction temperature.

24.9   Properties of calcium

Metallic calcium is silver-white in color, but a freshly-cut piece tarnishes to bluish-gray within a few hours. Calcium is somewhat harder than lead, but it is only about one-eighth as dense. If a piece of calcium is added to water, it reacts with the water and gives off hydrogen gas slowly.

$$Ca + 2H_2O \rightarrow Ca(OH)_2 + H_2(g)$$

Since calcium has a greater electrochemical activity than sodium, we might expect this reaction to be more violent. However, the reaction is much less violent than that of sodium or potassium with water. The calcium hydroxide produced is only slightly soluble and coats the surface of the calcium. This coating protects the metal from rapid interaction with the water.

Calcium is a good reducing agent. It burns with a bright, yellowish-red flame in oxygen. It also unites directly with chlorine. Calcium salts yield a yellowish-red color in flame tests. See Figure 24-6. Sodium contamination often changes the color to orange-yellow. The flame color becomes greenish when seen through cobalt-blue glass. It is masked by the yellowish-green flame of the barium salts. Thus, a calcium flame test must be used with caution.

Calcium is used in small amounts to reduce uranium tetra-fluoride to uranium, and thorium dioxide to thorium.

$$UF_4 + 2Ca \rightarrow 2CaF_2 + U$$

$$ThO_2 + 2Ca \rightarrow 2CaO + Th$$

Calcium is an effective deoxidizer for iron, steel, and copper. Some alloy steels contain it in small quantities. Lead-calcium alloys are used for bearings in machines. Calcium is also used to harden lead for cables and storage-battery plates.

24.10 Calcium carbonate

Calcium carbonate, $CaCO_3$, is an abundant mineral found in many different forms.

1. Limestone. This is the most common form of calcium carbonate. It was formed in past geologic ages by great pressures on layers of seashells. Limestone is found in layers, as a *sedimentary rock.* It is quarried in varying amounts in almost every state in the country. Pure calcium carbonate is white or colorless when crystalline. Most deposits, however, are gray because of impurities.

Limestone is used for making glass, iron, and steel, and as a source of carbon dioxide. It is a building stone, and large quantities are used for building roads. Powdered or pulverized limestone is used to neutralize acid soils. It is heated to produce calcium oxide, CaO. Calcium oxide, called *quicklime,* is one of the largest tonnage chemicals in industry.

A mixture of limestone and clay is converted to *cement* by heating strongly in a rotary kiln. Some limestone deposits contain clay and calcium carbonate naturally mixed in about the right proportions for making cement. Such deposits are called *natural cement.*

2. Calcite. The clear, crystalline form of calcium carbonate is known as calcite. Transparent, colorless specimens are called *Iceland spar.*

3. Marble. This rock was originally limestone. Later heat and pressure changed it into marble with a resulting increase in

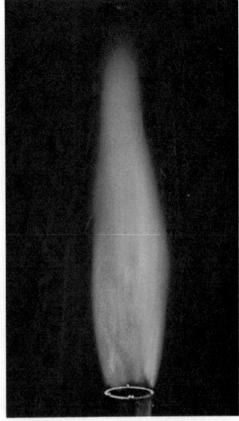

Fig. 24-6. Calcium salts impart a yellowish-red color to the Bunsen flame. The calcium flame is masked by the presence of barium salts.

Fig. 24-7. Calcite, a crystalline form of calcium carbonate.

Lee Boltin

Fig. 24-8. Marble is an excellent stone for the construction of buildings and monuments. Here it is shown being quarried in Vermont.

the size of the calcium carbonate crystals. Hence it is classed as a *metamorphic* (changed) *rock.*

4. Shells. The shells of such animals as snails, clams, and oysters consist largely of calcium carbonate. In some places, large masses of such shells have become cemented together and formed rock called *coquina* (koh-*kee*-nuh). It is used as a building stone in the southern states. Tiny marine animals, called *polyps,* deposit limestone as they build *coral* reefs. *Chalk,* such as that of the chalk cliffs of England, consists of the microscopic shells of small marine animals. Blackboard "chalk" is made of claylike material mixed with calcium carbonate; it should not be confused with natural chalk.

5. Precipitated chalk. This form of calcium carbonate is made by the reaction of sodium carbonate and calcium chloride.

$$Na_2CO_3 + CaCl_2 \rightarrow CaCO_3(s) + 2NaCl$$

It is soft and finely divided. Thus, it forms a nongritty scouring powder suitable for toothpastes and tooth powders. Under the name of *whiting* it is used in paints to fill the pores in the wood. When it is ground with linseed oil, it forms putty.

24.11   Hardness in water

Rainwater falling on the earth usually contains carbon dioxide in solution. As it soaks through the ground, it reaches deposits of limestone or dolomite. Some of the calcium carbonate and magnesium carbonate in these rocks react with the CO_2 solution. This reaction produces the soluble hydrogen carbonates of these metals. The ground water now contains Ca^{++} ions and Mg^{++} ions in solution. Such water is called "*hard water.*" This term indicates that it is "hard" to get a lather when soap is added to the water. Water that lathers readily with soap is called "soft" water. The terms are not precise, but they are in common use. Deposits of iron and other heavy metals in the ground may also produce hard water.

Water hardness is of two types. *Temporary hardness* results from the presence of HCO_3^- ions along with the metal ions. *Permanent hardness* results when other negative ions (usually SO_4^{--}) more stable than the HCO_3^- ion are present along with the metal ions.

The main ingredient of ordinary soap is water-soluble sodium stearate, $NaC_{18}H_{35}O_2$. When soap is added to water containing Ca^{++} ions, the large $C_{18}H_{35}O_2^-$ ions react with the Ca^{++} ions. The reaction produces the insoluble stearate, $Ca(C_{18}H_{35}O_2)_2$, which deposits as a gray scum.

$$Ca^{++} + 2C_{18}H_{35}O_2^- \rightarrow Ca(C_{18}H_{35}O_2)_2(s)$$

The metal ions in hard water react with the soap and form precipitates until all of these ions are removed. Until this occurs, no lasting lather is produced. Soft water does not contain these ions and therefore lathers easily when soap is added.

24.12 Softening of hard water

Hard water is a nuisance in laundering. The sticky precipitate wastes soap and collects on the fibers of the garments being laundered. In bathing, the hard water does not lather freely, and the precipitate forms a scum on the bathtub. In steam boilers, temporary hard water containing HCO_3^- ions has a still more serious fault. When this water is boiled, calcium carbonate collects as a hard scale inside the boiler and the steam pipes. It may form a thick crust, acting as a heat insulator and preventing efficient transfer of heat. Thus, for most purposes, hard water should be softened before it is used.

There are several practical methods of softening water. Generally, the nature of the hardness and the quantity of soft water required determine the best method.

1. Boiling (for temporary hardness). Hard water containing HCO_3^- ions can be softened by boiling. The metal ions precipitate as carbonates according to the following equation:

$$Ca^{++} + 2HCO_3^- \rightarrow CaCO_3(s) + H_2O + CO_2(g)$$

This reaction is reversible except for the fact that boiling drives off the CO_2.

2. Precipitation. When sodium carbonate, Na_2CO_3, is added to hard water, Ca^{++} and Mg^{++} ions precipitate as insoluble carbonates. The Na^+ ions added to the water cause no difficulties with soap.

$$Ca^{++} + CO_3^{--} \rightarrow CaCO_3(s)$$

$$Mg^{++} + CO_3^{--} \rightarrow MgCO_3(s)$$

The addition of a basic solution such as $NH_3(aq)$ or limewater to temporary hard water supplies OH^- ions. These ions neutralize the HCO_3^- ions and precipitate the "hard" metal ions as carbonates.

$$Ca^{++} + HCO_3^- + OH^- \rightarrow CaCO_3(s) + H_2O$$
$$Mg^{++} + HCO_3^- + OH^- \rightarrow MgCO_3(s) + H_2O$$

Other precipitating agents such as borax and sodium phosphate are sometimes used. Both produce basic solutions by hydrolysis, and the phosphate salts of calcium and magnesium are insoluble.

3. Ion exchange. Certain natural minerals called *zeolites* have porous, three-dimensional networks of silicate-aluminate groups. These networks act as large fixed ions carrying negative charges. Metallic ions such as Na^+ are attached to these complexes forming giant molecules. If hard water is allowed to stand in contact with sodium zeolite, Ca^{++} and Mg^{++} ions replace the

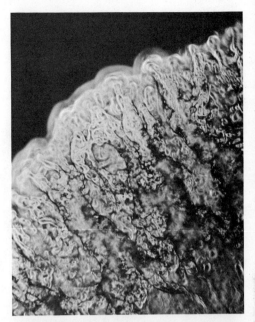

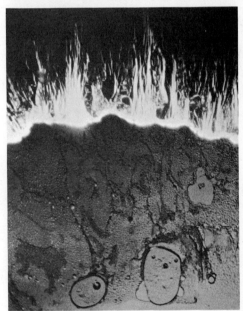

The Permutit Company

Fig. 24-9. Photomicrographs of soap in the process of dissolving in hard water (top) and in soft water (bottom). In hard water the solution process is inhibited by a barrier of sticky soap curd, but in soft water soap streamers extend into the water, forming a clear solution.

The Permutit Company

Fig. 24-10. The scale of calcium carbonate which has collected on the inside of these pipes cuts down the flow of steam and acts as an insulator. Thus, the scale prevents efficient transfer of heat.

Na^+ ions. Since the zeolite ions are immoble, the "hard" metal ions thus exchanged do not return to the water.

$$Ca^{++} + Na_2 \text{ zeolite} \rightarrow Ca \text{ zeolite} + 2Na^+$$

The law of mass action (Section 19.13) explains how zeolites can be used over and over again. Calcium zeolite is placed in a concentrated sodium chloride solution. The solution has a high Na^+ ion concentration, and the Ca^{++} ions are replaced by Na^+ ions. This reaction is the reverse of the one shown above. The equation is

$$2Na^+ + Ca \text{ zeolite} \rightarrow Na_2 \text{ zeolite} + Ca^{++}$$

A synthetic zeolite, known as *permutit*, acts more rapidly than natural zeolites. Permutit is used today in many household water softeners. Sodium chloride, the cheapest source of Na^+ ions, is used to renew the water-softening agent in these softeners.

Chemists recently have developed *ion-exchange resins* far superior to the zeolites. One type of resin is called an *acid-exchange resin* or a *cation exchanger*. This type has large negatively charged organic units whose neutralizing ions in water are H_3O^+ ions. A second type of resin is the *base-exchange resin* or *anion exchanger*. These resins have large positively charged organic units whose neutralizing ions in water are OH^- ions.

Used together, the two types of ion-exchange resins can remove both positive and negative ions from water. The cation exchanger removes metallic ions (cations) and replaces them with H_3O^+ ions. The water is then passed through the anion exchanger. Here, negative ions (anions) are removed and replaced by OH^- ions. The H_3O^+ and OH^- ions form water by neutralization.

Natural water or a water solution of salts treated by combinations of ion-exchange resins is made *ion-free*. (Only the small equilibrium quantities of H_3O^+ and OH^- ions remain.) This treated water is called *deionized* or *demineralized* water. Deionized water is now used in many processes that once required distilled water. Deionized water is as free of ions as the most carefully distilled water, although it may contain some dissolved carbon dioxide.

An acid-exchange resin can be renewed by running a strong acid through it. Similarly, a base-exchange resin can be renewed by using a basic solution.

24.13 Calcium oxide

Calcium oxide is a white, ionic solid with a cubic structure. It is *refractory* since it does not melt or vaporize below the temperature of the electric arc. It unites chemically with water and forms calcium hydroxide.

$$CaO(s) + H_2O \rightarrow Ca(OH)_2(s) \qquad \Delta H = -16 \text{ kcal}$$

During this process, called *slaking,* the mass swells and a large amount of heat is released.

A lump of quicklime exposed to air gradually absorbs water. It swells, then cracks, and finally crumbles to a powder. It first forms calcium hydroxide, and then slowly unites with carbon dioxide from the air and forms calcium carbonate. Thus, a mixture of calcium hydroxide and calcium carbonate is formed. Such a mixture is valuable for treating acidic soils. However, air slaking ruins lime for making mortar and plaster.

Calcium oxide is produced by heating calcium carbonate to a high temperature in a rotary kiln.

$$CaCO_3(s) \rightarrow CaO(s) + CO_2(g)$$

A high concentration of carbon dioxide would drive the reaction in the reverse direction according to Le Chatelier's principle. Such an equilibrium is avoided by removing the carbon dioxide from the kiln as it forms.

24.14 Calcium hydroxide

Calcium hydroxide, or *slaked lime,* is a white solid which is sparingly soluble in water. Its water solution, called *limewater,* has basic properties. A suspension of calcium hydroxide in water is known as milk of lime. Mixed with flour paste or glue, it makes whitewash.

Calcium hydroxide is the cheapest of the hydroxides. It is used to remove hair from hides before they are tanned, or made into leather. It is useful for treating soils, for freeing ammonia from ammonium compounds, and for softening temporary hard water. Large quantities are used for making mortar and plaster.

Lime mortar consists of slaked lime, sand, and water. Mortar of this type has been used for many centuries, but the process by which it sets to a hard mass is still not fully understood. The first step in the setting is loss of water by evaporation. It appears that the lime and sand slowly react according to the equation:

$$Ca(OH)_2 + SiO_2 \rightarrow CaSiO_3 + H_2O$$

Carbon dioxide from the air reacts with the lime also, as follows:

$$Ca(OH)_2 + CO_2 \rightarrow CaCO_3 + H_2O$$

Mortar becomes harder over many years as chemical changes occur in the center of the mass.

24.15 Calcium sulfate

Calcium sulfate occurs as the mineral *gypsum.* Transparent crystals of gypsum are called *selenite.* When gypsum is heated gently, it partially dehydrates and forms a white powder known as plaster of Paris. The equation is

$$2CaSO_4 \cdot 2H_2O(s) \rightarrow (CaSO_4)_2 \cdot H_2O(s) + 3H_2O(g)$$

When plaster of Paris is mixed with water, it forms a paste useful in making molds and casts. Plaster of Paris unites with water readily thereby "setting" the paste rapidly. This setting reaction is the reverse of the above dehydrating reaction. Gypsum is mixed with lime to make the finish coat of plaster. Large quantities are used in making wallboard or plasterboard.

STRONTIUM
AND BARIUM

24.16   Strontium compounds

The sulfate and the carbonate are the chief strontium minerals. Since all compounds of strontium give a beautiful scarlet color to a flame, they are used in fireworks displays. See Figure 24-11.

Fig. 24-11. Strontium salts color the Bunsen flame scarlet. The strontium flame is masked by barium salts and is violet through cobalt-blue glass.

Fig. 24-12. Barium salts impart a yellowish-green color to the Bunsen flame.

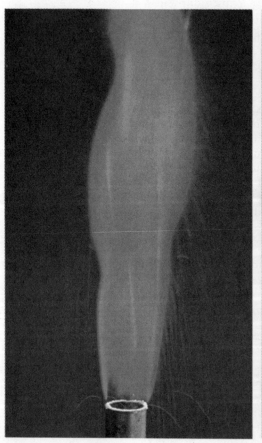
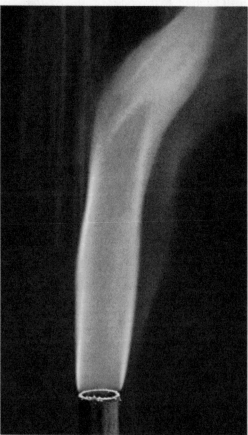

Strontium nitrate mixed with powdered shellac makes a red light for fireworks and flares. Strontium salts give an intense scarlet color in flame tests. However, the color is not easily obtained with dilute solutions. The inexperienced observer usually finds it hard to tell lithium flames from strontium flames.

24.17   Compounds of barium

Both the sulfate and carbonate of barium are found in nature. The compounds of barium are similar in chemical properties to the compounds of calcium. The following are most widely used.

Barium sulfate, $BaSO_4$, is a dense white solid used as a filler in making heavy paper and paints. It gives paper more body and reduces its transparency. Barium sulfate also increases the durability of paint.

Barium peroxide, BaO_2, is used in fireworks and to some extent in making hydrogen peroxide. It is a vigorous oxidizing agent.

Barium nitrate, $Ba(NO_3)_2$, is a white crystalline solid. It is generally used in making flares and fireworks.

All barium compounds give a yellowish-green color to a flame. See Figure 24-12. This color, however, may be masked by sodium impurities. In turn, the barium color masks a calcium flame.

The oxides of both barium and strontium are used to coat the filaments of vacuum tubes. A single layer of barium atoms on a filament may increase the yield of electrons given off by the filament more than a hundred million times.

QUESTIONS

Group A

1. What useful alloy is made from beryllium and a heavy metal?
2. List some of the common uses for asbestos.
3. (*a*) What is dolomite? (*b*) For what purposes is it used?
4. Since magnesium is an active metal, why is it that objects made from it do not corrode rapidly as iron does?
5. Compare the preparation of elementary calcium with that of elementary sodium.
6. What are the important uses for metallic calcium?
7. In what forms is calcium carbonate found in nature?
8. (*a*) What does the term *hard water* mean? (*b*) What does the term *soft water* mean? (*c*) What is the difference between temporary and permanent hardness of water?
9. What principle is employed to regenerate a zeolite water softener?
10. Distinguish: (*a*) limestone; (*b*) quicklime; (*c*) slaked lime; (*d*) lime; (*e*) hydrated lime.
11. For what gas is limewater used as a test solution?
12. How could you demonstrate that a piece of coral is a carbonate?

13. Write an empirical equation to show the action of water containing dissolved carbon dioxide or limestone.
14. How is cement manufactured from clay and limestone?
15. How are "red fire" and "green fire" made for fireworks?

Group B

16. Write three balanced equations to show the steps in the preparation of magnesium from sea water.
17. Why must the reduction of magnesium oxide by ferrosilicon be carried out in a vacuum?
18. How do beryllium compounds differ from those of the other Group II elements?
19. Why are the members of the Calcium Family denser and harder than the corresponding members of the Sodium Family?
20. Why does calcium chloride exist as a hydrate, $CaCl_2 \cdot 2H_2O$, while sodium chloride does not occur as a hydrate?
21. Give two reasons why the reaction of calcium with water is not as vigorous as that of potassium and water.
22. (a) What metallic ions cause water to be hard? (b) What negative ion causes temporary hardness? (c) What negative ion causes permanent hardness?
23. What type of chemical reaction occurs between soap and hard water?
24. Write an empirical equation to show the softening action of sodium carbonate on hard water containing: (a) calcium sulfate; (b) magnesium hydrogen carbonate.
25. What are some uses for calcium chloride produced in large quantities as a by-product of the manufacture of Solvay soda?
26. (a) How is plaster of Paris made? (b) Why does it harden?
27. What are the uses for barium sulfate?
28. (a) What impurity may still remain in water that has been passed through both an acid exchange resin and a base exchange resin? (b) For what kind of solutions would such water be unsuited?
29. How can you account for the fact that temporary hard water, containing Ca^{++} ions, is softened by the addition of limewater, a solution containing Ca^{++} ions and OH^- ions?

PROBLEMS

Group A

1. How many kilograms of calcium oxide can be produced from 1.000 metric ton of limestone which contains 12.5% of impurities?
2. How much mass will 86.0 kg of gypsum lose when it is converted into plaster of Paris?
3. Calculate the percentage of beryllium in beryl, $Be_3Al_2Si_6O_{18}$.
4. What quantity of magnesium can be prepared from a metric ton of magnesium oxide, MgO?
5. A cubic kilometer of sea water contains in solution enough minerals to form about 4.0×10^6 kg of magnesium chloride. How much metallic magnesium could be obtained from this volume of sea water?

6. If dolomite is 95.0% a double carbonate of calcium and magnesium, together with 5.0% of impurities such as iron and silica, what is the percentage of magnesium in the sample? (Compute to 3 significant figures.)

7. How many kilograms of carbon dioxide can be obtained from a metric ton of oyster shells that are 81.0% calcium carbonate?

8. How many liters will the carbon dioxide produced in <u>Problem</u> 7 occupy at <u>STP</u>?

9. If the carbon dioxide of Problem 8 is measured at $72\overline{0}$ mm pressure and $2\overline{0}°$ C, what volume does it occupy?

10. The thermal decomposition of a charge of limestone produced $50\overline{0}$ m³ of carbon dioxide when stored at 28° C and $95\overline{0}$ mm pressure. How many moles of the gas was this?

Chapter 25

The Transition Metals

25.1 Transition subgroups

The transition metals are unique among the chemical elements. They consist of 10 subgroups between Group II and Group III in the periodic table, beginning with Period 4. This region of the periodic table is shown in Figure 25-1. The uniqueness of the transition metals results from the presence of electrons of d sublevel orbitals of the next-to-outermost shell. The number of d electrons increases with atomic number across each period.

The metallic character of the transition elements is related to the presence of one or two electrons in the outermost shell of

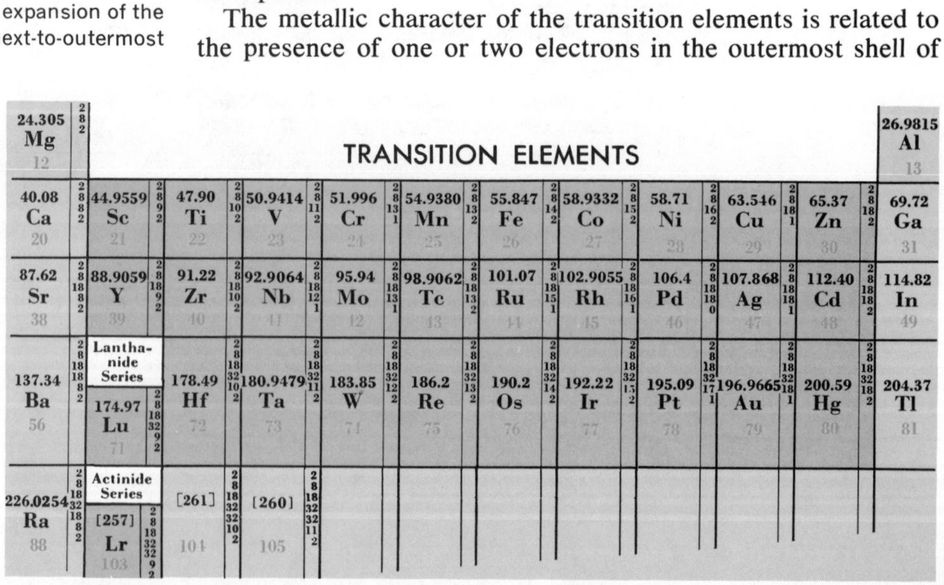

Fig. 25-1. Transition metals are characterized by the expansion of the d sublevel in the next-to-outermost shell.

TRANSITION ELEMENTS

24.305 **Mg** 12 (2,8,2)											26.9815 **Al** 13
40.08 **Ca** 20 (2,8,8,2)	44.9559 **Sc** 21 (2,8,9,2)	47.90 **Ti** 22 (2,8,10,2)	50.9414 **V** 23 (2,8,11,2)	51.996 **Cr** 24 (2,8,13,1)	54.9380 **Mn** 25 (2,8,13,2)	55.847 **Fe** 26 (2,8,14,2)	58.9332 **Co** 27 (2,8,15,2)	58.71 **Ni** 28 (2,8,16,2)	63.546 **Cu** 29 (2,8,18,1)	65.37 **Zn** 30 (2,8,18,2)	69.72 **Ga** 31
87.62 **Sr** 38 (2,8,18,8,2)	88.9059 **Y** 39 (2,8,18,9,2)	91.22 **Zr** 40 (2,8,18,10,2)	92.9064 **Nb** 41 (2,8,18,12,1)	95.94 **Mo** 42 (2,8,18,13,1)	98.9062 **Tc** 43 (2,8,18,13,2)	101.07 **Ru** 44 (2,8,18,15,1)	102.9055 **Rh** 45 (2,8,18,16,1)	106.4 **Pd** 46 (2,8,18,18,0)	107.868 **Ag** 47 (2,8,18,18,1)	112.40 **Cd** 48 (2,8,18,18,2)	114.82 **In** 49
137.34 **Ba** 56	Lanthanide Series / 174.97 **Lu** 71	178.49 **Hf** 72	180.9479 **Ta** 73	183.85 **W** 74	186.2 **Re** 75	190.2 **Os** 76	192.22 **Ir** 77	195.09 **Pt** 78	196.9665 **Au** 79	200.59 **Hg** 80	204.37 **Tl** 81
226.0254 **Ra** 88	Actinide Series / [257] **Lr** 103	[261] 104	[260] 105								

Table 25-1

ELECTRONIC CONFIGURATIONS OF FIRST-ROW TRANSITION ELEMENTS

Name	Symbol	Atomic number	Number of electrons in sublevels						
			1s	2s	2p	3s	3p	3d	4s
scandium	Sc	21	2	2	6	2	6	1	2
titanium	Ti	22	2	2	6	2	6	2	2
vanadium	V	23	2	2	6	2	6	3	2
chromium	Cr	24	2	2	6	2	6	5	1
manganese	Mn	25	2	2	6	2	6	5	2
iron	Fe	26	2	2	6	2	6	6	2
cobalt	Co	27	2	2	6	2	6	7	2
nickel	Ni	28	2	2	6	2	6	8	2
copper	Cu	29	2	2	6	2	6	10	1
zinc	Zn	30	2	2	6	2	6	10	2

their atoms. Their unique chemical properties are related to incomplete inner shells. In the fourth period, calcium has the electron configuration $1s^2 2s^2 2p^6 3s^2 3p^6 4s^2$. Beyond calcium the electron configurations expand (with increasing atomic number) from $3d^1$ to $3d^{10}$ through the transition subgroups. Following this $3d$ expansion, the regular buildup of $4p$ electrons occurs in Groups III through VIII.

In the fifth period there is a similar expansion of the $4d$ sublevel following strontium (-----$4s^2 4p^6 5s^2$), before the buildup of the $5p$ sublevel occurs to complete the period. In the sixth period, expansion of the electron configuration of the $5d$ sublevel following barium (-----$4s^2 4p^6 5s^2 5p^6 6s^2$) is interrupted by expansion of the $4f$ sublevel. These two expansions greatly complicate this period. There are seven $4f$ orbitals which can accommodate 14 electrons. In the *Lanthanide Series* of rare earth elements, the $4f$ electron population increases with atomic number.

In the seventh period, the $6d$ sublevel expansion is similarly interrupted by the buildup of the $5f$ sublevel characteristic of the *Actinide Series* of rare earth elements. The placement of lawrencium (at. no. 103) in the scandium subgroup marks the resumption of the $6d$ expansion. Elements 104 and 105, in the titanium and vanadium subgroups respectively, indicate a continuation of this $6d$ expansion.

The transition elements occupy the long periods in the periodic table as it is arranged in Chapter 5. The choice of the first and last elements in the series depends somewhat on the definition used. Based on d and s electron populations, the transition elements are considered to consist of the ten subgroups between Groups II and III. The first-row transition elements are the most important since they are the most abundant. Their electron configurations are shown in Table 25-1.

25.2 General properties of transition elements

We have stated that the transition elements have several unique properties related to their *d* sublevel electron populations. Examples are their *variable oxidation states, strong color, tendency to form complex ions,* and *attraction into a magnetic field* (paramagnetism).

All transition elements are distinctly metallic because there are not more than two electrons in the outermost shell. Their atoms are small compared to those of the metals of Groups I and II. Transition elements show some tendency toward covalent bonding among their particles. Thus, with a few exceptions, transition metals are hard and brittle. Their melting points are generally higher than those of other metals.

25.3 Oxidation states

The transition metals form compounds in which they exhibit several oxidation states. The energies of the outermost *d* and *s* electrons do not differ greatly. The ionization energies of these electrons are relatively low.

The *d* sublevel has five available orbitals which can hold ten electrons when all are filled. The *s* sublevel has one orbital and it can hold two electrons. Electrons occupy the *d* orbitals singly as long as unoccupied orbitals of similar energy exist. The *s* electrons and one or more *d* electrons can be used in chemical bonding.

In the first-row transition metals, several 4*s* and 3*d* electrons may be transferred to or shared with other substances. Thus, several oxidation states become possible. Remember that the maximum oxidation state is limited by the total number of 4*s* and 3*d* electrons present.

Table 25–2

OXIDATION STATES OF FIRST-ROW TRANSITION ELEMENTS

Element	Electron populations			Common oxidation states
	$1s^2 2s^2 2p^6 3s^2 3p^6$	3d	4s	
scandium	Each	⊘◯◯◯◯	⊗	+3
titanium	transition	⊘⊘◯◯◯	⊗	+2 +3 +4
vanadium	element	⊘⊘⊘◯◯	⊗	+2 +3 +4 +5
chromium	has	⊘⊘⊘⊘⊘	⊘	+2 +3 +6
manganese	all	⊘⊘⊘⊘⊘	⊗	+2 +3 +4 +6 +7
iron	of	⊗⊘⊘⊘⊘	⊗	+2 +3
cobalt	these	⊗⊗⊘⊘⊘	⊗	+2 +3
nickel	sublevels	⊗⊗⊗⊘⊘	⊗	+2 +3
copper	filled	⊗⊗⊗⊗⊗	⊘	+1 +2
zinc		⊗⊗⊗⊗⊗	⊗	+2

Table 25-2 gives the common oxidation states and $3d$ and $4s$ electron populations of these metals. This table uses orbital notations introduced in Chapter 4. In these notations ◯ represents an unoccupied orbital. The symbol ⊘ re resents an orbital occupied by one electron, and ⊗ represents an orbital with an electron pair.

Observe that the maximum oxidation state increases to $+7$ for manganese and then decreases abruptly beyond manganese. The difficulty of forming the higher oxidation states increases toward the end of the row. This increase in difficulty is caused by the general increase in ionization energy with atomic number. The higher oxidation states generally involve covalent bonding.

Manganese atoms lose two $4s$ electrons and become Mn^{++} ions. Higher oxidation states involve one or more of the $3d$ electrons. In the permanganate ion, MnO_4^-, manganese is in the $+7$ oxidation state. It is covalently bonded with the oxygen atoms.

When the electron configuration includes both $3d$ and $4s$ valence electrons, the $3d$ electrons are lower in energy than the $4s$ electrons. Thus, the first electron removed in an ionizing reaction is the one most loosely held, a $4s$ electron. This fact is illustrated by the step-by-step ionization of titanium. The ground-state configurations of the valence electrons are as follows:

$$Ti \text{———} 3d^2 4s^2$$
$$Ti^+ \text{———} 3d^2 4s^1$$
$$Ti^{++} \text{———} 3d^2 4s^0$$
$$Ti^{+3} \text{———} 3d^1$$
$$Ti^{+4} \text{———} 3d^0$$

25.4 Color

A striking property of many compounds of transition metals is their color. Color in these compounds is related to the presence of d electrons in the metallic element and to its oxidation

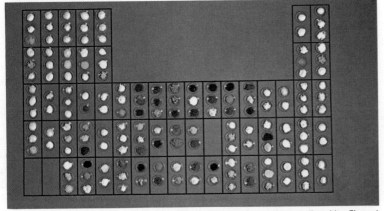

From the CHEM Study Film: *Vanadium, Transition Element*

Fig. 25-2. Most compounds of transition metals are colored. The color depends on the metal, its oxidation state, and the anion with which it is combined.

Table 25–3
COLORS OF COMPOUNDS OF TRANSITION METALS

Compound	Formula	Color
titanium(III) chloride	$TiCl_3$	violet
titanium(III) sulfate	$Ti_2(SO_4)_3$	green
titanium(IV) chloride	$TiCl_4$	yellow
vanadium(II) chloride	VCl_2	green
vanadium(II) sulfate, heptahydrate	$VSO_4 \cdot 7H_2O$	violet
vanadium(III) chloride	VCl_3	pink
vanadium(IV) chloride	VCl_4	violet
chromium(II) acetate	$Cr(C_2H_3O_2)_2$	red
chromium(II) sulfate, heptahydrate	$CrSO_4 \cdot 7H_2O$	blue
chromium(III) chloride	$CrCl_3$	violet
manganese(II) chloride	$MnCl_2$	pink
manganese(III) sulfate	$Mn_2(SO_4)_3$	green
manganese(IV) oxide	MnO_2	black
iron(II) chloride, dihydrate	$FeCl_2 \cdot 2H_2O$	green
iron(II) sulfate, heptahydrate	$FeSO_4 \cdot 7H_2O$	blue-green
iron(III) chloride, hexahydrate	$FeCl_3 \cdot 6H_2O$	brown-yellow
iron(III) sulfate,	$Fe_2(SO_4)_3$	yellow
iron(III) thiosulfate	$Fe(CNS)_3$	red
cobalt(II) chloride, hexahydrate	$CoCl_2 \cdot 6H_2O$	red
cobalt(II) nitrate, hexahydrate	$Co(NO_3)_2 \cdot 6H_2O$	red
cobalt(II) sulfate, heptahydrate	$CoSO_4 \cdot 7H_2O$	pink
cobalt(III) sulfate	$Co_2(SO_4)_3$	blue-green
nickel(II) hydroxide	$Ni(OH)_2$	green
nickel(II) nitrate, hexahydrate	$Ni(NO_3)_2 \cdot 6H_2O$	green
nickel(II) sulfate	$NiSO_4$	yellow
copper(I) carbonate	Cu_2CO_3	yellow
copper(I) oxide	Cu_2O	red
copper(II) oxide	CuO	black
copper(II) nitrate, hexahydrate	$Cu(NO_3)_2 \cdot 6H_2O$	blue
copper(II) sulfate, pentahydrate	$CuSO_4 \cdot 5H_2O$	blue

state. It is also related to the nature of the nonmetallic element or polyatomic group combined with the transition metal. The colors of compounds of several first row transition metals are listed in Table 25-3.

We know that the electrons of an atom can acquire energy only in discrete (definite) quantities. The energy of certain wavelengths of light may be just the amount needed to raise a *d* electron to a higher energy state. When white light strikes the substance, only these wavelengths are absorbed; the remaining light is reflected. It is no longer white light because some of the wavelengths are missing. Instead, the light now has a color which is the *complement* of the light removed.

25.5 The formation of complex ions

The NO_3^- ion, SO_4^{--} ion, and NH_4^+ ion are examples of *polyatomic* ions. They are charged particles made up of more than a single atom. These familiar ions are covalent structures. Their net ionic charge is the algebraic sum of the oxidation numbers of all the atoms present. Because of their small size and their stability, the common polyatomic ions behave just like single-atom ions. They *do not* themselves ionize and form simpler particles.

Transition metals have a strong tendency to form *complex ions,* with polyatomic groups. These complex ions *do* ionize slightly into simpler fragments. Because this ionization is slight, an equilibrium is quickly reached between the complex ions and their simpler fragments. Table 25-4 lists some complex ions formed by the transition metals.

Ammonia (NH_3), cyanide ions (CN^-), thiosulfate ions ($S_2O_3^{--}$), and thiocyanate ions (SCN^-) commonly form complex ions with transition metals. In each case the transition metal is the central atom. The number of groups attached to, or *coordinated* with, the central atom is called the *coordination number.* See Figure 25-3.

When silver nitrate and ammonia-water solutions are mixed, a silver-ammonia complex is formed.

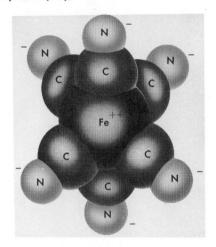

Fig. 25-3. A possible space model of a complex ion, the hexacyanoferrate (II) ion $Fe(CN)_6^{----}$.

$$Ag^+ + 2NH_3 \rightarrow Ag(NH_3)_2^+$$

$$Ag^+ + 2\,\overset{\displaystyle H}{\underset{\displaystyle \ddot{H}}{:\!\ddot{N}\!:\!H}} \rightarrow \left[\,\overset{\displaystyle H \quad\quad H}{\underset{\displaystyle \ddot{H} \quad\quad \ddot{H}}{H\!:\!\ddot{N}\!:\!Ag\!:\!\ddot{N}\!:\!H}}\,\right]^+$$

		Table 25–4	
	SOME COMMON COMPLEX IONS		
Coordinating atom	*Coordinating group*	*Typical complex ions*	*Color*
N	H :Ṅ:H H	$Ag(NH_3)_2^+$ $Ni(NH_3)_4^{++}$ $Co(NH_3)_6^{+++}$	— blue blue
C	:C:::N:⁻	$Fe(CN)_6^{----}$ $Fe(CN)_6^{---}$	yellow red
S	:Ö: :S̈:S̈:Ö:⁻⁻ :Ö:	$Ag(S_2O_3)_2^{---}$	—
N	:Ṅ: :C̈: :S̈:⁻	$FeNCS^{++}$	red

An equilibrium is reached between the silver-ammonia complex, silver ion, and ammonia molecule. The ionization constant K_i is approximately 6×10^{-8}.

$$\mathbf{Ag(NH_3)_2^+ \rightleftharpoons Ag^+ + 2NH_3}$$

$$K_i = \frac{[\mathbf{Ag^+}][\mathbf{NH_3}]^2}{[\mathbf{Ag(NH_3)_2^+}]} = 6 \times 10^{-8}$$

Further additions of NH_3 reduce the Ag^+ ion concentration according to Le Chatelier's principle.

When metallic ions in solution form complexes, they are, in effect, removed from the solution as simple ions. Thus, the formation of complex ions increases the solubility of metallic ions. The solubility of a precipitate may also be increased if cations of the substance form complex ions. For example, the formation of chloride complexes may *increase* solubility where, by common ion effect (Section 20.6), a *decrease* would be expected.

Let us consider the equilibrium of sparingly soluble AgCl.

$$\mathbf{AgCl(s) \rightleftharpoons Ag^+(aq) + Cl^-(aq)}$$

A small addition of Cl^- ions *does* shift the equilibrium to the left and lower the solubility as expected. However, if a large concentration of Cl^- ions is added, *the solid AgCl dissolves.* This apparent contradiction is explained by the formation of soluble $AgCl_2^-$ complex ions.

The very slight ionization of complex ions is indicated by the small values for the ionization constants, K_i. See Table 25-5. The smaller the value for K_i, the more stable is the complex ion and the more effectively it holds the simple metal ions as part of the soluble complex.

Table 25-5
IONIZATION OF COMPLEX IONS

Complex ion	Equilibrium reaction	K_i
$Ag(NH_3)_2^+$	$Ag(NH_3)_2^+ \rightleftharpoons Ag^+ + 2NH_3$	6×10^{-8}
$Co(NH_3)_6^{++}$	$Co(NH_3)_6^{++} \rightleftharpoons Co^{++} + 6NH_3$	1×10^{-5}
$Co(NH_3)_6^{+++}$	$Co(NH_3)_6^{+++} \rightleftharpoons Co^{+++} + 6NH_3$	2×10^{-34}
$Cu(NH_3)_4^{++}$	$Cu(NH_3)_4^{++} \rightleftharpoons Cu^{++} + 4NH_3$	5×10^{-14}
$Ag(CN)_2^-$	$Ag(CN)_2^- \rightleftharpoons Ag^+ + 2CN^-$	2×10^{-19}
$Au(CN)_2^-$	$Au(CN)_2^- \rightleftharpoons Au^+ + 2CN^-$	5×10^{-39}
$Cu(CN)_3^{--}$	$Cu(CN)_3^{--} \rightleftharpoons Cu^+ + 3CN^-$	1×10^{-35}
$Fe(CN)_6^{----}$	$Fe(CN)_6^{----} \rightleftharpoons Fe^{++} + 6CN^-$	1×10^{-35}
$Fe(CN)_6^{---}$	$Fe(CN)_6^{---} \rightleftharpoons Fe^{+++} + 6CN^-$	1×10^{-42}
$FeNCS^{++}$	$FeNCS^{++} \rightleftharpoons Fe^{+++} + NCS^-$	8×10^{-3}
$Ag(S_2O_3)_2^{---}$	$Ag(S_2O_3)_2^{---} \rightleftharpoons Ag^+ + 2S_2O_3^{--}$	6×10^{-14}

25.6 Paramagnetism

Substances that are attracted into a magnetic field are said to be **paramagnetic**. Paramagnetism among elements and their compounds is related to the presence of unpaired electrons in the structure. Some transition metals have unpaired *d* electrons.

Manganese atoms, for example, have 5 unpaired $3d$ electrons as do Mn^{++} ions. Electron sharing in covalent complexes may reduce the number of unpaired electrons to the point where the substance is not paramagnetic. Most compounds of transition metals are paramagnetic in all but the highest oxidation states.

25.7 Transition metal similarities

The electron population in the outermost shell of the transition elements remains fairly constant. It never exceeds two electrons as the *d* sublevel expansion proceeds across a period. Thus, similar properties often appear in a horizontal sequence of transition elements as well as vertically through a subgroup.

The first five subgroups are those headed by Sc, Ti, V, Cr, and Mn. The greatest similarities among these elements appear within each subgroup. The 6th, 7th, and 8th subgroups are headed by Fe, Co, and Ni. Here, the similarities *across* each period are greater than those down each subgroup. Iron, cobalt, and nickel resemble each other more than do iron, ruthenium, and osmium, the members of the iron subgroup.

The 9th and 10th subgroups are headed by Cu and Zn. Here we again find the greatest similarity within each subgroup. We will now examine some common and important transition metals within the framework of their similarities.

THE IRON FAMILY

25.8 Members of the Iron Family

The Iron Family consists of the heavy metals *iron, cobalt,* and *nickel.* These metals are all in the fourth period. Each is the first member of a subgroup of transition metals which bears its name. The iron subgroup includes *iron* (at. no. 26) in the fourth period, *ruthenium* (at. no. 44) in the fifth period, and *osmium* (at. no. 76) in the sixth period. The cobalt subgroup includes *cobalt* (at. no. 27) in the fourth period, *rhodium* (at. no. 45) in the fifth period, and *iridium* (at. no. 77) in the sixth period. The nickel subgroup includes *nickel* (at. no. 28) in the fourth period, *palladium* (at. no. 46) in the fifth period, and *platinum* (at. no. 78) in the sixth period.

As stated in Section 25.7, the similarities between iron, cobalt, and nickel are greater than those within each of the three subgroups they head. The remaining six members of these three

Table 25–6
THE IRON FAMILY

Element	Atomic number	Atomic weight	Electron configuration	Oxidation number	Melting point (°C)	Boiling point (°C)	Density (g/cm³)
iron	26	55.874	2,8,14,2	+2, +3	1535	3000	7.87
cobalt	27	58.9332	2,8,15,2	+2, +3	1495	2900	8.9
nickel	28	58.71	2,8,16,2	+2, +3	1453	2732	8.90

Table 25–7
ELECTRON POPULATION OF THE IRON FAMILY

Sublevel	1s	2s	2p	3s	3p	3d	4s
Maximum population	2	2	6	2	6	10	2
iron	2	2	6	2	6	:....	:
cobalt	2	2	6	2	6	::...	:
nickel	2	2	6	2	6	:::..	:

subgroups have properties similar to platinum. Thus, they are considered to be members of the *Platinum Family*. They are called *noble metals* because they show little chemical activity. They are rare and expensive.

Iron is by far the most important member of the Iron Family. Alloys of iron, cobalt, and nickel are important structural metals. Some properties of the Iron Family are listed in Table 25-6.

The Iron Family is located in the middle of the transition elements. Atoms in this region have fewer than the maximum number of 3d electrons. Each member exhibits the +2 and +3 oxidation states. The +3 oxidation state of iron tends to be more stable than the +2 state. This tendency decreases through cobalt to nickel, which occurs only rarely in the +3 oxidation state. The electron populations of iron, cobalt, and nickel sublevels are shown in Table 25-7. In this table paired and unpaired electrons of the 3d and 4s sublevels are represented by paired and unpaired dots.

The two 4s electrons are removed easily, as is usually the case with metals. This removal forms the Fe^{++}, Co^{++}, or Ni^{++} ion. In the case of iron, one 3d electron is also easily removed since the five remaining 3d electrons make a half-filled sublevel. (Recall that filled and half-filled sublevels have extra stability.) When two 4s and one 3d electrons are removed, the Fe^{+++} ion is formed. It becomes increasingly more difficult to remove a 3d electron from cobalt and nickel. This increasing difficulty is partly explained by the higher nuclear charges. Another factor is that neither 3d sublevel would be left at the filled or half-filled stage. Neither Co^{+++} nor Ni^{+++} ions are common. However, cobalt atoms in the +3 oxidation state occur in many complexes. See Section 25.5.

All three metals of the Iron Family have a strong magnetic property. This property is commonly known as *ferromagnetism* because of the unusual extent to which it is possessed by iron. Cobalt is strongly magnetic, while nickel is the least magnetic of the three. The ferromagnetic nature of these metals is thought to be related to the similar spin orientations of their unpaired 3d electrons.

Each spinning electron acts like a tiny magnet. Electron pairs are formed by two electrons spinning in opposite directions.

The electron magnetisms of such a pair of electrons neutralize each other. In Iron Family metals, groups of atoms may be aligned and form small magnetized regions called *domains*. Ordinarily, magnetic domains within the metallic crystals point in random directions. In this way, they cancel one another so that the net magnetism is zero. A piece of iron becomes magnetized when an outside force aligns the domains in the same direction. Figure 25-4 illustrates the mechanism of electron spin for paired and unpaired electrons.

25.9 Occurrence of iron

Iron is the fourth element in abundance by weight in the earth's crust. Nearly 5% of the earth's crust is iron. It is the second most abundant metal, following only aluminum. Meteors are known to contain iron. This fact and the known magnetic nature of the earth itself suggest that the earth's core may consist mainly of iron.

Unfortunately, much of the iron in the crust of the earth cannot be removed profitably. Only minerals from which iron can be profitably recovered by practical methods are considered iron ores.

Great deposits of *hematite*, Fe_2O_3, once existed in the Lake Superior region of the United States. They were the major sources of iron in this country for many years. These rich ores are now used up. Today the iron industry depends on medium- and low-grade ores, the most abundant of which is *taconite*.

Taconite has an iron content of roughly 25% to 50% in mixtures of chemically complex ores. The main iron minerals present are hematite, Fe_2O_3, and magnetite, Fe_3O_4. The rest of the ore is rock. Modern blast furnaces for reducing iron ore to iron require ores containing well above 60% iron. Thus, the raw ores must be concentrated by removing much of the waste materials. This process is performed at the mines before the ores are transported to the blast furnaces.

Taconite ores are first crushed and pulverized. They are then concentrated by a variety of complex methods. The concentrated ores are hardened into pellets for shipment to the smelters. Ore concentrates containing 90% iron are produced by the chemical removal of oxygen during the pelletizing treatment.

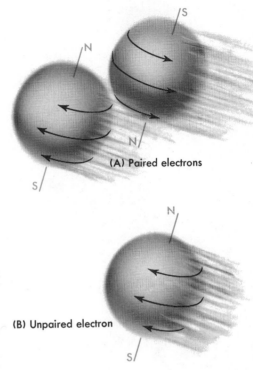

(A) Paired electrons

(B) Unpaired electron

Fig. 25-4. Magnetism in matter stems basically from the spin of electrons.

Fig. 25-5. Enrichment of low-grade iron ores. Today nearly all iron ore mined in the United States is concentrated before shipment to the blast furnace.

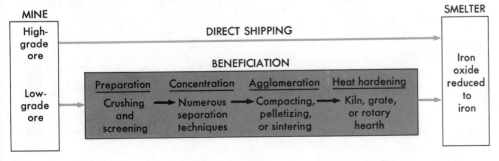

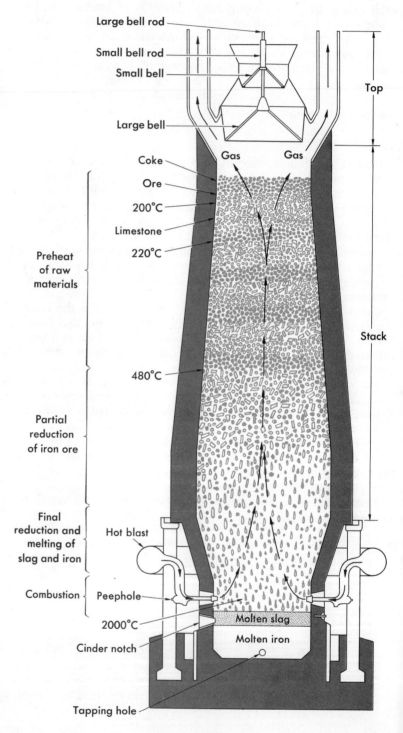

Fig. 25-6. A sectional view of a blast furnace.

25.10 The blast furnace

Iron oxide is reduced to iron in a giant structure called a blast furnace. The charge placed in the blast furnace consists of iron oxide, coke, and a flux (which causes mineral impurities in the ore to melt more readily). The proper proportions for the charge are calculated by analyzing the raw materials. Usually the flux is limestone, because silica or sand is the most common impurity in the iron ore. Some iron ores contain limestone as an impurity and, in such cases, the flux added is sand. See Figure 25-6. A blast of hot air, sometimes enriched with oxygen, is forced into the base of the furnace.

Iron ore is reduced in the blast furnace to iron. The earthy impurities are removed as slag. Coke is required for the first function and limestone for the second. The products of the blast furnace are *pig iron, slag,* and *flue gas.*

The actual chemical changes which occur are complex and somewhat unclear. The coke is ignited by the blast of hot air and some of it burns, forming carbon dioxide.

$$C(s) + O_2(g) \rightarrow CO_2(g)$$

The carbon dioxide comes in contact with other pieces of hot coke when the oxygen is blown in and is reduced to carbon monoxide.

$$CO_2(g) + C(s) \rightarrow 2CO(g)$$

The carbon monoxide thus formed is actually the reducing agent that reduces the iron oxide to metallic iron.

$$Fe_2O_3 + 3CO \rightarrow 2Fe(l) + 3CO_2(g)$$

This reduction probably occurs in steps as the temperature increases toward the bottom of the furnace. Possible steps are

$$Fe_2O_3 \rightarrow Fe_3O_4 \rightarrow FeO \rightarrow Fe$$

The white-hot liquid iron collects in the bottom of the furnace. Every 4 or 5 hours it is tapped off. It may be cast in molds as *pig iron,* or converted directly to steel. See Figure 25-7.

In the middle region of the furnace, the limestone decomposes to calcium oxide and carbon dioxide.

$$CaCO_3(s) \rightarrow CaO(s) + CO_2(g)$$

The calcium oxide combines with silica and forms a calcium silicate slag. This slag melts more readily than silica.

$$CaO + SiO_2 \rightarrow CaSiO_3(l)$$

This glassy slag also collects at the bottom of the furnace. Since it has a much lower density than liquid iron, it floats on top of the iron. It prevents the re-oxidation of the iron. The melted slag is tapped off every few hours. Usually it is thrown away, although it is sometimes used for making Portland cement.

Fig. 25-7. A basic-oxygen furnace receives a charge of molten iron directly from the blast furnace.

Inland Steel Company

25.11 Steel production

The relatively high carbon content of iron recovered from the blast furnace makes it very hard and brittle. Two other impurities are phosphorus and sulfur. The phosphorus makes pig iron brittle at low temperatures. The sulfur makes it brittle at high temperatures.

The conversion of iron to steel *is essentially a purification process in which impurities are removed by oxidation.* This purification process is carried out in a furnace at a high temperature. Scrap steel which is being recycled is added to the charge of iron. Iron ore may be added to supply oxygen for oxidizing the impurities. Often, oxygen gas is added directly for very rapid oxidation. Limestone or lime is included in the charge for forming a slag with nongaseous oxides. Near the end of the process, selected alloying substances are added. By using different kinds and quantities of these alloys, the steel is given different desired properties.

The impurities in the pig iron are oxidized in the following way:

$$3C + Fe_2O_3 \rightarrow 3CO(g) + 2Fe$$

$$3Mn + Fe_2O_3 \rightarrow 3MnO + 2Fe$$

$$12P + 10Fe_2O_3 \rightarrow 3P_4O_{10} + 20Fe$$

$$3Si + 2Fe_2O_3 \rightarrow 3SiO_2 + 4Fe$$

$$3S + 2Fe_2O_3 \rightarrow 3SO_2(g) + 4Fe$$

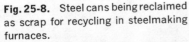

Fig. 25-8. Steel cans being reclaimed as scrap for recycling in steelmaking furnaces.

The limestone flux decomposes as in the blast furnace.

$$CaCO_3 \rightarrow CaO + CO_2(g)$$

Carbon and sulfur escape as gases. Calcium oxide and the oxides of other impurities react and form slag.

$$P_4O_{10} + 6CaO \rightarrow 2Ca_3(PO_4)_2$$

$$SiO_2 + CaO \rightarrow CaSiO_3$$

$$MnO + SiO_2 \rightarrow MnSiO_3$$

Despite large imports from Japan and Western Europe, steel production in the United States exceeds 100 million tons each year. Present technological developments deal mainly with improving steel quality and production efficiency, rather than with increasing output. Examples of these improvements are:

1. Continuous casting, in which freshly made liquid steel is cast directly into slabs ready for the rolling mills.

2. Vacuum degassing, in which steel is melted in a high vacuum and gases are removed.

Most steel produced in the United States is made by the *basic-oxygen process,* or *BOP.* The *open-hearth process* is another major producer. Special steels are made by the *electric-furnace process.* Of the two major ways of making steel, the

U.S. Steel

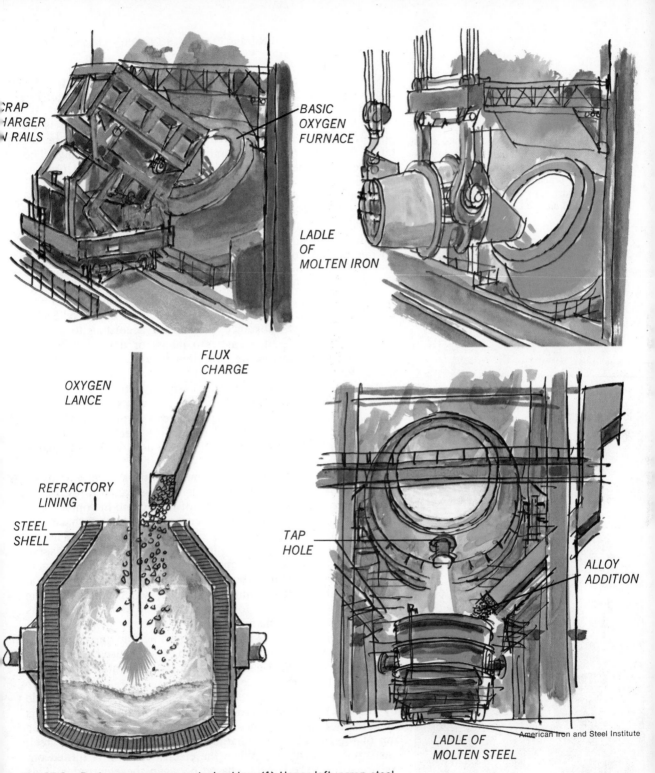

CRAP
HARGER
N RAILS

BASIC
OXYGEN
FURNACE

LADLE
OF
MOLTEN IRON

FLUX
CHARGE

OXYGEN
LANCE

REFRACTORY
LINING

STEEL
SHELL

TAP
HOLE

ALLOY
ADDITION

LADLE OF
MOLTEN STEEL

Fig. 25-9. Basic-oxygen process steelmaking: (1) Upper left, scrap steel charge, (2) upper right, molten iron charge, (3) lower left, oxygen blow and flux charge, (4) lower right, BOF cap and alloy addition.

basic-oxygen process is the more recent development. It is capable of producing steel at about eight times the rate of the older open-hearth process.

1. Basic-oxygen process. The basic-oxygen furnace is an open-top vessel lined with heat-resistant bricks. It can be rotated through 360° for charging, tapping, and relining. The furnace is charged with scrap steel, molten iron, and lime as required.

A water-cooled lance is inserted over the charge from above and oxygen is blown in at about twice the speed of sound. A tremendous turbulence is produced by the oxygen crashing into the molten metal at this speed. The oxygen is delivered for 20 minutes. It combines with carbon and other unwanted elements, eliminating these impurities from the charge. During the oxygen "blow," lime is added to remove the oxidized impurities as a floating slag. The operation takes about 45 minutes to produce as much as 300 tons of steel. The steel is poured into a ladle and alloying substances are added according to precise specifications. It is then cast into ingots or delivered directly to a continuous casting unit for immediate working. See Figure 25-9.

An improved version of the basic-oxygen process, called *Q-BOP,* has been developed. In this process, oxygen is blown in from the bottom of the furnace instead of the top. The time required for refining a "heat" (batch) of steel is reduced by 10%. Also, 20% more scrap steel can be used with each charge of pig iron.

2. Open-hearth process. The open-hearth system employs a huge oven with a curved roof. This oven is called a *reverberatory furnace* because flames, but not fuel, come in contact with the charge by reflection from the curved roof. Such furnaces are capable of producing from 50 to 200 tons of steel in 5 to 8 hours. The charge consists of molten iron from the blast furnace, scrap steel, iron ore, and limestone. The iron ore supplies oxygen, which combines with carbon and other impurities in the liquid iron. The limestone decomposes to lime, which unites with the oxides of impurities and forms a slag. Scrap steel may form as much as 50% of the charge.

A high temperature is required to burn out the impurities from the iron and to melt the steel scrap. Gas is used to heat the furnace. Both the fuel gas and air for its combustion are heated before entering the furnace.

3. Electric-furnace process. Very high quality steels are made by the electric-furnace process. A common type of furnace is lined with dolomite. Large carbon electrodes extend through the top of the furnace. The charge usually consists of scrap steel, cast iron, and iron ore. When the electric current is turned on, an arc forms through the charge between the electrodes. This arc provides the heat necessary to carry out the process. There is no electrolysis.

Fig. 25-10. Dust and smoke emissions from an open-hearth furnace are virtually eliminated by electrostatic precipitators. (Top) Precipitator turned off. (Bottom) Precipitator turned on.

U.S. Steel Corp. 1971 Annual Report

There are several advantages to using the electric-furnace process: (*1*) The steel can be tested at various stages before it is finished. (*2*) High quality raw materials are used. (*3*) A reducing atmosphere can be maintained to prevent oxidation of the steel.

Fig. 25-11. Clean air, the result of replacing an open-hearth facility with basic-oxygen process equipment with integrated air quality controls. (Left) Smoke emissions from an open-hearth steelmaking shop. (Right) The same shop after conversion to the basic-oxygen process.

Fig. 25-12. A machined forging made from a stainless steel ingot for a power plant nuclear reactor core support.

U.S. Steel Quarterly

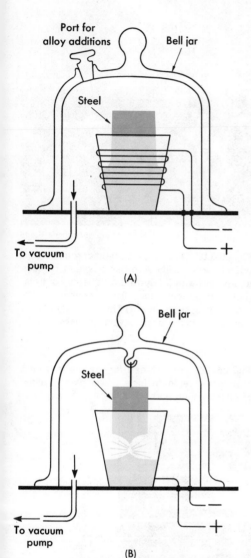

Fig. 25-13. Laboratory models of vacuum degassing methods: (A) by induction, and (B) by electric-arc melting.

25.12   Vacuum-degassing processes

Special steels for gas turbine blades, rocket motor cases, and parts for spacecraft must meet very strict requirements. Such requirements place these metals in a "superalloy" category. Gases such as hydrogen, nitrogen, and oxygen remain in ordinary steel and cause the center of the solid metal to be porous. These gases also give ordinary steel its uneven structural qualities.

Two highly successful methods are used to remove unwanted gases from steel under vacuum conditions. These *vacuum-degassing processes* produce special steel alloys of the highest quality. They also differ in the manner of melting the steel; the metal is heated by *induction* or an *electric arc* as shown in Figure 25-13.

1.   Vacuum-induction process. The steel is melted and refined in a crucible surrounded by an electric coil. This coil induces a current in the steel that provides the melting heat. The entire furnace is contained in a highly evacuated chamber. Vacuum pumps remove the unwanted gases. Alloying substances are added through vacuum locks. The final product is cast into ingots under vacuum conditions also.

2.   Vacuum-arc process. The steel to be melted serves as one electrode and a crucible serves as the other electrode. The entire furnace is enclosed in an evacuated chamber. An electric arc between the two electrodes melts the steel. Gaseous impurities are removed by the vacuum pumps. The crucible serves as an ingot mold in which the metal solidifies under high-vacuum conditions.

25.13   Pure iron

Pure iron is a metal that is seldom seen. It is silver-white, soft, ductile, tough, and does not tarnish readily. It melts at 1535° C. Commercial iron contains carbon and other impurities that alter its properties. Cast iron melts at about 1150° C. All forms of iron corrode, or rust, in moist air, so it is not a self-protective metal. The rust that forms is brittle and scales off, exposing the metal underneath to further corrosion. Iron does not rust in dry air or in water that is free of dissolved oxygen.

The corrosion of iron is an electrochemical process. A carbon particle in contact with moist iron causes the iron to rust rapidly. The carbon acts as the positive electrode of a miniature electrochemical cell. The iron becomes the negative electrode. This cell action is illustrated in Figure 25-15. Rain water containing dissolved carbon dioxide speeds up the reaction. Iron(II) hydroxide is formed and is readily converted to iron(III) hydroxide. With loss of water the familiar red rust, $Fe_2O_3 \cdot xH_2O$, is formed.

Dilute acids generally act readily on iron. Alkalies do not react with it. Concentrated nitric acid does not react with iron. In fact, dipping iron into concentrated nitric acid makes the iron *passive,* or *inactive,* with other chemicals. Concentrated sulfuric acid has little effect on iron.

25.14 Three oxides of iron

Of the three oxides of iron, *iron(II) oxide,* FeO, is of little importance. It oxidizes rapidly when exposed to air and forms *iron(III) oxide,* Fe_2O_3. This oxide is the important ore of iron. It is used as a cheap red paint pigment (coloring material) known as red ocher, Venetian red, or Indian red. It is also used for grinding and polishing glass lenses and mirrors. When used for this purpose it is referred to as rouge.

Limonite is a natural *hydrated iron(III) oxide* which is powdered to make pigment called yellow ocher. When heated or roasted, it forms pigments known as *siennas* and *umbers.* *Magnetic iron oxide,* Fe_3O_4, is an important ore. It is composed of Fe_2O_3 and FeO. Thus, it may be considered to be iron(II,III) oxide, and can be written $FeO \cdot Fe_2O_3$.

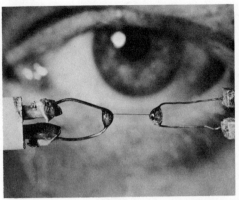

Westinghouse

Fig. 25-14. A tiny "whisker" of pure iron, free of the structural imperfections of the ordinary metal, provides scientists with a means of studying the nature of the enormous forces which bind atoms tightly together.

25.15 Reactions of the Fe⁺⁺ ion

Hydrated iron(II) sulfate, $FeSO_4 \cdot 7H_2O$, is the most useful compound of iron in the +2 oxidation state. It is used as a reducing agent and in medicine for iron tonics. Iron(II) sulfate can be prepared by the action of dilute sulfuric acid on iron. The crystalline hydrate loses water of hydration when exposed to air and turns brown because of oxidation. Iron(II) sulfate in solution is gradually oxidized to the iron(III) state by dissolved oxygen. The brown precipitate of basic iron(III) sulfate that forms is evidence of this change:

$$4FeSO_4 + O_2 + 2H_2O \rightarrow 4Fe(OH)SO_4(s)$$

The Fe⁺⁺ ions can be kept in the reduced state by making the solution acidic with sulfuric acid and adding pieces of iron. Hydrated iron(II) ammonium sulfate, $Fe(NH_4)_2(SO_4)_2 \cdot 6H_2O$, is a better source of Fe⁺⁺ ions in the laboratory because it is stable in contact with air.

Iron(II) salts are readily oxidized to iron(III) salts by the corresponding acid and an oxidizing agent. In the case of the nitrate, nitric acid meets both requirements:

$$3Fe(NO_3)_2 + 4HNO_3 \rightarrow 3Fe(NO_3)_3 + NO(g) + 2H_2O$$

Crystals of hydrated iron(II) chloride, $FeCl_2 \cdot 2H_2O$, are blue as long as the reduced state is maintained. Gradual oxidation to the iron(III) state is evident as a green color develops. Iron(II) chloride can be prepared by the action of hydrochloric acid on iron.

Fig. 25-15. Iron and steel contain impurities and corrode readily unless covered by a protective coating. The miniature electro-chemical cell formed between the carbon and iron surfaces speeds up the rusting action.

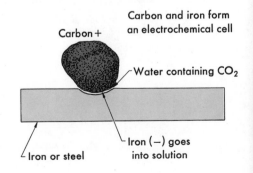

Carbon and iron form an electrochemical cell

Carbon +

Water containing CO_2

Iron or steel

Iron (−) goes into solution

Iron(II) hydroxide forms as a white precipitate when sodium hydroxide is added to a solution of an iron(II) salt. Exposed to air, the precipitate is first green and finally brown as the iron(III) hydroxide is formed. We can observe the oxidation of Fe^{++} ions by adding a solution of iron(II) sulfate to a solution of tannic acid. The nearly colorless compound, *iron(II) tannate,* is formed. It slowly oxidizes to the black compound, *iron(III) tannate.*

25.16 Reaction of the Fe^{+++} ion

Hydrated iron(III) chloride, $FeCl_3 \cdot 6H_2O$, is the most useful compound of iron in the +3 oxidation state. It is used as an oxidizing agent. The anhydrous salt can be recovered as black crystals in the composition reaction between iron and chlorine. The hydrated Fe^{+++} ion, $Fe(H_2O)_6^{+++}$, gives a pale violet color. This color usually is not seen, however, because of hydrolysis. Hydrated iron(III) chloride has a yellow-brown color.

The Fe^{+++} ion undergoes hydrolysis in water solutions of iron(III) salts. The solutions are acidic.

$$Fe^{+++} + 2H_2O \rightleftarrows FeOH^{++} + H_3O^+$$
$$FeOH^{++} + 2H_2O \rightleftarrows Fe(OH)_2^+ + H_3O^+$$
$$Fe(OH)_2^+ + 2H_2O \rightleftarrows Fe(OH)_3 + H_3O^+$$

The hydrolysis is extensive when it occurs in boiling water. A blood-red colloidal suspension of iron(III) hydroxide is formed.

Iron(III) ions are removed from solution by adding a solution containing hydroxide ions. A red-brown jelly-like precipitate of iron(III) hydroxide is formed. By evaporating the water, red Fe_2O_3 remains. This is the Venetian red pigment, or the rouge polishing powder referred to in Section 25.15.

$$Fe^{+++} + 3OH^- \rightarrow Fe(OH)_3(s)$$

25.17 Tests for iron ions

Potassium hexacyanoferrate(II), $K_4Fe(CN)_6$ (also called potassium ferrocyanide), is a light yellow crystalline salt. It contains the complex hexacyanoferrate(II) ion (ferrocyanide ion), $Fe(CN)_6^{----}$. The iron is in the +2 oxidation state. It forms when an excess of cyanide ions is added to a solution of an iron(II) salt.

$$6CN^- + Fe^{++} \rightarrow Fe(CN)_6^{----}$$

Suppose KCN is used as the source of CN^- ions and $FeCl_2$ as the source of Fe^{++} ions. The empirical equation for the reaction then becomes

$$6KCN + FeCl_2 \rightarrow K_4Fe(CN)_6 + 2KCl$$

CAUTION: *Solutions containing cyanide ions are deadly poisons and should never be handled by inexperienced chemistry students.*

The iron of the $Fe(CN)_6^{----}$ ion can be oxidized by chlorine to the +3 state. This reaction forms the hexacyanoferrate(III) ion (ferricyanide ion) $Fe(CN)_6^{---}$.

$$2Fe(CN)_6^{----} + Cl_2 \rightarrow 2Fe(CN)_6^{---} + 2Cl^-$$

As the iron is oxidized from the +2 oxidation state to the +3 state, the chlorine is reduced from the 0 state to the −1 state.

Using the potassium salt as the source of the $Fe(CN)_6^{----}$ ions, the empirical equation is

$$2K_4Fe(CN)_6 + Cl_2 \rightarrow 2K_3Fe(CN)_6 + 2KCl$$

$K_3Fe(CN)_6$, potassium hexacyanoferrate(III) (known also as potassium ferricyanide), is a dark red crystalline salt.

When Fe^{++} ions and $Fe(CN)_6^{---}$ ions are brought together, a deep blue precipitate forms. *The color is caused by the presence of iron in two different oxidation states.* This insoluble substance forms when the potassium salt is the source of the $Fe(CN)_6^{---}$ ions. It is called *Turnbull's blue.*

$$FeSO_4 + K_3Fe(CN)_6 + H_2O \rightarrow KFeFe(CN)_6 \cdot H_2O(s) + K_2SO_4$$

or simply

$$Fe^{++} + K^+ + Fe(CN)_6^{---} + H_2O \rightarrow KFeFe(CN)_6 \cdot H_2O(s)$$

Similarly, the Fe^{+++} ions and $Fe(CN)_6^{----}$ ions form a deep blue precipitate. Again the color is caused by the presence of *two different* oxidation states of iron. The precipitate in this reaction is called *Prussian blue.* It is identical to the Turnbull's blue formed with Fe^{++} and $Fe(CN)_6^{---}$ ions. The composition of both precipitates is $KFeFe(CN)_6 \cdot H_2O$.

$$Fe^{+++} + K^+ + Fe(CN)_6^{----} + H_2O \rightarrow KFeFe(CN)_6 \cdot H_2O(s)$$

Fe^{++} ions and $Fe(CN)_6^{----}$ ions form a white precipitate of $K_2FeFe(CN)_6$. This precipitate remains white if measures are taken to prevent the oxidation of any Fe^{++} ions. Of course, on exposure to air, it begins to turn blue because of oxidation. Fe^{---} ions and $Fe(CN)_6^{----}$ ions give only a brown solution. These reactions provide us with ways to detect the presence of the two oxidation states of iron.

1.   *Test for the Fe^{++} ion.* Suppose a few drops of $K_3Fe(CN)_6$ solution are added to a solution of iron(II) sulfate (or iron(II) ammonium sulfate). The characteristic dark blue precipitate, $KFeFe(CN)_6 \cdot H_2O$, forms

$$Fe^{++} + SO_4^{--} + 3K^+ + Fe(CN)_6^{---} + H_2O \rightarrow KFeFe(CN)_6 \cdot H_2O(s) + 2K^+ + SO_4^{--}$$

The two potassium ions and the sulfate ions are merely spectator ions. The net reaction is

$$Fe^{++} + K^+ + Fe(CN)_6^{---} + H_2O \rightarrow KFeFe(CN)_6 \cdot H_2O(s)$$

The formation of a blue precipitate when $K_3Fe(CN)_6$ is added to an unknown solution serves to identify the Fe^{++} ion.

2. Test for the Fe⁺⁺⁺ ion. Suppose a few drops of $K_4Fe(CN)_6$ solution are added to a solution of iron(III) chloride. The characteristic blue precipitate, $KFeFe(CN)_6 \cdot H_2O$, is formed. The net reaction is

$$Fe^{+++} + K^+ + Fe(CN)_6{}^{----} + H_2O \rightarrow KFeFe(CN)_6 \cdot H_2O(s)$$

The formation of a blue precipitate when $K_4Fe(CN)_6$ is added to a solution thought to contain iron(III) ions serves to identify the Fe⁺⁺⁺ ion.

Potassium thiocyanate, KSCN, provides another good test for the Fe⁺⁺⁺ ion. It is often used to confirm the $K_4Fe(CN)_6$ test. A blood-red solution results from the formation of the complex FeNCS⁺⁺ ion.

25.18 Cobalt

Cobalt is found in nature in many minerals, together with iron, nickel, copper, silver, and arsenic. It is ordinarily recovered as a by-product of the refining of various ores. Both cobalt and nickel often remain as oxides after the roasting and reduction processes. Cobalt is usually found combined with arsenic and sulfur. The principal ores are *cobaltite,* CoAsS; *smaltite,* $CoAs_2$; and *linnalite,* Co_3S_4. Metallic cobalt is produced by the reduction of its oxide with aluminum.

This metal so closely resembles nickel that the two metals are often spoken of as "twins." Cobalt sometimes is used to plate iron, but its most important uses are in making alloys.

Stellite, a very hard alloy of cobalt and chromium, is used for making metal-cutting tools. *Carboloy* is made by combining cobalt with a carbide of tungsten. It is one of the hardest materials manufactured. It is a tough alloy, not easily broken, and is used for high-speed cutting tools. *Alnico* is a very strongly ferromagnetic alloy composed of aluminum, cobalt, iron, and nickel. It is used widely in making small permanent magnets for loudspeakers, telephones, and hearing aids.

Fig. 25-16. Fused pellets of cobalt. For centuries its salts have given color to porcelains.

25.19 Compounds of cobalt

Cobalt forms cobalt(II) and cobalt(III) compounds. Its oxidation numbers in such compounds are +2 and +3, respectively. The cobalt(II) compounds exist as red crystals and form pink-colored solutions. They are more common than cobalt(III) compounds.

Cobalt(II) chloride hexahydrate, $CoCl_2 \cdot 6H_2O$, is red when it exists as the hydrate, but turns blue when dehydrated. Paper covered with a solution of cobalt(II) chloride can be used as a simple *hygrometer* to tell how much moisture the air contains. In damp weather, the paper appears pink. It changes to violet and then to blue as the air becomes less moist.

Cobalt(II) nitrate, $Co(NO_3)_2$, is used to some extent in analytical work. Cobalt compounds give a blue color to glass. Cobalt can be made radioactive and is used in treating certain types of cancer.

25.20 Cobalt nitrate tests

Cobalt(II) nitrate provides a test for the presence of aluminum, magnesium, and zinc. The test is based on the fact that the nitrate, when heated strongly, decomposes to the oxide. This oxide then combines with the oxides of the test metals, forming distinctly colored complexes. A compound of the unknown metal is first heated in the oxidizing flame of a blowpipe on charcoal or plaster of Paris. A drop of cobalt(II) nitrate is then added, and the mass is heated again. If *aluminum* is present, a blue color appears. *Magnesium* yields a pink-colored mass. *Zinc* produces a green color.

25.21 Nickel

Nickel is a hard, silvery-white metal capable of taking a high polish. It does not tarnish easily. Its chemical properties resemble those of iron, although it is less active.

Nickel is used for toughening steel and for nickel-plating. It serves as a catalyst in the hydrogenation of oils and many other chemical reactions. It also appears in several special alloys. The "nickel" coin used in the United States is composed of 25% nickel and 75% copper. A copper-nickel alloy is now used in "silver" coins. See Figure 25-17.

Monel metal contains about 67% nickel, 28% copper, and small quantities of iron and manganese. It is made directly from a complex ore of nickel and copper. This alloy is strong and tough. It resists the action of air, sea water, and acids. Monel metal is used in making valves for steam engines, decorative metal trimmings, and other objects requiring a metal that does not tarnish easily.

Nichrome is an alloy of nickel, chromium, iron, and manganese. It melts at a high temperature and has a high resistance to the passage of an electric current. It is used in making the heating units for electric irons, toasters, and other heating appliances.

25.22 Compounds of nickel

Nickel forms nickel(II) and (rarely) nickel(III) salts. Its oxidation numbers in these salts are +2 and +3, respectively. Nickel(II) salts usually crystallize as beautiful green crystals. The most common salts are nickel(II) chloride, nickel(II) nitrate, and nickel(II) sulfate. Nickel(II) sulfide, when prepared by precipitation, is a black, amorphous powder.

Fig. 25-17. Coinage metal for new "silver" coins. The metal has a copper core and surfaces of a cupro-nickel alloy.

Olin Mathieson

Nickel flakes and nickel(II) oxide are used in the positive plates of the Edison storage battery. When such a battery is charged, *the nickel(II) compound is oxidized to the nickel(III) compound*. The nickel(III) compound is reduced as the battery is discharged. Nickel(II) ammonium sulfate, a double salt, is used as the electrolyte for nickel plating. A piece of pure nickel is used as the anode of the plating cell. The object to be plated is the cathode.

THE COPPER FAMILY

25.23 Members of the Copper Family

The Copper Family consists of *copper, silver,* and *gold,* the copper subgroup of transition metals. All three metals appear below hydrogen in the electrochemical series. They are not easily oxidized and often occur in nature in the free, or *native,* state. Because of their pleasing appearance, durability, and relative scarcity, these metals have been highly valued since the time of their discovery. All have been used in ornamental objects and coins throughout history.

The atoms of copper, silver, and gold have a single electron in their outermost energy levels. Thus, they often form compounds in which they exhibit the +1 oxidation state. To this extent, they resemble the Group I metals of the Sodium Family.

Each metal of the Copper Family has 18 electrons in the next-to-outermost shell. The *d* electrons in this next-to-outermost shell have energies that differ only slightly from the energy of the outer *s* electron. Thus, one or two of these *d* electrons can be removed with relative ease. For this reason, copper and gold often form compounds in which they respectively exhibit the +2 and +3 oxidation states. In the case of silver, the +2 oxidation state is reached only under extreme oxidizing conditions.

Copper, silver, and gold are very dense, ductile, and malleable. They are classed as heavy metals along with other transition metals in the central region of the periodic table. Some important properties of each metal are shown in Table 25-8.

Table 25-8
THE COPPER FAMILY

Element	Atomic number	Atomic weight	Electron configuration	Oxidation numbers	Melting point (°C)	Boiling point (°C)	Density (g/cm³)
copper	29	63.546	2,8,18,1	+1, +2	1083.0	2595	8.96
silver	47	107.868	2,8,18,18,1	+1	960.8	2212	10.50
gold	79	196.9665	2,8,18,32,18,1	+1, +3	1063.0	2966	19.32

Kennecott Copper Corporation

25.24 Copper and its recovery

Copper, alloyed with tin in the form of bronze, has been in use for over 5000 years. Native copper deposits lie deep underground and are difficult to mine.

Sulfide ores of copper yield most of the supply of this metal. *Chalcocite,* Cu_2S, *chalcopyrite,* $CuFeS_2$, and *bornite,* Cu_3FeS_3, are the major sulfide ores. The minerals *malachite,* $Cu_2(OH)_2CO_3$, and *azurite,* $Cu_3(OH)_2(CO_3)_2$, are basic carbonates of copper. Malachite is a rich green, and azurite is a deep blue. Besides serving as ores of copper, fine specimens of these minerals are sometimes polished for use as ornaments or in making jewelry.

The carbonate ores of copper are washed with dilute sulfuric acid, forming a solution of copper(II) sulfate. The copper is then recovered by electrolysis. High-grade carbonate ores are heated in air to convert them to copper(II) oxide. The oxide is then reduced with coke, yielding metallic copper.

The sulfide ores are usually low-grade and require concentrating before they can be refined profitably. The concentration is accomplished by *oil-flotation.* Earthy impurities are wetted by water and the ore is wetted by oil. Air is blown into the mixture to form a froth. The oil-wetted ore floats to the surface in the froth. See Figure 25-18. This treatment changes the concentration of the ore from about 2% copper to as high as 30% copper.

Fig. 25-18. Froth flotation process of copper ore. The particles of ore are carried to the surface by air bubbles in the froth.

The concentrated ore is partially roasted to form a mixture of CU_2S, FeS, FeO, and SiO_2. This mixture is known as *calcine*. The roasting process, using oxygen-enriched air, yields high-quality sulfur dioxide. This gas is converted to sulfuric acid. Calcine is fused with limestone in a furnace. Part of the iron is removed as a silicate slag. The rest of the iron, together with the copper, forms a mixture of sulfides known as *matte*. Copper matte is processed in a reverberatory furnace, and the end product contains about 40% copper.

The melted matte is further refined in a converter supplied with oxygen-enriched air as the oxidizing agent. Sulfur from the sulfides, as well as impurities of arsenic and antimony, are removed as volatile oxides. Most of the iron is removed as slag. Some of the copper(I) sulfide is converted into copper(I) oxide. The copper(I) oxide then reacts with more copper(I) sulfide, forming metallic copper and sulfur dioxide. The following equations show the chemical reactions involved in this process:

$$2Cu_2S + 3O_2 \rightarrow 2Cu_2O + 2SO_2(g)$$
$$2Cu_2O + Cu_2S \rightarrow 6Cu + SO_2(g)$$

The molten copper is cast as *blister copper* of 98.5 to 99.5% purity. As the copper cools, dissolved gases escape and form blisters, hence the name. Impurities remaining are iron, silver, gold, and sometimes zinc. In the fourth step of the copper-refining process, blister copper is further purified in a fire-refining furnace. See Figure 25-19.

Processes for extracting copper and other metals from sulfide ores release large amounts of sulfur dioxide into the air. A non-polluting process for extracting copper from its ore has been developed. Instead of heat, this process uses liquid ammonia at low temperature and under pressure to extract the copper from

Fig. 25-19. The copper refining process.

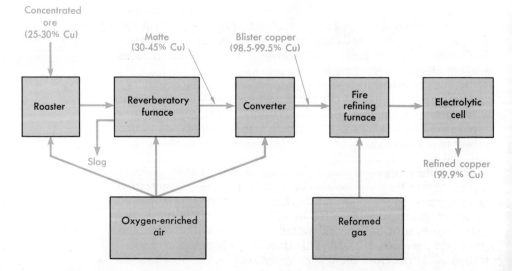

Concentrated ore (25-30% Cu)

Matte (30-45% Cu)

Blister copper (98.5-99.5% Cu)

Roaster | Reverberatory furnace | Converter | Fire refining furnace | Electrolytic cell

Slag

Refined copper (99.9% Cu)

Oxygen-enriched air

Reformed gas

concentrated ore. The first pollution-free plant is expected to be in operation by 1975. It will produce 36,000 tons of copper a year.

25.25   Electrolytic refining of copper

Unrefined copper contains fairly large amounts of silver and gold. Thus the cost of its refining is offset by the recovery of these precious metals. Copper is largely used for making electric conductors, and very small amounts of impurities greatly increase the electric resistance.

In electrolytic refining, sheets of pure copper are used as the cathodes in electrolytic cells. Large plates of *impure* copper are used as the anodes. The electrolyte is a solution of copper(II) sulfate in sulfuric acid. A direct current at low voltage is used to operate the cell. During the electrolysis, copper and the other metals in the anode which are above copper in the electrochemical series are oxidized. They enter the solution as ions.

$$Cu \rightarrow Cu^{++} + 2e^-$$
$$Fe \rightarrow Fe^{++} + 2e^-$$
$$Zn \rightarrow Zn^{++} + 2e^-$$

At the low voltages used, the less active silver and gold are not oxidized and so do not go into solution. As the anode is used up, they fall to the bottom of the cell as a sludge and are recovered easily.

We might expect the various positive ions of the electrolyte to be reduced at the cathode. However, H_3O^+ ions, Fe^{++} ions, and Zn^{++} ions all require higher voltages than Cu^{++} ions for reduction. At the low potential maintained across the cell, only Cu^{++} ions are reduced at the cathode.

$$Cu^{++} + 2e^- \rightarrow Cu$$

Of all the metals present, only copper plates out on the cathode. Electrolytic copper is over 99.9% pure.

25.26   Properties of copper

Copper is a soft, ductile, malleable, red metal with a density of 8.96 g/cm³. Next to silver, it is the best conductor of electricity.

Heated in air, copper forms a black coating of copper(II) oxide, CuO. Metallic copper and most copper compounds color a Bunsen flame green.

Copper forms copper(II) salts which dissociate in water and give blue solutions. The color is characteristic of the hydrated copper(II) ion, $Cu(H_2O)_4^{++}$. Adding an excess of ammonia to solutions containing this ion produces the deeper blue complex ion, $Cu(NH_3)_4^{++}$. Aqueous solutions of copper(II) salts are weakly acidic because of the mild hydrolysis of the Cu^{++} ion.

$$Cu(H_2O)_4^{++} + H_2O \rightarrow Cu(H_2O)_3OH^+ + H_3O^+$$

Copper Development Association

Fig. 25-20. The roof of the *Palace of the One Hundred Suns* in Mexico City is made of copper.

An excess of sulfur vapor forms a blue-black coating of copper(I) sulfide on hot copper. In moist air, copper tarnishes and forms a protective coating. This coating is a green basic carbonate, $Cu_2(OH)_2CO_3$. Sulfur dioxide in the air may also combine with copper. If so, a green basic sulfate, $Cu_4(OH)_6SO_4$, is produced. The green color seen on copper roofs is caused by the formation of these compounds.

Both copper(I) and copper(II) compounds are known. The copper(II) compounds are much more common. Copper(II) oxide is used to change alternating current to direct current. It is also used as an oxidizing agent in chemical laboratories.

Hydrated copper(II) sulfate, $CuSO_4 \cdot 5H_2O$, called *blue vitriol*, is an important copper compound. It is used to kill algae in reservoirs and to make certain pesticides. It is also used in electroplating and in preparing other copper compounds.

Because copper stands below hydrogen in the activity series (see Section 8.8), it does not replace hydrogen from acids. Thus, it is not acted on by nonoxidizing acids such as hydrochloric and dilute sulfuric except very slowly when oxygen is present. The oxidizing acids, nitric and hot concentrated sulfuric, react vigorously with copper. Such reactions produce the corresponding copper(II) salts. These chemical changes are typical oxidation-reduction reactions.

CAUTION: *All soluble compounds of copper are poisonous.*

25.27 Tests for the Cu++ ion

A dilute solution of a copper(II) salt changes to a very deep blue color when an excess of ammonia is added. This color change is caused by the formation of complex $Cu(NH_3)_4^{++}$ ions.

$$Cu^{++} + 4NH_3 \rightarrow Cu(NH_3)_4^{++}$$

The addition of $K_4Fe(CN)_6$ to a solution containing Cu^{++} ions produces a red precipitate of $Cu_2Fe(CN)_6$. This chemical is copper(II) hexacyanoferrate(II), also known as copper(II) ferrocyanide. If copper is present in a borax bead formed in an *oxidizing flame,* a clear blue color appears on cooling. The hot bead is green. A bead formed in a *reducing* flame is colorless while hot, and an opaque red when cool.

25.28 Silver and its recovery

Silver is obtained as a by-product in refining silver-bearing lead and copper ores. Silver is also found free in nature. Silver sulfide, Ag_2S, and silver chloride, $AgCl$, are common silver ores.

Extraction processes are the following:

1. By-product silver. When copper is refined by electrolysis, a sludge containing silver and other metals falls to the bottom of the electrolytic tank. See Section 25.25. This sludge is treated with dilute sulfuric acid to remove impurities more active than silver and gold. The remaining sludge is then treated with concentrated sulfuric acid. This treatment separates the silver from the gold as silver sulfate. Scrap copper is then added to the silver sulfate solution to precipitate the silver.

$$2Ag^+ + Cu \rightarrow Cu^{++} + 2Ag(s)$$

2. *Cyanide process.* Crushed silver ore is roasted with common salt to convert the silver to silver chloride. This sparingly soluble salt ($K_{sp} = 1.2 \times 10^{-10}$) is added to a dilute solution of NaCN. On standing, soluble complex $Ag(CN)_2^-$ ions are formed.

$$Ag^+ + 2CN^- \rightarrow Ag(CN)_2^-$$

Silver is precipitated from the filtered sodium argenticyanide solution by adding metallic zinc.

$$2Ag(CN)_2^- + Zn \rightarrow Zn(CN)_4^{--} + 2Ag(s)$$

3. *Parkes process.* In this process, lead containing silver and gold as impurities is melted in a large kettle. Zinc is then added, and the mixture is stirred. Both silver and gold are much more soluble in molten zinc than in lead. The zinc rises to the surface, carrying with it almost all of the silver and gold. This zinc alloy is scraped off, and the zinc is vaporized in a retort. The residue consists of silver, gold, and a little lead. It is heated in a crucible made of bone ash. The lead oxidizes, and the lead oxide is absorbed by the crucible, leaving a button of silver and gold. Nitric acid reacts with silver but not with gold. In this way, the silver is separated from the gold.

25.29 Properties and uses of silver

Silver is a soft, white, lustrous metal. Its density is 10.50 g/cm^3. It is the best conductor of heat and electricity known.

Silver is an inactive metal. It does not unite with oxygen in the air, even at high temperatures. Traces of hydrogen sulfide in the air cause a brownish-black coating of silver sulfide to form on the surface of silver. The sulfur compounds present in such foods as mustard and eggs cause silverware to tarnish rapidly.

Silver reacts readily with oxidizing acids such as nitric acid and hot concentrated sulfuric acid. Hydrochloric acid does not react with silver, nor does fused sodium hydroxide or potassium hydroxide.

For many years, United States silver coins contained 90% silver and 10% copper. Today, these "silver" coins contain no silver. Instead, they consist of a copper-nickel alloy with a core of pure copper. A solution of a silver compound mixed with a reducing agent such as formaldehyde is used for silvering mirrors. The mixture is poured on the clean glass, and a film of metallic silver deposits on the glass as the reduction occurs.

Fig. 25-21. Ancient silver coins.

Fritz Goro for LIFE Magazine © TIME INC.

The main use for silver is in photography. The halogen compounds of silver are sensitive to light, especially if organic matter is present. These compounds include silver chloride, AgCl; silver bromide, AgBr; and silver iodide, AgI. When light strikes these compounds, a reduction reaction takes place. A black, finely divided deposit of silver is formed. Silver bromide is the most light-sensitive of the halogen compounds of silver. However, all three are used in photography.

Silver nitrate, $AgNO_3$, crystallizes in colorless scales. It is sometimes used, under the name *lunar caustic,* for cauterizing (searing) wounds and bites. *Argyrol* is a compound of silver with a protein, silver vitellin. Argyrol is used in medicine as an antiseptic.

25.30 Test for the silver ion

Certain solubility properties of the silver ion, Ag^+, enable us to recognize its presence in solutions. The chlorides of silver, mercury(I), and lead are very slightly soluble. If a soluble chloride is added to a solution containing silver ions, silver chloride forms as a white precipitate. If lead and mercury(I) ions are present, they too precipitate as chlorides. Certain other metallic oxy-chloride complexes also tend to precipitate. These complexes do not precipitate if the solution is first made acidic with HNO_3.

Lead chloride is soluble in hot water. Thus, it can be removed from the precipitate by washing with hot water. Silver chloride and mercury(I) chloride remain. The silver chloride is separated by washing this remaining precipitate with an ammonia-water solution. Silver ions and ammonia molecules form soluble complex ions, $Ag(NH_3)_2^+$. The filtrate contains these silver-ammonia ions and chloride ions dissolved in the ammonia-water solution. By neutralizing the hydroxide ions of this basic filtrate with nitric acid, silver chloride again precipitates. *The formation of a white precipitate when this filtrate is made acidic with HNO_2 indicates the presence of silver.*

25.31 Gold and its recovery

Gold was probably the first metal known to man. Primitive people collected gold for its ornamental value before any metallurgical processes were known.

Gold occurs in stream beds as fine particles mixed with sand. It is also found in underground deposits mixed with quartz. While it is usually found as the native metal, compounds of gold with tellurium sometimes occur. Sea water contains 0.1 to 0.2 mg of gold per metric ton. However, it would cost many times its value to separate this gold by known processes.

Fig. 25-22. A nugget of native gold.

Lee Boltin

The gold from low-grade ores is recovered by a cyanide process similar to that used for silver. The soluble complex $Au(CN)_2^-$ ion is formed.

$$Au^+ + 2CN^- \rightarrow Au(CN)_2^-$$

Metallic zinc is used to precipitate gold.

$$2Au(CN)_2^- + Zn \rightarrow Zn(CN)_4^{--} + 2Au(s)$$

Gold is sometimes separated from crushed ore with moist chlorine gas. Gold unites with chlorine and forms gold(III) chloride, $AuCl_3$, which is soluble in water. The solution of gold(III) chloride is reduced by iron(II) sulfate to metallic gold, which precipitates.

25.32 Properties and uses of gold

Gold is a soft, yellow metal that is highly ductile. It is so malleable that it can be hammered into sheets $\frac{1}{250}$ the thickness of this page. Gold is a very good conductor of heat and electricity and has a density of 19.32 g/cm³.

Pure gold is too soft for use in jewelry, so copper is almost always alloyed with it for this use. The purity of gold is expressed in *carats*. Pure gold is 24 carats. Jewelry metal that is 18 carats contains 18 parts by weight of gold and 6 parts by weight of copper.

Gold does not tarnish when exposed to the air, even at high temperatures. Hydrofluoric acid reacts with it slowly. Such strong acids as hydrochloric, nitric, and sulfuric do not react with gold when used separately. However a mixture of 1 part nitric acid and 3 parts hydrochloric acid (called *aqua regia*) reacts vigorously with it. In this reaction, the gold is oxidized by HNO_3 in the presence of Cl^- ions, forming complex $AuCl_4^-$ ions.

In some compounds, gold exhibits the +1 oxidation state. More often, gold is in the +3 oxidation state in compounds. Gold(III) chloride is used in photography to give prints a "warmer" brown-tinted shade. The complex $Au(CN)_2^-$ ion as $NaAu(CN)_2$ is used for gold plating.

Engineering and Mining Journal

Fig. 25-23. The cascade method of pouring gold.

THE ZINC SUBGROUP

25.33 Metals of the zinc subgroup

The last subgroup of transition elements is composed of the metals *zinc, cadmium,* and *mercury.* Like the metals of the copper subgroup, these metals have 18 electrons in their next-to-outermost shells. Zinc and cadmium form ions in which they exhibit the +2 oxidation state. Mercury exhibits both the +1 and +2 oxidation states. The mercury(I) ion has the $(Hg:Hg)^{++}$ structure. Each Hg^+ ion has a single electron remaining in the valence shell. Two such ions share their odd electrons and form a covalent bond. This electron sharing produces greater stability and results in the structure Hg_2^{++}.

Ions of mercury are much more difficult to form than those of zinc and cadmium. In fact, mercury has a strong tendency to form covalent bonds. In some ways, it resembles metals of the Copper Family more closely than zinc and cadmium. Properties of the metals of the zinc subgroup are listed in Table 25-9.

25.34 Zinc and its recovery

Zinc ores were used for making brass centuries before the discovery of zinc as a metal. Zinc is thought to have been produced first in 1746 from a silicate ore heated with charcoal.

Zinc does not occur as the native metal because of its chemical activity. The principal ore is *sphalerite*, ZnS, also called *zinc blende*. *Zincite*, ZnO, and *smithsonite*, $ZnCO_3$, are also important ores. Two silicate ores of zinc are *willemite*, Zn_2SiO_4, and *calamine*, $Zn_2SiO_4 \cdot H_2O$. The mineral *franklinite*, a complex mixture of oxides of zinc, iron, and manganese, is found at Franklin, New Jersey.

Two methods are used to recover zinc.

1.   By reduction with coal. The zinc ores are first roasted to convert them into oxides.

$$2ZnS + 3O_2 \rightarrow 2ZnO + 2SO_2(g)$$

The oxides are mixed with powdered coal and heated in earthenware retorts.

$$ZnO + C \rightarrow Zn + CO(g)$$

Zinc has a low boiling point (907° C), and is distilled from the retorts as a vapor. It is then condensed in iron or earthenware receivers. Some of the zinc is deposited as *zinc dust* in the upper part of the receivers. Liquid zinc collects at the bottom of the

Table 25-9
THE ZINC SUBGROUP

Element	Atomic number	Atomic weight	Electron configuration	Oxidation numbers	Melting point (°C)	Boiling point (°C)	Density (g/cm³)
zinc	30	65.37	2,8,18,2	+2	419.4	907	7.13
cadmium	48	112.40	2,8,18,18,2	+2	320.9	764.9	8.65
mercury	80	200.59	2,8,18,32,18,2	+1, +2	−38.87	356.6	13.55

receivers and is drawn off and cast in molds. Such *spelter*, as it is called, may contain arsenic, cadmium, and carbon as impurities. If so, it can be purified by redistillation.

2. *By electrolysis.* In the electrolytic process, the ore is first roasted. It is then extracted with sulfuric acid to produce a solution of zinc sulfate. Iron and manganese are removed as impurities by adding lime and blowing air through the solution. Sheets of aluminum are used as cathodes in the electrolytic cells. An electric current is passed through the cell. Zinc ions are reduced at the cathode and the metallic zinc plates out on the aluminum. Zinc that is 99.9% pure is then stripped off the aluminum cathodes. Electrolytic zinc is preferred for making brass and other alloys because of its high purity.

25.35 Properties and uses of zinc

Metallic zinc is bluish-white in color. At room temperature it is somewhat brittle, but at about 100° C it becomes malleable and ductile. It is a moderately hard metal, slightly less dense than iron.

Zinc burns in air with a bluish-white flame and forms white clouds of zinc oxide. At room temperature dry air does not affect zinc. Moist air reacts with zinc and forms a coating of basic zinc carbonate, $Zn_2(OH)_2CO_3$. This tarnish clings to the surface and prevents further action. Hence, zinc is a self-protective metal.

Zinc stands well above hydrogen in the activity series. Therefore, it reacts readily with acids, replacing hydrogen. *Mossy* zinc is produced by pouring molten zinc drop by drop into water. Mossy zinc is commonly used in the laboratory to displace hydrogen from nonoxidizing acids. Pure zinc reacts very slowly with acids. Thus spelter, rather than electrolytic zinc, is preferred for preparing mossy zinc.

The active hydroxides, such as sodium hydroxide, react with zinc and set free hydrogen gas. Soluble zincates, which may be considered as the salts of zincic acid, H_2ZnO_2, are formed.

$$Zn + 2NaOH \rightarrow Na_2ZnO_2 + H_2(g)$$

This behavior indicates that the hydroxide of zinc is amphiprotic. It acts as the hydroxide, $Zn(OH)_2$, in the presence of a strong acid. On the other hand, it acts as the acid, H_2ZnO_2, in the presence of a strong hydroxide. Thus:

$$2HCl + Zn(OH)_2 \rightarrow ZnCl_2 + 2H_2O$$
$$2NaOH + H_2ZnO_2 \rightarrow Na_2ZnO_2 + 2H_2O$$

Zinc hydroxide dissolves readily in ammonia water because of the strong tendency of zinc to form complex ions. This tendency is common to all transition metals. With $NH_3(aq)$, a stable zinc-ammonia complex, $Zn(NH_3)_4^{++}$, is formed. Similarly, with cyanide solutions, a very stable zinc-cyanide complex, $Zn(CN)_4^{--}$, is formed.

$$Zn^{++} + 4NH_3 \rightleftarrows Zn(NH_3)_4^{++}$$

$$Zn^{++} + 4CN^- \rightleftarrows Zn(CN)_4^{--}$$

Large quantities of zinc are used for *galvanizing* iron. In this process, a thin protective covering of zinc is placed over the iron. This is done by dipping, by electroplating, or by condensing zinc vapor on the surface of the iron.

CAUTION: *All soluble salts of zinc are poisonous. Foods should never be stored in galvanized iron containers.*

From the activity series, it is clear that zinc is a strong reducing agent. This property makes it well suited for use as the negative electrode in an electrochemical cell. Here electrolytic zinc is preferred, because particles of carbon in the electrode cause local electrochemical action between the impurity and the zinc.

The most important alloy of zinc is *brass,* which contains zinc and copper. The proportions vary, but ordinary brass contains about 60% copper and 40% zinc. *Bronze* contains copper and tin; usually some zinc is added. *German silver* is an alloy containing 55% copper, 25% zinc, and 20% nickel. The name is misleading, since there is no silver in the alloy.

25.36 Cadmium and its uses

Cadmium was discovered in 1817 as an impurity in zinc carbonate. In nature, it is usually found associated with zinc. It also occurs as the sulfide, CdS, in the rare mineral known as *greenockite.* It is a bluish-white metal resembling zinc and magnesium in its chemical properties. Cadmium is used in making alloys that melt at a low temperature. It forms an even tougher coating than zinc for iron and steel. For this reason, a large amount of cadmium is used for plating small hardware such as screws and bolts. Cadmium metal is used for making the negative plates of the *nickel-cadmium* storage battery. Cadmium sulfide is a fine yellow pigment used as an artist's color called cadmium yellow. *The soluble salts of cadmium are poisonous.*

Cadmium is becoming increasingly important in industry. Because of its low coefficient of friction and resistance to fatigue, it is used in bearing alloys. Production of cadmium in the United States has been stimulated by its use in control rods for nuclear reactors.

B. M. Shaub

Fig. 25-24. Cadmium. It is found in nature with zinc.

25.37 Mercury and its uses

Mercury was known in ancient China and India. It has been found in Egyptian tombs built nearly 3500 years ago.

Most of the world's supply of mercury comes from California and Texas, and from Spain and Italy. Mercury may occur as tiny globules scattered through rock. However, the chief ore of mercury is a red mineral known as *cinnabar,* mercury(II) sulfide. The metal can be obtained by simply heating the ore:

$$HgS + O_2 \rightarrow Hg + SO_2(g)$$

Mercury is the only metal that is a liquid at room temperature. It is silver-white, lustrous, and about 13.6 times as dense as water. It freezes to a hard, brittle solid at approximately $-39°$ C, and boils at a temperature of nearly $357°$ C.

Mercury is found far down in the activity series of metals. Thus, most metals replace it from its compounds. It is a poor reducing agent. Therefore, it does not combine readily with oxygen and does not displace hydrogen from nonoxidizing acids. Nitric acid and hot concentrated sulfuric acid react with it and form mercury(II) nitrate and mercury(II) sulfate, respectively. These are typical oxidation-reduction reactions.

An alloy of mercury with one or more other metals is known as an *amalgam.* Mercury forms amalgams with most metals, although not with platinum and iron. An amalgam of silver, tin, zinc, and mercury is used for fillings in teeth. When freshly prepared, it is soft enough to be pressed into the cavity of a tooth, but it hardens very quickly.

25.38 Compounds of mercury

Mercury forms two series of compounds. Its oxidation number is $+1$ in one series of compounds and $+2$ in the other.

Mercury(I) chloride, a white solid with the molecular formula Hg_2Cl_2, is insoluble in water. It is known as *calomel* in medicine. Exposure to sunlight causes mercury(I) chloride to change slowly to mercury and mercury(II) chloride:

$$Hg_2Cl_2 \rightarrow Hg + HgCl_2$$

Fig. 25-25. Mercury(I) chloride and mercury(II) Chloride are covalent structures. The mercury(I) ion is also covalent.

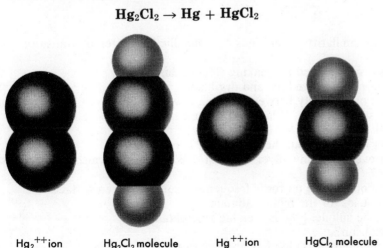

$Hg_2{}^{++}$ion Hg_2Cl_2 molecule Hg^{++}ion $HgCl_2$ molecule

Mercury(I) nitrate, $Hg_2(NO_3)_2$, is fairly soluble in water. Mercury(I) chloride is precipitated when chloride ions are added to a solution of mercury(I) nitrate. Ammonia reacts with this precipitate. The reaction forms the insoluble white mercury(II) complex, $HgNH_2Cl$, and metallic mercury as a black suspension. *The mixture of these two products gives a gray residue which serves to identify the Hg_2^{++} ion.*

$$Hg_2Cl_2 + 2NH_3 \rightarrow HgNH_2Cl(s) + Hg(s) + NH_4Cl$$
$$\text{white} \qquad\qquad \text{black}$$

CAUTION: *Hg, Hg vapor, and all the soluble salts of mercury are extremely poisonous.*

The whites of eggs or milk are used as antidotes for mercury poisoning. With mercury, these substances form an insoluble mercury albuminate. The use of Hg_2Cl_2 (calomel) in medicine is safe even though the Hg_2^{++} ion is very poisonous. This is because the compound is only very slightly soluble.

Mercury(II) chloride is commonly called *bichloride of mercury* or *corrosive sublimate*. It is covalent and has the molecular formula $HgCl_2$. It forms white crystals that can be purified by sublimation. It is an extremely poisonous compound.

Mercury(II) oxide, HgO, is used as an antiseptic under the name *red precipitate*. Priestley obtained oxygen by heating this compound. Sublimed *mercury(II) sulfide*, HgS, forms a red pigment known as *vermilion*. It is used as a paint to slow the growth of barnacles on ships.

QUESTIONS

Group A

1. What structural similarity determines the metallic character of transition elements?
2. Which process is most used for making steel in this country?
3. Explain why iron inks write blue and dry black.
4. List five points of similarity between copper, silver, and gold.
5. A gold ring is stamped 14K. What does this mean?
6. (*a*) What is blister copper? (*b*) How did it get its name?
7. How is copper obtained from the native ore?
8. (*a*) Have you ever seen any silver oxide? (*b*) What is the tarnish on a piece of old silverware?
9. Why does the copper trim on roofs frequently acquire a green surface?
10. What are some uses for the metal cadmium?
11. Starting with zinc sulfide, how is metallic zinc obtained?
12. What is an amalgam?
13. Explain why the mercury(I) ion has a +2 charge.

14. Why does impure iron rust more rapidly than pure iron?

Group B

15. How can you detect an iron(II) and an iron(III) compound, if both are present in the same solution?
16. Identify three factors which make the basic oxygen process attractive in steel production.
17. Why were some metals used in very early times, while many other metals were obtained only within the last century?
18. Suppose you have a powdered mixture that contains 90% gold and 10% silver. How can you obtain pure gold from such a mixture?
19. How can silver be obtained from the *anode sludge* that collects in a tank used for the electrolysis of copper?
20. What metals are alloyed in German silver?
21. How can lead chloride be separated from silver chloride?
22. Why does it usually pay to refine copper by electrolysis?
23. What is the cyanide process of extracting gold?
24. Describe the cyanide process of extracting silver from silver ore.
25. What is meant when we say that zinc hydroxide is amphiprotic?

PROBLEMS

1. How much iron(II) chloride can be produced by adding 165 g of iron to an excess of hydrochloric acid? Compute to 3 significant figures.

Group A

2. How much iron(III) chloride can be prepared from the iron(II) chloride in the preceding problem if more hydrochloric acid is added and air is blown through the solution?
3. What is the percentage of iron in a sample of limonite, $2Fe_2O_3 \cdot 3H_2O$?
4. How many grams of silver nitrate can be obtained by adding 100 g of pure silver to an excess of nitric acid?
5. A sample of hematite ore contains Fe_2O_3 87.0%, silica 8.0%, moisture 4.0%, other impurities 1.0%. What is the percentage of iron in the ore?
6. What will be the loss in mass when 1.0×10^6 metric tons of the ore in the preceding problem are heated to 200° C?

7. How much limestone will be needed to combine with the silica in 1.0×10^6 metric tons of the ore of Problem 5?

Group B

8. (*a*) How much carbon monoxide is required to reduce 1.0×10^6 metric tons of the ore of Problem 5? (*b*) How much coke must be supplied to meet this requirement? (Assume the coke to be 100% carbon.)
9. Iron(II) sulfate is oxidized to iron(III) sulfate in the presence of sulfuric acid using nitric acid as the oxidizing agent. Nitrogen monoxide and water are also formed. Balance the equation.
10. Silver reacts with dilute nitric acid and forms silver nitrate, water, and nitrogen monoxide. Balance the equation.
11. Copper reacts with hot concentrated sulfuric acid and forms copper(II) sulfate, sulfur dioxide, and water. Balance the equation.

Chapter 26

Aluminum and the Metalloids

26.1 Nature of metalloids

Fig. 26-1. The metalloids are the elements *boron, silicon, germanium, arsenic, antimony, tellurium,* and *polonium.*

The elements with properties intermediate between metallic and nonmetallic are called *metalloids* or *semimetals.* They occupy a diagonal region from the upper center toward the lower right of the periodic table. See Figure 26-1.

METALS					NON METALS				VIII
				III	IV	V	VI	VII	4.00260 **He** 2 (2)
				10.81 **B** 5 (2,3)	12.011 **C** 6 (2,4)	14.0067 **N** 7 (2,5)	15.9994 **O** 8 (2,6)	18.9984 **F** 9 (2,7)	20.179 **Ne** 10 (2,8)
				26.9815 **Al** 13 (2,8,3)	28.086 **Si** 14 (2,8,4)	30.9738 **P** 15 (2,8,5)	32.06 **S** 16 (2,8,6)	35.453 **Cl** 17 (2,8,7)	39.948 **Ar** 18 (2,8,8)
58.9332 **Co** 27 (2,8,15,2)	58.71 **Ni** 28 (2,8,16,2)	63.546 **Cu** 29 (2,8,18,1)	65.37 **Zn** 30 (2,8,18,2)	69.72 **Ga** 31 (2,8,18,3)	72.59 **Ge** 32 (2,8,18,4)	74.9216 **As** 33 (2,8,18,5)	78.96 **Se** 34 (2,8,18,6)	79.904 **Br** 35 (2,8,18,7)	83.8 **Kr** 36 (2,8,18,8)
102.9055 **Rh** 45 (2,8,18,16,1)	106.4 **Pd** 46 (2,8,18,18,0)	107.868 **Ag** 47 (2,8,18,18,1)	112.40 **Cd** 48 (2,8,18,18,2)	114.82 **In** 49 (2,8,18,18,3)	118.69 **Sn** 50 (2,8,18,18,4)	121.75 **Sb** 51 (2,8,18,18,5)	127.60 **Te** 52 (2,8,18,18,6)	126.9045 **I** 53 (2,8,18,18,7)	131.30 **Xe** 54 (2,8,18,18,8)
192.22 **Ir** 77 (2,8,18,32,15,2)	195.09 **Pt** 78 (2,8,18,32,17,1)	196.9665 **Au** 79 (2,8,18,32,18,1)	200.59 **Hg** 80 (2,8,18,32,18,2)	204.37 **Tl** 81 (2,8,18,32,18,3)	207.2 **Pb** 82 (2,8,18,32,18,4)	208.9806 **Bi** 83 (2,8,18,32,18,5)	[210] **Po** 84 (2,8,18,32,18,6)	[211] **At** 85 (2,8,18,32,18,7)	222 **Rn** 86 (2,8,18,32,18,8)

Table 26-1

PROPERTIES OF ALUMINUM AND METALLOIDS

Element	Atomic number	Electron configuration	Oxidation states	Melting point (°C)	Boiling point (°C)	Density (g/cm³)	Atomic radius (Å)	First ionization energy (kcal/mole)
boron	5	2,3	+3	2300	2550	2.34	0.82	191
aluminum	13	2,8,3	+3	660	2467	2.70	1.18	138
silicon	14	2,8,4	+2,+4,−4	1410	2355	2.33	1.11	188
germanium	32	2,8,18,4	+2,+4,−4	938	2825	5.36	1.22	187
arsenic	33	2,8,18,5	+3,+5,−3	sublimes		5.73	1.20	242
antimony	51	2,8,18,18,5	+3,+5,−3	631	1380	6.69	1.40	199
tellurium	52	2,8,18,18,6	+2,+4,+6,−2	450	987	6.24	1.36	208
polonium	84	2,8,18,32,18,6	+4,+6	254	962	9.32	1.46	196

The metalloids include the elements *boron, silicon, germanium, arsenic, antimony, tellurium, and polonium.* Aluminum is included in this chapter because of its unique position in the periodic table with respect to the metalloids.

Aluminum is distinctly metallic and we recognize it by the familiar properties of metals. However, aluminum can appear with oxygen in negative aluminate ions. Its hydroxide is amphiprotic. Its oxide is ionic, yet its hydride is polymeric. Taken together, these characteristics tend to place aluminum among metalloids.

Boron, silicon, arsenic, and antimony show typical metalloidal behavior. They will be considered separately as representative elements. Table 26-1 lists some of their important properties, together with those of aluminum and the other metalloids.

Germanium is a moderately rare element. Its compounds until recently had little importance. With the development of the transistor, germanium became important as a semiconductor material. It is chemically similar to silicon, which stands above it in Group IV. Germanium is more metallic than arsenic, which is just to its right in Period Five. The major oxidation state of germanium is +4.

Tellurium, a semiconductor, is most stable in a hexagonal metal-like form. Its chemistry is typically metalloidal. It appears with oxygen in both tellurite and tellurate ions. In these ions, tellurium shows respectively the +4 and +6 oxidation states. Tellurium combines covalently with the more electronegative oxygen and halogens in which the +2, +4, and +6 oxidation states are observed. It forms tellurides (−2 oxidation state) with such elements as gold, hydrogen, and lead. In fact, tellurium is the only element combined with gold in nature.

Tellurium (at. no. 52) appears just before iodine (at. no. 53) in the periodic table. However, its atomic weight (127.60) is

See Problem 11 at the end of this chapter.

higher than that of iodine (126.90). This seeming irregularity is cleared up if you remember that *the atomic weight of an element depends on the atomic masses and natural abundance of its isotopes.* While iodine has one naturally occurring isotope (I-127), tellurium has several, the two most abundant being Te-128 and Te-130.

Polonium is a radioactive element. It was discovered by Pierre and Marie Curie in 1898 just prior to their discovery of radium. Polonium is so rare in nature that little is known of its chemistry. It appears to be more metallic than tellurium.

ALUMINUM

26.2 Aluminum as a light metal

Aluminum, atomic number 13, is the second member of Group III. This group is headed by boron and includes gallium, indium, and thallium. All are typically metallic except boron, which is classed as a metalloid. Boron as an element and in compounds differs from aluminum and the other Group III elements. These differences result mainly from the small size of its atoms. Its chemistry resembles that of silicon and germanium more than it does that of aluminum.

Aluminum is a low-density metal. It is used to build many light and sturdy things such as the frame of airplanes or storm windows. In these applications, it may be used as the pure metal or it may be alloyed with other metals such as copper, manganese, and magnesium. Aluminum is similar to its corresponding alkaline-earth metal, magnesium, in chemical behavior. The Group III metals below aluminum are separated from the corresponding Group II elements by the transition metals.

Fig. 26-2. Aluminum-sheathed transit cars operating over the San Francisco Bay Area Rapid Transit system.

HR&W photo by Brian Hammill

Aluminum is the most abundant metal in the earth's crust. It is found in many clays, rocks, and other minerals. The aluminum industry is working on processes for profitably separating aluminum from clay. However no process has yet proved practical. Such a process would make the United States less dependent on foreign sources of aluminum ore. Bauxite, an impure aluminum oxide ore, presently is imported from Jamaica, Surinam, and Guyana. It is also mined in Georgia, Alabama, Tennessee, and Arkansas.

26.3 Discovery of aluminum

The first isolation of aluminum is usually credited to a German chemist, Friedrich Wöhler, in 1827. However, chemical historians now believe that the metal was first isolated in impure form in 1825 by Hans Christian Oersted, a Danish chemist. As late as 1855 the price of aluminum was $90 per pound, but by 1870 it was selling for $12 per pound. In 1886 an improved process of reduction with sodium brought the price down to about $2 per pound. Still, the metal was too expensive for structural and household use.

In 1886 a young American, Charles Martin Hall (1863–1914), developed a cheap practical method for producing aluminum. While a student at Oberlin College, Hall discovered that aluminum could be separated from its oxide by electrolysis. His process, first used commercially in 1889, lowered the price of aluminum to about 20¢ per pound. A similar process was developed independently in France at about this same time by Paul Héroult. Today aluminum is one of the most widely used metals.

26.4 Recovery of aluminum

Fused-salt electrolysis has great commercial value. It is used to produce alkali and alkaline-earth metals as well as aluminum and related metals.

Aluminum is extracted by electrolyzing aluminum oxide (refined bauxite) dissolved in molten cryolite, Na_3AlF_6. The process requires a temperature slightly below 1000° C. It is basically the process developed by Hall in 1886.

In the electrolytic cell, an iron box lined with graphite serves as the cathode. Graphite rods serve as the anode, and cryolite-aluminum oxide is the electrolyte. Heat produced by a large current in the cell melts the cryolite, which dissolves the aluminum oxide. This heat keeps the aluminum metal in the bottom of the cell in the liquid phase. This liquid aluminum is easily drawn off. Figure 26-3.

The electrode reactions are complex and are not understood completely. Aluminum is reduced at the cathode, possibly from a complex ion structure composed of aluminum, oxygen, and fluorine. The anode is gradually used up. This fact suggests that

Anaconda

Fig. 26-3. Batteries of electrolytic cells for the recovery of aluminum from aluminum oxide. In the foreground molten aluminum is being poured into a transfer ladle.

oxygen is formed at the anode by oxidation of the O^{--} ion or some complex containing oxygen in the negative oxidation state. The following equations for the reaction mechanism may be overly simple. However, they serve to summarize the oxidation-reduction processes.

cathode: $\quad 4Al^{+++} + 12e^- \rightarrow 4Al$

anode: $\quad\quad\quad\quad 6O^{--} \rightarrow 3O_2 + 12e^-$

$$3C + 3O_2 \rightarrow 3CO_2(g)$$

Efforts to replace the Hall process for recovering aluminum have been in progress for many years. Wastes from the bauxite-to-aluminum oxide process and fluorine from the electrolysis create serious pollution problems. The huge quantity of electric energy consumed during electrolysis contributes to the energy shortage. For example, the average amount of electricity required to produce 1 kg of aluminum would operate an ordinary 100-watt lamp 6 hours a day for about 1 month.

A new method for aluminum recovery is now being tested. The tests have shown it to be less polluting and to require less electric energy. In this process, aluminum oxide is combined with chlorine in a chemical reactor and aluminum chloride is formed. The compound is separated into aluminum and chlorine in a closed electrolysis cell. The chlorine is recycled to the reactor. The first commercial aluminum produced by this technique is expected in 1975. Variations of the chlorination method are under development. One, called the *Toth process*, may make possible greater use of aluminum-bearing minerals found in the United States.

26.5 Properties of aluminum

Aluminum has a density of 2.7 g/cm³. It is ductile and malleable, but is more easily pulled apart than brass, copper, or steel. Only silver, copper, and gold are better conductors of electricity. Aluminum can be welded, cast, or spun, but can be soldered only by using a special solder.

Aluminum takes a high polish, but soon becomes covered with a thin layer of aluminum oxide. This oxide layer is not affected by air or moisture. Hence, aluminum is a self-protective metal. At high temperatures, the metal combines vigorously with oxygen and releases a great deal of heat.

Aluminum is a very good reducing agent, but is not as active as the Group I and Group II metals.

$$Al \rightarrow Al^{+++} + 3e^-$$

The Al^{+++} ion is quite small and carries a large positive charge. The ion hydrates vigorously in water solution and is usually written as the hydrated ion, $Al(H_2O)_6^{+++}$. Water solutions of aluminum salts are generally acidic because of the hydrolysis of $Al(H_2O)_6^{+++}$ ions.

$$Al(H_2O)_6^{+++} + H_2O \rightarrow Al(H_2O)_5OH^{++} + H_3O^+$$

Water molecules are amphiprotic but are very weak proton donors or acceptors. However, water molecules which hydrate the Al^{+++} ion give up protons more readily. This increased activity results from the repulsion effect of the highly positive Al^{+++} ion. In the hydrolysis shown above, a water molecule does succeed in removing one proton from the $Al(H_2O)_6^{+++}$ ion.

Hydrochloric acid reacts readily with aluminum, forming aluminum chloride and releasing hydrogen.

$$2Al(s) + 6H_3O^+ + 6H_2O \rightarrow 2Al(H_2O)_6^{+++} + 3H_2(g)$$

The simple empirical equation is

$$2Al(s) + 6HCl \rightarrow 2AlCl_3 + 3H_2(g)$$

Nitric acid does not react readily with aluminum because of its protective oxide layer.

In basic solutions, aluminum forms aluminate ions, AlO_2^-, and releases hydrogen.

$$2Al(s) + 2OH^- + 2H_2O \rightarrow 2AlO_2^- + 3H_2(g)$$

The soluble aluminate ion is often represented as $Al(OH)_4^-$, which is the same as $AlO_2(H_2O)_2^-$. Each formula probably oversimplifies the ionic species that actually exists in solution.

Aluminum reacts rapidly in a solution of sodium hydroxide. Sodium aluminate, $NaAlO_2$, is the soluble product. The empirical equation can be written as

$$2Al(s) + 2NaOH + 2H_2O \rightarrow 2NaAlO_2 + 3H_2(g)$$

Fig. 26-4. This top-charging aluminum melting furnace receives a charge of 30,000 pounds of metal in less than two minutes.

Kaiser Aluminum and Chemical Corp.

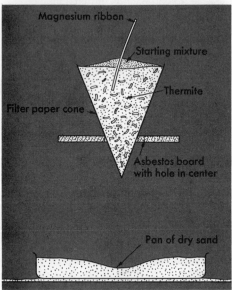

Fig. 26-5. The thermite reaction. Dry sand protects the table top. Spectators must stand at a safe distance. Sharp black and white contrast shows the brilliance of the molten iron.

This reaction is used in some commercial products for opening plugged sink drains. A mixture of granulated aluminum and solid sodium hydroxide is added to the water in a plugged drain. The vigorous release of H_2 gas agitates the water and raises pressure in the drain. Excess sodium hydroxide converts grease in the pipe to a water soluble soap. Hopefully, the combined actions unplug the drain.

26.6 The thermite reaction

When a mixture of powdered aluminum and an oxidizing agent such as iron oxide is ignited, the aluminum reduces the oxide to the free metal. This reduction is rapid and violent, and yields a tremendous amount of heat. The sudden release of this heat energy produces temperatures from 3000 to 3500° C, enough to melt the iron. Such a reaction between aluminum and the oxide of a less active metal is called the *thermite reaction*. See Figure 26-5.

The formation of aluminum oxide is strongly exothermic. The reaction releases 399 kilocalories of heat per mole of aluminum oxide formed. The heat of formation of iron(III) oxide is 196 kilocalories per mole. In the thermite reaction, the amount of heat released per mole of aluminum oxide formed equals the difference between these values. The net thermite reaction is considered to be the sum of these two separate reactions.

$$2Al + \tfrac{3}{2}O_2 \rightarrow Al_2O_3 \qquad \Delta H = -399 \text{ kcal}$$
$$\underline{Fe_2O_3 \rightarrow 2Fe + \tfrac{3}{2}O_2 \qquad \Delta H = +196 \text{ kcal}}$$
$$2Al + Fe_2O_3 \rightarrow 2Fe + Al_2O_3 \qquad \Delta H = -203 \text{ kcal}$$

It is not practical to use aluminum to reduce cheaper metals. However, the thermite reaction is often used to produce small quantities of carbon-free metal. A more important use of this reaction is to reduce metallic oxides which are not readily reduced with carbon. Chromium, manganese, titanium, tungsten, and molybdenum can be recovered from their oxides by the thermite reaction. All of these metals are used in making alloy steels. Uranium, used to produce nuclear energy, can also be reduced by the thermite reaction.

The very high temperature produced by the thermite reaction makes it useful in welding. Large steel parts, such as propeller shafts and rudder posts on a ship or the crankshafts of heavy machinery, are repaired by thermite welding. A mold is formed around the metals to be welded. A mixture of powdered aluminum and either Fe_2O_3 or Fe_3O_4 is placed in a cone-shaped crucible above this mold. A starting mixture of barium peroxide and powdered magnesium is placed on top of the aluminum-iron oxide mixture. Seconds after the starting mixture is ignited, white-hot iron flows out through the bottom of the crucible. The liquid iron fills the preheated mold and welds the broken ends of the steel.

26.7 Uses of aluminum oxide

Bauxite, the chief ore of aluminum, is an oxide. *Corundum* and *emery* are also natural oxides of this metal, and are used as abrasives. Emery is used in emery paper, emery cloth, or emery grinding wheels.

Rubies and sapphires are aluminum oxide colored by traces of other metallic oxides. Synthetic rubies and sapphires are made by fusing pure aluminum oxide in the flame of an oxyhydrogen blowtorch. In making clear sapphires, no coloring matter is added. Synthetic rubies are colored by adding a very small amount of chromium.

Scientists are finding new ways to strengthen and stiffen structural materials. One important development involves monocrystalline strands or fibers of one substance embedded in and held in place by some other material. An aluminum rod containing very hard, strong sapphire "whiskers" is quite unlike ordinary soft, ductile aluminum. Such a structure is six times stronger than aluminum and twice as stiff. These *fiber composites* may enable engineers to improve the strength-to-weight ratio of structural materials greatly. See Figure 26-7.

Alundum is an oxide of aluminum made by fusing bauxite. It is used for making grinding wheels and other abrasives. It is also found in crucibles, funnels, tubing, and other pieces of laboratory equipment.

26.8 Aluminum hydroxide

When a little sodium hydroxide solution is added to a solution of an aluminum salt, such as aluminum chloride, these substances react, forming a jelly-like white precipitate of aluminum hydroxide.

$$Al^{+++}(aq) + 3OH^-(aq) \rightarrow Al(OH)_3(s)$$

Aluminum hydroxide is insoluble in water. However, if an excess of sodium hydroxide is added, the precipitate dissolves and soluble sodium aluminate is formed. In this reaction aluminum hydroxide acts as an acid. The net reaction is

$$Al(OH)_3(s) + OH^- \rightarrow AlO_2^- + 2H_2O$$

The aluminum hydroxide precipitate also dissolves if hydrochloric acid is added. Soluble aluminum chloride is formed. In this reaction the aluminum hydroxide acts as a base. The net reaction is

$$Al(OH)_3(s) + 3H_3O^+ \rightarrow Al(H_2O)_6^{+++}$$

These reactions show the amphiprotic nature of aluminum hydroxide.

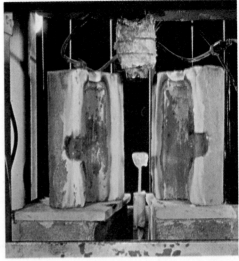

Union Carbide

Fig. 26-6. Verneuil flame fusion furnace for synthetic sapphire.

Fig. 26-7. Cross section of a fiber composite magnified 245 times. The experimental composite shown here consists of sapphire whiskers in a silver matrix.

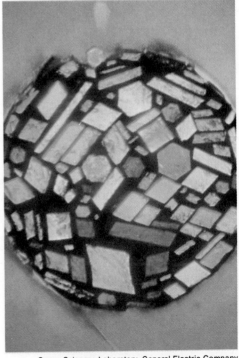

Space Sciences Laboratory, General Electric Company

Aluminum hydroxide is so weakly basic that its salts with weak acids are almost completely hydrolyzed. If sodium carbonate is added to a solution of aluminum chloride, aluminum hydroxide precipitates. A precipitate of aluminum hydroxide always forms when a soluble carbonate or soluble sulfide is added to a solution of an aluminum salt.

Aluminum hydroxide is used to precipitate suspended matter from drinking water. It also finds use as a *mordant,* an insoluble jelly-like material used to treat cotton fabrics in the dyeing process. Aluminum hydroxide is usually precipitated on the fibers before they are dyed.

Colored pigments for use in paint are sometimes made by precipitating a dye with aluminum hydroxide in a large vat. The insoluble compound, which contains the dye, is then filtered off.

26.9 Double salts of aluminum

If solutions of potassium sulfate and aluminum sulfate are mixed, the double salt $KAl(SO_4)_2 \cdot 12H_2O$ forms. This salt crystallizes when some of the water is evaporated. Any double sulfate formed in such a manner and having similar properties is called an *alum.*

Instead of potassium sulfate, either ammonium sulfate or sodium sulfate can be used. The sulfates of such metals as chromium or iron can be used instead of aluminum sulfate. The general formula used to represent alums is $M^+M^{+++}(SO_4)_2 \cdot 12H_2O$. Here, the M^+ stands for an alkali metal or the ammonium group. The M^{+++} represents some trivalent metal.

26.10 Some silicates of aluminum

Fuller's earth, a silicate of aluminum, is a good absorbent. It is used for removing suspended impurities from oils by filtration and for removing spots and stains from textile fabrics.

Mica is a potassium aluminum silicate which is translucent and melts only at high temperatures. It is used for the translucent tops of electric fuse plugs. As an electric insulator, it is used in the commutators of motors and generators.

The *feldspars* are complex silicates which usually contain aluminum silicate and silicates of either sodium or potassium. They are found in all granitic rocks. Natural waters containing dissolved carbon dioxide react slowly with the feldspars and form soluble compounds of the alkali metals. Thus, the weathering of a feldspar sometimes adds potassium to the soil. The insoluble portion remains as a fine white clay. This clay is a hydrated aluminum silicate known as *kaolin.* Colored clays usually owe their color to traces of iron compounds.

BORON

B.M. Shaub

Fig. 26-8. Boron, a metalloid, is best known as a constituent of borax.

26.11 Boron as a metalloid

The first member of a periodic group often has properties somewhat different from those of the rest of the group. This is true because the outer electrons of its atoms are shielded from the nucleus only by the K shell. The first member of Group III, boron, is a metalloid while all other Group III elements are metals. Boron also has the highest electronegativity of any element in Group III. Boron atoms are small, with an atomic radius of only 0.82 Å. Their valence electrons are quite tightly bound. Thus, boron has a relatively high ionization energy for a Group III element. The properties of boron indicate that it forms only covalent bonds with other atoms. At low temperatures boron is a poor conductor of electricity. As the temperature is raised, its electrons have more kinetic energy and its conductivity increases. This behavior is typical of a *semiconductor*.

26.12 Occurrence of boron

Boron is not found as the free element. It can be isolated in fairly pure form by reducing boron trichloride with hydrogen at a high temperature. Elemental boron is important in monocrystalline fiber research (see Section 26.7), but at present it has little commercial value. Hence, it is seldom seen except in compounds.

Boron filaments, embedded in and held in place by an epoxy plastic, form a very strong and stiff structural material. Such materials are much lighter than structural metals. They are called "advanced fiber composite materials." These composite materials are of great interest to aircraft and aerospace engineers. However, many difficult problems still face technologists in this field.

Fig. 26-9. Boron filaments being produced in a research laboratory.

Colemanite is a hydrated borate of calcium with the formula $Ca_2B_6O_{11} \cdot 5H_2O$. It is found in the desert regions of California and Nevada. Sodium tetraborate, $Na_2B_4O_6 \cdot 4H_2O$, is found as the mineral *kernite,* also in California. The salt brines of Searles Lake, California, yield most of the commercial supply of boron compounds today. Some hot springs contain small amounts of boric acid, H_3BO_3, in solution.

26.13 Useful compounds of boron

Boron carbide, B_4C, known as *Norbide,* is an extremely hard abrasive. It is made by combining boron with carbon in an electric furnace. Boron nitride, BN, has a soft, slippery structure similar to graphite. Under very high pressure, it acquires a tetrahedral structure similar to diamond. This form of boron

United Aircraft Photo

Fig. 26-10. An alcohol flame has green edges when boric acid is present. This serves as a qualitative test for boric acid.

nitride, called *Borazon,* has a hardness second only to diamond. It is used industrially for cutting, grinding, and polishing. Alloys of boron with iron or manganese are used to increase the hardness of steel.

Boric acid can be prepared by adding sulfuric acid to a concentrated solution of sodium tetraborate in water. The acid is only moderately soluble and separates as colorless, lustrous scales. It is a mild antiseptic. *Boric acid colors an alcohol flame green.* See Figure 26-10.

Borax is sodium tetraborate with the formula $Na_2B_4O_7 \cdot 10H_2O$. It is used alone and in washing powders as a water softener. Because it dissolves metallic oxides, leaving a clean metallic surface, it is also used in welding metals. The borates of certain metals are used in making glazes and enamels. Large amounts of boron compounds are used to make borosilicate glass, of which Pyrex is an example.

Boron combines with hydrogen and forms several boron hydrides, such as B_2H_6, diborane, and B_4H_{10}, tetraborane. Methyl and ethyl groups can be substituted for the hydrogen atoms. These boron compounds have positive heats of formation. Thus, when they are oxidized, they release unusually large amounts of energy.

Fig. 26-11. The melting and boiling points of the boranes rise with increasing molecular weight (Left) Pentaborane, B_5H_9. (Right) Decaborane, $B_{10}H_{14}$.

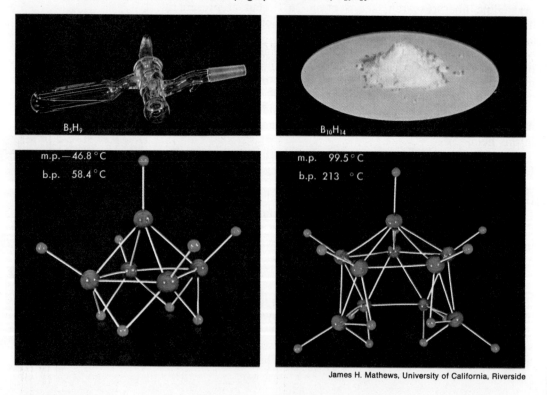

B_5H_9

m.p. —46.8 °C
b.p.   58.4 °C

$B_{10}H_{14}$

m.p.   99.5 °C
b.p. 213   °C

James H. Mathews, University of California, Riverside

26.14 Borax bead tests

Powdered borax held in a burner flame on a platinum wire loop swells and then fuses into a clear, glass-like bead. This bead can be used to identify certain metals. The bead is contaminated with a tiny speck of metal or metallic compound and heated again in the oxidizing flame. The metallic oxide formed fuses with the bead. Certain metals give characteristic transparent colors to the borax bead. Such colors serve to identify the metal involved. For example, cobalt colors the bead *blue;* chromium produces a *green* bead; and nickel yields a *brown* bead. Other metals that can be identified by means of the borax bead test are manganese, copper, and iron. The borax bead colors are shown in Figure 26-12.

SILICON

26.15 Silicon as a metalloid

Silicon atoms have four valence electrons. Silicon crystallizes with a tetrahedral bond arrangement similar to that of carbon atoms in diamond. Atoms of silicon also have small atomic radii and tightly held electrons. Thus, their ionization energy and electronegativity are fairly high. Silicon is a metalloid. It forms covalent bonds when combining with all other elements, except possibly the halogens. The electric conductivity of silicon is similar to that of boron; it, too, is a semiconductor. Unlike carbon, silicon forms only single bonds. It forms silicon-oxygen bonds more readily than silicon-silicon or silicon-hydrogen bonds. However, much of its chemistry is similar to that of carbon. Silicon has much the same role in mineral chemistry as carbon has in organic chemistry.

Boron and silicon atoms have roughly similar small radii. This similarity allows them to be substituted for one another in glass, even though boron is a member of Group III and silicon belongs to Group IV.

26.16 Silicon and its compounds

Silicon ranks second in abundance by weight among the elements of the earth's crust. Like boron, it does not occur free in nature. Silicon of high purity can be produced by reducing silicon dioxide, SiO_2, with magnesium.

The chief use for elemental silicon is in an alloy with iron, called *ferrosilicon,* for making silicon steel. Ferrosilicon can be prepared directly by reducing a mixture of silicon dioxide and iron oxide with carbon. Specially prepared silicon is used in making transistors and other semiconductor devices.

The compounds of silicon, such as silicon dioxide and many different silicates, are widely distributed in nature. The abun-

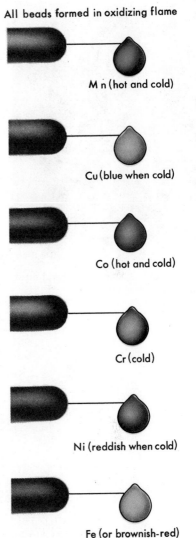

All beads formed in oxidizing flame

M n (hot and cold)

Cu (blue when cold)

Co (hot and cold)

Cr (cold)

Ni (reddish when cold)

Fe (or brownish-red)

Fig. 26-12. Borax bead tests for certain metals. Color is due to a minute trace of a certain metal.

B.M. Shaub

Fig. 26-13. Silicon, the second most abundant element.

dance of these compounds gives silicon its high rank among the elements of the earth's crust.

Silicon dioxide, SiO$_2$, is commonly called *silica.* It is one of the most widely distributed mineral compounds in the world. Four of its many forms are:

1. Sand. Ordinary sand or silicon dioxide is used in great quantities in glass-making. It is mixed with lime and water to make mortar, and with crushed stone and cement to make concrete.

2. Sandstone. This mineral is a sedimentary rock formed under water from particles of sand. These particles are bound together by a kind of natural cement. Sandstone is used mainly as a building stone.

3. Quartz. The transparent crystalline variety of silica is known as quartz. Quartz crystals are tetrahedral in structure. A central silicon atom is bonded to four oxygen atoms at the corners. Each oxygen atom serves as the corner of two such tetrahedra. Quartz is fairly hard because, in order to break it, strong silicon-oxygen bonds must be broken. Pure quartz is colorless, but impurities may give it different colors, yielding forms such as amethyst, smoky quartz, rose quartz, and milky quartz.

Quartz can be softened by an oxyhydrogen blowtorch and shaped into tubing, crucibles, and other laboratory equipment. It is also melted in a graphite crucible in an electric furnace and then extruded from the furnace under high pressure. This material is no longer crystalline, because the regular tetrahedral structure is disturbed by the heating. The random arrangement that results resembles that of a liquid. Fused quartz of this type is a super-cooled liquid or glass.

Quartz transmits ultraviolet rays much better than glass does. It is not as easily acted upon by acids and alkalies as ordinary glassware. If equal lengths of glass and quartz are heated to the same temperature, the quartz expands about one-eighteenth as much as glass. Thus, quartz is not likely to break when suddenly heated or cooled.

4. Amorphous silica. Such minerals as flint, jasper, chalcedony, sard, carnelian, onyx, and agate consist largely of silica. Onyx and agate are made up of bands of different colors. Fine specimens of crystallized and amorphous silica are used as semiprecious gems.

Silicon dioxide is insoluble in water and ordinary acids, but hydrofluoric acid reacts with it as follows:

$$SiO_2 + 2H_2F_2 \rightarrow SiF_4(g) + 2H_2O$$

The silicon tetrafluoride, SiF$_4$, formed by the reaction is a gas. Sodium carbonate reacts with silica at high temperatures and forms sodium silicate as follows:

$$Na_2CO_3 + SiO_2 \rightarrow Na_2SiO_3 + CO_2(g)$$

Silicon carbide, SiC, is made by heating sand and coke in an electric furnace. Salt is usually added to the mixture to make the mixture easier to melt. Sawdust is used to make it more porous. The main reaction is

$$SiO_2 + 3C \rightarrow SiC + 2CO(g)$$

On cooling, crystals of silicon carbide, called *Carborundum,* form around the central core of the furnace. The crystals are crushed, graded by size, and mixed with a binder that holds them together. They are then made into grinding wheels and sharpening stones. Silicon carbide has a structure like diamond with alternate carbon atoms replaced by silicon atoms. The rigid structure and strong covalent bonds give it great hardness.

26.17 Silicones

Silicon resembles carbon in the ability of its atoms to link together and form chains. A group of compounds called *silicones* has alternate silicon and oxygen atoms. Hydrocarbon groups are attached to the silicon atoms. Thus, the silicones are part organic and part inorganic. By using different hydrocarbon groups, a variety of silicones can be produced. One silicone chain has the structure

B.M. Shaub

Fig. 26-14. Crystals of silicon carbide.

The silicones are not much affected by heat. They have very good electric insulating properties, and are water repellents. Some silicones have the character of oils or greases and can be used as lubricants. Silicone varnishes are used to coat wires for the windings of electric motors. This insulation permits the electric motor to operate at high temperatures without short circuits. Water does not penetrate cloth treated with a silicone. Silicones are used in automobile and furniture polishes.

26.18 Manufacture of glass

Glass was made by the Egyptians many centuries before the Christian era. Glass is hard and very brittle when cold but softens when heated. It becomes so soft when very hot that it can be blown, rolled, or pressed into any shape. It is transparent and almost entirely insoluble in water.

Ordinary glass is made up of the silicates of sodium and calcium. In making the many different kinds of glass, potassium can be substituted for sodium. Barium, lead, aluminum, boron, and even zinc can be substituted for all or part of the calcium or silicon.

For making *ordinary glass,* the raw materials are sand, limestone, and sodium carbonate. A certain amount of broken glass is added to make the whole batch melt more rapidly. The mixture is heated in a long, tanklike furnace to a temperature of about 1400° C. The process is continuous. Raw materials are dumped in at one end, and liquid glass is withdrawn from the other end.

Some of the sand reacts with the limestone, forming calcium silicate and carbon dioxide.

$$CaCO_3 + SiO_2 \rightarrow CaSiO_3 + CO_2(g)$$

The remaining sand reacts with the sodium carbonate according to the following equation:

$$Na_2CO_3 + SiO_2 \rightarrow Na_2SiO_3 + CO_2(g)$$

Optical glass is made by heating sand, potassium carbonate, and lead oxide in pots made of a special clay. Such glass is made in small batches of a few hundred pounds each. Glass for cut glass tableware is also made in small batches from the same raw materials in a fire-clay pot.

Pyrex glass is made in a tank furnace by fusing sand, borax, and aluminum oxide. It is a sodium aluminum borosilicate glass that expands only one-third as much as ordinary glass. Ordinary glass can be softened in a Bunsen burner flame. Pyrex glass has a much higher softening temperature. It can be worked only in the flame of a blast lamp.

Research in glass-making processes has produced several new kinds of glass. These glasses have improved strength and flexibility and unusual properties. Among them are:

1. Glass-ceramic materials which have unusual thermal shock resistance and high mechanical strength. These are important today in making nose cones for rockets, and cooking utensils.

2. Chemically strengthened glass which is very flexible in sheet form. Flexible sheet glass is used in the rear windows of convertible tops for automobiles instead of the vinyl windows.

3. Glass fibers that have very high strength. Their use increases the structural strength of glass-fiber-reinforced plastics by 50%.

4. Photosensitive glass which produces an image when developed by heating.

5. Glass with special optical and radiation-absorbing properties that can be used for many special technical services.

After liquid glass has been formed into a finished article, it is cooled very slowly to prevent brittleness. The slow cooling process is called *annealing.* It is accomplished by passing the glass through a long, narrow chamber. The temperature in the

Fig. 26-15. A convertible rear window made of flexible glass.

Corning Glass Works

chamber is regulated carefully to keep it hot at one end and at room temperature at the other.

Many clear glasses can be colored by the presence of colloidally suspended metals or their oxides. The glass usually acquires the color desired with proper heat treatment. For example, the bright red glass used in danger signals and traffic lights usually contains a suspension of finely divided selenium as an impurity. The liquid glass is a pale yellow; when first cooled it is still only slightly colored. However, when the glass is reheated, the clear red color appears. If the selenium particles are too large, the color is maroon or even a muddy orange.

A small quantity of iron compounds as impurities in sand gives a pale-green color to finished glass. Manganese gives an amethyst or red color to glass. Small quantities of a manganese compound are sometimes added to a batch of glass to neutralize the pale-green color given by iron. Chromium in glass gives it a deep-green color. Cobalt produces a deep blue. Silver is used to make yellow glass. White or milky glass is made by adding calcium fluoride to the raw materials. The "old look" of glass describes a surface iridescence or rainbow effect. It is sometimes produced by spraying iron(II) or tin(IV) chloride on the surface of hot glass.

ARSENIC

26.19 The recovery of arsenic

Some arsenic is found free in nature. It is also found combined with sulfur. It is prepared from these sulfide ores by roasting them to form oxides. The oxides are then reduced with carbon, producing elemental arsenic. Arsenic is also present as an impurity in many metallic ores. It is recovered from the chimney stacks of the plants where these ores are processed. This is the largest source of arsenic in the United States.

26.20 Properties and uses of arsenic

Metallic arsenic is a brittle, gray solid. When freshly cut, it has a bright metallic luster which rapidly tarnishes in moist air. It exists in three allotropic forms. Chemically, it may act as a metal and form oxides and chlorides. It may also act as a nonmetal and form acids. When heated, arsenic sublimes and forms a yellow vapor, As_4, which has the odor of garlic. Metallic arsenic has few commercial uses except as a hardening agent in certain alloys. For example, a trace of arsenic in lead used for making lead shot hardens the shot.

When ignited, arsenic burns with a pale-blue flame and forms diarsenic trioxide, As_4O_6. (The name is taken from the empirical formula, even though the molecular formula is As_4O_6.) Arsenic unites indirectly with hydrogen, forming arsine, AsH_3. This com-

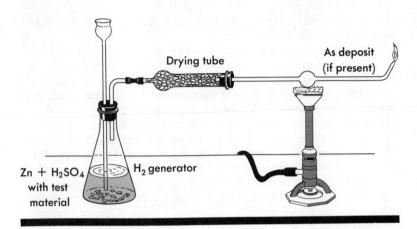

Fig. 26-16. The Marsh test for arsenic.

pound is chemically similar to ammonia. However, arsine is a deadly poisonous gas.

Diarsenic trioxide is used in producing other compounds of arsenic and in making some kinds of glass. Another use is as a preservative of animal skins that are to be mounted. Some medicines contain small quantities of arsenic compounds.

CAUTION: *While very small amounts of arsenic have limited value in medicine, larger quantities are extremely poisonous.*

Compounds of arsenic have long been known as poisons. A sensitive test for arsenic, called the *Marsh test,* depends on the formation and decomposition of arsine gas, AsH_3. Hydrogen gas is generated, dried, and ignited at the end of a glass delivery tube as pictured in Figure 26-16. The material to be tested for arsenic is placed in the hydrogen generator. If arsenic is present, AsH_3 is formed and escapes along with the hydrogen. Some point along the delivery tube is heated. At this point, arsine is decomposed and a mirrorlike deposit of arsenic forms. The reactions are

(generator)

$$HAsO_2 + 3Zn + 6H^+(aq) \rightarrow AsH_3(g) + 3Zn^{++} + 2H_2O$$

(tube)　　　　　　$$2AsH_3 \rightarrow 2As(s) + 3H_2(g)$$

ANTIMONY

26.21　Recovery of antimony

Some antimony is found free in nature. Its most important ore is *stibnite,* a sulfide of antimony, Sb_2S_3. Antimony is usually prepared from stibnite by reduction with iron. While China has been the chief source of antimony, deposits in Bolivia and Mexico are now being developed. Very little antimony is found in the United States. Most of what we need is imported.

26.22   Properties and uses of antimony

Antimony is a dense, brittle, silver-white metalloid with a bright metallic luster. It is less active than arsenic, and exists in several allotropic forms. When strongly heated in air, antimony forms a white oxide, Sb_4O_6. This compound is amphiprotic. It reacts with hydroxides and forms antimony(III) salts. Pure antimony is not affected by hydrochloric acid, but reacts readily in aqua regia, forming $SbCl_5$. Antimonates, which correspond to the phosphates and arsenates, are also known.

Type metal contains antimony, tin, and lead. The antimony is important because it causes the molten alloy to expand as it solidifies. Hence, the edges of the type cast from this alloy are sharp and distinct.

Clevite Corporation

An alloy of lead and antimony is used to reduce friction between the surfaces of moving parts in machinery. The friction of steel sliding over this "antifriction" alloy is much less than the friction of steel sliding over steel.

Another alloy of lead and antimony is used for the plates in storage batteries. This alloy is stronger and more resistant to acids than lead alone. Thus, battery plates made from the alloy last longer.

Only a few of the compounds of antimony are used widely. The sulfides are used in matches and as pigments. Red rubber contains diantimony trisulfide. Tartar emetic, potassium antimonyl tartrate, $KSbOC_4H_4O_6$, is used as a mordant in the dyeing of cotton goods.

Fig. 26-17. The bearings shown here are made of anti-friction alloy to help reduce friction produced when a shaft turns inside them.

CAUTION: *The soluble compounds of antimony are nearly as poisonous as the compounds of arsenic.*

QUESTIONS

Group A

1. In what materials does aluminum occur in nature?
2. What are the important physical properties of aluminum?
3. What is the chemical nature of corundum and emery?
4. Why must aluminum oxide be dissolved in molten cryolite before it can be decomposed by electricity?
5. Why are certain metallic oxides reduced with aluminum rather than with carbon?
6. Write the chemical formulas for four different alums.
7. What is the main source of boron compounds in the United States?
8. Why can borax be used to prepare metals for welding?
9. Name some of the varieties of amorphous silica.
10. (*a*) How does silicon rank in abundance among the elements? (*b*) What accounts for this rank?
11. (*a*) From what raw materials is silicon carbide made? (*b*) Write the equation for the reaction by which it is prepared.
12. Of what substances is ordinary glass composed?
13. What are the raw materials used in making ordinary glass?

14. (*a*) How does Pyrex glass differ in composition from ordinary glass? (*b*) How does it differ in properties?
15. Should the preparation of arsenic be classed as a product or a by-product of refining operations?
16. Why must extreme care be used in handling arsenic and its compounds?

Group B　　17. What reaction occurs when aluminum is placed in: (*a*) hydrochloric acid solution; (*b*) sodium hydroxide solution?
18. Write equations to show the net anode and cathode reactions during the electrolysis of aluminum oxide.
19. Write equations to show the amphiprotic nature of aluminum hydroxide.
20. Why do we import bauxite from the West Indies and South America when almost any clay bank in the United States contains aluminum?
21. What geographic conditions affect the location of plants for the production of aluminum from purified bauxite?
22. Describe the properties characteristic of metalloids such as boron and silicon in terms of (*a*) atomic radius; (*b*) ionization energy; (*c*) electronegativity; (*d*) type of bonds formed; (*e*) electric conductivity.
23. Explain how the test for boric acid is performed.
24. (*a*) What is the structure of a quartz crystal? (*b*) What characteristic of this structure gives quartz its hardness? (*c*) How does fused quartz differ in structure from quartz crystals?
25. (*a*) What is a silicone? (*b*) What are some of the important uses for silicones?
26. Compare the structures of silicon carbide and diamond.
27. Why is sand of very high purity desired by glass manufacturers?
28. How is glass of different colors obtained for use in "stained glass" windows in churches and public buildings?
29. Why is quartz not damaged by rapid temperature changes?
30. When a red crystalline compound was tested by means of a borax bead, the bead turned blue. What metal was probably present in the compound?
31. Borazon, a form of boron nitride, and diamond have similar crystal structures. Is there any relationship between this fact and the similarity of their hardness?
32. (*a*) In what form does boric acid usually exist in water solution: as molecules, or as hydronium and borate ions? (*b*) What experimental evidence supports your answer?
33. Why is silicon dioxide usually not classified as an acid anhydride?
34. Why would you expect silicones to be water repellent?

PROBLEMS

Group A　　1. How much aluminum and how much iron(III) oxide must be used in a thermite mixture to produce 10.0 kg of iron for a welding job?
2. What is the percentage of aluminum in sodium alum which crystallizes with 12 molecules of water of hydration?
3. How many liters of hydrogen can be prepared by the reaction of 50.0 g of aluminum and $10\overline{0}$ g of sodium hydroxide in solution?
4. Calculate the percentage of boron in colemanite, $Ca_2B_6O_{11} \cdot 5H_2O$.

5. What quantity of sodium silicate can be prepared from 1.000 kg of sodium carbonate by reacting it with an excess of silica?
6. How many liters of carbon dioxide are given off in Problem 5?
7. How many grams of $SbCl_3$ can be prepared by the reaction of 10.0 g of antimony with chlorine?

Group B

8. A compound contains 96.2% arsenic and 3.85% hydrogen. Its vapor is found to have a density of 3.48 g/liter. What is the molecular formula of the compound?
9. Boric acid, H_3BO_3, is produced when sulfuric acid is added to a water solution of borax, $Na_2B_4O_7$. How much boric acid can be prepared from 5.00 g of borax?
10. What quantity of silicon dioxide and what quantity of carbon are needed in order to prepare 1.00 metric ton of silicon carbide in an electric furnace?
11. Using the following data, show that the atomic weight of tellurium is higher than that of iodine.

Isotope	Atomic mass	Distribution
Te-122	121.903	.2.46%
Te-123	122.904	0.87%
Te-124	123.903	4.61%
Te-125	124.904	6.99%
Te-126	125.903	18.71%
Te-128	127.905	31.79%
Te-130	129.907	34.48%
I-127	126.904	100.00%

27

Nitrogen and Its Compounds

NITROGEN

27.1 Occurrence of nitrogen

About four-fifths by volume of the earth's atmosphere is elemental nitrogen. Combined nitrogen is also widely distributed. It is found in the proteins of both plants and animals. Natural deposits of potassium nitrate and sodium nitrate are used as raw materials for producing other nitrogen compounds.

27.2 Discovery of nitrogen

In 1772, Daniel Rutherford (1749–1819), a Scottish physician, published a study of the respiration products of small animals. The animals were confined in closed vessels. After removing the carbon dioxide from the air exhaled by the animals, Rutherford found that a colorless gas remained. This remaining gas would support neither life nor combustion. Rutherford's experiment marked the first separation of relatively pure nitrogen from the air.

27.3 Preparation of nitrogen

1. By fractional distillation of liquid air. Air condenses to a liquid if it is cooled enough. Small amounts of liquid air were first produced in France in 1877. Today it is made in large amounts as a first step in separating the various gases of the atmosphere. The physical principles involved in liquefying gases were discussed in Section 11.7.

Liquid air resembles water in appearance. Under ordinary atmospheric pressure, liquid air boils at a temperature of about −190° C. Its boiling temperature is not constant, because liquid air is mainly a mixture of liquid nitrogen and liquid oxygen. Liquid nitrogen boils at −195.8° C, while liquid oxygen boils at −183.0° C. The lower boiling point of the nitrogen causes it to separate in the first portions evaporated. Fractional distillation of liquid air is the commercial method for producing nitrogen, oxygen, and the noble gases (except helium.)

2.   *By decomposing ammonium nitrite.* Pure nitrogen can be prepared by gently heating ammonium nitrite, NH_4NO_2. However, ammonium nitrite is too unstable a compound to store safely.

The usual laboratory preparation of pure nitrogen involves gently heating a mixture of ammonium chloride and sodium nitrite solutions. The dissolved ammonium ions and nitrite ions form ammonium nitrite, which then decomposes and yields nitrogen.

$$NH_4Cl(aq) + NaNO_2(aq) \rightarrow NH_4NO_2(aq) + NaCl(aq)$$

$$NH_4NO_2(aq) \rightarrow N_2(g) + 2H_2O(l)$$

Or, writing only the net ionic equation for these reactions,

$$NH_4^+(aq) + NO_2^-(aq) \rightarrow N_2(g) + 2H_2O(l)$$

Fig. 27-1. A plant in which liquid air is produced. The towers at the left are fractional distillation towers in which the gases of the air are separated. The trucks with insulated tanks are used to transport liquefied gases.

Fig. 27-2. Pure nitrogen can be prepared by the decomposition of ammonium nitrite in solution. The flask must be heated gently to prevent too rapid decomposition.

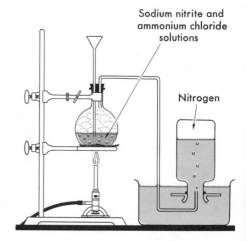

Sodium nitrite and ammonium chloride solutions

Nitrogen

27.4   Physical properties of nitrogen

Nitrogen is a colorless, odorless, and tasteless gas. It is slightly less dense than air, and is only slightly soluble in water. Its density shows that its molecules are diatomic, N_2. Nitrogen condenses to a colorless liquid at $-195.8°$ C and freezes to a white solid at $-209.9°$ C.

27.5   Chemical properties of nitrogen

Nitrogen atoms have the electron configuration $1s^2 2s^2 2p^3$. Nitrogen atoms share $2p$ electrons and form nonpolar diatomic molecules with a triple covalent bond.

$$\overset{..}{N} \!:\!:\!: N \!:$$

This triple covalent bond is very strong. Even at $3000°$ C, nitrogen molecules do not decompose measurably. The nitrogen molecule bond energy is very large, 227 kcal/mole. Hence elemental nitrogen is rather inactive. It combines with other elements only with difficulty. Many nitrogen compounds have positive heats of formation.

At a high temperature, nitrogen combines directly with such metals as magnesium, titanium, and aluminum. Nitrides are formed in these reactions.

Nitrogen does not burn in oxygen. However, when nitrogen and oxygen are passed through an electric arc, nitrogen monoxide, NO, is formed. Similarly, NO is formed when lightning passes through the air. Oxides of nitrogen are also formed in the high temperature and high pressure combustion in automobile engines. By use of a catalyst, nitrogen can be made to combine with hydrogen at a practical rate. Ammonia, NH_3, is formed in this reaction.

27.6   Uses of elemental nitrogen

An important use of pure nitrogen is in the commercial preparation of ammonia. It is also used in making calcium cyanamid, $CaCN_2$. Other uses of pure nitrogen are based upon its inactivity.

Substances burn rapidly in pure oxygen, but nitrogen does not support combustion. In the air, therefore, nitrogen serves as a diluting agent and lowers the rate of combustion. Its inactivity makes pure nitrogen useful in food processing and metallurgical operations. As a "blanket" atmosphere, it prevents unwanted oxidation in these processes. It is used similarly in the chemical, petroleum, and paint industries to prevent fires or explosions. Electric lamps are filled with a mixture of nitrogen and argon.

Liquid nitrogen is used for cooling foods to about $-100°$ C for preservation during storage and transportation.

27.7 Test for nitrogen

The best test for nitrogen depends on the fact that magnesium combines with it when heated. Magnesium nitride, Mg_3N_2, is formed. If water is added to magnesium nitride, the odor of ammonia can be detected.

$$Mg_3N_2 + 6H_2O \rightarrow 3Mg(OH)_2 + 2NH_3(g)$$

27.8 Nitrogen fixation

All living things contain nitrogen compounds. The nitrogen in these compounds is called *combined* or *fixed* nitrogen. *Any process that converts free nitrogen to nitrogen compounds is called **nitrogen fixation**.* Such processes are important because nitrogen compounds in the soil are necessary for plant growth. There are both *natural* and *artificial* nitrogen fixation methods.

1.   One natural method is to grow crops which restore nitrogen compounds to the soil. Most crops rapidly remove such compounds from the soil. On the other hand, certain plants called legumes actually restore large amounts of nitrogen compounds. These plants include beans and peas. They have small swellings or *nodules* on their roots. Organisms known as **nitrogen-fixing bacteria** grow in these nodules.

In alkaline soil, the nitrogen-fixing bacteria take free nitrogen from the air and convert it to nitrogen compounds. Chemists do not yet understand how this is done. If these plants are plowed under or if their roots are left to decay, the soil is enriched by nitrogen compounds.

2. Another *natural method* of nitrogen fixation occurs during electrical storms. Lightning supplies energy which enables some of the nitrogen and oxygen of the air to combine. An oxide of nitrogen is formed. After a series of changes, nitrogen compounds are washed down into the soil in rain.

3. The chief *artificial method* of nitrogen fixation involves making ammonia from a mixture of nitrogen and hydrogen. This ammonia is then oxidized to nitric acid. The nitric acid, in turn, is converted to nitrates suitable for fertilizer.

4. Another *artificial method* is the manufacture of calcium cyanamid, $CaCN_2$. In this process, nitrogen is passed over white-hot calcium carbide.

$$CaC_2 + N_2 \rightarrow CaCN_2 + C$$

The cyanamid is used directly as a nitrogen fertilizer or converted to ammonia by superheated steam.

$$CaCN_2 + 3H_2O \rightarrow CaCO_3 + 2NH_3(g)$$

The ammonia can then be converted to suitable nitrates.

Calcium cyanamid is also an important starting compound for preparing certain explosives and melamine resins.

Fig. 27-3. These black-eyed pea roots have nodules containing nitrogen-fixing bacteria.

U.S. Department of Agriculture, Soil Conservation Service

5. Scientists are developing ways of combining atmospheric nitrogen and oxygen in the radiations of nuclear reactors. Reactors have been designed exclusively for nitrogen fixation. Other designs combine nitrogen fixation with electric power production. This process may be very important in the near future. Because of the rapid growth of world population, much greater amounts of fixed nitrogen will be needed for fertilizers in food production.

AMMONIA AND AMMONIUM COMPOUNDS

27.9 Occurrence of ammonia

Very small traces of gaseous ammonia, NH_3, are found in the air. Some of this ammonia is produced by decomposition of the complex proteins in the bodies of dead plants and animals. An odor of ammonia always occurs around buildings where animals are housed. Bacteria break down the nitrogen compounds in manures and form ammonia.

27.10 Preparation of ammonia

1. *By decomposing ammonium compounds.* In the laboratory, ammonia is prepared by heating a mixture of a moderately strong hydroxide and an ammonium compound. Usually, calcium hydroxide and ammonium chloride are used.

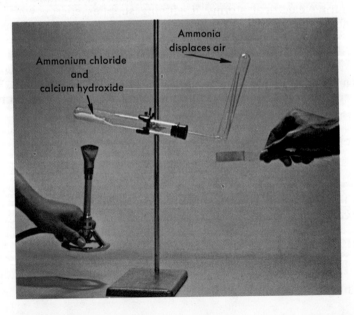

Fig. 27-4. When the mixture of ammonium chloride and calcium hydroxide in the test tube is heated, ammonia is evolved.

$$Ca(OH)_2(s) + 2NH_4Cl(s) \rightarrow CaCl_2(s) + 2NH_3(g) + 2H_2O(g)$$

The mixture is heated in a test tube fitted with an L-shaped delivery tube, as shown in Figure 27-4. Ammonia is so soluble in water that it cannot be collected by water displacement. Instead, it is collected by downward displacement of air in an inverted container. In what way would moist red litmus paper show when the test tube is full?

In this reaction, ammonium ions, NH_4^+, from the ammonium compound react with hydroxide ions, OH^-, from the strong hydroxide. The products are ammonia and water.

$$NH_4^+ + OH^- \rightarrow NH_3(g) + H_2O(g)$$

Since ammonia and steam are both gases, heating drives the reaction to the right.

2. *By destructive distillation of bituminous coal.* When bituminous coal is heated in a closed container without air, ammonia is one of the gaseous products. The ammonia is then converted to ammonium sulfate by reacting it with sulfuric acid.

$$2NH_3(g) + H_2SO_4(aq) \rightarrow (NH_4)_2SO_4(aq)$$

3. *By the Haber process.* Chemists long ago discovered that ammonia is formed when an electric spark passes through a mixture of nitrogen and hydrogen. But the reaction is reversible:

$$N_2(g) + 3H_2(g) \rightleftarrows 2NH_3(g) + 22 \text{ kcal}$$

Only a very small percentage of ammonia is produced at equilibrium. The problem of increasing that percentage was solved in 1913 by Fritz Haber (1868–1934), a German chemist.

The reaction between nitrogen and hydrogen is exothermic. Higher temperatures increase the rate at which the molecules of nitrogen and hydrogen react. But, *higher temperatures shift the equilibrium toward the left.* On the other hand, four volumes of reactants produce only two volumes of products. Thus, *increased pressure shifts the equilibrium toward the right.* Haber used a catalyst to increase the speed of reaction. He used a temperature of about 600° C and a pressure of about 200 atmospheres. These conditions resulted in a yield of about 8% ammonia.

Today, the yield from the Haber process has been raised to about 40% to 60%. This was done by using pressures as high as 1000 atmospheres, and an improved catalyst. This catalyst is a mixture of porous iron and the oxides of potassium and aluminum. It enables the reaction to proceed at a satisfactory rate at the lower temperature of 400°-550° C. The pressures and temperatures used in various Haber-process plants vary widely.

The ammonia is produced in special chrome-vanadium steel converters designed to withstand the tremendous pressure. It is

Fig. 27-5. A flow diagram of the Haber process. Ammonia gas produced in the catalyst chamber is condensed into a liquid in the cooler. The uncombined nitrogen and hydrogen are re-circulated through the catalyst chamber.

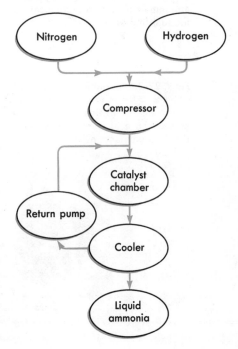

German Information Service

Fig. 27-6. Fritz Haber, a German chemist, determined the conditions under which the nitrogen-hydrogen-ammonia equilibrium could yield useful quantities of ammonia.

Fig. 27-7. Ammonia reacts with water and forms ammonium ion and hydroxide ion. In this reaction, water acts as an acid (proton donor) and the ammonia acts as a base (proton acceptor).

separated from the unreacted nitrogen and hydrogen by being dissolved in water, or by being cooled until it liquefies. The uncombined gases are returned to the converters and exposed again to the action of the catalyst.

27.11 Physical properties of ammonia

Ammonia is a colorless gas with a characteristic, strong odor. It is less dense than air and is easily liquified when cooled to the proper temperature. Liquid ammonia, which boils at $-33°$ C at atmospheric pressure, is sold in steel cylinders. The melting point of ammonia is $-78°$ C.

An important property of ammonia is its great solubility in water. One liter of water at $20°$ C dissolves about 700 liters of ammonia. At $0°$ C nearly 1200 volumes of ammonia can be dissolved in one volume of water.

The electron-dot formula for ammonia is

$$H\!:\!\overset{\overset{\circ\circ}{}}{\underset{\underset{H}{\cdot\cdot}}{N}}\!:\!H$$

The hydrogen atoms bond covalently to the nitrogen atom. In this bonding, the $1s$ hydrogen electrons occupy the half-filled $2p$ nitrogen orbitals. The hydrogen nuclei in ammonia molecules form an equilateral triangle 1.6 Å on a side. The nitrogen nucleus is 0.38 Å vertically above the midpoint of this triangle. This pyramid structure is evidence of sp^3 hybridization in the molecule. (See Figure 6.7.)

For a compound with such a simple molecular structure and low molecular weight, ammonia has a high boiling point and a very high melting point. In Chapter 11, we noted that water shows these properties to an even greater degree. The high melting and boiling points of both ammonia and water are explained as resulting from hydrogen bonds between their molecules in the solid and liquid phases. Ammonia molecules are polar because the three hydrogen atoms are not symmetrically bonded to the nitrogen atom. Hydrogen atoms from one ammonia molecule form hydrogen bonds to the nitrogen atom in adjacent ammonia

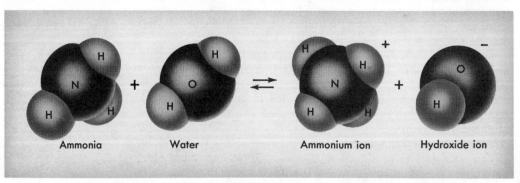

Ammonia   Water   Ammonium ion   Hydroxide ion

molecules. The polar nature of both water and ammonia molecules is also believed to cause the high solubility of ammonia in water.

Ammonia's high heat of vaporization is also evidence of its hydrogen bonding. Much energy is required to break the hydrogen bonds between molecules and to separate the molecules in the boiling of ammonia.

Liquid ammonia shows many of the solvent properties of water. Many salts dissolve and dissociate in liquid ammonia.

27.12 Chemical properties of ammonia

Gaseous ammonia does not support combustion or burn in air, but it burns in pure oxygen.

$$4NH_3 + 3O_2 \rightarrow 2N_2 + 6H_2O$$

At ordinary temperatures it is a stable compound. However, it decomposes into nitrogen and hydrogen at high temperatures. When ammonia is dissolved in water, most of the ammonia forms a simple solution. A small part of the ammonia, however, reacts with water and ionizes. The equation for this reaction is

$$NH_3 + H_2O \rightleftharpoons NH_4^+ + OH^- \qquad K_i = 1.8 \times 10^{-5}$$

This mixture of molecules and ions is commonly called *ammonium hydroxide;* a better name is *ammonia-water solution.* Ammonia-water solution is weakly basic.

Do not confuse *ammonium ions,* NH_4^+ with *ammonia molecules.* While ammonium ions may act like metallic ions in compounds, they cannot be isolated as NH_4^+. In all attempts to separate ammonium from ammonium compounds, the compounds decompose to ammonia and other products. The hydrogen atoms in ammonium ions are linked to the central nitrogen by s-sp^3 hybrid bonds. In this arrangement ammonium ions have a tetrahedral structure like methane.

The unshared pair of nitrogen electrons in NH_3 molecules enables them to bond to metallic ions. Thus, NH_3 appears in complex ions such as $Cu(NH_3)_4^{++}$ and $Ag(NH_3)_2^+$.

27.13 Uses of ammonia and ammonium compounds

1. As fertilizers. Ammonium compounds have long been used to supply nitrogen to the soil for growing plants. Recently, methods have been worked out for using ammonia directly as a fertilizer.

2. As a cleaning agent. Ammonia-water solution makes a good cleaning agent. It is weakly basic, emulsifies grease, and leaves no residue to be wiped up.

3. As a refrigerant. Ammonia is used as a refrigerant in frozen food production and storage plants. A compressor is

(Top) Inter Agriculture: Arthur Paulsmeyer (Bottom) Weil

Fig. 27-8. (Top) This farmer is applying liquid ammonia directly to the soil as a fertilizer. (Bottom) Using household ammonia to clean windows.

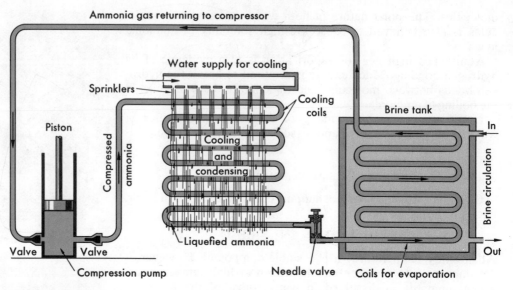

Fig. 27-9. The absorption of the heat needed to evaporate the liquid ammonia and expand the resulting gas lowers the temperature of the brine pumped through pipes to freezing and storage rooms.

used to liquefy ammonia gas, as shown in Figure 27-9. The heat released during the compression is absorbed by water which flows down over the cooling and condensing coils. At this high pressure and lowered temperature, the ammonia liquefies. The cold, liquid ammonia then flows through a valve into coils of pipe submerged in a tank of brine. Low pressure is maintained in the pipe coil. As the liquid ammonia passes the valve, it evaporates and the resulting gas expands. Heat energy is absorbed by this expansion, cooling the brine to about −20° C. Then the cold brine is pumped through pipes to the freezing and storage rooms.

4. *For making other componds.* Great quantities of ammonia are oxidized to make nitric acid, as explained in Section 27-15. It is also used in producing nylon and one type of rayon, and as a catalyst in making several types of plastic. Ammonia is used to make sulfa drugs, vitamins, and drugs for treating the tropical disease malaria. It is also used as a neutralizing agent in the petroleum industry. In the rubber industry, it prevents the rubber in latex from separating out during shipment.

27.14 Hydrazine: another compound
of nitrogen and hydrogen

Hydrazine, N_2H_4, is produced by oxidizing ammonia-water solution with sodium hypochlorite. It burns readily, and is used as a fuel for rockets. It also serves as a strong reducing agent.

NITRIC ACID

27.15 Preparation of nitric acid

Two methods are commonly used to prepare this important acid.

1. From nitrates. Small amounts of nitric acid are prepared in the laboratory by heating a nitrate with sulfuric acid. The reaction is carried out in a glass-stoppered retort because nitric acid oxidizes rubber stoppers or rubber connectors.

$$NaNO_3(s) + H_2SO_4(aq) \rightarrow NaHSO_4(aq) + HNO_3(g)$$

The ionic equation:

$$NO_3^- + H^+(aq) \rightarrow HNO_3(g)$$

The nitric acid vapor is condensed in the side arm of the retort and collected in the receiver.

2. From ammonia. Wilhelm Ostwald (1853–1933), a German chemist, discovered how to oxidize ammonia to nitric acid with a catalyst. Ostwald made his discovery at about the same time that Haber developed the process for the synthesis of ammonia. These two processes fit together perfectly. Ammonia is made by synthesis from nitrogen and hydrogen. The ammonia is then oxidized to nitric acid in another part of the same plant. Some of the nitric acid may be neutralized with more ammonia, producing ammonium nitrate. This compound is a useful fertilizer as well as an ingredient in explosives.

The Bettmann Archive, Inc.

Fig. 27-10. Wilhelm Ostwald, a German chemist, developed the ammonia oxidation process for preparing nitric acid.

Fig. 27-11. Nitric acid may be prepared in the laboratory by the action of sulfuric acid on sodium nitrate.

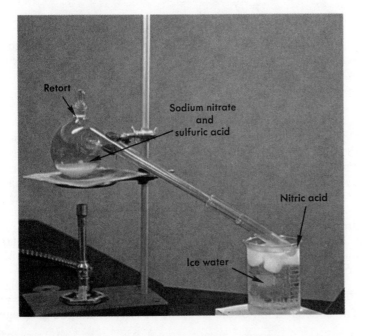

Retort

Sodium nitrate and sulfuric acid

Nitric acid

Ice water

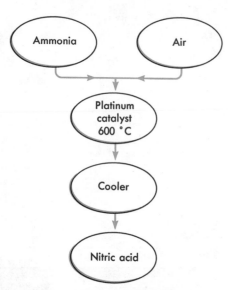

Fig. 27-12. Flow diagram of the Ostwald process for the oxidation of ammonia into nitric acid.

Fig. 27-13. The reactions of concentrated nitric acid with copper and zinc. What is the reddish-brown gas? What salt is in solution in each beaker?

From the CHEM STUDY Film: *Nitric Acid*

In the Ostwald process, a mixture of ammonia and air is heated to a temperature of 600° C. It is then passed through a tube containing platinum gauze, which serves as the catalyst. On the surface of the platinum, the ammonia is oxidized to nitrogen monoxide, NO.

$$4NH_3 + 5O_2 \rightarrow 4NO + 6H_2O$$

This reaction is exothermic and raises the temperature of the mixture of gases to about 1000° C. Then more air is mixed with nitrogen monoxide to oxidize it to nitrogen dioxide, NO_2.

$$2NO + O_2 \rightarrow 2NO_2$$

The nitrogen dioxide is cooled and absorbed in water, forming nitric acid.

$$3NO_2(g) + H_2O(l) \rightarrow 2HNO_3(aq) + NO(g)$$

The nitrogen monoxide produced is recycled to oxidize it to nitrogen dioxide and absorb it in water.

Today almost all of the nitric acid used in industry is made by the oxidation of ammonia.

27.16   Physical properties of nitric acid

Pure HNO_3 is a colorless liquid, about 1.5 times as dense as water. It fumes in moist air and boils at 86° C. Pure HNO_3 is unstable. For this reason, commercial concentrated nitric acid is a 68% solution of HNO_3 in water. The solution boils at 120° C.

27.17   Chemical properties of nitric acid.

1.   Stability. Nitric acid is not very stable. When boiled, or even when exposed to sunlight, it decomposes to some extent. Water, nitrogen dioxide, and oxygen are the decomposition products.

$$4HNO_3 \rightarrow 4NO_2 + 2H_2O + O_2$$

Concentrated nitric acid stored in laboratory bottles exposed to light gradually turns a deep yellow. This color change is caused by small amounts of dissolved nitrogen dioxide formed by decomposition. In dilute water solution, HNO_3 is more stable.

2.   Acid properties. Dilute nitric acid has the usual properties of acids. It reacts with metals, metallic oxides, and metallic hydroxides, forming salts known as *nitrates.*

Nitric acid stains the skin yellow, forming xanthoproteic (zan-thoh-proh-*tee*-ik) acid. It produces the same effect with many proteins, and for that reason is used as a *test* for proteins.

3.   As an oxidizing agent. Nitric acid is a powerful oxidizing agent. It may react as an oxidizing agent in a variety of ways. The concentration of the acid, the activity of the reducing agent mixed with it, and the reaction temperature determine what products are formed. Under ordinary conditions, moderately dilute nitric acid is reduced to nitrogen monoxide. If concentrated nitric acid is reduced, nitrogen dioxide is the product. Other reducing agents and different reaction conditions may produce N_2O, N_2, or NH_3. Dinitrogen monoxide, N_2O, is usually called nitrous oxide.

4. *Action with metals.* Nitric acid is such a vigorous oxidizing agent that hydrogen gas is *not* produced in significant amounts when the acid is added to common metals. *Very dilute nitric acid* reacts with such active metals as sodium, calcium, or magnesium. The reaction forms a nitrate and produces hydrogen.

$$Mg(s) + 2HNO_3(aq) \rightarrow Mg(NO_3)_2(aq) + H_2(g)$$

In reactions with less active metals such as zinc and copper, the hydrogen appears in the water product. In these reactions, the nitrogen of the nitric acid is reduced. Copper reacts with cold, dilute nitric acid as shown by this equation:

$$3Cu(s) + 8HNO_3(aq) \rightarrow 3Cu(NO_3)_2(aq) + 2NO(g) + 4H_2O(l)$$

The ionic equation:

$$3Cu(s) + 8H^+(aq) + 2NO_3^-(aq) \rightarrow 3Cu^{++}(aq) + 2NO(g) + 4H_2O(l)$$

With concentrated nitric acid, copper reacts as follows:

$$Cu(s) + 4HNO_3(aq) \rightarrow Cu(NO_3)_2(aq) + 2NO_2(g) + 2H_2O(l)$$

Ionic:

$$Cu(s) + 4H^+(aq) + 2NO_3^-(aq) \rightarrow Cu^{++}(aq) + 2NO_2(g) + 2H_2O(l)$$

Nitric acid does not react with gold or platinum because of the stability of these metals. Very concentrated nitric acid reacts with aluminum and iron very slowly. The reactions probably are slowed by the formation of semi-protective surface coatings.

When nitric acid reacts with a metal, the nitrate of that metal is usually formed. The nitrates of the various metals are crystalline compounds which are readily soluble in water.

Fig. 27-14. The brown layer formed when sulfuric acid is added slowly to a solution of iron (II) sulfate containing nitrate ions serves as a test for the nitrate ion.

27.18 Test for a nitrate

To several milliliters of the solution to be tested in a test tube, an equal volume of a solution of iron(II) sulfate, $FeSO_4$, is added. The test tube is tilted and a few milliliters of concentrated sulfuric acid is added slowly. The sulfuric acid is added in such a way that it runs down the tilted wall of the test tube very gradually. It settles to the bottom, not mixing with the other mixture in the tube. If the solution tested does contain a nitrate, a *brown layer* containing nitrosyl iron(II) sulfate, $Fe(NO)SO_4$, forms where the acid and the other mixture meets. (See Figure 27-14.)

27.19 Uses of nitric acid

1. For making fertilizers. About 75% of the nitric acid produced in the United States is used in the manufacture of fertilizers. Ammonium nitrate is the most important nitrate so used. It is manufactured in plants using the combined Haber-Ostwald processes. Sodium nitrate and potassium nitrate are also used as fertilizer ingredients.

2. For making explosives. Many explosives are made directly or indirectly from nitric acid. The acid itself is not an explosive. However, some of its compounds form the most violent explosives known. Among these are nitroglycerin, smokeless powders, and TNT (trinitrotoluene).

3. For making dyes. Nitric acid reacts with several products obtained from coal tar, forming *nitro compounds.* One of these coal tar products is benzene. Benzene reacts with nitric acid and forms nitrobenzene, $C_6H_5NO_2$. (See Section 17.19.) Aniline, $C_6H_5NH_2$, is used in making many different dyes. It is made by reducing nitrobenzene with hydrogen.

4. For making plastics. Cotton consists mainly of cellulose, $(C_6H_{10}O_5)_n$. When treated with a mixture of nitric acid and sulfuric acid, cellulose forms nitrocellulose plastics. A variety of products can be produced. The product depends on the amount of nitric acid used, the temperature, and how long the acid is allowed to act on the cellulose. Manufacturers use sulfuric acid to absorb the water formed in the reaction. Celluloid, pyroxylins, and many other products are made from nitrocellulose plastics.

E.I. DuPont de Nemours, & Co.

Fig. 27-15. Setting off 1,250,000 kilograms of explosive sends rock and water 365 meters into the air. This explosion cleared a channel in Seymour Narrows on the inland waterway to Alaska about 200 kilometers northwest of Vancouver, Canada.

QUESTIONS

Group A

1. (*a*) Where are large quantities of elemental nitrogen found? (*b*) In what kinds of compounds does combined nitrogen occur naturally?
2. (*a*) Who first isolated relatively pure nitrogen? (*b*) How was this done?
3. (*a*) Which has the higher boiling point, liquid nitrogen or liquid oxygen? (*b*) What practical use is made of this difference in boiling points?
4. (*a*) Write the balanced formula equation for the production of nitrogen from ammonium chloride and sodium nitrite. (*b*) Of what type of reaction is this an example?
5. How can you test a bottle of colorless gas to determine whether or not it is nitrogen?

6. What is meant by *nitrogen fixation?*
7. (*a*) What are two natural methods of nitrogen fixation? (*b*) Name two artificial methods.
8. (*a*) What is the purpose of high pressure in the Haber process? (*b*) What is the function of the catalyst?
9. (*a*) Describe the shape of NH_3 molecules. (*b*) What type of bonding occurs in these molecules?
10. Why is *ammonia-water solution* a better name for the solution of ammonia in water than *ammonium hydroxide?*
11. Give two reasons why ammonia-water solution makes an excellent window cleaner.
12. Why is a completely glass apparatus used for the laboratory preparation of nitric acid?
13. What condition must be met for the reaction between sodium nitrate and sulfuric acid to run to completion?
14. Write three equations to show the steps in the production of nitric acid from ammonia.
15. Why does concentrated nitric acid turn yellow in the laboratory?

16. (*a*) Why does compressing a gas raise its temperature? (*b*) Why does a gas become colder when it is allowed to expand?

Group B

17. What structural feature of nitrogen molecules accounts for the stability of this element?
18. (*a*) Name three uses for nitrogen. (*b*) For each use, give the related physical or chemical property of nitrogen which makes the use possible.
19. What must be the condition of the soil for nitrogen-fixing bacteria to be most effective?
20. Why might a farmer alternate crops of corn and lima beans on one of his fields in successive years?
21. (*a*) Write the balanced equation for the reaction between calcium hydroxide and ammonium nitrate for producing ammonia. (*b*) Write the net ionic equation for this reaction. (*c*) How does the net ionic equation for this reaction compare with the net ionic equation for the reaction between calcium hydroxide and ammonium chloride? between sodium hydroxide and ammonium sulfate?
22. Why is the boiling point of ammonia, $-33°$ C, so much higher than the boiling point of methane, $-161°$ C, when molecules of both have nearly the same molecular weight?
23. Why is ammonia so soluble in water, while methane is nearly insoluble in water?
24. What solvent and complexing properties does ammonia have?
25. Why can zinc be used with either hydrochloric or sulfuric acids for producing hydrogen, but not with nitric acid?
26. The equation for the reaction of copper and dilute nitric acid indicates that colorless nitrogen monoxide gas is one of the products. Yet when we carry out this reaction in an evaporating dish, dense reddish-brown nitrogen dioxide gas flows over the rim of the dish. Explain.
27. What is the oxidation number of nitrogen in (*a*) NH_3, (*b*) N_2H_4, (*c*) N_2, (*d*) HNO_2, (*e*) HNO_3?
28. You are given a colorless solution of a salt. Tell how you would test it to determine whether or not the salt is a nitrate.

PROBLEMS

Group A

1. How many grams of ammonia can be produced by the reaction of steam with $16\overline{0}$ g of calcium cyanamid?

2. How many liters of nitrogen and hydrogen are required for the preparation of $20\overline{0}$ liters of ammonia?

3. If 15 g of HNO_3 is needed for a laboratory experiment, what mass of sodium nitrate is required for its preparation?

Group B

4. What volume, in liters, of nitrogen at STP can be prepared from a mixture of $1\overline{0}$ g of NH_4Cl and $1\overline{0}$ g of $NaNO_2$?

5. How many grams of nitric acid can be prepared from 50.0 g of potassium nitrate of 80.0% purity?

6. (*a*) What mass of copper(II) nitrate may be prepared from 254 g of copper by reaction with nitric acid? (*b*) How many liters of nitrogen monoxide at STP are also produced?

Chapter 28

Sulfur and Its Compounds

SULFUR

28.1 Occurrence of sulfur

Sulfur is one of the elements known since ancient times. It occurs in nature as the free element or combined with other elements in sulfides and sulfates.

The United States is the greatest producer of sulfur. Huge deposits of nearly pure sulfur occur between 500 and 2000 feet underground in Texas and Louisiana, near the Gulf of Mexico. These deposits are now the world's largest source of sulfur.

Sulfur is also obtained from deposits in Sicily and from South America and Asia.

28.2 The production of sulfur

The sulfur beds in Texas and Louisiana are as much as 200 feet thick. Between the surface of the ground and the sulfur there is usually a layer of quicksand. This makes it difficult to sink a shaft and mine the sulfur by ordinary methods.

The American chemist, Herman Frasch (1852–1914), developed a method for obtaining the sulfur without sinking a shaft. This method uses a complex system of pipes. Superheated water (170° C, under pressure) is pumped into the sulfur deposit. The hot water melts the sulfur, which is then forced to the surface by compressed air. See Figure 28-1. The melted sulfur may be shipped as a liquid in tank cars or ocean-going tankers. Or, it

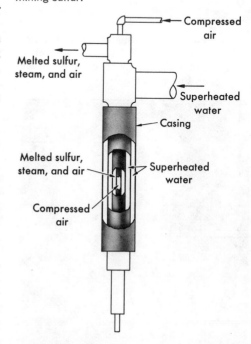

Fig. 28-1. The system of concentric pipes used in the Frasch process of mining sulfur.

Compressed air

Melted sulfur, steam, and air

Superheated water

Casing

Melted sulfur, steam, and air

Superheated water

Compressed air

Fig. 28-2. Melted sulfur being spread on a storage vat.

Fig. 28-3. Elemental sulfur is a yellow nonmetallic solid. What other physical property of sulfur is shown by this photograph?

may be allowed to solidify in large wooden molds and then be broken into pieces for shipment. See Figure 28-2.

Elemental sulfur is also obtained by chemical processes from pyrite (FeS_2), coke oven gas, smelter gases, petroleum, and natural gas.

28.3 Physical properties of sulfur

Common sulfur is a yellow, *odorless* solid. It is practically insoluble in water and is twice as dense as water. It dissolves readily in carbon disulfide and less readily in carbon tetrachloride.

Sulfur melts at a temperature of 114.5° C, forming a pale-yellow easily flowing liquid. When heated to a higher temperature, instead of flowing more easily as liquids usually do, it becomes thicker (more *viscous*). At a temperature above about 160° C, melted sulfur becomes so thick that it hardly flows at all. As the temperature rises, the color changes from a light yellow to a reddish-brown, and then almost to black. Near the boiling point the liquid again flows freely. Sulfur boils at 445° C. This unusual behavior is caused by the properties of different allotropic forms of liquid sulfur. These different forms exist at different temperatures.

28.4 Allotropic forms of sulfur

Sulfur exists in several different solid and liquid allotropic forms. These forms are produced by different arrangements of groups of sulfur atoms.

1. Rhombic sulfur. This form of solid sulfur is stable at ordinary temperatures. It consists of eight-membered puckered rings of sulfur atoms connected in these rings by single covalent bonds. See Figure 28-4. Crystals of rhombic sulfur are prepared by dissolving sulfur in carbon disulfide and then allowing the solvent to evaporate slowly. The density of rhombic sulfur is 2.07 g/cm³.

2. Monoclinic sulfur. Sulfur can also be crystallized in the form of long needle-like monoclinic crystals. This allotropic form is prepared by first melting some sulfur in a crucible at as low a temperature as possible. It is next allowed to cool slowly until a crust begins to form. The crust is broken and the liquid sulfur remaining is poured off. A mass of monoclinic crystals is then found lining the walls of the crucible. Heat energy must be added to produce this type of sulfur. When such crystals cool below 95° C they gradually change back into the rhombic form. The arrangement of sulfur atoms in monoclinic sulfur is eight-membered rings in a monoclinic crystal pattern. The density of monoclinic sulfur is 1.96 g/cm³.

3. λ-sulfur. (*Lambda-sulfur.*) This is the liquid allotropic form of sulfur produced at temperatures just above the melting point of sulfur. It flows easily and has a straw-yellow color. It is believed to consist of eight-membered rings of sulfur atoms. The rounded shape of these S_8 molecules enables them to roll over one another easily, giving this form of sulfur its fluidity.

4. *μ-sulfur*. (*Mu-sulfur*.) If λ-sulfur is heated to about 160° C, it darkens to a reddish and then almost black liquid. The melted sulfur becomes so viscous that it does not flow. It is thought that the heating gives enough energy to the sulfur atoms to break some of the eight-membered rings. When a ring of sulfur atoms breaks open, the sulfur atoms on either side of the break are each left with an unshared electron. These sulfur atoms form bonds with similar sulfur atoms from other open rings. In this way, long chains of sulfur atoms are formed. These chains are another allotropic form of sulfur, μ-sulfur. The dark color of μ-sulfur arises from the greater absorption of light by electrons from the broken ring structure. In μ-sulfur these electrons are free to migrate along the chain structure.

The high viscosity of μ-sulfur is caused by tangling of the chains of sulfur atoms. As the temperature is raised, however, these chains break up into smaller groups of atoms. The mass then flows more easily. The color becomes still darker because breaking the chains produces more free electrons.

Sulfur vapor, produced when sulfur boils at 445° C, also consists of S_8 molecules. If sulfur vapor is heated to a higher temperature, these molecules gradually dissociate into S_6 and then into S_2 molecules. Monatomic molecules of sulfur are produced at very high temperatures.

5. *Amorphous sulfur*. Amorphous sulfur is a rubbery, plastic mass made by pouring boiling sulfur into cold water. It is dark-brown or even black in color, and is elastic, like rubber. At the boiling point of sulfur, the long tangled chains of μ-sulfur have largely broken down, and the sulfur is fluid again. Eight-membered rings of sulfur atoms and chains are in equilibrium. The S_8 rings are evaporating. When this boiling mixture is suddenly cooled, the chains of μ-sulfur have no time to re-form into rings. Instead, amorphous sulfur is produced. A mass of amorphous sulfur soon loses its elasticity and becomes hard and brittle. In room-temperature amorphous sulfur, the changes into successive allotropic forms occur in reverse order. Finally, it

Fig. 28-4. The structure of S_8 molecules of sulfur.

Fig. 28-5. A chain of sulfur atoms as found in μ sulfur (mu-sulfur).

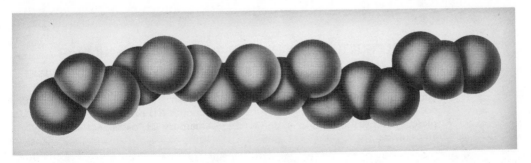

Fig. 28-6. The sudden cooling of mu-sulfur produces amorphous sulfur.

once again becomes the S_8 ring configuration of stable rhombic sulfur. Amorphous sulfur is insoluble in carbon disulfide.

28.5 Chemical properties of sulfur

At room temperature, sulfur is not very active chemically. When heated, it combines with oxygen and produces sulfur dioxide.

$$S_8(s) + 8O_2(g) \rightarrow 8SO_2(g)$$

This equation is written using the molecular formula for sulfur, S_8. Usually, however, sulfur is represented by the symbol S. The less complicated but stoichiometrically correct equation is

$$S(s) + O_2(g) \rightarrow SO_2(g)$$

Traces of sulfur trioxide, SO_3, also form when sulfur burns in the air. Sulfur can be made to combine with non-metals, such as hydrogen, carbon, and chlorine. However, such compounds are formed with difficulty and are not very stable. The differences in electronegativity between sulfur and hydrogen, carbon, and chlorine are small. Thus, the bonding in such compounds is mostly covalent.

The formulas SO_3, SO_2, and H_2S indicate that sulfur can have oxidation numbers of $+6$ or $+4$ when combined with oxygen, and of -2 when combined with hydrogen. Electron-dot formulas for these compounds are shown below.

Sulfur trioxide   **Sulfur dioxide**   **Hydrogen sulfide**

The actual molecules of sulfur trioxide and sulfur dioxide are resonance hybrids of the possible structures given. Sulfur resembles oxygen in the ways in which it combines with other elements. This similarity can be seen from Table 28-1.

Table 28–1
SIMILARITIES OF SULFIDE AND OXIDE FORMULAS

hydrogen sulfide	H_2S	hydrogen oxide	H_2O
carbon disulfide	CS_2	carbon dioxide	CO_2
copper (I) sulfide	Cu_2S	copper (I) oxide	Cu_2O
copper (II) sulfide	CuS	copper (II) oxide	CuO
mercury (II) sulfide	HgS	mercury (II) oxide	HgO
zinc sulfide	ZnS	zinc oxide	ZnO

Sulfur combines directly with all metals except gold and platinum. Powdered zinc and sulfur combine vigorously. The heat produced when iron filings and sulfur unite causes the whole mass to glow red hot. Copper unites with the vapor of boiling sulfur and forms copper(I) sulfide. If the oxide of any metal is insoluble in water, the sulfide of that metal is usually insoluble in water also.

28.6 Uses of sulfur

Sulfur is used in making sulfur dioxide, carbon disulfide, sulfuric acid, and other sulfur compounds. Several million tons are used annually to make sulfuric acid. Matches, fireworks, and black gunpowder all contain either sulfur or sulfur compounds. Sulfur is also used in the preparation of certain dyes, medicines, and fungicides. It is also used in the vulcanization of rubber. (See Section 17.26.)

HYDROGEN SULFIDE

28.7 Hydrogen sulfide formed by natural processes

When sulfur-containing proteins decay, hydrogen sulfide is one of the products formed. The odor of decayed eggs is caused by the formation of hydrogen sulfide. Coal is seldom entirely free of sulfur. When coal burns, sulfur dioxide and some traces of hydrogen sulfide pass off into the air. Some mineral waters also contain hydrogen sulfide.

28.8 Preparation of hydrogen sulfide

A metallic sulfide and either hydrochloric or sulfuric acid can be used to prepare hydrogen sulfide. Iron(II) sulfide, FeS, is suitable for the purpose. Exchange reactions occur when these acids are used.

$$FeS(s) + 2HCl(aq) \rightarrow FeCl_2(aq) + H_2S(g)$$
$$FeS(s) + H_2SO_4(aq) \rightarrow FeSO_4(aq) + H_2S(g)$$

Ionically for either reaction,

$$FeS(s) + 2H^+(aq) \rightarrow Fe^{++}(aq) + H_2S(g)$$

Hydrogen sulfide is a gas, and the exchange reactions go to completion. The gas is denser than air and moderately soluble in water. Thus, it is usually collected by upward displacement of air.

28.9 Physical properties of hydrogen sulfide

The gas is colorless and has the very disagreeable odor of decayed eggs. *Hydrogen sulfide is poisonous.* In concentrated form, it is a violent poison which may cause death if inhaled. When diluted with air, it causes nausea, headache, and dizziness.

28.10 Chemical properties of hydrogen sulfide

1. Hydrogen sulfide burns. The products formed depend on the relative amounts of hydrogen sulfide and oxygen present. If more than enough oxygen is available, 2 volumes of hydrogen sulfide react with 3 volumes of oxygen. Sulfur dioxide and water vapor are the products.

$$2H_2S(g) + 3O_2(g) \rightarrow 2SO_2(g) + 2H_2O(g)$$

When hydrogen sulfide reacts with an equal volume of oxygen, some of the sulfur does not oxidize to sulfur dioxide. A possible equation is

$$2H_2S(g) + 2O_2(g) \rightarrow 2H_2O(g) + SO_2(g) + S(s)$$

2. Hydrogen sulfide is a good reducing agent. Reducing agents give up electrons to oxidizing agents. The sulfide ions in hydrogen sulfide do this readily. Its properties as a reducing agent are shown by bubbling hydrogen sulfide through a solution of hydrogen peroxide. The oxygen in hydrogen peroxide is reduced from peroxide to oxide. Meanwhile, the sulfide ions are oxidized to sulfur in the form of a white colloidal suspension in the water.

$$\overset{-1}{H_2O_2}(aq) + \overset{-2}{H_2S}(g) \rightarrow 2\overset{-2}{H_2O}(l) + \overset{0}{S}(s)$$

Note the oxidation-number changes of the sulfur and the oxygen.

3. Hydrogen sulfide forms a weak acid. Dissolved in water, hydrogen sulfide forms a weak diprotic acid called hydrosulfuric acid.

$$H_2S + H_2O \rightleftarrows H_3O^+ + HS^-$$
$$HS^- + H_2O \rightleftarrows H_3O^+ + S^{--}$$

This weak acid turns blue litmus red. It reacts with hydroxides, forming sulfides and water.

$$Cu(OH)_2(s) + H_2S(g) \rightarrow CuS(s) + 2H_2O(l)$$

For the two stages of ionization of hydrogen sulfide solution, the ionization constants are

$$K_{ion\,1} = \frac{[H_3O^+][HS^-]}{[H_2S]} = 5.7 \times 10^{-8}$$

$$K_{ion\,2} = \frac{[H_3O^+][S^{--}]}{[HS^-]} = 1.2 \times 10^{-15}$$

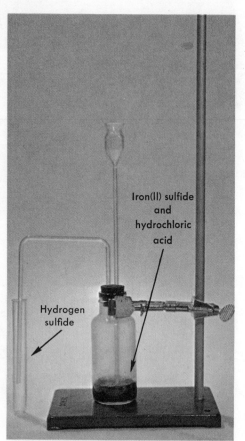

Fig. 28-7. The laboratory method of preparing hydrogen sulfide. This preparation should be performed in a hood because hydrogen sulfide has a foul odor and is poisonous.

Iron(II) sulfide and hydrochloric acid

Hydrogen sulfide

The following calculations show the relationship between $[S^{--}]$ and $[H_3O^+]$ in such solutions:

$$K = K_{\text{ion 1}} \times K_{\text{ion 2}}$$

$$K = \frac{[H_3O^+][HS^-][H_3O^+][S^{--}]}{[H_2S][HS^-]}$$

$$K = 5.7 \times 10^{-8} \times 1.2 \times 10^{-15}$$

$$K = 6.8 \times 10^{-23}$$

or

$$K = \frac{[H_3O^+]^2[S^{--}]}{[H_2S]} = 6.8 \times 10^{-23}$$

Saturated solutions of H_2S in water are approximately 0.1 M H_2S solutions. Hence, we can substitute $[H_2S] = 10^{-1}$,

$$\frac{[H_3O^+]^2[S^{--}]}{10^{-1}} = 6.8 \times 10^{-23}$$

and then

$$[S^{--}] = \frac{6.8 \times 10^{-24}}{[H_3O^+]^2}$$

Thus, the sulfide ion concentration in saturated hydrogen sulfide solutions varies inversely as the *square* of the hydronium ion concentration. Table 28-2 gives sulfide ion concentrations in mole/liter for various hydronium ion concentrations, also in mole/liter. Thus, it is possible to vary the sulfide ion concentration in solutions of H_2S by adjusting the pH, and thus the hydronium ion concentration, to an appropriate value.

4. *Hydrogen sulfide acts on metals.* Some metals tarnish when a coating of a sulfide of the metal is formed. Such foods as eggs and mustard form enough hydrogen sulfide to tarnish silver tableware with black silver sulfide.

Table 28-2

SULFIDE ION CONCENTRATIONS
IN SATURATED HYDROGEN
SULFIDE SOLUTIONS

$[H_3O^+]$	pH	$[S^{--}]$
10^{-1}	1	6.8×10^{-22}
10^{-3}	3	6.8×10^{-18}
10^{-5}	5	6.8×10^{-14}
10^{-7}	7	6.8×10^{-10}
10^{-9}	9	6.8×10^{-6}
10^{-11}	11	6.8×10^{-2}

28.11 Tests for the presence of a sulfide

Any soluble sulfide supplies sulfide ions, S^{--}, in solution. Such ions combine with silver, lead, or copper and form black precipitates. A drop of a soluble sulfide solution applied to a piece of silver forms a brownish-black stain.

When hydrochloric acid is added to a moderately insoluble sulfide, hydrogen sulfide is set free. It can usually be recognized by its odor.

A strip of filter paper wet with a solution of lead acetate, $Pb(C_2H_3O_2)_2$, turns brownish-black when exposed to H_2S in water solution or as a gas.

$$Pb(C_2H_3O_2)_2(aq) + H_2S(g) \rightarrow PbS(s) + 2HC_2H_3O_2(aq)$$

Table 28-3
PROPERTIES OF COMMON SULFIDES

Table 28-3

Compound	Color	K_{sp}
As_2S_3	yellow	
As_2S_5	yellow	
HgS	black	3.5×10^{-52}
CuS	black	8.7×10^{-36}
Sb_2S_3	orange	
Sb_2S_5	orange	
Bi_2S_3	brown-black	6.8×10^{-97}
SnS_2	yellow	
CdS	yellow	7.8×10^{-27}
PbS	black	8.4×10^{-28}
ZnS	white	1.1×10^{-21}
CoS	black	8.7×10^{-23}
NiS	black	1.8×10^{-21}
FeS	brown-black	4.9×10^{-18}
MnS	pink	5.1×10^{-15}

28.12   Hydrogen sulfide in chemical analysis

Hydrogen sulfide is often used in analyzing minerals or metals. When it is added to solutions containing the ions of certain metals, insoluble sulfides of those metals precipitate. Table 28-3 lists common sulfides and their colors. Solubility-product constants are given where known.

The list gives the experimental order in which sulfides are precipitated by H_2S from solutions containing the metallic ions as the hydronium ion concentration is decreased. The solubility-products for the sulfides are not very reliable. But roughly, it is clear that the solubility-product constants increase going down the table.

In the classical scheme of analysis, the sulfides listed are separated into two groups by sulfide precipitations under different pH conditions. The sulfides of arsenic through lead are precipitated at pH = 1. The sulfides of zinc through manganese are precipitated at pH = 9.

Two sample calculations show why this separation is possible. Suppose in the same solution we have $[Pb^{++}] = 0.001\ M$ and $[Zn^{++}] = 0.001\ M$. We add HCl until $[H_3O^+] = 10^{-1}\ M$, and pass in H_2S until the solution is saturated. At this $[H_3O^+]$, $[S^{--}] = 6.8 \times 10^{-22}$. (See Table 28-2.) Then $[Pb^{++}][S^{--}] = 10^{-3} \times 6.8 \times 10^{-22} = 6.8 \times 10^{-25}$. The K_{sp} of PbS is exceeded; PbS precipitates. But $[Zn^{++}][S^{--}] = 10^{-3} \times 6.8 \times 10^{-22} = 6.8 \times 10^{-25}$ also. However, the K_{sp} of ZnS is not exceeded, and Zn^{++} remains in solution.

The sulfides listed *above* lead sulfide all have *smaller* solubility products than lead sulfide. Therefore, these sulfides are precipitated by H_2S in a solution where pH = 1. The sulfides listed *below* zinc sulfide have *larger* solubility products than zinc sulfide. Hence, none of these sulfides is precipitated by H_2S in a solution having pH 1. The theoretical pH conditions for separating any pair of sulfides with suitably different solubility products can be found by similar calculations.

OTHER SULFIDES

28.13   Metallic sulfides found in nature

Many important ores found in nature are sulfides. Large quantities of copper sulfide are found in Montana. Zinc sulfide is a major source of zinc. Nearly all lead comes from lead sulfide. The sulfides of such metals as silver, nickel, arsenic, antimony, and iron are found in nature. Sulfides of iron are a profitable source of sulfur and sulfur compounds. However, they are not important as a source of iron.

28.14 Preparation and properties of carbon disulfide

When sulfur vapor is passed over hot charcoal in an electric furnace, carbon and sulfur combine. They form a vapor which condenses to an almost colorless liquid. Its formula is CS_2, similar to that of carbon dioxide. The commercial product has an odor rather like that of boiled cabbage. The liquid does not dissolve in water. It has a very low kindling temperature and burns rapidly. Its vapor burns explosively when ignited in air.

$$CS_2(l) + 3O_2(g) \rightarrow CO_2(g) + 2SO_2(g)$$

Carbon disulfide is a good solvent for rubber, phosphorus, waxes, and resins. It is used in making varnishes and matches, and in one step of the production of viscose rayon.

Fig. 28-8. Sulfur dioxide may be prepared in the laboratory by reducing hot, concentrated sulfuric acid with copper. This preparation should be performed in a hood to prevent the escape of sulfur dioxide with its suffocating, choking odor.

THE OXIDES OF SULFUR

28.15 Occurrence of sulfur dioxide

Traces of sulfur dioxide get into the air from several sources. Sulfur dioxide occurs in some volcanic gases and in some mineral waters. Coal and fuel oil may contain sulfur as an impurity. As these fuels are burned, the sulfur burns to sulfur dioxide. Coal and fuel oil of low sulfur content produce less sulfur dioxide air pollution than similar fuels having high sulfur content. The roasting of sulfide ores converts the sulfur in the ore to sulfur dioxide. In modern smelting plants, this sulfur dioxide is converted to sulfuric acid.

28.16 Preparation of sulfur dioxide

1. By burning sulfur. The simplest way to prepare sulfur dioxide is to burn sulfur in air or in pure oxygen.

$$S(s) + O_2(g) \rightarrow SO_2(g)$$

The gas produced by burning sulfur in air is mixed with nitrogen. This impurity is not objectionable for many operations.

2. By roasting sulfides. Huge quantities of sulfur dioxide are produced by roasting sulfide ores. The roasting of zinc sulfide ore is typical.

$$2ZnS(s) + 3O_2(g) \rightarrow 2ZnO(s) + 2SO_2(g)$$

Sulfur dioxide is a by-product in this operation. Iron pyrite, FeS_2, is roasted to produce sulfur dioxide for making sulfuric acid.

3. By the reduction of sulfuric acid. In one laboratory method of preparing this gas, copper is heated with concentrated sulfuric acid (see Figure 28-8). The hot, concentrated acid is a vigorous

Fig. 28-9. An acid added to a sulfite forms unstable sulfurous acid which decomposes into sulfur dioxide and water. This preparation should also be performed in a hood.

oxidizing agent. The copper is oxidized and the sulfur in sulfuric acid is reduced.

$$Cu(s) + 2H_2SO_4(aq) \rightarrow CuSO_4(aq) + 2H_2O(l) + SO_2(g)$$

4. By the decomposition of sulfites. In this second laboratory method, pure sulfur dioxide is formed by the action of a strong acid on a sulfite. When sodium sulfite reacts with sulfuric acid, the following reaction occurs:

$$Na_2SO_3(aq) + H_2SO_4(aq) \rightarrow Na_2SO_4(aq) + H_2O(l) + SO_2(g)$$

Sulfurous acid, H_2SO_3, is first formed. It then decomposes into water and sulfur dioxide (see Figure 28-9).

28.17   Physical properties of sulfur dioxide

Pure sulfur dioxide is a colorless gas with a suffocating, choking odor. It is more than twice as dense as air, and is very soluble in water. It is one of the easiest gases to liquefy, becoming liquid at room temperature under a pressure of about three atmospheres. (See Sections 11.7 and 11.8.) Liquid sulfur dioxide is commercially available in steel cylinders.

28.18   Chemical properties of sulfur dioxide

1. It is an acid anhydride. Sulfur dioxide is the anhydride of sulfurous acid. As it dissolves in water, it also reacts with the water:

$$SO_2(aq) + H_2O(l) \rightleftarrows H_2SO_3(aq)$$

This reaction partly accounts for the high solubility of sulfur dioxide in water. Sulfurous acid is a weak acid. It turns litmus paper red, neutralizes hydroxides, and forms hydrogen sulfites and sulfites.

$$H_2SO_3 + H_2O \rightleftarrows H_3O^+ + HSO_3^- \qquad K_i = 1.2 \times 10^{-2}$$
$$HSO_3^- + H_2O \rightleftarrows H_3O^+ + SO_3^{--} \qquad K_i = 5.6 \times 10^{-8}$$

Both of these reactions are reversible. The acid decomposes into water and sulfur dioxide again when the water solution is warmed. If exposed to the air, a solution of sulfurous acid reacts slowly with oxygen and forms sulfuric acid.

2. It is a stable gas. Sulfur dioxide does not burn. With a suitable catalyst and at a high temperature, it can be oxidized to sulfur trioxide.

$$2SO_2(g) + O_2(g) \rightleftarrows 2SO_3(g)$$

28.19 Uses for sulfur dioxide and sulfurous acid

1. For making sulfuric acid. In the chemical industry, great quantities of sulfur dioxide are oxidized to sulfur trioxide. The sulfur trioxide is then combined with water, forming sulfuric acid. (See Section 28.21.)

2. As a preservative. Dried fruits such as apricots and prunes are treated with sulfur dioxide, which acts as a preservative.

3. In the petroleum industry. Liquid sulfur dioxide is used in treating kerosene and light lubricating oils.

4. For making sulfites. Sulfurous acid is diprotic and reacts with hydroxides, forming hydrogen sulfites and sulfites.

5. For bleaching. Sulfurous acid does not harm the fibers of wool, silk, straw, or paper. Thus, it can be used to bleach these materials. It is believed that sulfurous acid converts the colored compounds in these materials to colorless sulfites. The bleaching is not permanent, and the natural yellow color of the fiber reappears after some time.

6. In preparing paper pulp. Sulfurous acid reacts with limestone and forms calcium hydrogen sulfite, $Ca(HSO_3)_2$. Wood chips are heated in calcium hydrogen sulfite solution as a first step in paper-making. The hot solution dissolves the lignin which binds the cellulose fibers of wood together. The cellulose fibers are left unchanged and are processed to form paper.

28.20 Sulfur trioxide

Sulfur trioxide is the anhydride of sulfuric acid. It is an intermediate product in the manufacture of sulfuric acid. Sulfur trioxide is a white, crystalline solid at room temperature. It reacts vigorously with water and forms sulfuric acid.

$$SO_3 + H_2O \rightarrow H_2SO_4(l)$$

SULFURIC ACID

28.21 Preparation of sulfuric acid

Most of the sulfuric acid produced in the United States today is made by the contact process. In this process, sulfur dioxide is prepared by burning sulfur or by roasting iron pyrite, FeS_2. Impurities which later might combine with the catalyst and ruin it are removed from the gas. The purified sulfur dioxide is mixed with air and passed through heated iron pipes. These pipes contain the catalyst, usually divanadium pentoxide, V_2O_5. This close "contact" of the sulfur dioxide and the catalyst gives the *contact process* its name. Sulfur dioxide and oxygen of the air are both adsorbed on the surface of the catalyst. There, they react and form sulfur trioxide. See Figure 28-10.

Fig. 28-10. A flow diagram of the contact process for manufacturing sulfuric acid.

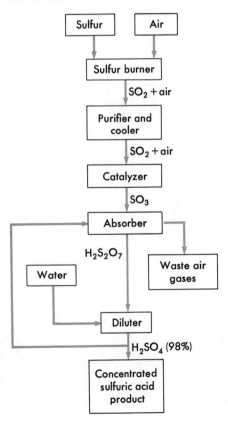

Although the oxidation of sulfur dioxide is an exothermic process, it is carried out at about 400° C. This temperature is high enough to cause the reaction to proceed at a practical rate. The heat given off by the reaction is used to preheat the entering reactants. This preheating regulates the temperature in the catalyst chamber. The catalyst chamber temperature is thus prevented from becoming so high as to cause too much decomposition of the sulfur trioxide produced.

Gaseous sulfur trioxide does not dissolve in or unite readily with pure water. Usually, sulfur trioxide is dissolved in approximately 98% sulfuric acid. The sulfur trioxide combines readily with sulfuric acid, forming pyrosulfuric acid, $H_2S_2O_7$.

$$SO_3(g) + H_2SO_4(l) \rightarrow H_2S_2O_7(l)$$

Pyrosulfuric acid, when diluted with water, yields sulfuric acid.

$$H_2S_2O_7(l) + H_2O(l) \rightarrow 2H_2SO_4(l)$$

Very pure, highly concentrated sulfuric acid is produced by the contact process.

28.22 Physical properties of sulfuric acid

Concentrated sulfuric acid is a dense, oily liquid. It contains about 2% water, has a density of about 1.84 g/ml, and a boiling point of 338° C. Pure sulfuric acid is colorless. Commercial acid may be yellow or brown or almost black because of the presence of impurities, especially organic matter.

When sulfuric acid is added to water much heat is released as the hydrates $H_2SO_4 \cdot H_2O$ and $H_2SO_4 \cdot 2H_2O$ are formed. **CAUTION:** *Never add water to sulfuric acid.*

28.23 Chemical properties of sulfuric acid

1. Its acid properties. Sulfuric acid is a diprotic acid. It ionizes in dilute water solution in two stages:

$$H_2SO_4 + H_2O \rightleftarrows H_3O^+ + HSO_4^-$$
$$HSO_4^- + H_2O \rightleftarrows H_3O^+ + SO_4^{--}$$
$$K_i = 1.26 \times 10^{-2}$$

At 18° C, 0.1-N H_2SO_4 is 90% ionized in the first stage and 60% ionized in the second stage. Sulfuric acid reacts with hydroxides and forms hydrogen sulfates and sulfates. It reacts with metals and with the oxides of metals. Dilute sulfuric acid is more highly ionized than cold, concentrated sulfuric acid. Thus, the dilute acid reacts more vigorously than the cold, concentrated acid with metals above hydrogen in the oxidizing and reducing agents series. See Table 21-3 for this series.

2. Its oxidizing properties. Hot, concentrated sulfuric acid is a vigorous oxidizing agent. The sulfur is reduced from the +6 oxidation state to the +4 or −2 oxidation state. The extent of the reduction depends on the strength of the acid and on the reducing agent used. With copper, sulfur dioxide is produced (see Section 28.16). With zinc and hot, slightly dilute acid, hydrogen sulfide is produced.

$$4Zn(s) + 5H_2SO_4(aq) \rightarrow 4ZnSO_4(aq) + H_2S(g) + 4H_2O(l)$$

3. Its dehydrating properties. The strong attraction of sulfuric acid for water makes it a very good *dehydrating* agent. Gases which do not react with sulfuric acid can be dried by bubbling them through the concentrated acid. Lumps of pumice stone, a porous volcanic rock, soaked in sulfuric acid may be used in the lower part of a desiccator. Sulfuric acid is such an active dehydrating agent that it takes hydrogen and oxygen *directly and in the proportion found in water* from certain substances. It does so, for example, with sucrose, $C_{12}H_{22}O_{11}$, and cellulose, $(C_6H_{10}O_5)_n$, leaving the carbon uncombined. The equation for this process with sucrose is

$$C_{12}H_{22}O_{11} + 11H_2SO_4 \rightarrow 12C + 11H_2SO_4 \cdot H_2O$$

In the same way concentrated sulfuric acid chars wood, paper, cotton, starch, and other organic compounds.

In some commercial chemical processes, water is formed as a by-product. The reaction for making nitroglycerin, $C_3H_5(NO_3)_3$, is such a process.

$$C_3H_5(OH)_3 + 3HNO_3 \rightarrow C_3H_5(NO_3)_3 + 3H_2O$$

Concentrated nitric acid is used in making this explosive. Since the nitric acid is reacting with a nonelectrolyte, the reaction is slow. Dilution of the acid would cause the reaction to proceed still more slowly. To prevent this, sulfuric acid is always mixed with the nitric acid. The sulfuric acid acts as a dehydrating agent. It absorbs the water as fast as it is formed and thus maintains the rate of the reaction.

In the laboratory preparation of carbon monoxide, sulfuric acid is used to dehydrate formic acid. See Section 16.20.

CAUTION: *Sulfuric acid burns the flesh severely.* Great care must be used in handling sulfuric acid so that it does not come in contact with the skin.

28.24   Uses of sulfuric acid

Calcium phosphate, $Ca_3(PO_4)_2$, is found in great amounts especially in Florida and Tennessee. This rock phosphate is treated with sulfuric acid (about 4 million tons/year) to make it more soluble. The soluble form is used as *superphosphate* fertilizer.

Sulfuric acid is used also in making other acids, various sulfates, and many other chemicals.

The iron and steel industries consume large quantities of sulfuric acid. The acid removes oxides from the surface of iron or steel before the metal is plated or coated with an enamel.

In petroleum refining, sulfuric acid is used to remove certain organic impurities. The electrolyte in lead storage batteries is dilute sulfuric acid.

Sulfuric acid serves as a dehydrating agent in the production of smokeless powder and nitroglycerin. It is used in making photographic film, nitrocellulose plastics, and rayon. It is useful in producing paints and pigments, cellophane, and thousands of other commercial articles.

Fig. 28-11. When a white precipitate that is insoluble in hydrochloric acid is formed after the addition of barium chloride solution, the presence of a sulfate is indicated.

28.25   Importance of some sulfates

Sulfuric acid reacts with many metals and forms sulfates. Some of the most important sulfates are those of copper, iron, zinc, calcium, barium, and aluminum. Copper(II) sulfate is used in copper plating and in dyeing processes. Iron(II) sulfate is used in water purification and in making ink. Zinc sulfate is used to make lithopone, a white paint pigment. Hydrated calcium sulfate is the mineral gypsum. Barium sulfate and aluminum sulfate are used in preparing other compounds of these elements. Nearly all sulfates are soluble in water. Those of calcium, strontium, barium, and lead(II) are the chief exceptions. The hydrogen sulfates are not very important.

28.26   Test for a sulfate

A solution of barium chloride added to sulfuric acid or any soluble sulfate produces a white precipitate of barium sulfate.

$$Ba^{++}(aq) + SO_4^{--}(aq) \rightarrow BaSO_4(s)$$

Barium sulfate is insoluble in hydrochloric acid. Several other anions react with barium ions and form white precipitates closely resembling barium sulfate. Among these precipitates are barium oxalate, barium carbonate, barium sulfite, and barium phosphate. However, these precipitates are all soluble in hydrochloric acid. Thus, adding hydrochloric acid to the test solutions prevents these precipitates from forming and avoids confusion.

QUESTIONS

Group A

1. Where are sulfur deposits located in the United States?
2. (*a*) What is the function of the superheated water in the Frasch process? (*b*) the function of the compressed air? (*c*) Why is this process used instead of more common mining methods?
3. (*a*) What is the odor of sulfur? (*b*) of hydrogen sulfide? (*c*) of sulfur dioxide?

4. A pupil prepared some nearly black amorphous sulfur in the laboratory. When he examined it the following week, it had become brittle and much lighter in color. Explain.
5. What are the uses of elemental sulfur?
6. Write the formulas for: (a) iron(III) sulfide; (b) diarsenic pentasulfide; (c) copper(II) sulfide; (d) mercury(II) sulfide; (e) silver sulfide; (f) tin(IV) sulfide; (g) diantimony trisulfide.
7. Describe two natural processes which release hydrogen sulfide into the air.
8. (a) Write balanced formula equations to show the reactions between hydrogen sulfide and solutions of the chlorides of mercury(II), lead(II), and antimony(III). (b) Write the net ionic equations for these reactions.
9. What metals have important sulfide ores?
10. (a) Give several uses for carbon disulfide. (b) What property of carbon disulfide is involved in each case?
11. Sulfur dioxide may be found as an impurity in the air. From what sources does it come?
12. Write the balanced formula equations for: (a) a commercial preparation of sulfur dioxide; (b) a laboratory preparation of sulfur dioxide.
13. (a) What method of gas collection is used in a laboratory preparation of sulfur dioxide? (b) What properties of sulfur dioxide determine this choice?
14. What is the principal use for sulfur dioxide?
15. Write balanced chemical equations to show the formation from sulfurous acid and sodium hydroxide of: (a) sodium hydrogen sulfite; (b) sodium sulfite.
16. Why is the contact process for producing sulfuric acid so named?
17. What is the proper method of diluting sulfuric acid?
18. Why are large quantities of sulfuric acid used in the iron and steel industry?
19. Why is a mixture of nitric acid and sulfuric acid used in making nitroglycerin?
20. Name four important sulfates and give their uses.
21. How can you test a soluble salt to determine whether it is (a) a sulfide? (b) a sulfate?
22. What is the purpose of the concentrated hydrochloric acid in the test for a soluble sulfate?

Group B

23. (a) What is the molecular formula for rhombic sulfur? (b) Why is this molecular formula not usually used in equations?
24. Explain the changes in color and fluidity of sulfur between its melting point and boiling point.
25. Is the change from rhombic sulfur to monoclinic sulfur exothermic or endothermic? Explain.
26. (a) Write a formula equation for the laboratory preparation of hydrogen sulfide. (b) What type of chemical reaction is this? (c) Write the net ionic equation for the reaction.
27. How are the products of combustion of hydrogen sulfide related to the amount of oxygen available?
28. Balance the equation for the oxidation of hydrogen sulfide by hydrogen peroxide, using the electron-transfer method.
29. Draw electron-dot formulas to show the resonance structure of sulfur dioxide.
30. Is sulfur dioxide easy or difficult to liquefy? Explain.

31. Why is sulfur dioxide so soluble in water?
32. Balance the following oxidation-reduction equations:

$$(a)\quad Hg + H_2SO_4 \rightarrow HgSO_4 + SO_2(g) + H_2O$$

$$(b)\quad Cu_2S + O_2 \rightarrow Cu_2O + SO_2(g)$$

33. What test might be applied to determine whether a white crystalline powder is a sulfite or a hydrogen sulfite?
34. Explain the heat exchange needed in the catalyst chamber of a contact sulfuric acid plant.
35. In the contact process, why is sulfur trioxide dissolved in 98% sulfuric acid rather than in water?
36. Give two reasons why boiling concentrated sulfuric acid burns the flesh so badly.

PROBLEMS

Group A

1. How many kilograms of sulfur dioxide can be produced by burning 1.0 kg of pure sulfur?
2. (a) What volume of oxygen is required for the complete combustion of 5.0 liters of hydrogen sulfide? (b) Assuming the air to be 21% oxygen, what volume of air is required?
3. Calculate the percentage composition of lead sulfide, PbS.
4. How many liters of carbon dioxide at STP are formed by burning 39.0 g of carbon disulfide?
5. What is the percentage composition of H_2SO_4?
6. How many grams of sodium sulfite are needed to produce 1.00 liter of sulfur dioxide at STP by reaction with sulfuric acid?
7. A lead smelter processes $50\overline{0}$ metric tons of zinc sulfide, ZnS, each day. If no sulfur dioxide is lost, how many kilograms of sulfuric acid could be made in the plant daily?

Group B

8. Calculate the mass in grams of $50\overline{0}$ ml of hydrogen sulfide measured at 27° C and $74\overline{0}$ mm pressure.
9. How many kilograms of sulfuric acid can be prepared from 5.00 kg of sulfur that is 99.5% pure?
10. How many liters of sulfur dioxide at 25° C and $74\overline{0}$ mm pressure can be produced by roasting $120\overline{0}$ kg of iron pyrite, FeS_2?
11. (a) If $14\overline{0}$ kg of scrap iron is added to a large vat of dilute sulfuric acid, how many kilograms of iron(II) sulfate can be produced? (b) How many kilograms of 95% sulfuric acid are required?
12. How many liters of sulfur dioxide at STP can be prepared from a mixture of $10\overline{0}$ g of copper and $10\overline{0}$ g of H_2SO_4?
13. Calculate the sulfide ion concentration in saturated hydrogen sulfide solutions in water when the pH is 2, 4, 6, 8, and 10.

14. What must be the pH of the solution in order to separate the following pairs of ions in 0.01-M solutions by precipitation as sulfides with hydrogen sulfide? (a) Hg^{++} and Fe^{++}; (b) Bi^{+++} and Zn^{++}; (c) Co^{++} and Ni^{++}.

15. If a barium chloride solution is 0.01 M, what is the smallest sulfate ion concentration which can be detected by precipitation? K_{sp} $BaSO_4 = 1.5 \times 10^{-9}$.

16. If a lead acetate solution is 0.01 M, what is the smallest sulfide ion concentration which can be detected by precipitation?

29

The Halogen Family

29.1 The Halogen Family: Group VII of the Periodic Table

The Halogen Family consists of the nonmetallic elements fluorine, chlorine, bromine, iodine, and astatine. Table 29-1 gives some data about these elements.

From this table we see that the atoms of each of these elements have seven electrons in the outer shell. A halogen atom needs

Table 29–1
THE HALOGEN FAMILY

Element	Atomic number	Atomic weight	Electron configuration	Principal oxidation number	Melting point (°C)	Boiling point (°C)	Color	Density, 0° C	Atomic radius (Å)	Ionic radius (Å)
fluorine	9	18.9984	2,7	−1	−219.6	−188.1	pale-yellow gas	1.696 g/liter	0.72	1.33
chlorine	17	35.453	2,8,7	−1	−101.0	−34.6	greenish-yellow gas	3.214 g/liter	0.99	1.81
bromine	35	79.904	2,8,18,7	−1	−7.2	58.78	reddish-brown liquid	3.12 g/ml	1.14	1.96
iodine	53	126.9045	2,8,18,18,7	−1	113.5	184.35	grayish-black crystals	4.93 g/ml	1.33	2.20
astatine	85	21$\overline{0}$	2,8,18,32,18,7						1.45	

only one electron in order to have an outer octet of electrons and become a halide ion. Since the atoms of these elements are so strongly electronegative, they are all active elements. For this reason, they are very rarely found free in nature. In the elemental state they exist as covalent diatomic molecules.

Fluorine has the smallest atoms and the greatest attraction for electrons. Thus, it is the most highly electronegative element and the most active nonmetal. Because of these properties, fluorine cannot be prepared from its compounds by any purely chemical reduction.

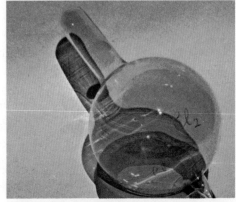

The other halogens, with increasingly larger atoms, are less electronegative than fluorine. As a result, the smaller, lighter halogens can replace and oxidize the larger, heavier halogens from their compounds. Astatine is a synthetic radioactive halogen.

Table 29-1 shows clearly the regular change in properties that occurs in this family. This change in properties proceeds from the smallest and lightest to the largest and heaviest. You should also refer to Figure 5-7 on page 85 and to Figure 6-10 on page 113. These tables provide ionization energy and electronegativity data for members of the Halogen Family.

Each of the halogens combines with hydrogen. The great electronegativity difference between hydrogen and fluorine makes hydrogen fluoride molecules so polar that they associate by hydrogen bonding. The remaining hydrogen halides have smaller electronegativity differences and do not show this property. All hydrogen halides are colorless gases which ionize in water solution. Except for hydrofluoric acid, these acids are highly ionized and are strong acids.

Each of the halogens forms ionic salts with metals. Hence the name *halogen,* which means "salt producer."

FLUORINE

29.2 Preparation of fluorine

Fluorine was first prepared in 1886 by Henri Moissan (1852–1907). He electrolyzed a solution of potassium hydrogen fluoride, KHF_2, in liquid anhydrous hydrogen fluoride. He used a platinum tube as the electrolytic cell, with platinum-iridium electrodes. Today it is prepared by electrolyzing a mixture of potassium fluoride and hydrogen fluoride. A steel and Monel metal electrolytic cell with a carbon anode is used. The fluoride coating which forms on these metals protects them from further reaction.

29.3 Properties of fluorine

Fluorine is the most active nonmetallic element. A fluorine atom has seven electrons in its outer L shell and strongly attracts

Carolyn Polese

Fig. 29-1. The halogens are colorful elements. Fluorine is a pale-yellow gas; chlorine, a greenish-yellow gas; bromine, a reddish-brown liquid; iodine, a grayish-black crystalline solid.

an additional electron to complete its octet. Such an electron is very strongly attracted by the positively charged nucleus because of the small size of fluorine atoms. This attraction accounts for the extreme electronegativity of fluorine. It unites with hydrogen explosively, even in the dark. It forms compounds with all elements except helium, neon, and argon. There are no known positive oxidation states of fluorine. It forms salts known as *fluorides*. Fluorine reacts with gold and platinum slowly. Special carbon steel containers are used to transport fluorine. These containers become coated with iron fluoride which resists further action.

29.4 Usefulness of fluorine compounds

The mineral fluorspar, CaF_2, is used in preparing most fluorine compounds. Sodium fluoride is used as a poison for destroying roaches, rats, and other pests. A trace of sodium fluoride, or the less expensive sodium silico-fluoride, is added to drinking water in many areas because fluorides help prevent tooth decay. Fluorides have also been added to some tooth pastes for this reason.

One of the Freons, dichlorodifluoromethane, CCl_2F_2, is used as a refrigerant. It is odorless, nonflammable, and nontoxic. It is also used as the propellant in spray cans of insecticides. In producing aluminum, melted cryolite, $AlF_3 \cdot 3NaF$, is used as a solvent for aluminum oxide. Uranium is changed to uranium hexafluoride gas, UF_6, for separating the uranium isotopes.

Fluorine combines with the noble gases krypton, xenon, and radon. The very high radioactivity of radon and its short half-life make experiments with radon fluorides very difficult to perform. Two fluorides of krypton, KrF_2 and KrF_4, are prepared by passing electricity through krypton-fluorine mixtures. This process is carried out at the temperature of liquid nitrogen. At room temperature the krypton fluorides are not stable and decompose quickly.

Three fluorides of xenon, XeF_2, XeF_4, and XeF_6, have been made. The method involves step-by-step additions of fluorine to the xenon atoms. All are white solids at ordinary temperatures; XeF_6 is the most highly reactive. The three compounds each react with hydrogen and produce elemental xenon and hydrogen fluoride. With water, XeF_2 produces xenon, oxygen, and hydrogen fluoride. The other two fluorides react with water and yield xenon trioxide, XeO_3, a colorless, highly explosive solid. Xenon trioxide dissolves in water and forms a stable solution which is a very strong oxidizing agent. The xenon fluorides may someday be useful as fluorinating agents.

29.5 Preparation and properties of hydrogen fluoride

Hydrogen fluoride is prepared both in the laboratory and in industry by treating calcium fluoride with concentrated sulfuric acid.

Fig. 29-2. Crystals of xenon tetrafluoride.

Argonne National Laboratory

$$CaF_2(s) + H_2SO_4(l) \rightarrow CaSO_4(s) + 2HF(g)$$

The colorless gas released by the reaction fumes strongly in moist air. It dissolves in water and forms hydrofluoric acid. This acid is very corrosive; it attacks the flesh and forms painful sores which heal slowly. The vapor is very dangerous if inhaled. Hydrofluoric acid reacts with most materials but not with wax, lead, platinum, and certain plastics.

At room temperature, the molar volume of hydrogen fluoride has a mass of about $5\bar{0}$ g. This measurement shows that hydrogen fluoride molecules have an average molecular weight of $5\bar{0}$. However, the molecular weight of an HF molecule is only $2\bar{0}$. Therefore, hydrogen fluoride at room temperature must contain some molecules more complex than HF. Some scientists believe that gaseous hydrogen fluoride is an approximately equal mixture of H_2F_2 and H_3F_3 molecules. These molecules have molecular weights of $4\bar{0}$ and $6\bar{0}$, respectively. There is some evidence, however, that still more complex molecules, up to H_6F_6, exist in gaseous hydrogen fluoride. At higher temperatures, the molar volume of the gas has a mass of only $2\bar{0}$ g. This mass change shows that dissociation into HF molecules occurs. As noted in Section 29.1, the association of hydrogen fluoride molecules is an example of hydrogen bonding. This hydrogen bonding is caused by the high electronegativity of fluorine and the resulting polarity of hydrogen fluoride molecules. The hydrogen-fluorine bond is estimated to have about 50 percent ionic character.

Water dipoles can cause some of the H_2F_2 molecules in hydrofluoric acid at room temperature to ionize:

$$H_2O(l) + H_2F_2(aq) \rightleftarrows H_3O^+(aq) + HF_2^-(aq)$$

The hydrogen difluoride ion, HF_2^-, contains the strongest hydrogen bond known. It is even stronger than the hydrogen bonds in H_2F_2 and H_3F_3. Because of its slight ionization, hydrofluoric acid is a weak acid. Because it is a diprotic acid, it forms both acid and normal salts.

$$H_2F_2 + KOH \rightarrow KHF_2 + H_2O$$

$$H_2F_2 + 2KOH \rightarrow 2KF + 2H_2O$$

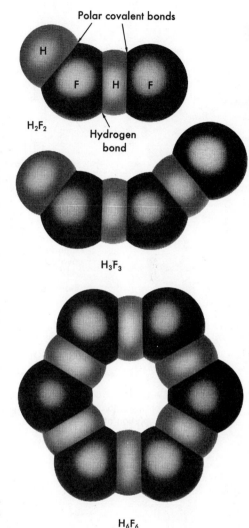

Fig. 29-3. Among the molecules found in hydrogen fluoride at room temperature may be H_2F_2, H_3F_3, and H_6F_6 molecules.

29.6 Uses of hydrofluoric acid

Hydrofluoric acid is used chiefly as a catalyst. It performs this role in the manufacture of high-octane gasoline and in making synthetic cryolite for aluminum production.

For many years hydrofluoric acid has been used for etching glass. Glassware is frosted by exposing it to hydrogen fluoride fumes.

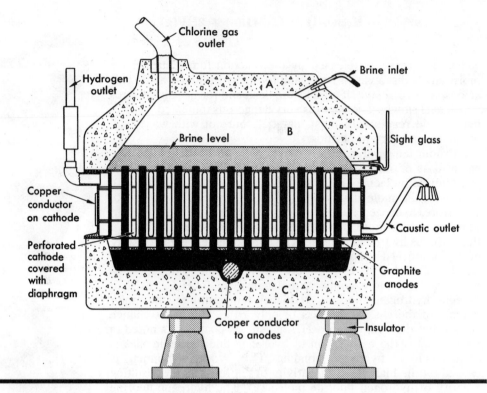

Fig. 29-4. The Hooker cell is used for preparing chlorine by the electrolysis of a solution of sodium chloride.

CHLORINE

29.7 Wide occurrence of compounds

Because chlorine is so strongly electronegative, it very rarely occurs uncombined in nature. Elemental chlorine is found in small amounts in some volcanic gases. Chlorides of sodium, potassium, and magnesium are fairly abundant. Common table salt, sodium chloride, is widely distributed. It is found in sea water, in salt brines underground, and in rock salt deposits. Sodium chloride is the commercial source of chlorine.

29.8 Preparation of chlorine

The element chlorine was first isolated in 1774 by Carl Wilhelm Scheele, a Swedish chemist (1742–1786). There are several ways to prepare it. Here we shall discuss three.

1. By the electrolysis of sodium chloride. Chlorine is most often prepared by the electrolysis of sodium chloride in water solution. The concentration of the solution is such that hydrogen from the water is released at the cathode, and chlorine is set free at the anode. The hydrogen and chlorine gases are kept separate from each other and from the solution by asbestos partitions. The sodium and hydroxide ions remaining in the solution are recovered as sodium hydroxide.

$$2NaCl(aq) + 2H_2O(l) \xrightarrow{\text{(electricity)}} 2NaOH(aq) + H_2(g) + Cl_2(g)$$

The ionic equation is:

$$2Na^+(aq) + 2Cl^-(aq) + 2H_2O(l) \xrightarrow{\text{(electricity)}} 2Na^+(aq) + 2OH^-(aq) + H_2(g) + Cl_2(g)$$

Electrolysis of fused sodium chloride is an important sodium-producing process. Small amounts of chlorine are formed as a by-product.

2. *By the oxidation of hydrogen chloride.* This method involves heating a mixture of manganese dioxide and concentrated hydrochloric acid. The manganese oxidizes half of the chloride ions in the reacting HCl to chlorine atoms. Manganese is reduced during the reaction from the +4 oxidation state to the +2 state.

$$MnO_2(s) + 4HCl(aq) \rightarrow MnCl_2(aq) + 2H_2O(l) + Cl_2(g)$$

This is the method used by Scheele in first preparing chlorine. It is a useful laboratory preparation.

Fig. 29-5. One method of preparing chlorine in the laboratory is by heating a mixture of manganese dioxide, sodium chloride, and sulfuric acid. The preparation should be performed in a hood.

Carolyn Polese

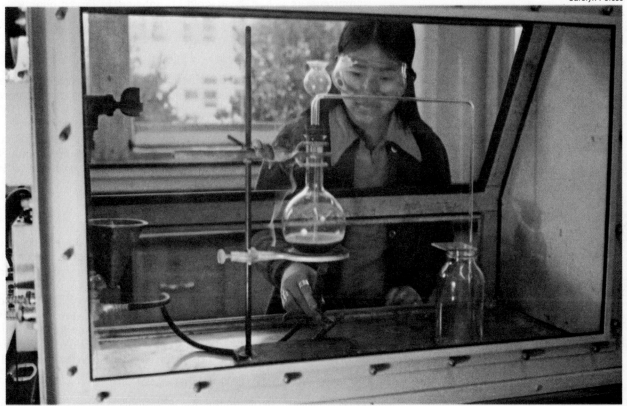

An alternate process involves heating manganese dioxide mixed with sodium chloride and sulfuric acid.

$$2NaCl(s) + 2H_2SO_4(aq) + MnO_2(s) \rightarrow Na_2SO_4(aq) + MnSO_4(aq) + 2H_2O(l) + Cl_2(g)$$

3. By the action of hydrochloric acid on calcium hypochlorite. This method is convenient in the laboratory, because heat is not required. Also, the chlorine can be produced in small quantities as needed. Hydrochloric acid is added drop by drop to calcium hypochlorite powder. Chlorine is released and calcium chloride and water are formed.

$$4HCl(aq) + Ca(ClO)_2(s) \rightarrow CaCl_2(aq) + 2Cl_2(g) + 2H_2O(l)$$

29.9   Physical properties of chlorine

At room temperature chlorine is a greenish-yellow gas with a disagreeable, suffocating odor. It is about 2.5 times as dense as air and is moderately soluble in water, forming a pale greenish-yellow solution. Chlorine is easily liquefied and is usually marketed in steel cylinders.

When inhaled in small quantities, chlorine affects the mucous membranes of the nose and throat. It produces about the same symptoms as a bad head cold. If inhaled in larger quantities, chlorine is so poisonous that it may cause death.

29.10   Chemical properties of chlorine

The outer shell of a chlorine atom contains seven electrons. There are many reactions by which chlorine atoms may acquire an additional electron and complete the octet. We will discuss the chemical properties of chlorine under the following subtopics.

1. Action with metals. When powdered antimony is sprinkled into a jar of moist chlorine, the two elements combine spontaneously, emitting a shower of sparks. Antimony trichloride is formed. See Figure 21-1.

$$2Sb(s) + 3Cl_2(g) \rightarrow 2SbCl_3(s)$$

In a similar manner, hot metallic sodium burns in chlorine and forms sodium chloride. Chlorine combines directly with such metals as copper, iron, zinc, and arsenic, if they are heated slightly.

2. Action with hydrogen. If hydrogen and chlorine are mixed in the dark, no reaction occurs. But such a mixture explodes violently if it is heated or exposed to sunlight. The heat or sunlight provides the activation energy. A jet of hydrogen, burning in air, continues to burn if it is inserted into a bottle of chlorine.

$$H_2(g) + Cl_2(g) \rightarrow 2HCl(g)$$

This is an example of combustion without the presence of oxygen.

Chlorine has such a great attraction for hydrogen that it can take hydrogen from some of its compounds. Chlorine does not support the combustion of wood or paper. A paraffin candle, however, continues to burn in chlorine with a smoky flame. In this reaction the hydrogen of the paraffin combines with the chlorine, forming hydrogen chloride. The carbon is left uncombined. Turpentine is a hydrocarbon with the formula $C_{10}H_{16}$. A strip of filter paper moistened with hot turpentine burns in a jar of chlorine with a sooty flame. Hydrogen chloride is formed, and a dense cloud of soot is set free:

$$C_{10}H_{16}(l) + 8Cl_2(g) \rightarrow 10C(s) + 16HCl(g)$$

3. Action with water. A freshly prepared solution of chlorine in water is yellow-green in color. If the solution stands in sunlight for a few days, both the color and the strong chlorine odor disappear. The chlorine combines with the water and forms hypochlorous acid and hydrochloric acid. Hypochlorous acid is unstable and decomposes into hydrochloric acid and oxygen.

$$2H_2O(l) + 2Cl_2(g) \rightarrow 2HClO(aq) + 2HCl(aq)$$
$$\searrow$$
$$2HCl(aq) + O_2(g)$$

The instability of hypochlorous acid makes chlorine water a good oxidizing agent.

If no oxidizable material is present, hypochlorous acid decomposes and produces molecules of oxygen as shown by the above equation. However, if an oxidizable material is present, the released oxygen combines directly with the oxidizable material. In bleaching, the oxygen combines with the dye. If the dye can be oxidized to a colorless compound, it is bleached successfully. However, if the dye cannot be oxidized to a colorless compound, it is not bleached. Hypochlorous acid does not bleach all dyes or destroy all colors. Many dyes are not affected by it at all. Hypochlorous acid usually removes natural colors. It bleaches some ink spots by reacting with the ink and forming white or pale-colored oxides. It does not affect printer's ink because it cannot oxidize the carbon in it.

29.11 Uses of chlorine

1. For bleaching. Bleaching solution is usually a solution of sodium hypochlorite. It is made by electrolyzing sodium chloride solution. The released chlorine is allowed to react with the sodium hydroxide being produced at the same time. Sodium hypochlorite is also formed in a reaction between chlorine and sodium carbonate. Dry powdered chlorine bleaches are available. They generally contain sodium hypochlorite also.

CAUTION: Chlorine destroys silk or wool fibers. *Never use commercial bleaches containing hypochlorites on silk or wool.*

Weil

Fig. 29-6. This attendant is regulating the amount of chlorine being added to swimming pool water. Chlorine is used to lower the bacterial content of the water to a safe level.

2. As a disinfectant. Since moist chlorine is a good oxidizing agent, it destroys bacteria. Large quantities of chlorinated lime, $Ca(ClO)Cl$, are used as a disinfectant.

In city water systems, billions of gallons of water are treated with chlorine to kill disease-producing bacteria. The water in swimming pools is usually treated with chlorine. Chlorine is sometimes used to kill bacteria in sewage before it is pumped into lakes or rivers. This treatment reduces the harmful effects of this type of pollution.

3. For making compounds. Because chlorine combines directly with many metals and nonmetals it is used to produce many chlorides. Among these are chloroform, $CHCl_3$; carbon tetrachloride, CCl_4; aluminum chloride, Al_2Cl_6; and disulfur dichloride, S_2Cl_2.

29.12   Preparation of hydrogen chloride

In the laboratory, hydrogen chloride can be prepared by treating sodium chloride with sulfuric acid.

$$NaCl(s) + H_2SO_4(aq) \rightarrow NaHSO_4(aq) + HCl(g)$$

This same reaction, carried out at a higher temperature, is used commercially. Under this condition, a second molecule of HCl can be produced per molecule of H_2SO_4 if more NaCl is used.

$$2NaCl(s) + H_2SO_4(aq) \rightarrow Na_2SO_4(aq) + 2HCl(g)$$

Another commercial preparation involves the direct union of hydrogen and chlorine. Both are obtained by the electrolysis of concentrated sodium chloride solution. (See Section 29.8.)

A third important commercial source of hydrogen chloride is the chlorination of hydrocarbons. Hydrogen chloride forms as a by-product. (See Sections 17.10 and 17.19.)

Hydrogen chloride dissolved in pure water is sold under the name of hydrochloric acid.

29.13   Physical properties of hydrogen chloride

Hydrogen chloride is a colorless gas with a sharp, penetrating odor. It is denser than air and extremely soluble in water. One volume of water at 0° C dissolves more than 500 volumes of hydrogen chloride at standard pressure. Hydrogen chloride fumes in moist air. It is so soluble that it condenses water vapor from the air into tiny drops of hydrochloric acid.

29.14   Chemical properties of hydrogen chloride

Hydrogen chloride is a stable compound which does not burn. Some vigorous oxidizing agents react with it and form water and chlorine.

Carolyn Polese

Fig. 29-7. Bromine may be prepared in the laboratory by heating a mixture of sodium bromide, manganese dioxide, and sulfuric acid in a glass-stoppered retort. This preparation should be performed in a hood.

Hydrogen chloride gas does not act as an acid except in the sense that it may be a proton donor. This statement is also true of the liquid which is formed by compressing and cooling the gas. However, the water solution of the gas is a strong acid known as *hydrochloric acid*. Hydrogen chloride is a polar covalent compound. When it is dissolved in water, however, the water dipoles cause it to ionize extensively. Hydronium ions and chloride ions are formed. Thus the solution has acid properties. The concentrated acid contains about 38% hydrogen chloride by weight, and is about 1.2 times as dense as water. Hydrochloric acid is a typical nonoxidizing acid. It reacts with many metals and oxides of metals. It neutralizes hydroxides, forming salts and water.

29.15 Uses of hydrochloric acid

Hydrochloric acid is used in preparing certain chlorides and in cleaning metals. This cleaning involves removing oxides and other forms of tarnish. Many metals must be cleaned before they can be galvanized, enameled, tinned, or plated with other metals.

Some hydrochloric acid is essential in the process of digestion. The concentration of hydrochloric acid in gastric juice is $0.16\ M$.

29.16   Uses of chlorides

The metallic chlorides form an important group of salts. Nearly all of them are crystalline compounds, and most of them are soluble in water. The chlorides of lead, silver, and mercury(I) are insoluble. Sodium chloride is used for food preservation and seasoning. It is also a very important chemical raw material. Aluminum chloride is employed as a catalyst in cracking petroleum to increase the yield of gasoline. Chlorides of carbon, sulfur, and phosphorus have some important applications.

29.17   Test for a chloride

One test for a soluble chloride is based on the insolubility of silver chloride. When silver nitrate is added to the solution to be tested for chloride ions, a white precipitate may result. If this precipitate dissolves in ammonia-water solution, but precipitates again when excess nitric acid is added, chloride ions are present.

The ionic equations for the reactions involved in the test for the chloride ion are:

1.   Forming the white silver chloride precipitate:

$$Ag^+(aq) + Cl^-(aq) \rightarrow Ag^+Cl^-(s)$$

2.   Dissolving the silver chloride in ammonia-water solution:

$$Ag^+Cl^-(s) + 2NH_3(aq) \rightarrow Ag(NH_3)_2{}^+(aq) + Cl^-(aq)$$

3.   Reprecipitating the silver chloride by adding nitric acid:

$$Ag(NH_3)_2{}^+(aq) + Cl^-(aq) + 2H^+(aq) + 2NO_3{}^-(aq) \rightarrow Ag^+Cl^-(s) + 2NH_4{}^+(aq) + 2NO_3{}^-(aq)$$

BROMINE

29.18   Occurrence and discovery of bromine

Several bromides, especially those of sodium and magnesium, are found in nature. For many years the chief source of bromine has been the solution left after sodium chloride has been removed from the brine of salt wells. Chemists have also developed processes for removing bromine from sea water.

Bromine was discovered in 1826 by the French chemist Antoine-Jerome Balard (1802–1876). His method involved treating the solution left after sodium chloride had been removed from salt-well brine with chlorine gas.

29.19 Bromine from bromides

In the laboratory, bromine can be prepared by using manganese dioxide, sulfuric acid and sodium bromide.

$$2NaBr(s) + MnO_2(s) + 2H_2SO_4(aq) \rightarrow Na_2SO_4(aq) + MnSO_4(aq) + 2H_2O(l) + Br_2(g)$$

This method is similar to that for preparing chlorine.

The commercial production of bromine depends on the ability of chlorine to displace bromide ions from solution. Chlorine displaces bromide ions because it is more highly electronegative than bromine.

$$2Br^-(aq) + Cl_2(g) \rightarrow 2Cl^-(aq) + Br_2(l)$$

Large quantities of acidified brine are treated with chlorine. Bromine is released and then blown out of the solution by steam or air. It is condensed directly or absorbed in sodium carbonate solution, from which it can be recovered by treatment with sulfuric acid. Bromine is also prepared by electrolysis of soluble bromides.

29.20 Physical properties of bromine

Bromine is a dark-red liquid which is about three times as dense as water. It evaporates readily, forming a vapor which burns the eyes and throat and has a very disagreeable odor. Bromine is moderately soluble in water. Its reddish-brown solution is used in the laboratory under the name of bromine water. Bromine dissolves readily in carbon tetrachloride, carbon disulfide, and in water solutions of bromides.

CAUTION: *Use great care in handling bromine.* It burns the flesh and forms wounds that heal slowly.

29.21 Chemical properties of bromine

Bromine unites directly with hydrogen and forms hydrogen bromide. It combines with most metals and forms bromides. When it is moist, bromine is a good bleaching agent. Its water solution is a strong oxidizing agent and forms hydrobromic acid and oxygen in sunlight. However, bromine is not as electronegative as chlorine. The use of bromine in organic addition and substitution reactions was described in Sections 17.10, 17.13, 17.16, 17.19, and 18.1.

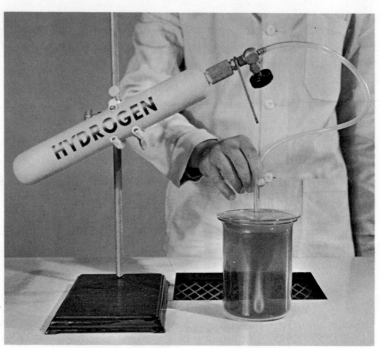

Fig. 29-8. Hydrogen burns in an atmosphere of bromine vapor.

From the CHEM Study Film: *Bromine—Element from the Sea*

29.22   Uses of bromides

The bromides of sodium and potassium are used in medicine as sedatives. Such medicines should not be used unless prescribed by a physician. Silver bromide, AgBr, is a yellowish solid. It is highly photosensitive and is widely used in making photographic films or plates. Ethylene bromide, $C_2H_4Br_2$, is used to increase the efficiency of lead tetraethyl, $Pb(C_2H_5)_4$, in anti-knock gasoline. Normally, the combustion of lead tetraethyl produces lead oxide. This substance is harmful to engine cylinder walls and to exhaust lines. The addition of ethylene bromide causes lead bromide to be formed instead. Lead bromide is volatile enough to go off with the exhaust gases. Other organic bromine compounds are used in making dyes.

29.23   Test for bromide ions

Tests for soluble bromides depend on two facts. First, bromine is very soluble in carbon tetrachloride, to which it gives an orange-red color. Second, chlorine displaces bromine from a bromide.

To the solution to be tested for bromide ions, carbon tetrachloride and several milliliters of chlorine water are added. The mixture is shaken vigorously. If *bromide* ions are present, *bromine* molecules are set free by the chlorine. The bromine is much more soluble in carbon tetrachloride than in water. It dissolves in the carbon tetrachloride producing the orange-red color. The carbon tetrachloride does not mix with the water but forms a separate layer below the water. *Br₂ molecules* color the carbon tetrachloride when the test is positive. But the only form in which bromine could have existed and be oxidized to free bromine by chlorine was as *Br⁻ ions*. Therefore, a positive test indicates the presence of bromide ions in the original solution.

IODINE

29.24 Discovery and occurrence of iodine

The element iodine was discovered in 1811 by Bernard Courtois (1777–1838), a French chemist. He noticed the purplish vapor of iodine when he added sulfuric acid to the solution obtained by mixing seaweed ashes with water. For many years nearly all iodine was prepared from seaweed.

At present, most iodine produced in this country is made from iodides found in natural underground brines. The iodine is freed from the brine by treatment with chlorine. Some iodine is obtained from Chile, where it occurs in nitrate deposits as calcium iodate, $Ca(IO_3)_2$.

29.25 Preparation of iodine

The laboratory preparation of iodine is similar to that of chlorine and bromine. An iodide is heated with manganese dioxide and sulfuric acid.

$$2NaI(s) + MnO_2(s) + 2H_2SO_4(aq) \rightarrow Na_2SO_4(aq) + MnSO_4(aq) + 2H_2O(l) + I_2(g)$$

The iodine is driven off as a vapor. It can be condensed as a solid on the walls of a cold dish or beaker.

Either chlorine or bromine can be used to displace iodine from a soluble iodide.

$$2I^- + Cl_2 \rightarrow 2Cl^- + I_2$$

$$2I^- + Br_2 \rightarrow 2Br^- + I_2$$

29.26 Physical properties of iodine

Iodine is a steel-gray solid. When heated, it sublimes (vaporizes without melting) and produces a violet-colored vapor. The odor of this vapor is irritating, resembling that of chlorine.

Iodine is very slightly soluble in water. It is much more soluble in water solutions of sodium or potassium iodide. With these solutions, it forms complex I_3^- ions. It dissolves readily in alcohol, forming a dark-brown solution. It is very soluble in carbon disulfide and carbon tetrachloride, giving a rich purple color. Free iodine colors starch paste blue. This color change

Fig. 29-9. Iodine is prepared in the laboratory by heating sodium iodide and manganese dioxide with sulfuric acid.

is caused by iodine being adsorbed on the surface of the starch particles. It serves as a test for free iodine. Conversely, an iodine solution can be used to test for starch.

29.27   Chemical properties of iodine

Iodine is active chemically, though less so than either bromine or chlorine. It combines with metals and forms iodides, and can also unite with some nonmetals. If a crystal of iodine is placed on a small piece of white phosphorus, the two elements combine spontaneously. Light and heat are given off.

29.28   Uses for iodine

Iodine is used for making certain iodides, especially AgI for photography. It is also used as an antiseptic for cuts and open wounds. Surgeons sometimes use a *tincture* (alcohol solution) of iodine to sterilize a patient's skin before an operation.

CAUTION: *Iodine is poisonous if taken internally. Starch paste or starchy foods can be used as an antidote.*

If a bottle containing tincture of iodine is left unstoppered, some of the solvent evaporates. The concentrated tincture which is left may blister the skin. Blistering may also result if a bandage or dressing is placed on the skin after the iodine is applied, or if more iodine is later applied.

29.29   Uses of iodide

Potassium iodide, KI, has some uses in medicine. Iodine is present in the thyroid gland of the body. The thyroid gland produces an iodine-containing compound, *thyroxine.* Thyroxine controls the rate at which the body uses food energy. If the diet contains too little iodine, the thyroid gland may become enlarged. This condition is known as simple goiter. Iodine compounds are added to the water in some areas where simple goiter is common. Either sodium iodide, NaI, or potassium iodide, KI, is added to common salt to make *iodized salt.*

29.30   Test for soluble iodides

To test a solution for a soluble iodide, add a few milliliters of carbon tetrachloride and a few milliliters of chlorine water. Shake the mixture vigorously. If an iodide is present, the carbon tetrachloride which sinks to the bottom is colored purple. This color results from free iodine. As in the test for bromides, the release of the *free halogen* indicates the presence of the corresponding *halide ion* in the solution tested.

QUESTIONS

Group A

1. Why are the halogens very rarely found in nature as free elements?
2. List the halogens in order of increasing activity.
3. What does the term *halogen* mean?
4. (*a*) What kind of container must be used for fluorine? (*b*) for hydrofluoric acid?
5. Write balanced formula equations for the step-by-step fluorination of xenon to XeF_2, XeF_4, and XeF_6.
6. What are the most important uses for hydrofluoric acid?
7. (*a*) What compound is the commercial source of chlorine? (*b*) For what other element is this compound the commercial source?
8. (*a*) Write the equation for the laboratory preparation of chlorine from manganese dioxide and hydrochloric acid. (*b*) Assign oxidation numbers and tell which element is oxidized and which element is reduced.
9. Describe the effects of chlorine on the body.
10. (*a*) List the physical and chemical properties of hydrogen chloride which must be considered in choosing a method of collecting this gas in the laboratory. (*b*) Which method of collection is necessitated by this combination of properties?
11. How could you test an unknown solution to determine if there are any chloride ions present in it?
12. Why is bromine produced in large quantities today?
13. (*a*) Write the ionic equation for the reaction involved in extracting bromine from sea water. (*b*) What type of reaction is this?
14. List the important physical properties of bromine.
15. What is the most important source of iodine in the United States?
16. What is the danger of using tincture of iodine that has been in the medicine cabinet for several years?
17. (*a*) For what purpose does the body require iodine? (*b*) From what sources can it be obtained?

Group B

18. Fluorine does not exhibit any positive oxidation state. Why?
19. Water reacts with xenon difluoride and yields xenon, oxygen, and hydrogen fluoride. (*a*) Write an equation for this reaction. (*b*) Assign oxidation numbers to each element, and balance the equation by a method used to balance oxidation-reduction equations.
20. What properties does dichlorodifluoromethane have which makes it useful as the propellant in aerosol spray cans?
21. Why do hydrogen fluoride molecules exhibit hydrogen bonding?
22. Why must the hydrogen, chlorine, and sodium hydroxide produced in a Hooker cell be kept separated from each other?
23. (*a*) For which does chlorine have greater attraction, carbon or hydrogen? (*b*) What experimental evidence can you give to support your answer?
24. (*a*) Why is freshly prepared chlorine water yellow-green in color? (*b*) Why does it become colorless after standing in sunlight?
25. When chlorine is added to water for bleaching purposes, what element is responsible for the bleaching effect?
26. Is liquid hydrogen chloride an acid? Explain.

27. Of what does a positive test for bromide ions in a solution consist?
28. Compare the colors of (a) solid iodine; (b) iodine in alcohol; (c) iodine in carbon tetrachloride; (d) iodine vapor.
29. Hydrogen forms binary compounds with each of the four common halogens. (a) Write the formulas you would expect for these compounds. (b) From electronegativity differences, compare the ionic characters of the bonds in each of these compounds. (c) Write equations for the reactions you would expect each to have with water.
30. The reactions between water molecules and molecules of the hydrogen halides (Question 29) are reversible. (a) Qualitatively, at equilibrium, what are the relative concentrations of the particles involved? (b) What does this indicate about the relative stability of the hydrogen halide molecules compared with the stability of the ions which can be formed from them?
31. Why are sodium chloride and calcium chloride ionic salts, while aluminum chloride is molecular?

PROBLEMS

Group A

1. What mass of sodium hydroxide is formed during the production of $71\overline{0}$ kg of chlorine by the electrolysis of sodium chloride?
2. Bromine (10.0 g) is needed for an experiment. How many grams of sodium bromide are required to produce this bromine?
3. Chlorine reacts with calcium hydroxide and produces bleaching powder, $Ca(Cl\overline{O})Cl$, and water. (a) What mass of calcium hydroxide is required for making $25\overline{0}$ g of bleaching powder? (b) What mass of chlorine is also required?
4. How many grams of zinc chloride can be produced from 11.2 liters of chlorine at STP?

Group B

5. How many grams of hydrogen fluoride can be obtained when $60\overline{0}$ g of 95% sulfuric acid acts on $39\overline{0}$ g of calcium fluoride?
6. What is the percentage of bromine in ethylene bromide, $C_2H_4Br_2$?
7. How many liters of chlorine at STP can be obtained from 468 g of sodium chloride by electrolysis?
8. A laboratory experiment requires five $25\overline{0}$-ml bottles of chlorine, measured at 27° C and $75\overline{0}$ mm pressure. What volume of 38% hydrochloric acid (density 1.20 g/ml) and what mass of manganese dioxide will be required?

Chapter 30

Radioactivity

NATURAL RADIOACTIVITY

30.1 Discovery of radioactivity

In 1896 the French scientist Henri Becquerel (bek-*rel*) (1852–1908) was studying the properties of certain minerals. He was particularly interested in their ability to *fluoresce* (give off visible light after being exposed to sunlight). Among these minerals was a sample of uranium ore. By accident, Becquerel found that uranium ore gives off invisible rays. He discovered that these rays penetrate the light-proof covering of a photographic plate and affect the film as if it had been exposed to light rays directly. Substances which give off such invisible rays are *radioactive,* and the property is called *radioactivity.* **Radioactivity** *is the spontaneous, uncontrollable breakdown of an unstable atomic nucleus with the release of particles and rays.*

30.2 Discovery of radium

Becquerel was very interested in the source of radioactivity. At his suggestion, Pierre Curie (1859–1906) and his wife Marie (1867–1934) began to investigate the properties of uranium and its ores. They soon learned that uranium and uranium compounds are mildly radioactive. But they also discovered that one uranium ore (pitchblende) had four times the amount of radioactivity expected on the basis of its uranium content.

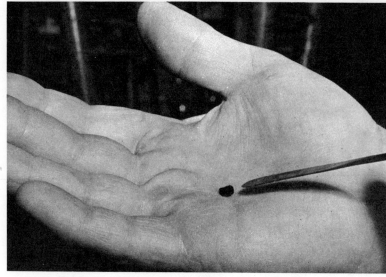
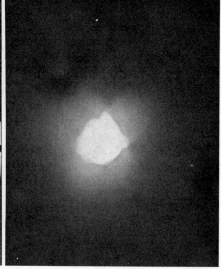

Matt Grimaldi and Mark Schupack

Fig. 30-1. Left, a fragment of metallic uranium, one of the radioactive elements; and right, a photograph produced when radiation from the same fragment of uranium penetrated the light-tight wrappings of a photographic plate.

Fig. 30-2. The activity of a radioactive material may be measured by the speed with which it discharges a goldleaf electroscope like this one. The material to be tested is placed in the hinged drawer at the bottom.

Welch Scientific Co.

In 1898 the Curies discovered two new radioactive metallic elements in pitchblende. These elements, *polonium* and *radium*, accounted for the high radioactivity of pitchblende. Radium is more than 1,000,000 times as radioactive as the same mass of uranium.

Radium is always found in uranium ores. However, it never occurs in such ores in a greater proportion than 1 part of radium to 3×10^6 parts of uranium. The reason for this proportion will be explained in Section 30.7. The production of radium from uranium ore is a long, difficult, and costly procedure. Radium is usually marketed as radium bromide rather than as elemental radium. The radioactivity of an element is not affected by chemical combination, because radioactivity is a nuclear property.

30.3 Properties of radium

Radium is the element of highest atomic weight in Group II of the periodic table. Its physical properties were listed in Table 24-1. It is the least electronegative and thus most metallic member of its group. Radium has chemical properties similar to those of barium.

Radium is important not because of its physical or chemical properties, but because of its radioactivity. Radium-226 is a naturally occurring radioactive nuclide. Because of its radioactivity, radium-226 and its compounds have several unusual properties. These properties are also observed in other radioactive elements. They include the following:

1. They affect the light-sensitive emulsion on a photographic film. Photographic film may be wrapped in heavy black paper and stored in the dark. Even so, radiations from radioactive elements penetrate the wrapping. They affect the film in the same way that light does when the film is exposed to it. When the film is developed, a black spot shows up on the negative where the invisible radiation struck it. The rays from radioactive elements penetrate paper, wood, flesh, and *thin* sheets of metal.

2. *They produce an electric charge in the surrounding air.* The radiation from radioactive elements ionizes the molecules of the gases in the air surrounding it. These ionized molecules conduct electric charges away from the knob of a charged electroscope, thus discharging it. The activity of a radium compound can be measured by the rate at which it discharges an electroscope. Similarly, the radiation given off by radioactive elements ionizes the low pressure gas in the tube of a Geiger counter. Electricity thus passes through the tube for an instant. The passage of electricity may be registered as a "click" in a set of earphones.

3. *They produce fluorescence with certain other compounds.* A small quantity of radium bromide added to zinc sulfide causes the zinc sulfide to glow. Since the glow is visible in the dark, the mixture is used in making luminous paint.

4. *Their radiations have special physiological effects.* The radiation from radium can destroy the germinating power of seed. It can kill bacteria or animals. People who work with radium may be severely burned by the rays which it emits. Such burns heal slowly, and can be fatal. However, radiations from radioactive materials often destroy cancerous cells more readily than normal cells. For this reason, they are used in the treatment of cancer and certain skin diseases.

5. *They undergo radioactive decay.* The atoms of all radioactive elements steadily decay into simpler atoms as they release radiation. For example, one half of any number of radium-226 atoms decays into simpler atoms in 1620 years. One half of what remains, or one fourth of the original atoms, decays in the next 1620 years. One half of what is left, or one eighth of the original atoms, decays in the next 1620 years, and so on. This period of 1620 years is called the *half-life of radium-226.* **Half-life** *is the length of time during which half of a given number of atoms of a radioactive nuclide decays.* Each radioactive nuclide has its characteristic half-life.

30.4 Other natural radioactive elements

The radioactive elements known to Becquerel were uranium and thorium. We have already noted that the Curies discovered two more, polonium and radium. Since that time the natural radioactive nuclides have been identified. See Table 30-1. All nuclides of the elements beyond bismuth in the periodic table

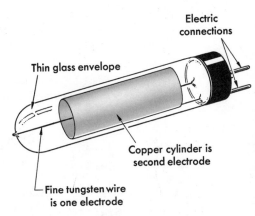

Electric connections

Thin glass envelope

Copper cylinder is second electrode

Fine tungsten wire is one electrode

Fig. 30-3. A diagram showing the construction of a Geiger-Müller counter tube. Radiation passing through the tube ionizes the gas it contains and enables current to flow.

Fig. 30-4. A uranium prospector using a Geiger counter in his exploration.

Ebony

Table 30-1

NATURAL RADIOACTIVE NUCLIDES
WITH ATOMIC NUMBERS LESS THAN 83

Nuclide	Abundance in natural element (%)	Half-life (years)	Nuclide	Abundance in natural element (%)	Half-life (years)
$^{40}_{19}K$	0.0118	1.3×10^9	$^{148}_{62}Sm$	11.24	1.2×10^{13}
$^{48}_{20}Ca$	0.18	2×10^{16}	$^{149}_{62}Sm$	13.83	4×10^{14}
$^{50}_{23}V$	0.24	6×10^{14}	$^{152}_{64}Gd$	0.200	1.1×10^{14}
$^{87}_{37}Rb$	27.85	4.7×10^{10}	$^{176}_{71}Lu$	2.59	2.1×10^{10}
$^{115}_{49}In$	95.72	6×10^{14}	$^{174}_{72}Hf$	0.18	4.3×10^{15}
$^{138}_{57}La$	0.089	1.1×10^{11}	$^{187}_{75}Re$	62.93	7×10^{10}
$^{142}_{58}Ce$	11.07	5×10^{15}	$^{190}_{78}Pt$	0.0127	7×10^{11}
$^{144}_{60}Nd$	23.85	5×10^{15}	$^{192}_{78}Pt$	0.78	10^{15}
$^{147}_{62}Sm$	14.97	1.1×10^{11}	$^{204}_{82}Pb$	1.48	1.4×10^{19}

are radioactive. However, only polonium, radon, radium, actinium, thorium, protactinium, and uranium have any natural radioactive nuclides. The rest of the elements beyond bismuth have only radioactive nuclides that have been artificially produced.

One important natural radioactive nuclide is the noble gas radon-222. Radon-222 is given off when radium atoms decay. It is collected in tubes and used instead of radium for the treatment of disease.

30.5   Nature of the radiation

The radiation given off by such radioactive elements as uranium, thorium, and radium is complex. It consists of three different kinds of particles and rays.

1. The α (alpha) particles are helium nuclei. Their mass is nearly four times that of a protium atom. They have a +2 charge, and move at speeds that are near one-tenth the speed of light. They have low penetrating ability mainly because of their relatively low speed. A thin sheet of aluminum foil or a sheet of paper stops them. However, they burn flesh and ionize air easily.

2. The β (beta) particles are electrons. They travel at speeds near the speed of light, with penetrating ability about 100 times greater than that of alpha particles.

3. The γ (gamma) rays are high-energy electromagnetic waves. They are the same kind of radiation as visible light, but of much shorter wavelength and higher frequency. Gamma rays can be produced when nuclear particles undergo transitions in nuclear energy levels. They are the most penetrating of the radiations given off by radioactive elements. Alpha and beta particles are seldom, if ever, given off at the same time from the same nucleus. Gamma rays, however, are often produced along with either alpha or beta particles.

Figure 30-5 shows the effect of a powerful magnetic field on the complex radiation given off by a small particle of radioactive material. The field is perpendicular to the plane of the paper. The heavy alpha particles are deflected slightly in one direction. The lighter beta particles are deflected more sharply in the opposite direction. The gamma rays, being uncharged, are not affected by the magnet.

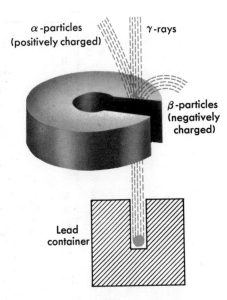

Fig. 30-5. The effect of a magnet on the different types of radiations. The north pole of the magnet is toward the reader and the south pole is away from the reader.

30.6 Decay of atoms of radioactive elements

Radioactive nuclides decay spontaneously, yielding energy. At first it was believed that they did not lose mass and would give off energy forever. However, more careful investigation proved that radioactive materials do lose mass slowly. The presence of electrons and helium nuclei among the radiations is evidence for the loss of mass.

A long series of experiments has shown that this energy results from the decay of nuclei of radium-226 and other radioactive nuclides. Alpha and beta particles are products of such nuclear decay. Certain heavy nuclei break down spontaneously into simpler and lighter nuclei, releasing enormous quantities of energy.

30.7 A series of related radioactive nuclides

All naturally occurring radioactive nuclides belong to one of three series of related nuclides. The heaviest nuclides of these series are called *parent* nuclides. They are, respectively, uranium-238, uranium-235, and thorium-232. Since radium-226 is in the series which has uranium-238 as its parent, let us trace this decay series. The various nuclear changes are charted in Figure 30-6.

The nucleus of a uranium-238 atom contains 92 protons (the atomic number of uranium is 92). It has a mass number (number of protons + number of neutrons) of 238. As this nucleus decays, it emits an alpha particle which becomes an atom of helium when its positive charge is neutralized. An alpha particle has a mass number of 4. Since it contains two protons, it has an atomic number of 2. The remainder of the uranium nucleus thus has an atomic number of 90 and a mass number of 234. This nuclide is

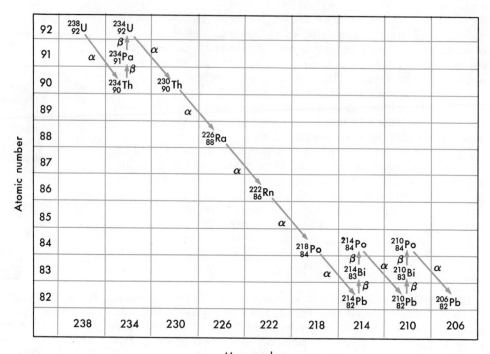

Atomic number

Mass number

Fig. 30-6. The parent element of the uranium decay series is $^{238}_{92}U$. The final element of the series is $^{206}_{82}Pb$.

an isotope of thorium. The *nuclear equation* for this *transmutation reaction* can be written:

$$^{238}_{92}U \rightarrow ^{234}_{90}Th + ^{4}_{2}He$$

A transmutation is a change in the identity of a nucleus because of a change in the number of its protons. Since the above equation is a nuclear equation, only nuclei are represented. The superscript is the mass number. The subscript is the atomic number. Alpha particles are represented as helium nuclei, $^{4}_{2}He$. The total of the mass numbers on the left must equal the total of the mass numbers on the right. The total of the atomic numbers on the left side of the equation must equal the total of the atomic numbers on the right side of the equation.

The half-life of $^{234}_{90}Th$ is about 24 days. It decays by giving off beta particles. The loss of a beta particle from a nucleus increases the number of positive charges in the nucleus (the atomic number) by one. The beta particle is believed to be formed by the change of a neutron into a proton and beta particle (electron). Since the mass of the lost beta particle is so small that it may be neglected, the mass number of the resulting nuclide stays the same.

$$^{234}_{90}Th \rightarrow ^{234}_{91}Pa + ^{0}_{-1}e$$

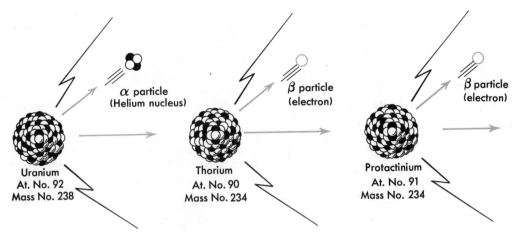

Uranium
At. No. 92
Mass No. 238

α particle
(Helium nucleus)

Thorium
At. No. 90
Mass No. 234

β particle
(electron)

Protactinium
At. No. 91
Mass No. 234

β particle
(electron)

Fig. 30-7. This diagram shows successive alpha and beta particle emissions in the decay of $^{238}_{92}U$.

The symbol $_{-1}^{0}e$ represents an electron with an atomic number of -1 and a mass number of 0. $^{234}_{91}Pa$ is an isotope of protactinium. This nuclide decays by releasing beta particles and producing $^{234}_{92}U$.

$$^{234}_{91}Pa \rightarrow \ ^{234}_{92}U + \ _{-1}^{0}e$$

The $^{234}_{92}U$ nuclide decays by giving off alpha particles.

$$^{234}_{92}U \rightarrow \ ^{230}_{90}Th + \ ^{4}_{2}He$$

The isotope of thorium produced also emits alpha particles, forming radium-226.

$$^{230}_{90}Th \rightarrow \ ^{226}_{88}Ra + \ ^{4}_{2}He$$

Now we can see why ores of uranium contain radium. Radium is one of the products of the decay of uranium atoms. The rates of decay of $^{238}_{92}U$ and of $^{226}_{88}Ra$ determine the proportion of uranium atoms to radium atoms in uranium ores.

The decay of $^{226}_{88}Ra$ proceeds according to the chart shown in Figure 30-6. The $^{226}_{88}Ra$ nuclide decays by giving off alpha particles, forming radon-222 as shown by the nuclear equation:

$$^{226}_{88}Ra \rightarrow \ ^{222}_{86}Rn + \ ^{4}_{2}He$$

The $^{222}_{86}Rn$ nuclei are unstable and have a half-life of about four days. They decay by giving off alpha particles.

$$^{222}_{86}Rn \rightarrow \ ^{218}_{84}Po + \ ^{4}_{2}He$$

The remaining atomic number and mass number changes shown on the decay chart are also explained in terms of the particles given off. When it loses alpha particles, $^{210}_{84}Po$ forms $^{206}_{82}Pb$. This is a stable, nonradioactive, isotope of lead. Thus, a series of spontaneous transmutations begins with $^{238}_{92}U$. It passes through $^{226}_{88}Ra$ and continues on down to $^{206}_{82}Pb$. These transmutations occur continuously and at unchangeable rates.

30.8 Applications of natural radioactivity

The age of any mineral containing radioactive substances can be estimated fairly accurately. Such an estimate is based on the fact that radioactive substances decay at known rates. The mineral is analyzed to determine the amount of long-lived parent nuclide and the amounts of shorter-lived *daughter* nuclides in the sample. Then, by calculation, scientists can determine how long it must have taken for these amounts of daughter nuclides to be produced. This time is assumed to be the age of the mineral. By this method the oldest known minerals on earth have been estimated to be about 3 billion years old. Dust from sites of moon landings has been found to be about 4.6 billion years old. The ages of moon rocks range from 3.2 to 4.1 billion years.

Some carbon atoms involved in the oxygen-carbon dioxide cycle of living plants and animals are radioactive. Radioactive $^{14}_{6}C$ is continuously being produced from $^{14}_{7}N$ atoms in the atmosphere. This change is brought about by the action of *cosmic rays*. (Cosmic rays are protons and other nuclei of very high energy. These particles come to the earth from outer space.) when living things die, the oxygen-carbon dioxide cycle no longer operates in them. They no longer replace carbon atoms in their cells with other carbon atoms. Thus, the level of radioactivity produced by the radioactive carbon in a given amount of non-living material slowly diminishes.

Carbon from a wooden beam taken from the tomb of an Egyptian pharaoh yields about half the radiation of carbon in living trees. The half-life of a $^{14}_{6}C$ atom is about 5600 years. Thus, the age of dead wood with half the radioactivity of living wood is about 5600 years. Objects up to about 30,000 years old have been dated by the use of this method.

ARTIFICIAL RADIOACTIVITY

30.9 Stability of a nucleus

On the atomic mass scale, the isotope of carbon with six protons and six neutrons in its nucleus is defined as having an *atomic mass* of exactly 12. (See Section 3.11.) On this scale, a $^{4}_{2}He$ nucleus has a mass of 4.0015. The mass of a proton is 1.0073 and the mass of a neutron is 1.0087. A $^{4}_{2}He$ nucleus contains two protons and two neutrons. Thus, we might expect its mass to be the combined mass of these four particles, 4.0320. [2(1.0073) + 2(1.0087) = 4.0320.] Note that there is a *difference* of 0.0305 atomic mass unit between the measured mass, 4.0015, and the calculated mass, 4.0320, of a $^{4}_{2}He$ nucleus. *This difference in mass is called the* **nuclear mass defect.** *The mass defect, converted into energy units by using Einstein's equation, $E = mc^2$ (see Section 1.11), is the energy released when a nucleus is* formed from the particles that compose it. This energy is generally referred to as the **binding energy.**

Calculations of binding energies of the atoms of the elements show that the lightest and the heaviest elements have the smallest binding energies per nuclear particle. Elements having intermediate atomic weights have the greatest binding energies per nuclear particle. The elements with the greatest binding energies per nuclear particle are the ones with the most stable nuclei. Therefore, the nuclei of the lightest and heaviest atoms are less stable than the nuclei of elements having intermediate atomic weights.

There are factors other than mass that are associated with the stability of atomic nuclei. These are the *ratio of neutrons to protons* and the *even-odd nature* of the number of neutrons and protons.

Many properties of nuclear particles indicate that energy levels exist *within* the atomic nucleus. Among atoms having low atomic numbers, the most stable nuclei are those whose proton to neutron ratio is 1:1. Nuclei with a greater number of neutrons than protons have lower binding energies and are less stable. In nuclei with an equal number of protons and neutrons, these particles apparently occupy the lowest energy levels in the nucleus. In this way, they give it stability. However, in nuclei that contain an excess of neutrons over protons, some of the neutrons seem to occupy higher energy levels, reducing the

Fig. 30-8. This graph shows the relationship between binding energy per nuclear particle and mass number.

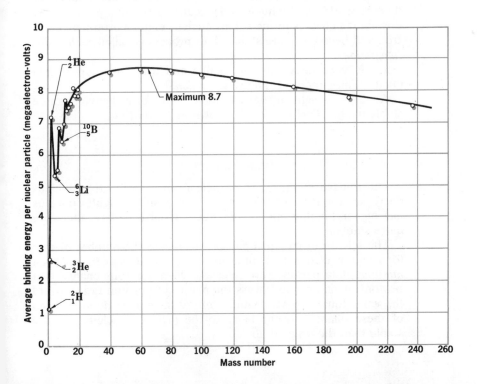

binding energy and consequently lowering the stability of the nucleus.

As the atomic number increases, the most stable nuclei have a neutron to proton ratio greater than 1:1. For example, $^{127}_{53}I$ with a $\frac{neutron}{proton}$ ratio of $\frac{74}{53}$ (about 1.40:1) is stable. On the other hand, $^{126}_{53}I$ $\left(\frac{73}{53}\right)$, $^{128}_{53}I$ $\left(\frac{75}{53}\right)$, and all other isotopes of iodine, are radioactive. The stable end-product of the uranium decay series is $^{206}_{82}Pb$. It has a $\frac{neutron}{proton}$ ratio of $\frac{124}{82}$ (about 1.51:1).

The even-odd relationship of the number of protons to the number of neutrons affects the stability of a nucleus. By far the greatest number of stable nuclei have even numbers of both protons and neutrons. Less often, stable nuclei have an even number of protons and an odd number of neutrons, or vice versa. Only a few stable nuclei are known which have odd numbers of both protons and neutrons.

Because of the difference in stability of different nuclei, there are four types of nuclear reactions. In each type, a small amount of the mass of the reactants is converted into energy, forming products of greater stability.

1. A nucleus undergoes ***radioactive decay***. The nucleus releases an alpha or beta particle and gamma rays, forming a slightly lighter, more stable nucleus.

2. A nucleus is bombarded with alpha particles, protons, deuterons (deuterium nuclei, ^2_1H), neutrons, or other particles. An unstable nucleus is formed. This nucleus emits a proton or a neutron and becomes more stable. This process is called ***nuclear disintegration***.

3. A very heavy nucleus splits and forms medium-weight nuclei. This process is known as ***fission***.

4. Light-weight nuclei combine and form heavier, more stable nuclei. This process is known as ***fusion***.

30.10   Stable nuclei from radioactive decay

The release of an alpha particle from a radioactive nucleus decreases the mass of the nucleus. The resulting lighter nucleus has higher binding energy per nuclear particle. It is therefore more stable.

The release of an alpha particle decreases the number of protons and neutrons in a nucleus *equally and also by an even number*. Beta particles are released when neutrons change into protons. This change lowers the neutron-to-proton ratio toward the value found for stable nuclei of the same mass number. Both of these changes occur because the product nucleus is more stable than the original nucleus.

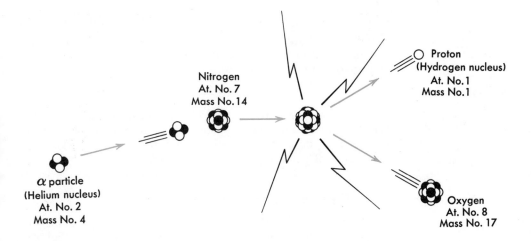

Nitrogen
At. No. 7
Mass No. 14

Proton
(Hydrogen nucleus)
At. No. 1
Mass No. 1

α particle
(Helium nucleus)
At. No. 2
Mass No. 4

Oxygen
At. No. 8
Mass No. 17

Fig. 30-9. This diagram shows the historic nuclear disintegration performed by Rutherford.

30.11   The first nuclear disintegration

After scientists discovered how uranium and radium undergo natural decay and transmutation, they worked to produce man-made transmutations. They had to find a way to add protons to a nucleus of an atom of an element, converting it to the nucleus of an atom of a different element. In 1919, Rutherford produced the first nuclear disintegration. His method involved bombarding nitrogen with alpha particles from radium. He obtained protons (hydrogen nuclei) and a stable isotope of oxygen. This first nuclear disintegration is represented by the following equation:

$$^{14}_{7}\text{N} + {}^{4}_{2}\text{He} \rightarrow {}^{17}_{8}\text{O} + {}^{1}_{1}\text{H}$$

30.12   Proofs of Einstein's equation

In 1932 two English scientists, J. D. Cockcroft (1897–1967), and E. T. S. Walton (b. 1903), experimentally proved Einstein's equation, $E = mc^2$. They bombarded lithium with high-speed protons. Alpha particles and a very large amount of energy were produced.

$$^{7}_{3}\text{Li} + {}^{1}_{1}\text{H} \rightarrow {}^{4}_{2}\text{He} + {}^{4}_{2}\text{He} + \textbf{energy}$$

There is a loss of matter in this reaction. One lithium nucleus (mass 7.0144) was hit by a proton (mass 1.0073). These formed two alpha particles (helium nuclei) each having a mass of 4.0015. Calculation, $(7.0144 + 1.0073) - 2(4.0015)$, shows that there is a loss of 0.0187 atomic mass unit. Cockcroft and Walton found that the energy released very nearly equaled that predicted by Einstein for such a loss in mass. Later experiments have further supported Einstein's equation.

30.13   Neutron emission in some nuclear disintegrations

We have already stated that neutrons were discovered by Chadwick in 1932. He first detected them in an experiment which involved bombarding beryllium with alpha particles:

$$^{9}_{4}\text{Be} + ^{4}_{2}\text{He} \rightarrow ^{12}_{6}\text{C} + ^{1}_{0}\text{n}$$

The symbol for a neutron is $^{1}_{0}\text{n}$. This symbol indicates a particle with zero atomic number (no protons) and a mass number of 1. The reaction described above proved that neutrons were a second type of particle in the nuclei of atoms.

30.14   The cyclotron and other "atom smashers"

Radium was used as a natural source of alpha particles in many early experiments. However, radium is not very efficient in producing nuclear changes. As a result, scientists sought more effective ways of producing high-energy particles for bombarding nuclei. This search resulted in the development of many large electric devices for accelerating charged particles.

The *cyclotron* was invented by Dr. E. O. Lawrence (1901–1958) of the University of California. It consists of a cylindrical box placed between the poles of a huge electromagnet. Air is pumped out of the box until a high vacuum is produced. The "bullets" used to bombard nuclei are usually protons or deuterons. They are introduced into the cylindrical box through its center.

Inside the box are two hollow, D-shaped electrodes called *dees*. These dees are connected through an oscillator to a source of very high voltage. When the cyclotron is in operation, the oscillator reverses the electric charge on the dees very rapidly. The combined effects of the high-voltage alternating potential and the electromagnetic field cause the protons or deuterons inside to move in a spiral course. They move faster and faster as they near the outside of the box, gaining more and more energy. When they reach the outer rim of the box, they are deflected toward the target. The energy of particles accelerated in a simple cyclotron may reach 15,000,000 electron-volts. This is the energy an electron would have if it were accelerated across a potential difference of 1.5×10^{7} volts. By studying the fragments of atoms formed by bombardment, scientists have learned a great deal about atomic structure. They also have discovered much about the products formed when atoms disintegrate. Other machines for bombarding atomic nuclei are the *synchrotron*, the *betatron*, and the *linear accelerator*.

The synchrotron works much like the cyclotron. By varying both the oscillating voltage and the magnetic field, particles are accelerated in a narrow circular path rather than in a spiral. A synchrotron can give an energy of more than 500 billion electron-volts to the protons it accelerates. The betatron ac-

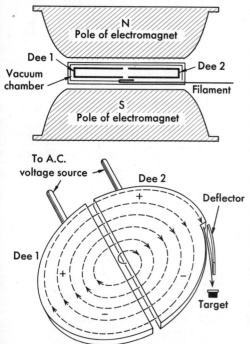

Fig. 30-10. A diagram of the cyclotron used to produce "atomic bullets" of very high energy.

Brookhaven National Laboratory

celerates electrons rather than positively charged particles. The accelerated electrons can be used as "bullets" for bombardment or for producing high-energy X rays. Still another type of particle accelerator is the linear accelerator. In this device the particles travel in a straight line. They are accelerated by passage through many stages of potential difference.

Fig. 30-11. The 60-inch cyclotron of the Brookhaven National Laboratory.

Brookhaven National Laboratory

Fig. 30-12. A portion of the huge synchrotron at the Brookhaven National Laboratory.

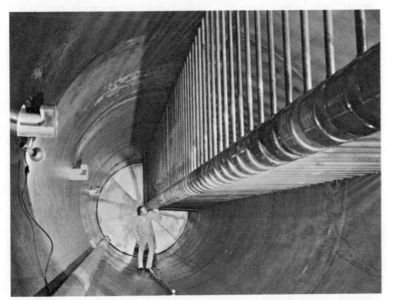

Lawrence Laboratory, Berkeley

Fig. 30-13. An interior view of the powerful linear accelerator at the Lawrence Laboratory, Berkeley, Calif.

30.15 Neutrons as "bullets"

Before the discovery of neutrons in 1932, alpha particles and protons were used in studying atomic nuclei. But alpha particles and protons are charged particles. It requires great quantities of energy to "fire" these charged "bullets" into a nucleus. Their positive charge causes them to be repelled by the positive nuclear charge. The various kinds of particle accelerators were developed to give charged "bullets" enough energy to overcome this repelling force.

When accelerated positive particles from an atom smasher strike a target material, usually lithium or beryllium, neutrons are produced. Neutrons have no charge. Thus, there is no repelling force, and they can easily penetrate the nucleus of an atom. Some fast neutrons may go through an atom without causing any change in it. Other fast neutrons, however, may cause nuclear disintegration. Slow neutrons, on the other hand, are sometimes trapped by a nucleus. This nucleus is then unstable, and may break apart. Fast neutrons are slowed down by passage through materials composed of elements of low atomic weight. Examples are deuterium oxide or graphite.

30.16 Man-made elements from neutron bombardment

The $^{238}_{92}\text{U}$ nuclide is the most plentiful isotope of uranium. When hit by slow neutrons, a $^{238}_{92}\text{U}$ nucleus may capture a neutron. This capture produces the nucleus of an atom of an unstable isotope of uranium, $^{239}_{92}\text{U}$. This nucleus emits a beta particle. In doing so, it becomes the nucleus of an atom of a man-made radioactive element, neptunium. Neptunium has atomic number 93.

$$^{238}_{92}\text{U} + ^{1}_{0}\text{n} \rightarrow ^{239}_{92}\text{U}$$

$$^{239}_{92}\text{U} \rightarrow ^{239}_{93}\text{Np} + ^{0}_{-1}\text{e}$$

Neptunium is itself an unstable element. The nucleus of a neptunium atom gives off a beta particle. This change produces the nucleus of an atom of still another man-made element, plutonium, atomic number 94.

$$^{239}_{93}\text{Np} \rightarrow ^{239}_{94}\text{Pu} + ^{0}_{-1}\text{e}$$

Neptunium and plutonium were the first man-made *transuranium* elements. **Transuranium elements** are those with more than 92 protons in their nuclei. As this is written, thirteen artificially prepared transuranium elements have been reported. In addition to neptunium and plutonium, there are americium, curium, berkelium, californium, einsteinium, fermium, mendelevium, nobelium, lawrencium, kurchatovium or ruther-

Table 30–2

REACTIONS FOR THE FIRST PREPARATION
OF TRANSURANIUM ELEMENTS

Atomic number	Name	Symbol	Nuclear reaction
93	neptunium	Np	$^{238}_{92}U + ^{1}_{0}n \rightarrow ^{239}_{93}Np + ^{0}_{-1}e$
94	plutonium	Pu	$^{238}_{92}U + ^{2}_{1}H \rightarrow ^{238}_{93}Np + 2^{1}_{0}n$
			$^{238}_{93}Np \rightarrow ^{238}_{94}Pu + ^{0}_{-1}e$
95	americium	Am	$^{239}_{94}Pu + 2^{1}_{0}n \rightarrow ^{241}_{95}Am + ^{0}_{-1}e$
96	curium	Cm	$^{239}_{94}Pu + ^{4}_{2}He \rightarrow ^{242}_{96}Cm + ^{1}_{0}n$
97	berkelium	Bk	$^{241}_{95}Am + ^{4}_{2}He \rightarrow ^{243}_{97}Bk + 2^{1}_{0}n$
98	californium	Cf	$^{242}_{96}Cm + ^{4}_{2}He \rightarrow ^{245}_{98}Cf + ^{1}_{0}n$
99	einsteinium	Es	$^{238}_{92}U + 15^{1}_{0}n \rightarrow ^{253}_{99}Es + 7^{0}_{-1}e$
100	fermium	Fm	$^{238}_{92}U + 17^{1}_{0}n \rightarrow ^{255}_{100}Fm + 8^{0}_{-1}e$
101	mendelevium	Md	$^{253}_{99}Es + ^{4}_{2}He \rightarrow ^{256}_{101}Md + ^{1}_{0}n$
102	nobelium	No	$^{246}_{96}Cm + ^{12}_{6}C \rightarrow ^{254}_{102}No + 4^{1}_{0}n$
103	lawrencium	Lr	$^{252}_{98}Cf + ^{10}_{5}B \rightarrow ^{258}_{103}Lr + 4^{1}_{0}n$
104	kurchatovium	Ku	$^{242}_{94}Pu + ^{22}_{10}Ne \rightarrow ^{260}_{104}Ku + 4^{1}_{0}n$
104	rutherfordium	Rf	$^{249}_{98}Cf + ^{12}_{6}C \rightarrow ^{257}_{104}Rf + 4^{1}_{0}n$
105	hahnium	Ha	$^{249}_{98}Cf + ^{15}_{7}N \rightarrow ^{260}_{105}Ha + 4^{1}_{0}n$

fordium, and hahnium. All of these were prepared by bombarding the nuclei of uranium or more complex atoms with neutrons, alpha particles, or other "nuclear bullets." See Table 30-2.

30.17   Artificial radioactive atoms

In 1934, Madame Curie's daughter Irène (1897–1956) and her husband Frédéric Joliot (1900–1958) discovered that stable atoms can be made radioactive by artificial means. This occurs when they are bombarded with deuterons or neutrons. Radioactive isotopes of all the elements have been prepared. For example, radioactive $^{60}_{27}Co$ can be produced from natural non-

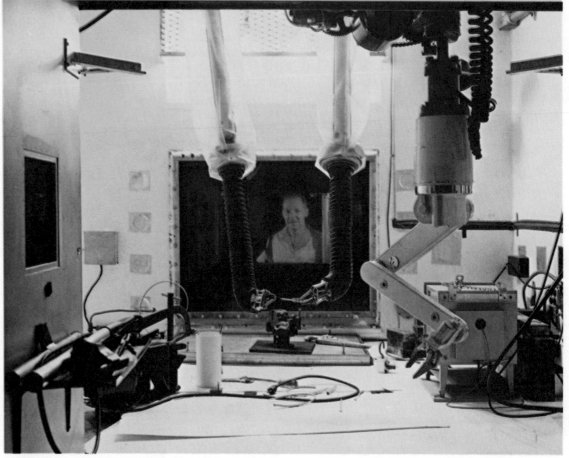

Fig. 30-14. Radioactive materials are handled by remote control in specially designed and shielded "cells."

radioactive $^{59}_{27}Co$ by slow-neutron bombardment. The nuclear equation is:

$$^{59}_{27}\text{Co} + ^{1}_{0}\text{n} \rightarrow ^{60}_{27}\text{Co}$$

The radiation from $^{60}_{27}Co$ consists of beta particles and gamma rays.

Radioactive $^{32}_{15}P$ is prepared by bombardment of $^{32}_{16}S$ with slow neutrons:

$$^{32}_{16}\text{S} + ^{1}_{0}\text{n} \rightarrow ^{32}_{15}\text{P} + ^{1}_{1}\text{H}$$

The radiation from $^{32}_{15}P$ consists only of beta particles.

Radioactive phosphorus, radioactive cobalt, and some other radioactive elements are used to treat certain forms of cancer. Also, many radioactive isotopes are used as *tracers*. Using them, scientists can determine the course of chemical reactions, the cleaning ability of detergents, the wearing ability of various products, the efficiency of fertilizers, and the flow of fluids through pipelines. Many new radioactive isotopes are made by slow-neutron bombardment in the nuclear reactor at Oak Ridge, Tennessee.

30.18   Fission of $^{235}_{92}$U

The element uranium exists as three naturally occurring iso-
topes, $^{238}_{92}$U, $^{235}_{92}$U, and $^{234}_{92}$U. Most uranium is the nuclide $^{238}_{92}$U.
Only 0.7% of natural uranium is $^{235}_{92}$U. The nuclide $^{234}_{92}$U occurs
in only the slightest traces. We have already stated that transuranium elements can be produced when $^{238}_{92}$U is bombarded
with slow neutrons. However, when $^{235}_{92}$U is bombarded with slow
neutrons, each atom may capture one of the neutrons. This extra
neutron in the nucleus makes it very unstable. Instead of giving
off an alpha or beta particle, as in other radioactive changes, the
nucleus splits into medium-weight parts. Neutrons are usually
produced during this *fission*. There is a small loss of mass, which
appears as a great amount of energy. One equation for the fission
of $^{235}_{92}$U is

$$^{235}_{92}\text{U} + ^{1}_{0}\text{n} \rightarrow \ ^{138}_{56}\text{Ba} + ^{95}_{36}\text{Kr} + 3^{1}_{0}\text{n} + \textbf{energy}$$

The atomic mass of $^{235}_{92}$U is slightly greater than 235. The atomic
masses of the unstable barium and krypton isotopes are slightly
less than 138 and 95 respectively. Thus, the masses of the reactants and the masses of the products are not equal. Instead,
about 0.2 atomic mass unit of mass is converted to energy for
each uranium atom undergoing fission. Plutonium, made from
$^{238}_{92}$U, also undergoes fission and produces more neutrons when
bombarded with slow neutrons.

30.19   Nuclear chain reaction

*A **chain reaction** is one in which the material or energy which
starts the reaction is also one of the products.* The fissions of
$^{235}_{92}$U and $^{239}_{94}$Pu can produce chain reactions. One neutron causes
the fission of one $^{235}_{92}$U nucleus. Two or three neutrons are given
off when this fission occurs. These neutrons can cause the fission
of other $^{235}_{92}$U nuclei. Again neutrons are emitted. These can
cause the fission of still other $^{235}_{92}$U nuclei. This is a chain reaction.
It continues until all the $^{235}_{92}$U atoms have split or until the neutrons fail to strike $^{235}_{92}$U nuclei. This is what happens in an uncon-
trolled chain reaction such as the explosion of a nuclear warhead.

30.20   Action in a nuclear reactor

*A **nuclear reactor** is a device in which the controlled fission of
radioactive material produces new radioactive substances and
energy.* One of the earliest nuclear reactors was built at Oak
Ridge, Tennessee, in 1943. This reactor uses natural uranium.
It has a lattice-type structure with blocks of graphite forming
the framework. Spaced between the blocks of graphite are rods
of uranium, encased in aluminum cans for protection. *Control
rods* of neutron-absorbing boron steel are inserted into the lattice
to limit the number of free neutrons. The reactor is air cooled.

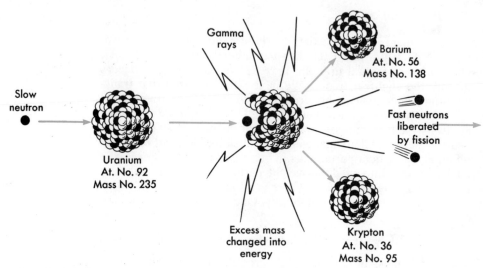

Fig. 30-15. Neutrons from fission of a $^{235}_{92}$U nucleus, when slowed down by a carbon moderator, can cause fission in a second $^{235}_{92}$U nucleus. This process makes a chain reaction possible.

Fig. 30-16. A cutaway view of the Oak Ridge reactor.

The rods of uranium or uranium oxide are the *nuclear fuel* for the reactor. The energy released in the reactor comes from changes in the uranium nuclei. Graphite is said to be the *moderator,* because it slows down the fast neutrons produced by fission. By doing so, it makes them more readily captured by a nucleus, and thus more effective for producing additional nuclear

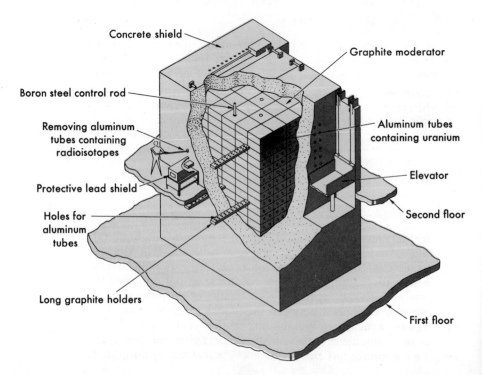

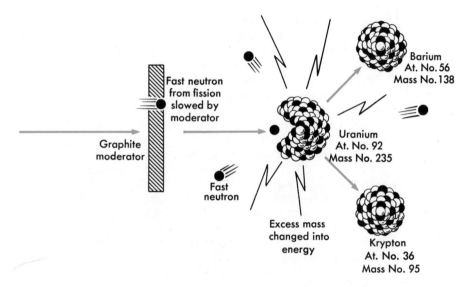

changes. The amount of uranium in such a reactor is important. Enough uranium must be present to provide the number of neutrons needed to sustain a chain reaction. This quantity of uranium is called the *critical size*.

Two types of reactions occur in the fuel in such a reactor. Neutrons cause $^{235}_{92}$U nuclei to undergo fission. The fast neutrons from this fission are slowed down as they pass through the graphite. Some strike other $^{235}_{92}$U nuclei and continue the chain reaction. Other neutrons strike $^{238}_{92}$U nuclei, starting the changes which finally produce plutonium. Great quantities of energy are released. For this reason, the reactor has to be cooled continuously by blowing air through tubes in the lattice. The rate of the reaction is controlled by the insertion or removal of the neutron-absorbing control rods. This type of reactor is now used to produce radioactive isotopes.

30.21   Fusion reactions

We have stated that nuclear stability can be increased by combining light-weight nuclei into heavier nuclei. This process was defined as *fusion*.

Fusion reactions are the source of the sun's energy. It is believed that there are two series of such reactions going on in the sun. One series occurs at the very hot center of the sun, while the other takes place in the cooler outer portion of the sun. These two reactions proceed by different pathways. However, their net effect is the combination of four hydrogen nuclei into a helium nucleus. A loss of mass occurs and a tremendous amount of energy is released.

The thermonuclear bomb, sometimes called the hydrogen bomb, or H-bomb, produces energy by a fusion reaction. More energy is released per gram of fuel in a fusion reaction than in a fission reaction. For this reason, the H-bomb is much more destructive than the atomic bomb, a fission bomb. Also, the quantities of reacting materials can be made much larger. In theory, there is no limit to the amount of reactants that can be used. Fusion reactions are not chain reactions and thus do not require a critical size of reacting materials.

One possible reaction in a hydrogen bomb involves the formation of alpha particles and tremendous energy from a specific lithium hydride. This special compound may be formed from lithium-6 and deuterium and have the formula $_3^6 \text{Li} _1^2 \text{H}$. Such a fusion reaction can be started only by placing $_3^6 \text{Li} _1^2 \text{H}$ under extremely high temperature and pressure. These conditions are created by using an atomic bomb to set off the hydrogen bomb.

Current research indicates that fusion reactions may be controlled. If so, such reactions may some day be used to produce electric power.

QUESTIONS

Group A

1. (*a*) Who discovered radioactivity? (*b*) How was the discovery made?
2. What evidence led Pierre and Marie Curie to suspect that there were radioactive elements other than uranium in pitchblende?
3. How does the radioactivity of radium compare with that of uranium?
4. What practical use is made of the fluorescence produced in zinc sulfide by a radium compound?
5. What is meant by the *half-life* of a radioactive nuclide?
6. From what part of a radioactive nuclide do the alpha or beta particles come?
7. What change in identity and mass number occurs when a radioactive nuclide gives off an alpha particle?
8. What change in identity and mass number occurs when a radioactive nuclide gives off a beta particle?
9. How is the age of a radioactive mineral estimated?
10. Name the four types of nuclear reactions which produce more stable nuclei.
11. In what ways does natural radioactive decay produce more stable nuclei?
12. How were neutrons first detected as nuclear particles?
13. Why are neutrons more effective particles than protons or alpha particles for bombarding atomic nuclei?
14. What may happen to a neutron that is fired at the nucleus of an atom?
15. For what purposes are radioactive isotopes used?
16. (*a*) What are the naturally occurring isotopes of uranium? (*b*) What is their relative abundance?
17. (*a*) What is fission? (*b*) How is it produced in $_{92}^{235} \text{U}$?
18. What is meant by the *critical size* of a reactor?
19. Why must a nuclear reactor be continually cooled?
20. (*a*) What reaction produces the sun's energy? (*b*) To what man-made reaction is this similar?

21. Why is radium studied separately rather than with the other elements of Group II?
22. Explain why the radioactivity of a nuclide is not affected by other nuclides with which it may be chemically combined.
23. Why can the radiation from a radioactive material affect photographic film, even though the film is well wrapped in black paper?
24. How does a radioactive material affect the rate of discharge of an electroscope?
25. Where are most of the radioactive nuclides found in the periodic table?
26. Give the mass, nature, and approximate speed of: (a) alpha particles; (b) beta particles.
27. What do scientists believe gamma rays to be?
28. Write the nuclear equation for the release of an alpha particle by $^{226}_{88}$Ra.
29. Write the nuclear equation for the release of a beta particle by $^{214}_{82}$Pb.
30. Write nuclear equations for successive releases of an alpha particle and a beta particle from $^{214}_{84}$Po.
31. (a) Which kinds of elements have the smallest binding energy per nuclear particle? (b) Which kind has the largest binding energy per nuclear particle? (c) How does the binding energy per nuclear particle affect the stability of a nucleus?
32. What factors affect the stability of a nucleus?
33. How does each type of nuclear reaction produce more stable nuclei?
34. (a) Who produced the first nuclear disintegration? (b) Write the equation for this reaction.
35. How was Einstein's equation for the relationship between matter and energy, $E = mc^2$, proved to be correct?
36. (a) Describe the path of the accelerated particles in a cyclotron. (b) What causes them to take this path?
37. Explain the changes occurring in the nucleus by which $^{239}_{94}$Pu is produced from $^{238}_{92}$U.
38. (a) How are artificially radioactive isotopes prepared? (b) Write a nuclear equation to show the preparation of such a nuclide. (c) What use is made of the nuclide whose preparation you have shown in this nuclear equation?
39. (a) Describe a chain reaction. (b) How does the fission of $^{235}_{92}$U produce a chain reaction?
40. How is a uranium-graphite reactor constructed?

APPENDIX

Table 1
METRIC-ENGLISH EQUIVALENTS

English to Metric	*Metric to English*
1 in = 2.54 cm = 2.54×10^{-2} m	1 cm = 0.3937 in = 3.281×10^{-2} ft
1 ft = 30.5 cm = 0.305 m	1 m = 39.37 in = 3.218 ft = 1.094 yd
1 yd = 91.4 cm = 0.914 m	1 cm^3 = 0.0610 in^3 = 3.53×10^{-5} ft^3
1 qt = 946 ml = 0.946 liter	1 liter = 1.06 qt = 3.53×10^{-2} ft^3

Table 2
ISOTOPES OF SOME ELEMENTS

(Naturally occurring nonradioactive isotopes are given in bold type. Naturally occurring radioactive isotopes are in bold-face blue italics. All other radioactive isotopes are in italics. Naturally occurring isotopes are listed in order of their abundance. All other isotopes are listed in order of length of half-life.)

Elements	*Mass Numbers of Isotopes*
H	**1**, **2**, *3*
He	**4**, **3**, *6*, *7*, *5*
Li	**7**, **6**, *8*, *9*, *5*
Be	**9**, *10*, *7*, *11*, *8*, *6*
B	**11**, **10**, *8*, *13*, *12*, *9*
C	**12**, **13**, *14*, *11*, *10*, *15*, *16*
N	**14**, **15**, *13*, *16*, *17*, *12*
O	**16**, **18**, **17**, *15*, *14*, *19*, *20*
F	**19**, *18*, *17*, *20*, *21*, *16*
Ne	**20**, **22**, **21**, *24*, *23*, *19*, *18*
Na	**23**, *22*, *24*, *25*, *21*, *26*, *20*
Mg	**24**, **26**, **25**, *28*, *27*, *23*
Al	**27**, *26*, *28*, *29*, *25*, *30*, *24*, *23*
Si	**28**, **29**, **30**, *32*, *31*, *27*, *26*
P	**31**, *33*, *32*, *30*, *34*, *29*, *28*
S	**32**, **34**, **33**, **36**, *35*, *38*, *37*, *31*, *30*
Cl	**35**, **37**, *36*, *39*, *38*, *40*, *33*, *34*, *32*
Ar	**40**, **36**, **38**. *39*, *42*, *37*, *41*, *35*
K	**39**, **41**, ***40***, *43*, *42*, *44*, *45*, *38*, *37*
Ca	**40**, **44**, **42**, ***48***, **43**, **46**, *41*, *45*, *47*, *49*, *39*, *38*
Cr	**52**, **53**, **50**, **54**, *51*, *48*, *49*, *56*, *55*, *46*, *47*
Fe	**56**, **54**, **57**, **58**, *60*, *55*, *59*, *52*, *53*, *61*
Ni	**58**, **60**, **62**, **61**, **64**, *59*, *63*, *66*, *57*, *56*, *65*
Cu	**63**, **65**, *67*, *64*, *61*, *62*, *66*, *60*, *59*, *68*, *58*
Zn	**64**, **66**, **68**, **67**, **70**, *65*, *72*, *62*, *69*, *63*, *71*, *60*, *61*
Br	**79**, **81**, *77*, *82*, *83*, *76*, *75*, *74*, *84*, *80*, *78*, *85*, *88*, *87*, *89*, *90*
Sr	**88**, **87**, **86**, **84**, *90*, *85*, *89*, *82*, *83*, *91*, *92*, *80*, *81*, *93*, *94*, *95*
Ag	**107**, **109**, *105*, *111*, *113*, *112*, *104*, *103*, *106*, *115*, *102*, *116*, *108*, *117*, *110*, *114*
Sn	**120**, **118**, **116**, **119**, **117**, **124**, **122**, **112**, **114**, **115**, *126*, *113*, *125*, *121*, *110*, *127*, *123*, *111*, *109*, *108*, *129*, *128*, *130*, *132*

Table 2
ISOTOPES OF SOME ELEMENTS (cont'd)

Elements	Mass Numbers of Isotopes
I	**127,** *129, 125, 126, 131, 124, 133, 123, 130, 135, 132, 121, 120, 134, 128, 119, 118, 117, 122, 136, 137, 138, 139*
Ba	**138, 137, 136, 135, 134, 130, 132,** *133, 140, 131, 128, 129, 126, 139, 141, 127, 142, 143*
W	**184, 186, 182, 183, 180,** *181, 185, 188, 178, 187, 177, 176, 179*
Pt	**195, 194, 196, 198,** *192, 190, 193, 188, 191, 197, 200, 189, 184, 186, 187, 199*
Pb	**208, 206, 207,** *204, 205, 202, 210, 203, 200, 212, 201, 209, 198, 199, 196, 211, 214, 195, 194*
Bi	**209,** *208, 207, 205, 206, 210, 203, 204, 202, 201, 212, 213, 200, 199, 214, 215, 196, 211*
Rn	*222, 211, 224, 210, 209, 221, 212, 208, 223, 207, 206, 204, 215, 220, 219, 218, 217, 216*
Ra	*226, 228, 225, 223, 224, 230, 227, 229, 222, 221, 220*
U	*238, 235, 234, 236, 233, 232, 230, 237, 231, 229, 239, 228, 227*
Np	*237, 236, 235, 234, 239, 238, 240, 231, 233, 241, 232*
Pu	*244, 242, 239, 240, 238, 241, 236, 237, 246, 245, 234, 243, 232, 235, 233*
Am	*243, 241, 240, 242, 239, 244, 245, 238, 237, 246, 247*
Cm	*247, 248, 250, 245, 246, 243, 244, 242, 241, 240, 239, 238, 249*
Bk	*247, 248, 249, 245, 246, 243, 244, 250, 251*
Cf	*251, 249, 250, 252, 248, 254, 253, 246, 247, 245, 244, 243, 242*
Es	*254, 252, 255, 253, 251, 250, 249, 256, 248, 246, 247, 245*
Fm	*257, 253, 252, 255, 251, 254, 256, 250, 249, 248, 247, 245, 246, 244*
Md	*258, 257, 256, 255, 252*
No	*255, 253, 254, 257, 256, 252, 251*
Lr	*256, 257, 258, 259*
104	*257, 259, 260*
105	*260*

Table 3
PHYSICAL CONSTANTS

Quantity	Symbol	Value
atomic mass unit	u	1.660531×10^{-24} g
Avogadro number	N_A	6.022169×10^{23}/mole
electron rest mass	m_e	9.109558×10^{-28} g
gas constant	R	8.2057×10^{-2} liter-atm/mole-°K
ideal gas volume at STP	V_0	22.4136 liters/mole
mechanical equivalent of heat	J	4.1868 joules/cal
neutron rest mass	m_n	1.67482×10^{-24} g
Planck's constant	h	6.626196×10^{-34} joule-sec
proton rest mass	m_p	1.672614×10^{-24} g
speed of light in vacuum	c	2.9979250×10^{8} m/sec
temperature of triple point of water		273.16°K = 0.01°C

Table 4

THE ELEMENTS, THEIR SYMBOLS, ATOMIC NUMBERS, AND ATOMIC WEIGHTS

The more common elements are printed in color.

Name of element	Symbol	Atomic number	Atomic weight	Name of element	Symbol	Atomic number	Atomic weight
actinium	Ac	89	[227]	mendelevium	Md	101	[256]
aluminum	Al	13	26.9815	mercury	Hg	80	200.59
americium	Am	95	[243]	molybdenum	Mo	42	95.94
antimony	Sb	51	121.75	neodymium	Nd	60	144.24
argon	Ar	18	39.948	neon	Ne	10	20.179
arsenic	As	33	74.9216	neptunium	Np	93	237.0482
astatine	At	85	[210]	nickel	Ni	28	58.71
barium	Ba	56	137.34	niobium	Nb	41	92.9064
berkelium	Bk	97	[247]	nitrogen	N	7	14.0067
beryllium	Be	4	9.01218	nobelium	No	102	[254]
bismuth	Bi	83	208.9806	osmium	Os	76	190.2
boron	B	5	10.81	oxygen	O	8	15.9994
bromine	Br	35	79.904	palladium	Pd	46	106.4
cadmium	Cd	48	112.40	phosphorus	P	15	30.9738
calcium	Ca	20	40.08	platinum	Pt	78	195.09
californium	Cf	98	[249]	plutonium	Pu	94	[244]
carbon	C	6	12.011	polonium	Po	84	[210]
cerium	Ce	58	140.12	potassium	K	19	39.102
cesium	Cs	55	132.9055	praseodymium	Pr	59	140.9077
chlorine	Cl	17	35.453	promethium	Pm	61	[147]
chromium	Cr	24	51.996	protactinium	Pa	91	231.0359
cobalt	Co	27	58.9332	radium	Ra	88	226.0254
copper	Cu	29	63.546	radon	Rn	86	[222]
curium	Cm	96	[245]	rhenium	Re	75	186.2
dysprosium	Dy	66	162.50	rhodium	Rh	45	102.9055
einsteinium	Es	99	[254]	rubidium	Rb	37	85.4678
erbium	Er	68	167.26	ruthenium	Ru	44	101.07
europium	Eu	63	151.96	rutherfordium	Rf	104	[261]
fermium	Fm	100	[255]	samarium	Sm	62	150.4
fluorine	F	9	18.9984	scandium	Sc	21	44.9559
francium	Fr	87	[223]	selenium	Se	34	78.96
gadolinium	Gd	64	157.25	silicon	Si	14	28.086
gallium	Ga	31	69.72	silver	Ag	47	107.868
germanium	Ge	32	72.59	sodium	Na	11	22.9898
gold	Au	79	196.9665	strontium	Sr	38	87.62
hafnium	Hf	72	178.49	sulfur	S	16	32.06
hahnium	Ha	105	[260]	tantalum	Ta	73	180.9479
helium	He	2	4.00260	technetium	Tc	43	98.9062
holmium	Ho	67	164.9303	tellurium	Te	52	127.60
hydrogen	H	1	1.0080	terbium	Tb	65	158.9254
indium	In	49	114.82	thallium	Tl	81	204.37
iodine	I	53	126.9045	thorium	Th	90	232.0381
iridium	Ir	77	192.22	thulium	Tm	69	168.9342
iron	Fe	26	55.847	tin	Sn	50	118.69
krypton	Kr	36	83.80	titanium	Ti	22	47.90
kurchatovium	Ku	104	[261]	tungsten	W	74	183.85
lanthanum	La	57	138.9055	uranium	U	92	238.029
lawrencium	Lr	103	[257]	vanadium	V	23	50.9414
lead	Pb	82	207.2	xenon	Xe	54	131.30
lithium	Li	3	6.941	ytterbium	Yb	70	173.04
lutetium	Lu	71	174.97	yttrium	Y	39	88.9059
magnesium	Mg	12	24.305	zinc	Zn	30	65.37
manganese	Mn	25	54.9380	zirconium	Zr	40	91.22

A value given in brackets denotes the mass number of the isotope of longest known half-life. The atomic weights of most of these elements are believed to have an error no greater than ±1 in the last digit given.

Table 5
COMMON ELEMENTS

Name	Symbol	Approx. at. wt.	Common ox. nos.	Name	Symbol	Approx. at. wt.	Common ox. nos.
aluminum	Al	27.0	+3	magnesium	Mg	24.3	+2
antimony	Sb	121.8	+3,+5	manganese	Mn	54.9	+2,+4,+7
arsenic	As	74.9	+3,+5	mercury	Hg	200.6	+1,+2
barium	Ba	137.3	+2	nickel	Ni	58.7	+2
bismuth	Bi	209.0	+3	nitrogen	N	14.0	-3,+3,+5
bromine	Br	79.9	-1,+5	oxygen	O	16.0	-2
calcium	Ca	40.1	+2	phosphorus	P	31.0	+3,+5
carbon	C	12.0	+2,+4	platinum	Pt	195.1	+2,+4
chlorine	Cl	35.5	-1,+5,+7	potassium	K	39.1	+1
chromium	Cr	52.0	+2,+3,+6	silicon	Si	28.1	+4
cobalt	Co	58.9	+2,+3	silver	Ag	107.9	+1
copper	Cu	63.5	+1,+2	sodium	Na	23.0	+1
fluorine	F	19.0	-1	strontium	Sr	87.6	+2
gold	Au	197.0	+1,+3	sulfur	S	32.1	-2,+4,+6
hydrogen	H	1.0	-1,+1	tin	Sn	118.7	+2,+4
iodine	I	126.9	-1,+5	titanium	Ti	47.9	+3,+4
iron	Fe	55.8	+2,+3	tungsten	W	183.8	+6
lead	Pb	207.2	+2,+4	zinc	Zn	65.4	+2

Table 6
COMMON IONS AND THEIR CHARGES

Name	Symbol	Charge	Name	Symbol	Charge
aluminum	Al^{+++}	+3	lead(II)	Pb^{++}	+2
ammonium	NH_4^+	+1	magnesium	Mg^{++}	+2
barium	Ba^{++}	+2	mercury(I)	Hg_2^{++}	+2
calcium	Ca^{++}	+2	mercury(II)	Hg^{++}	+2
chromium(III)	Cr^{+++}	+3	nickel(II)	Ni^{++}	+2
cobalt(II)	Co^{++}	+2	potassium	K^+	+1
copper(I)	Cu^+	+1	silver	Ag^+	+1
copper(II)	Cu^{++}	+2	sodium	Na^+	+1
hydronium	H_3O^+	+1	tin(II)	Sn^{++}	+2
iron(II)	Fe^{++}	+2	tin(IV)	Sn^{++++}	+4
iron(III)	Fe^{+++}	+3	zinc	Zn^{++}	+2
acetate	$C_2H_3O_2^-$	-1	hydrogen sulfate	HSO_4^-	-1
bromide	Br^-	-1	hydroxide	OH^-	-1
carbonate	CO_3^{--}	-2	hypochlorite	ClO^-	-1
chlorate	ClO_3^-	-1	iodide	I^-	-1
chloride	Cl^-	-1	nitrate	NO_3^-	-1
chlorite	ClO_2^-	-1	nitrite	NO_2^-	-1
chromate	CrO_4^{--}	-2	oxide	O^{--}	-2
cyanide	CN^-	-1	perchlorate	ClO_4^-	-1
dichromate	$Cr_2O_7^{--}$	-2	permanganate	MnO_4^-	-1
fluoride	F^-	-1	peroxide	O_2^{--}	-2
hexacyanoferrate(II)	$Fe(CN)_6^{----}$	-4	phosphate	PO_4^{---}	-3
hexacyanoferrate(III)	$Fe(CN)_6^{---}$	-3	sulfate	SO_4^{--}	-2
hydride	H^-	-1	sulfide	S^{--}	-2
hydrogen carbonate	HCO_3^-	-1	sulfite	SO_3^{--}	-2

Table 7
ELECTRONIC ARRANGEMENT OF THE ELEMENTS

	Shells	K	L		M			N				O				P				Q
	Sub-levels	1s	2s	2p	3s	3p	3d	4s	4p	4d	4f	5s	5p	5d	5f	6s	6p	6d	6f	7s
1	hydrogen	1																		
2	helium	2																		
3	lithium	2	1																	
4	beryllium	2	2																	
5	boron	2	2	1																
6	carbon	2	2	2																
7	nitrogen	2	2	3																
8	oxygen	2	2	4																
9	fluorine	2	2	5																
10	neon	2	2	6																
11	sodium	2	2	6	1															
12	magnesium	2	2	6	2															
13	aluminum	2	2	6	2	1														
14	silicon	2	2	6	2	2														
15	phosphorus	2	2	6	2	3														
16	sulfur	2	2	6	2	4														
17	chlorine	2	2	6	2	5														
18	argon	2	2	6	2	6														
19	potassium	2	2	6	2	6		1												
20	calcium	2	2	6	2	6		2												
21	scandium	2	2	6	2	6	1	2												
22	titanium	2	2	6	2	6	2	2												
23	vanadium	2	2	6	2	6	3	2												
24	chromium	2	2	6	2	6	5	1												
25	manganese	2	2	6	2	6	5	2												
26	iron	2	2	6	2	6	6	2												
27	cobalt	2	2	6	2	6	7	2												
28	nickel	2	2	6	2	6	8	2												
29	copper	2	2	6	2	6	10	1												
30	zinc	2	2	6	2	6	10	2												
31	gallium	2	2	6	2	6	10	2	1											
32	germanium	2	2	6	2	6	10	2	2											
33	arsenic	2	2	6	2	6	10	2	3											
34	selenium	2	2	6	2	6	10	2	4											
35	bromine	2	2	6	2	6	10	2	5											
36	krypton	2	2	6	2	6	10	2	6											
37	rubidium	2	2	6	2	6	10	2	6			1								
38	strontium	2	2	6	2	6	10	2	6			2								
39	yttrium	2	2	6	2	6	10	2	6	1		2								
40	zirconium	2	2	6	2	6	10	2	6	2		2								
41	niobium	2	2	6	2	6	10	2	6	4		1								
42	molybdenum	2	2	6	2	6	10	2	6	5		1								
43	technetium	2	2	6	2	6	10	2	6	5		2								
44	ruthenium	2	2	6	2	6	10	2	6	7		1								
45	rhodium	2	2	6	2	6	10	2	6	8		1								
46	palladium	2	2	6	2	6	10	2	6	10										
47	silver	2	2	6	2	6	10	2	6	10		1								
48	cadmium	2	2	6	2	6	10	2	6	10		2								
49	indium	2	2	6	2	6	10	2	6	10		2	1							
50	tin	2	2	6	2	6	10	2	6	10		2	2							
51	antimony	2	2	6	2	6	10	2	6	10		2	3							
52	tellurium	2	2	6	2	6	10	2	6	10		2	4							

Table 7

ELECTRONIC ARRANGEMENT OF THE ELEMENTS (cont'd)

Shells		K	L		M			N				O				P				Q
Sub-levels		1s	2s	2p	3s	3p	3d	4s	4p	4d	4f	5s	5p	5d	5f	6s	6p	6d	6f	7s
53	iodine	2	2	6	2	6	10	2	6	10		2	5							
54	xenon	2	2	6	2	6	10	2	6	10		2	6							
55	cesium	2	2	6	2	6	10	2	6	10		2	6			1				
56	barium	2	2	6	2	6	10	2	6	10		2	6			2				
57	lanthanum	2	2	6	2	6	10	2	6	10		2	6	1		2				
58	cerium	2	2	6	2	6	10	2	6	10	2	2	6			2				
59	praseodymium	2	2	6	2	6	10	2	6	10	3	2	6			2				
60	neodymium	2	2	6	2	6	10	2	6	10	4	2	6			2				
61	promethium	2	2	6	2	6	10	2	6	10	5	2	6			2				
62	samarium	2	2	6	2	6	10	2	6	10	6	2	6			2				
63	europium	2	2	6	2	6	10	2	6	10	7	2	6			2				
64	gadolinium	2	2	6	2	6	10	2	6	10	7	2	6	1		2				
65	terbium	2	2	6	2	6	10	2	6	10	9	2	6			2				
66	dysprosium	2	2	6	2	6	10	2	6	10	10	2	6			2				
67	holmium	2	2	6	2	6	10	2	6	10	11	2	6			2				
68	erbium	2	2	6	2	6	10	2	6	10	12	2	6			2				
69	thulium	2	2	6	2	6	10	2	6	10	13	2	6			2				
70	ytterbium	2	2	6	2	6	10	2	6	10	14	2	6			2				
71	lutetium	2	2	6	2	6	10	2	6	10	14	2	6	1		2				
72	hafnium	2	2	6	2	6	10	2	6	10	14	2	6	2		2				
73	tantalum	2	2	6	2	6	10	2	6	10	14	2	6	3		2				
74	tungsten	2	2	6	2	6	10	2	6	10	14	2	6	4		2				
75	rhenium	2	2	6	2	6	10	2	6	10	14	2	6	5		2				
76	osmium	2	2	6	2	6	10	2	6	10	14	2	6	6		2				
77	iridium	2	2	6	2	6	10	2	6	10	14	2	6	7		2				
78	platinum	2	2	6	2	6	10	2	6	10	14	2	6	9		1				
79	gold	2	2	6	2	6	10	2	6	10	14	2	6	10		1				
80	mercury	2	2	6	2	6	10	2	6	10	14	2	6	10		2				
81	thallium	2	2	6	2	6	10	2	6	10	14	2	6	10		2	1			
82	lead	2	2	6	2	6	10	2	6	10	14	2	6	10		2	2			
83	bismuth	2	2	6	2	6	10	2	6	10	14	2	6	10		2	3			
84	polonium	2	2	6	2	6	10	2	6	10	14	2	6	10		2	4			
85	astatine	2	2	6	2	6	10	2	6	10	14	2	6	10		2	5			
86	radon	2	2	6	2	6	10	2	6	10	14	2	6	10		2	6			
87	francium	2	2	6	2	6	10	2	6	10	14	2	6	10		2	6			1
88	radium	2	2	6	2	6	10	2	6	10	14	2	6	10		2	6			2
89	actinium	2	2	6	2	6	10	2	6	10	14	2	6	10		2	6	1		2
90	thorium	2	2	6	2	6	10	2	6	10	14	2	6	10		2	6	2		2
91	protactinium	2	2	6	2	6	10	2	6	10	14	2	6	10	2	2	6	1		2
92	uranium	2	2	6	2	6	10	2	6	10	14	2	6	10	3	2	6	1		2
93	neptunium	2	2	6	2	6	10	2	6	10	14	2	6	10	4	2	6	1		2
94	plutonium	2	2	6	2	6	10	2	6	10	14	2	6	10	6	2	6			2
95	americium	2	2	6	2	6	10	2	6	10	14	2	6	10	7	2	6			2
96	curium	2	2	6	2	6	10	2	6	10	14	2	6	10	7	2	6	1		2
97	berkelium	2	2	6	2	6	10	2	6	10	14	2	6	10	8	2	6	1		2
98	californium	2	2	6	2	6	10	2	6	10	14	2	6	10	10	2	6			2?
99	einsteinium	2	2	6	2	6	10	2	6	10	14	2	6	10	11	2	6			2?
100	fermium	2	2	6	2	6	10	2	6	10	14	2	6	10	12	2	6			2?
101	mendelevium	2	2	6	2	6	10	2	6	10	14	2	6	10	13	2	6			2?
102	nobelium	2	2	6	2	6	10	2	6	10	14	2	6	10	14	2	6			2?
103	lawrencium	2	2	6	2	6	10	2	6	10	14	2	6	10	14	2	6	1		2?
104		2	2	6	2	6	10	2	6	10	14	2	6	10	14	2	6	2		2?
105		2	2	6	2	6	10	2	6	10	14	2	6	10	14	2	6	3		2?

Table 8
WATER-VAPOR PRESSURE

Temperature (°C)	Pressure (mm Hg)	Temperature (°C)	Pressure (mm Hg)	Temperature (°C)	Pressure (mm Hg)
0.0	4.6	19.5	17.0	27.0	26.7
5.0	6.5	20.0	17.5	28.0	28.3
10.0	9.2	20.5	18.1	29.0	30.0
12.5	10.9	21.0	18.6	30.0	31.8
15.0	12.8	21.5	19.2	35.0	42.2
15.5	13.2	22.0	19.8	40.0	55.3
16.0	13.6	22.5	20.4	50.0	92.5
16.5	14.1	23.0	21.1	60.0	149.4
17.0	14.5	23.5	21.7	70.0	233.7
17.5	15.0	24.0	22.4	80.0	355.1
18.0	15.5	24.5	23.1	90.0	525.8
18.5	16.0	25.0	23.8	95.0	633.9
19.0	16.5	26.0	25.2	100.0	760.0

Table 9
DENSITY OF GASES AT STP

Gas	Density (g/liter)	Gas	Density (g/liter)
air, dry	1.2929	hydrogen	0.0899
ammonia	0.771	hydrogen chloride	1.640
carbon dioxide	1.977	hydrogen sulfide	1.539
carbon monoxide	1.250	methane	0.716
chlorine	3.214	nitrogen	1.251
dinitrogen monoxide	1.977	nitrogen monoxide	1.340
ethyne (acetylene)	1.172	oxygen	1.429
helium	0.1785	sulfur dioxide	2.927

Table 10
DENSITY OF WATER

Temperature (°C)	Density (g/ml)	Temperature (°C)	Density (g/ml)
0	0.99987	15	0.99913
1	0.99993	20	0.99823
2	0.99997	25	0.99707
3	0.99999	30	0.99567
4	1.00000	40	0.99224
5	0.99999	50	0.98807
6	0.99997	60	0.98324
7	0.99993	70	0.97781
8	0.99988	80	0.97183
9	0.99981	90	0.96534
10	0.99973	100	0.95838

Table 11
SOLUBILITY OF GASES IN WATER

Volume of gas (reduced to STP) that can be dissolved in 1 volume of water.

Gas	0° C	10° C	20° C
air	0.0292	0.0228	0.0187
ammonia	1176	902	702
carbon dioxide	1.713	1.194	0.878
chlorine	4.54	3.148	2.299
hydrogen	0.0215	0.0196	0.0182
hydrogen chloride	506.7	473.9	442.0
hydrogen sulfide	4.670	3.399	2.582
nitrogen	0.0235	0.0186	0.0155
oxygen	0.0489	0.0380	0.0310
sulfur dioxide	79.79	56.65	39.37

Table 12
SOLUBILITY CHART

S = soluble in water. A = soluble in acids, insoluble in water. P = partially soluble in water, soluble in dilute acids. I = insoluble in dilute acids and in water. a = slightly soluble in acids, insoluble in water. d = decomposes in water.

	acetate	bromide	carbonate	chlorate	chloride	chromate	hydroxide	iodide	nitrate	oxide	phosphate	silicate	sulfate	sulfide
aluminum	S	S	—	S	S	—	A	S	S	a	A	I	S	d
ammonium	S	S	S	S	S	S	—	S	S	—	S	—	S	S
barium	S	S	P	S	S	A	S	S	S	S	A	S	a	d
calcium	S	S	P	S	S	S	S	S	S	P	P	P	P	P
copper(II)	S	S	—	S	S	—	A	—	S	A	A	A	S	A
hydrogen	S	S	—	S	S	—	—	S	S	—	S	I	S	S
iron(II)	S	S	P	S	S	—	A	S	S	A	A	—	S	A
iron(III)	S	S	—	S	S	A	A	S	S	A	P	—	P	d
lead(II)	S	S	A	S	S	A	P	P	S	P	A	A	P	A
magnesium	S	S	P	S	S	S	A	S	S	A	P	A	S	d
manganese(II)	S	S	P	S	S	—	A	S	S	A	P	I	S	A
mercury(I)	P	A	A	S	a	P	—	A	S	A	A	—	P	I
mercury(II)	S	S	—	S	S	P	A	P	S	P	A	—	d	I
potassium	S	S	S	S	S	S	S	S	S	S	S	S	S	S
silver	P	a	A	S	a	P	—	I	S	P	A	—	P	A
sodium	S	S	S	S	S	S	S	S	S	S	S	S	S	S
strontium	S	S	P	S	S	P	S	S	S	S	A	A	P	S
tin(II)	d	S	—	S	S	A	A	S	d	A	A	—	S	A
tin(IV)	S	S	—	—	S	S	P	d	—	A	—	—	S	A
zinc	S	S	P	S	S	P	A	S	S	P	A	A	S	A

Table 13
SOLUBILITY OF COMPOUNDS

Solubilities given in grams of anhydrous compound that can be dissolved in exactly 100 grams of water at the indicated temperatures. Solid phase gives the hydrated form in equilibrium with the saturated solution.

Compound	Formula	Solid phase	0° C	20° C	60° C	100° C
aluminum sulfate	$Al_2(SO_4)_3$	$18H_2O$	31.2	36.4	59.2	89.0
ammonium chloride	NH_4Cl	—	29.4	37.2	55.2	77.3
ammonium nitrate	NH_4NO_3	—	118.3	192.0	421.0	871.0
ammonium sulfate	$(NH_4)_2SO_4$	—	70.6	75.4	88.0	103.3
barium carbonate	$BaCO_3$	—	$0.0016^{8°}$	$0.0022^{18°}$	—	0.0065
barium chloride	$BaCl_2$	$2H_2O$	31.6	35.7	46.4	58.8
barium hydroxide	$Ba(OH)_2$	$8H_2O$	1.67	3.89	20.94	$101.40^{80°}$
barium nitrate	$Ba(NO_3)_2$	—	5.0	9.2	20.3	34.2
barium sulfate	$BaSO_4$	—	1.15×10^{-4}	2.4×10^{-4}	—	4.13×10^{-4}
cadmium sulfate	$CdSO_4$	—	76.48	76.60	83.68	60.77
calcium acetate	$Ca(C_2H_3O_2)_2$	$2H_2O$	37.4	34.7	32.7	—
calcium carbonate	$CaCO_3$	—	—	0.0012	—	0.002
calcium fluoride	CaF_2	—	$0.0016^{18°}$	$0.0017^{25°}$	—	—
calcium hydrogen carbonate	$Ca(HCO_3)_2$	—	16.15	16.60	17.50	18.40
calcium hydroxide	$Ca(OH)_2$	—	0.19	0.17	0.12	0.08
calcium sulfate	$CaSO_4$	$2H_2O$	0.18	0.19	0.20	0.16
cerium sulfate	$Ce_2(SO_4)_3$	$8H_2O$	19.0	9.52	4.04	—
cesium nitrate	$CsNO_3$	—	9.33	23.0	83.8	197.0
copper(II) chloride	$CuCl_2$	$2H_2O$	70.7	77.0	91.2	107.9
copper(II) sulfate	$CuSO_4$	$5H_2O$	14.3	20.7	40.0	75.4
lead(II) chloride	$PbCl_2$	—	0.67	0.99	1.98	3.34
lead(II) nitrate	$Pb(NO_3)_2$	—	38.8	56.5	95	138.8
lithium chloride	$LiCl$	—	67	78.5	103	127.5
lithium sulfate	Li_2SO_4	H_2O	35.3	34.2	31.9	29.9
magnesium hydroxide	$Mg(OH)_2$	—	—	$0.0009^{18°}$	—	—
magnesium sulfate	$MgSO_4$	$6H_2O$	40.8	44.5	53.5	74.0
mercury(I) chloride	Hg_2Cl_2	—	0.00014	0.0002	$0.0007^{40°}$	—
mercury(II) chloride	$HgCl_2$	—	3.6	6.5	16.2	61.3
potassium aluminum sulfate	$KAl(SO_4)_2$	$12H_2O$	3.0	5.9	24.75	$109.0^{90°}$
potassium bromide	KBr	—	53.5	65.2	85.5	104.0
potassium chlorate	$KClO_3$	—	3.3	7.4	24.5	57.0
potassium chloride	KCl	—	27.6	34.0	45.5	56.7
potassium chromate	K_2CrO_4	—	58.2	61.7	68.6	75.6
potassium iodide	KI	—	127.5	144	176	208
potassium nitrate	KNO_3	—	13.3	31.6	110.0	246.0
potassium permanganate	$KMnO_4$	—	2.83	6.4	22.2	—
potassium sulfate	K_2SO_4	—	7.4	11.1	18.2	24.1
silver acetate	$AgC_2H_3O_2$	—	0.72	1.04	1.89	$2.52^{80°}$
silver chloride	$AgCl$	—	$8.9 \times 10^{-5\ 10°}$	1.5×10^{-4}	$0.0005^{50°}$	0.002
silver nitrate	$AgNO_3$	—	122	222	525	952
silver sulfate	Ag_2SO_4	—	0.573	0.796	1.15	1.41
sodium acetate	$NaC_2H_3O_2$	—	119	123.5	139.5	170
sodium chlorate	$NaClO_3$	—	79	101	155	230
sodium chloride	$NaCl$	—	35.7	36.0	37.3	39.8
sodium nitrate	$NaNO_3$	—	73.0	88.0	124.0	180.0
sugar (sucrose)	$C_{12}H_{22}O_{11}$	—	179.2	203.9	287.3	487.2
ytterbium sulfate	$Yb_2(SO_4)_3$	$8H_2O$	44.2	$21.0^{30°}$	10.4	4.67

Table 14
HEAT OF FORMATION

ΔH_f = heat of formation of the given substance from its elements. All values of ΔH_f are expressed as kcal/mole at 25° C. Negative values of ΔH_f indicate exothermic reactions. s = solid, l = liquid, g = gas.

Substance	Phase	ΔH_f	Substance	Phase	ΔH_f
aluminum oxide	s	−399.09	iron(II) sulfate	s	−220.5
ammonia	g	−11.04	iron(II) sulfide	s	−22.72
ammonium chloride	s	−75.38	lead(II) oxide	s	−52.07
ammonium sulfate	s	−281.86	lead(IV) oxide	s	−66.12
barium chloride	s	−205.56	lead(II) nitrate	s	−107.35
barium nitrate	s	−237.06	lead(II) sulfate	s	−219.50
barium sulfate	s	−350.2	lead(II) sulfide	s	−22.54
benzene	g	+19.82	lithium chloride	s	−97.70
benzene	l	+11.72	lithium nitrate	s	−115.28
calcium carbonate	s	−288.45	lithium sulfate	s	−342.83
calcium chloride	s	−190.0	magnesium chloride	s	−153.40
calcium hydroxide	s	−235.80	magnesium oxide	s	−143.84
calcium nitrate	s	−224.0	magnesium sulfate	s	−305.5
calcium oxide	s	−151.9	manganese(IV) oxide	s	−124.5
calcium sulfate	s	−342.42	mercury(I) chloride	s	−63.32
carbon (diamond)	s	+0.45	mercury(II) chloride	s	−55.0
carbon (graphite)	s	0.00	mercury(II) fulminate	s	+64
carbon dioxide	g	−94.05	mercury(II) nitrate	s	−93.0
carbon disulfide	g	+27.55	mercury(II) oxide	s	−21.68
carbon disulfide	l	+21.0	methane	g	−17.89
carbon monoxide	g	−26.42	nitrogen dioxide	g	+8.09
carbon tetrachloride	g	−25.5	nitrogen monoxide	g	+21.60
carbon tetrachloride	l	−33.3	oxygen (O_2)	g	0.00
copper(II) nitrate	s	−73.4	ozone (O_3)	g	+34.00
copper(II) oxide	s	−37.1	diphosphorus pentoxide	s	−720.0
copper(II) sulfate	s	−184.00	potassium bromide	s	−93.73
copper(I) sulfide	s	−19.0	potassium chloride	s	−104.18
copper(II) sulfide	s	−11.6	potassium hydroxide	s	−101.78
dinitrogen monoxide	g	+19.49	potassium nitrate	s	−117.76
dinitrogen pentoxide	g	+3.6	potassium sulfate	s	−342.66
dinitrogen pentoxide	l	−10.0	silicon dioxide (quartz)	s	−205.4
dinitrogen tetroxide	g	+2.31	silver acetate	s	−93.41
ethyne (acetylene)	g	+54.19	silver chloride	s	−30.36
hydrogen (H_2)	g	0.00	silver nitrate	s	−29.43
hydrogen bromide	g	−8.66	silver sulfide	s	−7.69
hydrogen chloride	g	−22.06	sodium bromide	s	−86.03
hydrogen fluoride	g	−64.2	sodium chloride	s	−98.23
hydrogen iodide	g	+6.20	sodium hydroxide	s	−101.99
hydrogen oxide (water)	g	−57.80	sodium nitrate	s	−101.54
hydrogen oxide (water)	l	−68.32	sodium sulfate	s	−330.90
hydrogen peroxide	g	−31.83	sulfur dioxide	g	−70.96
hydrogen peroxide	l	−44.84	sulfur trioxide	g	−94.45
hydrogen sulfide	g	−4.82	tin(IV) chloride	l	−130.3
iodine (I_2)	s	0.00	zinc nitrate	s	−115.12
iodine (I_2)	g	+14.88	zinc oxide	s	−83.17
iron(III) chloride	s	−96.8	zinc sulfate	s	−233.88
iron(III) oxide	s	−196.5	zinc sulfide	s	−48.5
iron(II,III) oxide	s	−267.0	zirconium oxide	s	−258.2

Table 15
HEAT OF COMBUSTION

ΔH_C = heat of combustion of the given substance. All values of ΔH_C are expressed as kcal/mole of substance oxidized to $H_2O(l)$ and/or $CO_2(g)$ at constant pressure and 25° C. s = solid, l = liquid, g = gas.

Substance	Formula	Phase	ΔH_c
hydrogen	H_2	g	-68.32
graphite	C	s	-94.05
carbon monoxide	CO	g	-67.64
methane	CH_4	g	-212.80
ethane	C_2H_6	g	-372.82
propane	C_3H_8	g	-530.60
butane	C_4H_{10}	g	-687.98
pentane	C_5H_{12}	g	-845.16
hexane	C_6H_{14}	l	-995.01
heptane	C_7H_{16}	l	-1151.27
octane	C_8H_{18}	l	-1307.53
ethene (ethylene)	C_2H_4	g	-337.23
propene (propylene)	C_3H_6	g	-491.99
ethyne (acetylene)	C_2H_2	g	-310.62
benzene	C_6H_6	l	-780.98
toluene	C_7H_8	l	-934.50

Table 16
PROPERTIES OF COMMON ELEMENTS

Name	Form/color at room temp	Density (g/cm³)	Melting point (°C)	Boiling point (°C)	Common oxidation numbers
aluminum	silv metal	2.70	660.2	2467	+3
antimony	silv metal	6.69	630.5	1380	+3, +5
argon	colorless gas	1.782*	−189.2	−185.7	0
arsenic	gray metal	5.73	(sublimes)	(sublimes)	+3, +5
barium	silv metal	3.5	725	1140	+2
beryllium	gray metal	1.848	1278	2970	+2
bismuth	silv metal	9.75	271.3	1560	+3
boron	blk solid	2.34	2300	2550 (sublimes)	+3
bromine	red-br liquid	3.12	−7.2	58.8	−1, +5
calcium	silv metal	1.55	842	1487	+2
carbon	diamond	3.51	(sublimes	4827	+2, +4
	graphite	2.26	above 3500° C)	4200	
chlorine	grn-yel gas	3.214*	−101.0	−34.6	−1, +5, +7
chromium	silv metal	7.18	1890	2482	+2, +3, +6
cobalt	silv metal	8.9	1495	2900	+2, +3
copper	red metal	8.96	1083.0	2595	+1, +2
fluorine	yel gas	1.695*	−219.6	−188.1	−1
gold	yel metal	19.32	1063.0	2966	+1, +3
helium	colorless gas	0.1785*	−272.2 (26 atm)	−268.6	0
hydrogen	colorless gas	0.0899*	−259.1	−252.5	−1, +1
iodine	blk solid	4.93	113.5	184.4	−1, +5
iron	silv metal	7.87	1535	3000	+2, +3
lead	silv metal	11.35	327.5	1744	+2, +4
lithium	silv metal	0.534	179	1317	+1
magnesium	silv metal	1.74	651	1107	+2
manganese	silv metal	7.3	1244	2097	+2, +4, +7
mercury	silv liquid	13.55	−38.9	356.6	+1, +2
neon	colorless gas	0.9002*	−248.67	−245.92	0
nickel	silv metal	8.90	1453	2732	+2
nitrogen	colorless gas	1.2506*	−209.9	−195.8	−3, +3, +5
oxygen	colorless gas	1.4290*	−218.4	−183.0	−2
phosphorus	yel solid	1.82	44.1	280	+3, +5
platinum	silv metal	21.45	1769	3800	+2, +4
potassium	silv metal	0.86	63.6	774	+1
radium	silv metal	5(?)	700	<1737	+2
silicon	blk solid	2.33	1410	2355	+4
silver	silv metal	10.50	960.8	2212	+1
sodium	silv metal	0.97	97.8	892	+1
strontium	silv metal	2.54	769	1384	+2
sulfur	yel solid	2.0	114.5	444.6	−2, +4, +6
tin	silv metal	7.31	231.9	2270	+2, +4
titanium	silv metal	4.54	1675	3260	+3, +4
tungsten	gray metal	19.3	3410	5927	+6
uranium	silv metal	19.05	1132.3	3818	+4, +6
zinc	silv metal	7.13	419.4	907	+2

*Densities of gases are given in grams/liter.

Table 17
FOUR-PLACE LOGARITHMS OF NUMBERS

n	0	1	2	3	4	5	6	7	8	9
10	0000	0043	0086	0128	0170	0212	0253	0294	0334	0374
11	0414	0453	0492	0531	0569	0607	0645	0682	0719	0755
12	0792	0828	0864	0899	0934	0969	1004	1038	1072	1106
13	1139	1173	1206	1239	1271	1303	1335	1367	1399	1430
14	1461	1492	1523	1553	1584	1614	1644	1673	1703	1732
15	1761	1790	1818	1847	1875	1903	1931	1959	1987	2014
16	2041	2068	2095	2122	2148	2175	2201	2227	2253	2279
17	2304	2330	2355	2380	2405	2430	2455	2480	2504	2529
18	2553	2577	2601	2625	2648	2672	2695	2718	2742	2765
19	2788	2810	2833	2856	2878	2900	2923	2945	2967	2989
20	3010	3032	3054	3075	3096	3118	3139	3160	3181	3201
21	3222	3243	3263	3284	3304	3324	3345	3365	3385	3404
22	3424	3444	3464	3483	3502	3522	3541	3560	3579	3598
23	3617	3636	3655	3674	3692	3711	3729	3747	3766	3784
24	3802	3820	3838	3856	3874	3892	3909	3927	3945	3962
25	3979	3997	4014	4031	4048	4065	4082	4099	4116	4133
26	4150	4166	4183	4200	4216	4232	4249	4265	4281	4298
27	4314	4330	4346	4362	4378	4393	4409	4425	4440	4456
28	4472	4487	4502	4518	4533	4548	4564	4579	4594	4609
29	4624	4639	4654	4669	4683	4698	4713	4728	4742	4757
30	4771	4786	4800	4814	4829	4843	4857	4871	4886	4900
31	4914	4928	4942	4955	4969	4983	4997	5011	5024	5038
32	5051	5065	5079	5092	5105	5119	5132	5145	5159	5172
33	5185	5198	5211	5224	5237	5250	5263	5276	5289	5302
34	5315	5328	5340	5353	5366	5378	5391	5403	5416	5428
35	5441	5453	5465	5478	5490	5502	5514	5527	5539	5551
36	5563	5575	5587	5599	5611	5623	5635	5647	5658	5670
37	5682	5694	5705	5717	5729	5740	5752	5763	5775	5786
38	5798	5809	5821	5832	5843	5855	5866	5877	5888	5899
39	5911	5922	5933	5944	5955	5966	5977	5988	5999	6010
40	6021	6031	6042	6053	6064	6075	6085	6096	6107	6117
41	6128	6138	6149	6160	6170	6180	6191	6201	6212	6222
42	6232	6243	6253	6263	6274	6284	6294	6304	6314	6325
43	6335	6345	6355	6365	6375	6385	6395	6405	6415	6425
44	6435	6444	6454	6464	6474	6484	6493	6503	6513	6522
45	6532	6542	6551	6561	6571	6580	6590	6599	6609	6618
46	6628	6637	6646	6656	6665	6675	6684	6693	6702	6712
47	6721	6730	6739	6749	6758	6767	6776	6785	6794	6803
48	6812	6821	6830	6839	6848	6857	6866	6875	6884	6893
49	6902	6911	6920	6928	6937	6946	6955	6964	6972	6981
50	6990	6998	7007	7016	7024	7033	7042	7050	7059	7067
51	7076	7084	7093	7101	7110	7118	7126	7135	7143	7152
52	7160	7168	7177	7185	7193	7202	7210	7218	7226	7235
53	7243	7251	7259	7267	7275	7284	7292	7300	7308	7316
54	7324	7332	7340	7348	7356	7364	7372	7380	7388	7396

Table 17
FOUR-PLACE LOGARITHMS OF NUMBERS (cont'd)

n	0	1	2	3	4	5	6	7	8	9
55	7404	7412	7419	7427	7435	7443	7451	7459	7466	7474
56	7482	7490	7497	7505	7513	7520	7528	7536	7543	7551
57	7559	7566	7574	7582	7589	7597	7604	7612	7619	7627
58	7634	7642	7649	7657	7664	7672	7679	7686	7694	7701
59	7709	7716	7723	7731	7738	7745	7752	7760	7767	7774
60	7782	7789	7796	7803	7810	7818	7825	7832	7839	7846
61	7853	7860	7868	7875	7882	7889	7896	7903	7910	7917
62	7924	7931	7938	7945	7952	7959	7966	7973	7980	7987
63	7993	8000	8007	8014	8021	8028	8035	8041	8048	8055
64	8062	8069	8075	8082	8089	8096	8102	8109	8116	8122
65	8129	8136	8142	8149	8156	8162	8169	8176	8182	8189
66	8195	8202	8209	8215	8222	8228	8235	8241	8248	8254
67	8261	8267	8274	8280	8287	8293	8299	8306	8312	8319
68	8325	8331	8338	8344	8351	8357	8363	8370	8376	8382
69	8388	8395	8401	8407	8414	8420	8426	8432	8439	8445
70	8451	8457	8463	8470	8476	8482	8488	8494	8500	8506
71	8513	8519	8525	8531	8537	8543	8549	8555	8561	8567
72	8573	8579	8585	8591	8597	8603	8609	8615	8621	8627
73	8633	8639	8645	8651	8657	8663	8669	8675	8681	8686
74	8692	8698	8704	8710	8716	8722	8727	8733	8739	8745
75	8751	8756	8762	8768	8774	8779	8785	8791	8797	8802
76	8808	8814	8820	8825	8831	8837	8842	8848	8854	8859
77	8865	8871	8876	8882	8887	8893	8899	8904	8910	8915
78	8921	8927	8932	8938	8943	8949	8954	8960	8965	8971
79	8976	8982	8987	8993	8998	9004	9009	9015	9020	9025
80	9031	9036	9042	9047	9053	9058	9063	9069	9074	9079
81	9085	9090	9096	9101	9106	9112	9117	9122	9128	9133
82	9138	9143	9149	9154	9159	9165	9170	9175	9180	9186
83	9191	9196	9201	9206	9212	9217	9222	9227	9232	9238
84	9243	9248	9253	9258	9263	9269	9274	9279	9284	9289
85	9294	9299	9304	9309	9315	9320	9325	9330	9335	9340
86	9345	9350	9355	9360	9365	9370	9375	9380	9385	9390
87	9395	9400	9405	9410	9415	9420	9425	9430	9435	9440
88	9445	9450	9455	9460	9465	9469	9474	9479	9484	9489
89	9494	9499	9504	9509	9513	9518	9523	9528	9533	9538
90	9542	9547	9552	9557	9562	9566	9571	9576	9581	9586
91	9590	9595	9600	9605	9609	9614	9619	9624	9628	9633
92	9638	9643	9647	9652	9657	9661	9666	9671	9675	9680
93	9685	9689	9694	9699	9703	9708	9713	9717	9722	9727
94	9731	9736	9741	9745	9750	9754	9759	9763	9768	9773
95	9777	9782	9786	9791	9795	9800	9805	9809	9814	9818
96	9823	9827	9832	9836	9841	9845	9850	9854	9859	9863
97	9868	9872	9877	9881	9886	9890	9894	9899	9903	9908
98	9912	9917	9921	9926	9930	9934	9939	9943	9948	9952
99	9956	9961	9965	9969	9974	9978	9983	9987	9991	9996

Index

PERIODIC TABLE

METALS

1 | 1.0080 **H** 1 ¹

TRANSITION ELEMENTS

	I	II						
2	6.941 **Li** 3 `2 1`	9.01218 **Be** 4 `2 2`						
3	22.9898 **Na** 11 `2 8 1`	24.305 **Mg** 12 `2 8 2`						
4	39.102 **K** 19 `2 8 8 1`	40.08 **Ca** 20 `2 8 8 2`	44.9559 **Sc** 21 `2 8 9 2`	47.90 **Ti** 22 `2 8 10 2`	50.9414 **V** 23 `2 8 11 2`	51.996 **Cr** 24 `2 8 13 1`	54.9380 **Mn** 25 `2 8 13 2`	55.847 **Fe** 26 `2 8 14 2`	58.9332 **Co** 27 `2 8 15 2`
5	85.4678 **Rb** 37 `2 8 18 8 1`	87.62 **Sr** 38 `2 8 18 8 2`	88.9059 **Y** 39 `2 8 18 9 2`	91.22 **Zr** 40 `2 8 18 10 2`	92.9064 **Nb** 41 `2 8 18 12 1`	95.94 **Mo** 42 `2 8 18 13 1`	98.9062 **Tc** 43 `2 8 18 13 2`	101.07 **Ru** 44 `2 8 18 15 1`	102.9055 **Rh** 45 `2 8 18 16 1`
6	132.9055 **Cs** 55 `2 8 18 18 8 1`	137.34 **Ba** 56 `2 8 18 18 8 2`	Lanthanide Series / 174.97 **Lu** 71 `2 8 18 32 9 2`	178.49 **Hf** 72 `2 8 18 32 10 2`	180.9479 **Ta** 73 `2 8 18 32 11 2`	183.85 **W** 74 `2 8 18 32 12 2`	186.2 **Re** 75 `2 8 18 32 13 2`	190.2 **Os** 76 `2 8 18 32 14 2`	192.22 **Ir** 77 `2 8 18 32 15 2`
7	[223] **Fr** 87 `2 8 18 32 18 8 1`	226.0254 **Ra** 88 `2 8 18 32 18 8 2`	Actinide Series / [257] **Lr** 103 `2 8 18 32 32 9 2`	[261] 104 `2 8 18 32 32 10 2`	[260] 105 `2 8 18 32 32 11 2`			

Lanthanide Series	138.9055 **La** 57 `2 8 18 9 2`	140.12 **Ce** 58 `2 8 18 20 2`	140.9077 **Pr** 59 `2 8 18 21 2`	144.24 **Nd** 60 `2 8 18 22 2`	[147] **Pm** 61 `2 8 18 23 2`	150.4 **Sm** 62 `2 8 18 24 2`	151.96 **Eu** 63 `2 8 18 25 2`

Actinide Series	[227] **Ac** 89 `2 8 18 32 18 9 2`	232.0381 **Th** 90 `2 8 18 32 18 10 2`	231.0359 **Pa** 91 `2 8 18 32 20 9 2`	238.029 **U** 92 `2 8 18 32 21 9 2`	237.0482 **Np** 93 `2 8 18 32 22 9 2`	[244] **Pu** 94 `2 8 18 32 24 8 2`	[243] **Am** 95 `2 8 18 32 25 8 2`